We're Not Going To Take It Anymore

Published in the United States by
Beckham Publications Group, Inc.
ISBN: 0-931761-84-0
10 9 8 7 6 5 4 3 2 1

We're Not Going To Take It Anymore

Educational and Psychological Practices
from an Africentric Paradigm of Helping

Gerald G. Jackson

Africana Studies & Research Center
Cornell University

THE Beckham
PUBLICATIONS GROUP, INC.

Silver Spring

Other Books by Gerald G. Jackson

Delimits of American Helping: Precursors of an African Genesis Model of Helping

Sankofa Helping: The African Genesis of an African-American Model of Helping

Njikoka: Towards an Africentric Paradigm of Helping

DEDICATION

You're my Ace Boon Coon,
My pride and joy,
Usa ugly muthafucka,
BUT, you still My Boy.

Back in the day, the above poem was recited when one African-American male wanted another to know that the friend was forgiven for a mistake. By citing it, I am neither trying to offend nor shock, its presence is to introduce culturally the dedication of this book, both the concept of redemption (Malcolm X) and language (ebonics). This book is dedicated to *my boys* in the past, and the present encompassing concept of the term. This decidedly African-American male notion is what determined my survival for countless years, drive, and ability to write this book. It does not denigrate African-American women, it is a distinct relationship that I have witnessed and experienced among African-American males. I believe its full appreciation and appropriate use can enhance African-American male relationships with others. Most importantly, it holds promise as a measure to produce more economically and socially productive African-American males, even if only fragments of the concept are generally in use.

My Boy is more than a best friend, and provides more than unconditional love. He equals your wife in devotion and is the last resort, when all else fails. I still recall when Jerry Killebrew and I were "jumped" and I was slated to be stabbed to death. What is still vivid and profoundly appreciated is Jerry returning with a butcher knife, by himself, to rescue me. Jerry named his son after me. Yeah, your boy is willing to die for you and vice versa, and in the streets of East Harlem it was impossible to grow up there and not have the concept tested. Your boy knows what to do without you saying anything. He knew and respected your boundaries and relationships. Your boy would never have an affair with either your girlfriend or wife, even if one of them made the advance towards you. Your boy's behavior is the measure of absolute trust. Your boy respects your pride. He would, therefore defend you even when you are not present and are wrong. Similarly, your boy exhibits admirable behaviors that you do not begrudge because you can take it as being a part of the circle of friendship.

Your boy is not envious of your accomplishments and does not take delights in your failures. You can trust your boy with your uncensored fears, anxieties, and fanciful ambitions, and without fear that he will throw them back in your face at an inopportune time. If overwhelmed by a painful situation or person that results in you breaking down and crying, your boy will not scorn your behavior so long as you keep such an occurrence rare. Your boy is the one that can tell you when your *do do* is *shaky.* You take heed in what he says, and tell him so because you are not embarrassed by his knowledge of the real you. You can go months and years without seeing your boy and when you get together to *talk shit,* it seems as it was the day before that you last met. Your wife knows that your boy has access to your time and confidentiality that no others can possess and grants this special space. She knows also that your boy, if he sanctioned the marriage, would be the greatest supporter of its maintenance. Your boy is the first godfather to your child, and if you and your wife should die, your boy would gladly assume responsibility and correctly raise your children. The term, therefore, should be used sparingly and explanatorily to the behaviors and actions of voiceless African-American men.

COVER EPIGRAPH

The titles of this book are based upon two Africentric educational and philosophical *value systems*. The first title is based upon a conscious and unconscious stimulus. Consciously, it is predicated upon a videotape of a confrontation in Elizabeth, New Jersey between the school board and primarily Black parents, teachers, ministers, Black and Dominican community leaders and concerned citizens. The contest was over the adoption of a Curriculum of Inclusion, developed by Gerald Jackson, and the leadership of Gerald Jackson in the implementation of his model. The Cornell students grasped that the charge of the multicultural and multiracial community advocates was broader than cited confrontational issues and it served to inspire them. It involved respecting concerns and needs. They understood clearly that the breadth of the community group was halting the miseducation of their children so that they progressed intellectually, socially, and politically. They demanded an education for their children that would result in economically, socially and politically viable Black adults.

This community group was steadfast in being heard and having their deeply felt needs addressed in a manner that indicated problem resolution and not simply problem identification. On an unconscious level, the title may be based upon an earlier work by Dr. Carroll L. Miller. In 1982, he published *Role Model Blacks Known But Little Known Role Models of Successful Blacks* (Indiana: Accelerated Development, Inc.). I knew him as Dean Miller, "the kind Dean," of the Howard University Graduate School. I worked several years as his student assistant and learned about the likes of Kelley Miller from his conversations. Dean Miller was a role model and his work probably reinforced my belief, nurtured in Harlem, NY and Anacostia, DC of great Black people from ordinary societal ranks.

The second title reveals a belief in the efficacy of an Africentric paradigm in the educational and psychological development of African-American students, in particular, and American students, in general. It too is rooted in the African-American experience; however, it includes a conceptual and theoretical base that is locus in traditional West African society. These titles are shorthand introductions to the book. The African motif demands more than words because it is a culture fraught with symbolism.

Akin to the symbolism associated with the Statue of Liberty's representation of freedom, the picture on the book cover is a representation of African-American dignity, social and political

7

achievements, and *Africentric culturalism*. The young and mature African-American males represent both an "endangered species," and the future of the race. More broadly, they say that African-Americans will not be denied their human rights. They will not be denied their place in the history of the United States, their social, communal and familial position as role models and icons, and the greatness of the physical sites of their communities (e.g., African burial grounds in New York City). Afrospace includes both time and space; therefore, contemporary cultural institutions are examined. Assessed are cultural institutions housed in structures specifically designed to convey African-American heritage, history, philosophy, legacy, and psychology. The continued presence of these structures connotes the viability of a world-view starting in Africa and growing in concept, design, and application in the Americas.

In short, the images on the book cover convey more than protest; they portray the celebration of a humane African spirit. Therefore, it encompasses as an ancestral core the cultural affirmation of African-American people. This is why it is deemed as primarily educational in thrust and evidently of the educational and psychological gains from an Africentric definition of reality.

CONTENTS

SECTION I
Dr. John Henrik Clark Group Research Project

SECTION II
You don't have to move mountains to make a difference: Leaders in the African Disapora and the way they shape our future

SECTION III
Afrospace Incubates Learning

SECTION IV
Harlem Experience Educational and Cultural Tour

FOREWORD

"How can we know where we're going to if we don't know where we've come from?" In Euro-American cultures there is a tendency to emphasize the present and the immediate future and disconnect it from the past, whereas the African and African-American perspective is much more comprehensive, complex and associative. In the Africentric paradigm, the past, present, and future are interconnected and interrelated. However, wisdom in the present and guidance for the future begins with an awareness of the past.

Most Africans and African Americans can easily trace their ancestry back through at least six or seven generations. Heritage is passed down orally at special family events such as reunions, weddings, and funerals. Through the experience of sharing the family history, one becomes embedded in the family and the African-American experience. Personal identity is no longer "earned" or simply a matter of an individual's achievements. It is also "ascribed," or given by others through the collective historical experience.

In the Africentric paradigm, who one "is" supersedes what one "does." We are who we are because of our interactions with others and the experiences and wisdom that have been passed down to us from one generation to another. Central to this approach is the idea of "context." While many modern psychotherapists emphasize strengthening the individual's ego often by separating from others in codependent relationships, the Africentric approach would argue that the individual is strengthened when he or she feels connected to others, and one actually gains ego-support from interdependency with others over time. Once we understand how we are contexted in a particular historical and cultural tradition, we can then transcend the present and move into the future.

Professor Jackson's Africentric paradigm combines a historical perspective with experiential learning. These are traditional ways of acquiring knowledge and discovering truth in African cultures. He challenges his students to examine not only the history of African Americans, but also their own personal histories. Rather than focusing on the lives of the extraordinary, his students consider the lives of ordinary African Americans. In turn, students gain insight into the connectedness between their ancestors and their personal lives and thereby develop greater self-awareness and cultural-awareness.

A major source of inspiration for this book began when Professor Jackson and his family attended the funeral in Harlem for Dr. John Henrik Clarke. The obituary, which appeared on the front page of *The*

Amsterdam News, listed a number of dignitaries who attended. When he shared this event with his students, Professor Jackson discovered that few of them knew any of these people or why the newspaper considered their attendance as newsworthy. He wanted them to understand the historical significance of Dr. Clarke's life and to explore the background of these people who were not well known by most Americans, although they were very well-known to people in Harlem and the greater African-American community.

Professor Jackson believed that this would be a good group project, where students could work together collaboratively and share the experience of historical and cultural discovery. The process of exploration and discovery, through cooperation with others rather than competition between individuals, is also traditional in African cultures. He therefore formed student teams to examine the histories of those who attended the funeral, with each team reporting to the entire class. This class assignment not only allowed students to understand who the dignitaries "were" and what they had "done," but more importantly they shared the experience with their teammates of contexting attendees, and finally themselves, in the African-American cultural experience.

Much of this book is a compilation of the histories of ordinary and extraordinary African Americans coupled with the experiences that the students had in exploring those histories. This, in turn, made the students more consciously aware of the African-American culture and its impact on their personal identities. However, this book is much more than self-discovery through a classroom assignment. It presents a model and approach for self-discovery that could be used by any teacher.

Professor Jackson's Africentric paradigm is based upon his diunital approach which is roughly akin to the idea of "union-of-opposites" found in many nonwestern traditions, such as the *yin-yang* of Confucian culture.[1] The *yin* in Chinese thought is the female, passive force or principle of life and being which is complementary to the *yang*, which is the masculine, active force or principle. The whole is greater than the sum of the parts and men can learn from women, just as women can learn from men. The male and female together become a force that is even greater than the two combined. In addition, the

---

[1] See Sudhir Kakar, "Western Science, Eastern Minds" in *Culture, Communication and Conflict: Readings in Intercultural Relations, revised second edition,* Gary R. Weaver, editor, Boston: Pearson Publishing, 2000, pp. 338-344.

relationship between women and men allows for greater self-awareness, synergy, and creativity.

This is a truly multicultural, pluralistic or diunital approach. The opposite approach is the assimilationist model where differences disappear when people throw their cultures into a "melting pot" or when they give up their differences to fit the cultural cookie-cutter mold of the dominant white, Anglo-Saxon, Protestant, male culture. For example, in the United States twenty years ago, women often went through "assertiveness training." These workshops and seminars were never intended for men. The assumption was that women, if they were to be truly successful in the workforce, had to learn to be assertive and aggressive—"just like men." The only thing wrong with women is that they were underdeveloped men or pathologically male. Given the right training, they would be just like males.

Professor Jackson would label this the "deficit model" in contrast to the "diunital model." Today, we might view this as "cloning." Clones contribute little to the overall society and certainly are not creative. Why would any organization want women who think like men sitting around a conference table? Today, most managers want the African-American, Euro-American, Asian-American, female, male, gay, straight, old and young and any others' perspectives brought to the table.

The tension between opposites, and the contrast and comparison of opposites, leads to creative conflict where both sides benefit. One could argue that countries such as the United States that have struggled with racism and multicultural and multiethnic conflict, have actually discovered how different ways of thinking and perceiving enhance the entire society with creativity. This is also true of the individual. For example, Nikos Kazantzakis wrote *Zorba the Greek* to depict the conflict between the West (Boss) and the non-West (Zorba). In fact, it was the struggle between two parts of Kazantzakis' own personality. Throughout his life he was trying to determine how to find "truth"—theoretically by becoming a monk (the Western intellectual way with the denial of the senses) or kinesthetically and experientially with the union of the sensual and intellectual. Moreover, this makes sense because Greece is between the so-called East and the West.

This struggle can also be found in much of the literature of the Mediterranean world. Even Michelangelo claimed that he wanted to dedicate his art to God, and yet on his deathbed he lamented his defeat because he found that every time he used a chisel he "crucified Christ." That is, he found that in his struggle to deny the humanistic to extol the aesthetic, he ended up glorifying the human body. However, one could argue that this very struggle produced the profound beauty and creativity of Michelangelo's frescos, paintings, and especially his sculpture.

Self-awareness often begins with the feeling of being lost. We often find our "selves" by losing our "selves." While many fear that they will lose their home cultures when they are immersed in another culture, in fact, exactly the opposite is true.[2] As long as we remain within our own culture surrounded by those who share our values, beliefs, assumptions and ways of thinking, we take our own culture for granted. But when we are surrounded by those who are different, we become more consciously aware of our own culture. The irony is that the best way to find your culture is to leave it. Fela, the great Nigerian jazz artist, once said that he didn't know what it meant to be an African until he left Africa. The Black Identity Movement of the mid-1960s did not begin on historically Black University campuses in the United States.[3] Rather, as large numbers of African-American students came on to predominately white university campuses where they were surrounded by white people, they did not become white. Instead, they were forced to ask the question, "What does it mean to be Black?" The interesting paradox is that as integration increases, black and white people become even more consciously aware of their cultural and sociological differences and the consequences of racism.[4]

The creativity and synergy of diunitality is caused by the conflict of different cultures and usually begins with *diversion*. And only after there is diversion can *conversion* and diunitality take place. Diversion must precede conversion, but the reverse is not true. That is, we can't deny or devalue differences and assume that everyone can come together harmoniously. Eventually, differences will emerge and must be acknowledged and even valued.

Not only are differences good for the society, the clash of cultures causes personal self-awareness and greater awareness of one's own culture, which becomes more valuable to the individual and a source of strength. Certainly, the Black Identity Movement provided a way of

---

[2] This was the reason given by the Department of State for rotating American diplomats every two or three year. There was concern that if they stayed in a country too long they would no longer represent the United States' interests and would "go native."

[3] Gary R. Weaver, "American Identity Movements", *Intellect* (March 1975), pp. 377-380. Also in Weaver, *Culture, Communication and Conflict*, pp. 60-65.

[4] See Orlando Patterson, "The Paradox of Integration" in *Ibid.* pp. 95-100.

reconciling the dilemma of being part of two entirely different cultures at the same time. Immediately after the 1964 Civil Rights Act was enacted, many young African Americans were faced with the question as to whether they had to give up their "blackness" to become a participant in the White World. This was not simply a matter of "acting White" or behavior. It was a much more profound existential question of giving up an identity that indeed had helped African Americans to survive the slavery and racism. Moreover, as African Americans increasingly interacted with White Americans on an interpersonal level, they became more consciously aware of African-American culture.

The significance of the Black Identity Movement, which became the *leitmotiv* of every "identity movement" since the 1960s including the feminist, Chicano and Gay Liberation movements, was that it was no longer an either-or proposition. One could be both—African-American and a full participant in the dominant or mainstream society. Moreover, the differences between cultures are a source of strength for both the individual and the overall society.

The Africentric paradigm provides a technique for raising the self-awareness of students to their African and African-American culture in the context of the American experience. While it provides the historical perspective, it also uses a deductive and Dionysian approach where the student extrapolates from the history of an individual or a family to the broader African-American community. It is basically nonlinear, comprehensive, and qualitative using a case-study technique which ties events and people together, almost poetically. This is very different from the Eurocentric approach found in contemporary social science research (especially sociology) which is highly linear, inductive, quantitative, and Apollonian. While the Africentric paradigm focuses on context, the Eurocentric approach or paradigm disconnects, isolates variables, fragments, and fictionalizes. It denies context.

Dr. Gary R. Weaver
Professor
American University

PREFACE

Professor Gerald Jackson in "We're not going to take it anymore" has presented a guide and a challenge to educators to educate their students about what they have lost that the generations before them had collectively as an African people. That which was lost was a sense of community that could evolve into self-knowledge.

Professor Jackson in detail took us through a process with his students in quest of community. This process was initiated with an examination and revelation of Dr. John Henrik Clarke, the Father of Black Studies, at the time of his funeral or crossing over. The students did not know the dignitaries who were listed in the *Amsterdam News* accounting of the funeral. Inspirationally, Professor Jackson assigned his students to research these notables—to them, unknown dignitaries. I believe that the hands and spirits of the ancestors (including John Henrik Clarke) were present in this inspiration.

John Henrik Clarke was the consummate scholar who had a passionate love for his people. His library filled nearly three floors of books in his Brownstone in Harlem. He had read all of them and could quote salient chapters from memory when he lectured. This memory was cultivated when he was a poor child in Georgia where his community recognized that he had special talents. For example, the local hustlers would take little "Bubba" John to the local bars and bet that Bubba could give the capital of any state in the union. He gave the right answer every time, won all the bets for the hustlers, and got a meal at the end of the day, as a reward for his performance. His total recall served him well when he went blind late in life. Going blind was tragic for this voracious reader, but his memory continued to serve him although he could not add new volumes of literature.

There is an illustrative anecdote on John Clarke's appetite for books. One day he called me at my office in Newark, New Jersey, saying that the Newark Public Library had a book he had to have; it was called *The Sociology of Dirt*. I wondered why this African scholar was hunting for this book. Then I scanned it before mailing it to him and I had my answer. It was filled with documentation by a British sociologist on the appalling, filthy conditions in England during the 15th and 16th centuries. It revealed how Madam Pompadour set her hair with sugar and it became infested with crawling maggots because she didn't wash, so the maggots came to dine on the sugar in her hair. There were other accounts on lack of basic sanitation of famous historical figures. I knew John was going to use this to counter British claims that Africans were filthy, in his next lecture or book. John believed that you should read what your enemies write. Professor Jackson included a bibliography of Dr. Clarke's works, providing students with the opportunity to learn the scope of Dr. Clarke's scholarship as a political/activist, philosopher, counselor and, of course, historian.

Our students must understand the depth and complexity of our people and biographies, even autobiographies, are a rich resource and can provide enlightenment. Integration has devastated our communities, as it was opened up. Segregation was indisputably evil but we were all together–the poor, the professional, the laborers, the fraternal organizations–the NAACP chapters. WE WERE CONNECTED!! For generations the elders in our communities were responsible for the young and gave whatever they had to the children, as did the hustlers to John Clarke. There were achievers who would urge, the nurturers who watched and protected, the laborers who taught the pride and satisfaction of honest work, the aged who shared the wisdom of their years and the hustlers who gave lesson in manipulation (a valuable lesson). These riches were all available.

Integration shuffled us all around to different places with new agendas, only the poor were left behind to fend for themselves and too many of us turned our backs and are embarrassed by them. The biographies bring back our past, our roots and recognition of the struggles that took place to make our lives easier. As educators, we are obliged to enlighten our students, to make them a part of our/the community.

Thirdly, Professor Jackson included Black fraternities in his analysis. They were part of the organizations during the years of segregation that sustained our community, gave fellowship, connections, culture and laughter. There were the Masons, National Council of Negro Women, Links, Black professional groups (NMA is the black counterpart of the American Medical Association), as well as the Black Greeks. Professor Jackson, however, moves on to illustrate how the Greek structure could be used to broaden the network with the inclusion of Latinos. There is a shared history that is frequently denied by African-Americans as well as Latinos. With his students, Professor Jackson demonstrated the positive effects of breaking the barriers and the resulting benefits. Our students must learn to reach out for new inclusive connections. The Latino community has experienced much of our problems, internally and externally, and could become a valuable ally in both of our struggles ahead.

Lastly and significantly was the trip/tour to Harlem, New York that Professor Jackson organized. It included an extensive Harlem bibliography and an itinerary touching base with significant institutions, i.e. The Studio Museum, a musical at the Apollo, bookstores, and "soul food." The students' accounts of the experience were bursting with enthusiasm. They were awed by the fact that they were walking the same streets that Baldwin, Malcolm X, and Ellington had walked–amazing! It reminded me again of John Clarke. While I was at Seton Hall a Japanese student enrolled for an independent study with me. I was perplexed until I asked her some questions and discovered that she knew African-American history (more than some of my American students). She wanted to learn more about Black people, their spirituality, and their music, but especially to see Harlem. She had read one of John's books, which had been translated into Japanese, so I arranged for us to meet John in Harlem for a walk and talk and, of course, eat. It was a memorable evening for all of us, as John thoughtfully educated us about his beloved Harlem. I was reminded again of how African Americans have impacted others who sense we have something of value for them, while we are too frequently unaware of our own richness.

Again, this creative guide is an inspiration for pedagogues to reach past the insularity of the campus, not abroad, but in our own backyards, applying the tools of the academy for rich academic adventures in learning. I am honored by Professor Jackson's invitation to write this Preface. It was a stimulating assignment experiencing Professor

Photo by Gerald G. Jackson.

Jackson's creativity, as well as affording me the opportunity to share my thoughts and memories of my beloved friend and mentor, Dr. John Henrik Clarke.

Dr. Julia A. Miller
Emeritus Professor and
former Director of Black Studies
Seton Hall University

ACKNOWLEDGMENTS

In my earlier books, I was so preoccupied with being "inclusive" that I generously acknowledged everyone who had the slightest bearing upon me. Here, I am slightly less comprehensive and will confine myself to noting individuals that took me over the edge in writing and producing this book. Who comes first reminds me of the chicken and egg proposition. Similarly, it may not matter who comes first because sequence is not the point; what is paramount is group composition. Practically, it was Bill Cross' affirmation of the concept of the book and suggestion that the initial book be made into smaller ones that resulted in this book. Starting this discussion on "my boys," therefore, does not imply most important. Spiritually, for instance, I continue to be indebted to my frat brothers of Kappa Alpha Psi. I am especially grateful for the way they have turned us away from our "wine, women and song" days and make our current meetings healing and professional development. Big shout-outs to Pinkard for suggesting books, ideas, resourceful people and providing an internship opportunity for my Cornell student at his Booker T. Washington Charter School. To the Wave, you are the Connector, Kappa chapter liaison, business consultant, and friend, thanks. Your generously given business expertise has been very helpful in my professional life, just as your modeling of an excellent regiment of exercise and spiritual development is meeting needs in my personal life. Both of you Nups have provided, through the vigorous support of your adult children, the needed space to dialogue on a challenging subject for divorced Black fathers. Phi Nu Pi til we die.

One recent "my boy" behavior of an African-American males is James Turner's. His emotional and physical support when I lay in pain, immobilized over three weeks from back problems, is an outstanding reflection of the concept. His support goes beyond crisis intervention, and his actions probably saved my life. Since the illness, he has been steadfast in the exchange of information and ideas and the sharing of his cumulative wisdom, and for the refinement of Black Studies theories and practices. Most importantly, he continues to serve as a role model of industry with students, teaching and serving the African-American and African Diaspora communities.

Similarly, Bob Harris' intervention in saving my car, a life-saving entity when you commute weekly, ranks very high. I deeply appreciate his intuitive understanding of my stressful state of being at that time, and willingness to inconvenience himself and his family to accommodate my circumstances. His apparent commitment to his family, scholarship and the Africana Studies and Research Center, is a commendable guideline for others to emulate.

Both James and Bob, former directors of AS&RC, embody diunital thinking: James, as creator and director of a summer Institute devoted to the study of Black women, and Bob, in having the AS&RC conduct programs with historically Black colleges and having the center qualified to increase the number of teaching slots of African scholars as professors.

In a germane sphere, I continue to be grateful to my former 171, 172 and 100.4 Africana Studies and Research Center students, and current 171 and 100.4 students for keeping the classroom discussion flow real. They are noteworthy in replacing an expectation for classroom perfection with one for joyous learning. Their willingness to take risks in sharing ideas, situations and experiences, has enabled us to create innovative moments and make pedagogical advances. Without such students, this book would not have been imaginable. Special shout-outs to Hope Jamison, Nafis Smith, David Ladd, and Funa for volunteering to conduct student programs, provide classroom lectures and consequently serve as peer role models, and continue a spirit I identified decades ago in African-American peer counselors.[5] Singular distinction to Dawn Darby, Shari Moseley, Shelby Senzer, and Tara Woods for volunteering, after the class was over, their time, energy, thoughts and enthusiasm to the production of this book. Relatedly, I would be remiss if I did not thank Hope for her unique support to me during her tenure and afterwards, and shout-outs to Tiffany and Donnell for continuing after graduation to be supportive campus children. Lastly, much respect is for the students who went beyond the Cornell environment comfort zone and allowed themselves to enjoy the Harlem Experience educational and cultural tour. Overall, the actions of these students truly reflect the Africentric concepts of reciprocity, spiral time, diunitality, and extended self. Akin to the crucial work of the students is the work of Tom Weissinger, former Director of the John Henrik Clarke library, and Eric Acree, current Director. In addition to compiling a bibliography published in this book, both directly enhanced the educational process noted in these pages by providing classroom lectures on research, library tours and resource material.

---

[5]Gerald Jackson (1972). "Black students as peer counselors." *Personnel and Guidance Journal*, 51, 280-285.

I have continuously explored new ways of teaching, even when the approach and content have been demonstrated to be successful. In this regard, the Africana Studies department and the John S. Knight Institute for Writing in the Disciplines program deserve note. The tremendous amount of potential flexibility in the classroom and learning environment, depending upon the professor's philosophical predilections, administrative overhead and cultural milieu, is dependent upon the institution's programs, philosophies and practices. Considering all of my teaching positions, being in AS&RC and the Knight program has been an instructive and insightful experience.

Another type of relationship that needs acknowledgment is a friendship springing from professional work. With a great sense of fraternity, I acknowledge Gary Weaver. He has always been on point and his vanguard professional and scholarly behaviors have been a source of professional assurance in my life. Our relationship affirms the powerful ends that are achieved through publishing scholarly articles. I can still recall the day when a female telephone caller asked if I was Gerald Jackson. When I replied yes, she subsequently made me feel as if I were Livingston. Dr. Weaver, she remarked, was in search of me because he wanted to republish my Black Backlash article in his book.[6] Learning this caused the coin to flip: now I was Livingston. It was an article that I thought was one of my most masterful pieces; however, I had received disappointingly little professional recognition. In addition, I was excited because I had used Gary's concept of abstractive and associative cultures in it and wondered about the person who proposed such a comprehensive map for configuring societies. We subsequently met, and I discovered a great similarity in experiences, ideas, and beliefs. Since then, Gary has provided me with a forum for my ideas by inviting me to present at his Institute. He recommended me to be a part of an international group of psychologists charged with developing a curriculum for psychologists interested in ending ethnoviolence around the world. What continues to strengthen our relationship is our professional and personal responsiveness to requests for assistance. Indicative of the process, he agreed to write the foreword and returned the stellar document in two weeks!

Special shout-out for the following Cornell Students for proofreading and commenting on the text – Danielle Williams, Melissa

---

[6]Gerald Jackson (1977). "The roots of the black backlash theory in mental health." *Journal of Black Psychology*, 6(1), 17-45; Gary Weaver (Ed.) (1991). *Culture, Communication and conflict: Readings in intercultural relations.* Massachusetts: Simon & Schuster.

Thompson, Azaria Tesfa, Jessica Barrett, Amanda Colon, John Rawlins, and Jennifer Kamara.

Dr. Julia Miller reminds me very much of the sculptor-engraver Elizabeth Catlett.[7] Typifying diunital thinking, she professed that her art "speaks for both of my peoples," meaning African Americans and Mexicans. I did not realize the resemblance when I first heard of Judy. I first heard of her as the Director of the Black Studies department at Seton Hall University. In that capacity, she hired me as an adjunct to teach a Black family course, my first teaching assignment in the Black Studies field. I got to know her, however, during an educational tour in Puerto Rico. I discovered that she was fluent in Spanish and had great rapport with Puerto Rican students, staff and administrators among S.H.U. people and education officials in Puerto Rico. Over the years, I have come to admire her for a number of reasons. Most prominent in my mind is her commitment to Black S.H.U. students, functions, institutions and issues. Whenever something was "going down," Dr. Miller's name was in the middle of "the stuff." Second, I like the way she has been able to be interdependent with her husband. The Farm she and her husband maintain in Upstate New York has been an informal retreat site for some of the notables in the Africana Studies field.

It is, therefore, not only her leadership in the Black Studies field[8] but several other things. It is her closeness to the late Dr. John Henrik Clarke. Most formative, it is her integration of many facets of life and limb into a warm, intelligent and generous individual. All these factors encouraged me to request her to write the book Preface. Personifying the diunital person, she knows the Black and Latino communities, is a model of heroic commitment and above the call of duty ardor, and a spirit I felt this book needed to unite cultural worlds.

---

[7]"My art speaks for both my people" (January 1970). *Ebony*, 94, 95, 98, 100, 101.

[8]Although officially retired, a picture of her appeared in the March issue of the New York Amsterdam News. It described her role as the keynote speaker for the African Women's Alliance annual reception for Women's History Month. The organization is women of African and Diaspora descent that are committed to fostering greater understanding of cultural diversity; promoting the visibility of African women's perspectives; addressing global issues; and strengthening the capacity of women, families and communities. They noted her former position of state director of communities in schools and how she established CIS in New Jersey and was for 7 years a part of a national network of dropout prevention programs. Gideon Manassen (March 18 – 24, 2004). *The New York Amsterdam News*, p. 8.

Integrating boundaries, Barry Beckham is more than a publisher; he has been a colleague, supporter and friend. His writer's ebullience is contagious and needed in the preparation of an Africentric book. He not only provided germane articles on the subject matter of the book; he gave additional vision to the book's objectives and goals. His inspirational notes, therefore, encouraged me to put forth those extra efforts that elevate the standards of success. He also can provide time lines, limitations and closure to the book writing process, essential management qualities.

Another person is Peaches (Ingrid Hill). As in my other books, she is mentioned as an indispensable help. She continues to be so; however, recently I had an experience that truly captured her essence. For quite some time, the oil gauge on my car was off-centered and I reported this observation to my mechanic. In his apparent professional opinion, a little oil leak was characteristic of Fords so there was not a real problem. Accepting his expertise, I felt it safe to drive if I had my oil replaced in a timely manner by the same mechanic. Then it happened, first a small explosion, then massive oil leakage and, I am told, the pistons fused together because there was no oil to enable them to run smoothly. Upshots, leave the car or purchase a new engine. Dear Peaches, I am watching the gauge and learned the importance of oil, similar to you, in maintaining the successful operation of myself, and my car and engine.

I have saved the last set of people to be acknowledged because these acknowledgments speak to a new and old realm in my life. Being an African-American with a self-consciousness about non-African-American "experts," I have been leery about becoming one for another group. This is my case with Latinos; I do not have "lived" knowledge. To avoid being considered an expert, I wrote an article in which I used an Africentric framework to remedy Latino problems. The article was rejected by the *Journal of Black Psychology* and published as a technical paper by an Afro-Latina in the Federal government. I never met her in person but she said the article aptly captured a point of view that needed publication. Her responses was sufficient endorsement of my approach; however, I neither had the time nor predilection to seek publication in a source with a wider readership. I am doing so now and there are people to acknowledge for getting me to this point.

I have to thank Lillian Comas-Diaz, Wilfredo Nieves, and Juan Flores for supporting my efforts to convey the plight and prospects for Afro-Latinos. I initially met Lillian through her citation of my work in her publications.[9] I was, of course, flattered by the recognition but was especially pleased because her publications not only complemented mine, they made me feel less alone in trying to get the psychology and mental health professions to accept other worldviews.[10] What was most impactful was sharing time with her and her husband, deepening my understanding of Afrilatinas, working together on projects and consults, and having a good time together.

I met Wilfredo when he was fresh out of graduate school. We laugh now at his interview and militant posture. He declared at the time that he would wear "red pants " to work if he wanted, and his tone almost resulted in me not hiring him (as a college President today, I wonder if he would allow someone to be hired who wore red pants?). He turned out to be a great hire who was able to work with all cultural and racial groups. He calls me Hermano and I now have been with his mother, father, sisters at numerous family and social events. In addition to our friendship, he has consistently and continuously provided me with his thoughts, readings and articles on the group now termed **Afro-Latinos**.

Juan Flores is acknowledged for expressing an appreciation, after reading a book draft, for my treatment of Afro-Latinos. He received this respect because of his publications, presentations, advisorship and marriage to an Afro-Latina. Before his book comment, I had thought my work was liberating for all Latinos; however, his remark caused me to reflect. Perhaps what I analyzed was more appropriate for a Latino that could not be White or allowed to accept the **racial bride,** to be defined shortly. I decided to concentrate on an inequitably downtrodden group that has experienced a similar history in the Americas. His pronouncement encouraged me, therefore, to think about my experiences with Afro-Latino/as.

My first contact with an Afro-Latino in East Harlem was a Black Puerto Rican named Ralph Delgado. We were both living in the projects, had a single mother and were only children. What stands out in my mind is that he was the only Puerto Rican male in the neighborhood that ever invited me to a dinner made especially for me. When I shared with my other Puerto Rican friends what I had for dinner, they informed me that I had received a special one. Maybe this

---

[9]Lillian Comas-Diaz (1981). "Effects of cognitive and behavioral group treatment on the depressive symptomatology of Puerto Rican women." *Journal of Consulting and Clinical Psychology*, 49(3), 627–632.
[10]Lillian Comas-Diaz & Greene, B. (Eds.) (1994). *Women of Color Integrating ethnic and gender identities in psychotherapy*. New York: Guiford Press.

friendship is a cornerstone of the foundation for my interest in what happens to Afro-Latinos?

Less buried in my subconscious is Milagros Dennis' efforts to augment my awareness and knowledge, and assist me in bringing the Afro-Puerto Rican dimension to my class at Cornell. The impact of her classroom work is revealed in my book *Njikoka: Towards an Africentric Paradigm of Helping.* The other areas I will acknowledge are awareness and knowledge. Her personal account of what it means to be a dark-skinned Puerto Rican in Puerto Rico paralleled my African-American experiences on the continent. The convergence helped me to understand our Pan-American cultural links as Diaspora people. Similarly, the bibliographical material, books and articles she shared were empowering. She exposed me to works written in Spanish and the specific names of people in Puerto Rico that had interests similar to my own. She captured and conveyed a point of view that the overwhelming majority of my Puerto Rican colleagues and friends have not been comfortable engaging in such an exchange. One implication of her work is how do we overcome the racial bribe, defined as:

> a strategy that invites specific racial or ethnic groups to advance within the existing black-white racial hierarchy by becoming "white." The strategy expands the range of physical characteristics that can fall within the definition of "white," in order to pursue four goals: (1) to defuse the previously marginalized group's oppositional agenda, (2) to offer incentives that discourage the group from affiliating with black people, (3) to secure high status for individual group members within existing hierarchies, and (4) to make the social position of "whiteness" appear more racially or ethnically diverse.[11]

A prerequisite to a genuine coalition between African-Americans and European-Latinos is building relationships that withstand racial bribes. She is a central part of my friendship and professional relationship with the late Italian-American Anthony Buonocore. It set the stage for the closing discussion on Italian-American and African-American relationships.

---

[11]Lani Guinier & Torres, G. (2002). *The miner's canary.* Massachusetts: Harvard University Press, p. 225.

INTRODUCTION

"I learned something reading that article. Of course, I knew about Dorothy Height, but I honestly didn't know the full richness of her legacy.[12] *One thing I have learned about life, just because you are out of school doesn't mean that the learning has stopped. Life is a continuous learning process. Speaking of learning new things and being inspired by the ancestors, my family reunion was in Charleston, SC last weekend. I went and had a ball. The reunion was great, but Charleston was even better. I always knew that Charleston was a southern city rich in history, but I really appreciated seeing it come to life. I saw Denmark Vessey's house; I passed through his church and I saw the jail where he was kept before being executed. I saw the slave market, which, by the way wasn't even opened up until 1854, right on the eve of the Civil War. We toured the Gullah islands and met some folks...that were very interesting. And here is one more fact that is interesting for you...did you knows that the Citadel was only founded after Denmark Vessey's slave revolt to "protect" the white citizens? Isn't that hilarious...they created an entire military college to try and hold us back, but freedom came just the same, lol. I chuckled to myself every time I thought about that. Well, that's my report for this week." (Tiffany Lynn Haliburton, July,14, 2003)*[13]

---

[12]In addition to a legacy, she continues to serve as a source for initiatives. She was a discussant in a program to mark a Women's Studies program at Howard University. According to Lakesha Robinson, president of the Alpha chapter of Delta Sigma Theta, Height's presence was important because "Courage is something that every woman needs to learn about and embody." Shara Taylor (November 25, 2003). "Height Encourages Women's Studies." *The Hilltop*. 1. Two decades ago, Dr. Height accepted Barnard College's highest honor, the Barnard Medal of Distinction. However, in 1929, after being accepted at the same college, she was denied admission because her attendance would mean the college would have to go beyond its two Blacks per year quota. She did not let the racism impede her pursuit of an education and went to receive a bachelor's and master's from N.Y.U. Ironically, it is only in 2004 that the college has given her an apology for their past racist admission program. Jamal Watson (June 10 – June 16, 2004). "Barnard apologizes to Dorothy Height." *The New York Amsterdam News*, p 4.

[13]Her quotation was originally an email to Professor Jackson, in response to an educational email he sent her on Dorothy Height. She was a student in his Black Family and Black Education courses. Tiff affectionately called Professor Jackson her "Campus Dad" and this is the basis of the continuation in the educational relationship.

Since my first professional position as a senior counselor at a Job Corps Center for Women and later staff developer administrator, I have been keenly interested in determining what works in counseling, training and education. A quest led to being rewarded for finding counseling techniques that worked with "disadvantaged" females.[14] I was elated by the accolades, and concerned that the reader might overlook the implied strengths, especially cultural, in such learners. I next reported, consequently, on the strengths of Black students, and how they could be used to facilitate the education process.[15] I was even quoted as far back as 1969 in a book called *I Heard A Scream in the Street* by Nancy Larrick. She quoted me as saying, "Somebody turned on a tap in these kids, and the poetry just kept coming."[16] To fathom my quest, I would learn that what was needed was an Africana Studies field.[17] Only it would meet my kindred need for a multicultural, multidimensional and multidisciplinary framework.

My focus then, as it is today, was to identify and publicize who and what inspires learning, and convey this information to those who are instrumentally involved in mental health and education fields. One way I have decided to disseminate information is this text. To illustrate, as a well-disciplined scholar and well-trained researcher who teaches in an Africana Studies Center in an Ivy League university, I was tempted to perpetuate a Black academic type book introduction. These influential sources tempted me to introduce book goals and objectives by quoting a famous Black person. Presumably, someone dead, venerated and widely acclaimed as a sagacious and prophetic person. I decided against the use of a prominent African-American scholar, celebrity, or spiritual leader because such a beginning would contradict basic book objectives and goals, and my published accounts of an Africentric

---

[14]Gerald G. Jackson (1972). "The use of role-playing job interviews with Job Corps females." *Journal of Employment Counseling*, 9, 130 - 39.

[15]Gerald G. Jackson (1972). "Black students as peer counselor." *Personnel and Guidance Journal*, 51, 280-285. Currently *Journal of Counseling and Development*.

[16]Nancy Larrick (1970). *I Heard A Scream in the Street Poems by Young People in the City* (p. 6). New York: J. B. Lippincott Company.

[17]William M. Banks & Kelly, S. (1997). "Guess who's coming to academies: The impact and current status of Black studies" (pp. 381–390). In Ishmael Reed (Ed.). *Multiamerica. Essays on cultural wars and cultural peace*. New York: Penguin Books

approach to helping.[18] Instead, I selected the thoughtful and vibrant expressions of a former student and campus daughter to capture and convey the *ethos* of this book.

This does not mean that this book advances a dichotomy between *drylongso* (ordinary) African Americans and acclaimed ones, the latter being the type that appears in such books as: *Black Profiles in Courage,*[19] *Fifty Black Women Who Changed America*[20], *Created Equal the lives and ideas of black American innovators,*[21] *THE AFRICAN AMERICAN A celebration of Achievement,*[22] *Black Heroes*[23] *African Americans, A Portrait*[24] *THEY HAD A DREAM The story of African-American Astronauts,*[25] *A CENTURY OF GREAT AFRICAN-AMERICANS,*[26] *THE AFRICAN AMERICAN CENTURY How Black Americans Have Shaped Our Country*[27]. It means that the emphasis will be on **unsung warriors** who are significant according to an African-American *agency*. Nor does it mean that other African Diaspora groups cannot use the achievements of African Americans as a source of inspiration. For example, I was privy to be the only male at a national convention dinner of Omega Phi Beta sorority. The point here is that the position enabled me to see a wonderful semblance of

---

[18]Gerald Jackson (2000). *Precursor of an African Genesis Model of Helping.* New York: Global Publications.

[19]Kareem Adbul-Jabbar, & Steinberg, A. (1996). *Black Profiles In Courage. A Legacy of African-American Achievement.* New York: William Morrow & Company.

[20]Amy Alexander (1999). *Fifty Black Women Who Changed America.* New Jersey: Birch Lane.

[21]James Brodie (1993). *Created Equal the lives and ideas of black american innovators.* New York: William Morrow & Company.

[22]Charles Collins & Cohen, D. (Eds.) (1995). *THE AFRICAN AMERICANS A celebration of Achievement.* New York: Vikings Books.

[23] Jesse Smith (Ed.) (1998). *Black heroes of the 20th century.* Michigan: Visible Ink Press.

[24]Richard Long (1985). *African Americans A Portrait.* New York: Crescent Books.

[25]Alfred Phelps. (1994). *They Had A Dream The story of African-American astronauts.* California: Presidio.

[26]Allison Schwartz (1999). *A CENTURY OF GREAT AFRICAN-AMERICANS.* New York: Gramercy Books.

[27]Louis Gates & West, C. (2000). *The African-American CENTURY How Black Americans Have Shaped Our Country.* New York: Free Press.

African Diaspora allegiance in a predominantly Latina setting. The speaker extolled *Black Genius*[28] as a great book to read and did so to a predominantly Latina group.

Essentially, what I aspire to accomplish is the publication of a book that models the application of Africentric helping in a variety of educational settings, and showcase distinct ways of doing education. This is something rarely done by educators and mental health professionals, regardless of race, gender, sexual orientation, philosophical base and age.[29] First, it will reveal heroes that are not necessarily widely known and offer more than a depiction of old African Americans. These remarkable foot soldiers in the war for human decency are the epitome of resiliency in the African-American and Afro-Latino communities. Second, more than report who they are, this book provides evidence of the instructive work they have performed, and the way such knowledge can be used in a variety of settings and ways. Most relevant to a concern with future generations or genocide, it models how similar books with guidance and instructional ends can be generated and maintained. Third, it is not a manifesto either to be replicated or assimilated. Its uniqueness as a work is that one emulates its thrust, and preferably the user adapts his efforts to existing educational circumstances. The reader is thereby encouraged, through concepts and models, to innovate, not perform as a cultist.

This book has five germane sections and three could stand on their own as a distinct book. However, they are published together to demonstrate a need to include an analysis of process in this educational work, and the companion need to take into account the interaction of people, places and things in an Africentric education. The threads that unite them are also some of the criticism made, based upon an Africentric frame of analysis, of conventional Eurocentric approaches to education, mental health, cross-cultural psychotherapy and research. An Africentric analysis integrates the historical, contextual, interpersonal, political, social, cultural and racial. In my Africentrically grounded cultural and psychological mindset, therefore, institutions, agencies and programs that are educationally designed and geared should impart, as a general rule, language and interpersonal skills, and a range of cultural knowledge and appreciation. These are not simply

---

[28]Donald Russell (1998). *Black Genius: And the American Experience*. New York: Carroll & Graff.

[29]Maulana Karenga (2002). *Introduction to Black Studies* (3rd edition). California: Sankore Press.

prerequisite skills to justify according to a reality of eventual job use; they are essential skills for a prosperous living among human beings. This is the realization that these sections aim to foster in the drylongso scholar, researcher, parent, business leader, teacher and political leader. To be tuned in means that they adhere to a spiritual and material DNA code, one that engulfs the way they problem-solve, dress, articulate and even dwell.

This angle of vision is psychology. To illustrate, the educational practices depicted in this book are more apparent since most readers have experienced some form of formal education. A formal knowledge of psychology is comparatively less known, and a Black psychology is even less known and understood. This psychology is a more recent evolutionary discipline starting with a Black psychology[30] and ending with an Africana one.[31] Its preliminary efforts aimed at adapting such sub-areas as clinical, counseling, experimental, educational, social, cognitive, and environmental psychology to the *Black experience*. Failing at this renovation approach, a number of psychologists grouped to form a Black, African and finally an Africana psychology to encompass the Black experience, African-derived culture and race-based socio-eonomic and political circumstance. In the behavioral sciences, it is one of the few movements to strengthen the field of psychology by fostering a paradigm shift. Similarly, it has had an interlocking relationship with the field of Black Studies.

A brief discussion on this subject will be given. It provides a guideline for comprehending the specific educational intervention used to enhance self and group worth, writing and research skills, African-American people, institutions, places and experiences.[32] Implicit in this overview is the Africana Helping notion of connecting to and

---

[30]Gerald Jackson. (1979). "The origin and development of black psychology: Implications for black studies and human behavior." *Studia Africana*, 270-293. Gerald Jackson (1982). "Black psychology as an avenue to the study of Afro-American behavior." *Journal of Black Studies*, 12(3), pp. 241-260.

[31]Gerald Jackson (2005). *Njikoka: Towards an Africentric paradigm of helping.* New Jersey: Africa World Press.

[32]Henry Gates (Ed.) (1985). *Race, writing, and difference.* Illinois: University of Chicago; Maryemma Graham, Pineault-Burke, S. & David, M. (Eds.) (1998). *Teaching African American literature.* New York: Routledge; Gerald Jackson (2005). *Delimits of American helping: Precursors of an African genesis model of helping.* New Jersey: Africa World Press; Art Young & Fulwiler, T. (Ed.) (1986). *Writing across the disciplines: Research into practice.* New Hampshire: Boynton/Cook.

augmenting relationships with Asian Americans,[33] European Americans,[34] Latino American,[35] as well as sub-groups within the African-American community.[36]

Black Studies, as the glossary reveals, is *the critical and systematic study of the thought and practice of African people in their current and historical unfolding. It stresses and offers a dynamic portrait of African life in which Africans are not simply people swept up in the experience of victimization or passive encounter in the world, but rather are active agents of their own life, engaging their environment, each other and other people in unique, meaningful and valuable ways.*[37] It is a relatively new field of intellectual inquiry with a rich and vibrant history. It is birthed in the 1960s, proclaimed as one of the most significant politically active and successful periods of Black history. It cannot, according to Dr. Karenga,[38] "be separated from it without severe damage to analytical clarity." It is part and parcel of an evolution of movements during this period that sequenced The Civil Rights Movement, The Free Speech Movement, The Anti-War Movement and the Black Studies Movement. In an updated version of his embryonic work on the field, Karenga noted that the changes that had occurred in the discipline had to be incorporated, presumably to

---

[33]Vickie Nam (Ed.) (2001). *Yell-oh girls!* New York: Quill; Frank Wu (2002). *Yellow race in America: Beyond Black & White.* New York: Basic Books; Visay Prashad (2001). *everybody was kung fu fighting Afro-Asian connections and the myth of cultural purity.* Massachusetts: Beacon Press.

[34]Cooper Thompson, Schaefer, E., & Brody, H. (Eds) (2003). *White Men Challenging Racism. 35 Personal Stories.* North Carolina: Duke University.

[35]Juan Flores (1999). *From Bomba to Hip Hop.* New York: Columbia University; Raquel Riveria (2003). *New York Ricans From the Hip Hop Zone.* New York: Palgrave Macmillan .

[36]Black Gay community - Earol Hutchinson (1999). "My gay problem, your Black problem" (pp. 303 – 305). In Devon Carbado (Ed.). *Black men on race, gender, and sexuality.* New York: New York University Press; Kim Howard & Stevens, A. (Ed.) (2000). *Out & About Campus.* New York: Alyson; Black Men - Lee Jones (Ed.) (2002). *Making It on Broken Promises.* Virginia: Stylus.

[37]Maulana Karenga (2000). *Introduction to Black studies* (2nd edition). California: University of Sankore Press, p. 352.

[38] James Turner (Ed.) (1984). *The next decade: Theoretical and reearch issues in Africana Studies.* New York: Cornell University Press; Maulana Karenga (2000). *Introduction to Black studies* (2nd edition). California: University of Sankore Press, p. 3.

foster its growth. He not only recognized a new body of literature but the "consultation and expansion of Black Studies professional organization, the emergence of Afrocentricity as a major intellectual concept, the expansion and growth of Black women's studies, the focus on classical African studies, and the rise and challenge of multiculturalism."[39]

Similarly, Black psychology has been defined by one of the progenitors of the field. According to Robert Williams (1981), then, Black psychology is *the study of human behavior conducted by Black people and for Black people. It is concerned, therefore, with the affirmation of Black people and not the negation of others. It is designed to provide a framework that will enable Black people to free our minds psychologically from oppression. It points out the problems and issues in such a way that it also has solutions attached. It is not a negatively oriented psychology; it is positively oriented. In fact, Black psychology must derive its energy from positive sources rather than from negative ones. Black psychology is not a protest psychology... It is more than a Black response to White racism. As many fields have been born out of protest, Black psychology did begin initially as a reaction to and a revolt against racism in mainstream and traditional psychology. But more importantly, it has evolved as an Afrocentric discipline that sets forth the appropriate frames of reference, concepts and research strategies for Black Americans.*[40] What shaped the discipline of Black psychology was its principles, as put forth by Dr. Williams:

Principles of Black Psychology

1. Black psychology theory must be based on African rather than European philosophy.
2. Black psychological theory must emphasize the unity of Black people. Unification is the natural state of Black people; disunity is the pathological state that is usually brought on by oppressive forces.
3. Black psychological theory must be a psychology of liberation. This means that it is a psychology of and for the Black community

---

[39]Maulana Karenga (2002). *Introduction to Black Studies* (3rd edition). California: University of Sankore Press, p. xiv.

[40]Robert Williams (1981). *The collective Black mind: An Afrocentric theory of Black personality.* Missouri: Williams & Associates (pp. 64-65).

and seeks to interpret psychological forces that are moving toward liberation.

4. Black psychological principles and theory must be transformational, i.e., they must deal with strategies designed to bring about changes in Black personalites and the broader society.
5. Black psychological theory must be pro-active rather than reactive, i.e., it must declare the status of Black people rather than engage in reactions.
6. Black personality theory must begin with positive assumptions about the basic nature of the Black man.
7. Black psychological theory must be non-comparative in nature.
8. Black psychological theory must generate new roles for professional psychologists as in the "life guard" approach. A life guard does not expect a drowning person to get out of the water and walk to the life guard tower to be saved; rather, he jumps into the water and attempts to save the drowning person. We, as psychologists, are the lifeguards; the Black community is our pool and our offices are our towers. We should not be afraid of the water, for our drowning sisters and brothers may not be able to make it to the towers (pp. 65-66).

As students of the mind, Black psychologists, especially the Africanist group, focused attention on the Eurocentric definition that enslaved the mind of African –Americans. Thus, they commenced a struggle to regain the Power to Define reality. In Jennifer Bothamley's Dictionary of Theories,[41] she defines "backlash theory as (20th century) Political Feminism Theory of male counterattack against Feminism." She further espouses:

> Women have made slow and steady, if relatively insubstantial, advances. But in response to this a semi-consciously articulated campaign, or "backlash" has developed in the last quarter of the 20th century to discredit women's aspirations and to remove their gains, and to do so by any means from propaganda to violence.

The contention here is not the legitimacy of a woman backlash theory, it is making gender the generic formulation of the backlash theory. In this book's forward, Gary notes how the Black struggle was the

---

[41] Jennifer Bothamley (1995). *Dictionary of Theories*. Washington, D.C.: Gale Research Interational Ltd, p. 43.

antecedent to all the other identity struggles, as have Akbar[42] and Karenga.[43] On the subject of backlash, he wrote:

> From the mid-1960s until the mid-1970s, racial, ethnic, cultural, gender and sexual orientation were considered important to the self-esteem of the individual. In both education and mental health, it was assumed that if we strengthen one's pride in his or her identity, it would allow for greater learning and better mental health...But, this all came to an end with the use of such phrases as "genderblind" and "colorblind." These words reflected a backlash to the various identity movements.
>
> Gerald Gregory Jackson describes this backlash in his article "The Roots of the Backlash Theory in Mental Health." He begins by providing evidence that there is indeed a black culture in the United States with its own particular set of values. While many of these values appear to be in opposition to dominant white values, they are actually complimentary and, in fact, create a form of "diunitality," where not only is there a "union of opposites," but even more, the whole is greater than the sum of the parts. That is, blacks can learn a great deal from whites and vice versa.[44]

My backlash treatise was written earlier than the feminist one and included as the source of its analysis decades of Eurocentric backlash. I did not, however, stop at revealing the backlash phenomena; I provided a conceptual and theoretical foundation for its elimination. My way of fulfilling the charge to reclaim the Power to Define, while consistent with an Africentric Helping paradigm, is an unorthodox practice even for the Africana Studies field and Black/African psychology discipline.

I was compelled, however, by a pioneering leadership spirit nurtured at Howard University during my college days. This involved attending school with Stokely, Alton Maddox, John Brittain, Sharon Pratt, Larry and Alfonso Mizell, Donny Hathaway, Caine Felder,

[42]Na'im Akbar (2000). Foreword (pp. xv-xix). In Gerald Jackson. *Precursors of an African Genesis Model of Helping.* New York: Global Publications

[43]Maulana Karenga (2000). *Introduction of Black Studie* (2nd editon): University of Sankore Press.

[44]Gary Weaver (1994). *Culture, communication and conflict Readings in intercultural relations.* Massachusetts: Simon & Schuster.

Madison Richardson, Togo West, Glegg Watson, Paula Giddings, Leon Dash, Therman Evans, Freddie Perren, Edison Jackson, Floyd Atkins, Harry Simmons, Sanford Cloud, George Smith, Patrick Swygert, Richard and Valerie Wesley, Phylicia Allen, Larry Gibson, Shirley Clarke-Franklin, Charlene Moton, Houston Baker, Ming Smith and Eileen Boyd, to name a few.

All areas of academia, therefore, need an upgrade because even the students of the 60s, who started the innovative Black Studies field, are now the elders who have been faulted for not encouraging enough their replacements.[45] At Cornell, the landmark for Black student protest, we continue to do progressive things such as getting our students involved in presenting scholarly papers at Black professional conferences and managing such events, supporting students learning about the conservative elements on campus and speaking at campus rallies. What is not prominent is the Africentric pedagogy that surrounds such efforts and demonstrative proof of the efficacy of such experiences in the classroom.

In the end, its pertinence is what it all means for inspiring and educating African Americans and related African Diaspora groups (e.g., Afro-Latino). Many know that there is a long history of books on the subject of educating African Americans and a stream that explicates an Africentric approach.[46] Despite the waxing volumes on Black/Africana Studies, the field has been characterized as "surviving but not thriving."[47] What is frequently missing from these works and others on the education of Blacks is the nexus between concepts, theories and practices. Step 1 in this delineation is the presentation of the syllabus I used to guide the Africentric teaching discussed in this book.

---

[45] See Bakari Kitwana (2002). *The Hip Hop Generation*. New York: BasicCivitas; Russell Simmons (2001). *Life and Def.* New York: Crown.

[46] Jacqueline Bobo, Hudley, C. & Michael, C. (Eds.). (2004). *The Black studies reader*. New York: Routledge; Mwalimu Shujaa (Ed.) (1994). *Too much schooling Too Little Education*. New Jersey: Africa World Press; Willy D. Smith & Chunn, E. (Eds.) (1993). *Black education. A quest for equity and excellence*. New Jersey: Transaction Publishers; Carter G. Woodson (1933). *The miseducation of the Negro*. Washington, DC: Associated Publishers; Maulana Karenga (2002). *Introduction to Black Studies* (3rd edition). California: University of Sankore Press.

[47] Herb Boyd. (February 12, 2003). *The Black World Today*, p. 1.

Syllabus for Whom? Some of My Cornell Students

A prerequisite discussion to my course syllabus one is the nature of the intended students. As I have detailed elsewhere,[48] I am not an adherent of the Doctrine of Colorblindness, and I do believe there are universal virtues to the notion of diversity. Before I had a well-defined philosophy to guide my actions, I was attracted to institutions and students that reflected cultural, ethnic, geographical, age and religious differences. It can be documented, therefore, that I have been dealing with special populations of students my entire professional life. Briefly, I cut my teeth on students that "dropped-out" of public schools and sought advancement through a combination of job training and compensatory education.[49] I successfully administered educational programs at Yale University that aimed to prepare visible minority and economically disadvantaged students to be students at elite White colleges and universities.[50]

Moreover, to deepen my appreciation of differences, I have consciously selected teaching and administering positions at State, Catholic, Presbyterian and community colleges and universities. My experience at Cornell, consequently, is best viewed as another dot in a spiral definition of time, and another "special student population." It is within this context that a succinct discussion on my students is viewed as pertinent. There are few discourses and studies on the educational process of African-American students at elite White colleges and universities.[51] I wrote on the pre-college and post-high school

---

[48]Gerald Jackson (2000). *Precursor of an African genesis model of helping.* New York: Global Publications.

[49]Gerald Jackson (1972). "The use of role playing job interviews with job corps females." *Journal of Employment Counseling*, 9, 130-139.

[50]Ren Frutkins (October, 1969). "Mysteries of a mixed success, Yale Summer High School, 1969." *Yale Alumni Magazine,* pp. 26-33; Nancy Larrick (1970). *I heard a scream in the streets: Poems by young people in the city.* New York: M. Evans and Company.

[51]See Walter Allen, Epps, E. & Haniff, N. (Eds.) (1991) *College in Black and White.* New York: State University of New York Press; Carter G. Woodson (1919). *The education of the Negro* (first published by Associated Publisher). New York: A & B Book Publishers.

There are even rarer studies of White students in Africana Studies courses, especially devoted to Black literature and writing. See Victoria Boynton (2001). "Whiteness studies and literature classrooms: Confronting Denial and defensiveness in White students" (pp. 199–209). In Seth Asumah & Johnston-

experience and wanted to conduct and write a follow-up study that would help determine the educational advantages of Black and White colleges for African-American students. However, my proposed study was not deemed paramount enough to fund by the authorities I contacted. There have been studies since then; however, they have not included either a worldview perspective or African psychology framework.[52]

The syllabus is a discussion on what kind of person took this course and participated in other reported experiences. Noting that the majority of students are from Cornell University and that background information on them can be found in the biographical sketch section is not enough. Such information does not capture group differences found relevant to teaching Africana Studies courses. While my students are not posed as representative because they do not include Black students who have internalized a negative stigma of Black Studies courses and refuse to take any, nor students who are not attracted to my courses, they have been a disproportionate representation of the Black campus leadership. I have observed, when I look at the list of the 25 Most Influential Cornellians, that a majority of the Black students have taken one or more of my courses. What have intrigued me have been the subculture types. There are emerging subculture configurations that shape the classroom expectations, preferences and propensities of my students.

There are American-African students. They are the first-generation offspring of African parents. Many of these students report internalized negative stereotypes of African Americans that they have learned from their parents. The Black experiences that guide African-American students frequently elude American-African students and can create disharmony when such students define and react to Blackness as just biogenetic.

Another set of students, not totally exclusive from the American-African, is African-American students schooled in predominantly White Prep and Catholic schools. Often, they have little Black experiential knowledge and appreciation of Afrospace, African-American social, cultural, religious and political institutions.

Anumonwo, I. (Ed.). *Issues in Africa and the African Diaspora in the 21st Century*. New York: Global Publications.

[52]See William Bowen & Bok, D. (1998). *The shape of the river*. New Jersey: Princeton University Press; Richard Zweigenhaft & Domhoff, G. (2003). *Blacks in the White elite*. New York: Rowan & Littlefield Publishers.

Less cohesive, but in existence and gaining in identification, are Afro-Latinos. An increasing number have taken my courses and one result has been a change in assignments and use of books to incorporate an Africana Studies perspective. A number are beginning to wrestle with gaining a voice that reflects their African subculture and experience in the Latino worlds in South and Central America, the United States and the Caribbean.

There are varieties of biracial students on campus that have formed an organization to meet their needs. Many of these students are culturally different from such students in the past because they have not grown up in Afrospace. Therefore, they are not psychologically, culturally and spiritually Black. On rare occasions, I have had students who are White and non-White and non-Black. For the most part, the biracial students taking my courses have been children from Black and White parents. They typically express more dissatisfaction with the Africana Studies configuration of an African-American or Black individual. They claim to be in a province that is neither Black nor White but frequently exhibits Eurocentric thinking. The Jewish students are usually socially conscious and express an attraction to the subject because of its similarity to anti-semitism, and the course opportunity to touch on homophobia, sexism and classism.

One such illustration is the following extra-credit report by Jared Wolf, a White Jewish male Cornell student. He wrote, in response to a lecture by Dr. Manning Marable, a renowned African-American scholar:

> Malcolm X was basically the anti-Martin Luther King, a man who devoted his life to teaching Black people to hate and resent Whites and to have no relationship with Whites unless it involved being violent towards them. He devoted his life to preaching this anti-social ideology until he got what was coming to him, when he was assassinated for being so hateful. At least, this is always what I had been taught growing up in school and through the people in my community. It is astonishing to me how much his legacy has been manipulated and misconstrued in the White community, and I'm fortunate to have had the opportunity to attend Dr. Manny Marable's lecture on the fallacies in mainstream America concerning Malcolm X and his untimely death.
>
> Marable began by discussing some injustices that exist for minorities in society today, especially politically. He stated that out of five million Americans who lost the right to

44

vote because of felony convictions that led to their disenfranchisement, 50% were Black and 25% Latino. He then stated how Bush had weaseled his way into winning the Presidential elections by less than a thousand votes in some places, which would not have occurred had the disenfranchised been allowed to vote. This got me thinking about how frustrating America could be, minorities are more likely to be punished more harshly by the American judicial system than Whites, and therefore more of them are more likely to lose the right to vote. Consequently, minorities have less power politically, and cannot muster up enough votes to go against the corrupt politicians that held them back in the first place. This is just a vicious cycle that leads to minorities having less and less of say about how their government is run and what rights they deserve to have.

Right after discussing this, as if to show the contrast between the megalomania of Bush and the self-sacrificing nature of Malcolm X, Marble talked about what the latter actually was like as a person. He stated that Malcolm X was clearly intelligent and charismatic, but also had an acute ability to critique himself and really think about what was good for society, something that Marble said was conspicuously missing from most of today's politicians. This made me think of Bush, and how yesterday on the news I heard him talk about how attending the Constitution to prevent gay marriages was what was right society because most Americans agreed with him. Had he pulled a Brother Malcolm and actually took a minute to think of whether this really what was right and not just what would increase his popularity rating, maybe he would have taken a different stance on the issue.

Marable alluded to Malcolm's involvement with selling drugs, which reminded me of how a lot of people I know would always make mention of the illegal activities he took part in such as dealing drugs and prostitution. I went on the official Malcolm X website and found out that Malcolm actually was at the top of his class in junior high school, having aspirations of becoming a lawyer, but when his teacher told him this was "no realistic goal for a nigger," he gave up this dream and soon dropped out of school. Malcolm X's life could actually be seen as a paradigm for how many White people view minorities who commit crimes; everybody mentions the illegal activities he took part in, but are either ignorant or just don't care that it was society that put him in the position in the first place.

The majority of Marable's lecture discussed the actual assassination: how it looks as though it is possible that certain groups may have been involved in the shooting and how the media was guilty of misconstruing the events in order to reaffirm middle-America's erroneous perception of all Blacks in order to make a profit. When Marable said that Malcolm X was written in the White media as a segregationist and racist hate-monger, most of the people at the lecture made gestures at how ridiculous this was and laughed at the absurdity of the media. I felt so ignorant at this moment because although I never really believed this to be true (I have always been cynical of what my teachers would tell me about topics not concerning middle-class white people), I never really took the time to find out the truth about Malcolm X, either. Marable said that the media portrayed the assassination as a feud between two rival hate groups, when this was not the case and only served to hurt the public's view of Malcolm X and his followers even more.

Marable went over plenty inconsistencies and suspicious actions on the part of various groups concerning the assassination, such as the NYPD, who actually planted agents in the Nation of Islam and Malcolm's group. Not surprisingly, the media never discussed this and no inquiry was ever made to see if the NYPD was involved in the murder. Marable also pointed out many other facts concerning the assassination that make one question whether there was actually more than one group involved, whether the government played a direct role, and whether Malcolm X actually knew that the murder might take place that day.

What touched me the most about Dr. Manny Marable's lecture was that even though his whole talk about the injustices that have occurred and continue to occur concerning minorities in society, Malcolm X's assassination, and middle America's perception of the man himself, his tone was never really one of bitter as much as pride. Marable said that "Malcolm was our manhood...Dr. King belonged to the entire world, but Malcolm belonged to us." If his assassination was indeed inevitable like my teachers always insinuate, it would have been because he had no fear in standing up for what was right, unlike Bush who stands up for what is White. Maybe facing intense opposition just goes with the territory for people like Malcolm, but how else can you really stand up for minorities without going against the majority? I'm glad that I had the opportunity to attend Dr. Manny Marable's lecture and finally got to find out the truth behind Brother Malcolm.

My writing seminar attracts more White lesbians than homosexual males, at least in terms of classroom presentation. My Asian-American students have been increasingly of South Asian descent.[53] They have been verbal about being Brown people and experiencing struggles related to culture and color. They have not, however, used their differences to avoid learning and appreciating the Black experience offered by my courses. The Korean and Chinese students have been less disclosing about their motivation and more typically in the realm that was revealed in Nam's book[54] and others on Asian Americans (e.g., footnote 515). The unique struggles of a representative sample of these students are hinted in the close of this book and appear in one of my Africentric Helping books.[55]

Empowering Black Students

Regrettably, too few of my Black male students attended the lecture. To foster such behavior, an empowerment process for African-American males must start in their first year. On a college level, a program can be advanced by having males participate in off-campus leadership program conferences. The following informal note gives evidence of its role, especially when the leaders are individuals that students have studied in Africana courses. In this instance, Kevin Powell's writings and life experiences[56] have been pivotal considerations in my First Year Writing Seminar, detailed in several of

---

[53]See, Vickie Nam (Ed.) (2001). *Yell-Oh Girls!* New York: Quill; Vijay Prashad (2000). *The Karma of Brown Folk.* Minnesota: University of Minnesota Press.

[54]Vickie Nam (Ed.) (2001). *Yell-Oh Girls!.* NewYork: Quill.

[55]Gerald G. Jackson (2005). *Njikoka: Towards an Africentric Paradigm of Helping.* New Jersey: Africa World Press.

[56]Kevin Powell (2003). *who's gonna take the weight?* New York: Three Rivers Press; Kevin Powell (Ed.) (2000). *Step into a world.* New York: John Wiley & Sons; Keven Powell (1997). *keepin' it real.* New York: Ballantine.

my other books,[57] and touched upon earlier. What follows is an informal note and writing seminar essay by a first year African-American male student.

hey prof. Jackson,

how was the break? i wanted to email you to let you know what happened to me over the break. On jan. 8-11 i had the opp. to go to the national black leadership conference held in williamsburg, va. it was phenomenal! best of all was that i had the chance to hear kevin powell speak. He spoke about leadership and how it was important to reach success. afterwards i also bought his new book, whose gonna take the weight now? and got it signed by him after he spoke. What was better about the whole experience was that while he was signing my book he asked me where i was from and i said without hesitation "atlanta" he said oh yeah, and he told me to take his business card because he was coming to atlanta on jan 18 to speak about the state of black men in america. i went and it was great. i emailed him and he told me about the event and requested that i come out. i thought the whole experience was rather ironic considering that we had just spent a whole semester talking about the influence of his book, keeping it real. also at the conference was nikki giovanni, i got a book signed by her too. elaine johnson, lorrain (sic Lerone) bennet jr. author of before the mayflower, and harriet tubbs jones first black woman in congress. i had a great time but most of all i really learned the value of leadership and how adversity does not hinder but help us to reach our goals by making us stronger. Also this semester i am in prof. blacksheer's class on black women writers.

thanks seeya soon,

Justin Davis

---

[57]See Gerald Jackson (2005). *Delimits of American Helping: Precursors of an African Genesis Model of Helping.* New Jersey: Africa World Press; (2005) *Njikoka: Towards an Africentric Paradigm of Helping.* New Jersey: Africa World Press. For a synopsis of Powell, see Lynda Richardson (April 7, 2004). The real world, real life, can be redefining. *The New York Times Metro*, p. B2.

Do not let the informality of Justin's prose fool you into thinking that he has a limited command of the English language. Much more indicative of his level of functioning is an essay he submitted on Kevin Powell in my first year writing seminar course. It reveals writing skills and insightfulness that match the approach in the book Identity Lessons.[58] I am including the essay because it shows the merits of encouraging students to write about out-of-class experiences. Powell is a transgenerational intracultural communication writer and I use his autobiography to promote creative writing and clearer thinking. This is manifested in the ensuing essay on Powell by Justin.

Justin Davis
FWS
10-3-03

Keeping it real enough for you?

I really admire Kevin Powell. He tells it like it is. To you or me, it may seem too boisterous or too farfetched but nonetheless he keeps it real. He also understands that being black is real too. Whether Caribbean, African or African American; being black is a reality that we as people of color must face. Powell addresses the notion of blackness in his book keeping it real. Before I move on let me explain what I mean by blackness. Blackness to me is the culture, the language, the trials, the tribulations, and most of all the mentality. The mindset of common black folk is truly very different from that of any other race. We like to consider ourselves as one connected unit body functioning to show to the world what being black is and ain't. Being black is most times very rewarding, hence select ones that are not black often mock our way of slang and fashions, as well as very odd when you continuously stand out from others whether you want to or not sometimes to be seen as a thief, poor, a thug, a hoe, a nigger or just simply black. In fact the true name to call African-Americans is Nubian, just as the proper name to call whites is Caucasian.

---

[58]Marta Gillan & Gillan, J. (Eds.) (1999). *Identity lessons*. New York: Penguin Books.

In Powell's book, he talks about his life and the ways in which his less than accepted lifestyle enabled him to become real. In order for him to become what one refers to as real he had to allow himself to live through the various levels of blackness commonly referred to as nigresence. Nigrescence is the stage throughout an African American's or person of color's life in which his concept of himself and the world around him change to fit his corresponding level of blackness. Powell goes through these stages as he recounts his life from the time he and his best friend were young kids, to the time where his heart constantly yearned for the love of his ex-girl Nina. Powell enters the first of the four stages called the pre-encounter stage where the esteem of the black face drapes over the thought that the black life is not as good as other lives, just as he moved away from what is considered the ghetto. He and his mother, who if you have been reading is not the wealthiest person in the world, along with his boy Anthony and his mother moved to a predominately white area. The fact is, and Powell mentions this in his story, that most blacks saw access to white schools, white neighborhoods, and job opportunities previously reserved for whites as the key to freedom. In addition, of course they were not alone in believing this because even the people that graduated from college felt this way. It was a commonly accepted thought for those blacks that spent most of their lives in the pre-encounter stage. Powell in this area began to take on white tendencies, as well as lusted to be white and to live the white life, which stereotypically is seen as being wealth, two parents, and in an upstanding living area. At this point Powell felt as if his life was not worth as much as the white life and thereby would lead him to look at himself in disgust and wonder why he had the irregular facial features and why he never had any money, and how his color was not as good as their color, and how his family was embarrassing to him, and how…. I could go on. The question is, is it that as long as Kevin looked at himself and his blackness he only wanted to change? No, he was just confused or was he?

The best part about reading this story was how he was able to capture the reader's best interest and use it to prolong his story for what may seem short but is actually over a length of 5-6 pages. An example would be the story earlier referred about his move out of the life unyielding to sociological activity. The story also leads into the second stage of nigrescene called the encounter state. The encounter stage is where an experience in the life of the journeymen pushes him to begin to dislike others unlike him and becomes motivated to be more black (if you will). It was somewhat interesting to hear him speak about the experiences within the neighborhood that led him to become more aware that he was not assimilating but slowly being ostracized from what in the beginning, he thought was good. He uses the BONES story, which is an acronym for Beat On Niggas Every Second, to tell about how this group of white guys would taunt the blacks and at times beat them. Powell feared that his world of white surrounding was beginning to feel as a world of hardships and confusion, keep in mind this is a world he and his mother left before. This not what he wanted, this is not what he needed and he now is confused about the people around as well as the person within him. This term "nigga" has been laden upon him and now what is he to do? He does just what any kid in his situation would do he conceals it and focuses on what he secretly wants to be white.

It wasn't until his days at Rutgers University when he found that this concept of being white was a pipe dream and that it was a way to give closure to what confusion still existed from his big move out of the ghetto. He then realized that his life was progressing quickly to the next stage of nigrescence called the immerging and emerging stage. This is where the person has taken the experiences of the past and used them to submerge him into blackness. Powell recounts that his white American heroes fell by the wayside, and that he within this neo-Reagan era was vast becoming more and more submerged in the black Diaspora, and how he now says he sees the world in a different set of eyes and how he grew to despise everything he was taught. It's a different world, and UPN and other broadcasting networks were not the only ones to see that change was coming. After getting kicked out of college and wondering where he belonged in the world, just as Ralph Ellison's character did in *Invisible Man*, he was almost alone.

This now leads to the final stage of nigrescence, the internalization stage. This stage, as Powell writes it, is somewhat vague because he jumps to a point in his life where he just wants to get away from what he grew up around. The last stage made him feel compassionate about those he left behind especially his mother. Instead or going back to deal with those who have not traveled his journey, he backs away and starts a new chapter of his life. His now famous life beckons him to return to see just what he missed by running away, by letting his selfishness get the best of him, and by moving on without his people. The question that really gets me is that, yeah his friend Anthony experienced just about the same things he did, (don't think I forgot about his best friend), but as Kevin was matriculating into being what black is defined as, was Anthony? As he went on into the military, did his thoughts for the home in Jersey ever remind him of his life before he began to travel?

After reading and then reflecting on what and how I felt, I came to the conclusion that most of us here today feel as though we have significantly moved throughout the stages of nigrescene. To keep it real with you, no we have not. We are at the very beginning stages of this concept of identity. If you don't agree and most of you won't then I ask you to look back throughout your life and pin point the times where you were in a certain stage. And then ask yourself the question "what stage led me to Cornell?" What stage led me on one of the biggest decisions of my life to come here? A school highly accredited amongst the white community and naively talked about amongst some black communities. It feels as if I am at a point where I am confused about exactly where I stand on certain issues, or what I think about the idea of being black. In truth, the concept of blackness is confusing, especially to those who are at the brink of believing that once you go black you can never go back. When I look at what all I have accomplished and what it took to get to this point, I still wonder for whom is the work benefiting beside me. Keepin it real for me conveys truth within a world of false people and false values. Powell's idea about keeping it real is what the black community needs. I think the reason behind his truthfulness is that as a child it seemed as if his life lacked reality and was more focused around surviving everyday with the hopes that one day moving on up, and at times missed the truth that most people who are not living in that lifestyle were given. Nevertheless, the question still comes up, what does this all mean? To answer that all I can say is just keep it real.

Student Reaction to Kevin Powell as Black History Month Speaker[59]

I must admit that before attending his lecture on Sunday afternoon my image of Powell was limited to the angry black man with all the trimmings of sexism, anger, and an uncontrollable temper. I was not overly excited or looking forward to the rants and raves of another "successful" African American man attempting to find excuses for his actions. I didn't want him to brainwash me telling me about the faults of the system. I did not want to hear that it was society that had made him erupt that it was the news, the music, and his upbringing that had produced this stereotypical black male. I had read the first chapter of his book, a letter to his estranged cousin Anthony and it was plagued with societal clichés. I wasn't sympathetic to his cause and I found his writing simplistic and boring, in other words I had heard it all before and I wasn't in the mood to hear it again.

One may ask then, why did I attend? Well there are two reasons; one was because Professor Jackson made it seem mandatory (but then again is there really anything mandatory in college) and the second reason being that I wanted to be proven wrong. To my surprise, it wasn't mandatory and I was proven wrong. Kevin Powell is a successful black man who understands the faults with society but refuses to be a product of society. He is an individual who realizes his past mistakes and understands that to move on to become a better person there is a level of shame and pride that is needed of one's notorious and sometimes painful past. Kevin Powell can now be seen as a successful black leader and one of the answers to Martin Luther King's speech "Where do we go from here?" Powell doesn't have all the answers, he is neither a God, nor

---

[59]Program was held on February 29, 2003 at Goldwinsmith Hall, Cornell University. It was sponsored by The LINK and Alpha Phi Alpha fraternity. The title of Powell's talk was "The New Underground Railroad." The power of these presentations are based upon the interracial classroom discussion and unconventional discussion of such things as racism in White women. See, Lawrence Bloom (November/December, 1998). "Can we talk? Interracial dialogue in the university classroom." *Change,* pp. 27–37; Mario Anderson (January 28, 2002). "My enounter with White feminist racism." *Konch Magazine,* pp. 1-5.

the God but he is undoubtedly a mechanism for positive change within the African American Community, a Moses of the African American Community.

It was the last day of Black History Month when Kevin Powell came to speak, and I must admit that this time it flew by faster than usual. I could blame it on the University, that there wasn't enough emphasis on the importance of this month. But what more could I want than a speech on Affirmative Action, another on Malcolm X, a few movies in Cornell Cinema featuring black actors, and of course my favorite a soul food dinner. The truth of the matter is that the disappearance of the importance was undoubtedly no fault but my own. Now in my own defense I must say I was busy, taking 20 credits, working, weekly debate trips to the other Ivies, did not leave much time for sleep much less recognizing the efforts and achievements of my brothers and sisters. Regardless, I was ashamed sitting in front of Kevin Powell, calling myself a strong black woman when I felt like he was talking about me. I passively knew that I wasn't really helping the African American cause but I never really said it aloud. I reasoned that I was going to Cornell, going to make a lot of money, what more could the community want from me? What I so desperately needed was someone to tell me that I needed a radical revolution of values. As he spoke those words…Radical Revolution of Values I wanted to hide my face. He knew exactly what my problem was; I was sitting at the table of diversity and not knowing anything of my past. How did I expect to create a future if I didn't know my past? I saw flaws and as I looked around the room, I wondered if everyone else saw their flaws? If they had any? Was I the only one? Was I the only one who wasn't tired nor exhausted because they hadn't tried, or because they had no vision? What had I created or achieved that I could pass onto future generations? I know I am young but these questions plagued my mind as I ran out of the room, not wanting to face anyone for fear of them seeing through my transparency. I knew Kevin was right, far too many of black youth shared my mentality, and I feared for the future of the black race.

As I sat in Uris, trying to settle my thoughts so I could actually be productive, Kevin's words echoed in my head. I recalled the old Kevin and the fact that I thought I was so much different from that Kevin but the fact of the matter was that I wasn't. I was mentally living the life Kevin had left behind. I was adding more poison to the system. Here I was, studying at such a prestigious University thinking I was a real leader that I had made it…but in reality I had barely began the journey. When I lived my life, I was under the impression I was living it for me, and maybe my present and future family. Kevin opened my eyes to the hard facts of life, I have to represent, take hold of the responsibilities that come along with this privilege. Yes, I am not a thug, and yes I know that my contribution won't be overnight, and transitions such as this have to be taken in small steps but as a promise to myself I will change. I will think about the life I want my future race to be in 100 years and I will make it so. After hours of contemplation, a new question plagued my mind…Would I be doing this alone?

Sorbrique Grant

Striving for Africentric Balance, not Eurocentric Dichotomy

The informal note and essays reveal a balance between the experiential and the cognitive components of learning that is a derivative of my Africentric cultural approach to teaching. My delight in seeing the connection I thought was based upon my student affairs background. However, a development initiated by Howard students reminded me of the education and inspiration I received at HU. My daughter Melissa introduced me to the materials she had received from a former classmate who expressed pride in the work of her *Howard ambassadors*. Howard undergraduate men developed a website called DCC Collegelife.com. Demonstrative of the *extended self-affirmation*, it is a holistic guide for all college students in the DC metropolitan area. The creators of the website did not focus exclusively on Howard or Black colleges in the area; they conducted research on each campus. The final product includes articles, music reviews, shopping, art galleries, museums, performance art, education, health/beauty, organizations and entertainment information, and opportunities. The website is *fluid and flexible* and offers readers several ways to add, correct and modify the website. I was taught, therefore, to stimulate the sharing of knowledge. In general, I find Cornell students to be extremely hardworking, intelligent, dutiful, open-minded, humorous and prone to be creative, when encouraged. Many are warm and caring individuals who have not given up on the older generation, although elitist about cohorts in the non-Ivy League colleges. My course syllabus reflects my appreciation for their minds, relative venturesome nature and diligent ways. It is an organic document. It develops by adjusting to changes in student populace, such as including the post Hip-Hop generation starting in college in 2003.Essentially, it is an educational proposal that explains what I hoped to do, how I expected to do what I proposed, and why I do what I do. As an additional guide, presented is the course syllabus that frames the majority of the material described in this book. Similarly, background on the conceptual base of the course and co-curricula outside classroom learning is outlined. This discussion consists of a review of a worldview chart and the place of Africana Studies in Africentric helping education.

The practical application of this work Is illustrated in a January 7, 2005 e-mail from a former Cornell student. Several years after graduation and obtainment of a master's degree, David Ladd wrote:

> I work as a counselor in the program services department . . . My main duty is to create and run programs and classes for the boys when they are not in school . . . I will soon be starting a TV production class . . . In addition, my bosses were intrigued by my educational background and abilities, and so I was put in charge of establishing an independent living program for all residents. While this is a huge task to undertake, I am kind of excited by this because I am getting a chance to create something I wrote much about at Cornell .
> . . a multicultural educational curriculum. Instead of following the "traditional" setup for an independent living program (which is supposed to teach the residents how to "survive" in the real world), I am going to establish classes that follow the multicultural philosophies that I learned so much about at Cornell . . . In other words . . . your afrocentric chart is going to find some real-world application ☺. . .
>
> In addition to the programs I create, I am also assigned to mentor and help some of the residents at the facility, working in conjunction with their various therapists. I really enjoy those interactions, and the boys I have begun working with have really warmed up to me quickly. All three of the kids I work with at the moment are 14 years old. Two are African American, one is Hispanic. Ninety-five percent of the kids at the placement are actually Hispanic or African American. The staff at the lodge is pretty diverse though. All

the kids originally went to juvenile hall for gang activity, theft, drug use, minor forms of assault or carrying weapons . . . There isn't any real violence or outrageously bad behavior at the facility . . . probably because the kids can actually walk off the grounds and leave anytime they want, because there are no gates, and the staff is not allowed to physically stop them . . .

Anyway, the job . . . makes me feel like I am positively contributing to society and helping these boys out. The pay is very little and I have to work weekends on occasion, but . . .

Africana Studies & Research Center 172

The Education of Black Americans:
Historical and Contemporary Issues
Spring, 2003 Semester
Cornell University

PROFESSOR: Gerald G. Jackson
TA ags@cornell.edu
OFFICE: B12 Africana Studies & Research Center
PHONE: 617-255-8379
E-MAIL: GGJI@cornell.edu and Cutthroatgener@cs.com
CLASS MEETINGS: MW – 2:55 p.m. - 4:10 p.m., UH
OFFICE HOURS: M – 1:30 - 2:30 and W – 1:00 - 2:30 p.m.

COURSE OVERVIEW

This course examines the African-American struggle for an education that enhances their group's social, economic and psychological well-being. Critical attention is given to various cultural approaches to an African-American education in the USA. Subjects of study include historical debates and analysis over the type of education that would most benefit Black peoples and contemporary struggles over culturally and politically appropriate educational programs and institutions. In addition, attention is given to educational efforts by an elite group of African Americans to secure economic and social success for the masses of Black people, compensatory educational programs and institutions to rehabilitate Blacks, and educational institutions championed by Black political, religious and cultural groups.

COURSE OBJECTIVES AND OUTCOMES

Students will be provided with an Africentric perspective for interpreting efforts to educate African Americans. Similarly, they will be provided Africentric experiential learning opportunities and activities to deepen their understanding of the educative process undergirding an Africentric analytical framework. In the end, successful students can identify groups, programs, institutions and concepts that will optimally educate African Americans.

COURSE REQUIREMENTS

The course requirements listed below are designed to measure subject comprehension through a variety of modes of instruction. The student will be expected to show, through group projects and written examinations, the course mastery of class lectures and discussions. Attendance is mandatory, and it is the responsibility of the student to report to the professor class lateness.

Spontaneous quizzes (no make-ups)	10%
Prelim one (classroom lectures and discussions)	
February 25, 2002	15%
Prelim two (based upon class discussions, film	
Viewing and readings)	15%
Course participation (speaking and attending	
outside interactive programs & films)	15%
Group Presentation, library assignment and	
Journal April 24, 29 and May 2, 2002	20%
Final Prelim (class discussions, lectures, group	
presentations May 14th)	25%

EXTRA CREDITS

Book Report - Required typed submission (including 11/2 inch margins, double-spaced, Times Roman font), and should be between two and three pages. This synopsis entails a use of a book on the recommended reading list and should include a discussion of the relevance of the book to 172 course, your learnings and recommendations for use by other students.

Outside talks and events - Required typed submission (including 11/2 inch margins, double-spaced, Times Roman font), and between two and three pages in length. This summary should be related to the Africana Studies and Research Center and on campus that pertains to objectives and content of the 172 course.

Research Paper - Required typed submission (including 11/2 inch margins, double-spaced, Times Roman font), and should be between 10 and 15 pages in length. The research paper topic has to be approved by the professor by the third week of the semester, and has to focus on an aspect of the 172 course.

GROUP PRESENTATION PROJECT OVERVIEW

Objectives
1. To enhance the experiential learning of the African concept of the group.
2. To provide a personal opportunity to explore course areas in a way that produces creative and innovative academic results.
3. To provide a review of the course material in preparation for the final prelim.

Requirements:
1. 6 or more individuals are required to form a group.
2. Group presentation based upon 172 course topic areas.
3. Each member of the group is to write an individual chronological account of their group experience and submit this journal at the close of the last class. It is developmental in structure and includes observations made of group developments, struggles, triumphs and personal insights gained.
4. The group presentation should stay within the time constraints set forth by the Professor while fulfilling points 1-3.

Evaluation
1. Assessment reports completed by the class.
2. Overall evaluation by the professor, based primarily upon an Africentric definition of a group (e.g., group oneness of being, fluidity, creativity, group self-knowledge revealed, journals) and class assessments.

REQUIRED COURSE TEXTS

1. Akoto, K. Agyei (1992). *NATION BUILDING Theory and Practice in Afrikan Centered Education.* Washington, D.C.: Pan Afrikan World Institute.
2. Woodson, Carter G. (1933). *The Mis-education of the Negro.* New Jersey: Africa World.
3. Shujaa, Mwalimu J. (1998). *Too much schooling Too Little Education: A Paradox of Black Life in White Societies.* New Jersey: Africa World.
4. Course package (obtain from KC copy in college town)

RECOMMENDED COURSE READINGS

Banks, James A. (1970). *Teaching the Black Experience*. California: Fearon.

Barrett, Paul (1999). *The Good Black - A True Story of race in America*. New York: Dutton. Bowen

William G. & Bok, Derek (1998). *THE SHAPE OF THE RIVER: Long-Term Consequences of Considering Race in College and University Admissions*. New Jersey: Princeton University.

Carnoy, Martin (1977). *Education as Cultural Imperialism*. New York: Longman.

Clark, Reginald C. (1983). *Family Life and School Achievement Why Poor Black Children Succeed or Fail*. Illinois: University of Chicago.

Franklin, J. (1969). *From Slavery to Freedom*. New York: Vintage.

Gary, Lawrence E. & Favors, Aaron (Eds.) (1975). *Restructuring the Educational Process: A Black Perspective*. Washington, D.C.: Howard University Institute for Urban Affairs and Research.

Gordon, Edmund W. & Wilkerson, Doxey A. (1966). *Compensatory Education for the Disadvantaged*. New York: College Entrance Examination Board.

Goggins, Lathardus (1996). *African Centered Rites of Passage and Education*. Illinois: Images.

Kunjufu, Jawanzaa (1993). *Hip-Hop vs. Maat: A Psycho/Social Analysis of Values*. Illinois: African-American Images.

Hale, Janice E. (1986). *Black Children Their Roots, Culture, and Learning Styles*. Maryland: John Hopkins University.

Hare, Nathan & Hare, Julia (1991). *The Hare Plan*. California: The Black Think Tank.

Jackson, Gerald G. (2000). *The African Genesis of a Black Perspective in Helping*. New York: Global.

Johnson, Roosevelt (Ed.) (1974). *Black Scholars on Higher Education in the 70's*. Ohio: Education-Community Counselors Association.

Ladson-Billings, Gloria (1994). *The Dreamkeepers Successful Teachers of African American Children*. California: Jossey-Bass.

Osa, Osayimwense (Ed.) (1995). *The All White World of Children's Books & African American Children's Literature*. New Jersey: Africa World.

READING REQUIREMENT SCHEDULE

January 21, 2002
Introduction to the course

HISTORICAL PERSPECTIVE

January 23, 2002
Carter Woodson, 1-5

January 28, 2002
Woodson, Chapters 9-18

January 30, 2002
Quiz on Carter Woodson

Classroom selection of groups and group project members.

February 4, 2002
Africentric and Eurocentric worldviews and their implications for the education of African Americans

February 6, 2002
Asa Hilliard, Sebait: African Indigenous Pedagogy from the Nile to the Niger, 69-98, Reprint package.
Hilliard, Pedagogy in Ancient Kemet, pp. 83-102 and Kemetic Concepts in Education, pp. 117-127.

February 11 and 13, 2002
Marin Camoy, Education and the Colonization of West Africa, 113-143, Reprint package.
Anderson, Ex-Slaves and the Rise of Universal Education in the South, 1866-1880, pp. 1-32.
Anderson, The Hampton Model of Normal School Industrial Education, 1868-1950, pp. 33-78 and Education as the Race Problem in the New South: The Struggle for Ideological Hegemony, pp. 79-I10.

February 18 and 20, 2002
Shujaa – Foreword, Introduction, Chapter 1, 2, 3, 4,5,6

LEADERSHIP DEVELOPMENT

February 25, 2002
Shujaa, Introduction to Part 3, Chapters 7, 8, 9, 10
Barbara A. Sizemore, pp. 185-195, Reprint package.

February 27, 2002
Prelim I (lectures, class discussions, film and readings)
Group project library assignment due.

March 4 and March 6, 2002
Hilliard, The Maroon With Us.... pp. 50-70.
Shujaa, Introduction to Part 4, Chapters 11, 12, 13

RACIAL GROUP IDENTITY AND EDUCATION

March 11, 2002
Hilliard, Socialize Our Children for the Resurrection of African People,
pp. 128-144.
Hilliard, Conceptual Confusion and the Persistence of Group Oppression Through
Education, pp. 142-159.

March 13 , 2001
Robert T. Carter, Racial Identity and Education, pp. 291-335, Reprint package.

SPRING BREAK - March 16 – 24

Black Education as Innovation

March 25 and 27, 2002
Carol Tavris (1 976). Compensatory Education Is The Glass Half Full,
pp. 63, 65, 66, 69, 70, 73, 74. Reprint package.
Gordon & Wilkerson, Compensatory Education for the Disadvantaged,
pp. 122-153. Reprint package.
Randolph Bracy, Compensatory Educational Programs, Is there a Place in Higher Education, pp. 27 -284. Reprint package.

April 1, 2002
Anderson, Training the Apostles of Liberal Culture: Black Higher Education, 1900 1935, pp. 238-278.
Ren Frutkin (I 969). Mysteries of a Mixed Success: Yale Summer High School, pp. 26-33, Reprint package.
(Gerald Jackson, Book Review of The High School Revolutionaries, p. 1 Reprint package.
Bowen & Bok, The Shape of the River, pp. 1-15; 275-290, Reprint package.
April 3, 2002
Outside lecturer – Black Studies – Where it has been and where it is going.
Reading to be assigned

April 8 and 10, 2002
Shujaa, Introduction to Part 5, Chapters 14, 15

April 15 and 17, 2002
Shujaa, Chapters 16 and Afterword.

- Extra credit material due

April 22, 2002
Hillary, Do We have the 'Will' to educate all children, pp. 194-206 and The Meaning of KIT (Ancient Egyptian) History for Contemporary African Americans, pp. 207-218.
Group Presentation delivered (Group 1)

April 24 and 29, 2002
Group Presentations delivered (Groups 2, 3, 4 and 5)

May 2, 2000
- Journals due
- Final Examination distributed (Take home final – Due May 14, 2002 by 12:00 noon – Incomplete given only after prior arrangements with Professor Jackson

DISTINGUISHING PEOPLE BY WORLDVIEW

The next section introduces the linking concept of *world-view*. The notion recognizes a global dimension of human compatibility and cultural clashes. In the latter case, it provides a cultural lens for interpreting racial and ethnic conflicts and the extrapolation of clashes between Black and White Studies. Most importantly, it leads to a method for analyzing the varied group interpretations of people, places and things.

The second step, then, is the presentation of a design that enables the reader to conceptualize world-view differences so that racial, ideological, group and personal conflicts are temporized, contextualized and theorized. A world-view chart first published by the African Psychology Institute faculty in a training module handbook is provided to enhance cross-cultural understanding.[60] More recently reported by McPhail, it provides a philosophical and cultural base for assessing paradigm differences between Black and White Studies that are rooted in cultural and racial differences.[61] In a marked way,[62] the chart epitomizes observable and documentable differences between African Americans and European Americans in thoughts, behaviors and social institutions.

Third, background on the conceptual base of the course and co-curricula outside classroom learning is outlined. This discussion consists of an examination of the application of the world-view chart in measuring the intellectual facility of students in analyzing and proposing solutions for African-American and Afro-Latino problems. It is believed that the evaluation of individual performance tends to support material analysis, while the evaluation of concepts and ideas encourages spiritual connections and relationships. Moreover, the measurement of Africentric concepts and practices is crucial in the advancement and proliferation of the Africana Studies helping field and

---

[60]The African Psychology Institute, North Florida and Atlanta Chapters, (1982).

[61]Irving McPhail (2002). "Culture, Style, and Cognition: Expanding the boundaries of the Learning paradigm for African American learners in the community college." In Lee Jones (Ed.). *Making it on broken promises.* Virgina: Stylus.

[62]Jacob Carruthers (1999). *intellectual warfare.* Illinois: Third World Press; Kobi Kambon (2003). *Cultural misorientation.* Florida: Nubian Nation Publication; Wade Nobles (1986). *African psychology.* California: Black Family Institute.

Africana psychology discipline. Currently, there is too much emphasis on what scholars say rather than what they do. In the current situation, the "doing" is the measurement of the *extended self*. The object is a group project in which there is one grade for each member of the group. The assessment of the groups was based upon journals kept by each group member, student evaluation of each group, group evaluation questions on the take home final and the professor's group evaluation. Each undertaking is intended to show how the Africentric Helping approach is more than either a theory or practice. To illustrate, McPhail's use of the world-view chart to explicate the Nairobi method is from the viewpoint of the scholar. We learn about the philosophy of the program and the techniques; however, we do not see the work of the students who are no longer *miseducated* and are motivated through *intellectual excitement*, knowledge of the educational system and their history. This is not an attack on the model; it is more of a suggestion that it is insufficient in combatting the Eurocentric *deficit model*. Despite the heroic deeds of African-American students in the 60s, they are not typically described in terms of their strengths. The eye of the clinician is usually seen and they are given pathologically based typologies, syndromes and personality flaws. In contrast, various means will be used to reveal the strengths of African-American, American-African and Afro-Latino students. What will be shown is their analytical skills, capacity to include empathy in their thinking without forfeiting reason, an appreciation of an African-American subculture, recognition of the strengths of the African-American family and social institutions, and adult clarity about their role in the resolution of human relations problems.

The next discussion extends this idea into several Africentric crevices. This pivotal work in Section I on Dr. John Henrik Clarke, akin to most of my professional pursuits, has a spiritual, pedagogical, educational, psychological and cultural component. These areas are essential elements of my definition of an Africentric Helping, to be detailed more in the text.

A decidedly European world-view differs from an African one in ways that are indicated on the world-view chart. Both are found present in the course syllabus, indicative of a diunital approach. To elaborate, a European world-view is evident in the negative stereotypes of African-Americans and the resulting *miseducated Negro/Black* that the course reveals and corrects. The orientation of African-Americans is presumed to be Eurocentric and exclusive of a distinct subculture, psychology and religious component. It birthed a plethora of Black scholarship to counteract it, and the springing of the Black Studies field. The

Eurocentric idea that any distinguishing norm that Blacks may possess is grounded in a slave experience, and based upon the actions of lower-class Black males, is repetitiously challenged. It is done by African Americans because of the perennial nature of the charge by principally White scholars and racists. In White Studies, all Blacks are considered to have a damaged sense of self because the ego ideal has to be a White, middle-class male. This postulate spearheaded the creation and development of Black mental health organizations and a Black psychology discipline. The Eurocentric human goal of hedonism, pictured as a drive for excessive sexual gratification, fancy cars and clothes, is projected upon Blacks, based upon a belief that they can't manage time well enough to build viable communities and democratic political organizations. This is so because such structures are believed to be the result of a Eurocentric culture and temporal orientation. This cultural bias is evident in the ensuing philosophical outlooks.

WORLDVIEW CHART

AFRICAN   EUROPEAN

Orientation	NATUROCENTRIC	EUROCENTRIC
Norms	HUMAN NATURE	MIDDLE CLASS, MALE CAUCASIAN
Conception of Self	EXTENDED SELF	INDIVIDUAL SELF
Human Goal	EXTENDED SELF-AFFIRMATION	GRATIFICATION
Conception of Time	CYCLICAL, PHENO-MENA	LINEAR, FUTURISTIC
Ontology (What is)	1.SPIRITUAL ESSENCE 2.COLLECTIVISM-WE-NESS 3.INTERDEPENDENCE 4.SURVIVAL OF THE COMMUNITY 5.ONENESS OF BEING/WITH NATURE	1.PHYSICAL/MATERIAL 2.INDIVIDUALISM-I-NESS 3.INDEPENDENCE 4-SURVIVAL OF THE FITTEST 5-DICHOTOMY OF BEING/CONTROL OVER NATURE
EPISTEMOLOGY (Knowledge of "What is")	1-.AFFECT/ SYMBOLIC 2.IMMERSION IN EXPERIENCE 3.FLUID AND FLEX-IBLE 4.DIUNITAL LOGIC 5.COMPLEMENTARITY OF DIFFERENCES	1.OBJECT MEASURE 2.OBSERVATION OF EXPERIENCE 3.RIGID AND FIXED 4.DICHOTOMOUS LOGIC 5.DUALITY OF OPPOSITES
Axiology (Value of "What is")	1.COOPERATION/ HARMONY 2.PRESERVATION OF LIFE 3.AFFILIATION (HUMAN-TO-HUMAN) 4.COLLECTIVE RESPONSIBILITY 5.SELF-KNOWLEDGE	1.COMPETITION/ CONFLICT 2.CONTROL OF LIFE 3.OWNERSHIP (MAN-TO- MAN) 4.INDIVIDUAL RIGHTS 5.ACQUIRING INFORMATION

Ontologically, as Americans, Blacks are perceived to think in dichotomous or either/or ways, and honor individualism, independence and the survival-of-the-fittest concept; conversely, it dishonors foreigners, the disabled, the sexually different and women. Similarly, as Americans, they are conceived to be just as dissatisfied with the vicissitudes of nature as other Americans, and seek and applaud studies that result in the maximum control over nature.

Epistemologically, they infer knowledge through "objective" measures that are based primarily upon the observation of experience. Success is determined by fixed and rigid standards that can be best understood through dichotomous logic or duality-of-opposites thinking. *Axiologically*, they would support the notion that conflict and competitiveness are the ideal motivations for family development, learning, work and religion. They would support, consequently, a value system that regards the control of life, ownership of people and things. The healthiest African Americans, in this mode of analysis, would be Blacks that advocated individual rights and the acquisition of information and data to justify actions.

A different view of African Americans emerges from an African world-view. This outlook is guided by a naturocentric orientation. Its concept of self is an *extended self* that is supported by a human goal that is an extended self-affirmation. Temporal notions, reported by Weaver earlier, are guided by spiral, phenomenon and "in-time" concepts.

Ontologically, a spiritual essence defines the people and their attraction to others and various religions. This ontological reality is manifested in a view that is collective, interdependent and perceives a survival of the community and a oneness with nature as the highest ideals. Capturing the essence of this philosophical outlook, Tempels[63] wrote:

> This concept of separate being, of substance (to use the scholastic terms again) which find themselves side by side, entirely independent created beings preserve a bond one with another, an intimate ontological relationship, comparable with the causal tie which binds creature and Creator...(p. 58)
>
> Just as Bantu ontology is opposed to the European concept of individual things existing in themselves, isolated from others, so Bantu psychology cannot conceive of man as

---

[63]Placide Tempels (1959). *Bantu Philosophy*. France: Presence Africaine, p. 103.

an individual, as a force existing by itself and apart from its ontological relationships with other living beings and from its connection with animals, or intimate forces around it.

Epistemologically, knowledge is based upon an immersion in experience, diunital logic and a complementarity of differences. One understands the universe through an affective-symbolic mode described as:

> In Black use, the thought is generated through the use of a picture concept (visualization), rather than through the use of a notion or theoretical statement, or a theoretical formula. In Black imagery, a picture of the thing as it really exists is put before the mind and imagination. In the Black method, one proceeds through visual thinking as against non-visual thinking. One may wish to represent this position as the concrete vs. the abstract, but this would not be accurate. In the concrete presentation of the Black concept, there is a whole lot of abstract thinking. On the other hand, it is not correct to talk about the Western thing as exclusively analytic, because it is not more analytic in method than the Black image.[64]

Axiologically, Black people are viewed as having a cooperative outlook that allows for the inclusion of all types of individuals and groups that can differ widely in phenotypic type. African Americans have a penchance to oppose politically based wars. A preservation for life is historically seen in the comparatively lower suicide rate and attraction to social organizations and institutions. A sense of collective responsibility is at the hub of the identification of Black professional organizations with all classes of African Americans, child adoptions and respect for knowledge gained through personal experiences and age. Iceberg Slim's and Malcolm X's autobiographies are the biggest-selling works on Black male growth and development in the United States, and they are based on the *Black experience* of these African-American males and not the synopsis of scientific studies and quantitatively derived data.

The John Henrik Clarke assignment in the ensuing section, therefore, is appropriately understood within the Black Studies field

---

[64]George Matthews (1977). "Voices of Africa in the diaspora." *New Directions* 4(2), p. 16.

context. This provides the basis of the course content and forges a space for the consideration of an archetypal person. Dr. Clarke's breadth, partially reflected in the section on his publications, interviews and works by others on him (see Sect. I), is the way he modeled the African Activist-intellectual tradition. This tradition, noted Dr. Maulana Karenga, dates back to ancient Egypt and "its model of the socially conscious and activist intellectual, the sesh, who understood themselves in both moral and social terms and constantly expressed a commitment to using their knowledge and skills in the service of the people."[65] Predating and grounding the Black Studies cry for service to the Black community to Egypt, the Africentric social service entailed ensuring justice, caring for the vulnerable and the environment, respecting persons as bearers of dignity and divinity, and working for future generations.

Barring the view that Egypt was the only source for educational edification, guidelines were used from other regions. Again, Dr. Karenga revealed that the sage and teacher, Orunmila in Yorubaland, "taught that the fundamental criterion for a good world and the key instrument in creating the good word is effective knowledge of things, a moral wisdom which enables human beings to come together for the purpose of increasing and sustaining good in the world."[66] Clearly, and exhibiting the African axiology noted in the world-view chart, Karenga summarized learning in African societies as: "based on the conception of knowledge which values knowledge not simply to enjoy oneself or even simply to get a job, but because of its value and role in improving the human condition and enhancing the human prospect for human future."[67]

This diunital approach, a hallmark of *Black Studies*, contrasts with the dichotomous approach to White Studies or European norms and orientation. The latter splits thoughts from actions, and scholars are credited when they detach their work from political actions. Given this historical and cultural backdrop, it can be affirmed that Dr. Clarke is the embodiment of diunital thinking and professional/scholar behaving. He is neither an activist nor intellectual, but both. Homage, therefore, at

---

[65]Maulana Karenga (2003). *Introduction to Black Studies*. California: University of Sankore Press.

[66]Maulana Karenga (2003). *Introduction to Black Studies* (p. 7). California: University of Sankore Press.

[67]Maulana Karenga (2003). *Introduction to Black Studies* (pp. 7-8). California: University of Sankore Press.

his funeral was given to him by all segments of the African-American community. His broad-based popularity, however, stemmed from his publication of his research in forms that the Black masses could comprehend and from his public display of political actions. Similarly, it was believed that the noted people at his funeral would also reflect the activist/scholar Africentric tradition. My pedagogical efforts and steps, consistent with the critical role students played in the development of Black studies, aimed at the empowering of students and the nurturing of their leadership and followship capacities.

In short, a broad objective of this work is to put the enterprise of learning in a philosophical, cultural, historical, environmental and temporal (process) context. Africana learning is predicated upon data from an Africana Studies, Writing in the Disciplines at Cornell and African Helping concept, theory and practice. Viewed as organic in nature, the approach is based upon self-knowledge gained from a variety of sources. These sources included my Harlem village and Howard University, Job Corps, Ivy Leagues (Yale and Cornell Universities), State and Catholic universities and community colleges in Newark and Connecticut (South Central Community College), and a sundry of consulting jobs. An immediate illustration of the application of these philosophically based cultural differences is the following section on the John Henrik Clarke Research assignment.

SECTION I
Dr. John Henrik Clarke Group
Research Project

The first project stems from my actual attendance at the funeral in Harlem for Dr. John Henrik Clarke. I attended the ceremony out of respect for him and rituals of the African-American community. So

GGJ & daughter Melissa. Photo of Gerald G. Jackson.

much so, that I brought my family. I wanted all of us to share and be a part of a great ritualistic moment in the life of a premiere African-American community. For my daughter, it meant being a part of the African ethos and learning how to preserve it after I am deceased.

His unusual youth appeal is captured in the following account by a former Cornell student in an extra-credit assignment essay on Dr. Clarke.

Keith Cherry
AS&RC 171
Assignment 2

"History is not everything, but it is the starting point. History is a clock that people use to tell their time of day. It is a compass they use to find themselves on the map of human geography. It tells them where they are, but more importantly, what they must be."

I was walking to the Africana Studies and Research Center one summer afternoon getting ready for my 1:25 class with professor Ohadike when I realized I left the dining hall too early and had to wait for class to commence. I sat there at first annoyed that I arrived so early, I mean after all who really wants to be early to class? I started thinking about how I misjudged the time and then I though I probably got there early because I was walking too fast to compensate for a building that was too far. I took up and scan the room similar to the behavior when waiting at the dentist's office. I see hung prominently on the wall a picture of a stern, yet seemingly kind, older man, with the familiar face of a grandfather, someone you would listen to. I did not know who he was.

John Henrik Clarke is the name of the man in the picture, more than someone to listen to, but someone with a story worth hearing. I started researching and amongst the accolades and abridged biographical accounts, I saw an article with a grabbing line, "John Henrik Clarke remembered as Master Griot." I thought back to my summer Africana course, and I remembered what a Griot was. The great storyteller of African, specifically West Africa and Nigeria were known as Griots. More than a storyteller, the Griot is to the oral tradition what any well renowned author or poet is to the literary world. The Griot is a messenger, a proponent of culture, ideas, family, events, worlds lost and history often forgotten. The oral tradition is dying if not already dead and buried.

Clarke is probably one of the most under-recognized historians of modern time. Born into sharecropping and self educated he took on a responsibility to share a history that challenges what most accept as truth. A history book is opened and the majority it serves appreciates the subtleties of race-guided historical accounts of Black people dating back to Herodotus. Probably the most formidable tool of oppression, a history is received that nearly erases the contributions and significant roles of African people, to which its absence would have been detrimental to the world we live in today so blindly. Clarke dared to challenge that by traveling, researching, teaching, rediscovering, but more importantly sharing the African history with each and every corner of the world that is relevant to the history of black people and vice versa. Clarke is the patron librarian of African people and their children. He was described by the Daily Challenge as "one of the world's foremost authorities on African history." We lost him in 1998.

Observing the attendance list from his funeral I initially could not see the connection aside from obvious admiration for some of the individuals. Wesley Snipes stood out the most to me partially because he jumped out as one of the most contemporary celebrity/socialite individuals who attended. I wondered what other connections Wesley Snipes, actor, had to the "Master Griot." Snipes is also a director and sad to say one of his lesser know projects could arguably be one of his most important, similar to a knowledge of Clarke among many young adults, my age and younger.

The 1997 Sundance Film Festival I was privileged enough to review and ultimately critique the film *John Henrik Clarke: A Great and Mighty Walk,* produced by Wesley Snipes. The film is a lesson and a tribute documenting John Henrik Clarke's life and the work he dedicated it to within the context of African history. The film uses Clarke as a centerpiece in a chronology of the African experience that could be edited to fit on film in viewing time. Aside from producing the film, it is Snipes who conceived its idea, and it is through this effort that his attendance at the funeral becomes more and more clear. A Great and Mighty Walk is a proponent to Clarke's mission, a modern multimedia spirit reincarnate. At least, Snipes was there to pay respect not just to a man but to a purpose and to a tradition that we cannot let die, making *history "our"* story.

Geoffrey Gilmore's account of that year's Sundance Festival describes Snipe's Film as "an engrossing biography of a formidable thinker and scholar whom most people have probably never heard of." Possibly it is not that most people did not know about Clarke but more than likely it may be that people like Gilmore just did not always have their ears in the right places. Snipes is a black actor in a liberal, politically correct, progressive society that perpetuates systematic oppression from films to history books. I appreciate Snipes' effort for moving behind the camera to take control just like Clarke did and I think that is the connection between him and the subject of his visual tool that was born from an oral tradition and marks the importance of the great orator, the Master Griot.

"The Setting"

As expected, given the symbolic African *extended self* of Dr. Clarke, his political activism, groundbreaking scholarship and

Long line awaiting entry to Clarke funeral at
Abyssinian Baptist church. Photo by Gerald G. Jackson.

humanitarian spirit, the line was long for people to give tribute to the Man. As a teacher, researcher and diversity consultant I was curious to learn how the event was portrayed in the media. For an answer, I turned to the authoritative source *The New York Amsterdam News*. Not surprising, the account of his funeral made front page. In the account was a list of dignitaries who attended. I was knowledgeable of most of the names but pondered how many of these "noteworthy individuals would be known to students taking an Africana studies course at a leading historically White university?"

This was not idle speculation; a great deal of chagrin had been shared among colleagues over the paucity in Black historical perspective that existed among contemporary college students, despite the celebration of MLK birthday and Black History month annual programs. For my part in this struggle for the minds of youth, I was searching for ways to provide them with educational experiences that gave realistic instruction in a cooperative versus competitive model of learning. I had introduced past classes to the Africentric concept of group, and experience had shown that I needed to provide them with more opportunities to fathom and internalize what the concept meant in theory and practice.

Innocently, I combined my two aims and divided the list of important African-American people attending the Dr. Clarke funeral according to the number of groups for a larger intragroup project. The groups were assigned equally the task of writing an essay on why the people on their list were assessed noteworthy by *The New York Amsterdam News*. To aid them in their research process, the librarian for the Africana Studies & Research Center gave a tour of the library and lecture. When the group projects were completed, I noted the group with the best package, and had outstanding student essays read to the class. It seemed to work, although I long suspected that there was more to be achieved from this exercise. To my dismay momentarily, time constraints and teaching demands kept me from delving more into innovations. However, last year I was spirited into action through student instigation for change. They expressed an interest for an opportunity to read and learn more about the other individuals on group lists. This section carries this request a step further, and makes the icon research from the student groups available to a larger audience.

To reiterate, the JHC assignment was more than a learning exercise. It pays tribute to African-American ancestors, keeps Dr. Clarke alive in a functional way, and extends his legacy for others to replicate. Dr. Clarke's widow, for example, revealed in an Amsterdam News article an aim to maintain his legacy, and there are no reasons why, thinking diunitally, she should shoulder this charge alone. In the African tradition, as long as his name is recalled, he is alive and can continue to educate and inspire the living. This book, conceived of as a conduit, is designed to add to the JH Clarke educational process.

Gerald G. Jackson

Dr. John Henrik Clarke Group Research Project

Professor G. Jackson
Africana Studies and Research Center 172

Group II – Miseducation

February 25, 2003

Alexandra Carlin, Rachelle Dubuche, Charles Fick,
Alexandra Jean-Francois, David Morales, Tracy Noisette,
Kareen Waite, Diamaris Welch

Overview

"The ultimate purpose of heritage and heritage teaching is to use peopled talents to develop awareness and pride in themselves so that they themselves can achieve good relationships with other peoples." —John Henrik Clarke

A July 1998 Amsterdam News headline reads "Father History Passes." A 'master griot' as he was called, John Henrik Clarke, a celebrated historian, was honored by many remembrances on his behalf at his Service of Commemoration and Initiation into Eternity. Among the honorary were such as educator and historian James Anderson, Ruby Dee, Schomburg Center head Howard Dodson, Les Edmonds, historian and professor Asa Hilliard, Ralph Carter, historian Molefi Asante, Nsinga Ratibisha Hem, Mari Evans, and Dr. Jacob Carruthers. In the search for a deeper understanding of the wide expanse of Africana Studies through the lens of those in attendance as aforementioned, an outlined biography of each follows.

John Henrik Clarke was born in Union Springs, Alabama, and died on July 16, 1998. He studied at New York University and Columbia University. Then he dedicated his life to the African American Community through both scholarly pursuits and community involvement. He served as a professor and lecturer, primarily at the new school for social research and Hunter College of the City University of New York, but lectured everywhere from Harlem community centers to African universities. Serving as the director for the heritage teaching program for the Harlem Youth Associated Community Team and as a teacher of African and African American history in Harlem community centers are just two examples of John Henrik Clarke's contributions. Clarke has also authored seven books and contributed to at least seventeen.

He "dedicated his life to countering widely held stereotypes and misconceptions"(www.africanpubs.com/Apps/bios/0295ClarkeJohn.ap ?pic=none). He said "Until quite recently, it was rather generally assumed, even among well educated persons in the west, that the African continent was a great expanse of land mostly jungle, inhabited by savages and fierce beasts. It was not thought of as an area where great civilizations could have existed.

Clarke established the department of Black and Puerto Rican Studies at Hunter College to help in his quest to disseminate knowledge about minority communities. He had a nontraditional career path in comparison to other full time professors. He dropped out of school in eighth grade to help support his family and found himself in New York when he hopped a train out of his hometown due to his frustration with segregation. He spent hours in the New York City Public Library studying black history and racial oppression. Clarke's radically Afrocentric scholarship became well known and began to generate controversy in academic circles. He responded by accusing "white scholars of having disguised their own Eurocentric propaganda as historic fact." Clarke's influence is inestimable.

When John Henrik Clarke died several prominent members of the African American community that revered him and sought to carry on his vision were in attendance at his funeral- A few of them follow.

Howard Dodson

Howard Dodson grew up in rural Chester, Pennsylvania. Dodson's mother was a silk presser, while his father was a general laborer, doing every conceivable kind of job to keep food on the table for Howard and his sisters. His father was such a fine worker that despite having no education past ninth grade, he got offered several promotions, all of which he turned down. Dodson did not understand this and one day asked his father why he kept turning down promotions that would mean less work and more pay? His father's response was "... Look son, the unions and the construction companies are corrupt. Any time you move into that level of management you move into a corrupt structure while I could make a few dollars more, I prefer to work for every dollar I earn to ensure that you and your sisters have a stable living situation." After hearing this, Dodson realized that in order to keep his dignity and set a positive example, his father had to turn down these promotions. To this day, Dodson speaks highly of his parents (Shuler, p. 16). From the foundation that his parents laid for him, Howard Dodson has built a prestigious career. He was in the top 5% of his class in high school and was deemed the boy who was most likely to succeed. Dodson went to Westchester State College where he received a degree in secondary education with a major in social studies and a minor in English. Next, Dodson enrolled at Villanova College, where he earned a dual master's degree in political science and history. Dodson finished his education by getting his Ph.D. in history, having done some work in physiology as well (Shuler p. 16).

In 1964, the new Dr. Dodson joined the Peace Corps, traveling to Ecuador to teach English and coach basketball. While there, Dr. Dodson started some fifteen credit unions, and many of them continue to do business up to the present day (Shuler, p. 16). After serving in

Ecuador for several years, Dr. Dodson returned home to America and was eventually given the job of Deputy Director of Recruitment and Director of Minority Specialized Recruiting for the Peace Corps. Dodson also worked alongside Martin Luther King Jr. in the 1968 Poor People's Campaign, which was still being organized when King was assassinated (Shuler, p. 16).

In 1984, Dr. Dodson became the chief of the Schomburg Center for Research in Black Culture of the New York Public Library. Since he assumed his leadership role, Dr. Dodson has raised funds for renovations including the addition of the Langston Hughes auditorium. Today Dr. Dodson is looked up to as a specialist in African American history. He is a noted author, a consultant, and an educator ("4 recommended for Black museum commission" (p. A5). He has also increased the library's collection, which now exceeds five million items. His fundraising efforts have allowed the center to have around seventy-five annual events and six exhibitions. Through his hard work, he has made the Schomburg Center the most comprehensive public research library devoted primarily to the documentation of African American and African history and culture. To give back to his community, Dr. Dodson started a Scholarship-in-Residence program, which has provided fellowships to over eighty scholars over the last fourteen years (Shuler, p, 16).

Ralph Carter

Unfortunately, African American accomplishments are not celebrated as much as they should be within and out of the Black community. It took the death of a great man to bring within one room, many well-accomplished Blacks who have contributed to their communities in various forms. The funeral of Dr. Henrick Clarke filled the Abyssinian Church of Harlem with family, friends, and accomplished individuals who helped to mold the African American community into a more positive image. Besides Dr Henrick Clarke's many accomplishments over a lifetime, another person who has accomplished a great deal, but is not in the spotlight for his fabulous talent and influence in the Black community is Ralph Carter.

Ralph Carter was born on June 30, 1961 in New York City. He became a well acclaimed actor that not many have heard of besides knowing him for his role on the 70's sitcom, Good Times, at a tender age of 13 (Mapp, p. 284). He played the young character of Michael Evans from 1974 to 1979 (Mapp, p. 284). This character was wise beyond his years, voicing the problems of the Black Communities and praising the accomplishments of great leaders like Martin Luther King Jr. and Malcolm X. Although Carter was a well known character to many Americans for his acting career on this sitcom, his talent also shone on Broadway. His talent exceeded acting, for he was also a talented singer. At the age of 14, and in the middle of his first year on Good Times, he starred in his first Broadway play, Raisin in the Sun (Mapp, 1974, p. 284).

Besides Raisin, for which Ralph Carter won the Drama Desk Award for most promising young actor in Theater World Award, he performed in other Broadway as well as Off- Broadway shows, such as Tough to Get Help, Dude, The Karl Marx Play, The Me Nobody Knows (1971), Via Galastica (1973), as well as Denny's House (1987) (Mapp, 284). His career in performing arts has also won him acclaim and awards such as a Tony nomination (Mapp, 284).

Ralph Carter is also known for being one of Dr. Henrick Clarke's students. Within an industry where Blacks are often portrayed as "sidekicks and jesters," Ralph Carter along with another one of Dr. Henrick Clarke's students, Wesley Snipes, offer the portrayal of Blacks as "positive and forceful characters" (Sacramento Observer, All). Ralph Carter is also a familiar face to conventions and other events held, in attempt to uplift the Black community. Ralph Carter, along with Al Sharpton, Dr. Henrick Clarke's wife, as well as many other influential leaders in the Black Community were present at he celebration for Imhotep Gary Byrd's return to the radio, for he is referred to as a "fixture in the Black Community" (Timms, p.2). Ralph Carter was also present at the ceremony held in honor of Sonia Sanchez who is a well-known poet and activist for the Black Arts Movement (Yusef, p. 21). At this ceremony, Carter sang a song that was inspired by one of Sona Sanchez's famous "be" poems (Yusef, p.21). Carter attended the conference for Brooklyn Reggae Day and he was noted as an important person in the entrepreneurial community (Fuller, p.30). Ralph Carter even attended the award ceremony held in honor of the well-accomplished Ruby Dee at Columbia University in 2001 (Amsterdam News, p. 30).

Black entertainers and other well accomplished individuals that showed up to honor Dr. John Henrick Clarke at his funeral, are not celebrated as often and as much as they should be for their various contributions to the Black Community. Blacks like Ralph Carter, Wesley Snipes, Ruby Dee, and Dr. John Henrick Clarke have been a part of the uplifting of the Black community, and should be more recognized, and celebrated by Blacks and all other races.

Prominent Africentric scholars Asa Hilliard and Jacob Carruthers
at Clarke's funeral inside of Abyssinian Baptist church.
Photo by Gerald G. Jackson.

Jacob Carruthers[68]

Jacob Carruthers is a socially active academic. He is a firm believer that a large part of liberating African American people comes from understanding and connecting history, culture, and heritage. He has earned respect as one of the world's leading experts in classical African civilizations. His interests have carried him throughout the continent of Africa, conducting study tours to Egypt, Ethiopia, the Nile Valley, Zimbabwe, Senegal, the Ivory Coast, and other parts of West Africa. Carruthers served as founding president of the Association for the Study of Classical African Civilizations for five years. In that capacity, he led a group of 1,000 black teachers, students, artists and scholars from the United States to the Nubian Cultural Center in Aswan, Egypt for a two week conference and tour of Nubia and Egypt. He is a founding member and priest of the temple of African Community of Chicago and founding member and director of the Kemetic (Egyptian) Institute, which sponsors the annual "Teaching About Africa" program for schoolteachers and administrators. He is the acting director of the

---

[68]Dr. Carruthers died on Monday, January 5, 2003. Kobi Kambon had dedicated his most recent book to Jake (Kobi Kambon (2003). *Cultural Misorientation.* Florida: Nubian Nation).

Center for Inner City Studies, Northeastern Illinois University, where he also serves as a professor (www.thehistorymakers.com).

He has written many important articles and books concerning oppression, education and the destruction of African civilization. Some of his well known publications include Science and Oppression, The Irritated Genie, and MDW NTR Divine Speech. As the founding member and director of ASCAC, Carruthers provides assistance to communities, schools and teachers who opt to move in the direction of African centered education. The program also attempts to help educators teach about African correctly by exposing the truths of African history, provides a body of knowledge that continuously contributes to the "rescue, reconstruction and restoration of African history and culture." He believes in African centered education for many reasons. For one, the population of the United States is too diverse and multiethnic to continue using the Eurocentric curriculum that is now in place and African centered education can provide the leadership for educational reform. He also believes that one reason that western culture has been able to remain dominant in our diversifying country is because whites control economic, political and social capital such as educational policy and are able to convince both blacks and whites of the absence of black history and prominence. Carruthers said, "The European intellectuals had fabricated a theory of the absence of African civilization; African thinkers found the reverse." He says Africans history must be based on an African centered paradigm that used "African historiography and an African worldview." Blacks need to create a literature to educate children instead of using the literature used by their oppressors to debase Africans, (www.africawithin.com)

Jacob Carruthers has dedicated his life to teaching blacks about the greatness of African civilization and challenging the Eurocentric notions that are taught in American schools to date. He has founded many institutions whose purposes are to distribute knowledge about Africa from an African worldview. He takes the historical accounts of whites and looks at them from an African worldview, thus bringing truth to the history of the continent and making it applicable to the experiential education of Africans.

Nzinga Ratibisha Heru

Nzinga Ratibisha Hem is an influential advocate for the study and promotion of African history. While computer technology is her vocation, her passion lies in preserving the ancient African heritage. Her name could not better express the impact she is making throughout the world. She took the name of Nzinga (a warrior Queen who unified her people and fought for forty years to keep the Portuguese out of Angola), and Ratibisha which means "she who corrects things and makes things right." Heru attended the University of Minnesota, California State University of Los Angeles and the institute of Pan African Studies. Sister Nzinga devotes an enormous amount of love to her people and serves the people of the African community as both a consultant and advisor for various community based organizations. Her devotion to the African community is portrayed in her significant involvements and diverse experiences in the field of African and African American studies ("Association for the Study of Classical African Civilizations," www.ascac.org/president.html).

Sister Nzinga serves on the Advisory Board of Uhuru Shule, an alternative school for African children and the Urban League Training Center in Los Angeles. This school has received national attention from the black community and has served as a template for similar schools throughout the country. One such school is a charter school in Philadelphia, which follows the principles that are honored in ASCAC. Imani Education Circle Charter School provides K-8 students with a rigorous math, science and technology intensive program in an African-centered, child-centered environment (www.gpuac.org/csprofile.pdf). Sister Nzinga is also instrumental in planning and organizing many conferences. This includes, the First Annual Ancient Egyptian Studies Conference held in Los Angeles, February 1984. Heru is currently the International President of the Association for the Study of Classical African Civilizations (ASCAC) and chairperson of its executive committee and has served in that position since 1990. She also served as Technical Consultant to the national office of ASCAC for the Fourth Annual ASCAC Conference in Aswan, Kemet, 1987. In addition, she is also a charter member of ASCAC and the former National Treasurer and a member of the National Council of Negro Women and Black Women's Forum ("Association for the Study of Classical African Civilizations," www.ascac.org/presidenthtml).

ASCAC is an association that promotes the study of African civilizations for the development of an African worldview. It was founded by many scholarly intellectuals and among them was Dr. John Henrik Clarke (Wright, p. A2). He was a major force behind the creation of ASCAC and amongst his closest co-partners in the "quest to emancipate the African mind," was Nzinga Hem (Daniels, p. A7). President Nzinga describes the aim and thrust of ASCAC as, "bringing together scholars, thinkers, planners, artists, students, scientists, teachers, technicians and most significantly, dedicated workers to promote and preserve our ancient African heritage as well as issue an urgent call to the African World community about our morally compelling responsibility to respond collectively, immediately and effectively to our current situation" (Los Angeles Sentinel, p.B5). The organizations commitment is to the truth and aims to build African centered study groups while strengthening existing institutions ("Association for the Study of Classical African Civilizations," www.ascac.org/ president .html). Amongst others, Dr. Clarke and President Nzinga would get together in local African centered study groups throughout the country. The study groups resemble reading circles, where individuals are responsible for reading selected texts and coming together in a group to discuss content and meaning (Wright, p. A2). Their goal was to utilize the study groups and institutions to accumulate knowledge and raises consciousness for the liberation of Africans in the Diaspora.

President Sister Nzinga had a profound respect for her friend and colleague, Dr. Clarke. Their relationship was so beautifully evidenced when she introduced Dr. Clarke at the "Race Women and Race Men" national conference. During this symposium, Heru portrayed Dr. Clarke as the epitome of an African man living in America. When describing one man, who followed Dr. Clarke's philosophy, she introduced him as, "A black man from the Nile, walking in the footsteps, standing on the shoulders of Dr. John Henrik Clarke (Mullen)." From this quote it shows that Dr. Clarke was a figure that was adored and respected by President Nzinga.

Mari Evans

Mari Evans was born in Toledo, Ohio on July 16, 1923. Growing up in a very traditional black family, her father served as a rock for her to lean on. He provided her with guidance, strength, and encouragement in her endeavors. After attending a public high school, she went on to study fashion design at University of Toledo. There, the subject matter did not truly grab her attention, and she left without finishing her degree (www.africanpubs.com).

Being a renaissance woman, Evans holds many different titles including: poet, playwright, storyteller, screenwriter, television producer, college professor, and editor. She is critically acclaimed and very well appreciated throughout the African American community. She has strived to make everyone aware of the Black struggle in America. Mari Evans has made some very great accomplishments during the course of her life and career. She has been associated with many reputable academic institutions and organizations. Her first introduction into the world of academia was in 1969, when she was an instructor of African American literature as well as a writer in residence at Indiana University-Purdue. She later accepted a position as assistant professor of African American literature and writer in residence in Bloomington's Indiana University. Other universities where she has made an impact include: Northwestern University from 1972 to 1973, Purdue University from 1978 to 1980, Washington University in St. Louis in 1980, Cornell University from 1981 to 1985, and State University of New York-Albany from 1985 to 1986. She has also left her mark at Miami University-Coral Gables, and Spelman College (www.africanpubs.com).

She wrote, produced, and directed a television show called, "The Black Experience" for WTTV in Indianapolis, Indiana, from 1968 until 1973. This show served as a tool in order to enlighten others on the lifestyle of Blacks in America; Evans strived to depict Blacks and their lifestyles and traditions as accurately as possible. While she wanted to shed light on the struggles of Blacks, she also wanted to show the magnificence and greatness of the culture. While Evans was very accomplished in many different arenas, it was not until 1970 when her name began to create a buzz, with the publication of her second collection of poetry entitled, I Am a Black Woman. It seemed that this book really got her point across. Her thoughts and emotions were being heard. Although her first book of poetry may not have originally received as much acclaim, she was soon recognized for her great efforts to distinguish herself from the poets typical of the Harlem Renaissance. Although this was the time in which she was raised, she resented the black sentiment of assimilation and compromise that was typical of the time. In Contemporary Poets, Alan R. Shucard wrote, "Quite the contrary, her work is informed by the uncompromising black pride that burgeoned in the 1960's" (Shucard, www.arncanpubs.com). In a poem, "Who Can Be Born Black," she distinguished herself from the typical Harlem Renaissance poets. This poem was in response to that of Countee Cullen's sonnet from the mid-1920's, "Yet Do I Marvel." In his sonnet, Cullen wrote a long list of horrors that God has created, the worst of which is "To make a poet black, and bid him sing" (www.africanpubs.com). Evans' frustration shone through in her poem, when she says, "Who/can be born black/and not/sing/the wonder of it/the joy/the/challenge... Who/can be born black/and not exult (Evans, www.africanoubs. com)!" Mari Evans puts a high value upon culture, which makes the language of a poem and the alleged commercialism of other poets' cause for battle. She does an excellent job of instilling a sense of pride in the hearts of her black readers. Where others may tear them down, Mari Evans brings them up, making Blacks realize that they are a beautiful people (college.hmco.com).

Evans shared many of the same views of the distinguished Dr. John Henrik Clarke. Throughout the both of their careers, they staved to accomplish many of the same things. Having many things in common, including their teaching careers and associations with Cornell University, these two eminent individuals shared a bond unbreakable by anything of this world. An illustration of their bond was shown in Clarke's autobiographical obituary in which he speaks kind words to many people that he holds dear. Mari Evans is among the prominent black leaders described as being on a walk "anointed by God" (Clarke, www.mumia.org).

Ruby Dee

"We are the crumb snatchers of theater and entertainment in general—we are not mainstream." The famous actress Ruby Dee uttered these words. In a time when in the theatrical arts, talented Black actors and actresses were carefully isolated, exploited and forced to play menial roles such as maids and other servants, few artists were able to rise above this trend. One such person is Ruby Dee.

An actress known for her works on stage, screen, television, and radio, as well as her PBS appearances, recitals, and recordings with her husband, actor and playwright Ossie Davis, Ruby Dee is probably best known for her performance in the film version of *A Raisin in the Sun*. She broke the mold and paved a way for other Black actors to play meaningful roles. In 1965, she was the first Black actress to play major classical roles at the American Shakespeare Festival in Stratford, Connecticut. She played Katherine in *The Taming of the Shrew* and she appeared as Cordelia in *King Lear* (Ryan, p. 40).

Ruby Dee was born as Ruby Ann Wallace on October 27, 1924 in Cleveland, Ohio. She developed the name Ruby Dee as a stage name for her performances when she attended college. She was the third of four children of Marshall and Emma Benson Wallace. Soon after her birth, her family moved to Harlem in New York City. Ruby's mother was so determined not to have her children to fall prey to the ghetto to which Harlem was fast becoming, that she at the time, "coerced" her family into studying literature and music. Most times at night, the family would read aloud poetry from Longfellow, Wordsworth, and Paul Lawrence Dunbar (Hine, p. 88; Smith, p. 260). According to her mother, the arts were the only means for Blacks to escape the ghetto.

When Ruby Dee was in her teens, she was adept at art and she began submitting poetry to the New York Amsterdam News, a Black Weekly newspaper (Hine, pp. 88-89). During this time, Ruby became involved in political affairs. While in high school she spoke at a mass meeting protesting the cancellation of a federally funded music program, the result of which had been the suicide of a teacher whose job has just ended. Ruby's political activity did not end here. She continued her political activities throughout her years at Hunter College to the present day. Following the 1963 church bombing in Montgomery, Alabama, and the Assassination of President Kennedy, Dee and her husband (Ossie Davis) mounted a campaign that encouraged people to donate to the promotion of civil rights instead of buying Christmas presents (Hine, p. 90).

Ruby Dee has dedicated her life to helping others achieves their goals. For more than twenty years she has devoted herself to racial equality, giving much other time serving on national committees and performing in benefit shows to raise money for the legal defense of civil rights workers arrested in demonstrations and for other related activities. Some of the national committees that she has been affiliated with are the NAACP, the Congress of Racial Equality (CORE) and the Student Nonviolent Coordinating Committee (SNCC). She has also given benefits for the Black Panthers and the Young Lords. She has even developed the Ruby Dee Scholarship in Dramatic Art. This scholarship is targeted towards helping young Black women become established in the acting profession. Some of her other activities include making recordings for the blind, raising money to combat drug addition, and speaking out against the United States military involvement in Southeast Asia.

James Anderson

There are members of the African American community who strongly believes in giving back to their people, to benefit the community as a whole. Giving back to the community could be accomplished by various means. Both Dr. John Henrik Clarke, and James D. Anderson accomplished such a task through gaining a thorough education of the situation of Blacks and dedicating their lives to educating Black people of such facts for the betterment of the community.

James Anderson was born on November 21,1944 in Eutaw, Alabama (http://www.ed.uiuc.edu/EPS/people/Anderson_Vita.html). He spent time doing research on the history of African American education in the South from 1860-1935 (http://www.uiuc.edu/research). His dedication and work did not go unnoticed for he was the recipient of awards and honors including Spencer Mentor Award (1998-1999), and he was appointed Honorary Professor of Southwest China Normal University (1998-1999), as well as Guest Honorable Professor of Yunnan University (1998-1999) (http://www.ed.uiuc.edu/EPS/people/ Anderson.Vita.html).

The many books and articles of Anderson that were published, deal with his area of expertise, which is Black education (http://www.ed.uiuc. edu/EPS /people/ AndersonVita.html). Some of his books include The Education of Blacks in the South, 1860-1935, and New Perspectives on Black Educational History, while a couple of his many articles include topics such as higher education within the Black community as well as the miseducation of Blacks (http://www.ed.uiuc.edu/ EPS/people/ Anderson Vita. html).

As a Black intellectual who dedicates his life to researching the educational system with the intent of facilitating the growth of the Black community, he should be celebrated by all who are aware of his many accomplishments.

Dr. John Henrik Clarke and James Anderson are comparable, for they both value the progression of the African American community. Both are educated men who taught, and spread their knowledge to as many as possible, which aided in educating Blacks on their culture and accomplishments throughout history. Both of these leaders serve as prime examples of powerful figures who used their knowledge, and their capability to help others for the progression of Blacks.

Molefi Kefe Asante

Molefi Kefe Asante, also known as Arthur Lee Smith, Jr. is a brilliant educator, writer, and scholar. Born on August 14, 1942, in Valdosta, GA, he has been educated in many schools including Pepperdine University, Southwestern Christian College, Oklahoma Christian College, and University of California, Los Angeles where he obtained his Ph.D. in 1968. A man of many capabilities and a vast knowledge in the Afrocentric movement, he has taught across the United States from 1969 to the present where he resides and teaches in the Department of African American Studies at Temple University. While being a leading authority in African culture and philosophy, his studies and participation in the Afrocentric movement has helped teach his peers and students a comprehensive view of human beings and their behavior in an opposing field of the Eurocentric model of anthropology, much like the late John Henrick Clarke. Among his many awards including the William Wells Brown Award for Black Writers in 1981, for the three decades he has been an active teacher and has written over three dozen books thus becoming one of the most prolific African American scholars of the century (http://www-africanpubs-com/Apps/bios/0408AsanteMolefi-asp?pic=none).

Through his early years in Georgia, he attended school and work in cotton and tobacco fields to help support his parents who never finished elementary school themselves. His ambitions and support from his parents helped in educating himself and striving to feed his thirst for knowledge. He was so involved in the Civil Rights movements in the late '50's and early '60's, that during his high school years he participated in the Fisk University student march in Nashville, Tennessee (http://www.africawithin.com/griots.htm).

A short time later while attending Southwestern Christian College, a small junior college in Texas, Asante met a man from Nigeria named Essien Essien. Warm, gracious, and intelligent, Essien Essien went on to become a doctor. He made a profound impression on Asante, inspiring in the young student a hunger to learn more about Africa. Thus, by the age of 20, Asante had already embarked upon his crusade to delve into the history and culture of the African people. (http://kalamumagazine.com/ contours_of african_ amencan_ culture. htm).

Les Edmonds

Students could not find accurate information so biographical sketch was taken from another 172 group.[69] His name is an example of one of the man influential and prominent African American individuals that remain nameless within mainstream white America. Les Edmonds, also known as Ed, was a professor of African American Studies at Seton Hall University in South Orange, New Jersey. Known for his African Studies classes by some and his whiskey drinking by others, Les Edmonds is nameless in white America. I find it very ironic that the voice, or memory, of such an educated man is so easily silenced by the cheers and knowledge of Seton Hall's basketball team. Thus, the question of who Les Edmonds is should be rephrased to say, why is he not known? This individual, once influential in the 1970s, is now unrecognized among white America, as well as by many other African Americans. Les Edmonds possessed enough power among the educated

---

[69]AS&RC 172. Group 2 – Mupalia Wakhisi; William West; Danielle Williams; Anya Litvak; Tommy Monson and Mark Kendall.

black community that he was able to allow Professor Jackson to sit among the family at the funeral of the late great John Henrik Clarke, and inadvertently displacing Wesley Snipes to a less easily noticed seat. I find it hard to believe that such a man, so widely known among the educated African American community, does not exist in mainstream white America.

Asa Hillard

A founding member of the Association for the Study of Classical African Civilizations, Dr. Asa Grant Hilliard currently serves as the Fuller E. Callaway Professor of Urban Education at the Georgia State University. A historian, psychologist and teacher, Hilliard has concerned himself with the inadequacies of African-American education among a slew of his own research efforts. This efforts spring from his scholarly beginnings in the Denver Public Schools – having earned a Bachelor of Arts degree in Educational Psychology, a Master of Arts degree in Counseling and an Educational Doctorate degree also in Educational Psychology from the University of Denver.

His background in education continues as he served on the faculty at San Francisco State University for 18 years and was concurrently a consultant to the Peace Corps and Superintendent of Schools in Monrovia, Liberia two of those years. Referencing Africa, he and his wife were just recently made development chiefs at Mankranso Village in the Ashanti Region of Ghana.

His research, which included a tour of the Kemet along side such other such "great thinkers" as Dr. Jacob Carruthers and the revered late Dr. John Henrik Clarke (Hall 3), has taken Hilliard to explorations on the foundation of Black Education traced back to Egypt (specifically the Kemet) as well as to developing theories on assessment very widely referenced. His writings span the topics of Ancient African History to testing and test validity. Additionally, he has consulted on several issues including teacher development and training, curriculum equity for leading school districts, universities, and government agencies. In a recent speech captured by a February 22, 2002 article in the Philadelphia Tribune, Dr. Hilliard states relating to his areas of expertise and research that "the challenges that African people face in America, and throughout the world, as we enter the twenty-first century is to create programs, strategies, and institutions that will reclaim and preserve our rich culture" (Worrill 7A).

Along side his many speaking engagements addressing various and widespread areas in education, Hilliard's most recent writings include

Young, Gifted, and Black, co-authored with Theresa Perry and Claude Steele, in which Hilliard highlights those schools where African Americans are high achievers. His own self-identity is captured in this well-distributed quote, "I am a teacher, a psychologist and a historian. As such, I am interested in the aims, the methods and the content of the socialization processes that we ought to have in place to create wholeness among our people."

Bibliography

"4 recommended for Black museum commission." *New Pittsburg Courier.* V. 93, N. 43, 5/29/2002, p. A5.

Asa Hilliard. "Africa Within." 22 Feb. 2003 http://www.africawithin. com/hilliard/ asa_ hilliard.htm.

"African Voices magazine honors award-winning actress Ruby Dee at Columbia University," taken from *The Amsterdam News.* V. 92, N. 3. p. 30.

"Association for the Study of Classical African Civilizations." Available online: www.ascac.org/president.html.

Boyd, Herb. "Father History Passes: Dr. John Henrik Clarke; 1915-1998." *New York Amsterdam News.* 29 July 1998: 1.

"Ethnic News Watch." Proquest. Cornell University Library, Ithaca, NY. 25 Feb. 2003 http://enw.softlineweb.com/searchFrame.asp.

Clarke, John Henrik. "John Henrik darkens Autobiographical Obituary." Afrikan.net. Available online: www.mumia.org/wwwwboard/messages.

Daniels, Ron. (1998) "John Henrik Clarke: The Passing of a Great and Mighty Warrior." *The Michigan Citizen.* V. XX, N.3 7, p. A7.

Hall, Corey. "John Henrik Clarke's words, wisdom recalled by readers and listeners." *Chicago Citizen.* 30 July 1998: 3.

"Ethnic News Watch." *Proquest.* Cornell University Library Ithaca, NY. 25 Feb. 2003 http://enw.sottlineweb.com/searchFrame.asp.

"Harlem Honors Dr. Henrick Clarke" taken from *Sacramento Observer*, Volume 38 Number 5. P. All.

Hine, Darlene. Facts on File *Encyclopedia of Black Women in America.* New York: Facts on File Inc., 1997.

"John Henrik Clarke. Africa Within." 25 Feb. 2003 http://www.africawithin.com/clarke/tribute1.htm. http://kalamumagazme.com/contours_of_afncan_amencan_culture. htm.

Los Angeles Sentinel: ASCAC National Conference in L.A. (2001) V. 66, N. 49, p. B5.

Mapp, Edward. Directory of Blacks in the Performing Arts second edition. The Scarecrow Press, Inc., 1990

"Mari Evans: 1923-." Available online: www.africanpubs.com.

Joyce, Joyce, and John Reilly Ed. "Mari Evans" Available online: college.hmco.com.

Mullen, Leah. "Race Men of the Nineties" Available online: www.cwo. com/~lucumi/clarkethtml.

"Marcus Garvey: An Overview." Available Online: www.isop.ucla.edu/mgpp/intro.htm.

"Marcus Garvey, Jr. Denied Entry to U.S." The Sun Reporter. V. 28, N.L p. 7. 2/13/1971.

Mason, Bryant. "Garvey's son reflects on father's legacy." The New York Amsterdam News. V. 89, N. 52, p. 30. 12/30/1998.

"Profiles: A Directory of Philadelphia Charter Schools, 2000.2001." Available online: www.gpuac.org/csprofile.pdf.

Reyes, Pam. "Marcus Garvey, Jr. Visits Los Angeles." Los Angeles Sentinel. V. 59, N. 15, p. A.12, 7/22/1993.

Ryan, Elizabeth. The Biographical Dictionary of Black Americans. New York: Facts on File Inc., 1992.

Shuler, Deardra. "Howard Dodson: The Man Behind the Schomburg Center." Hyde Park Citizen. V. I2, N. 35, p. 16, 8/2/2001.

Smithy Jessie. Notable Black American Women. Detroit: Gale Research Inc., 1992.

Steel, Debora. "New party gives B.C. voters another option." Raven's Eye. V. 4, N. 10, p. 3. 2/28/2001.

Timms, Cynthia Moran. "Imhotep: A Fixture in Our Community," taken from The New York Observer. V. 6, N. 46. p. 2.

Worril, Conrad W. "We Suffer From Cultural Surrender: Dr. Asa G. Hilliard, III Explains Our Ignorance." The Philadelphia Tribune 22 Feb. 2002: 7A.

"Ethnic News Watch." Proquest. Cornell University Library, Ithaca, NY. 25 Feb. 2003 http://enw.softlineweb.com/searchFrame.asp.

Wright, Michelle D. (2000) "Baltimore—Afro-American:" ASCAC Conference to Be Held in Baltimore. V. I09, N. I7, p. A2.

Yusef, Salaam. "Sonia returns victorious and honored," taken from The New York Amsterdam News. V. 90, N. 48, p. 21.

University of Illinois-Educational Policy Studies, http://www.ed.uiuc.edu/ EPS/people/AndersonVita.html. 1997.

University of Illinois at Urbana Campaign-College of Education. http://www.uiuc.edu/research.

Alexandra Carlin and group. Photo by Gerald G. Jackson.
Miseducation

Diamaris Welch in center of group members.
Photo by Gerald G. Jackson.

Gerald G. Jackson

AN ETERNAL LEGEND:
John Henrik Clarke's Legacy
and the Dignitaries Who Loved Him

Deven Gray
Faith Harris
Meredith Howell
Shari T. Moseley
Tara L. Wood

Group III: Black Studies Education as Innovation

Overview

John Henrik Clarke was a great man! At a young age, he questioned the masses about the history all Blacks, not just African Americans or Caribbeans. He felt that just knowing he was Black did not tell him who he was or where he came from. He felt that Black history did not just begin with slavery. Whites told him that his people had no History, but that answer was not sufficient for him. He set out on a quest to find what he called "Negro History". Throughout his life he researched, wrote books, taught classes, and gave speeches to inform the world of Negro History. He felt Negro History was the missing history of the world.

He taught about Blacks in Africa having prosperous civilizations long before the Greeks and Romans. Contrary to what historians have said and taught, the Egyptians were Africans. Most of the Greek and Roman inventions came from these Africans. He also taught that Africa was invaded throughout history due to its abundant resources and not because Africans were inferior and needed to be "cultivated."

He believed that all Blacks should have some ties to Africa reaching back and restoring their "geographical reference." They should learn, be proud, and embrace their history, beliefs, and values of African culture. They should unify among each other from city to city, country to country, etc. He believed that if all Blacks received this information they would know that they are somebody, they came from proud people, and they should continue to strive. Furthermore, he believed that artists should use their talents to improve the world and that leaders should take a stand on the grounds of bettering, educating, housing, and defending Black people. In addition, he agreed with Malcolm X in his ideas of overcoming the struggle "by any means necessary."

Clarke inspired and touched so many individuals over his lifetime. He wanted to unveil the hidden history of the African people, not only to Blacks but also to the world. He wanted society in its entirety to recognize all the contributions Blacks made to civilization and to give them their due credit and accolades. He no longer wanted Blacks to be oppressed because of lack of information or misconstrued information. John Henrik Clarke was an activist teacher, historian, Pan-African, author, scholar and legend. John Henrik Clarke died July 16, 1998 at age 83. At his funeral, many were in attendance to celebrate his life and legacy. Some of these attendees included such prominent people such as Leonard Jeffries, Rosalind Jeffries, Quincy Jones, Bob Law, Tilden Lemelle, Alton Maddox, Vemon Mason, Judy Miller, Amiri Baraka, and Amina Baraka. This paper is a collection of biographies of the prominent individuals mentioned above.

Biographies

Leonard Jeffries

Leonard Jeffries was born on January 19, 1937 in Newark, New Jersey. An African proverb says, "It takes a village to raise a child." Newark provided this needed collective parenting for Jeffries. Newark consisted of many African villages; Leonard's particular village was on 14th street part of a neighborhood in the Roseville Section. His mother's family lived on 13th Street and his father's family lived on 12th Street. In this community all of the families were family to each other and they took care of each other.

Most of the families in the neighborhood attended a neighborhood church including the youth, Mount Sinai Baptist Church. Like a lot of spiritual followers, who attended primarily black churches, they developed a sense of self-worth and pride in the black race. This experience gave Lenny a sense of purpose as a teen. He developed an interest in the development of young black men and young black women. He himself received his education in the Newark Public School System where he excelled, he was the President of his graduating class in middle school, and he graduated high school with honors. He was building himself up in order to be able to do the same for others.

As a college student, Jeffries developed a great interest in Africa. After listening to Dr. Robinson in the chapel of Lafayette College, he was '"transformed." Tears were brought to his eyes when he heard of the work needed in Africa. He felt much compelled as if the speaker were talking to only him. After this speech, Jeffries took his first trip to Africa. Because of his many qualifications, leadership and being a French speaker Jeffries became a staff member of a program called Crossroads. He later became a group leader and to date he has traveled to Africa over forty times, taking along with him young people who would be able to benefit from the experience of Africa has he had. He hoped that the experience would touch their lives. His experience in Africa had such a great impact on his life that he changed his academic path; reshaping his career goals.. He became a political scientist instead of a lawyer and he received a master's degree in international affairs instead of pursing a law degree.

In his continued commitment to Africa Jeffries worked on his PhD in the Ivory Coast where he did field work for his study of African Studies, Economics and Politics. He was taken aback by the way that African Studies was taught in educational institutions He found that African Studies was taught from a very imperialistic point of view. This caused him to begin to question the integrity of those who claimed to be "authorities" on Africa. While teaching at City College, Jeffries began to meet people who could offer legitimate information that he could use to formulate his own idea of what African Studies should be. He called this a curriculum that was based on the "African World Focus." His main objectives for his program were community orientation, outreach, overseas to Africa and outreach out to the Caribbean. He wanted to create uniquely organized programs that linked academics to the community and rooted Black history to its actual beginning, prior to slavery. Implementing his views, he along with historian John Henrik Clarke established the African Heritage Studies Association.

Dr. Leonard Jeffries has many achievements, and continues to provide a great service to humanity with his work. He is the founding director and current second vice president of the Association for the Study of Classical African Civilizations. He is a professor of Africana Studies and former chairperson of the Department of Black Studies at the City College of New York. He has received honors in government and African Studies. He is committed to research and publishing articles that concern the revision of black studies curriculum, the urban crisis and the plight of the African American. Jeffries also as a commitment to informing students of his work, he has lectures at Universities all over the world including Columbia, Harvard, The University of Bahia Brazil, and University of the West Indies and the University of Paris.

Rosalind Jeffries

Leonard Jeffries married someone after his own heart, a prominent figure in her own right. Rosalind Jeffries specializes in art history; the cultural determiners of behavior and the course of the events of history. She speaks powerfully on these topics. She explores the art of countries all over the world; she evaluates paintings, sculptures, and other forms of visual art. Her study of art forms focuses mainly on that of Africa and countries in the Diaspora. She fulfills many roles in this capacity; she is a museum curator, educator, and lecturer. As part of her work, Jeffries goes further than academics, she is conscious of god and she desires to serve as an inspiration to her listeners. She works to uplift the oppressed, give new insights to the intellectual and to spark a commitment to the plight of the community. Jeffries earned her Ph.D. from Yale University. She is currently a faculty member of the School of Visual Arts in New York City. In the previous year, she earned an Arthur Schomburg position informing both students and faculty about African American History, racism, and the importance in the participation in arts and other cultural displays. Dr. Jeffries has been employed by many facilities in New York City such as the Metropolitan Museum of Art. She too has great commitment to the needs of Africa, as does her husband, and she has done both field research and lived in Africa to pursue these interests. As a respected speaker, she has also lectured all over the world including countries in Europe and Asia.

Due to her great work in Africa, Dr. Jeffries was made Queen Mother in a special ceremony in celebration of Queen Mother's Day that took place during the PanaFest and Emancipation Ceremonies in Ghana. Rosalind was named Queen Mother of Education, Development, and Social Services. This ceremony took place near what used to be a slave castle where thousands of enslaved Africans were held before being shipped to the US and the Caribbean. This honor places emphasis on one of the most important aspects of the Africa worldview, oneness, and connectedness with others. Due to her great efforts to be a help to the black and African communities, Rosalind is embraced as a mother emphasizing her role as a part of angus working together to advance a people who struggle and succeed not as individual units but as a collective.

Quincy Delight Jones Jr.

Quincy Delight Jones Jr. or as most call him, Quincy, or simply Q, is a musical and film genius and legend throughout the world. Not only has he gained success and recognition in the every aspect of mainstream American society, he has also done it not at the usual expense of "selling out" the Black community. As a master of musical hybrids, Quincy Jones has shuffled pop, soul, hip-hop, jazz, classical, African and Brazilian music into many dazzling and distinctive fusion's, encompassing virtually every medium, including records, live performances, movies and television. He is a 26-time Grammy Award winner (second on the all-time list) and is the all-time most-nominated Grammy artist with 77 nominations. Having been in nearly all aspects of the music and film industry for over half a century, he has set the standard for young Black artists, entrepreneurs, business executives, owners, producers, and film makers. He is a leader in his field and has changed the face of music for Black people all over the world. Quincy Jones was born in Chicago on March 14, 1933, and grew up in Seattle. While in junior high school, he began his musical career by studying trumpet and sang in a gospel quartet. His musical studies continued at the prestigious Berkley College of Music in Boston, where he remained until the opportunity arose to tour with Lionel Hampton's band as a trumpeter, arranger, and sometime-pianist. In 1951, he moved on to New York and the musical big leagues, where his reputation as an arranger grew. By the 1950s, he was arranging and recording for such diverse artists as Sarah Vaughan, Ray Charles, Count Basie, Duke Ellington, Big Maybelle, Dinah Washington, Cannonball Adderly and LeVern Baker.

In the early 1960's Quincy won his first Grammy award for his arrangement with Count Basie. He also became vice-president of Mercury records in 1961, and became the first Black high-level executive of a major record company. Toward the end of his association with the label, Quincy turned his attention to another musical area that had been closed to blacks—the world of film scores. In 1963, he started work on the music for Sidney Linnet's *The Pawnbroker*, the first of his 33 major motion picture scores. In 1985, he co-produced Steven Spielberg's adaptation of Alice Walker's *The Color Purple*, which won 11 Oscar nominations, introduced Whoopi Goldberg and Oprah Winfrey to film audiences, and marked Quincy's debut as a film producer. In 1991, Quincy and his company QJE (Quincy Jones Entertainment) helped launch the acting career of rapper and film star Will Smith on NBC-TV's hit series *The Fresh Prince Of Bel Air*, for which Jones acted as an executive producer. Also QJE, in conjunction with David Salzman, produced the currently running UPN's In The House and Fox Television's Mad TV. Quincy Jones is also the founder and chair of *VIBE* Magazine and part owner of *SPIN* Magazine.

As a record company executive, Quincy remains highly active in the recording field as the guiding force behind his own Qwest Records, which boasts such important artists as New Order, Tevin Campbell, Milt Jackson, Tamia, Andraé Crouch, Young Americans, Shannon and Catero. New Order's album Substance earned Qwest a gold record in 1987. Tevin Campbell's debut T.E.V.I.N. was both a critical sensation and major commercial success, with his follow-up release, I'm Ready, going double platinum. The label's release of the *Boyz N The Hood* soundtrack album was among the most successful recordings of 1991. Qwest Records has also released soundtrack albums from the major motion pictures *Sarafina!* and *Malcolm X.* However, as producer and conductor of the historic "We Are The World" recording (the best-selling single of all time) and Michael Jackson's multi-platinum solo albums *Off The Wall*, *Bad* and *Thriller* (the best-selling album of all time, at more than 45 million copies and counting), Quincy Jones stands as one of the most successful and admired creative artist/executives in the entertainment world.

In 1994, Quincy Jones led a group of businesspersons that included football Hall of Famer Willie Davis, television producer Don Cornelius, television journalist Geraldo Rivera and Sonia Salzman in the formation of Qwest Broadcasting. A minority-controlled broadcasting company; it has purchased television stations WATL in Atlanta and WNOL in New Orleans. establishing it as one of the largest minority-owned broadcasting companies in the United States. Quincy serves as chair and CEO of Qwest Broadcasting. In addition to forming the Quincy Jones media group, Inc. in 1998, which is currently producing series on HBO, TNT, and several other broadcast stations?

Quincy Jones is also a lifelong activist. He was a major supporter of Dr. Martin Luther King Jr.'s Operation Breadbasket, and after King's death, he served on the board of Jesse Jackson's People United to Save Humanity. An ongoing concern throughout his life has been to foster appreciation of African-American music and culture and to this end he helped form the Institute for Black American Music, which was instrumental in establishing a national library of African-American art and music. Jones is also the founder of the annual Black Arts Festival in his hometown of Chicago.

Quincy's life and career were chronicled in the critically-acclaimed WamerBros- film, *Listen Up: The Lives of Quincy Jones*, This film helped illuminate not only Quincy's music and Spirit, but also revealed much about the development of the African American musical tradition. Reflecting on the changes in pop music over the years, Quincy says, "If there are any common denominators; they are spirit and musicality. I go for the music that gives me goose bumps, music that touches my heart and my soul." Over the years, Quincy Jones has reached the essence of music and art — the ability to touch people's feelings and emotions.

Bob Law

Bob Law is a man whose voice for many is the educated, thought provoking, and uplifting consciousness that reigns in the urban cultures of New York City. His political thought and opinions on the state of Black America have encouraged many men and women to become active in their communities to combat racism, political oppression, and economic and social inequality. Bob Law was one of the first African Americans to host his own national syndicated radio talk show, broadcast out of Queens. The 20 year long running program "Night Talk" aired daily on the National Black Network, giving urban listeners a voice they had never had on America's airwaves. He paved the way for many Black radio talk show hosts such as Tom Joyner's morning show, and many others. Being Vice President/Programming of WWRL in New York City, he was able to strengthen the Black and Latino community's in urban New York City, with programs often discussing entrepreneurship, and leadership in the minority community.

Bob Law not only talked about being successful in the Black community, he led by example. Mr. Law has founded the Namaskar Capital Assistance Program which develops and manages a loan program for Black-owned businesses. He has launched and led Recycle Your Black Dollars tours and campaigns to enhance African American businesses. Recently; in September 2002, he opened a seafood restaurant in Prospect Heights just three doors down from his health food store, which had been on the same block for a decade. However; Bob Law's Seafood Cafe is not just a carryout diner. Its purpose is part of a two-fold response to Black eating trends and to the buying powder of the local demographic. In an interview with Law from the KIP business report, he admits to having "always talked about economic development...[and] at the center of that is ownership." Through his involvement with the PowerNomics campaign in conjunction with the Washington-based think tank and the Harvest Institute, he found that research revealed that the primary consumers of seafood are African Americans. Thus, he decided to launch a business that would prove to be a success in the Black community. Law eventually wants to open a chain of restaurants that provide more in terms of quality and service to African Americans. However, he knew a good starting place would be Prospect Heights in Central Brooklyn, where a middle class group of Black urban professionals resides. He had been politically active there, and knew that they would be receptive to his business. Law's intelligent, and friendly and customer satisfying business ethics have been confirmed by his accomplishment with the restaurant. Bob Law asserts, "What I'm talking about is ownership, not renting someone else's name. If we franchise, then people can buy a franchise name from a Black company. This is what I said people ought to do, and now I'm doing it."

Bob Law, also a community activist has been involved with several events that have brought Black people together, not only in the New York City area, but nationwide as well. He was co-chairman of the citywide (NYC) Coordination Committee for the incredibly successful October 16, 1995 Million Man March and host of the actual event. He is founder of the national Respect Your Youth Organization which has been operating for over two decades. He, along with James L. Muhammad, are co-chairs of the National Leadership Alliance (NLA), a group of Black individuals and organizations, whose primary focus is effective use of Black political and economic strength. They recently hosted a conference in Washington D.C., at the National Black Theater, where the Nation of Islam Leader, Louis Farrakhan addressed political success.

Bob law is an incredible motivational and empowering lecturer who influences masses. Bob fore fronted the lawsuit against the New York City Board of Education for the miseducation of our society's children. His work has led to Saturday Academies nationwide, which emphasize academics and culture. His Agenda 2000 health, business and personal development seminars and retreats have been making a difference in the Black community, in the way we teach, learn, and prepare ourselves and our children for competition in mainstream society, and success within our own communities.

Bob Law not only talks about ways in which we can develop our business, leadership, political, and community skills, he also writes about these issues. In his book, "Appreciating the Past in Order to Understand the Present, While Planning for the Future", his broad ideas of the state of Black America economically and socially are really captured and discussed. In chapter six, *"From Black Rage to a Blueprint for Change,"* Law asserts that middle class Black America has finally "seen" the glass ceiling of corporate White America, and are starting to form their own businesses as a result. Socially, he feels that Black Americans have talked a great deal about overcoming racism and political oppression and building strong communities, and as a result have elected young Black officials to office, and called for certain plans to take action. However, Blacks never "stay angry long enough to effectively set any of these ideas in motion." The violence within the Black communities is coming from that same exact anger, which is used directly against us. In conclusion, Bob Law's philosophies of where Black Americans stand as far as political and social contexts are pertinent to describe reasons why Black Americans are in the those very situations to begin with. This quote from his book accurately verbalizes the mentality of many Black Americans today. The "take-low" philosophy survived even as we began to achieve these "unrealistic" goals. It was simply updated to fit the realities of each generation. It went from "you can't do it" to "now that you're here, don't rock the boat." Don't seek or expect recognition and don't be too ambitious". This advice was internalized, because the people who offered it were not enemies (except in the case of Malcolm whose White teacher was trying to break his spirit). For the most part, the people passing along this advice were family, friends, and neighbors, and they were passing along a survival tradition.

For many African Americans, the effects of those ideas linger on and are still being passed along. Black politicians say they cannot identify too closely with the African American community as their careers reach new heights. Black professionals avoid political causes, and Black entrepreneurs desire nice little businesses, "nothing too big, just enough to feed my family and pay my bills." Each generation of African Americans is told in one way or another to expect that their success will be less than other racial groups.

We must replace negative thinking with a new perspective. Alice Walker is correct when she says, "No person is your friend who demands your silence or denies your right to grow." We must develop and utilize all of our skills; nothing less is acceptable. In school we are expected to learn reading, math, history, and science; we must continue to learn throughout life—Geoffrey Holder illuminates the need to develop yourself as he has become a dancer, actor, painter, cook, choreographer, and clothing designer.

Dr. Tilden J. LeMelle

Tilden LeMelle has spent forty years in higher education as a faculty member and administrator. He taught at public universities in Louisiana, Illinois and New York as well as at Fordham in New York; University of Denver and Harvard University. He has lectured across the United States, Africa, and the Caribbean. He serves as Chairman of The Africa Fund, Chairman of the Advisory Board the Fulbright Senior Scholar Program, founding member of the African Heritage Studies Association, and member of the Boards of the American Committee on Africa, the Institute of International Education, and the Social Science Foundation. He is also a member the Council on Foreign Relations and the Phelps Stokes Fund. He is a member of Africa Today Associates, which has published and owned the magazine *Africa Today* since 1966. His publications include numerous articles on African affairs, and US foreign policy, international and domestic race relations and public education. His books include *Race among Nations*, and *The Black College.* Dr. LeMelle held the presidency of Hunter College and New York Technical College, both of the City University of New York, and the presidency of the University of the District of Columbia. He holds a BA and MA in Comparative Languages and Literature from Xavier University of Louisiana; and a Ph.D. in International Relations from GSIS at the University of Denver.

Dr. LeMelle was able to use these positions to their full potential without slighting his time; though a member of several professional and/or philanthropic organizations. An example of his involvement can be seen in the instrumental role that he played in establishing the first independent elections of Zimbabwe, subsequent to its battle for independence from British rule.

Throughout the late 1970's, LeMelle worked side by side in his capacity as treasurer of the American Committee on Africa and as an observer of the struggle that was taking place in then Rhodesia, with other members of the ACOA and other Africa-help orientated organizations, to see the people of that country gain autonomous control over their national affairs.[70] LeMelle took all opportunities to remain an active voice in Umted States – Africa relations. During the Clinton administration, LeMelle, as Africa Fund Chair, alongside others chastised the President in a letter "rejecting the administration's constructive engagement accommodation with the Nigerian military dictatorship and calling instead for economic sanctions on that repressive regime and greater political and diplomatic backing for that west African nation's democracy movement."[71]

Despite LeMelle's deep involvement in the affairs of Africa, he took time to incorporate his passion for the betterment of race relations in American education as well. In his book, co-authored with his brother Wilbert, *The Black College: A Strategy for Relevancy* LeMelle proposes new goals for black colleges along the lines of service and leadership; in this way the college and the students would connect with the whole Black American community. In this new capacity the colleges' focus was to be on the emphasis of "socialization" and "tooling" in education.

By "socialization," they mean a "socializing and politicizing function which is aimed at creating, maintaining and propagating the political and social values and ideals from which the society's institutions derive their legitimacy" (p. 61). The "tooling" function "is aimed at producing trained and qualified personnel to man successfully the society's economy" (p. 61). The "socialization" and "tooling" functions, if used correctly by the black colleges in the interests of the black community, will breathe new life into these institutions.[72]

The thoughts and philosophies expressed by the authors in *The Black College* were very much in line with those of Dr. John Henrik Clarke. If the LeMelles' collegiate revolution were to take place, it

---

[70] http://richardknight.homestead.com/files/zimletmarch80.htm.

[71] http://africanation.org/docs98/nig9805b.htm.

[72] http://www.tcrecord.org/Content.asp?ContentID=1812.

would be built on Clarke's pillar of the strength and power of education. Clarke believed that an educated person was much more advantaged and competitive than an uneducated one could ever be.

Alton Maddox

Alton Maddox is a renowned civil rights attorney; especially among Blacks. He holds this title due to his lifelong fight for justice, equality, and loyalty to the Black community. Throughout his law career, he battled against racism, police brutality, and racial equity in the judicial system, racial profiling, and economic and political empowerment among other issues; which he continues to combat until this day.

He was born July 21, 1945. He grew up in Newnan, Georgia. He attended Howard University and Boston College Law School. He graduated in 1971 and was admitted to practice law in the state of New York on March 15, 1976.

However, fourteen years later in 1990, he was suspended from practicing law on the federal level for eleven years. He will be recorded in history for having his license to practice law suspended longer than any attorney has in US history. He was suspended because he refused to breach attorney-client privilege in the Tawana Brawley case-1987. This case consisted of a young teenage black girl being abducted and raped by six white males, whom she claimed, were police officers. During the trial Maddox, Tawana, other attorneys on the case, and other witnesses kept quiet to protect her and the case. They wanted arrests to be made and a Charles Haynes appointed as prosecutor. The media and courts misconstrued their silence and tried to make them look like liars to the pubic by stating it was a hoax and they made the entire incident up. Since she would not talk and Maddox would not let the courts question her, they suspended him. His suspension was a duration of eleven years.

He was suspended on the grounds of professional misconduct and immediately threatening the public interest. During his suspension, he had to refrain from practicing law in any form, from giving any legal advice or opinion, from appearing as an attorney or counselor, among other things.

During these eleven years, he stood strong on his beliefs. He would not give in. He believed Tawana. He also believed he did nothing wrong but tried to protect his client. Yet white lawyers who had committed illegal crimes were often suspended but was back in practicing a year later. He stated he was under investigation for suspension long before this case because of his past high-profiled cases, most of them dealing with racism and police brutality. He felt that the state got tired of Black people receiving justice for brutality and discrimination due to him. He said he knew they were going to make him pay and the suspension was not a surprise.

For those eleven years many Blacks protested and demonstrated in his honor. They even fund-raised for him because he had no steady income due to his suspension and no one would hire him. At one banquet in honor of his re-instatement and support, John Henrik Clarke attended. They appreciated him for taking a stand to represent Black clients who have been denied justice and due process in the courts, and he appreciated their support. He said in an interview during his suspension, *"If anything, it makes me want to up the ante to make the message clear that this Black Man does not intend to be a victim of racial subjugation. There is no way that suspension, or even disbarment would interfere with what I think my role is with respect to the struggle for justice of Black people"* (City Sun, May 23-39, 1990). He was re-instated to practice law on the federal level in 2001. Besides being a civil rights lawyer, he is a political activist, a leader of SNCC, a founder of Pan-Africanism, a poet, civil rights activist in Both the USA and in Africa. He is the founder and leader of the United African Movement, an organization that focuses on Black unity in the entire world, focuses on social and political changes for Blacks, and focuses on family and the Black community as a whole.

Alton Maddox is a great man that has always fought against the courts and political systems injustices targeted against Blacks. As he continues his pursuit of justice he stated, *"You see, I love legal combat, and I have not found another niche. What makes a person great is a love and passion for what they do, and I love the law."*

Vernon Mason

Vernon Mason is a civil rights attorney. He is a political activist that throughout his legal career challenged the judicial and political systems of New York State. He took a stand for justice and equality for Blacks. He has a history of activism in the Black community.

He grew up in Georgia. He has an M.B.A. from the Indiana University School of Business; J.D.(Juris doctor), Doctor of Law, Columbia University and a B.A., Morehouse College.

He is a friend of Alton Maddox and they often defended cases together, such as the Tawana Brawley case-1987. Due to his involvement, he was disbarred from practicing law in 1995. After being disbarred, Mason said: *"They will not silence us. We will continue to fight for our rights and justice for our community. We will continue to speak truth to power and organize our people to change the balance of political power in New York State. This is not the end, it is a new beginning."* (http://enw.softlineweb.com/record). He had 66 charges of misconduct, which included abandoning cases, lying to clients, fee gouging, and misuse of clients' funds. The charges were made by 22 past clients but he had represented over thousands because he had been in practice over 22 years, which half his cases were free of charge because the clients had no income to pay him.

During his disbarment, he went through a lot. His law firm was designated as a "sensitive location" by the NYPD. According to their definition, a sensitive location was as an area that may be subject to demonstration or may result in diplomatic or political confrontation. However, he was unaware that his office was a sensitive location and did this label violate any of his rights. Rights such as not being informed, did illegal surveillances occur, and were his former clients' rights violated. He, as well as Alton Maddox and the rest of the council of the Tawana Brawley case were sued by Steven Pagones, one of the acquitted white officer's accused of rape in the case. Pagones sued for $410 million on the grounds of defamation. He said the entire case was made up by the council and they intentionally defamed him, knowing that their information accusations were false. Pagones won the case but he did not receive that amount of money. Mason, Maddox, and the rest of the council are also in the process of appealing that jury's decision,

He also protested and demonstrated for his honor, Maddox's honor, Tawana's honor. He still believes her story until this day. He is no longer disbarred but he does not practice law. He is currently Reverend Vernon Mason and Director of Project Youth Turn at New York Theological Seminary. He is an advocate for family unity and progress in all Black communities. He has stopped practicing law but he has not giving up the fight for Black equality.

Dr. Judy Miller

Dr. Julia "Judy" Miller was the director of the Black Studies/ African-American Studies Department at Seton Hall University for twenty years. She is now a Professor Emeritus of Seton Hall University. She is the wife of famous painter Don Miller.[73] It can only be inferred that in her capacity as director of the Black Studies/African-

---

[73] http://libraryiShu.edu/gallery/donl.htm

American Studies Department that she strove to perpetuate Dr. Clarke's belief in the power and criticalness of Black education for all people, but especially Black Americans. The Millers were well known for hosting friends on their ranch in Moravia, New York.

Amiri Baraka

A famous writer poet and political activist, Imamu Amiri Baraka was born LeRoi Jones on October 7, 1934 in Newark, New Jersey. He was the child of Anna Lois Russ and Coyette LeRoi Jones. As a young boy, he lived with not only his parents, but also his grandparents and uncle in the same household. This unity shaped his view of life and the world around him.

Although his mother and father both worked, they made time for their children enrolling them in voice, music, and art lessons at a young age. In addition, Jones and his siblings would occasionally visit the famous Dr. George Washington Carver's laboratory at Tuskegee. This immersion in the arts and education eventually contributed to Jones' decision to pursue higher education at Howard University in 1952.

Although he eventually got a Bachelor's and a Master's degree, he was initially kicked out of college due to poor grades. In 1954, he enlisted in the United States Air Force developing a passion for poetry during that period. In an interview in 1985 Jones stated, "The air force made me think about what I really wanted to do with my life." After discharging in 1957, he began to read literature by Kafka, Hemingway, Proust, and Thomas Hardy and moved to Greenwich Village in New York.

As Jones continued to study the works of White intellectuals, he internalized their belief systems. He even married a White woman named Hettie Cohen and had two children from that marriage. However, his relationship ended in divorce in 1965, as Jones became increasingly "aware of himself." During the Civil Rights Movement, he came to realize that "White America" was not where his heart was. He said, "I began to feel less and less like I needed to be where I was."

Jones resolved his feeling of dislocation by moving to Harlem, a historical center of Blackness and Black culture. It was there where he established The Black Arts Repertory Theater School in 1965 leading to an influx of Jazz musicians and performers to the area. In addition to living in a new place, Jones also took on a new name. His official name became Amiri Baraka to symbolize his cultural awakening. "Imam" was an Islamic title that Baraka added to his name that meant "spiritual priest." Fundamentally, he was embracing a more African ideal system through the concepts of revitalizing his spiritual essence and forming closer ties with the Black community. As Barrack increasingly started thinking of himself as a part of the Black collective, he became more active in politics and social transformation.

Baraka often used his poetry and essays as a means of communicating his political opinions. In some instances, he called on Blacks to take action against the powers that were holding them back or he blatantly described the greed and cruelty of White people. He demanded that Blacks wake up and stop trying to follow a Martin Lurther King model of non-violent political activism. A strong advocate of Malcolm X's philosophy, Baraka wanted Blacks to stand up for themselves and fight back against their oppressors. For example, in *The Music* he has a poem that states:

> No be bullshit only for word noise
> No be dry dull stuff but war war war war war
> *Fuck a bourgeois alligator*
> Lyin he tryin to be help {p.93-94}

In this poem, Baraka voices his strong beliefs of self-defense by repeating "war" opposed to "words" which he refers to as "noise." Not only does he call the mere use of words noise, but he also calls it "bullshit." This generates the idea that there is something inherently wrong with words also. He calls for "war" as a direct consequence of the "lyin bourgeois alligator." He uses the term "alligator" to show how fierce the many Whites and others who worked against Blacks were.

Of course, his political stand was not widely accepted among White politicians and government officials. This obvious bias was apparent in 1981 when he was arrested for "resisting arrest." The incident occurred as he was double-parked near a shoe store arguing with his wife Amina Baraka about the outlandish cost of one of their child's shoes. Police attacked Baraka pulling him out of his car as more police arrived on the scene. Although the police claimed that they were "protecting Mrs. Baraka," they were clearly doing nothing of the sort. Mrs. Baraka said, "I am a strong woman. If he was attacking me, the police would have had to pull me off of him!" Amiri Baraka told the media, "The government doesn't like my nationality and my opinions." Although a grand jury threw Baraka's case out and charged two police with harassment, he inevitably was convicted and served ninety days in prison.

While he was in prison, Baraka managed to write his autobiography, LeRoi Jones. By 1998, Baraka had 13 volumes of poetry, 9 non-fiction books, and 2 fiction books. He also had written numerous plays some of which he discussed in the college courses that he instructed. Today, Baraka is no longer teaching at universities, but he does travel often, giving lectures all over the country.

Although Amiri Baraka was not one of the main speakers in John Henrick Clarke's over "six- hour- long [funeral] celebration," the similarities between the two are clear. They are both legends in their own time. Education and the liberation of Black people politically, socially, and culturally all tie into the unique connection between Clarke and Baraka. They realized that the struggle for equality encompasses the redistribution of power and knowledge throughout the Black community.

Amina Baraka

Amina Baraka is most commonly known as the wife of the famous, Amiri Barrack; however, she has an identity all her own. Although she, like her husband, is also interested in poetry, politics, art and literature, she adds a "twist" to her works. Many of her poems are written in a Blues form. Rarely does she recite her poetry without sounds of Blues music floating in the background because it is an integral pail of her presentation. Like any passion, the love for her work developed overtime.

Baraka was raised by her grandmother and grandfather because her mother was only fourteen when she had her. Her grandmother had a wonderful voice and loved to sing the Blues. Her grandfather, on the other hand, played the harmonica and guitar. This made a lovely match for a musical family. Although she could not play an instrument, Baraka had no trouble singing. Singing at an early age fostered the type of poetry that she would end up reciting later in life. Aside from taking an interest in poetry, she was also interested in knowing what made her so different from other people. In an interview with Mrs. Baraka, she recalls, "As a young kid, I understood there were class differences among Blacks." Some parents did not allow their kids to play with Baraka because she was considered lower-class. This sense of stratification and rejection within the Black community was carried with her to adulthood. Her husband told an interviewer, "She has no respect for the Black bourgeoisic at all." Mrs. Baraka affirms that she has no "trust" for them, but claims to have friends of the Black bourgeoisie class. This is a defining factor between her and her husband because he addresses Blacks collectively and can "tolerate" the bourgeoisie because that is the class from which his family originated.

In addition to the trauma of being rejected as "lower-class" at a young age, Mrs. Baraka encountered the trauma of being viciously raped by three boys when she was fourteen. Although one of the males was old enough to be considered an adult, all three individuals were acquitted of the charges. This might have been the beginning of Mrs. Baraka's political and social equality awareness. For a long time, she did not want to go to school or even leave the house because she thought that being raped was her fault. When she was finally able to return to school, she ended up having to drop out because she became pregnant with her first child.

Although she did eventually get her high school diploma, her pregnancy devastated her family because they had very high hopes for her education. With all of the tension at home, she left and stayed with a friend before marrying her first husband. Although she was married with a child, Baraka's dream was to become a movie star. She went to every play opportunity that she could find. She even formed the Jazz Arts Society with a group of musicians because she enjoyed the beauty of music, dance, and fine arts all together.

When Amiri Baraka came to her town to make a film, she jumped at an open position. Naturally, she landed the part due to her passion for the position and various acting experiences. After play practice, Amiri and Amina used to go out to get drinks. This was a peculiar situation because they both liked each other; but they were both in relationships as well. Amiri Baraka was dating a woman named Bumi who was pregnant with his child. Although Amina Baraka was married, she left her husband and moved her children in to her mother's home. Mrs. Baraka, on the hand, went to live in a polygamous relationship with Amiri Baraka and Bumi upon their persistence.

After two weeks, Mrs. Baraka left the polygamous situation citing that there were "tensions" in the home. Perhaps the tensions and arguments were the catalyst for the premature stillborn birth of Bumi's child. Bumi went into a coma after delivery, but was not able to be revived. This sad situation opened the door to the reunion of Amina Baraka with her future husband. In the new marriage between Amina and Amiri Baraka, they had five children: Obalaji Malik Ali, Ras Jua Al Aziz, Shani Isis, Amiri Seku, and Ahi Mwenge. All of their children are out of the house and in their own occupations now.

Like her husband, Amina Baraka did not make a speech at John Henrick Clarke's funeral "celebration." However, there is no question to the degree in which their lives were interrelated. They were both consumed with the betterment of the whole (versus the individual) through collective responsibilities. Clarke taught African history and culture in the classroom as well as lecturing outside of the class. Likewise, Baraka taught her children to be empowered and also used her poetry as a way to connect with people of all occupations.

They also both represented the African philosophy of self-knowledge. As Mrs. Baraka analyzed her place as part of the lower-class, but overcame the biases and obstacles in front of her, so Clarke proved that bias imposed by colonial conquerors can be overcome showing that Africans do have history beyond slavery and bondage. In addition, he exposed a wealth of information that children do not learn in school, but that is important when it comes to attaining self-understanding. Even at Clarke's funeral "celebration," one of his admirers said, "He was a giant for freeing us from racist lies and helping us confront the truth about ourselves and the world. We love him." Although Clarke was a dynamic person and was mourned by thousands of people, it is good to know that his legacy lives on not only in Mrs. Baraka, but also in all of the distinguished individuals presented in this work.

Bibliography/Works Cited

Baraka, Amiri and Amina. *The Music: Reflections on Jazz and Blues*. New York: William and Morrow Company Inc., 1987.

Boyd, Herb. "Father History Passes: Dr. John Henrick Clarke; 1915-1998." *New York Amsterdam News* 80, 30 (1998): 1.

Buffalo, Audreen. "A Revolutionary Life Together." *Essence* 16, 1 (1985) 82.

Daily Challenge: Voicing the Black View. Vol. 21, #284, weekend ed. (May 21-23 1993).

Horne, J.W. Robinson. "Blues according to Baraka." *Richmond AfroAmerican* 114, 14 (1994) A14.

Hudson, Theodore. *From LeRoi Jones to Amiri Baraka: The literary works*. North Carolina: Duke University Press, 1973.

Leild, Utrice. "Maddox Suspended for Failure To Comply with Committee's Demands." *The City Sun*. (May 23- 29, 1990).

Perry, Jean. "Amiri Baraka Keeps It Going On." *Los Angeles Sentinel* 66, 49 (2001) B3.

Woodard, Komozi. *A Nation within a Nation: Amiri Baraka (LeRoi Jones) & Black Power Politics*. Chapel Hill and London: The University of North Carolina Press, 1999.

Gerald G. Jackson

Websites Cited

www.google.com

http://www.stg.brown.edu/projects/CreativeNonfiction/fall00/bockian.html

http://www.unu.edu/unupress/unupbooks/uul2ee/uul2ee0o.htm

http://www.blackvoices.com/feature/pillars/report.html

http://enw.softlineweb.com/record.asp?move=l&biblio=&recNum=4&CurrentHit=0&hitCount=6&textSelected=&returnPage=record.asp

http://enw.softlineweb.com/record.asp?move=l&biblio=&recNum=8&CurrentHit=0&hitCount=2&textSelected=&returnPage=record.asp

http://enw.softlineweb.com/record.asp?move=l&biblio=&recNum=17CurrentHit=0&hitCount=2&textSelected=&returnPage=record.asp

http://www.finalcall.com/national/youth_summit10-01-2002.htm

http://enw.softlineweb.com/record.asp?msel_from=l0&msel_to=l9&preview=&move=&returnPage=list.asp&articleID=278571&recNum=19

http://enw.softlineweb.com/record.asp?move=l&biblio=&recNum=66&CurrentHit=0&hitCount=l&textSelected=&returnPage=record.asp

www.blackspectrum.com/about.htm Black spectrum theater

http://www.kennedyenter.org/programs/specialevents/honors/history/honoree/jones.html

www.wbr.com/quincyjones/index_bio.html

http://www.kenrobinson.com/fame.html radio hall of fame

http://www.nbufront.org/html/FRONTalView/BookExcerpts/BobLawl.html

Tara, Kate, Shari, Meredith, Faith and Deven.
Photo by Gerald G. Jackson.

Kimberly Jones is sharing her food, a behavioral rule for the course and
lesson in an African philosophical principle.
Photo by Gerald G. Jackson

Gerald G. Jackson

"We're Not Going to Take It Anymore" Biographical Sketches of Prominent Black Activists

February 26, 2003
AS&RC 172

Ricardo Arguello
Dawn Darby
Kimberly Jones
Jamy Rodriquez
Shelby Senzer
Gerald Souders
Phela Townsend
Rahim Wooley

Overview

Khalid Abdul Muhammad, Derrick Bell, Dr. Yosef A.A. Jochannan, Benjamin Chavis Muhammad, Conrad Muhammad, Kefa Nephthys, Gil Noble, Viola Plummer, Sonia Sanchez, Adelaide Sanford, and Al Sharpton. While some of these names were extremely familiar, others were virtually unknown to us until we researched them. Upon reading the material available on the different activist leaders in our community, as a group we realized that there was an overall theme that connected these individuals; they have all made significant contributions to the struggle for equality and continue to feel that it is their mission to make public the disparities that exist within our society. While others remain silent about the injustices Blacks, Latinos, and other marginalized groups are subject too, leaders such as Dr. Ben, Derrick Bell, and the Reverend Al Sharpton vociferously advocate for the welfare of our people.

On December 21, 1987, people from all lifestyles united in a massive demonstration to protest the surge of racially motivated incidents that were sweeping New York City. The murder of Yusuf Hawkins, a young man whose assassination was reminiscent of Emmet Till's lynching in the 1950's, was one such event. On this day, which later became known as "the day of outrage and mourning," Ben Chavis, Adelaide Sanford, and others rallied in an act of civil disobedience that ended in a violent clash between the city's police and the demonstrators. This tragedy did not diminish the persistence and determination of these leaders to achieve social justice. They continued to speak out against the discrimination that oppresses minority groups.

The "Day of Outrage and Mourning" March is just one of many historic events that connect these activists. Because the circle of social activists is small, the individuals who make it up are often dependent on one another for support as they strive to overcome obstacles. What becomes clear upon learning about these great activists is that they all have consistently and selflessly served as effective agents of change on behalf of the masses of historically oppressed groups.

We also discovered that some of the less renowned activists such as Sister Kefa Nephthys and Viola Plummer are the forces behind well-known, eminent leaders such as Rev. Al Sharpton and Benjamin Chavis Muhammad. Additionally, some of these less-known actors have been integral to the success of many internationally recognized protests and events. Such events include: The Million Man March, The Million Youth March, and Women in Support of the Million Man March; under organizations such as the First World Alliance, the New Black Panther

Party, CEMOTAP (Committee to Eliminate Media Offensive to African People), Harlem History Club and the Harlem Writers Guild. All of these individuals share in the same plight as they struggle to achieve equality and justice for the black community. They have actively challenged societal norms while attempting to create a society where social and economic justice actuallyexists. One of the primary arenas where these leaders have confronted ideas of discrimination and inequality is in the sphere of education. In renewing this commitment to education, these activists hope to send out a wake up call to the Black community enlightening them on the dispossession and devaluing of their history and the inadequacies of the education system.

John Henrik Clarke

From SBA to SIA: A Great and Mighty Walk. July 16, 1998. When the European emerged in the world in the 15th and 16th centuries, for the second times, they not only colonized most of the world, they colonized information about the world, and they also colonized images, including the image of God, thereby putting us into a trap, for we are the only people who worship a God whose image we did not choose!

A father, brother, husband, mentor, teacher and leader are but few words that can describe John Henrik Clarke's presence and the impact that he left on society. Born on January 1, 1915, in Union Springs, Alabama, Clarke was raised in a world full of racism and discrimination. At a young age, John Henrik knew very well that the power of knowledge could change the world. Rather than become one of the first land owners in Alabama, John Henrik decided to migrate to Harlem to further his search for the truths of his heritage. He describe Harlem as "the laboratory where I would search for the true history of my people" (Clarke, *Eulogy)*.

Clarke's goal in life was to propagate the advancement of African Americans through the advancement of education. He explains, "I could not stomach the lies of world history, so I took some strategic steps in order to build a life of scholarship and activism in New York. I began to pave strong roads towards what I envisioned as a mighty walk where I would initiate, inspire and help found organizations to elevate my people" (Clarke, *Eulogy*). Clarke began his search for knowledge at New York and Columbia Universities, and continued this quest at the League for Professional Writers. His life-long goal was "to deliver a message of renewal, redemption and rededication for young people all over the world" (Clarke; *Eulogy*). Dr. Clarke became an inspiration to many and is revered as, a symbol of defiance to conventional institutions. Dr. Clarke has authored many books and articles which in 1991 the Los Angeles Times cited him as one of the five distinguished "elder statesmen," the five "black historians known for rewriting history to reclaim black people's place in it" (Hitchcock, 12).

Consequently, Dr. John Henrik Clarke has been the source of inspiration for countless movements, protests, and individuals who believe that they can change the conditions of African Americans. Without John Henrik Clarke, countless numbers of African American leaders would not have been able to break down the walls of oppression and say, "We are not going to take it anymore!"

Dr. Clarke was a monumental influence on several generations of African American leaders including those we have studied. Sadly, the most prominent occasion that has united all of these activists and educators was the memorial service of Dr John Henrik Clarke, who died at age 83 of a heart attack.

Sister Kefa Nephthys

Born in the 1920's, Sister Kefa Nepthys is one of the founders of the First World Alliance. During the early part of this decade, Clarke spoke often of the First World Alliance meetings in Harlem. He was a comsmopolite who could debate points of history with the best minds in the world, but his great love was Harlem and her people (Karium, 1998).

Derrick Bell

Derrick Bell is one of the leading voices on issues of race and class in American society. Throughout his 40-year career as a lawyer; activist, teacher; and writer, he has written extensively on social justice and the importance of being active in the civil rights struggle. His progressive views and uncompromising sincerity make him a leading figure in the fight for equality in the United States. Not only does he write on such issues, but also he practices what he preaches. Bell has made several personal protests against the lack of occupations available to underrepresented minorities in the labor market. His most famous act of resistance occurred in 1980 when he decided to take a stand against Harvard University for the lack of women of color on the faculty.

Bell was born in 1930 in Pittsburgh, and went on to be the first member of his family to attend college. After serving in the U.S. Air force in Korea, he enrolled in the University of Pittsburgh Law School where his main objective was to learn the structure and dynamics of the

U.S. governmental system in order to implement changes as a future civil rights lawyer. His legal career began as an intern in the Justice Department when Thurgood Marshall recruited him to join the Legal Defense and Education Fund of the NAACP. When Bell became the first black tenured professor at the Harvard Law School in 1971; it was a monumental accomplishment not only in his professional life, but also in the progressive advancement of African-Americans. He nonetheless relinquished his position in 1992 to demonstrate the institution's failure to add women of color to the faculty. His act of protests are Afro-centric in the sense that he is not content simply with his own individual success, but believes it necessary for the marginalized group as a whole to have equal opportunities. Bell's belief was that the cause for equal opportunity was more important than financial gains He demonstrated this when he refused to return from his two-year, unpaid leave of absence, following the Harvard protest.

Derrick Bell launched a similar protest earlier while serving as dean of the Oregon Law School. He resigned his position in 1985 after the faculty directed that he did not extend an employment offer to an Asian-American women candidate who was third on the list for a faculty position. When the top two candidates declined the offer, the institution decided to reopen the search instead of hiring the Asian-American applicant. This is another indication of Bell's integrity, dignity, and passion towards the fight for justice in this country. Although the fate of this woman did not affect him directly, he felt a sense of interdependence between himself and the women. His reaction is characteristic of the Afro-centric perspective of collectivity, which asserts that we are all connected and must therefore look out for each other.

As a writer Bell is best known for his books, which feature the fictional civil rights leader, Geneva Crenshaw. The books include *And We Are Not Saved, Faces at the Bottom of the Well*, and *Gospel Choirs*. His message of activism is more effective because of the manner in which he conveys it. His use of fictional literature makes his works even more unique, rich and empowering. At the age of 70, Bell wrote *Ethical* Ambition: Living a Life of Meaning and Worth. The book begins with the statement "How can I maintain my integrity while seeking success? Those of us with dreams of success struggle with this question everyday" (Bell, Derrick; 2002). The book renders the lives of civil rights leaders such as Martin Luther King Jr., Paul Robeson; and Medgar Evers, as well as Bell's own life to answer this question. This question is essential in our understanding of who we are. Many of us, especially students of color in Ivy League universities; grapple with finding a way to arrive at success while simultaneously positively contributing to our respective communities. Bell believes that "we live in a system that espouses merit; equality; and a level playing field; but exalts those with wealth; power; and celebrity; however gained." This paradox is often the case of those who reach success, he states. Bell's accomplishments are proof, however, that one can be both successful and conscience at the same time.

Derrick Bell is presently a professor at New York University's School of Law. He continues to write about the need for activism and social justice in a variety of professional journals published by the leading academic institutions, national magazines, and newspapers of the country.

Dr. Yosef A. A. Ben Jochannan

The proceeding is a very standard biographical sketch on Dr. Ben and it is listed just about everywhere his name appears. However, what is not listed is that he was a close friend of Dr. John Henrik Clarke. During an interview on "Like It Is", Dr. Ben recalls how he and Dr. Clarke met. They came along during the same period in Harlem and they were both "struggling historians." They were looking for a voice, a platform and they found it through Sister Kefa Nepthys and the First World Alliance, a group that she was a cofounder. They carried a unified mission to put the true history of the origins of civilization and the origin of America, in its appropriate place within the annals of world history.

Dr. Ben's contribution to the Black Studies movements has been unparalleled. Together with Dr. Clarke and Sister Nepthys. They formed the core of the First World Alliance and began in the eighties taking trips and to the Nile Valley. In a 2000 article in the New Amsterdam, Sister Nepthys recalls, "When we were floundering around and not sure what path to take, Dr. Ben opened his home (House of Justice in Harlem) to us. He introduced us to the history of the Nile Valley; but more than introducing us, he took us there." These tours grew into conferences attended by thousands and lectures through the First World Alliance, the Harlem History Club and it was there that both Clarke and ben-Jochannan cemented their place in the field of Black Studies and Black Movements. He has taught thousands of students in various communities, authored over thirty books including Africa: Mother of Western Civilization, Black Man of the Nile Valley and We the Black Jews. Upon his retirement from Cornell, the graduate students within Africana sent a memo to the then Director, Dr. Robert

Harris, charging him with the responsibility of immediately assuming the task of replacing the "irreplaceable" Dr. Ben. His loss was felt immediately and every year there was an annual banquet honoring his unforgettable contributions. On the steering committee, for his banquets were logically others included within this paper: Gil Noble, Adelaide Sanford, and Dr. John H. Clarke. On all accounts, to work with him is considered life changing and motivating. He still holds office hours at Pan-Pan on 135th and Malcolm X Boulevard in Harlem, NY. He will be leading a tour in fall 2003 to Egypt further illustration his life commitment to this cause.

"Born December 31, 1918 in Gondar, Ethiopia, Dr. Yosef Alfredo Antonio ben-Jochannan ("Dr. Ben," as he is affectionately known) has devoted the better part of his life to the illumination of the indigenous origins of African civilizations. By profession, he is a trained lawyer, engineer, historian, and Egyptologist. Ben-Jochannan went to Egypt for the first time in 1939, and moved to Harlem, New York in 1945. Dr. Ben knew Malcolm X personally, and was a student and colleague of George G.M. James. He was exceptionally close to the late Dr. John Henrik Clarke. Since 1957, he has coordinated regular study tours and pilgrimages to the Nile Valley, hence directly educating and exposing thousands of Africans to the still visible splendors of ancient Egypt.

Formerly a professor at Cornell University's Africana Studies Department; Dr. ben-Jochannan has also been a professor-at-large at Al Azar University in Cairo" (Rasdi, 2002).

Benjamin Chavis Muhammad

Benjamin Chavis Muhammad is a multi-dimensional man. He is a preacher, a theologian; a chemise a political; civil and human rights activist, a writer, an environmentalist, a gifted speaker, a leader, and perhaps above all, an educator. With his many facets, Muhammad has managed – and continues – to leave a historic, and in some ways, controversial mark on the Black community, America, and the world.

Hoping to leave a positive imprint on his community in the theological context of being obedient to God; Benjamin Franklin Chavis Jr., in the early 1960's, began to develop his leadership abilities. From the time that he was a young toddler, inculcated in Benjamin, was the realization of the plight and dispossession of the Black American community. He was from a long line of civil rights leaders, dating back to his great-great grandfather, Rev. John Chavis, who two hundred years prior was ordained as the first African American Presbyterian minister in the U.S. and an activist against slavery. In 1960, at the age of twelve, Benjamin became a member of the NAACP in his hometown, Oxford, North Carolina, this was the first of many organizations, which he would later head, that was committed to the mission of racial and economic justice. Also during this time Chavis joined the Congress on Racial Equality (CORE); the Southern Christian Leadership Conference (SCLC), and the American Federation of State, County and Municipal Employees (AFSCME) – all groups that challenged "institutionalized racism," and "promoted progressive self transformation of American Society."

In February of 1971, Chavis experienced firsthand the nationally plaguing racism, consequently springing him to the forefront of global civil rights controversy. Chavis and nine others, while in Wilmington, North Carolina, for a desegregation demonstration, were wrongly convicted on false charges in the case of a white-owned grocery store in a black neighborhood that was firebombed. Consequently, Chavis and his colleagues, infamously known as "The Wilmington Ten," were unjustly incarcerated for four and a half years. On December 4, 1980, due to the case's garnering of worldwide attention and the ample vigilance on the part of human rights agencies, like Amnesty International, the U.S. Fourth Circuit Court of Appeals overturned the trumped up charges, clearing all names and records.

Emerging from his prison experience with an even deeper commitment to eradicating racial and economic injustice, Chavis immersed himself in the civil rights movement. Continuing his dedication to the education of the African people, he wrote his second book, called *Psalms from Prison* (1983). It documented his false imprisonment (His first book was entitled *An African American Political Prisoner: Appeals for Human Rights* (1979) – written while he was still incarcerated).

From 1885-1993, Chavis wrote, produced, and hosted a weekly nationally syndicated newspaper column and radio show, both entitled the "Civil Rights Journal." In 1993, at the age of 45, he became the seventh and youngest member to be elected as the Executive Director and CEO of the NAACP. Coinciding with this leadership position was his appointment also as Executive Director and CEO, of the Commission for Racial Justice, an extension of the United Church of Christ. Under his leadership, the CRJ sponsored "Freedom Rides" to the Alabama Black Belt and to Chicago to ensure voter rights and voter mobilization. Chavis and the CRJ were additionally instrumental in coining the term, "environmental racism." Chavis, who also had a degree in chemistry, issued a study of a clandestine, national environmental scandal: three of the five largest toxic waste landfills in the country were in minority neighborhoods.' The CRJ and NAACP are only two on the following list of the plethora of organizations which Chavis either held membership or headed: Vice President of the National Council of the Church of Christ (NCC); CEO and Founder of the National African American Leadership Summit (NAALS); Chairman of the Prophetic Justice Unit of the NCC; Co-Chair of the Southern Organizing Committee for Economic/Social Justice; President of the Angolan Foundation; Co-Founder of the National Black Independent Political Party; President of the Board of the Washington Office on Africa; and a member of the Clinton/Gore Transition Team for National Resources Center, which was in accord with the Departments of Energy, Interior, Agriculture and the Environmental Protection Agency (EPA). Clearly, Chavis' functional presence in the civil and human rights movement has been national and global in scale.

In the wake of officially changing his surname to Muhammad, on February 23, 1997, Dr. Benjamin F. Muhammad announced in Chicago that "God has called me to into the Nation of Islam and I have accepted God's call to the ministry of Islam... I affirm the oneness of God and the oneness of humanity. It is God, not the forces of this world, and God only who discloses God's self today as Allah" (Powerhouse, 2001). Benjamin Chavis Muhammad has grown to be an influential figure within the infrastructure of the NOI, even being rumored to be the next in line to head the Nation. Despite criticism for his involvement in the NOI, he has still managed to remain an active part of the civil rights and human movement, and as mentioned he directed the Million Man March which has been to date the greatest attempt in American history to uplift, educate, and empower the African community. In heading this attempt to "renew the Black sense of purpose," and to "end Black destruction" (New Journal, 2000). Muhammad affirms his activist and educator principles: "One of the responsibilities of the civil rights movement," he preaches, "is to define the postmodern manifestations of racism. We must not only point to overt forms of racism, but also to institutionalized racism" (Powerhouse, 2001).

Conrad Muhammad

Conrad Muhammad, founder and executive director of A Movement for CHHANGE (Conscious Hip Hop Activism Necessary for Global Empowerment), "an organization dedicated to correcting negative stereotypes in the media and pop culture" (Williams, *Republicans Stumble with Outreach*), has often found himself against top music moguls such as Russell Simmons, Clive Davis, and Sean "Puffy" Combs in hopes of cleaning up hip-hop. At first Mr. Muhammad started his public career as minister for the Nation of Islam under the tutelage of Minister Louis Farrakhan who is currently the nation's leader. "Once considered an heir to Farrakhan," Conrad now focuses his time and attention on destroying the violence and misinterpretation of African Americans in main stream media, especially in the world of Rap (Noel, *Hip-Hop War*).

"After nearly 20 years of shuttle diplomacy between warring factions of the hip hop nation, many feel that Muhammad has earned the title of 'Hip-Hop Minister'" (Noel, *Hip-Hop War*). Muhammad has gathered groups together such as A Tribe Called Quest, Wrecks-n-Effects, and Afrika Bambaata's Zulu Nation in order to settle differences and disputes. Before the rapper Tupac Shakur was assassinated in 1996, Muhammad "repeatedly requested to leave his 'thug for life' gangsta image" and focus on the thousands of teens that join rival gangs, the Bloods and Crips in order to be like their role model (Noel, *Hip-Hop War*). In addition, upon Marion "Suge" Knight's (President of Death Row Records) first visit to Harlem several years ago, Muhammad, requested Mr. Knight to stop terrorizing Sean "Puffy" Combs and Andre Harrell, another music executive.

Muhammad now is on a crusade to change the lyrics of rap music in order to stop the portrayal of young black males as violent gang members while at the same time stopping the humiliation of the black women by calling them "hoes." Muhammad has confronted and portrayed Russell Simmons as "someone who has exploited hip hop for the benefit of white fans, who he claims represents 70 percent of the rap consumer market" (Noel, *Hip-Hop War*). Simmons has portrayed the black male as "penny-chasing, champagne-drinking, gold-teeth-wearing, modern-day Sambos, pimps and playas" (Noel, *Hip-Hop War*). Violent portrayal of Black men, Muhammad believes, has often given police or other government authorities reason for racial profiling. An example of this would be with the Jamaal "Shyne" Barrows when he was brought up on for shooting in a nightclub and illegal possession of a weapon. "Prosecutors are threatening to introduce Barrow's lyrics as evidence against him" (Noel, *Taking the Rap*). Muhammad goes on to add, "When you talk about people who have projected images of themselves as gangstas and find themselves involved with violent incidents, that's not racial profiling. If you go out and say you are a gangsta and the police trail you, that's not profiling you-you told them you are a gangsta" (Noel, *Taking the Rap*).

As a result, Conrad Muhammad has been on an ongoing battle to change the image of Rap so that society's view of the African American youth can change. He does not want African American women to be seen as only symbols of sex and he wants to stop the portrayal of Black men as violent gun-toting, felons. Recently, Muhammad tried to gain the Republican support for New York's 15th Congressional District in Harlem, but has failed to find any success. He has found little success because of his past actions where he denounced the American democratic system. Conrad Muhammad feels disappointed because he "supports Republican values of empowering small business and injecting market dynamics into the public school system" (Williams; Republicans Stumble with Outreach). Muhammad continues his active involvement in CHHANGE and still strives to change the economic and political situation of African-Americans.

Khalid Abdul Muhammad

Khalid Abdul Muhammad was born Harold Moore Jr. in Texas in 1948. He lived with his aunt in Texas and was raised with strong Christian backgrounds. Muhammad was involved with his Methodist church Fellowship group and even practiced delivering sermons to cars that drove by his aunt's porch (Cheshire 1994). At his all black high school, he served many leadership roles ranging from quarterback of his football team to captain of the debate team. Dillard University in New Orleans offered him a full scholarship where he spent several semesters before heading to Harvard.

It was at Dillard that Khalid was introduced to Minister Louis Farrakhan, who was Elijah Muhammad's top aide at the time. It was here, after Farrakhan's speech, that he became interested in the black liberation movement. Farrakhan's words were so touching to Khalid that he decided to join the Nation of Islam (Hunter 1994). Farrakhan gave Khalid his name after the Arab general Khalid ibnal-Walid who united Islam after Muhammad, its leader, passed away.

Khalid worked hard in the Nation throughout his first decade of service, and in 1981, he became Farrakhan's top aide. Muhammad was named one of Farrakhan's top lieutenants in the Nation of Islam in 1981 and in 1985 he conducted many fund raising events for the nation including some in Libya. He served at Nation of Islam mosques in New York and Atlanta throughout the decade and in 1991 became Farrakhan's personal assistant.

In the following few years, Muhammad became progressively more radical in his ideas and in delivering speeches. His views on the role of certain groups in society became increasingly controversial until a climax on November 29, 1993 when he delivered a speech at Kean College in New Jersey. Here is an example of the statements made by Muhammad during the speech:

Condemning Nelson Mandela: "We don't owe the white man nothing in South Africa... If we want to be merciful at all, when we gain enough power from God Almighty to take our freedom from him, we give him 24 hours to get out of town by sundown. That's all. If he don't get out of town by sundown, we kill everything that ain't right that's in sight in South Africa. We kill the women. We kill the babies. We kill the cripples. We kill 'em all. We kill the faggot. We kill the lesbian. We kill 'em all!"

This controversial speech came only a few months after other significant black leaders such as Jesse Jackson took steps toward forging some sort of partnership with the NOI to work on passing legislation. Many of these leaders demanded that the Nation of Islam take some sort of action against such commentary arising out of their organization if the partnership was to remain strong. On February 3, 1994, Minister Farrakhan made a statement to the press stating that he has ousted Khalid Muhammad not for the messages he delivered, but for the method he chose to deliver them. He was quoted as saying, "even though these quotes were malicious, there were many truths to be found in them."

Muhammad continued to speak out about the injustices that have plagued the black people for years and he gave many speeches at various academic institutions.

While some embraced his theories, others shunned him and vehemently opposed his views. In 1998, Muhammad made his most radical attempt to get the Black youth involved in his movements by organizing the Million Youth March, which took place on March 5, 1998. This march was fervently opposed by Mayor Rudolph Gulliani, but was allowed to commence by the New York City court system. Sadly, this march ended in a riot that ensued after a bottle was thrown at the police after they attempted to end the riot.

Armed with his views on protecting the Black people at any cost, Muhammad went on to found the New Black Panther Party. This organization was established in the city of Dallas in 1989. Muhammad, serving as the initial National Chairman, launched most of the 26 chapters in America and Europe along with the headquarters in Washington. With his new group, he continued his militant ways at getting his point across. One event that stuck out in his experiences was a march he led in Jasper, TX in 1998. He was there to protest the death of James Byrd Jr., a black man who was killed by three men who tied him to the back of a truck and dragged him around town.

At age 53, Muhammad died on February 20, 1998 at Wellstar Kennestone Hospital in Marietta, Ga. from a brain hemorrhage. He was often seen as the future black militant leaders and his speeches have arguably been some of the most influential in his story.

Gil Noble

A great deal of reporters report the news but few give you the truths For the past 34 years, Gil Noble has made it a point to report the news from the Black perspective. Mr. Noble "is responsible for the longest-running African American-produced television program in the US, *Like It Is*" (Aidi, *Gil Nobel*). *Like It Is* was created in 1968 after the Kemer Commission, which concluded that white racism was responsible for the riots in urban America and warned that the country was "moving towards two societies, one black, one white – separate and unequal" (Aidi, Gil Nobel). Some of the recommendations that arose from the Kerner Report were to show an increase in the representation of African Americans in the media and to show their problems and issues through television programming.

Gil Noble has been able to keep the show running for over 34 years with over 600 local awards and seven New York area Emmy awards. The greatest impact that Gil Nobel has had on the community· is his pressing need to educate African Americans on not only the state of African Americans affairs but to educate the world about the state of African people through out the world. "His one-hour Sunday afternoon program offers analysis of current political, economic, and cultural issues through interviews, profiles and documentaries" (Aidi, *Gil Nobel*). Noble is able to interview a rap artist such as "Treach from Jersey's Naughty by Nature; followed by an interview with brilliant neurosurgeon Dr. Ben Carson" (Arinde, *Gil Noble Calls...*). In addition, Noble has used his show to interview any number of Caribbean and African heads of state in order to address the issue of reparations to Africa and those that were displaced during the slave trade.

In addition to interviewing leaders of the African communities throughout the world, Noble has also produced documentaries such as "The Odyssey of Jesse Jackson," which showed the civil rights movement of African Americans as well as Jesse Jackson's national and international activism. Noble has also uncovered government institutions that have committed crimes such as the trafficking of illegal drugs through military installations in drugs into the US: The Quiet Route (Arinde, Gil Noble Calls...). In addition, Noble has made it an effort to portray the African American experience by producing documentaries on Martin Luther King, Jr., Malcolm X, Fannie Lou Hamer, and Adam C. Powell Jr. because most of their documentaries were produced by those that were not African American (American Entertainment, *Gil Noble*).

Even though the show has left a deep positive impact on the African American community, Disney, the owners of Channel 7-ABC did not want to continue the show due to the fact that they believed that the show was not profitable. Disney was "not willing to give Noble a full and extended contract or ensure that the show will not be canceled" (Arinde, Gil Noble Calls...). As a result, Noble did not take this lightly; he managed to gain political and economic support from leaders in the African American community. Noble supported by the "the African Poetry Theater, Million Man and Woman Coordinating committee of Queens, N'Cobra, National Black United Front, United African Movement, National Action Network, the December 12th movement and the New Black Panther Party (NBPP)," planned on boycotting Disney (Arinde, *Gil Noble Calls...*). Since the beginning of the boycott Disney stocks plummeted from 24.02, to 14.76 showing the impact that a minority community can have on a mainstream mega-media giant.

Gil Noble has proven the power of a collective effort through activism. He has not only been able to cripple a multi-billion dollar company but he has also opened doors for countless students to aspire to professional careers. He has not only influenced the world of journalism but every profession by introducing to the nation African community leaders, like himself, which has advanced the African American community.

Viola Plummer

Viola Plummer is a longtime movement activist organizer and leader who sprang out of the 1960's. Viola Plummer is a member of the New York 8+, co-founder of the December 12th Movement, the Sunrise Collective, the African Liberation Support Committee and the Harriet Tubman Fannie Lou Hamer Collective (Worrill; 1999). The activist/educator has confounded the December 12th Movement; is her main vehicle to increase awareness and catalyze change for Black people all over the world.

The December 12th Movement, a grassroots activist organization based in New York, has a strong commitment to the struggle against imperialism which has enabled them to bring the issue of human rights violations against black people to the international stage. Their mission is to expose these human rights violations domestically and build upon a national agenda to encourage social change and a total eradication of racism in our culture (Peam, 2000).

Viola Plummer, as an educator, is a strong supporter of academic freedom as well as enlightening black youths about their rich ancestry. Plummer, ispart of a coalition of organizations are active in planning a grand return home to Africa for the burial of 24 skeletons found at the African American Burial Ground in downtown Manhattan. The skeletons would be shipped on a course retracing the Middle Passage. A part of this effort is the Save the Children Campaign, in which 10,000 students will be enlisted to go on the trip to spend the summer working and learning in Ghana (Egyt, 1995). Plummer also contributes to the sustininence of black culture in Brooklyn where her coffee house, Sista's Place, is located. The coffee house which is named in honor of the many Black women participating in local and national politics, provides a safe and enriching environment for all.

Plummer the activist, started, after the murder of Amadou Diallo, to catalyze a People's Militia to protect and defend the Black and Latino community. Plummer, an anti-death penalty activist, helps to defend Black men on Death Row whom she feels had not been given a fair trial. She has also spoken out about the untimely deaths of rappers Tupac and Biggie Smalls; and how she suspects a governmental cover-up of their murders. Plummer recognizes that Black men are becoming increasingly expendable and has done all in her power to protect their human rights and safety.

Perhaps Plummer's biggest goal is to secure reparations for the descendants of African slaves. Plummer is the National Coordinator of the Millions for Reparations Rally. "The African slave trade greatly enriched the coffers of the US capitalist economy, helping to propel the US to its position as the dominant imperialist country in the world. At least 4 million African people were brutally exploited by not being paid one penny for all the great wealth they created" (Moorhead).

In addition to ensuring the safety and education of Blacks in America, Plummer is also deeply involved in international relations as they relate to Africa. She attends conferences across the globe to increase awareness of the Black plight and to gain support in the aid of it. She addresses critical issues in Zimbabwe and Congo. She was also in support of such issues as the ceasing of the Cubans trade sanctions (because of Cuba's strong support of the changes in Africa) and Israeli-

Palestine issues (believing that land is the basis of independence, a philosophy of Malcolm X (Salaam, 2002).

Viola Plummer is a truly strong black woman. She has an undying spirit that has enabled her to fight for the rights of Blacks for the past forty years. "Plummer draws her inspirations from former heroes like Malcolm X, Martin Luther King Jr., and Harriet Tubman, to name a few" (Wilkins, 1998).

Sonia Sanchez

Sonia Benita Sanchez was born Wilsonia Driver in Birmingham, Alabama on September 9, 1934. After her mother's death while Sonia was still an infant; Sonia and her older sister went to live with her grandmother, who she called Mama. At the age of six her grandmother died. Her relationship with Mama and this tragic incident unmasked Sanchez's gift of poetry (Uminski, 1997). Mama's strength and unconditional love, described by Sanchez, provided the security she needed to withstand childhood traumas and adult pain. As a means of expressing her feelings, Sanchez began writing poetry.

At the age of nine, Sonia moved to Harlem to live with her father, Wilson, who was the drummer of a jazz band. She attended public school in New York, and in 1955, attended Hunter College, where she earned her Bachelor's Degree in political science. It was when she attended New York University that her writing career began. After studying poetry under the teaching of Louise Bogan, she discovered that writing was her forte. Amiri Baraka (Leroi Jones) and Larry Neale also inspired Sanchez with their poetry and political activism.

In 1965 Sonia's teaching career began at the Downtown Community School in San Francisco. She continued her career at San Francisco State, where she helped to found one of the first Black studies programs in the country. In the early part of her career, Sanchez's ideas promoted integration, but in the early 1960's, after hearing a moving speech by Malcolm X outside of a New York coffeehouse, her thoughts changed dramatically. During her years in New York City, Sanchez became active in the civil rights movement and was a member of the New York activist group CORE. During this time she met Malcolm X, an activist who was also working in Harlem (Uminski, 1997). She soon became a revolutionary spokesperson for the African American Civil Rights Movement.

The early works of Sanchez focus on the political and personal problems that many black Americans faced during the 1960's, such as drug abuse, relationships, and racial oppression. Her first work, a book of poetry called Homecoming, was written in 1969. This book consisted of very blunt poems that targeted white Americans and black Puritans as the enemies, while praising Malcolm X and others like him. In Homecoming, as well as in her other works, Sanchez expresses a deep pride of being an African American, especially an African American woman. In 1972 Sonia joined the Nation of Islam; an event that significantly influenced her second book of poetry, Blue Black Magical Women, which is clearly a spiritual biography about her conversion and dedication to the Black Muslims. In the end, however, her ideas of women being strong and independent conflicted with the views of the Nation of Islam. The religion views women's roles as secondary to those of their male counterparts.

During the early part of her writing career Sonia Sanchez wrote many plays that focused primarily on the topics of drug use, racial discrimination, and most notably feminine pride. These plays usually displayed militant themes. Her first play, *The Bronx is Next*, traces the plot of residents to burn up a run-down Harlem ghetto. Through this play, Sonia Sanchez describes the journey and the rebirth of a black woman.

Even in her children's books Sanchez tries to convey her important message. She has written three: *It's A New Day; The Adventures of Fathead, Smallhead,* and *Soaphead*; and *A Sound Investment*. In each, she makes an effort to educate young Black children about their history, heritage, and culture. Although Sanchez's novels are few, they are extremely powerful. One of her most recent novels, written in 1998, *Does Your House Have Lions?*, is written in epic form. It addresses the issues of homosexuality and one of the most deadly epidemics facing the world today, AIDS. It is about the struggle that her brother experienced being a black, homosexual male dying of AIDS. After this novel was published, Julie Chance, editor of Vibe magazine stated in all her words, "Sanchez grabs your heart."

In 1985 a group of black political radicals were barricaded against the police in their place of residence. The group of citizens called themselves "MOVE." In retaliation to the uncooperative members, the police dropped a bomb on the residential building.

The drastic and catastrophic actions of the police resulted in fires that grew from the explosion and wiped out an entire city block. Many MOVE members, including children, were killed. In the midst of all the chaos, Sanchez recalls what others forgot: that the victims of this violent act were people. "Are you saying to me that we are at war with each other in this country? Is the message to be given to people that if we speak out and become non-conformists that certainly we can be killed? Or are you saying that in a black neighborhood anything goes?" (A Moveable Feast). In response to this unforgettable tragedy Sanchez wrote "Elegy: For Move and Philadelphia." Sanchez wanted people to see the horrible significance of this tragedy and to never forget that it happened. She waited three years to present this poem to the people of Philadelphia because she believed they needed time to heal in order to understand the poem and realize it wasn't a personal attack. Sanchez took on the heavy responsibility of this elegy because she believes "we must never let this happen again" (Uminski; 1997).

Currently Sonia Sanchez is a tenured professor at Temple University in Philadelphia, Pennsylvania where she currently lives. She teaches English and women's studies and holds workshops/lectures about women studies, civil rights and poetry.

Adelaide Sanford

Adelaide Sanford is an inspiration to us all. A genuine pioneer in the 20th century, she is an educator, teacher, and community activists. In 2002, there were more than 29 people whom were influential to the education field in their own right; many of them cite Adelaide Sanford as their source of major inspiration. These are teachers, community leaders, superintendents; and doctors. All of them attribute their beginnings to her. She was the main driving force behind their decisions to overcome adversity in order to make great strides personally and professionally.

Born during a time when there was major civil unrest; Sanford persevered to be known as "New York State's Top Educator;" a title she has earned after decades of tireless work on behalf of the voiceless masses of youth in the state of New York – many of whom are low-income, mis-educated, under educated and overlooked.

She began her professional career as a teacher in 1950. Upon her retirement in 1985 she had already been hailed as a statewide leader in education through her work helping many families successfully matriculate through what was and remains to be a public educational system, showing blatant and sometimes, subtle, prejudices against low-income, traditionally marginalized youth. On several occasions, Regent Sanford has described the past and present state of education as unchanged since the 1950's with the same schools that were neglected then as still failing and neglected. Her consistent message to the masses is that the only way to change this systemic failure is through community activism, something that she has dedicated her life. A noted example of her activism occurred in 1992 when the City College

135

System announced cutbacks, she was instrumental in organizing a grassroots effort to monitor the process in order to insure consistency, justice and fairness be upheld.

One of Sanford's defining moments came when she was elected to the Board of Regents of New York State. Amazingly, she was retired but working to make a difference in the lives of the New York youth. As a Regent, she has been able to further her causes to progress these youth to the forefront agenda of New York legislators.

Currently, Adelaide Sanford is second in command of the Board of Regents. This is groundbreaking, as she is the first African-American woman to hold this office for two terms, ending in 2005.

Sanford remains present in community activism; which has galvanized the formation of many grassroots efforts like the Million Youth March, and Women Working In Support Of the Million Man March. She has also been honored by many groups, including honorary doctorates from Mercy College and the Bank Street College of Education.

Reverend Al Sharpton

The Reverend Al Sharpton is best known as a civil rights activist, social advocate, and preacher. Throughout his life, he has attached himself with causes that he sees as a threat to basic rights, fairness, and equality. Most of the views he's represented have dealt with bettering the lives of black Americans. He has been extremely successful in addressing the concerns of many people and bringing these matters into the public arena where they receive a great deal of publicity and media attention.

Sharpton was born in 1954 in Brooklyn and began preaching at the young age of Four. By the time he was nine years old, he was an ordained minister and the junior pastor of a local congregation of 5,000 members. At about this time, Sharpton's parents got divorced and he went from living in a 10-room house in Hollis, Queens to a housing project in Brownsville, Brooklyn. He says that this is when he began to ask, "How do you make things fair?" He knew of a better life, and was aware that life in the projects was unfair (Garner, 2003).

One of the most significant and influential events in Sharpton's life was when he met Jesse Jackson at the age of fourteen. Jackson was a protege of Martin Luther King Jr. and became a father figure and mentor for the young preacher. Sharpton became involved in Operation Breadbasket under the supervision and leadership of Jackson, which was an organization that sought to spawn private-sector jobs for blacks

(Newfield, 2002). From this point on, Sharpton has become increasingly involved in the affairs of the people; specifically in the minority community of New York City. He has, however, allied himself with causes both nationwide and on an international scale.

Over the years Sharpton has aligned himself with many issues including police brutality, racism, economic inequality, and community empowerment. His most significant achievement has probably been the foundation of the National Action Network (NAN) in 1991, which is based out of Harlem, New York. The mission statement of this organization is "to be the voice of empowerment for the disenfranchised throughout America. NAN offers a committed national advocacy network of activists, volunteers, and religious leaders guided by the non-violent civil protest doctrines of Mahatma Gandhi and Dr. Martin Luther King Jr., that speak against racism, bigotry, and bias." Since its establishment NAN has supported many movements that affect communities throughout the United States and worldwide. "Reverend Al Sharpton heads an organization that fights for progressive, people-based policies against the rising conservative trend of cutting human services and balancing budgets at the expense of working class people" (NAN website).

Some of these issues include the assistance to pro-democracy movements in Haiti; peaceful protests against violence and racism, and the launch of anti-crime campaigns. One of the foremost issues that Sharpton has been a spokesperson for has been the issue of police brutality against members of the minority community. There have been several cases that have received a great deal of attention nationwide including those of Rodney King in Los Angeles, and of Abner Louima. Sharpton has provided spiritual guidance and to both the victims themselves and the victims' families while bringing their cases to the public's attention to create awareness among members of the community and influential political leaders about the problem that exists.

There are several committees within NAN that focus on different areas of the community. One of these committees is the education committee, which aims to provide all students, regardless of race, ethnicity, or background, talented teachers that come from diverse backgrounds. This committee also promotes the implementation of a curriculum that puts a greater emphasis on African history and on the contributions of people of African descent. Lastly, the initiative aims to provide better facilities and educational materials to disadvantaged and disregarded communities nationwide (NAN website). Although Sharpton promotes community empowerment and wants to represent the people, he is often seen as a very controversial character and is often not taken seriously due to some of his past actions. He has a tendency to exaggerate events in order to fight for certain points he believes in. Although his intentions may be peaceful, many civil protests that have been spearheaded or supported by Sharpton have ended in violence and even death. Nonetheless, Sharpton maintains that since he got stabbed at a protest in Bensonhurst, he has re-evaluated his tactics in order to be taken more seriously by the general public and be a more effective leader for the people he is trying to help.

Most recently, Sharpton has announced his plans to run for President in the democratic seat. He has run for office twice in the past as has shocked many political actors in the large number of votes he attracted from New York City and the minority communities in particular. Sharpton is a noteworthy competitor in this electoral race given the significant number of votes he has received in the past and the growing concern over many of the issues that he represents.

Works Cited

Associated Press. "Sanford on Diversity Education." *The New York Beacon* 21 Oct 1998: p 41.

Baillou, Charles. "Adelaide Sanford interprets Million Man March message." *New York Amsterdam News* 15 Nov. 1995: p. 6.

Cheshire, M.R. "Muhammad stresses unity in Nation of Islam." *Washington Afro-American* Nov 1998: p Al Egyir, W. (1995).

"Elaborate Rites are Being Planned for Burial of 24 Skeletons in Ghana." *New York Amsterdam News* 86. Retrieved on February 10, 2003, from *ProQuest* database.

Gamer, Dwight. "The Salon Interview: Al Sharpton: online." http://www.salon.com/weekly/sharpton.html (18 Apr. 1998).

Hunter, Jehron X. "Who is Dr. Khallid Muhammad?" *The Philadelphia Tribune* 17 Dec 1999: p. 2.

Juliet, Kaye. "School Failure Feeds the Prison System Contends Longstanding State Regent." *New York Voice Inc./Harlem USA* 22 May 2002: p 59.

Karriem, Bruce. "Kefa Nephthys." *New York Amsterdam News* 29 Jul. 1998: p. 12.

Moorehead, M. (June 11) Re: Drive a stake in slavery's rotten heart "Pay reparations, free political prisoners." Message posted to http://www.mumia2000.org/reparations/reparations-7.html.

Muhammad, Benjamin F. "Benjamin F. Muhammad." http://www_powerhousespeakers_com/Bios/Benjamin_Muhammad.htm. (Jan_ 2002).

Muhammad, Benjamin F. "Benjamin Chavis Muhammad."
http://africanpubs.com/Apps/bios/0739MuhamadBenjamin.html
(Feb 2002).

Muhammad, Benjamin F. "Minister Benjamin Chavis Muhammad
Speaks on the Million Man March." http://www. njournalg. com/
news/2000/09/ chavis_muhammad_speaks.html. (Sept. 2000).

Newfield, Jack. "Rev Vs. Rev. New York Magazine: online."
www.newyorkmetro.com/nymetro/news/politics/national/features/5
570/index2.html (7 Jan. 2002).

Noble, Gil. "Like It Is" interview with Dr. John Henrik Clarke (1987).

Noel, Peter. "The Minister vs. the Mogul: Hip Hop War."
http://www.villagevoice.com/issues/0117/noel.php. (21 Feb. 2003).

Noel, Peter. "Taking the Rap: Are Civil Rights Leaders Frontin' for
Hip-Hop Gangstas?"
http://wwvv.counterpunch.org/pipermail/counterpunch-list/2001-
January/005276.html. (16 Jan.2001).

Peam.C. (2000, November 2) Re: Massive Conference Planned Against
Racism. Message posted to
http://www.tbwt.com/views/specialrpt/special%20report-1_11-02-
00.asp.

Rahsidi, Runoko. The Global African Community History Notes: "In
Egypt with Yosef A.A. Ben-Jochannan." Icon of African
Biography. 2002.

Salaam, Y. (2002). Conference in Harlem focuses on Israeli-Palestinian
Issues. *New York Amsterdam News*, 93. Retrieved on February 10.
2003, from ProQuest database.

Sanford, Adelaide. "A New View." *The New York Beacon* 2 Oct. 1996:
p. 14.

Unknown. "Adelaide Sanford to speak against senseless violence." *The
New York Amsterdam News* 15 Mar. 1997: p. 5.

Wilkins, D.(1998). "Sistas1 Place is Good to the Last Drop in Bedford-
Stuyvesant." *New York Amsterdam News*, 89. Retrieved on
February 10. 2003, from ProQuest database.

Williams, Armstrong. "Republicans Stumble with Outreach. Again."
http://www.townhall.com/columinists/Armstrongwilliams/printlaw
20020724.shtml. (24 Jul. 2002).

Williams, Lakisha N. "Beyond Fear." National Action Network
website.
http://www.nationalactionnetwork.org (Feb.2003).

Worrill, C. (1999). Re: [BRC-NEWS] African Liberation Day
Symposium in Chicago. Message posted to

Gerald G. Jackson

http://www.blythe.org/nytransfer-subs/99rac/%5BBRC-
NEWS%5D_African_Liberation_Day-Chicago-Viola_Plummer.
Zamgba, Browne. "Sanford warns against hasty decisions on Ebonics."
The New York Amsterdam News 28 Dec. 1996: p. 1.

Ricardo Arguello and Rahim Wooley.
Photo by Gerald G. Jackson.

Shelby Senzer, Jamy Rodriguez and Phela Townsend.
Photo by Gerald G. Jackson.

AS&RC 172 Group Project #5

Overview

The system of oppression that has plagued black people around the world is based upon falsehood and negative psychological images. In various societies, the repetitive theme of black inferiority has been driven into people's minds. Common stereotypes show blacks as being lazy, stupid, violent, ignorant, savage, and having many other negative characteristics. The truth is that Africa is the birthplace of humankind and that blacks have made significant contributions to human society. In essence, the negative portrayal and complete exploitation of blacks shows the true sense of savage in the very oppressors who have continued to hold blacks down. In order to break this oppressive attitude; the true history of Black people needs to be known. One of the great historians who have accomplished much in this effort is John Henrik Clark.

Clark was born in Alabama in 1915 to a family of sharecroppers. Noticing that hypocrisies between the bible's teaching of events that took place in Africa and the lack of Africans illustrated in the bible, Clark began to study the history of Africa only to find out that he has been deceived his whole life. He learned that Africa's history is one of long success and excellent achievement. It has only been denied in order to enslave and degrade a group of people whose culture, achievements, and influence has been felt all around the world. He was a self-educated man who immersed himself in libraries, reading books that told the true history of Africa and its people. He taught in countries around the world, educating people that the history of black people is one that should be celebrated. After living 83 years learning about and teaching black history, John Henrik Clark died of a heart attack on July 16, 1998. There was a funeral service in remembrance of a great scholar whose work benefited and sparked intellectual thought amongst many black people. Notable figures in the current black community were present at the funeral including Cornel West, Wyatt Walker, Preston Wilcox, Wesley Snipes, Ivan Van Sertima, James Turner, and Percy Sutton. These people each had a connection to Clark and a similar connection and interest in the furthering of expressing the genuine history of black people.

Gerald G. Jackson

Cornel West

West was born June 2nd 1953 in Tulsa, OK as the grandson of a reverend and son of an elementary school teacher (mother) while his father was a civilian air force administrator. Much of his upbringing was derived from influences from his parents, grandparents, siblings, and community. In his autobiographical introduction to his book, "The ethical dimensions of Marxist thought," West reveals that the basis of his life vocation lies in three essential components of a Christian outlook that is viewed most clearly by Martin Luther King Jr. These are "a Christian ethic of love informed service to others, ego-deflating humility about oneself owing to the precious yet fallible humanity of others and politically engaged struggle for social betterment." West defines the "Age of Europe" as the descent of seven generations of Africans who were "enslaved and exploited, devalued and despised" by European whites as well as three more generations that were demeaned and terrorized by the Jim Crow laws and racist social practices of the South. He doesn't consider himself as an entire part of the "Age of Europe." Partially, yes but being a child of the "American Century," defined as a youth of the time that witnessed the overturning of discriminatory segregationist laws in the US. At the age of 17, West enrolled in Harvard; he graduated one year early with achievement of magna cum laude. During his time, there he participated in many influential activities outside the classroom, such as Black Student Organization takeover at Massachusetts Hall to protest Harvard's involvement in investing Gulf Oil. He volunteered at Norfolk State Prison and continued to intellectually challenge himself.

After his time at Harvard, he pursued a doctorate in philosophy at Princeton University. It was here that West discovered the values that were most precious to him: individuality and democracy. West began to publish books in the early 80's but many of them were written in the late 1970's. During his mid-twenties, he left Princeton, returning to Harvard to finish his dissertation. He then went to begin his tenure-track-teaching job as an assistant professor of philosophy of religion at Union Theological Seminary in NYC. While at Union, West traveled to many different countries, indulging himself in "national progressive multiracial and religious activity." While he was at Union he also wrote "The ethical dimensions of Marxist thought" but it wasn't published until 1991. The book he traces is Marx's intellectual development to see how he incorporated growing conscious of modem history. This was representative of West's awareness and values intellectually and socially. In 1984 West assumed a position at Yale Divinity School. He was jailed for protesting in Yale's investments in South African companies. West was punished by administration by having his scheduled planned of absence of leave to be substituted by a full load of two courses that spring semester.

West has continued to write and edit books on philosophy throughout the 1980s and early 1990s. He has also ventured attempts successfully addressing topics such as black male-female dialogue and suggestions to practical solutions to communication problems.

West continued his explorations into race relations and cultural diversity, in his widely acclaimed 1993 book, "Race Matters" which according to Ellis Cose in Newsweek is "salvation in a renewal of love, empathy and compassion in a radical redistribution of power and wealth- and in facing difficult truths." More recently, West had completed a spoken-word CD, which was distributed to major record stores. He was asked by the dean at Harvard (the school he was teaching at the time), that he was concentrating on being a Professor. In an ensuing argument through a couple meetings and media coverage, he decided to return to Princeton; where his intellectual endeavors were accepted and welcomed in any form. This was another example of the strong beliefs and various talents of Cornel West.

Wyatt Tee Walker

The Reverend Wyatt Tee Walker has made many contributions to the African American Community. His accomplishments began in 1950 when he decided to join VUU's seminary. As a seminarian and president of the student body, Walker attended a meeting of the Inter-Seminary Movement. At this meeting, he met another seminarian and student body president, Martin Luther King, Jr., from which a lasting friendship was formed. He received his Master of Divinity degree from VUU in 1953. That same year, he became minister of the Gillfield Baptist Church in Petersburg, Virginia. Walker was among one of a few young activist ministers. He acquired many leadership roles in a number of organizations. Along with his ministerial duties, Walker was president of the local chapter of the NAACP, state director of the Congress for Racial Equality, and founder of the Petersburg Improvement Association, a group patterned after the organization King had led to victory in the Montgomery bus boycott of 1955-1956. In 1958, at the request of Martin Luther King Jr., Walker became a member of the board of the Southern Christian Leadership Conference. Within the following two years, Walker organized an effort with other activist clergy that eventually led to the creation of the SCLC's *organizational structure in that state.*[1] In 1960, Dr. Martin Luther King Jr. again turned to his longtime friend. King asked Walker to accept the role of Executive Director of the SCLC. At that time, the SCLC was highly disorganized, and King looked to Walker to help bring some stability to the organization. Walker accepted, and from 1960 to 1964 he established order and stability in the SCLC.

Walker left the SCLC in 1964. That year, he became the marketing specialist for the Negro Heritage Library, for which he later assumed the role of president. The Negro Heritage Library's main focus was to convince school boards to include roles of black people in their curriculum. During this time, Walker served as the New York State governor's Special Assistant on Urban Affairs. In 1967 Walker became the pastor of Canaan Baptist Church of Christ in Harlem. While acting as pastor; Walker also completed his doctoral dissertation, and received his Ph.D from Colgate Rochester Divinity School in 1975.

Due to Walker's extensive research over the years, he has become one of the world's foremost authorities on the music of the African-American religious experience. In all, Walker has produced twenty-one published works on African-American music since 1979. Some of his most popular works are: Somebody's Calling My Name, *Road to Damascus: A Journey of Faith*, Millennium End Papers: The Walker File '98-'99, and Prophet from Harlem Speaks; Sermons and Essays. Walker's activism in the African American community has earned him distinction and praise. In the 1993 Ebony Magazine poll, he was named one of the fifteen greatest African-American preachers in the nation. Today, not only has Walker been noted for being the single largest developer of affordable housing in New York City, he serves as the President of the American Committee on Africa and Chairman of the Board of the National Action Network, the civil rights organization founded by Rev. Al Sharpton.

Preston Wilcox

Preston Wilcox stands among the very notable African American figures that attended the funeral of Dr. John Henrik Clarke. Born on December 17, 1923, he embarked his education in his hometown Youngstown, Ohio. Following his instruction at Youngstown College; he continued his academic merits and community service at other universities, such as Morehouse College, the City University of New York, New York University, and Columbia University.[2] Dr. Wilcox's influential experiences in New York, as well as inspiration by prominent Black leaders were crucial factors that shaped his future contributions to

African American society and culture. One such experience was his close friendship with Malcolm X, whose acquaintance he made while teaching a Community Organization seminar at Columbia University. Other influential figures that Wilcox admires are Dr. Martin Luther King Jr. and the late Dr. John Henrik Clarke.

With a source of inspiration and encouragement from various leaders in African American society, Preston became a representative and founder of many organizations and schools. He was the founding chairman of the National Association for African American Education, and executive director for AFRAM Associates Inc., an association that focuses on the preservation of African culture and improvement of the community with collections such as JAZZ, African American Figures in History; Social Work; Community Research & Organization, Housing Development, African American Education, Early Childhood through Higher Education, and drug treatment programs. Dr. Wilcox has a profound belief that the progression and representation of blacks and other minorities within the United States begins in the institution of education and schooling. With the aim of submerging children, youths, and adults to the true aspects of their culture, Dr. Wilcox is the chairman and founding board member of the College of Human Services, the Manhattan Country School and in 1990 became the co-chair member of the Borough President's Task Force on Education and Decentralization.

Dr. Wilcox developed a copyrighted and tested education model known as the Parent implementation in Education. He was also the consultant to The New Approach Method Reading Program and the Shawn A. Lambert Scholarship Fund. In providing youths with support programs, Dr. Wilcox was a member of the New York State Task Force on Youth Gangs and the New York State division of Youth in 1991. One of his honorable projects includes an evaluation of the Massachusetts Experimental School System.[3]

Collecting books, photographs, and articles of the Black experience in America, Dr. Preston Wilcox is an urban archaeologist and social worker who pursues the objective of "identifying the proper propaganda, so that people can get the information that they need to do what they have to do to empower, to think, and act for themselves." [4] Dr. Wilcox documents and preserves one of the largest bodies of information pertaining to African American society, and has been doing so for over three decades, starting in 1965. Dr. Wilcox is currently working with the Malcolm X Memorial Museum, and the Committee to Preserve the Works and Images of Malcolm X. He is in hopes of establishing a foundation that will exhibit his work as well as the work of other scholars. All of his contributions have been an effort, as he articulates, of "sharing information, and not hoarding it. Spreading it around, not necessarily telling people what to think, but have them exposed to the knowledge."[4]

Wesley Snipes

Born to an aircraft engineer and teacher's aide in Orlando, Florida, Wesley Snipes started his acting career at a very early age. His first minor role in an off-Broadway play was at the age of 12. It is said that because he was not very tall throughout high school, he substituted for his short stature with charm and confidence that helped him throughout his career. Later, moving to the southern section of the Bronx allowed him to enroll in New York's High School for the Performing Arts where he pursued his strong interest in dance.

When his mother decided it was time for a change of atmosphere and a move back down to Florida, it was not an easy transition for Snipes. He was used to the fast-paced life of the city and could not deal with the humdrum life of the South. He is quoted as saying, "They're just moseying along; like lemonade on the porch on a Sunday afternoon; and you're like yo; I can't stand this. Let me outta here." He does admit however the life in the city often leads to a dead end. In the New York Times he states, "Moving to Florida was the best thing that could have happened to me. A lot of the cats I grew up with in the South Bronx found themselves in sticky situations." [5]

After doing exceptionally well in high school, Snipes enrolled at SUNY Purchase in a prestigious theater arts program. Being one of the only four African-American students in the program, Snipes talks about how isolated he felt. Snipes states in Ebony magazine, "I felt like mold on white bread... what saved me was being exposed to Malcolm X."

He claims his faith in Islam was short-lived though highly important to his overall character. He sees Islam as "the log [that kept me afloat and made] me more conscious of what African people have accomplished, of my self-worth, [and gave] me some self-dignity." David Garfield, an acting teacher at Purchase, calls Snipes, "obviously gifted," and states, "He also exhibited a strong black consciousness."[5] After college, Wesley Snipes career as an actor soared to great heights. Because he had the natural grace of a dancer, he was often cast in martial arts and athletic roles, but it was his cameo in Michael Jackson's *Bad* video that caught the eye of director Spike Lee for his new movie *Do the Right Thing*. Although Snipes turned down this role, he would later work with Lee in movies such as *Jungle Fever* and *Mo'*

Better Blues. A talented mimic, Snipes memorized scales and fingering for all of the music played in *Mo Better Blues*. The characters in both *Jungle Fever* and *New Jack City* were both written with Snipes in mind. Mario Van Peebles, the director of *New Jack City*, cast Snipes in the role of Nino Brown, a Harlem drug lord, after his appearance in Jackson's *Bad* video. The movie was designed to be an anti-drug and anti-violence gangster film, but a wave of shootings and violence erupted briefly at some theaters across the country after it opened. Although most of the violence had to do with the oversell of tickets, it was also stated that Snipes' portrayal of Nino Brown might have been *too effective*. His controversial roles in *Jungle Fever* and movies like *New Jack City* and *Sugar Hill* didn't stop Snipes from winning numerous awards for his roles. Snipes was also applauded for his in-depth research for the roles he played. To research his role as a paraplegic in *The Waterdance*, Snipes spoke with patients at rehabilitation centers to understand their physical limitations and collect emotional insight as well. He also shows his political beliefs as the executive producer and narrator of *John Henrik Clarke: A Great and Mighty Walk*. Snipes is known for his role as a community activist and is not ashamed to do so. Snipes also appears in *Down in the Delta*, a film directed by Maya Angelou and produced by Snipes' production company, Amen Ra Films. A deeply spiritual movie, Snipes has often said, "[spirituality] is the only way I've been able to survive."

Ivan Van Sertima

Ivan Van Sertima, perhaps best known for his work *They Came Before Columbus: The African Presence in Ancient America*, was born in Kitty Village, Guyana in South America. Sertima grew up with his father in the deep woods of Guyana separated from things what many at the time took for granted, and he recounts on his distorted view of the world saying, "I grew up believing there were only three great civilizations in the world: Greek, Roman, and British...I believed all the myths of black inferiority." Sertima did, though, rise from somewhat humble beginnings to end up studying at the School of Oriental and African Studies in London. Sertima wanted to study Africa and the African population; however, he realized that the field was interested solely in Africa's primitive cultures. Sertima graduated, and continued his study of Africa in the United States at Rutgers University resolving to document the careers and achievements of Africans. Some of his research, most notably on Christopher Columbus, has attacked the long-standing ideas that society has held over time.

Sertima has made several lectures speaking on the largely under appreciated contributions made by Africans in the field of science. At one such lecture, Sertima states that, "We [Africans] are shut off from our own genius... we have grown up on incredible myths." One of these myths is the notion that Africans over time have been uncivilized savages though Sertima's research proves the contrary. The Caesarean Section, for example, has been one significant contribution made to science by Africans. The process was being performed at an almost perfect success rate in Uganda. British scientists took note of the procedure and materials used by the Ugandans, and improved vastly on their own techniques for doing the same operation. Speaking about his findings, Sertima says, "Where did they [British] get this knowledge from? They [Ugandans] were supposed to be Bugaboos running around in the jungle." Besides this development of medicine, Sertima has also found that Astronomy was another field that Africans have pioneered. Discouraged that a lot of the information he has found has been left out of history books over time, Sertima started *The Journal of African Civilizations*, devoted to promoting African achievement and culture in science.

In his career, Sertima has made a name for himself as in anthropology, literary criticism, and he is currently a professor of African Studies at Rutgers University. Sertima has written critical essays, nominated works for the Nobel Prize, and his findings have led to his inclusion in UNESCO'S International Commission for Rewriting the Scientific and Cultural History of Mankind where he shared his research on the misconceptions of the impact of Africans in history. Sertima's work on the Christopher Columbus myth entitled *They Came Before Columbus: The African Presence in Ancient America*, is in its 21st printing, and has garnered Sertima perhaps his most fame. About the myth that Columbus was the first to arrive to North America Sertima says, "The African presence in America before Columbus is of importance not only to African and American history, but to the history of world civilizations. The African presence is proven by stone heads, terra cottas, skeletons, artifacts, techniques and inscriptions, by oral traditions and documented history, by botanical, linguistic and cultural data." Sertima continues to work to uncover the contributions to society that have been largely overshadowed for years.

James Turner

James Turner is a Professor of African and African American Politics and Social Policy at Cornell University. Turner earned a B.S. from Central Michigan University, an M.A. from Northwestern

University, a certificate in African Studies from Northwestern's African Studies Center, and a Ph.D. from the Union Graduate School in Cincinnati. During an interview with Professor James Turner, he describes consciousness as a process. Whom you meet. What you experience. What you do. Turner's process is more than personal. His process is his mission – a mission that affects all those involved in Africana studies.

As the interview began Turner became comfortable and relaxed in his chair. A reflective and pensive air seemed to surround him. His story started in Brooklyn – Kings County, New York, as he spent the first ten years of life there. His times in Manhattan were more memorable though. Yet, before Turner digressed into his Manhattan adolescence, he discussed his family. Dr. Turner's parents and aunts were a part of the Second Great Migration. This migration occurred between the years 1939 and 1944, when many blacks left the conditions in the south for northern opportunities presented by the war. Turner's mother and her four sisters came to New York as a collective to take advantage of this opportunity. His mom found work in a factory making war uniforms. She attended school as well and received more education than she would have received in the south. With an emphasis on the value on education, Turner's mother set out an objective for her children to graduate high school. Thus, the value of an education became a part of Turner's process of consciousness when he was still very young. Education it its many forms entered Turner's life and affected his development most while he lived in Harlem In Brooklyn, both immediate family and his aunt's family lived together in a cold water flat. Because of the crowded and poor conditions that came with living in tenement housing. Turner's family had their name put on the Public housing list in New York City. Finally, his family received word of the availability of a five-room apartment in Harlem. This would give the family more space.

It was there in Harlem, that Turner met many of the people that would eventually help him continue to develop his consciousness. His mother-in-law was one of those people as she was a proud and encouraging figure. She came into his life when he met his wife-to-be during mid-adolescence. Turner's mother-in-law was very race conscious and did not allow for any slandering against Black people. Her influence helped to further reinforce what he observed in his own mother's positive attitudes towards Black people.

One Hundred and Twenty Fifth Street between seventh and eighth Avenues in Harlem became the black equivalent to Hyde Park in London. It was there where loud speakers would be put on the comers and Blacks would lecture to both those who passed by and stopped to listen. Turner was one of those who stopped and on one occasion was deeply inspired. As Professor Turner reminisced on this memory, he motioned as if he was there again, standing on the corner in awe.

With Turner's eyes now looking from more than one angle, he began to rise and seek out answers to questions that he long had in his mind. Turner wondered: *Why are our people so different? Why is there so little pride in our identity?* Why were blacks always making fun of each other? (Skin, hair, nose) Why do we fight so much with each other? Why do we interact so differently with whites than we do with our own people? It was those inspired years that Turner met a writer named J.A. Rodgers, and began reading his books. While JA Rodgers was writing, Malcolm X was speaking, and Turner began to listen to him speak. As Professor Turner fell deeper into his memories, he recalled the experiences of listening to Malcolm X as a mind opening and mind-bending experience. Turner remembered John Herick Clarke to be from the same condition as Rodgers – they were Non-professional scholars. They both taught and learned with people in the community. Turner was twenty and recently married to a young woman from Harlem named Janice when he first met Clarke at a lecture.

Around the same time, Richard B. Moore had become an important mentor to Turner. Moore always kept the young developing scholar well supplied with books. Moore gave Turner exposure to works of great men such as W.E.B. Dubois and Paul Robeson.

After gaining such exposure to Black thought, Turner and his wife decided that they needed to get away. They wanted to further their education, and after saving for a year, they began attending school in the Mid-West. Just then, a ray of sunlight entered the office and brightened the room during Professor Turner's interview. He then recalled the day he and his wife were leaving for school. It was on that day that he and his wife met Malcolm X. Malcolm X was very impressed that this young black couple was going to school and urged them to come back to the community when they were done advancing their education. He told them that Black people needed those educated to build the communities. After Professor Turner was done recalling this memory, he thought again and stated matter of fact that Malcolm X was a good person on a personal level. Soon after that encounter, James and Janice Turner headed to Michigan to attend school. At this point, it was the 1960's. While in school, Turner often told Blacks that they needed to be proud. As the Black consciousness movement expanded, Turner and his wife became popular. As Janice Turner pursued studies in psychology and academic counseling, James Turner wanted to pursue African American Studies. Unfortunately, there was no African American department where he attended. It was then that Turner and others took action and demanded that there be a black studies department. With the national movement, it seemed like an extremely necessary and appropriate change. Turner was now at the center of the student and the black studies movement.

Students at Cornell began scouting for faculty to build a Center for Black Studies. They recommended Turner and although he had no experience in designing an entire center of studies; he managed to found the Africana Center at Cornell University in 1969. The uniqueness of the Africana Center today is its autonomy from the university; it's bigger than a department but smaller than a college. This autonomy allowed the Center to develop its own courses and hire its own faculty and so Turner turned back to the community for resources. He approached Dr. Clarke who agreed to help and draw up a basic plan for the courses offered, as well as teach. Professor Turner was sure to mention strongly how Dr. Clarke was very instrumental in helping to develop the program and very critical in getting the Africana Studies and Research Center started.

Dr. Clarke eventually left the Center to take a position running Black and Puerto Rican studies at Hunter College in New York City. Throughout the relationship between Turner and Clarke, they worked together in many organizations outside of Cornell. Together they created the African Heritage Studies Association, that which Clarke was the first president and Turner was the third. Although Clarke was now faculty at Hunter, he was often invited back to Cornell and would often give lectures there. When Clarke retired, the Africana Library was named after him.

This Library in essence was named after a man who dedicated himself to education at the community level. His main goals included spreading knowledge, fighting against the mass of ignorance, increasing self-worth among Blacks, and increasing pride, self-respect, and self-knowledge. Through Dr. Turner's process of consciousness, he has done the same and continues to achieve these things. At this time of the day, the interview was reaching its closing stages and the sunlight now seemed to illuminate Turner's expansive book collection on the North wall of his office. He assured that, his career at Cornell University has never strictly been a vocation; it is rather more who he is. He enjoys it all, and through his work, Turner is carrying a vision to Black people. Turner will continue to answer those questions that rose and continue to rise in him through out his observations in life. The process of his consciousness, of all Black consciousness will not end.

151

Percy Sutton

Marked with dignitary status, Percy Sutton sat in Abyssinian Baptist Church and watched as his beloved friend and colleague John Henrik Clarke was laid to rest on the 21st of July 1998. Sutton obtained his VIP status the same way in which Clarke did, by being an effective participant in the Civil Rights Movement and accomplishing feats that moved the Black race closer to equality. Born on November 4th, 1920, Percy E. Sutton was the youngest of fifteen children. Samuel J. and Lillian Smith were residing in San Antonio when they brought Percy into the world. Since they were both educators, his parents were determined to provide the best academic opportunities for Percy and his siblings. As each child successfully completed their education, they began to support the family financially to ensure the proper education of the remaining siblings.

Following the completion of his education, Sutton began what was to be an extremely successful and admirable career. Before his retirement, Sutton held a plethora of jobs and positions. He was an attorney, a civil rights activist, an advisor, a counselor, a human rights activist, a US Air Force pilot, a politician, and a businessperson. During his occupancy of these various jobs, his focused remained centered on the betterment of the Black race.

While in the Air Force, Sutton was a pilot for the Tuskegee Airmen. His political career involved holding many different positions in the New York branch of the NAACP including being elected its president in 1961 and 1962. He was elected to the Lower House of the New York legislature in November of 1964, taking his seat the following January. Voted Assemblyman of the Year by the intercollegiate legislative assembly in 1966 Sutton was elected to be the president of the Manhattan Borough andheld the position from 1966 to 1977.

Practicing law in a few states, Suttonwas hired to be Malcolm X's lawyer, and after his death continued to represent his widow and the Shabazz family. One of Harlem Hospital's and the United Black Association's top advisors, Sutton was also used as a counselor and confidante by Jesse Jackson while he was trying to win the presidential election. Sutton served as a mentor and role model to many younger African American men and women during his career and continues to today.

Sutton, being the epitome of a true Renaissance man, not only had a substantial political career but an extensive business one also. Being a major founder of the Street Literacy Clinic and Magic of Learning, he was able to pass on his education beliefs and provide a computer-based learning system that helps kids to read and write. Sutton was also Chairman of the Queens Inner Unity Cable System. In 1971, he co-founded the Inner City Broadcasting Corporation, which upon its purchase of WLIB-AM became the first black owned radio station in New York City. During the same year, he formed AMNEWS an organization that bought the New York Amsterdam news. Sutton and one of his companies were even responsible for the survival of the Apollo Theatre in 1981, and for turning it into the historical non-profit organization it is now.

Percy Sutton's fame and honor will clearly surpass his years and the legacy he has created will continue to thrive within his successors. Totaling over seven hundred and fifty international, national, and local awards, his trophy case alone illustrates the love and appreciation many feel he deserves. Sutton was a man of intelligence, charisma, honor, and one who was committed to perpetuating the advancement of a people.

Clark's funeral brought together a group of distinguished black people whose goals are all similar. Each has been committed to the advancement of a people who have been oppressed and wrongly imaged. In order for black people to elevate the race's status in the world, a factual sense of self is necessary. John Henrik Clark is a man who has understood the history of black people as it really is, and as it should be commonly known. There is a glorious, colorful and highly intellectual history of black people, complete with accomplishments that have changed the world. It is sad that current history books all contain the same names such as Dr. Martin Luther King Jr., Malcolm X, and Rosa Parks, portraying a sense that there are few black leaders and innovators that have made a mark on the world. The truth is that there are many names out there, such as John Henrik Clark, who stands out as scholars, thinkers, and intellectuals. Through reading and researching, much like how Clark did throughout his whole life, answers to who these people are can be found and later dispersed to the rest of the world.

Haki Madhubuti

Haki Madhubuti, born Don Lee in Little Rock, Arkansas in 1942, first made a name for himself in the literary world in the late sixties. Madhubuti's work, from his first to his most recent has focused on various aspects of Black life in America, and is even written in slang. Madhubuti can be described as a socially conscious poet as his work can be characterized by anger at social and economic injustices and also a rejoicing in African American culture. Madhubuti's mother, Maxine, who raised him in Detroit, died of a drug overdose when Haki was sixteen, and he still sites his mother as the driving force of his literary creativity.

In early adulthood, besides focusing his work on Blacks in America, Madhubuti also physically participated in groups aimed at fighting the social injustices prevalent during the civil rights movement. Madhubuti has participated in the Student Non-Violent Coordinating Community (SNCC), the Congress of Racial Equality (CORE) and the Southern Christian Leadership Conference (SCLC) proving that Haki has always had a great interest in helping the situation for all Blacks. Much has been said of Madhubuti's work. One critic says his work is "like a razor; it's sharp and will cut deep, not out to wound but to kill the inactive Black mind."

Madhubut's message is clear: if you are not for the betterment of society for Blacks then you are against it, plain and simple. A testament to his influence, Madhubuti sold about 250,000 books of poetry in 1971, alone which could be more than any other Black poets before him, combined could. After a short stint in the military, Madhubuti's literary career began to rise. Madhubuti earned professional degrees at several colleges, and moved on to teach his idea of a Black cultural value system as a guest professor at schools across the country. As a writer, Madhubuti has written nineteen books, and has reached out to other fledgling writers by founding the Third World Press. Some notable authors published by the independent press include celebrated playwright and essayist Amiri Baraka, scholar Chancellor Williams, and renowned poet Gwendolyn Brooks, who has published the second volume of her autobiography and several books of poetry with Madhubuti's press. Madhubuti has also helped to influence the education of young Blacks by helping to establish the Institute of Positive Education in Chicago, a school for black children, in 1969.

Works Cited

1. Aldon D. Morris. *The Origins of the Civil Rights Movement*. New York: The Free Press, 1984, p. 183.
2. *Who's Who among African Americans*. 15th edition. Detroit: Gale Group, 2001.
3. Spradling, Mary Mace. *In Black and White. Third edition: a guide to magazine articles, newspaper articles, and books concerning*

more than 6,700 Black Individuals and Groups. Detroit, Michigan: Gale, 1985, p. 405.

4. http://www.harlemlive.org/community/peeps/wilcox/
    "Snipes, Wesley." *Contemporary Black Biography*. Vol. 24. pp. 55-159.

Collage in background created by the group. Student is Catherine Soto.
Photos by Gerald G. Jackson.

Left to Right Keven, Stefun and Joe. Photos by Gerald G. Jackson.

Missing Biographical Essays[74]

LaTasha Richardson
Professor Gerald Jackson
AS&RC 172
May 1, 2002

Camille Yarbrough

Camille Yarbrough is known for her contribution to the arts. She is involved in theater, film, dance, and music. She has also written books for children. In any event, she is known for her involvement in the Black Arts Movement, and she has paved the way for many Black women into the entertainment and arts division at large. Her CD is entitled "Iron Pot Cooker."

She taught in the Black Studies department of City College of New York, and at Dunham Technique at Southern Illinois University.

She is an advocate of preserving African and African American culture through the arts. In addition, Yarbrough teaches about pride in racial heritage and physical features. Two of her books are examples of her attempt to instill a sense of taking pride in African and African American culture to Black children and their parents. One children's book she has written is entitled "Cornrow." It gives the historical significance of wearing cornrows, and depicts those who still wear them today, as courageous African Americans. Her book, "The Shimmershine Queens," is a children's book that examines the differences between being light-skinned and dark-skinned and having "good" and "bad" hair.

Rashad Harris[75]
Africana 171

Research Paper on Dr. Robert L. Harris

Dr. Robert L. Harris is a Professor in the Africana Studies program at Cornell University. He teaches the courses entitled, "The Survey of

---

[74]Individuals inadvertently omitted from this class' project. Not presented is Marcus Garvey Jr.

[75]Group II – Michelle Evans, Rashad Harris, Stacy-Ann Elvy, Amanda Glover,and Ericka Gibson.

African American history," Black Leaders and Movements," and a graduate seminar on African American Historyography. He describes the latter as basically the writing, and interpretation of black history.

As a child growing up in Chicago, Dr. Harris remembers always having a keen interest in the Black person in history. Much like John Henrik Clarke, at a young age Professor Harris, hoping to expand his knowledge on the subject, took it upon himself to go to places like the library and read about people like Frederick Douglas, Booker T. Washington, W.E.B. Dubois, George Washington Carver and other prominent figures in Black history. Professor Harris remembers reading the *Chicago Defender,* a Black newspaper, and more specifically, a feature written by J. A. Rogers that was titled: "Know Your History." It was at this stage of his life that he became interested in African Studies.

Later on, during the 1960's, Dr. Harris became active in the Civil Rights Movement. He became part of an organization called C.O.R.E. (the Congress of Racial Equality), and organization whose primary focus was to improve living conditions in the projects of the inner city.

My interview with the Professor became more of a discussion of sorts in which we talked about many current issues faced by black youth today, and during which he shared with me some insightful information. I asked him what he thought about current race relations on campus and one thing he said was that he's not surprised. "Cornell's campus is a microcosm of society," he said and added, "why would one suspect it to be any different" One of the things I found most interesting about Dr. Harris was that he is an avid watcher of BET, and also a listener of Rap music. On these matters, he said, "I think that you have to try to keep up with popular culture." Professor Harris also says that although it has been "corrupted for commercial purpose," and that much of Rap tends to illustrate many of the baser aspects of urban life (e.g., drugs, crime, and sex), he still believes "it is as interesting musically as it is lyrically," and that it is most definitely a "vehicle of communication for today's black youth." Surprisingly, he noted that it also reflects the music of his era in the sense that the Rhythm and Blues music he listened to as a youth, just as rap is today, was scorned and ridiculed by his parents. In short, according to Dr. Harris, the conflict is a "generation thing." We sort of agreed upon the idea that ignorance, is also another thing that plagues my generation. We started discussing the entertainment industry and how it is often one sided in terms of the way it portrays black people. He says "There's a certain image of black people that's projected [by Hollywood and the rest of the entertainment industry]" and "if you don't also see this image, then you're often seen by others as not *real*." This ignorance is best illustrated in the lack of support shown for black movies by the black community. Movies like "Eve's Bayou," "Amistad," and "Soul Food," which portray blacks in a variety of roles other than the "pimp," the "hustler," or the "gangbanger" are not as popular because they don't feature again, the baser aspects that we, in a sense, are almost used to seeing.

My interview with Professor Harris was very interesting. In fact, I came away with a very good piece of advice, which is never to let others define **who I am**. And also to: know my own history.

Thanks for giving me the extension and I'll see you in 172 next semester.

GROUP I
AS&RC 171
Prof. Jackson
1 November, 2000

Dr. Reverend Calvin O. Butts

Reverend Calvin O. Butts, III, D. Min. is one of the foremost activists for the equal treatment of African-Americans in the New York City area. While the majority of his projects are focused there, his tremendous work in the area of social justice, community building, and empowerment has received nationwide attention. He is involved in the majority of major fights that take place in New York, alongside other famous political rights activists, such as Rev. Al Sharpton and Jesse Jackson. He slowly works towards his dream of creating a world that has all people on a common ground.

Dr. Butts was born and raised originally in New York City, New York. For his college education, he traveled down South and graduated from the historically Black Morehouse College in Atlanta, GA. Here his major of study was philosophy. It was also here that he became a member of Kappa Alpha Psi fraternity, Incorporated. Soon after, he returned to New York to seek further educational training. His calling to the church urged him into seeking and receiving a Master of Divinity degree in church history from Union Theological Seminary. Soon after, he went to study at Drew University and earned a Doctor of Ministry in Church and Public Policy from there.

Currently, Dr. Butts is the Pastor of the Abyssinian Baptist Church in New York City. His commitment to the glorification of his Lord and his Earthly kingdom has brought Dr. Butts and his church into the neighboring streets of New York City. Integrated into the daily duties of Dr. Butts are things that go to eliminate social problems such as homelessness, senior citizen and youth empowerment, cultural awareness, and ecumenical outreach. Under his direction, the Abyssinian Church has completed the following projects: the acquisition and renovation of apartment units for the homeless across the street from the church; construction of senior citizens housing on West 131st Street; moderate income condominiums for purchase on 131st Street; acquisition of the Renaissance Ballroom and Small's Paradise: two major historic landmark facilities in Central Harlem. The Church has also worked on building a solid foundation for the intermediate and high school, which would operate under the control of the Abyssinian Development Corporation. This school has been named Thurgood Marshall Academy for Learning and Social Change, in honor of the great advances that Thurgood Marshall has made for the African-American race in this country.

Dr. Butt's efforts to improve the lives of Blacks do not stop with the activities in which he engages his church. He, himself, holds many prominent positions with which he tries to get the voice of an African-American heard. Dr. Butts has taught African studies at City College, New York, Church History at Fordham University, as well as lectured at man other universities around the country. He still now teaches and lectures even after he has assumed the role of the President of SUNY College at Westbury. He is also President of the Council of Churches of of the City of New York, as well as the Chairman of the Board of Managers for the C. T. Walker Housing Corporation. Dr. Butts has served as the Chairman of the Board for the Harlem Branch YMCA, an and is now the Vice-chair of the Board of Directors of the United Way of New York City. He serves as a member on The Central Park Conservancy Board, as well as many other committees that try to raise the standards of New York City. He contributed to the founding of, and now serves as Chairman of the National Affiliate Development Initiative of the National Black Leadership Commission on AIDS. He also has served as the President of an independent organization, which sought to improve the living conditions in rural Africa, Africare.

Dr. Butts also spearheads many of the local gight, which threaten the rights of Blacks in his neighborhood and around the country. In New York City, he has taken a stand against the Brutality and Racial Profiling done by the New York Police Department. He has also incited huge boycotts of establishments who had racist tendencies against African-American people. Dr. Butts was also a central figure in the fight against drug abuse and exploitative billboards that were posted in the Central Harlem district. He is also a big advocate against the prominence of negative images of women and violence featured in hip-hop music. He believes that his taking stands in all of these circumstance makes a big difference in the uplift of his people around the world.

For all of his dedication to making a better life for his and all people, Dr. Butts has received a multitude of awards. His commendations include Man of the Year, and the Morehouse Candle Award from his alma mater. He has also received The William M. Moss Distinguished Brotherhood Award and The Louise Fisher Morris Humanitarian Award. In total, Dr. Butts has received more than 300 other awards for his outstanding work. He is also a Prince Hall Mason, and has received the final degree in Masonry. Dr. Butts was recognized as a living treasure by the New York City Chamber of Commerce and Industry, and has ben twice named a New York Power Broker.

Bibliography

http://www.moravian.edu/Newsinfo/NewsReleases/NR142.htm
http://www.upenn.edu/chaplain/pucfsn/buttsbio.html

Afterthoughts

In the end, the research effort and actual group presentations reveal approaches that are pedagogically sound for classroom assignments, reading and researching skills and enhancing a greater sense of community. Pedagogical issues in the United States typically center on color and not subculture. Yet, if conflict were simply a matter of color there would have been no wars exclusively among Africans, Europeans and Asians. It was this historical and global view that resulted in my development of the concept of *culturalism*.[76] It acknowledges an observable difference in thought and practice between African, European and Asian world-views without claiming inherent superiority in either cultural or philosophical systems.[77] This concept does not deny the existence and practice of racism.[78] One must be cognizant that using skin color to predict behavior is not necessarily woeful as a survival mechanism. It is a short-hand reaction to historical precedent and the continuation of racial crimes.[79] Its utility is most apparent when a Black person is driving, buying, learning and dealing with the police, while Black. What is presented is a more replete and balanced view. Included in this book, for instance, is a long-hand script that encompasses a broader range of race relations' factors.

Predictably, based upon an Africentric cultural system of thought, the approach recommends an appreciation of the strengths of different cultural systems and permits a freedom to use functional elements from many. This framework has allowed Africentric educators to recognize and appreciate the historical and contemporary contributions from an oral and literate culture.[80] In seeking concepts and theories, therefore, it enabled an Africana psychology, and pedagogy to see parallels in the works and movements of innovative Eurocentric writers, scholars,

---

[76] Gerald Jackson (1986). "Conceptualizing Afrocentric and Eurocentric Training" (pp. 131-150). In Harriet Lefley & Pedersen, P. (Eds.). *Cross-cultural Training for Mental Health Professionals.* Massachusetts: Charles C. Thomas.

[77] Hazel Weidman (1986). "Attaining The Transcultural Perspective in Health Care" (pp. 311-330). Implications for Clinical Training. In Harriet Lefley & Pederson, P. (Eds.). *Cross-cultural Training For Mental Health Professionals.* Massachusetts: Charles C. Thomas.

[78] The two ideas are linked in the a work by Sowell. See, Thomas Sowell (1994), Race and Culture A world view. New York: Basic Books.

[79] See James Byrd discussions in Sect. III.

[80] Walter Ong (1982). *Orality and Literacy: The technologizing of the word.* New York: Methuen.

scientists and researchers. These individuals included the individuals and works of Robert Ornstein's *Multimind*,[81] Daniel Goleman's *Emotional Intelligence*,[82] Howard Gardner's theory of multiple intelligence,[83] Edward O. Wilson's *Consilience*,[84] Gregory Bateson's *Steps To An Ecology of Mind*,[85] and Arnold Lazarus' *Multimodal Behavior Therapy*.[86] Viewed from an Africentric concept termed diunitality, the approach enabled opportunities for students to exercise their affective intellectual self, supported by the recent "emotional intelligence" work of Daniel Goleman.[87] Similarly, the ongoing critique of the concept of intelligence by Black psychologists[88] and proposal for alternative multiple intelligence concepts has been united. It enabled me to integrate the critique and Black proposals into the theory of multiple intelligence and use students' multiple intelligence in examining and detailing their course work. Overall, it gives instruction on how to use effectively the "Black aesthetic"[89] in an academic setting.

---

[81]Robert Ornstein (1986). *Multimind*. Massachusetts: Houghton Mifflin Company.

[82]Daniel Goleman (1995). *Emotional Intelligence*. New York: Bantam Books.

[83]Howard Gardner (1983). *Frames of Mind The theory of Multiple Intelligences*. New York: Basic Books.

[84]Edward O.Wilson (1998). *Consilience The Unity of Knowledge*. New York: Alfred A. Knope.

[85]Gregory Bateson (1972). *Steps To An Ecology of Mind*. New York: Ballantine Books.

[86]Arnold Lazarus (1972). *Multimodal Behavior Therapy*. New York: Springer.

[87]Daniel Goleman (1998). *Working with Emotional Intelligence*. New York: Bantam Books.

[88]Gerald Jackson (1979). "The origin and development of black psychology: Implications for black studies and human behavior." *Studia Africana*, 1, 270-293; Gerald Jackson (1982). "Black psychology as an avenue to the study of Afro-American behavior." *Journal of Black Studies*, 12(3), pp. 241-260.

[89]Addison Gayle (Ed.) (1971). *The Black aesthetic*. New York: Doubleday; Maulana Karenga (1993). *Introduction to Black Studies* (2nd edition). California: The University of Sankore Press; Sterling Stuckey (1994). *Going through the storm. The influence of African American art in history*. New York: Oxford University Press; Greg Tate (Ed.) (2003). *EVERYTHING BUT THE BURDEN What Whites are taking from Black culture*. New York: Random House; Jon Spencer (1995). *The rhythms of Black folks. Race, religion and Pan Africanism*. New Jersey: African World Press.

Gerald G. Jackson

Thinking diunitally, the exercise had a Eurocentric and Africentric component. In terms of the former, it provided an opportunity for individual achievement, self-gratification and futurism in the form of planning, independence, "objective" measurements, observation of experiences and the acquisition of information (cognitive).

Its uniqueness, however, was the inclusion of an Africentric component. The research task was to gather celebratory information on African-Americans. It was designed as an opportunity to learn about people whose lives reflected an extended self-concept, extended self-affirmation and oftentimes spiral sense of time. Each assigned person exhibited and demonstrated an *African ontology, epistemology, and axiology.* Typifying an Africentric epistemology, minimum direction was given on how and what information should be gathered and through what type of organizational structure.

There were no requirements on where and how many times the students should meet outside of class. One class was usually devoted to the assembled groups meeting, and it was common, based upon reading student journals at the end of the presentations, for the group to meet in the libraries, dormitories and student apartments.

Rickie & group in J.H. Clarke library preparing for group presentation.
Photo by Gerald G. Jackson.

Comparatively greater emphasis was placed upon student interdependence, creativity fluidity and adaptability than adherence to fixed forms and measurements. The research project, therefore, went beyond the acquisition of information, memorization of facts; it included mastery of the human interaction and communication process. The group exercises sought to enhance the value of (axiology) cooperation, preservation of life, human relations, collective responsibility and self-knowledge. This is seen in the individual members of the group working together responsibly and cooperatively to acquire and disseminate knowledge on Black historical figures. Shaping this effort was my requirement that each individual would receive the same grade. An assumption of this grade equity was that the process enhanced "emotional intelligence" or affective learning and that such learning served as a foundation for the group presentation, deemed beneficial for the small and large groups.

To illustrate, my approach uncovered that the process leading up to the group presentations contributed greatly to students examining areas not commonly dealt with in the formal classroom setting, especially topics researched and presented by students. Some of these areas are: Diaspora relationship between countries such as Haiti and the Dominican Republic; within racial group gender issues such as the female hatred popularized by some Hip-Hop leaders; and privileges bestowed by phenotypic and geographic differences. The group design and format made discussions of these things possible. Similarly, taking some ownership in the process led the students to point out additional areas for conceptual and theoretical growth.

Engrossed in the Africentric concept of helping, the students mastered the group concept so well that they detected an unforeseen contradiction. Many reported that while they appreciated an exercise that brought them closer to being a functional unit, they acknowledged simultaneously that they became more competitive with the other classroom student groups. Thus, they revealed that competitiveness was ultimately created by the group presentations and depreciated the Africentric concept of the **helpful** and **cooperative** group. Their charge reminded me of a similar sentiment that I had felt and heard from my predominantly Black classes at an urban Community College in New Jersey, and the converse at a predominantly White Catholic University in the same vicinity. In the latter case, the students initially reacted negatively to the task by charging that it smacked of communism. However, at the close of the semester such students recanted the allegation and acclaimed the virtues of group work.

I rejoiced for a moment at the constructive classroom result. The creative and curious mind prevailed and a while later I allowed myself to wonder about the Africentric group concept extension into the larger community, society and globe. Immediately, I reasoned that an inability to function well with racial, cultural and geographical differences is a terrible indictment of collegiate education and a blatant shortcoming in the education of many students. So, in the end I returned to the drawing

Gerald G. Jackson

board and designed a learning that would ameliorate intergroup competitiveness, viewed as the cynosure of poor campus race relations. The road to this solution, Section II will show, is the *guided* practice of a total group work.

A Bibliography of John Henrik Clarke
Compiled by Thomas Weissinger

Magazines Articles by Dr. Clarke
Journal Articles by Dr. Clarke
Books About Dr. Clarke
Journal/Magazine Articles About Dr. Clarke
Edited Books by Dr. Clarke
Monographs by Dr. Clarke.
Pamphlets by Dr. Clarke
Newspaper Articles About Dr. Clarke
Interviews of Dr. Clarke
Speeches by Dr. Clarke
Book Reviews by Dr. Clarke

Magazine articles by Dr. Clarke

Clarke, John Henrik. "Africa in Early World History (long before Rome, continent had scientists, scholars, builders)." *Ebony* (August 1976): 125+.

_____. "African American Historians and the Reclaiming of Black History." Excerpt. *Words Work*, vol. 1, no. 4 (1992): 3-4.

_____. "The Afrikan World at the Crossroads: Notes for an Afrikan World Revolution." *Black Collegian* (Jan./Feb. 1991): 112+.

_____. "American Scene." *Crisis*, 48 (January 1941): 29.

_____. "The Black Woman: A Figure in World History." *Essence* (May 1971): 42-43.

_____. "Image and Mind Control in the African World." *Black Collegian* (April 1991): 106-107.

_____. "In Our Image." *Essence*, vol. 20, no. 5 (September 1989): 159.

Journal articles by Dr. Clarke

Browne, Robert S. and John Henrik Clarke. "The American Negro's Impact." *Africa Today* (Jan. 1967): 16-18.

_____. "African and the American Negro Press." *Journal of Negro Education* (Winter 1961): 64-68.

Clarke, John Henrik. "Africa: New Approaches to an Old Continent." *Freedomways*, vol. 11, no. 2 (1971): 298-306.

_____. "African Cultural Continuity and Slave Revolts in the New World." *Black Scholar*, vol. 8, no. 1 (September 1976): 41-50.

_____. "African Cultural Continuity and Slave Revolts in the New World: Part Two—Conclusion." *Black Scholar*, vol. 8, no. 2 (October-November 1976): 2-10.

_____. "African Studies in the United States: An Afro-American View." *Africa Today*, (April-May 1969): 10-12.

_____. "Ancient Nigeria and the Western Sudan." *Presence Africaine* (English ed.), nos. 32-33 (1960): 11-18.

_____. "Bambata (of Southern Africa) a Zulu chief." In French. *Presence Africaine*, 1st quarter (1963): 175-181.

_____. "Black Power and Black History." *Negro Digest* (February 1969): 35-44.

_____. "La celebration d'une veillee funebre dans la tribu ga du Ghana." *Presence Africaine* (December, 1958-January 1959): 107-112.

_____. "The Fight to Reclaim African History." *Negro Digest* (February 1970): 10.

_____. "The History of the Black Family (The Black Family in Historical Perspective)." *Journal of Afro-American Issues*, vol. 3, no. 3, and 4 (Summer/Fall 1975): 336-342.

_____. "The Impact of the African on the 'New World:' a Reappraisal." *Presence Africaine*, 3rd quarter (1971): 3-16.

_____. "The Impact of the African on the New World: A Reappraisal." *Black Scholar* (February 1973): 32-39.

_____. "In Search for Timbuctoo." *Journal of Negro Education* (spring 1964): 125-130.

_____. "Journey to the Sierra Maestra (in Cuba)." *Freedomways* (spring 1961): 32-35.

_____. "Kwame Nkrumah: His Years in America." *Black Scholar*, vol. 6, no. 2 (October 1974): 9-17.

"Kwame Nkrumah: the measure of the man." *Presence Africaine*, 1st quarter (1973): 140-147.

_____. "Lerone Bennett: Social Historian." *Freedomways*, vol. 5 (fall 1965): 481-492.

_____. "Marcus Garvey: The Harlem Years." *Black Scholar*, vol. 5, no. 4 (December 1973/January 1974): 17-25.

_____. "The Meaning of Black History." *Black World*, vol. 20, no. 4 (February 1971): 27-36.

_____. "Mohammed Ahmed, (The Mahdi) Messiah of the Sudan." *Journal of Negro Education*, vol. 30, no. 2 (spring 1961): 156-162.

_____. "Morning Train to Ibadan (Nigeria)." *Journal of Negro Education*, vol. 31 (fall 1962): 527-530.

_____. "Neglected Dimensions of the Harlem Renaissance." *Black World*, vol. 20, no. 1 (November 1970): 118-129.

_____. "The New Afro-American Nationalism." *Freedomways* (fall 1961): 285-295.

_____. "Le Nigeria ancient et le Soudan occidental." *Presence Africaine* (June-September 1960): 187-193.

_____. "On 'the Cultural Unity of Africa.'" *Black World*, vol. 24, no. 4 (February 1975): 12-28.

_____. "Pan-Africanism: A Brief History of an Idea in the African World." *Presence Africaine*, no. 145, 1st Quarter (1988): 25-56.

_____. "The Passing of Patrice Lumumba." *Journal of Human Relations* (summer 1962): 383-393.

_____. "The Old Congo." *Phylon*, vol. 23, and no. 1 (1962): 61-65.

_____. "Revolt of the Angels. A Short Story." *Freedomways*, vol. 3 (summer 1963): 355-40.

_____. "The Rise of Racism in the West." *Black World*, vol. 19, no. 12 (October 1970): 4-11.

_____. "A Search for Identity." *Social Casework*, vol. 51, no. 5 (May 1970): 259-264.

_____. "Third Class on the Blue Train to Kumasi (Ghana)." *Phylon*, vol. 23, 3rd quarter (fall 1962): 294-301.

_____. "Transition in the American Negro Short Story." *Phylon*, vol. 21, no. 4 (1960).

_____. "Tom Mboya: The World's Youngest Statesman." *Journal of Human Relations* (autumn 1960): 58-66.

_____. "West Indian Partisans in the Fight for Freedom." *Negro Digest*, vol. 15 (July 1966): 18-25.

Books about Dr. Clarke
Adams, Barbara Eleanor. *John Henrik Clarke: Master Teacher*. Brooklyn, NY: A & B Publishers Group, 2000.

_____. *John Henrik Clarke: The Early Years*. Hampton, VA: United Brothers and Sisters Communications, 1992.

Ball, Jared A. *Still Speaking: An Intellectual History of John Henrik Clarke (Africana Thesis)*. Ithaca, NY: Cornell University, 2001.

Crowe, Larry F. *Reflections on the Life of John Henrik Clarke: January 1, 1916 to July 16, 1998*. Chicago, Ill: Kemetic Institute, 1998.

Thompson, Julius E. *John Henrik Clarke: A Pan-Africanist Thinker, Historian, and Poet*. Trenton, NJ: African World Press, 2002.

Journal/Magazine articles about Dr. Clarke
"Gets one of 3 of Chicago's Kuumba Workshop's 3rd Annual Awards in 1974 given to those persons who have made significant contributions to Afrikan people." *Black World* (April 1975): 29-30.

"In Memoriam: Dr. John Henrik Clarke." *The Black Scholar* (fall 1998): 50-52.

"The Power of Legacies of Two Giants: John Henrik Clarke." *American Visions* (October/November 1998): 30-32.

"Received the Marcus Garvey Annual Lectureship award from the organizers of the 1st annual Conference on the State of the Race,

Oct. 28-30, 1977 at Pepperdine University, Los Angeles, Calif."
Black Scholar (March 1978): 35-38.

"A Remarkable Person We Have Known: John Henrik Clarke, 1915-1998." *The New Crisis* (Sept./Oct. 1998): 40.

"Remembrance: John Henrik Clarke." *Transition* (1998): 4-8.

"Self-made Angry Man." *New York Magazine* (Jan. 3, 1999): 17-18.

"Writer and Lecturer. Biography." *Negro History Bulletin* (January 1960): 91-91.

Edited Books by Dr. Clarke

Clarke, John Henrik, Ed. *American Negro Short Stories*. New York, NY: Hill and Wang, 1966.

_____, Ed. *Black American Short Stories: One Hundred Years of the Best*. 1993.

_____, Ed. *Black Families in the American Economy. Washington, DC*: An E.C.C.A. Publication, Community Counselors Associates, 1975.

_____, Ed. *Dimensions of the Struggle against Apartheid: A Tribute to Paul Robeson: Proceedings of Special meeting of the Special Committee against Apartheid on the 80th anniversary of the birth of Paul Robeson, 10 April 1978*. New York, NY: United Nations Centre Against Apartheid and the African Heritage Studies Association, 1979.

_____, Ed. *Harlem, A Community in Transition*. Citadel Press, 1964.

_____, Ed. *Harlem, U.S.A.: The Story of a City within a City*. Edited with an introduction by John Henrik Clarke. 1964. 361p.

_____, Ed. *Harlem: Voices from the Soul of Black America*. New York, NY: New American Library, 1970.

_____, Ed. *Malcolm X: The Man and His Times*. New York, NY: Macmillan, 1969.

_____, Ed. *Marcus Garvey and the Vision of Africa*. 1974.

_____, Ed. *Pan-Africanism and the Liberation of Southern Africa: A Tribute to W.E.B. DuBois*. New York, NY: United Nations Centre Against Apartheid and the African Heritage Studies Association, 1978.

_____, Ed. *William Styron's Nat Turner: Ten Black Writers Respond*. 1968.

Clarke, John Henrik and Vincent Harding, Eds. *Slave Trade and Slavery*. New York, NY: Holt, Rinehart and Winston, 1970.

_____, Eds. *What's It all About?* New York, NY: Holt, Rinehart and Winston, 1969.

Clarke, John Henrik, et al, Eds. *Black Titan: W.E.B. DuBois: An Anthology by the editors of* Freedomways*: John Henrik Clarke, et al*. Boston, MA: Beacon Press, 1970. 333p.

_____, et al, Eds. *Paul Robeson: The Great Forerunner.* New York, NY: Dodd, Mead and Co., 1978.

Jackson, John G. *Introduction to African Civilizations.* Introduction and bibliographical notes by John Henrik Clarke. 1970. 384p.

Rogers, J.A. *World's Great Men of Color.* Vols. 1-2. Revised and updated with commentary. New York, NY: Collier-MacMillan, 1972.

Monographs by Dr. Clarke

Ben-Jochannan, Yosef and John Henrik Clarke. *New Dimensions in African History: The London Lectures of Dr. Yosef Ben-Jochannan and Dr. John Henrik Clarke.* Trenton, NJ: Africa World Press, 1990.

Clarke, John Henrik. *African People in World History.* Philadelphia, PA: Black Classic Press, 1991.

_____. *Africans at the Crossroads: Notes for an African World Revolution.* Trenton, NJ: Africa World Press, 1991.

_____. *Christopher Columbus and the Afrikan Holocaust: Slavery and the Rise of European Capitalism.* Brooklyn, NY: A and B Books, 1992.

_____. *The Early Years. As told to Barbara Eleanor Adams.* Hampton, VA: United Brothers and Sisters Communication, 1992.

_____. *Harlem, a Community in Transition.* 1969.

_____. *History and Culture of Africa.* New York, NY: Aevac, Inc., Educational Publishers, 1969.

_____. *The Lives of Great African Chiefs.* Pittsburgh, PA: Pittsburgh Courier Publishing Co., 1958.

_____. *My Life in Search of Africa.* Ithaca, NY: Africana Studies and Research Center, Cornell University, 1994.

_____. *Rebellion in Rhyme.* Prairie City, IL: The Dicker Press, 1948. 105p.

Pamphlets by Dr. Clarke

_____. *Africans away from Home.* Washington, DC: Institute for Independent Education, 1988. 13p.

_____. *Black Americans: Immigrants against their Will.* 1974. 38p.

_____. *Black-White Alliances: A Historical Perspective.* Chicago: Institute of Positive Education, 1976.

_____. *The End of the Age of Grandeur and the Beginning of the Slave Trade.* New York, NY: New York University, Institute of Afro American Affairs, 1981.

_____. *The Image of Africa in the Mind of the Afro-American: African Identity in the Literature of Struggle.* 1973. 32p.

_____. *The State of the Race*. Los Angeles, CA: Los Angeles Chapter, The Pan-African Secretariat, 1980.

_____. *Thoughts on the African World at Crossroads*. Guyana, South America: N.E.R.A.C., Educational Pamphlet, 1980.

Newspaper Articles by Dr. Clarke, arranged chronologically

"Famous African chiefs." *Pittsburgh Courier*, 9/7/57, page 4.

"Famous African chiefs." *Pittsburgh Courier*, 9/14/57, Magazine section, page 1.

"Famous African chiefs." *Pittsburgh Courier*, 9/21/57, page 14.

"Ja Ja of the Ibos, African chief." *Pittsburgh Courier*, 10/5/57, Magazine Section, page 1.

"Ja Ja of the Ibos (conclusion) ." *Pittsburgh Courier*, 10/12/57, Magazine Section, page 1.

"Kwaja Dua III." *Pittsburgh Courier*, 10/19/57, Magazine Section, page 1.

"African chiefs. Kwaja Dua III (continued)." *Pittsburgh Courier*, 10/26/57, Magazine Section, page 1.

"African chiefs. Nana Sirofori Atta." *Pittsburgh Courier*, 11/2/57, Magazine Section, page 1.

"African chiefs. Samory, the Mandingo." *Pittsburgh Courier*, 11/9/57, Magazine Section, page 6.

"Chaha of the Zulus." *Pittsburgh Courier*, 11/23/57, Magazine Section, page 6.

"Dingoan—Chaka's Successors." *Pittsburgh Courier*, 11/30/57, Magazine Section, page 3.

"Cetewago, nephew and disciple of Chaha." *Pittsburgh Courier*, 12/7/57, Magazine Section, page 6.

"Nobengala of the Matabele." *Pittsburgh Courier*, 12/14/57, Magazine Section, page 1.

"Nobengala (continued)." *Pittsburgh Courier*, 12/21/57, Magazine Section, page 1.

"Moshedi of the Basutos." *Pittsburgh Courier*, 12/28/57, Magazine Section, page 6.

"Moshedi of the Basutos (part 2)." *Pittsburgh Courier*, 1/4/58, Magazine Section, page 6.

"Sechele of the Bakivaria." *Pittsburgh Courier*, 1/11/58, Magazine Section, page 7.

"The Black Empire. A Heritage Series (part 1)." *NY Daily Challenge*, 5/31/72, page 15.

"Bambati of the Zondi. Last of the Zulu rebel chiefs (part 2)." *NY Daily Challenge*, 6/1/72, page 16.

"The Black Empire Series. Patrice Lumumba." *NY Daily Challenge*, 1/4/73, page 12.

"Harlem: A brief history the world's most famous black community."
Amsterdam News, Bicentennial issue, summer 1976, Section B,
page 9.

"From African grandeur to the slave trade (part 1)." *Black American*,
3/4-10/82, pages 20-21.

"Text of 3-27-82 statement by John Clarke on Schomburg Center."
Amsterdam News, 4/17/82, page 23, column 1.

"Editorial on W. Wray's defense of hiring white man for Schomburg."
Amsterdam News, 1/15/83, page 12, column 1.

"The Africans and the Conquest of Spain (part 1)." *Black American*,
10/27-11/2/83, page 24.

Newspaper Articles about Dr. Clarke, arranged chronologically

"Weds Eugenia A. Evans in Miami." *NY Amsterdam News*, 1/20/62,
page 13.

"Honor writer on new book (Harlem: A Community in Transition)."
NY Amsterdam News, 4/3/65, page 8.

"Honored by New York Support Committee of African Heritage
Studies Association." *Amsterdam News*, 10/19/74, Section A, page
15.

"Biographical note." *National Scene*, 8-9/75, page 10.

"Biography." *Amsterdam News*, summer 1976, Bicentennial issue,
Section B, page 9. >/P>

"Scholar and humanitarian. 62 years old." *Bilalian News*, 4/8/77, page
7.

"His column in NY Daily Challenge starts Monday, May 23, 1977." *NY
Daily Challenge*, 5/12/77, page 1.

"John Henrik Clarke calls for new look at black history." *Amsterdam
News*, 4/22/78, Section B, page 1, column 1.

"King Tut, teen ruler of Egypt was black, exhibit viewed." *Amsterdam
News*, 12/16/78, Section A, page 1, column 2.

"John Henry Clark, black historian featured." *Amsterdam News*, 3/3/79,
page 37, column 1.

"2nd in series on Black American Delegation visiting Libya." *New
Pittsburgh Courier*, 10/6/79, Section 1, page 1, column 1.

"Hood column on John Clarke speech about Afro-American history."
Michigan Chronicle, 2/21/81, Section A, page 7, column 3.

"Lte on 3-27-82 Clarke statement on Schomburg Center." *Amsterdam
News*, 5/1/82, page 38, column 1.

"Lte on 1-15-83 editorial on the Schomburg Center." *Amsterdam News*,
2/19/83, page 12, column 2.

"Hunter College group sponsors tribute to historian, John Clarke."
Amsterdam News, 10/1/83, page 36, column 1.

"Advises CIA joins 'beat the Russians' band—speech on Oct. 12, 1982 at the Harlem YMCA." *Daily World*, 11/12/82, page 9.

"Parents & activists criticize NYC Community School Board 17." *Amsterdam News*, 7/28/84, page 9, column 1.

"M. Gumbs says aide to his campaign opponent wrote 7-28-84 story." *Amsterdam News*, 8/4/84, page 9, column 1.

"Elizabeth Hood column on Black History Month.*" Michigan Chronicle*, 2/23/85, Section A, page 6, column 4.

"Tabernacle Christian Academy and Institute for Independent Education sponsor conference." *Chicago Defender*, 4/11/87, page 40, column 1.

"John Henrik Clarke speaks at Schomburg Center in New York about Marcus Garvey's Life." *Amsterdam News*, 8/22/87, page 15, column 1.

"Dr. John Henrik Clarke, historian and professor emeritus of African World History at Hunter College, spoke in Chicago about African American history and culture." *Chicago Defender*, 4/8/89, page 43, column 1.

"An editorial features black scholars John Henrik Clarke and Yosef A.A. ben-Jochannan." *Michigan Chronicle*, 6/10/89, page 6, column 1.

"Conrad Worrill applauds the work of black historian John Henrik Clarke." *Chicago Defender*, 9/13/89, page 10, column 1.

"Conrad W. Worrill comments on the beliefs of John Henrik Clarke on the importance of the media in the struggle for black liberation." *Chicago Defender*, 11/8/89, page 12, column 1.

"Conrad W. Worrill discusses report by Hunter College professor John Henrik Clarke concerning the movement for the empowerment of the black media." *Chicago Defender*, 8/15/90, page 10, column 1.

"History professors John Henrik Clarke and George Simmonds agree with Leonard Jeffries' controversial speech about the Jews having a hand in the enslavement of Africans in the Western world." *Amsterdam*, 8/31/91, page 27, column 1.

"In the second of two articles, the teachings of John Henrik Clarke are examined. At a forum dealing with Christopher Columbus, he blasted Columbus for his misdeeds and his role in slavery." *Amsterdam*, 10/26/91, page 8, column 1.

"Conrad Worrill praises the recently released book 'Notes for an African World Revolution: Africans at the Crossroads' by African-American scholar, writer and researcher John Henrik Clarke." *Chicago Defender*, 11/27/91, page 12, column 1.

"African historian John Henrik Clarke said that communism, the economic system that was claimed and touted by European intellectuals in the 19th century, came out of African societies,

adding that 'Communism didn't fail; the communists failed.'"
Amsterdam, 2/8/92, page 2, column 4.

"The day the KKK openly declared support for presidential GOP candidate Patrick Buchannan, Alfred Sharpton, a black candidate for the US Senate, won an endorsement from John Henrik Clarke, one of the most respected educators in the nation." *Amsterdam*, 3/7/92, page 1, column 1.

"John Henrik Clarke, the man who many consider the dean of black historians, told WLIB radio listeners the betrayal of all aspects of the African revolution lay with the leaders who failed to develop consistently independent values and urged people to develop a value system of their own." *Amsterdam*, 6/13/92, page 3, column 1.

"Scholars Yosef ben-Jochannan, Leonard Jeffries and John Henrik Clarke were honored on July 9, 1992 as three of America's greatest champions for the psychological and educational liberation of African people." *Amsterdam*, 7/11/92, page 5, column 1.

"More than a dozen prominent witnesses appeared before a subcommittee concerning African-American burial grounds, including New York City Mayor David Dinkins and Professor John Henrik Clarke." *Amsterdam*, 8/1/92, page 3, column 1.

"Historian John Henrik Clarke said he is glad remains of early Africans excavated from the African Burial Ground in New York City will be curated for four years at Howard University in Washington DC under the care of a host of anthropologists." *Amsterdam*, 6/19/93, page 36, column 5.

"John Henrik Clarke and George Edward Tait assailed the evils of white supremacy during separate speeches in New York on Nov. 20, 1993." *Amsterdam*, 11/27/93, page 10, column 5.

"John Henrik Clarke and Yosef ben-Jochannan were honored at the Boys and Girls High School in Brooklyn, NY in Nov. 1994." *Amsterdam*, 11/19/94, page 24, column 1.

"The role 80-year-old John Henrik Clarke, a retired history professor at the City University of New York, is playing in restructuring the education of black children is examined." *Amsterdam*, 2/11/95, page 10, column 1.

"The words of inspiration spoken by John Henrik Clarke during an engagement of the Global Black Experience at Harlem NY's Apollo Theater are recounted. Musical performances were part of the engagement, which was hosted by Imhotep Gary Byrd, but Clarke's words noting the achievements of such blacks as Adam Clayton Powell and Booker T. Washington, as well as criticism of Louis Farrakhan, drew a mixed response from the crowd." *Amsterdam*, 8/26/95, page 28, column 1.

"John Henrik Clarke, Black Studies Advocate, Dies at 83." *New York Times*, 7/20/98, Section A, page 13, column 3.

"Standing at the Crossroads: A Kwanzza Message." *Michigan Citizen*, 1/2/99, page 8.

"The Lives They Lived: John Henrik Clarke; Self-Made Angry Man." *New York Times*, 1/3/99, Section 6, page 17, column 2.

Interviews of Dr. Clarke

"Interview by Helen Mendes." *Black Caucus* (Association of Black Social Workers) (spring 1972): 12-14.

"We Need to Celebrate Our Survival." Interview with John Clarke. *CORE Magazine*, Bicentennial issue (1976):12-15.

Speeches by Dr. Clarke

"Afro-American Search" (speech at A.S.A. Eleventh Annual meeting, Los Angeles, Calif.). *Pan-African Journal*, vol. 1, no. 4 (fall 1968): 182-183.

"Beyond Pan-Africanism: an African World union." *Black Books Bulletin*, vol 2, no. 2 (fall1974): 10-17.

Who Betrayed the African World Revolution? And Other Speeches. Kent, OH: Institute for African American Affairs, Kent State University, 1994.

Book Reviews by Dr. Clarke

"Reviews (in French and English) of Langston Hughes' First Book of Africa and N.R. Richardson's Liberia's Past and Present." *Presence Africaine*, vols. 34-35 (October 1960-January 1961): 238-244.

"Reviews African novels of Tutuola, Beti, Achebe." *Pittsburgh Courier*, 6/11/60, page 20.

"Reviews Books for the Bulletin." *Negro History Bulletin* (January 1957): 86.

"Reviews of 4 novels about Africa." *Negro History Bulletin* (October 1959): 18-19.

SECTION II
You don't have to move mountains to make a difference:[90]
Leaders in the African Diaspora and the way they shape our future

Believing the criticism of the cumulative negative effect of the individual group assignment approach to be true, I decided on a less competitive measure to restore the espoused virtues of teamwork. It entailed giving a class group assignment as the last project before the final examination. The assignment was to teach how a situation can benefit a person as an individual and group member. The entire class would write a book devoted to students. Theoretically, it was designed to support and stimulate a desire in students to achieve in education and life. The class assignment consequently was to design and develop an electronic book that would be suitable for publication. Participation was mandatory; however, other aspects of development would be voluntary. This meant that participants could contribute ideas for a book cover, and select, based upon interests and skills, such roles and positions as publisher, writer and editor.

The rationale for this allocation needs some amplification, based on insights gained from my earlier Cornell teaching experience. In 1986, I taught at Cornell University, after having taught at a Community College, private sectarian four-year college, and Catholic University. I worked also as a dean at both a community college and state university. In most instances, I successfully used a group project component in these teaching positions, and gained knowledge and experience from my student affairs and corporate diversity work. Therefore, when I taught at Cornell I used a similar course requirement. One of the memorable experiences I had was being a part of the transformation process of a senior, preppy, rich New England White male. In describing himself during his group presentation, he declared several

---

[90]Taken from a portion of an essay written in this book by Catherine Soto. The profoundness of her comment is reflected in Montel Williams book *Mountain Get Out of My Way* (2003). New York: New American Library. According to the television personality, he used to want to move mountains; now what he sees as significant is to be able to be on top of a mountain and gain perspective.

177

defining occurrences or realities. First, he was reared in a New England town where everyone looked like him. Second, he attended a New England Prep school where everyone looked like him. Third, although a senior, he only associated at Cornell with people who looked and behaved like him. He reasoned, therefore, that he did not have an opportunity to learn of the existence of other viable perspectives (i.e., world-view).

One could think, being facetious, it was his background that resulted in him being baffled and vexed by a polyglot group that did not accept his leadership. He, on the other hand, in the early stages of interaction would not dare conjecture. It was clear that the group problem had nothing to do with his personality, cultural training, and learning. Consequently, he could not discern what he had done incorrectly that caused him to be rejected by the group, since he had honorable intentions for it. His sporadic attendance at group meetings was his way of coping with his mitigated displeasure. He said he would not have returned to the group, had he not forced himself to accost me at a fastfood store, where he shared his group membership concerns. He added that it was not only his perceived predicament but also the fact that he was drunk from drinking beer all day. Both conditions gave him the courage to reveal his sorrow. His group, composed of African Americans, Latinos, and White ethnic groups, responded that he presumed, from the start of the first meeting, that he should lead. They, presuming equality in knowledge and ability, resented his underlying assumption that they were inferior. He, in turn, acknowledged that an encompassing learning for him was that other valid viewpoints existed in the world and on campus.

As a finale, he made an effort to demonstrate to all his transformational process. He invited the class to visit him at his Lake Front home and water ski. Many jumped at the apparent opportunity to live like the Rich and Famous. However, others saw the requested association as a gratuitous gesture, and voiced disbelief that he could just be learning that there are different viewpoints in the world. This event and others greatly influenced what I did and supported why I returned to Cornell to teach.

The book ends on the Publisher's outline of the ramification of the book project. It continues the effort that espouses that the greater need and demand is to demonstrate that the educational and mental health value of being good is a place beyond self and family satisfaction. This idea is grounded in the Black Student leadership model and protest of the 1960s and the legacy of student empowerment and activism. This model, in turn, resulted in my fervent belief in the need for youth to experience and be assisted in handling power and its allocation. This place fundamentally is the focus of the ensuing sections on the Educational Context supporting the writing of the student-based book and the **Harlem Experience.** Both discussions give pertinence to the relationship between physical and mental health space to Africentric helping.

Overview

Collectively, these stories reveal the ways humans do overcome potentially insurmountable obstacles. They belie two other instructive stories. The first has to do with surpassing racial, ethnic and gender barriers that have been affirmed by years of unchallenged exposure to White Studies. The other symbolizes the process of turning a regrettable situation into an opportunity for problem resolution.

Two of the writers are White. One could rightly ask how they could fulfill a requirement involving writing about Black warriors from their home community. Although writing from another racial and cultural experience, is a part of the *democratic sanity* that Black students are expected to follow, the converse is rarely true and never officially mandated in the United States. Neither Charles nor Alexandra was encouraged nor forced to abandon their racial and gender identities; they were provided space to be creative and opportunistic. To their credit, they did not let their racial and gender backgrounds dissuade them from full participation in the project. They found in their home community African Americans to describe and did so without fanfare. Similarly, Rachelle, of Afro-Caribbean descent, wrote commendably on her Hatitan mother's altruistic medical assistance to Haitians in the Dominican Republic.

The other case is an omitted report. It would have been facile to drop the author and only the students would have known. In this case, the reader would have made a perusal of the book without suspicion. I ruminated on this prospect and decided to deal directly with the implication of the missing case. In the African way, something is subtract from the group soul when family members die and are forgotten. A writer, for example, gave an account of an inspirational religious leader with a sincere commitment to ministering to the community. His story would have added to our memory the countless religious spokespersons, of all religious persuasions, that practice daily what Dr. Rev. Martin Luther King, Jr. modeled and advocated.[91] Rather than either denying their existence or bemoaning my plight in not getting it published, I decided to deal with a broader subject of the shortage of Black males in the college classroom.[92] In the next section is my take on how we might gain from the situation. The Africentric approach detailed elsewhere, views struggle as an antecedent to personal and group growth.[93]

The Missing Black Male Student

One essay that appeared in the class project electronic book has not been included in this book version because the writer was not in school the semester of book preparation and publication. Moreover, he did not respond to requests to submit publication permission slips. I was more than saddened by his omission because he is a Black (Afro-Latino) male at Cornell, and his could be seized upon by individuals interestsed in Black male bashing.[94] As a Black male, they represent a group with a comparatively high attrition rate, in comparison to Black female students. Nationally, along with other Black male cohorts, he is a member of a group that has been overlooked, until recently, in higher education discourses and studies.[95]

---

[91]Walter Dean & Jenkins, L. (2003). *I've seen the promised land: The life of Dr. Marin Luther King.* New York: Amistad; Donald Philips (2000). *Martin Luther King, Jr. on leadership; inspiration and wisdom for challenging times.* New York: Warner Business Books; Kris Shepard, Carson, C. (2002). *A call to conscience; The landmark speeches of Dr. Martin Luther King, Jr.* New York: Warner Books; James Melvin (1991) *A testament of hope: The essential writings and speeches of Martin Luther King, Jr.* California: Harper; Michael Dyson. *I may not get there with you: The true Martin Luther King.*

[92]James Dunn (1988). "The shortage of Black male students in the college classroom: Consequences and Causes." *The Western Journal of Black Studies,* 12(2), pp. 73-76.

[93]Gerald Jackson (2004). *Delimits of American Helping: Precursors of an African Genesis Model of Helping.* New Jersey: Africa World Press.

[94]For a discussion of this phenomena, see Dr. Julia Hare, Thomas Dortch, Dr. Julianne Malveaux, Dr. Harry Edwards, Tom Joyner (April, 2004). "Is it open season on Black men?" *Ebony,* pp. 126–128.

[95]Cyrus Ellis (2002). "Examining the pitfalls facing African-American males" (pp. 61-72). In Lee Jones (Ed.). *Making it on broken promises leading African American male scholars confront the culture of higher education.* Virginia: Stylus; Nathan McCall and Anderson, T. (2002). "The role of Black colleges

I first published about the plight of Black College age males in 1974,[96] following up with a post high school pre-college program in the 1980's. It was for EOF students in New Jersey, and titled the "Male Machine."[97] It was designed to alleviate barriers to their collegiate academic and social success so that they would at least be on parity with African-American females in terms of G.P.A. and graduation rate. A difficulty in maintaining program support for the idea, despite the relative success of the program, resulted in another publication that included an analysis of ideological and institutional problems besetting such programs.[98]

I pined for more than just written material on ways to combat the dilemmas entailed in recruiting, retaining and graduating Black men. I learned that my alma mater Howard University was moving in this direction. Beyond sponsoring a program on the absence of Black men

---

in educating African-American men: An interview with Nathan McCall" (pp. 133-140). In Lee Jones (Ed.). *Making it on broken promises leading African American male scholars confront the culture of higher education.* Virginia: Stylus; Molefi Asante (2002). "Afrocentricity and the African-American Male in College" (pp. 141-148). In Lee Jones (Ed.). *Making it on broken promises leading African American male scholars confront the culture of higher education.* Virginia: Stylus; Wade Nobles (Nana Kwaku Berko I aka Ifagbemi Sangodare) (2002). "From Na Ezaleli to the Jegnoch: The force of the African family for Black men in higher education" (pp. 173-188). In Lee Jones (Ed.). *Making it on broken promises leading African American male scholars confront the culture of higher education.* Virginia: Stylus; Felicia Lee (February 1, 2003). "New topic in Black Studies debate: Latinos." RaceMatters.org.http://www.racematters.org/Newtopicblackstudieslatinos.htm

[96] Gerald Jackson (1974). "Project D.E.E.P.: An innovative adult education program." *Adult Student Personnel Journal,* 6(1), 10-15. First publication appeared in 1957 in an East Harlem Boy's Club newspaper article.

[97] Gerald Jackson, (June, 13, July 7, 14, 28 1988). "Male Machine." E.O.F. Program, Upsala College, East Orange, New Jersey; Gerald Jackson & Velasquez, C. (April 13, 1989). "The Male Machine." Twentieth Annual Conference of E.O.F. "Excellence Through Access," New Jersey; Gerald Jackson (July 30, 1989). "Male Machine." E.O.F., Fairleigh Dickinson University, Rutherford, New Jersey; Gerald Jackson (August 11, September 3, 24, 1993). "Male Machine." Cook College E.O.F. Program, Rutgers University, and New New Brunswick, New Jersey.

[98] See Gerald Jackson (2000). "The invisible Black male in an innovative adult education program" (pp. 83-100). In Gerald G. Jackson. *Precursor of an African Genesis model of helping.* New York: Global; Gerald G. Jackson (2004). *Delimits of American Helping: Precursors of an African Genesis model of helping.* New Jersey: Africa World Press.

in higher education, the administration is designing programs specifically to increase the number of Black men with college degrees.[99] Similarly what is personally heartening is my former college mate at Howard and the person I served as Associate Dean, president of Medgar Evers College Dr. Edison O. Jackson. He is giving the problem of Black men in higher education his intellectual, personal and institutional support.

Two aspects of his charge deserve accolades because they bear upon the culturally specific *pedagogy* noted in this book and the subtle oppression of diunital thinking by *Eurocentric culturalism*.[100] Edison's stance is laudatory for "not" being politically correct. All Black male schools, and presumably programs emanating from such settings, while shown successful in increasing academic performance and decreasing inappropriate behaviors, have been vehemently attacked and destroyed. It was bold, therefore, for Medgar Evers, in general, and E.O.J., in particular, to directly take on the challenge of developing programs and classes for Black males. Coincidentally, the newspaper article on the program summarized some decidedly cultural practice cues and beliefs that this book extols.[101]

Dr. Edison O. Jackson has not espoused an Africentric philosophical orientation. Given his strong Black southern cultural roots, he would probably not view his ideas and efforts as stemming from Africa. For illustrative purposes then, I am extrapolating from a newspaper account those elements that fit into an Africentric conceptual configuration. Indicative of a diunital analytical mode, his decision-making rests upon an axiology of both *self-knowledge* and *acquiring data*. The program selection is based upon data from the American Council on Education, the African-American Male Initiative

---

[99]For a worldview analysis of different types of training and educational efforts, see Gerald Jackson (2005). *Sankofa Helping: The African Genesis of an African-American model of Helping*. New Jersey: Africa World Press.

[100]Marimba Ani (1994). *YURUGU An Africen-centered critique of European cultural thought and behavior.* New Jersey: African World Press; Molefi Asante (1999). *The Painful Demise of Eurocentrism.* New Jersey: Africa World Press; Jacob H. Carruthers (1999). *intellectual warfare.* Illinois: Third World Press; Asa Hilliard (1995). *The Maroon Within Us.* Maryland: Black Classic Press; Kobi Kazembe Kalongi Kambon (2003). *Cultural Misorientation The Greatest Threat to the Survival of the Black Race in the 21st Century.* Florida: Nubian Nation.

[101]Karen W. Arenson (December 30, 3003). "Colleges struggle to help Black men stay enrolled." *The New York Times.*

program at the University of Georgia and his teaching a course offered by his institution's Male Development and Empowerment Center. His election to teach a course rather than simply observe the situation is a clear reflection of an Africentric epistemological outlook that is based upon an *immersion in an experience* and *affective/symbolic* evaluation.

In a Eurocentric culture that traditionally defines science as aloofness, distance and depersonalization, his undergraduate field of study and a counseling profession, his graduate training, that cautioned against revealing personal things to clients, he has surprisingly followed an African-American cultural pattern. Edison's class, pivots on the instructive use of the personal. When students reported debilitating encounters with racism, he revealed similar encounters. He did not resort to blaming and changing their perceptions. He shared, from an *extended self* of a group, his similar encounters. However, from an *extended self-affirmation*, he modeled coping strategies. First, he defined racism and racist behavior as a challenge. Second, he noted they could be surmounted in a constructive way. He neither preaches nor teaches victimology; conversely, he admonishes his students to use racial encounters to serve as one basis for achievement.

Demonstrating the essence of being *fluid and flexible*, rather than *fixed and rigid*, the epistemological realm in philosophy, he shifted the time for his direct involvement in the program. Originally, he was going to teach for a semester; however, he adjusted his schedule to teach another course. He elected to do this because he "felt" the students needed more coaching and he wanted to stay with his group until the end of the program. He could have easily used the demands of his position as President to escape this teaching obligation. Instead, what we witness is the axiology of *affiliation, collective responsibility, and harmony* in practice.

Predictably, from an Africentric way of thinking, the person Dr. Jackson selected to head the Male Development and Empowerment Center, would give evidence of Africentric beliefs and behaviors. In guiding and interacting with students, Mr. Holman notes his mercurial behavioral past, as an example of his "realness," and to show the positive results of *consequential thinking*. His self-disclosure reveals an ontology of *spiritual essence*, going beyond titles and positions, *collectivism,* and *interdependence.* Similarly, he did this when he reportedly encouraged students to trade telephone numbers and find ways to study together. Ironically, in my study of the failure of an educational program to meet the needs of Black men, Holman's suggestion meant a small group of men being integrated into predominantly female groups. The men did not like the "Buddy" system that meant female domination in cultural outlook and familial circumstances, a shortcoming the MEC emerging model would not experience.

The program recognizes income level differences; however, it did not discriminate according to a classification on income class. It does not follow a Eurocentric *democratic sanity* model and follows an Africentric one that includes Black males in the program from all economic strata. Similarly, I have found income difference categories to bear very little culturally in the allocation of support to Black male students at Cornell. Lectures, workshops, courses and aversive administrative acts and regulations, taken singly or combined Eurocentrically, will be of fleeting success from an Africentric notion of education. The African Psychology Institute defined such an education as: *the process of transmission of particular values, skills, knowledge and understanding which: 1) supports the process of transformation, 2) results in the goal of mental liberation, and 3) directs the attainment of self-knowledge (knowledge of self as an individual, as a member of a group, and as a cosmic being* (See glossary). Dr. Shujaa, educator and author of the classic book *Too Much Schooling Too Little Education A Paradox of Black Life in White Societies*, added to an Africentric definition of education that *it was the process of transmitting from one generation to the next knowledge of the values, aesthetics, spiritual belief, and all things that give a particular cultural orientation its uniqueness. Every cultural group must provide for this transmission process or it will cease to exist* (see glossary). Black men have been perennially called an "endangered species,"[102] and the works to liberate him have been cyclical.[103]

---

[102]Gerald Jackson (April 10, 1990). *Panelist. Black Issues Forum: The Black Male–An Endangered Species?* University of North Caroline Public Television. Johnson C. Smith University, Charlotte, North Carolina.

[103]Na'im Akbar (1991). *Visions for Black men.* Tennessee: Winston-Derek; Tonya Bolden (Ed.) (1999). *Strong men keep coming. The book of African American men.* New York: John Wiley & Sons; Herb Boyd & Allen, R. (Eds). (1995). *Brotherman.* New York: Ballantine; Geoffrey Canada (1998). *Reaching up for manhood.* Massachusetts: Beacon Press; Devon Carbado (Ed.) (1999). *Black men on race, gender, and sexuality.* New York: New York University Press; Anderson Franklin (2004). *From brotherhood to manhood. How Black men rescue their relationships and dreams from the invisibility syndrome.* New York: John Wiley & Sons; Lawrence Gary (Ed.) (1981). *Black men.* California: Sage; Jawanza Kunjufu (1984). *Countering the conspiracy to destroy Black boys.* Illinois: Afro-Am Publishing; Haki Madhubuti (1990). *Black men Obsolete, single, dangerous?* Illinois: Third World Press; E.

Out of the Mouth of Babes comes a Truth

I was prompted to write about the subject from my dialogues with my youngest daughter. Melissa is a 2001 *magna cum laude* Howard University graduate and as alumni, we share information continuously on the school's growth and development. When I learned that Howard had achieved tier 2 status, I shared what I thought would be lauded information. I was surprised to observe that she seemed neither impressed nor excited by my announcement. She responded that she hoped the more prestigious classification did not remove one of Howard's paramount strengths. In her eyes the Mecca, as it is called popularly, admitted proficient students and turned them into competitive graduates. She was well versed in my less than stellar academic performance at Howard, and that of my boys. In fact, it might be said that it was her recognition of our post-graduate career and professional success that informed her ambivalence about whether the tier 2 assignment was a gain. Another wrinkle then in the fabric of the false dichotomy drawn between Black and White schools is based upon a difference in world-views and missions. A dichotomous approach blankets this from such an analysis. In essence, Howard did not strive to admit the best of the best; it took solace in graduating the best. It selected students with promise and produced from this lot individuals and groups who would excel in society, according to moral ideals and concerns about group oppression. White elite schools were designed for a profiled upper class, forty-two long suit-sized White male Anglo-Saxons who favored the left hemisphere of the brain in conceptualizing and interpreting reality. A primary goal of students applying to these schools is eventually to make a lot of money, irrespective of race, as revealed in Sorby's essay on on pages 53-55. The educational processes at this type of school weeded out individuals and groups that did not conform to the WASP profile. Successful graduates were, therefore, schooled to excel in a society that professed to be color-blind.

Ethelbert Miller (2000). *Fathering Words*. New York: St. Martin's Press; Robert Staples (1982). *Black Masculinity. The Black male's role in American society*. California: The Black Scholar Press; Kristin Taylor (2003). *Black fathers A call for healing*. New York: Doubleday; Cliffor Watson & Smitherman, G. (1996). *Educating African American males: Detroit's Malcolm X Academy solution*. Illinois: Third World Press; Doris Wilkinson & Taylor, R. (Ed.) (1977). *The Black male in America. perspectives on his status in contemporary society*. Illinois: Nelson-Hall; Raymond Winbush (2001). *The warrior Method: A Program for Rearing Healthy Black Boys*. New York: Amistad.

Conversely, Black schools embraced all types of cultural and racial groups and prepared its graduates for a color conscious and multilingual world.[104]

Howard University Leadership Development

I did not attend Howard University to be a leader. Before H.U., I had typically resigned from bestowed leadership positions because I enjoyed being rebellious and recalcitrant. I was highly motivated to attend Howard; however, not because I wanted to be a leader. My intent came primarily from my father's thought that I should attend the school and let the "old timers" show me the way, based upon their training and experiences in the White world. His Generation of Black male speakers was terse, so although I did not know exactly what he meant, I dare not share the ambiguity because it would mean I was stupid. Being perceived as stupid was the least enviable place to be seen by one's father. Functionally, I trusted that older Black professors and administrators had wisdom to foster, and it would translate into knowledge that would enable me to be successful in life. It felt right, and tied into my secret thought that I had survived the streets of Harlem and D.C. to reveal to the world the humanity of my urban Black people. I did not feel guilty about making it to college, as the Eurocentric notion of "survivors' guilt" would suggest. On the contrary, I believed my place in college was a certain indication that the Supreme Being had selected me to help advance a constructive view of African-Americans.

The Howard experience caused me to continue my goal and change my outlook about leadership. At Howard, I learned that being a leader had a lot more rewards than simply being rebellious. Stokely Carmichael, for example, was revered for not only his courage in the Civil Rights limited war in the south but by many of the Ladies who adored him. Activism was not only coming into vogue, it was yielding conventional rewards. Consequently, Stokely created a new campus role model to emulate and eke out a career. Being a *Phi Beta Kappa* was still respected, but a true role model during this period was

---

[104]Tiffani Bell (November 4, 2003). "Student leadership at the Mecca." *The Hilltop*, pp. 1–3; Ayesha Roscoe (January 30, 2004). "Students find their calling at panel discussion." *The Hilltop*, pp. 1, 2; A. Rahmad Ford (February 24, 2004). "How Americans underdeveloped Haiti." Contemporary implications of *The Hilltop*, p. 1, 2; Melanie Holmes (November 4, 2003). "HU named among most politically active campus." *The Hilltop*, pp. 1, 2.

someone who maintained a balance between the personal and the racial. I was most impressed with a *Madison Richardson* type African-American male.[105] He was a star athlete, pre-med student with a high GPA, officer in ROTC, a Kappa and dated the head cheerleader for the football team. He was the multiplicity man that could lead and follow. The times and an African-American historical connection would include the political dimension.

In addition, I admired my boy Glegg. He attended college full-time, worked from 12:00 midnight until the morning at the *Washington Post*, was a varsity soccer player, Kappa, brilliant political science major, ladies' man, and generous to people in distress. He was of Jamaican ancestry; however, he could socialize with people from the Pike, DC, and Russia. The Kappas strongly encouraged us to assume leadership roles; however, our skills were honed by Dr. Carl Anderson, a Kappa man, and at the time Director of Student activities. The emphasis we undergraduates received was not so much on being a leader, as much as it was to support efforts for superior performance in our field of interest, model superior performance, and to make sure that things are done appropriately and correctly. My leadership efforts have been propelled, therefore, by training that says, make sure it is done right, even if it means you have to take command to make it happen.

Ivy League Schooling?

At Yale, it was different. The Black students were selected based on superior cognitive performance in high school, especially verbal skills. They were, as I had noted in a newspaper article in 1968, before coming to Yale, consciously Black and proud,[106]

---

[105]There was also a Howard female type and I married one. She was attending Howard University on an academic scholarship, member of AKA sorority, queen of Alpha Phi Alpha fraternity, a great dancer, participated in Civil Rights marches, served as an intern for her State Senator, was voted one of the top Best Dressed college student in America, participated in so many extra-curricular activities that she was elected to Who's Who Among College Students, and was a double for Lena Horne. We had the same major and she not only tutored me in French, after completing her language requirements, she took Spanish, a language quite helpful in our Latin American sub-specialty.

[106]Mildred Cole (December 7, 1968). "Panel would keep differences." *The Lewiston (Maine) Daily Sun*, p. 10.

...the black student is seeking fulfillment in the university. He does not want to reject all principles of blackness.

...Today, he wants to be a human being on the campus, not just a token. The Black student on the campus is no longer a clown, nor is he willing to sell his soul for acceptance. When education is not relevant or meaningful, they don't want it. There is a beauty in being Black, just as there is a beauty in being White.

They represented the largest class of Black students in Yale's history, and the times supported their belief that college should adjust to African-American culturally based education needs. They saw themselves as the apex of the apex and assumed a leadership stance without needing faculty endorsement or direction. This was the Yale undergraduate days of Skip Gates, Shirley Jackson, Ben Carson, Kurt Schmoke, and Warrington Hudlin. These students came to Yale before the generation of Black students who were first sent to Prep/Catholic schools. Larry Thompson, from Harlem and a public high school, inspired students in YSHS through his literary skills to write poetry. As a role model, he was publishing in the prestigious *Black World* magazine/journal,[107] and served as chairperson of a magazine[108] that published such notable Yale scholars as Drs. James Comer, Richard Goldsby, Clyde Blassingame, Austin Clarke, and Roy Bryce-Laporte.[109] At this time, many of the faculty and administrators had

---

[107]Larry Thompson (April, 1975). "The Black image in early American drama." *Black World*. pp. 54–60.

[108]In a biographical sketch in Renaissance II magazine, it was written: "Mr. Thompson was born in South Carolina in 1950 and raised and educated in New York City. He has been editor-in-charge-of-issue and the chairman of the **Yale Literary Magazine,** a founder and contributing editor of **Expression Magazine**, as well as being a founder and the chairman of this journal. Mr. Thompson has published in **Negro Digest (now Black World), Yale Literary Magazine and Expressions**. His work has also appeared in an anthology entitled, *Black is Best* and will be included in another anthology that is to be released this fall. Presently he is Scholar of the House at Yale University."

[109]These men and other Black scholars on campus at the time achieved endowed chairs; however, the majority did not do so at Yale. This is strange since Reeder in a proposed book on Blacks at Yale reported, "Since the early 1970s black enrollments have been strong but faculty levels have remained unchanged at a low level." See Gary Reeder (Winter 1999/2000). "The history of Blacks at Yale University." *The Journal of Blacks in Higher Education*, p.

graduated from historically Black colleges and universities or taught there before coming to Yale (e.g., Arna Bontemps, Clyde Blassingame). They brought a certain African-American cultural flavor to the Yale milieu. Their presence did not account for the pioneering boldness of the Black Yale Undergraduates. It would be a group of Yale students, for example, that hosted the first national conference on Black studies and edited the first book on the subject.[110] At almost the same time interval, Black Cornell students were making demands and historical marks.[111] However, over time the Cornell faculty and staff have assumed much of the leadership responsibilities that Yale students appear to still have vested in themselves.[112]

There is something distinct about a Yale student that continues to the present. The Black student at the Yale Law School would produce a report on the South African apartheid leader DeClerk. It would help Cornell students in understanding why it was an affront to pay him handsomely to speak at Cornell and served as one basis for challenging his lectureship. During the same epoch, Yale students designed and conducted an annual conference that linked Black Ivy League students. They reduced a destructive rivalry among Black students at different Ivy League schools that I saw in the late sixties and early seventies. The year I participated,[113] the group introduced Black students from Ivy League and historically Black colleges and universities to such

---

125. For a sample of individuals, I am referring to: **Dr. Houston Baker** (Susan Fox Beischer and George D. Beischer Arts and Sciences Professor English, Duke University); **Roy S. Bryce-Laporte** (John D. and Catherine T. MacArthur Professor of Sociology, Colgate University); **James P. Comer** (Maurice Falk Professor of Child Psychiatry, Yale University); **Richard A. Goldsby** (John Woodruff Simpson Lecturer and Professor of Biology, Amherst College). Chuck Stone (Autumn, 2001). "A roster of African-Americans who hold endowed university chairs." *The Journal of Blacks in Higher Education,* pp. 121–125.

[110] Armstead Robinson, Foster, C., & Ogilvie, D. (Eds.) (1969). *Black studies in the university*. Connecticut: Yale University Press.

[111] Charles White (Ed.) (1998). *The 20th Anniversary of the Willard Straight Hall Takeover. Commenorative Book.* Ithaca: New York.

[112] Yale undergraduates designed and implemented an annual Black Solidarity Conference, the event described by Danielle Williams.

[113] Gerald Jackson (November 3, 2001). "Black on Black Liberation: Freedom from the chains of anti-self disorder." In the 7th Annual Black Solidarity Conference, Perceptions of Self: The Black Psyche in the 21st Century, Yale University, New Haven, Connecticut.

stellar role models as Dr. Na'im Akbar and professor Kathleen Cleaver. They apparently did not need "no stinkin" faculty members to direct them. They had faculty assistance but the students were observably the leaders and conducted the majority of their program affairs.

The Praised False Dichotomy in Eurocentric Thought

What remains a contending issue and question is whether historically Black institutions have a sui generis purpose? One answer to this question is embedded in the definition of leadership development. The testing field for developing tomorrow's leaders, I have been told, is different in Latin America. Whereas the college years in the United States is considered an extension of adolescence, or temporal interval between childhood and adult functioning, in Latin America it is considered a part of adult life. Therefore, the political actions of students is regarded and treated as a real threat to the ruling regime. Similarly, the Howard I recollect was a part of the period in which students and near ones took the helm of the Black political leadership in the United States, as adult players who happened to be full-time college students. While some pictures Howard as a parallel universe that aspired to be Harvard, Howard leaders went beyond the social needs of the campus and the rule of the administration. One of our heroes, Stokely Carmichael, popularized and modeled the term "Black Power."[114]

Most telling of a Howard Tradition, it has been claimed that "a defiant young Stokeley gave rise to a waning Civil Rights Movement"[115] for the entire Black world, not simply Howard's campus. This does not mean he forsook one for the other or dichotomized. He also included his Howard home in his political ideology and actions. I witnessed his power when he confronted the Howard University administration about the all-White construction company building the new Howard University gym. He established picket lines and the company reactively found and employed Black workers. Similarly, Amiri Baraka, who also studied at Howard, is the penultimate scholar-activist. Even after being castigated by the governor of New Jersey for writing a characteristically thoughtful and provocative poem, the type he marveled students and faculty with at

---

[114]Stokely Carmichael & Hamilton, C. (1967). *Black power: the politics of liberation in America.* New York: Vintage Books. See also Richard Wright (1954). *Black power.* New York: Harper & Row.
[115]Charlie Cobb (June, 1997). "Black Power." *Emerge,* p. 38.

Cornell University,[116] Sarah Lawrence hosted a 3 day conference based solely on his works. With reference to him as a scholar, they noted that his book *Blue's People* [117] elevated jazz to a scholarly subject.[118]

Years later Kwame Ture's peers would continue in his footsteps and provide a nation with a variety of forms of leadership. Lawyers such as John Brittain (Kappa Alpha Psi), A. Dwight Pettit (Kappa Alpha Psi), and Alton Maddox continued the Thurgood Marshal H.U. Civil Rights lawyer tradition. One of the positions held by Togo West was Secretary of the Army. Two women from this period, Sharon Pratt (AKA) and Shirley Clarke-Franklin, would become the first Black women to head such major cities as Washington, DC and Atlanta, Georgia. Patrick Swygert (Omega Psi Phi) became President of Howard University, following the presidency of Franklin Jennifer (Kappa Alpha Psi) from the previous generation. This cohort had a number of writers who wrote seminal books and performers, such as Claude Brown (1966),[119] Leon Dash (1996)[120] (Omega Psi Phi), Paula Giddings (1984)[121] (Delta Sigma Theta), Cain Felder (1994, 1993)[122] (Alpha Phi Alpha), Glegg Watson (1978)[123] (Kappa Alpha Psi), Michael Thelwell (2003)[124] Therman Evans (1999)[125] (Kappa Alpha

---

[116]Amiri Baraka and The Blue Ark Band (February 28, 2000). *Funk Lore: A musical drama covering the history of African-American people.* Alice B. Statler Auditorium. New York: Cornell University.

[117]Leroi Jones (1963). *Blues people. The Negro experience in White America and the music that developed from it.* New York: Morrow Quill.

[118]."Amiri Baraka's Blues People: 40 Years later a symposium on jazz criticism and the music." February 6-Sarah Lawrence College (Yonders, NYP. http.//www.sic.edu//news.events/

[119]Claude Brown (1966). *Manchild in the promise land.* New York: Bantam Books.

[120]Leon Dash (1996). *Rosa Lee.* New York: Basic Books.

[121]Paula Giddings (1984). *When and where I enter. The impact of Black women on race and sex in America.* New York: William Morrow & Company.

[122]Cain Felder (1994). *Trouble Biblical Waters Race, class and family.* New York: Orbis; Cain Felder (Ed.) (1993). *The original African heritage study bible.* Iowa: World Bible Publishers. Michael Thelwell & Thelwell, M.

[123]George Davis & Watson, Glegg (1978). *Black life in corporate America. Swimming in the mainstream.* New York: Anchor.

[124]Stokely Carmichael with Ekwueme Michael Thelwell (2003). *Ready for Revolution.* New York: Scribner; Michael Thelwell (1988) *The harder they come.* New York: Grove Press; Michael Thelwell & Thelwell, M. (1987).

Psi), Houston Baker (1979), 1993, 1993, 1982, 1991, 1990, 1989, 1987, 2001[126] (Kappa Alpha Psi), and Phylicia Allen,[127] to name a few and some of their books and accomplishments.

Some may still ponder, has the place changed since the arrival of the Hip-Hop and the post Hip-Hop generations?[128] Will these generations be grounded enough in Africentric culture to continue to force the United States to strive for an incomparable higher moral ground in the world?[129] Less broad, now that the Ivy Leagues are fighting over the best Black students, is a Howard woman or man an

---

Duties, pleasure, and conflicts: Essays on struggle. Massachusetts. University of Massachusetts Press.

[125] Sara Reese, Johnson, K. & Evans, Therman (Eds.). (1999). *Staying strong: Reclaiming the Wisdom of African-American Healing.* New York: Avon.

[126] These are some of Houston's books: Houston Baker (1979). *No matter where you travel, you still be Black.* Michigan: University of Michigan Press; Houston Baker, Diaware, M. and Lindeberg, M. (Eds.). (1966*). Black British Cultural Series: A reader.* Illinois: University of Chicago Press; Houston Baker (2001). *Turning South again: Re-thinking Modernism/re-reading Booker T.* North Carolina: Duke University press; Houston Baker (1987). *Blues, Ideology and Afro-American Literature.* Illinois: University of Chicago Press; Dana Nelson and Houston Baker (Eds.). (2001). *Violence, the body and "the South".* Illinois: University of Chicago Press; Houston Baker and Patricia Redmond (Eds.). (1992). *Afro-American Literary study in the 1990s.* Illinois: University of Chicago Press; Houston Baker (1983). *Singers of daybreak: Studies in Black American Literature.* Washington, D.C.: Howard University Press. Leslie Fielder and Houston Baker (1981). *English Liteature: Opening up the Canon, Selected Papers from the English Institute*, 1979. Maryland: John Hopkins University Press; Houston Baker (1980*). The Journey Back: Illues in Black Literature and Criticism.* Illinois: University of Chicago Press.

[127] She became the first African-American actress to win the coveted Tony Award in the 58 year history of the award, for Best Leading Actress in a Play. The play was Lorraine Hansberry' classic drama *A raison in the Sun.* Puff Daddy, a Howard man, had a leading role in the play. Linda Armstrong (June 10–16, 2005). "Phylicia Rashad makes Tony history." *The Amerterdam News* pp. 1, 34.

[128] Authorities on Hip-Hop indicate that the Hip-Hop generation includes births from 1968–1984. See Bakari Kitwana (2002). *The Hip Hop generation Young Blacks and the crisis in African American culture.* New York: BasicCivitas Books.

[129] See Ralph Ellison (1986). "What America would be like without Blacks" (pp. 104–112). In Ralph Ellison, *Going to the Territory.* New YorK: Random House.

obsolete concept?[130] Do Howard and like schools provide an Afrospace that could be emulated, replicated or assimilated by PWU?[131] Is it enough to hire Black undergraduate college graduates such as Houston Baker, Toni Morrison, Leon Dash and graduate school graduate James Comer, and give them endowed chairs at prestigious PWC?[132] Complete answers to these questions are, of course, the basis of future works. In the interim, there is a value in Black universities that can be exported partially, just as there are values that Black universities have adapted syncretically from White ones.

Such an appreciation comes, however, from the use of the concept of diunitality. Admittedly, this book has been a discourse on the ways Blackness and Whiteness can be useful concepts that are applicable in educable ways and in different settings. Greater attention was applied to the educational advantages of Blackness for Blacks, Whites, Latinos and Asians because a Eurocentric educational thrust is widely known and accepted as the only paradigm from which to derive pedagogical approaches. It has consequently obscured the notion of a broad educational range to Blackness. Consistent with an Africentric educational imperative, this section will end by highlighting the broad educational reaches of the practice of Blackness and, realistically, on

---

[130]The question is being posed in the popular Black media. James A. Anderson (December, 2003/January, 2004). "It's a wonderfully brave new different life" *Savoy,* pp. 75, 76, 78.

[131]Salient issues at Howard that are typically not examined extensively at PWS: Kristal Knight (February 3, 2004). "Does attending a HBCU change your perspective?" *The Hilltop,* pp. 1, 2; Danielle Scrugg (October 7, 2002). "Cultural divide Students speak out on differences." *The Hilltop,* pp. 1-3; Khaila Edward (January 30, 2004). "A day in the life of Arthur Alexander." *The Hilltop,* p. 1, 2; Ayesha Rascoe (March 5, 2004). "HAS hosts forum on Haitian Uprising." *The Hilltop,* pp. 1, 2; Khaila Edward (January 23, 2004). "Egyptian fraternity works to fly African flag on the yard." *The Hilltop,* pp. 1, 3; Christoper Walls (February 3, 2004). "Lack of recognition for non-Pan Hellenic organization." *The Hilltop,* pp. 1, 2; Chad Bishop (February 24, 20004). "TURNGAIT entertainment works to inspire the Black community." *The Hilltop,* pp. 1, 2.

[132]Houston Baker (Susan Fox Beisccher and George D. Beischer Arts and Sciences Professor of English, Duke University); James Comer (Maurice Falk Professor of Child Psychiatry, Yale University); Leon Dash (Swanlund Professor of Journalism, University of Illinois at Urbana-Champaign); Toni Morrison (Robert Goheen Professor in the Humanities Council, Princeton University).

Gerald G. Jackson

ways of capitalizing on Whiteness within an Africentric educational construct.

Reaffirmation

If not patent at this point, my attraction to Africana Studies is more than a reaction to White Studies or nationalism;[133] it is based upon an Africentric paradigm and a racio-cultural survival imperative.[134] Specifically, what sustains the efforts resulting in the ensuing sections is the way it fulfills:

a concern for the betterment of a downtrodden group that I was personally familiar with and emboldened by;

a curiosity about the resilience of African Americans in the face of institutional, group, personal and modern racism;

a desire to pursue a subject in a multidimensional, multicultural and holistic way;

a human family need to discuss and foster the humanity of other racial, cultural and ethnic groups in the process of learning about Africana's history, development and practices.

Consequently, it can be espoused that the subsequent Africentric examination will continue without being preoccupied with the demise of Eurocentrism.[135] Much broader in scope, this discourse gives evidence of the educational efficacy of an Africentric model. The successful application of such a model would:

stimulate innovations in Black history month;

expand the definition and expanse of Black role models;

[133]Ronald Walters (2003). *White nationalism/Black interests.* Michigan: Wayne State University Press.
[134]Kobi Kambon (2003). *Cultural misorientation.* Florida: Nubian Nation Publications; Ama Mazama (Ed.) (2003). *The Afrocentric paradigm.* New Jersey: Africa World Press.
[135]Molefi Asante (1999). *The painful demise of Eurocentrism.* New Jersey: Africa World Press.

reinforce the value of faculty diversity in the classroom,[136] and promote quantitative and qualitative action research;

diminish barriers and enhance relationships among Blacks based upon gender, age, geographical location, income level, sub-cultural values, sexual orientation and experiences and

reveal the educational and psychological benefits of an Africana Studies for all students.

---

[136]"Survey reinforces value of faculty diversity in the classroom." *Black Issues in Higher Education*, (August 14, 2003), p. 13.

Gerald G. Jackson

You don't have to move mountains to make a difference:
Leaders in the African Diaspora and the way they shape our future

Submitted by: spring, 2003 Africana Studies and Research Center class 172 on Black Education.
Publisher: Professor Gerald G. Jackson Editor: Shelby Senzer
Cover Design: Dawn Darby, Shari Moseley and Professor Gerald G. Jackson

FOREWORD

The cover page displaying hands shaking and individuals united in a circle is symbolic of unity, strength, and togetherness. These ideas come together to create a new concept of what Blacks have done in the past, are doing now, and can do in the future. Not only are these notions shown through illustrations, but the entire book is dedicated to dismissing the stigmatic myths that plague the African race through acknowledging the value of significant leaders of the Diaspora who have never before been recognized for their tireless work in the community. Community service among these individuals is not limited to assisting Blacks, but helps people of various backgrounds. Thus, hands shaking and people forming a circle connotes more than just the need for unity, strength, and togetherness among Blacks alone, but in fact among all humankind. Only when we realize this truth can we all be victorious in our journey towards a brighter future.

Shari Tenielle Moseley
Undergraduate Student
Cornell University

PREFACE

AS&RC 172 really reminded us of a Real World meets Survivor with an Afro-centric flavor! From the first group assignment to the end, we were trying to be as collective and diunital as possible. The first assignment was very vague, we had a list of people who all had one thing in common, and they attended the funeral of the late Dr. John Henrik Clarke. Many of us were somewhat familiar with Dr. Clarke and with some of the names on the list but clearly, we had a task before us. Some of the people on the list were celebrities, some were leaders of national organizations, and some were only known within the black communities of Harlem. So as we began to research the names that had been divided up to our group, we searched for some commonalties because our overall assignment was to write biographical sketches on these funeral guests. What we found was that all of our leaders were activists for civil rights and had seen adversity on all sides of their public lives but were achievers who were not sick and tired but who were fed up with xenophobia, sexism and class-ism. After exhaustively searching, we realized that these leaders had all lived a life that boldly announced "We're Not Gonna Take It Anymore!" Our group was proud to be done and that set a tone within our group that turned this course into a life changing experience for most of us. Our work on our final presentation was an homage to the families of the New Jersey School district who stood up against the Jersey school board and told that group of predominantly white people that Elizabeth, New Jersey school district "was not gonna take it anymore either." While our group laughed at the acid wash overalls and the very stereotypical clergymen who were donned with corsages, the wisdom that each person had and the steadfastness with which they confronted the school board's racist decision to not proceed with the Curriculum of Inclusion introduced by Professor Jackson, stunned and inspired our group.

We were proud of the father who stood and acknowledged his academic failures, appropriately blaming them on that same school systems inept and substandard curriculum. He went on to plead with the board to rectify the substandard teaching for the sake of his children. It was probably the teacher, who was the most courageous person most of us had ever seen that led us to recreate that board meeting to show what should have happened. She was just an ordinary woman who had worked within that school system for many many years and spoke her peace without fear that she would lose her job. She told the truth even though she felt that her job would be lost as a result.[137] She dared to educate those in attendance of the mis-education that she had witnessed for all of those years and even though Al Sharpton nor Johnnie Cochran had her back, she told it so the title and our contribution to the book is really our way of taking the first steps at joining to support and thank Dr. Jackson for being a true messenger.

Dawn Darby
Graduate Student

---

[137]Her name is Ella Hopkins and she earned this special recognition through her courageous acts and supportive behaviors of Gerald Jackson.

Gerald G. Jackson

EDITOR'S INTRODUCTION

Looking through Cornell's gigantic course catalog just a few short months ago, I stumbled upon a course titled The Education of Black America. This was going to be the last chance I had to take classes at Cornell, and I was excited to take courses that reflected my interests and were not simply requirements for my major that seemed irrelevant to my future plans and unimportant to me personally. As I am planning to go into education, in some form or another, hopefully as a member of the Teach for America Corps, I enrolled in this class with no knowledge of what it was going to be like. I knew nothing about the professor or the requirements, and all I had to go on was the short blurb written about it in the course catalog. I figured, worst comes to worst, I would drop the class if it was not what I expected.

Entering the classroom the first day, I realized I didn't know anyone and was a little intimidated because, besides being one of three white students in the class, many of my other classmates seemed to be friends already or had previously taken classes with Professor Jackson. However, as the semester progressed, I felt increasingly comfortable in the classroom and actually began to make some friends through working in a group setting and talking to other students outside of class. The class was a wonderful experience; specifically how honest everyone was in their own personal anecdotes and experiences. I ended up coming out of this class with the knowledge of a different world view, a better understanding of black culture and reasons behind the problems that plague many black Americans today, a foundation to think about ways to improve our education system in a way that will benefit blacks and other minority students, and some new friends.

Editing this book has been a great way to reflect on the course as a whole, as I read my classmates' accounts of notable characters from their hometowns. It reminded me of how important it is for young students, and older ones, like us alike, to realize that there are people within our own communities, who come from backgrounds similar to our own, making significant contributions to individual communities, and even to society as a whole. Just because a person isn't "famous," it doesn't devalue their achievements and contributions. Many individuals who are on the covers of magazines or who appear on TV or in the movies have not given back to their communities. I hope that this book provides accounts of noteworthy community leaders that young students can relate to, and ideally, be inspired by.

Recently, I had the chance to visit my own high school, and I was able to speak with one of my favorite teachers. I had always had certain teachers that I was very fond of while I was in high school, but I never realized how influential some of those teachers would be, and how their presence would affect decisions I made in my own life. However, this all became clearer after talking to my former American history teacher, Mrs. Vogt. As I told her of my plan to join the Teach for America Corps, I realized that she was one of my inspirations to want to pursue a career in teaching, where I can impact the lives of young children. Through editing this book, I have realized how important it is to acknowledge the efforts and successes of our community leaders, as they are integral in keeping our communities thriving.

Shelby Senzer, Editor
Graduating Senior
Cornell University

Gerald G. Jackson

The Actual Book
Table of Contents

Gerald G. Jackson

EDUCATION LEADERS

Faith Harris

Kenneth Moore Lenon

Kenneth M. Lenon is one of Chicago's unsung heroes. He is a great man that inspires many. Kenneth M. Lenon has taught vocal and choral music in the Chicago Public Schools for 29 years. He himself is a product of the Chicago Public Schools System, attending Chicago Public Schools from adolescence through high school. He obtained

Kenneth Lenon. Photo by Faith Harris.

undergraduate training from Northern Illinois University. He holds graduate degrees from Vandercook College and Governors State University. He is the System-wide Staff Development Coordinator for the Bureau of Cultural Arts of the Chicago Public Schools, a member of the Music Educators National Conference, Alpha Phi Alpha Fraternity, Inc., National Association of Negro Musicians, and the American Choral Directors Association. He is also the founder of the Northern Illinois University Black Choir Alumni Foundation. Currently, he serves as the Director of the Concert Choir and Chairman of the Music Department and Coordinator of Student Activities at Kenwood Academy High School.

It is there where he takes students under his wings and gives them tough love, guidance, counseling, teachings, mentoring, speeches, and reproaches during their four years of attendance. He helps them through

Gerald G. Jackson

that awkward stage of life where they are questioning who they want to be, where they want to be, who they can trust, what to do or not to do, if their parents really know what is best, and so on. He cares for his students and never allows anyone to hurt or violate them. He tries to make sure that all of them are mentally, physically, and spiritually healthy. He forces his students to not only meet his standards and expectation of their capabilities but to exceed them. He does not allow students to quit nor make excuses. He builds their pride, gives them a certain confidence that they are somebody, and can accomplish anything.

He is known throughout the school as the "teacher who means business and don't play." He is also remembered after those four years of developing into adulthood "as the teacher who cared and gave his all." Many students who have been in his choir, who have worked with or for him, been in any of his classes, have gone on to do some great things. He is an unsung hero and his life should be celebrated. He truly is a "Dedicated and innovative Teacher and Educator." For more info. on the Choir: http://kaconcertchoir. com/.

Alexandria Jean-Francois

Ruth Simmons

"Ruth Simmons is to college presidents what Michael Jordan is to basketball players (1)." Ruth Simmons made history when she became the first African-American woman to lead an Ivy League institution. Once told by a colleague that she would never become a president of an Ivy League school, Simmons shattered that glass ceiling last fall when she was unaimosly elected president of Brown University. By doing so, she became Brown's 18th president, its first female president, and the first African American to lead one of the nation's prestigious Ivy League institutions (3). She is a one-of-a-kind leader who has and is presently steering new paths for Brown.

Dr. Ruth Simmons was born in Grapeland, Texas. She is the youngest of twelve children born to sharecropping parents. When her family later moved to Houston, her father worked in a factory and her mother was a maid (3). She grew up during a time where the South was racially divided due to segregation, a time when a college education for a poor black girl seemed impossible. She had three strikes against her: growing up African American, female, and poor. Somehow, Simmons used the strength and support given to her by her family and managed to beat the odds. She attended Dillard University in New Orleans, and with the support of her high school teachers, she graduated with honors.

Later, she earned her masters and Ph.D. in romance languages and literature from Harvard where she became a professor and an administrator. With those degrees under her belt, Simmons began pursuing her dream to become a college administrator. Keeping her dream clear in her mind, Simmons successfully served in various positions of progressive responsibility at the University of New Orleans, California State University, Butler College, Princeton University, and Spelman College before accepting her current post at Smith. Simmons became the first African American women president of Smith College in 1995 and currently, she is the president of Brown.

Simmons accepted the position at Brown, because she believed that it would enable her to better participate in educational reform on a national level, something that is very dear to her (3). In addition, she expects to take a significant leadership role in higher education as "the country is trying to reform education and asking pertinent questions about how to provide opportunities for (poor) children (3)." Ruth Simmons has earned many titles through her hard work and dedication. Despite all the obstacles that she has faced, she has managed to triumph as a leader at Brown University. During the beginning of her presidency, Simmons kicked off a program she called Initiatives for Academic Enrichment, which is a plan designed to add faculty and increase staff salary, improve graduate learning, provide new funds for libraries and technology and to build new academic space (4). Many officials at Brown considered the plan to be one of the biggest single moves to invest in academics at Brown University. In addition, she has made Brown's admissions policy blind to financial aid requests. The need-blind policies mean the college will not take into account a family's financial needs when considering an application for admission (4). Brown, up to that point, had been the only Ivy League school that wasn't considered need-blind to domestic applicants.

Ruth Simmons has demonstrated her leadership style in many ways. "First, she passionately believes in the transcendental importance of education, both to individuals and to society. Second, she has a vision and a clear set of priorities. Third, she listens, she learns and she leads. Fourth, she has tenacity and boundless energy. Fifth, she inspires (1)." Not all that she has accomplished was easier for her. There have been people who have tried to discourage her by telling her that she would never be president. These people were obstacles that turned out to be a way for her to develop and become a better person. Simmons advises: "Never assume when something (negative) happens, if you don't get an opportunity that you are not going to achieve anything in your life (3)."

Ruth Simmons has many goals and one of her goals is to make education accessible to everyone, especially minority students. "Education is a tool." She contends, "that it enables poor and minority students to bridge the economic gap to success. For education to be accessible, however, it must be affordable (3)." Therefore, there is the need for scholarships, internships, and other financial assistance. In addition to financial concerns, Simmons believes in five other areas where minorities should concentrate on and they are: setting general goals, selecting a broad liberal arts education, choosing appropriate mentors, learning how to respond to criticism, and being open to new opportunities (3). Simmons is a strong advocate for liberal arts education because many first generation college students and minority students are encouraged to go into a narrow education to get a good job. Minorities are especially prone to entering more traditional and less innovative fields. Not everyone agrees with this idea, but Simmons thinks that a liberal arts education helps poor children get basic knowledge in a lot of areas, like she did.

Today, Simmons' leadership style is currently received by almost everyone. Despite the fact that some believe that a liberal arts is not practical, Ruth Simmons believes that it is important to cover a broad range of knowledge. In settling general goals, Simmons reminds those students "ought to work very hard to get the skills needed to enable them to do a variety of occupation (3)." Brown Chancellor Stephen Robert, who introduced Simmons to the trustees and fellows following the corporation's vote, believes that, "We have selected an extraordinary leader, a person of character, of integrity, and of depth. I believe the broader campus community will welcome Dr. Simmons with great enthusiasm (2)." Ruth Simmons is currently impacting her community and hopefully, she will continue to do so in the future.

Gerald Souders

Ms. Askins

Unfortunately, I never thought of doing something like this and the assignment came a few years too late. During my second year in Philadelphia public schooling, 8th grade, I had an advisory teacher Ms. Askins. She was always hard on us especially me cause she expected so much out of me. Things went her way in the class until she felt that we completely respected her and then we could have say in what happened. She was an older woman who had seen a lot in her time because she grew up in the south while it was legal to segregate. She would always tell us her stories and tell us that we had not seen anything as bad as some of the stuff that she faced at our age in the south.

She was our social studies teacher. The classroom walls were plastered with black faces and accomplishments of people that I had never heard of. There were posters of Black inventors, scientists, poets, activist, leaders, etc. She also had more posters of Africa than I had ever seen at the time: names of countries, capitols, populations, and geography. We never really talked about Amerikkkan history too often it was mostly about ancient Africa. The class was never too much fun because we were always taking notes on stuff that did not seem too relevant to what we were interested in. The information was rather boring cause we always had to read from papers she handed out or listen to her go on about some land long lost and people we would never see. Thinking back I wish that I spent more time listening to what she said instead of trying to fit in with the rest of the kids cause I was the "new kid on the block" trying to make friends. Early in the year, I would be made fun of for actually paying attention and answering her questions when no one else would raise their hands. She would almost always keep me after class and ask me how things were going in general and how I felt about the information that she was giving me. I was usually indifferent to what she was teaching but it gave me a new perspective on Africa that I never got from previous education in private and suburban public schools. Now that I think about she was my first African Amerikkkan woman teacher and she taught us what she basically wanted to.

She was trying to give us a sense of what our history was trying to make us stand up straight and not lay back to what we would be learning the next year in high school in world and Amerikkkan history which denies Black people their history. She was not only a teacher but also a disciplinarian. This may have been another reason that students did not enjoy her class. If you missed her class or acted up in it, you could expect a call home that night to your parents. If she could not get in contact with them, she made you stand in front of the class, apologize, and stand in the corner for the rest of the period. Throughout the period she would look out the door and holler at students that were running through the halls or going to their lockers at the wrong time of the day. She was known around the school as the teacher that you did not mess with... thankfully I had her for homeroom teacher because she would not let anyone mess with any of us in her class.

My favorite day for class with her was Friday. She was the last class of the week and everyone was tired of being in that schoolhouse.

For some reason we had bars on the window of our room, we were on the third floor, and the windows only opened a couple of inches. To allow everyone time to chill out since we had gym the class before she would play jazz while we did work or while she read aloud from one of her books. Many of us had been forced to listen to jazz because of our parents so we did not really like it. She would tell us some of the history of artists that were playing so most of us began to appreciate it. That was the first time that I actually liked jazz and started asking my parents to turn the radio to their jazz station when I was in the car.

After graduation, we had a reception in the library for the graduates, parents, and teachers. She gave me a huge gift: $50 dollar gift certificate to some bookstore and $50 cash. I was amazed. I was shocked. All the animosity that I might have had for her had left me especially when I read her card. It said something about how she felt no fear of leaving the earth now cause the world would be in good hands. I almost wanted to cry. Every year during high school I would come back to visit and speak to kids in classes of my former teachers but I could never catch up to her. Every time that I came back, she was out sick or left early. Thankfully I did give her a big hug after I got her card and said my good-byes then because I never got to see her after that day. Teachers told me that she actually had a nervous breakdown the year after I left because the kids were so out of control. I really wanted to hurt somebody. They drove away one of the best teachers that I ever had. I keep going back to the school and it does not feel the same. I see kids running the halls at top speed and teachers afraid to confront them. How can we expect the kids to learn anything when the teachers are too afraid to talk them? She made us respect her and in turn we respected her. There are not too many teachers made of that character anymore… at least not at Roosevelt Middle School. I do not know how to end this so I will just say thank you Ms. Askins for all that you taught me even though it took another 6 years for it to finally take hold and mold me. I love you.

Alexandra Carlin

Fred Birkett

"In my job, there are no Mondays. I look forward to every day."

Fred Birkett is a conservatively dressed, soft-spoken man. He has over twenty years of experience as a senior administrator and educator. He was the executive director of Benjamin Banneker Charter School and was the Assistant Headmaster for the Boston Renaissance Charter

School in Boston. After receiving his Masters in Educational Administration from the Harvard University Graduate School of Education, he stayed on to serve as a Program Recruiter and University Supervisor for student teachers. Mr. Birkett was also a leader in the University of California's Upward Bound Program, serving first as a Teacher and then as its Program Director. He was a sixth grade classroom teacher in Brooklyn and spent seven years in the United States Air Force, attaining the rank of Captain.

After Birkett left the Air Force, he joined the charter school movement. Charter schools are public schools that operate independently of the regulations governing traditional schools. They are becoming increasingly popular with parents who are unsatisfied with their child's public school and are looking for a better education. The charter school movement took speed in the late 1990's as increasing attention to the failing public school system forced educators and parents to find alternative solutions. Congress appropriated one hundred million dollars to expand the number of charter schools across the country. Birkett was an integral part of this movement serving many leadership roles involved in all levels of the school.

When Birkett served as the executive director of the Benjamin Banneker Charter School in Cambridge, Mass., he called the time between the issuing of a permit and the opening of a school "a daunting task" that includes finding space, hiring administrators, teachers and other staff, and selecting students. He said, "The key is to make sure there is a clear delineation of responsibilities of the board, the school operator and other officials." "If it's not done, you have chaos, too many cooks things will get messy." Birkett believes it is best to hire teachers on a year-to-year basis rather than offering multi-year contracts so non-effective teachers can be dismissed more easily. Another piece of wisdom that Birkett has acquired from his involvement in charter schools is the importance of a sense of discipline and structure. He says, "We developed a culture at the school where there is an explicit link in rules, policies, and incentives." For instance, students who behaved badly in or outside the classroom weren't allowed to play on the newly formed basketball team. To reward students for good behavior, Birkett and his staff created an activity session during the last period of the day when students could pursue interests like chess, dance, reading, computers, or even singing in a gospel choir. He learned this lesson when he was the Assistant Headmaster the Boston Renaissance Charter School beginning in 1996. He believed that children who took advantage of facilities and teachers didn't have ownership of the school. Consequently, in his subsequent ventures he has instilled a sense of pride and community in his students and teachers. In order to enhance the educational experience, Birkett emphasizes making the children feel safe and showing the children that the staff is there for them, "My number-one goal was finding teachers who cared for kids. If the students think their teachers don't care, they turn them off. I didn't want that to happen."

Birkett is now the principle of The Sisulu Children's Academy in Harlem, New York. It was the first charter school to open in New York on September 8, 1999. It continues to expand every year by adding on new grade levels. Parents, students, and teachers alike thinks that Sisulu Children's Academy has been a great success.

Birkett has co-authored a book on charter schools entitled, *Charter Schools: Everything You Need To Know to Make the Right Decision for Your Child.* Its an instructional book that informs parents about the mission of charter schools and whether or not sending their child to a charter school is the best option for them.

Diamaris Welch

Mr. Bernard

As a child, I had many positive influences in my life. Well-accomplished individuals who loved me dearly and always guided me in the right direction surrounded me. Never was I discouraged from attaining any goals that I set for myself, nor was I ever told that I couldn't accomplish my dreams. I was always encouraged to do well in whatever I chose to do; therefore, there were no negative enforcement in my life informing me on what I could not do. That was beneficial to my upbringing.

Although such wonderful people have enlightened me, there is one person who still stands out for his efforts to push his students into a positive direction, within a school system that did not care. That is my seventh grade biology teacher, Mr. Bernard Forbes. I went to a junior high school that was run-down, with poor facilities, and teachers that did not really care about their students. Mr. Forbes was a new teacher to the public school in Brooklyn New York, and he took it upon himself to make some serious changes once he had arrived.

Mr. Forbes was from Grenada, and he was not used to the American school system, but he realized that there was definitely a need for change. He noticed that I, along with a few other students in the class were not being challenged by the work provided. Instead of leaving us in the science classes that were not challenging, he created an after school class, that taught biology given to high school students. Every Monday, Wednesday, and Friday afternoon he would stay in school with us for an extra three hours to go over Biology that would prepare us for the New York City Regents Examination. An examination that was to be taken by students in the 9th grade, but he was preparing us to take it in the seventh. He created tapes for us with helpful information for the examination and spoke to us whenever we needed to talk. All the students knew Mr. Forbes for his, "Thought for the Day." He'd put up a "Though for the Day," which was usually inspirational, and the students would each have to write in their own words what he meant by this, and follow this for the day.

Mr. Forbes did all of this extra work with no extra pay. This after school program that he brought to the school was taught by him alone, for no other teachers cared to put in these extra hours free. This is a sad situation, but it made him shine above all the rest and he was truly appreciated for it. All of his students excelled in the class and passed the Regents examination with good grades.

In a school system where many youths are forgotten, or simply ignored, Mr. Forbes meant a lot to his students. He instilled in us faith that there were still teachers in the school system that cared about their students enough to actually spend extra time with them with no personal profit other than gaining immense satisfaction from the success of his students.

Azaria Tesfa

Sheila Dixon

Progress for many begins with a bold step by one. Council President Sheila Dixon took her first step when she decided to enter politics sixteen years ago. Elected as the youngest woman ever to hold a seat on the Baltimore City Council in 1987, Council President Dixon represented the 4th Council District for three consecutive terms. In 1999, she was elected by a large margin to serve as the first African-American woman to lead the Baltimore City Council and preside over the Board of Estimates.

Instilled with an appreciation for education by her mother and the determination of her father, Ms. Dixon excelled in Baltimore City public schools. She earned her bachelor's degree in early childhood education from Towson University and obtained her master's degree in educational management from Johns Hopkins University. Dixon's work on several local political campaigns during her tenure as an elementary school teacher and Head Start instructor inspired her to seek public office and raise funds to improve the quality of education through the legislative process.

In addition to her civic duties as Council President, Ms. Dixon presides over the Board of Estimates, and serves as a member of numerous community organizations including the NAACP, the African-American Women's Caucus, the National Forum for Black Public Administrators, the National Black Caucus of Local Elected Officials, the Baltimore BELIEVE Campaign, Revitalizing Baltimore Advisory Panel, the Baltimore City Tobacco Community Health Coalition and the Retired Senior Volunteers Program Advisory Council. She is a board member of the Housing Authority Drug & Substance Abuse Committee and the Baltimore Public Markets Corporation.

Council President Dixon's honors include being named one of Baltimore's Most Influential Leaders, and selected twice as one of Maryland's Top 100 Women by Warfield's Business Record. Her most recent achievements include creating the Baltimore City Council Commission on Council Restructuring to develop recommendations to restructure the Council, the Baltimore City Council Commission on HIV/AIDS Prevention and Treatment to assess statistical information and develop a strategy to generate additional funding to counter the deadly pandemic; and sponsoring the inaugural of Bea Gaddy Day, an annual citywide collection of non-perishable food items, toiletries, clean winter coats, hats and gloves to honor the late Councilwoman's legacy of giving.

Ricardo Arguello

Mr. Brunell Griffith

What does it mean to be a leader in the community? Does it mean that you have to hold a prestigious position at a corporation or a state office? Is being a leader a person that has money and influence, whether negative or positive, on the community? A leader in my opinion is a person that leaves an indelible mark in the lives of an individual or a group. Brunell Griffith is a man of character who has left a positive impact on countless high school students at All Hallows High School.

Brunell Griffith was born on November 10, 1965 to Paul and Monica Griffith on the small West Indian Island of Montserrat. His parents raised Brunell in a strict, stern, and traditional West Indian household. Mr. Griffith grew up in the South Bronx where he attended All Hallows High School and became a track star throughout New York City. He managed to graduate third in his class at All Hallows as well as earn a full athletic scholarship in track at St. John's University. While attending St. John's Brunell managed to excel in track, earn a BA in marketing and communications, and become president of St. John's chapter of Phi Beta Sigma Fraternity, Incorporated.

Out of college, Brunell managed to receive a high paying job working for an advertising company but to his surprise, he was not happy. He did not care about the money or the job, he was not happy with the lack of connection with his community because his job demanded long and strenuous hours from him. Even though they were paying Brunell a great deal of money he was not able to enjoy it because he was always working. As a result, Brunell quit his job and became what he always wanted to be a high school teacher and track coach for All Hallows high school.

The first time I met Brunell was in my first year when I went to a track meeting to become part of the team. To this day, I did not know why I went to the meeting. Before the meeting, I had never thought about joining a school team, let alone running track. I believe that something told me to go because it was meant to be by some unknown force wanting to give me a positive role model in my life. Upon entering the track team I did not only manage to gain new friends but new family members.

The All Hallows track team consisted of mostly first generation immigrant students whose parent work over 40 hours a week to pay the tuition of the school. Some even came from single parent households where the parents could not spend most of the day with their children because they had to work. As a result, Brunell managed to create a tutoring program where the track students could stay in All Hallows until 8 p.m. doing their home work or getting projects or assignments done while at school. Even though he was a track coach he did not exclusively leave the library open for track students, he left it open to any student who needed to get their work done or anyone who did not want to go home or roam the streets late at night. Mr. Griffith quickly became the mentor of not only the track team but of countless, other students who were in search of a positive male role model.

Mr. Griffith did not only become a role model to me; he became my second father. While at All Hallows, Mr. Griffith always made sure that I got my work done, behaved my self well, made sure that I was doing well at home because at the time I was having problems with my father, and that if I ever needed a shoulder to lean on he was there to support me. I knew that coaches at time did help their students but Mr. Griffith went far above and beyond the call of duty. He spoke to me and my best friend about the importance of adult relationships, money management, and college. My brother Juan and my self were the first members of my family to finish high school consequently; my parents knew little about the college system in the United States. Mr. Griffith took Paul, my best friend, and myself to college campuses around the East Coast so that we would be able to make a good selection in our choice of college. He took his time and spent his money because he knew that we could not afford it and that our parents did not know how to inform us about college. He was one of the helping hands that molded this boy into a man.

Even though I went to a predominantly Black and Latino all boys' high school, I received little assistance in college preparation. The administration and guidance counseling office advised me to apply to community colleges or colleges that "were in my range of understanding." They did not encourage me to go to any Ivy League institutions because they did not consider that I had the tools to get in or even compete with the Caucasian students at these institutions. Even when I received my acceptance letters most of my professors at the time only thought that I got in due to Affirmative Action. The basketball coach even told me that the reason why I got into Cornell University and received a good financial aid package was because my last name was Arguello while his daughter, a white Irish girl from New Rochelle with a last name of Carey, received little assistance. He was implying that I was under qualified and because of Affirmative Action, I received not only entrance to Cornell but also a good package. What impact does that leaves on a child that is happy to be the first member of his family to go to college? I began to believe that I did get into Cornell because of my race rather than because I was the valedictorian of my class, captain of the track team, and because I tutored elementary school children on weekends. Mr. Griffith on the other hand reinforced my self-confidence by making me understand racist ideologies that existed in my school and in the world. He prepared me for college and the outside world.

Mr. Griffith did not only become a role model for me he was able to gain the trust of students who lost trust in themselves. He has managed to save countless students of All Hallows high school from dropping out or quitting their goals in life such as attending college. Although he is not on television as a political activist or a city assembly member, he has still managed to turn boys into men. He has lit the flames of success and encouraged countless men to go and break down the barriers that America has imposed on its colored youth.

Currently Mr. Griffith is still working for All Hallows high school as their religious studies teacher as well as coach to the All Hallows' cross-country, indoor and out door track teams. He is still taking students under his wing and mentoring them either in academics or just in lessons in life. He manages every year to take a busload of students to college campus throughout the East Coast so that inner city high school students can get a sense of what it is like to go to college outside of New York City. Brunell Griffith has lived the old Chinese proverb of "give a man a fish and he eats for a day, teach him how to fish and he eats for a life time" by making his students "angeles" of life.

Jamy Rodriguez

Mr. Rodney Harris

When I think of someone who has made a significant impact on my life, one individual comes to mind—Mr. Rodney Harris. His presence in my life completely changed the way I viewed the world and those around me. He taught me to take into consideration the backgrounds, lifestyles, and experiences of others before making judgments. He showed me the importance of accepting people for who they are instead of what they are. Ultimately, he instilled in me the belief that I was capable of accomplishing everything I set my mind too because, according to him, I was blessed.

I met Mr. Harris as a freshman in high school. Back then, I was disquietingly quiet; very rarely did I speak in class and this was due to my extreme shyness, which caused me to become isolated from the rest of the students and teachers. One day in algebra section, I got fed up with the students' disruptive behavior and I complained to the teacher; he suggested that I take it up with the assistant principal of the mathematics department and this is exactly what I did. This person was Mr. Harris, who after listening to my complaints gently reassured me that he would take care of it while commending me on the courage I demonstrated by approaching him in the first place. During our meeting, I had confessed to him that I was a terrible at math and he offered to help me get over my so-called "impediment." We met everyday during my lunch periods and after tutoring me for the entire year, I ended up scoring the highest grade on the math regent that year and every year thereafter. Mr. Harris became more than my teacher, he became a father figure, a friend.

Mr. Harris was instrumental in helping me overcome my insecurities as a student. He helped me realized that instead of being a mediocre student I should excel in order to be accepted into a prestigious university. After listening to him incessantly discuss the importance of doing well so that I could one day uplift my family and my community, I decided that I wanted to achieve bigger and greater things in my life. I began to do better academically and participated in the social events my school sponsored. By my sophomore year, I had been elected as class president and joined the swimming team. My senior year I was accepted into Cornell University and many other well-known institutions. If it were not for him, I would not have applied to these schools in the first place. He later convinced my parents to let me go away to school because this would be best for my development as an individual. Today he continues to help other students reach their potential and provides leadership and guidance to those who have no one to turn to. When I speak to him today, he tells me that the only thing I owe him is to one day provide my assistance and support to someone who needs it. He is in large part responsible for opening my eyes to the importance of giving back to where I came from.

My most vivid memory of him however, was on one particular day when I was feeling down because of an argument I had had with my father. The relationship with my father had gradually begun to deteriorate during my adolescence. I resented him because of the choices he had made during his life and how these had affected our family and most importantly my mother. After sitting down and telling Mr. Harris about the way I felt about my father, he urged me to see my father in all of his facets. I was to remember that my father was human and because of this was entitled to commit mistakes and be forgiven for them. Mr. Harris forced me to accept my father with his virtues and his vices – something I could not conceive of before. In order to comfort me, he told me about the hardships he endured growing up poor in the projects with only his mother and three sisters to look up to. He had never experienced the presence of a father figure to lead him in the right direction. Because I was fortunate enough to have my father in my life, he convinced me to open my heart and accept him.

Finally, Mr. Harris taught me to examine everything I was taught in school. He bought me books that he thought were necessary for me to read, but that I would not hear about in the classroom. He believed that the educational system was poor in that it was one-sided in its curriculum and that in order to combat years of mis-education it was necessary to take it upon myself to read about other histories, cultures, and values. He exposed me to a completely new fountain of information I had no idea existed. In class, he would incorporate these principles by being innovative and bringing to light information, which he felt, was necessary for us students to know about. For Malcolm X's birthday instead of teaching us a math lesson he showed a documentary on the life of this civil rights figure and made us write a reaction paper afterwards. He blatantly defied the school's program by teaching us about the greatness of the Egyptian civilization and calling Pythagorean theorem the Egyptian theorem after its real place of origin. He often was involved in predicaments with the principal of the school for his outlandish behavior, but this still did not deter him from doing what he believed was right.

The reason I admire this man so much is that he is one of those rare individuals that was able to change my outlook on the world because of his inherent goodness and selflessness. Because of him, I now understand that many of the things that happen around me have less to do with individuals themselves, but more to do with structural forces, which they have no control over. He came into my life at a very important time, when I needed someone's direction the most. He was able to see in me the potential that I could not see in myself and for that, I will always be grateful. I love him for believing in my dreams and believing in the dreams of others, for having a vision, and sharing with his students this vision despite the risks involved. Mr. Harris provided me with an entire new way of looking at the world around me. He is to me, more than a former teacher is. He is like a father.

Gerald G. Jackson

RELIGIOUS LEADERS

Kareen Waite

Brother Joseph Higgins

A native Jamaican, Brother Joseph Higgins now resides in Brooklyn. Brother Higgins is a leader of the community because he always encourages the youth of the community to strive for the best. A youth minister of Good Hope Missionary Church, he serves as a father, a male role model, and a friend for the youth members of the community and to the church.

He constantly preaches to the youth, urging them to finish their education and to obtain the degrees that are necessary to enable them to be successful in their careers. To further promote this idea, he has even made a promise to all the youth within the church, to award each person who graduates from college with scholarship money. He believes that if youth were provided with incentives, they would be motivated to strive for more and the public announcement of awarding of youths will serve as positive reinforcement. Instead of complaining about their negative actions, adults are congratulating them.

Brother Higgins is about the youth. He tries to make sure that the youth of the community have an outlet to release their "negative energies" instead of committing unruly acts. He encourages the men to treat women with respect, and the women to carry themselves with pride; he wants the youth to remain focused on their goals at all times. His motto is, "If the church can't hold their attention, then someone or something else will." Since the streets provide our youth with incentives to commit mischievous acts, then it is both the church's and the community's job to provide incentives to keep the youth of today along the straight and narrow path. Some other programs he has been involved with are as follows: the director of the youth choir, coordinator of youth meetings, and the coordinator of youth group outings. Some of the outings include volunteering at women and men shelters; outdoor church services, trips to Washington D.C. for youth conventions every September, and trips to adventure parks.

When the elders of the church and the community dismiss thoughts and opinions from adolescents because according to them "...youths do not know anything thing," Brother Joseph Higgins always tries to turn the ideas of adolescents into actions. For example, instead of having the elders of the church play musical instruments for services, Brother Higgins was an influential person in allowing members of the church to make adolescents play instruments such as the bass guitar, the drums, the keyboard and the clarinet. Most of these instruments are non-traditional instruments in the Pentecostal church. Also if any adolescent was interested in playing one of these instruments, Brother Higgins made sure that child was provided with musical lessons. In fact, when the original church drums were damaged, Brother Higgins donated a new drum set to the church.

Brother Higgins takes a new approach to leadership; one in which he is "one" with the group he services. A good leader is one who takes into account everyone's opinion and makes decisions after weighing the negative and the positive sides of the decisions. He reaches out to the community and in turn, everyone in the community reaches out to him. Although at times, his work may seem to go unwarranted, throughout his time as a youth minister at Good Hope Missionary church (30 years) he has impacted the lives of several youth members. His primary goal within the church is to raise the level of youth involvement within the community. Once again, he is a youth minister, a paternal figure, a role model, and a friend.

Tara Leigh Wood

Gregory J. Jackson

Pastor Gregory J. Jackson of Mount Olive Baptist Church has been one of the most influential people in the Hackensack and Northern New Jersey communities. He has influenced many people and has helped

Photo of Gregory Jackson. Photo by Tara Woods.

even more to attain success in their lives through faith in the Lord. He has set up many programs to help the community youth and adults live productive lives inside and outside of the church. His vision for Mount

Olive Baptist Church is that it will provide the kind of worship service that will be informative and inspiring. The church offers a variety of classes and seminars that meet the needs of the community. His dream is that as people grow numerically they will also grow deeper in their care for the lonely, aged, the hurting, depressed and that they will find love, acceptance, help, and encouragement. Mount Olive developed a social ministry that is global in perspective that attempts to help the hurting, hungry, homeless and hopeless people, not only in our Hackensack community but also all over the world. Mount Olive also serves as an advocate for the rights of the poor, and those who have been locked out or locked up as they seek justice. The church is a haven for youth as they seek to find themselves as individuals and as they seek to develop as young Christians. Mount Olive Baptist Church welcomes people regardless of race or background. The vision of Mount Olive Baptist Church is to be a culturally relevant African American church that provides dynamic worship of God, while extending his transforming Grace to reach the unchurched community.

Pastor Jackson has set up a myriad of programs that serve the community and follow the vision of the church. They provide a variety of classes, workshops, seminars, retreats, and small groups that will facilitate the biblical, spiritual, and cultural growth and transformation of our members. He, along with other members and staff at the church administer what is called a Christian education, which involves not only Bible classes, but may also involve Black History, parenting skills, economic development workshops, health seminars, and financial planning. Mount Olive is interested in ministering to the whole person. In addition, the church plans to build a new Family Life Center that would provide adequate space for Sunday school, fellowship, and community programs. The new Family Life Center will also have a Christian Bookstore, a computer-learning center, and a library.

Mount Olive is dynamic in that it serves many purposes throughout the community. One of which is commitment to youth empowerment, involving youth in a transforming relationship with Jesus Christ at an early age. Pastor Jackson always says that it is easier to build a boy or girl than it is to mend a man or a woman. Therefore, he is committed to ministry to youth. Being committed to the education of youth is equally important, so the church decided to tithe $50,000 a year toward the continued education of youth who plan to attend college. He has an exciting, relevant and dynamic ministry for youth that meets their spiritual, academic, cultural, and economic needs.

Photo of Tara Woods.

Pastor Jackson is a great leader in the community who is looked up to by many people. His kind ways and wise words have influenced the coldest of hearts to turn to the warmest of smiles.

Dawn Darby

Bishop F.D. Patterson Sr.

During a time when trust in the clergy is failing, as a community, Black people are losing the core of our communities. The Church and the Clergy are considered the cornerstone of Black communities, and

Photo of Bishop Patterson. Photo by Dawn Darby.

historically stood for what was right and good. Carter G. Woodson speaks of a mass exodus by the Black educational elite from the neighborhood storefront churches to the more pristine, affluent cathedrals. The elite felt that if they were away from the neighborhood clergy they could build state of the art worship centers and basically alienate themselves from the less educated Black churches whose members unfortunately could not complete the assimilation into the Euro-centric Middle class lifestyle.

Naturally this shift did influence those who remained in the churches of the neighborhood and the clergy men and women were left with the burden of being one of few role models, teachers, parents, bondsmen, etc. that Black people could easily call upon. This became, for many in the Black church, too much of a burden and many clergy began, at one time or another, to fall prey to traps, mishaps like drugs, sex and money. The Black people turned away from them and many are still searching for the place within the community that should represent faith, love, beauty and hope. One man's record of accomplishment has remained unstained, literally for the 30 plus years he has been a pastor. He is 78 years old, has never been involved in any scandal, and has never shamed his community and through sacrifices no one may ever know, he has been an example to men and women of how to live an honest life. As a human being, he has managed to never be convicted or charged with any crime. He has been married to the same woman for over 35 years, has no children out of wedlock and remains faithful to his wife in an almost newlywed way; they dote over each other. He has gained respect from the thugs, dealers, hustlers and pimps and corner drunks and is the one who gets called by the big time bishops and pastors for help and prayer when they succumb to the pressure of always being spotless in the eyes of the community.

Photo of Dawn Darby.

He is known as the Bishop's Bishop but because he keeps it real, he is not accepted into the public who's who of Black preachers. Because he refuses to forget his vow to God to take care of his people, he will not be bought, there is no price. There is no man that can make him refrain from giving the message from God. He fears no man and can help you better than any of the leading psychic reader or lotto-playing experts. I defy any person to research and find anything contrary to what I have reported.

His name is Frederick David Patterson Sr. He grew up in Indianapolis Indiana and moved to Winston-Salem, NC after graduating from Butler University with a seminary degree. He fully expected to be an ordained minister. With his degrees, he was also interested in becoming a schoolteacher but Winston-Salem had different plans for him. Called "Yankee boy" he was racially discriminated against and found himself in the early 60's as a janitor at a school he was more than qualified to teach in. He worked as if it were for God and not for the man, and took pride in his work. There he met Dorothy Douglas, who worked in the cafeteria. They called each other big brother and little sister. They married and he accepted her already four kids as his own and together they raised ten children (plus enormous extended family). With the help of God, Bishop Patterson, weathered many storms and always fed and clothed and cared for people. He took his life's mission as just that and his life and his work speak for him. He does not want the credit, many times, for all of the lives he has touched and helped, but he considers all he has influenced as stars in his crown when he gets to Heaven and that is what he lives for and is enough of a reward for him.

POLITICAL AND MILITARY LEADERS

Gerald G. Jackson

Phela Townsend

Colonel Margaret Bailey

Margaret Bailey was born on Christmas day, 1915, in Selma, Alabama. Not more than a couple of years passed when she and her family moved to Mobile, Alabama. There she received a basic public school education. Little did she know that the area where she grew up would be one of the most segregated and racially tense areas of the South. Moreover, she would have never envisioned that segregation, a racially discriminatory system, would lead her on the path to becoming one of the most respected and honored women in the nation's Armed Forces.

During the early '30s, it came time for Margaret to decide what she was going to do with her life. Yet, due to the racially pervasive restrictions Blacks had to adhere to, she, like many other young Black men and women, had to find a profession into which she could be accepted. That was how education, among other things, went during those times – Blacks went where they were allowed. Walking to class everyday, Margaret would pass by the local hospital and see all the nurses neatly dressed in their white suits, and she thought maybe she would like to be one as well. After all, most Black women infiltrated the career fields of cleaning, teaching, and nursing. She was accepted to The Fraternal Hospital School of Nursing in Montgomery, Alabama, and once she finished her education there, she found a job in New York City at the Sea View Hospital.

After Sea View, Margaret Bailey decided that she would join the military. As was everything else, the military was segregated. However, there was no doubt in her mind that that was what she wanted to do. While it did offer educational opportunities, in addition to the opportunity to see the world, Margaret had another more culturally specific reason for entering "the white man's army." She remarks, "I thought to myself: my people will be fighting as well as being killed; they would need my help."

During her time in the army, Bailey was able to make great educational advancements. She completed all her schooling at San Francisco University, receiving her BA in nursing. Additionally, Bailey was able to travel to 27 countries. All the while, she studied different destinations where she thought she might like to go; she learned the history of many countries through travel magazines and doing extensive research. Unheard of for blacks, especially a woman, Bailey saw the Louvre in Paris and the Taj Mahal in India.

Of her time in the military, Bailey recalls, "There were many different shades of color in the military, but we were alike in many ways. While I did encounter segregation, there were many nice people. Many of my friends were white, and it was strange – I would never be caught with any of them on the streets back home."

The most important thing that Bailey procured from her time in the military was that she was able to teach. She explains that even though she was away from the States for extended periods of time, she never felt like she lost her spiritual connection to her people there. In fact, she used the opportunity to spread knowledge of Black culture, especially in light of the racist views that proliferated throughout the world. "While in a foreign country," she says, "I had to adjust at first. Many foreigners were intrigued and weren't used to seeing black women. I have to know them, and they have to know me. You had to teach them about you, you know – Black women. It was very educational. I was so happy to teach about Blacks."

W.W.II was the only war in which Bailey was stationed. Initially, she and other Black nurses were told that there were no spaces for blacks. However, according to Bailey, "they underestimated the power of strong women, like Eleanor Roosevelt." And as time passed, eventually the need for nurses, Black or White became vital, so they had to be accepted on the front lines.

In her twenty-seven years in the military, Margaret Bailey rose throughout the ranks from a Second Lieutenant to Colonel. She was the first black nurse promoted to Colonel in the Army Nurse Corps. When she received this illustrious status there were no blacks, only whites in the Corps; furthermore, to begin with, there were not many colonels in the Nurse Corps.

Currently, Colonel Margaret Bailey resides in her home in Washington, D.C. When asked to comment on her life and what she thought was the most influential factor in her success, she recollects:

"If you look around at the most notable Blacks quite a few of them were from the South where there were Black schools and black teachers. We learned that you had to work hard and it wasn't an easy journey. You had to be better than your white counterparts. When given a task that is meant to be difficult, you must go home and burn the midnight oil. Segregation existed in the military so there were people who didn't even want me around. You had to learn how to cope or you would not make it."

The lesson she learned as a result of the book writing experience is that you can take a bad situation and make something good of it. Colonel Bailey didn't let segregation hinder her from doing something positive for the African American community. Perhaps without being racially restricted she wouldn't have had the drive. In true success, there is struggle.

Stefun Hawkins

Janet Jenkins

On March 12, 1960, Janet Jenkins was brought into this world and marveled for the first ever. Born to a poor couple that lived in a little town called Munford, AL, she was the fifth child of the family. Growing up she was very athletic and intelligent. She managed to graduate from high school ranked second in her class. Despite her high ranking the racist confines of the Deep South oppressed her and kept her from going to college. Her white guidance counselor suggested she go into the military with the rest of the Negroes. Thinking her counselor knew best and totally unaware of the opportunities in the world for someone with her intellect she joined the Air Force right out of high school.

Once in the service she found out about college through the Air Force and decided to go that route. After a few years she obtained her bachelors degree and continued working for the military. It was about this same time when she decided to wed her high school sweetheart Stephen Hawkins. Both in the military, they received orders for Dover Air Force Base in Dover, DE. Once there she began her fast track to a successful military career. Just before she was to be sent to Japan the most important thing in her life came, her only son. In 1984, after the birth of her son Janet got out of Active Duty and switched to the Air Force Reserves. She continued to earn her ranks just as she did before she became a mother.

It is evident that her hard work has paid off because she just received a promotion to Senior Master Sergeant. As the first African American female to earn that rank in the whole squadron and one of only two to be wearing it over all base her success is clear. Her family is very proud of her accomplishments and looks forward to the possibility of another promotion in the future.

Rahim Wooley

Ed McIntyre

It was a relatively easy decision to decide on a Black person who has had a lot of influence on my hometown. I come from the city of

North Augusta, SC. This is located in the Central Savannah River Area, otherwise known as the C.S.R.A. Augusta, GA is the largest city in this area and dictates much of what goes on in this area. Whoever is mayor of Augusta usually has a larger area to control besides Augusta.

Mayor Bob Young has been our mayor for several terms now spanning about 12 years. He has had an extensive track record for catering to the needs of the middle to upper class Whites in the area and has not done anything to help out the Blacks in the area. This is where Ed McIntyre comes in. Ed is a 70-year-old ex-real estate salesperson. He also holds the distinction of being Augusta's first Black mayor. His first and only term spanned from 1982-1984. During that time, his whole platform was based on revitalizing the state of downtown Augusta, home to over half the Black population within the city limits. McIntyre also lowered city property taxes in this area in an attempt to stimulate growth in the downtown area for Blacks.

Since McIntyre was removed from office in 1984, he has tried three other times to reclaim his mayor position, each time ending up unsuccessful. During this year's campaign, he has been a teacher, a chief executive and board member and a founder of countless nonprofit groups. He now operates the Augusta African American Historical Committee in the Bay Street Building. Many of his opponents in the past as well as the present have made countless attempts to encourage people to entrust more power in the hands of the mayor. McIntyre along with other Black Augustans believe this to be a bad idea, as they feel that the power should lie more within the people instead of one authority figure.

McIntyre was brought up on bribery and extortion charges in 1984 and was sentenced to a federal penitentiary for a term of two years. During his incarceration, he claims that his political views have been revolutionized and he believes now more than ever in bringing more power to the people rather than strengthening the office of the mayor.

The Blacks of this city have supported McIntyre ever since. We as a people have stood behind him for the last three elections, giving him the support he needs to get back into office to help us as a people. He has lost by narrow margins, especially in 2002, where the election became a runoff between him and Mayor Bob Young. McIntyre has given hope to the Blacks of Augusta. His beliefs in bettering education for the urban schools to providing free clinics in the downtown area have given the Blacks in my area something positive to look out for. McIntyre plans to continue running for mayor until his body is unable to handle the stress anymore. This won't be anytime soon because the politician always takes time out on Sundays to come to the North

Augusta Parks and Recreation center to play pick up games of basketball with the city's youth. This is just another reason why his Afro centric views will eventually pay off for the city of Augusta.

Shari Moseley

Col. Alphronzo Moseley: A Community leader

Alphronzo Moseley was born in Albany, Georgia on June 11, 1953 to Bessie Cole Moseley and Rev. Seminole Marvin Moseley. His father was a key figure in his life because he set the example for community leadership in the Moseley household. Rev. Moseley was the pastor of

Photo of Alphronzo Moseley. Photo by Shari Moseley.

three churches taking on the responsibilities as a spiritual leader in various communities. In addition, he met with Dr. Martin Luther King Jr. and other Christian leaders of the Southern Christian Leadership Conference (SCLC) during the civil rights movements to discuss church contributions in non-violent protests. Though Alphronzo was still too young to understand the importance of the events that were taking place in his community, watching the involvement of others ultimately influenced him to take on leadership responsibilities as well.

In 1971, Colonel Moseley entered the Air Force as an enlisted member. Two years later, he married Barbara DeLoyce Robinson. After graduating from Tuskegee University, in Alabama, the couple was stationed in a number of states. However, in each environment, they both retained a commitment to community service. They both operated on an afro centric idea of the betterment of the group and not the individual. As the Moseley's advanced in their education and in their job stability, they did as Paula Giddings suggested and "lifted as they climbed."

While stationed at Wright Patterson Air Force Base (AFB) in Fairborn, Ohio, Alphronzo took on the position of Youth Superintendent of the Sunday school at Shallow Missionary Baptist Church. From 1979 to 1982, he used this position to guide the preteens, teens, and young adults in their spiritual walk. He was there for the youth whether they needed support, counseling, or a little encouragement. Unfortunately, he could not stay in this position beyond 1983 because he received orders to go to Albuquerque, New Mexico.

He had not been in New Mexico long before he became a member of men's organization called the Shriners. This group sponsors a hospital that is named after their organization, but they also participate in other community related projects. Despite having a full time job as a software test manager, Alphronzo also became the President of the brotherhood (1984-1985) at his new church. In this position, he put together programs for the men in the church that reinforced spiritual and personal growth. Alphronzo's wife, Barbara, was very active in the church as well. She played an instrumental role in a church project that shipped food and clothing to Ethiopia. Outside of church centered events, Alphronzo also judged high school science fairs and encouraged youth to seek majors in technical fields. Although the Moseley family became a party of six by the beginning of 1983 with the addition of the couple's fourth child, they managed to balance community involvement with work and home responsibilities.

In 1986, the then Capt. Moseley received orders to work at the Pentagon. He bought a home in Springfield, Virginia for his family and commuted to Washington, D.C. daily. During the same year, Moseley became a founding member of the Air Force Cadet Officer Mentor Program (AFCOMAP) giving the program its name. This organization was centered on preparing younger members of the Air Force, who may have just entered, to get promotions. Thus, those of higher ranks mentored those of lesser ranking. This program has been implemented throughout the military and even internationally. It is based on a collective Afrocentric ideology and has been proven to be very effective in the armed forces because it creates a sense of family and friendship for cadets who may feel lonesome or unhappy because many are far away from their families and friends for the first time.

Capt. Moseley stayed in Virginia from 1986 until 1992. Over the course of these years, he did not give up his whole-hearted commitment to the church. He went on to be the superintendent of the entire Sunday school in Virginia and not just the youth classes as before mentioned in

Ohio. This position entailed waking up early in the morning to attend Sunday school each week because he was in charge of beginning the service in song. He also had a duty to dismiss the congregation into their designated classes, make sure Sunday school was over in a timely fashion, and to reconvene the people. This role took dedication, a love for God, and a love for the community.

In addition to being the superintendent of the Sunday school at Greater Little Zion Baptist Church, Moseley also served as a deacon of the church. In this role, he provided counseling on spiritual concerns and served communion. Moseley often lead prayers, read scriptures, and assisted with Baptisms. As a deacon, his primary task was to make the pastor of the church's position less stressful. Pastors have a great deal of responsibility. At times, they cannot aid the community in the way that they would like to because they have many issues to oversee. As a result, deacons take the pressures off the pastor, carrying the load collectively among one another. This makes the burden lighter for everyone.

Consequently, Moseley led the spiritual community as a deacon in his next two assignments. From 1992 to 1995, he served as a deacon at New Testament Baptist church in Sacramento, California. When he was transferred to Montgomery, Alabama in 1995, he became a member and a deacon of First Baptist Church despite the fact that he would only be staying in the state for one year. Although he stayed a very short time, the then Major Moseley began giving motivational speeches to junior high and high school students. He continued these speeches on into his next assignment in San Pedro, California.

Besides giving motivational speeches to school students, Major Moseley also gave a number of other speeches to benefit the community. He was a guest speaker at the McLauren Children's Center during a volunteer awards banquet. This center caters to disadvantaged children and provides volunteers who assist the children with their needs. Moseley's speech commended these volunteers for their time and effort identifying them as "true heroes" to the students. In other speeches, Moseley has fostered awareness of Martin Luther King, Jr. and his legacy during Black history month celebrations. He has been a guest speaker at the Veteran's Hospital and the keynote speaker on Los Angeles Air Force Base on the aforementioned topic.

Major Moseley's speaking ability carried on into the church when he was asked to be a guest speaker at the Western Baptist Convention. As a member of Mt. Sinai Baptist Church in San Pedro, California, he was honored to take on this task. He addressed spirituality and related Christian beliefs to what was being done in Baptist churches on the West Coast and what needed to be done in the future.

One important aspect of what Baptist church's do is educating its children. Major Moseley recognized the need for Black children to receive education beyond the schooling that their learning institutions were providing. He founded the first after school tutoring service at Mr. Sinai Baptist Church in 1996. This program consisted of community children and children who were members of the church going to Mt. Sinai after school so that they could master sciences, mathematics, English, social studies, and a variety of other subjects. Major Moseley was so committed to children's education that he allowed one calculus student to come to his home to be tutored for a longer period in a quieter atmosphere. This student was initially doing poorly in calculus but was able to attain a high mark in class after being tutored.

Major Moseley was also involved in a cancer walk-a-thon through his church. This took place in San Pedro close to the Pacific Ocean. The purpose of the walk-a-thon was raising money for cancer research. Moseley walked the 10K (6.3 miles) in support of the event.

In 2002, it was time to leave San Pedro for the Moseley family. The now Colonel Moseley received orders to go to Hanscom Air Force Base in Bedford Massachusetts. Since his arrival in June of 2002, he has joined the church choir at Hanscom Chapel and teaches Sunday school. The choir is a way for him to pass on the message to the congregation that they are not alone and it's a way to inspire them to pass on that message to others. As a Sunday school teacher, he clarifies and teaches the doctrines of the Bible providing spiritual guidance and understanding to the community.

Shari Moseley. Photo by Gerald Jackson.

Colonel Moseley is currently the system program director of the Global Air Traffic Operations/ Mobility Command and Control

Systems Program Office, Electronic Systems Center. He has a demanding career as a military officer, a husband, and a father, but he has found time over the years for to balance all of his roles. Thus, Colonel Moseley is much more than just an Air Force officer. Although he has faithfully served in the Air Force for more than thirty years, he will undoubtedly be dedicated to community leadership for a lifetime.

Kerby Samuels

Councilman Norman Oliver: Respected Community Leader

Norman Oliver is an African American resident of Wilmington, Delaware who happens to be the City Council representative of the fourth district of Wilmington. Throughout the course of his career so far, Oliver has made significant contributions to both the electorate and young adult population of his inner city community. Norman Oliver currently holds the positions of Chair of the Community and Economic Development Committee, and member of Wilmington Finance, Housing, Licenses and Inspectors, and Education/Youth and Family Services committees. In addition to this, Oliver owns a property company, Oliver Properties that aids non-profit organizations.

In 1980, Oliver founded a summer basketball league centered in Wilmington called Stormin's Classic/Summer Basketball League. The program was created to offer opportunities for young adults of the city to learn basketball skills while playing in a competitive league. Educational and computer training programs are also provided through the Boys and Girls Club of Delaware as an addition to this organization. Oliver encourages players to partake in community service activities to enrich their sense of responsibility and dedication to their community, and local community leaders are also invited to interact with players of the league in order to offer resources of guidance. With the funding of several generous corporations such as Dupont Inc. and several other administrators, the league has grown to include over 1,000 teens.

Oliver also uses his position in the city council to serve his community. His accomplishments include the construction of affordable housing complexes such as the Curlett Place and Quaker Village Townhouses, re-vitalization projects of downtown Wilmington, the construction of a new Justice Center and multi-use development center, and directed funding toward several other fourth district projects. Oliver has pushed for the adoption of gun ordinances for the city of Wilmington in an attempt to put an end to the steadily increasing shooting rate in the city. Concerning education, Oliver has supported the creation of new charter schools in Wilmington to supplement the current school system.

Norman Oliver caught my attention in doing research on the topic of a community leader who I respected because of his work to support young adults. In this day and age, many institutions are quick to provide easy but not necessarily effective solutions to problems of how to keep the young population from doing non-constructive activities. Oliver formed a program that not only entertained teenagers recreationally, but also allowed for the teaching of pertinent skills such as computer training, with an emphasis on community service. I believe that more devoted people like Norman Oliver are needed in our communities.

Gerald G. Jackson

LEADERS IN THE NON-PROFIT SECTOR

Rachelle Dubuche

AMHE

Its persistence and its accomplishments measure the value of an institution. AMHE, or L'Association des Medecins Haitiens a l'Etranger or the English translation, Association of Haitian Physicians Abroad, was founded in August 1972 by a group of Haitian physicians determined to mark their presence as a growing ethnic entity in America. They wanted to foster professional alliances as well as promote the health and interests of the Haitian immigrant community at large. The first official meeting took place on Sunday, November 12, 1972 in the Martin Luther King Auditorium of Harlem Hospital in New York. Sixty-four physicians with a common agenda were present that day. The association has been defined by its obligations towards its members, the Haitian community, and its homeland of Haiti,. The creation of AMHE was well received by Haitian physicians in several parts on the U.S. and soon after chapters was created. The New York Chapter was created in August of 1972 followed by the Baltimore/Washington Chapter in March 1973, the Chicago Chapter in April 1973, the St. Louis Chapter in May 1973, the Montreal Chapter in November 1974, the Florida Chapter founded in 1982 and the New Jersey Chapter in 1988.

The objectives of AMHE are to build ties between all physicians of Haitian origin, to help it's members in organizing and strengthening their professional life through continuing medical education, creating social bonds to provide cultural activities for personal enrichment, to cultivate ties with the Alma mater as well as the professional body and entire medical community in Haiti, and extend to the Haitian people the benefit of their collective experience.

AMHE hold annual scientific conventions, providing continuing medical credits to its members. These conventions in addition to keeping the practicing physician abreast of the latest advances in medicine provide a special opportunity for the preservation of Haitian culture. AMHE also participates in joint scientific programs with local medical societies and universities as a major part of its continuing medical education program. AMHE has a number of projects and programs that they have implemented to help the Haitian community as a whole. They have a Visiting Professor Program in which physicians from the U.S. aid the faculty of Medicine in Haiti in teaching advanced techniques in the practice of medicine. They also have a scholarship fund, which supports Haitian students pursuing degrees in the healthcare field. The most recent program is the Batey Relief Alliance (BRA). Bateyes are the name of the sugar cane plantations in the Dominican Republic where the majority of Haitian migrant laborers live and work. The condition of these living quarters has caused concern among many members of the association. Members of the association donate their medical services to the people living in the bateyes. The New York chapter is the lead promoter of this mission.

My mother, Carole Dubuche, M.D. a pediatrician, has been a member of the New York Chapter since 1993, and is currently the assistant secretary of the New York Chapter. My father, George Dubuche, an OB/GYN is a member of its Haitian affiliate, AMH (Association Medecin Haitiens). As a child, I never realized the significance of the organization. In my mind, all that AMHE did was have huge reunions in the summer at cool hotels. It was not until the annual convention this past summer in the Dominican Republic did I realize what an impact my mother and AMHE has. My mother as well as other members of the New York chapter gave up a week of their time to provide free health care consultations to the Haitian migrant workers living and working in the sugar cane fields of the Dominican Republic. The enormity of their act did not go unnoticed. They were written about in Dominican newspapers as well as featured on the news. For all her time and devotion to the planning of the Dominican Republic convention and the Batey Relief mission, my mother received an award from the association.

Recently I attended a fundraising gala thrown by the New York Chapter. I expected only physicians to attend however I was wrong. There were a number of New York City council members and officials in attendance. Several of them gave speeches discussing the impact AMHE had on each of their communities and districts. I was so proud of the fact that my parents were affiliated with such an influential organization. It also made me realize that instead of looking to famous people for inspiration I should look to the people I already know.

For more information about AMHE go to www.amhe.org.

Catherine Soto

Miriam Castillo

Miriam Yolanda Castillo was born on December 19, 1934 in Hague, Dominican Republic. She is the oldest of nine children and is the daughter of Alicia Rodriguez and Heliodor Castillo. Her mother is of Taino and African ancestry, while her father is a Spaniard. Miriam and her family lived in extremely poor conditions, and after her mother died she was left the responsibility at the age of 14 to care for her nine siblings, as well as take on all the household responsibilities. To help support her family, she sold food on the village streets, and thus, could not attend high school.

In 1974 she came to New York City, and is currently residing in Harlem. Although she did not attend high school or college, she felt that she had a vocation in life to help others, and bring their faith closer to God. As she says, "It was my faith in God that helped me to endure during bad times and I think faith can help many others as well." With this mission in her mind, heart, and spirit, she began her acts of philanthropy and community service.

Miriam is a very active member of St. Paul's church in Harlem. As one of the primary church leaders, she organizes groups that go to various prisons within the city and speak to prisoners, particularly Black and Latinos, providing them with hope, support, prayer, and an initiative to improve their lifestyles. In addition, she also makes trips to hospitals in the Bronx such as Lincoln Hospital and Harlem Hospital, giving the ill an opportunity to receive communion. She not only prepares the sick for their Holy Communion, but prepare illiterate children and adults who only speak Spanish as well.

Realizing what a gift it is to be her age and able to serve her community, she visits CASAVE, which is a center for people who are terminally ill, senile, elderly, and in extremely vegetative health conditions. During these visits she radiates her compassion, sense of humor, and prayer onto the residents in order to liven their spirits. Having much experience with marriages and building strong relationships, she touches the lives of many married couples from various minority communities in New York city, visiting their homes and giving them advice and encouragement for building a strong family.

Miriam has organized clothing and food drives for the poor in countries within the Caribbean, South America, and Africa. Her efforts not only have a religious nature, but she has also been involved in politics. During a trip to Miami, she made political reunions to collect money for the PLD, a political party in the Dominican Republic. This effort enabled Dominicans within the United States to practice dual-citizenship and participate in the governmental system that affects their families' back home.

There is nothing like being face to face with this inspiring woman, and better yet, there is nothing like having her as a grandmother. Her wisdom is awe striking and her smile, love, and compassion has always left me in admiration. More importantly, she is an exemplary figure within the community who demonstrates that leadership can come in all forms, and that you don't have to move mountains to make a difference.

Deven S. Gray

Vince Coleman

African American people are celebrated all throughout history for their great accomplishments, including social activism, athletic ability and academic accomplishments. There are those people that contribute to society that are not as widely acknowledged.

Photo of Vince Coleman. Photo by Deven Gray.

Mr. Coleman was a very successful lawyer in a large law firm. He was well paid and was doing some good for the community through his work. However, he felt that he was not doing enough and at the end of the day, he didn't feel good about the path his life was taking. After volunteering as a baseball coach for two years along with working at his firm he decided that he belonged more on the field coaching kids than he belonged behind a desk in an office. So Coach Coleman quit his job at the law firm and he made his volunteer coaching position a full time job.

Vince is now a full-time coach for an organization called Harlem R.B.I or the Revising Baseball in the Inner Cities a non-profit group that was started about 10 years ago. Coach Coleman directs over 350 boys and girls from his Harlem Community. Coach Coleman teaches the young people that he coaches to challenge them about their values and beliefs so they are on the right path. He is also teaching them the value of hard work and teamwork.

Though Vince Coleman is not widely recognized, he is having a large impact on his community. He is building future leaders who are learning now through their participation in his program about the real world and he hopes by giving his time to these young people that they will become responsible adults and will give back to the community when they are in the position to do so.

Lynn Thompson

Ms. Thompson is an actress and voice over artist. She wanted to use her talent to help others so she became involved with In Touch Network a division of the Jewish Guild for the Blind. In Touch is a radio readingof the New York Times for the blind.. She feels that her work is very pertinent to the community not only the visually impaired but also the elderly, so she does research and includes issues related to her audience in her shows including Medicare, Medicaid and general issues related to aging and medical issues. The information that she tries to convey through her work connects people not only to the disabled community but also to the community at large. This is what make her work so important; she is recognizing the importance of people that may usually be overlooked.

These two New Yorkers are not world famous but they deserve recognition for their work in the community and I hope that they serve as motivation to young people. You don't have to be well known to do something that helps others and you don't have to take part in large effort to make a difference. The small things do matter.

Kimberly Jones

Cary Jenkins

Paterson, New Jersey does not have the best public education. By the time youths are almost complete with their schooling and should be focusing on college, they are still working on their basic writing and mathematical skills. Finding teachers and counselors who actually care about the kids and their educational career after high school is a tough job. That is where Cary Jenkins comes in. Cary Jenkins, who majored in business, uses his business savvy to benefit the education of Paterson's youth.

As the founder and head of Operation Link-Up, a program that links high school students up with colleges, Jenkins has help send many students off to colleges and universities. Mr. Jenkins accomplishes linking teens with colleges by networking with individuals of power within post-secondary institutions. Mr. Jenkins informs the teens about the colleges and informs the colleges about the teens. He then proceeds to introduce the teens to college campuses by having them enroll in summer courses at institutions such as Syracuse University. He provides this invaluable experience to students cost-free; all the students must do is show initiative. Mr. Jenkins helps prepare the students for the SATs by scheduling weekly study group sessions; his goal is to get more teens to score 1000 points or more. When it is time to apply for college, he helps the teens fill out the numerous applications, provides them with fee waivers, and even sends the application to the schools. Teens in Operation Link Up have a very high acceptance rate in the schools that Mr. Jenkins is affiliated. Once the teens decide on which college they would like to attend, Mr. Jenkins uses his business savvy to help increase the amount of financial aid given to the students by their selected institutions.

Mr. Jenkins is a prime example of a community hero. By coming back to the community and using what he has learned to help Paterson's youth to have a fair chance in the world, Mr. Jenkins is displaying his concern for the survival of the community. Instead of leaving the education of the future in the hands of apathetic Europeans or miseducated minorities, Cary Jenkins has come back into the community and has taken the youth by the hand to lead them to a promising future.

Amanda Rabain

"You have to be able to work with the public"-Diane E. Rabain

This phrase was mentioned several times during a phone interview with Diane Rabain. Ms. Rabain is a Director of a Job Center in the South Bronx and has worked for the City of New York for twenty years. Challenges in her life have included earning Associates Degree and raising three children. Her latest challenge includes the recent developing and opening of the Transitional Opportunity Program (TOP Center).

Diane Rabain was the last of six children to be born to Frank and Rose Lee Brisbon in Lee County, South Carolina. She was the first child of the six to be born in a hospital. Ms. Rabain spent her first years of life in South Carolina until her family moved to 115th street and Broadway in New York City. While her father was the superintendent of their building, her mother was a homemaker.

As Ms. Rabain attended Brandies High school in 84th street and Columbus Avenue and at the age of seventeen, she moved out and rented her own apartment. While working two jobs to support her, she completed Brandies and enrolled in Bronx Community College. At

Photo of Diane Rabain. Photo by Amanda Rabain.

Bronx Community College Ms. Rabain earned an Associates Degree in Business Administration. After holding various other positions, Ms. Rabain took the Civil Service Exam of New York City and began working for the Human Resource Administration (HRA) of New York City in 1983 as a caseworker.

During Diane Rabain's twenty years of service to the people and city of New York, she steadily received promotions. Today she holds the title Administrative Job Opportunity Specialist M2, Director. This director's most recent challenge includes, forming, opening, and managing the TOP Center and running the Fordham Job Center at the same time. She ran both centers as the director for a year but after organizing the closing of the Fordham Center for renovations; her primary focus at work is the TOP Center.

The TOP Center is the only one of its kind in New York City. This center's primary goal is to aid people in getting off welfare and in beginning their careers. The TOP Center understands that these new jobs and careers may not offer enough compensation to help a household head or heads to support their family and offers transitional benefits and incentives to the families. The TOP center also offers seminars and job fairs. Diane Rabain often advertises to the surrounding community when such events are taking place. One event included bringing in bankers to inform the clients about saving, paying bills, and money markets. Another event includes a summer childcare informational and fair.

Another recent and very successful program at the TOP Center is the VITA Program. Ms. Rabain's sent her staff to the IRS to become proficient in preparing taxes. The center was then given official authorization by the government service the clients by preparing their taxes free of charge. Because the TOP Center is a paperless center – solely dependent upon computers – the VITA Program was executed successfully via computers. The concept of this program was derived from one of the biyearly conferences that Ms. Rabain attends to keep up on the new successful services that other communities have developed.

The TOP Center is the only center within the HRA of New York City that offers such outreach programs and benefits. Because other HRA centers such as welfare, Medicaid, and food stamp centers do not have the resources to do the outreach that the TOP Center can, Ms. Rabain collaborates with other center Directors to bring various seminars and fairs to these other places.

When asked about how she feels personally about her job, Ms. Rabain said that she is lucky to have such the perfect match between her personality, working style, and career. She loves to be able to lead, create, and manage. Diane Rabain is proud of being able to really use The City's resources for the South Bronx. She hires and brings in presenters within the community. If Ms. Rabain cannot offer a temporary staff member a permanent position at the time, she is often enthusiastic to refer him of her to another agency that would appreciate his or her labor.

Ms. Rabain loves the feeling that comes with knowing that she helped advance someone's job, life, or personal outlook.

> *"Whether it is a client or staff member, I like when people walk in office negative and down and leave with hope. Whether it's confidence, advice, benefits, or other resources that I offer, I give them a tool to make it through another part of their life and they walk out of my door surrounded with positive feelings."*

Ms. Rabain enjoys challenging her staff and pushing them fartherthan they imagined going in their job and career.

> *"I love giving promotions and bonuses. I want to staff to know that hard work does reap benefits and lead to further*

professional development. I enjoy showing people that the work that they do is important. Absolutely everyone in my center is important!"

Photo of Amanda Rabain.

This director knows the value in showing her staff that they are capable. Her appreciation pushes her staff to be more dedicated and work their hardest. Because Ms. Rabain has put so much time and dedication to the TOP Center – the clients and the staff – it has been very successful in its first year of full operation.

At the closing of the interview, Ms. Rabain repeats, "Everything isn't all smooth. In this career, you are dealing with many types of personalities, people, agencies, and organizations. You have to keep in mind that you are working for the good the people. You are working for the public."

Gerald G. Jackson

OTHER LEADERS IN THE COMMUNITY

Keisha Cummings

Gail F. Bridges

Gail was born and raised in Aliceville, Alabama. After graduating from Alabama A&M University with a major in Business and Education, she moved to New York City where she worked as a secretary at the prestigious Mount Sinai Hospital in Manhattan. During her employment there, Gail learned about social work and became genuinely interested in the field. She decided to go to Hunter College to get her masters degree in social work. While at Hunter, Gail worked as a social worker assistant at Mount Sinai. She was placed in an agency as part of her school requirements; involved in internship at various hospitals as well as continuing to work at Mount Sinai. Gail was required to work with an actual social worker and work on her problem solving skills. In addition, she worked with one of her professors at Hunter on a research project about nursing home patients. The project required her to interview nursing home patients at the Center for Nursing and Rehabilitation (then known as JHMCB Nursing and Rehabilitation). After the job was complete, Gail's professor recommended her for a job at the health-care facility. She has been working there for about twenty-five years.

Due to her exception work as a social worker, Gail was promoted to Director of Social Work at the Center for Nursing and Rehabilitation (CNR), a position she has held for fifteen years. As director, she supervises the social workers that provide services for residents and patients of Nursing and Rehab Center. Gail, along with her fellow co-workers, promotes the rights for the residents' to be treated with dignity and respect, and the right to receive the care they are entitled to. Gail's duties include helping the patients and residents safeguard their money and providing counseling and support for the patients and their families.

The Nursing Home Gail works for (CNR) is a non-profit health care network with many branches throughout the tri-state area. Although she has been a social for approximately twenty-five years and a director for about fifteen, she takes Continuing Education at various social work schools and organizations. Gail is also a part of the National Association of Social workers (NASW). Her participation in CNR, which is funded by the government through Medicaid, has allowed the proper help and healthcare to get to people who truly need it.

Gerald G. Jackson

Meredith L. Howell

Louis Graham

Born in Washington County, Sandersville, Georgia Louis Graham was raised by his grandmother and aunt. His mother had passed away when he was only thirteen years old. Louis matriculated through elementary and secondary as a bright student. Upon graduation from J. Elders High School, he made the decision to attend the police academy in Atlanta. He made this decision to attend the academy instead of going to college so that he could make a difference in the community and primarily to fulfill the police motto, "To serve and protect." He attended various police academies and received training in the law enforcement field. He also did some academic studies at Georgia State University. When he graduated from the academy, he became a member of the Fulton County Police Department. He was one of the first Blacks to join the force in Fulton County during integration/desegregation. While working his beat on Martin Luther King Jr. Road, formerly Hunter Street, he was shot at because of the racial tensions prevalent at the time he joined the force. He was the only Black on the streets then. He drew strength and encouragement from this experience and went on to become the first Black chief of investigation in Fulton County. Graham left the Fulton County force briefly to work in Texas, where he became the number on investigative detective. He then returned to Georgia as a police officer and worked his way through the ranks and became the first Black Assistant Chief and, later, Chief of the Fulton County Police Department. Chief Graham has subsequently served on the City of Atlanta and DeKalb County police forces in administrative capacity.

Because of his expertise and experience, Graham was sent to Barcelona, Spain to observe the organization of their police force during the Olympics so that he could employ their methods or improve upon their techniques for the 1996 Olympics in Atlanta. He has also traveled to Israel to observe their police system. After his retirement from the Fulton County Police Department, Graham served as a liaison for the Governor of Georgia in an advocacy program for imprisoned and at-risk youth. He also worked on the Dwayne Williams case in the 1970s, when several children where kidnapped—many of them later found murdered. Though Williams was convicted on circumstantial evidence, Graham did not believe that he was the culprit and did everything in his power to disprove the charges filed against him.

After the Williams case, Graham became intensely committed to mentoring to young Black males. He believes that he can be a role model to these youth, the role model that he did not have and many of them do not have presently. Graham is committed to any task that he is assigned or takes on, says his wife of 44 years, Leslie. He is a committed family man—husband, friend, and grandfather to his two children and one grandchild. So committed is Graham that even after his retirement, he continues to work daily because of his love for helping others.

I believe Chief Graham is a wonderful example of the Afrocentric ideals that we have learned is this course. Particularly, I believe he embodies the "We are, therefore I am" philosophy, as well as "It takes a village to raise a child." I met the Grahams about six years ago and they have welcomed me into their home, mentored to me and treat me as if I am a member of their immediate family. Chief Graham's continued commitment to his community and his people has inspired me and shown me how beneficial it can be to help others with your skills and talents.

Tracy Noisette

Bernadette E. Noisette

Upon receiving this assignment, I realized that I would have to follow my instincts and my passion to pursue the topic upon which I wanted to write. To me, a true leader is not one who receives critical acclaim and a great deal of public recognition for the great things that he or she has accomplished. The leader is simply content in setting an example for those whom he or she may have contact with, and this leader tries to bring out the best in everyone. That being said, I would like to give a brief explanation of what I have learned about the different worldviews. In the Eurocentric worldview, an "appropriate" leader to write about would be someone "famous" and well known, while in an Afrocentric worldview, a leader is someone who personally impacts people within their direct vicinity. While all leaders have been deemed that for legitimate reasons, some leaders have more of a personal touch behind their story. This is such a story.

Bernadette Noisette has many different aliases. Some common ones are Dr. Noisette, Mamadedette, Doc, and last but not least, I refer to her as Mom. Bernadette was born Bernadette Etienne on December 24, 1945 in Port-au-Prince Haiti. She grew up with three sisters and one brother who had the same mother as her, as well as two half sisters from another mother. Growing up in a very small house in the middle of the poverty-ridden city, Bernadette was determined to make much more for herself and her family. Bernadette was one of the very few people she knew to excel in her studies and really keep pursuing higher learning. She left Haiti at the age of 24 to come to America and further her studies. Bernadette arrived in the states by plane, with just ten American dollars to her name, and hardly knowing a word of English. She was in a very new and foreign place that did not seem to be very inviting, she knew no one and she was very afraid.

After trying to adjust herself to her surroundings, she eventually got a job cleaning hotel rooms at night, while she attended Long Island University's Brooklyn campus during the day. Bernadette was determined to become a doctor.

Her journey was filled with a great deal of heartache and abuse. This includes being subjected to both physical and mental abuse from her first husband, Clarel Leon. After she eventually escaped this relationship, she kept on pursuing her dreams. These dreams, she says, were at times the only things that kept her alive.

Eventually, Bernadette began to work in a box-making factory. In this factory, she was the administrative assistant to the factory's manager, George Steinitz. Mr. Steinitz played a very pivotal role in Bernadette's life. They immediately became very close, and George admired Bernadette's drive and ambition. He offered his assistance to help her through with her schooling and anything else that she needed. Bernadette decided to take George up on his offer, when she sent for all of her family to come America. Mr. Steinitz graciously and selflessly took a chance and vouched for each one of her family members, writing letters to the embassy guaranteeing jobs for all of them in his factory.

Bernadette eventually graduated from LIU and was well on her way to go to medical school. She had excelled in her coursework since she was such a dedicated student. Although she still hardly knew English, she says that the sciences spoke a universal language and she proved to understand this language with ease. Bernadette went on to attend Albert Einstein School of Medicine. Shortly after this graduation, she married Appolos Noisette, my father. She currently runs a pediatric office in Hempstead, New York.

Bernadette has served as a great inspiration to everyone that she meets. She provides unending support to anyone in need, whether it is financial, emotional, etc. She is always more than willing to lend a hand. This has been simply a small taste of the many accomplishments that she has achieved and hurdles that she has overcome. There is one hurdle, which is rather significant and very much worth speaking on.

My mother, Bernadette, on November 21, 1997, during the reception of her daughter's wedding, suffered from subarachnoid hemorrhages in her brain. She was immediately rushed to the hospital and was in very critical condition.

After days of being unconscious, neurologists at North Shore University Hospital of Manhasset decided to perform surgery in order to close the hemorrhages and avoid any further bleeding in her brain. This was a very risky procedure, but after many hours, it turned out to be a success. This success came with many "rules and regulations," however. Although this surgery was successful, Bernadette continued to be hospitalized for the following three months. She remained unconscious and unaware of her surroundings for the majority of that time.

When she did finally arise, she was not the same person that she once was. After much physical and occupational therapy, she re-learned many of her everyday activities. These included: walking, reading, speaking, and driving (eventually), as well as potty training. This entire process took many long and doubtful months.

Through it all, she remained very positive and determined to resume her regular activities. Surely, enough, much like a miracle, Bernadette's "medicine" never left her. Once she relearned the basics, it simply came right back to her. By the following year, she was driving again, as well as practicing medicine and carrying on her normal activities.

Although this is a very short depiction of the life of my mother, there is much more that can be shared, but I simply do not have enough space. I thought this was one instance that should be shared because of the impact it has had on my life. Her determination and perseverance has served as a great inspiration to me. She is the foundation and rock upon which my life is based. Every day I thank God that she is still in my life. I truly believe that He could have taken her that night, but He did not because He realized that there was so much better she had to do, and too many people would be missing their angel on Earth.

Charles Fick

Herman Russell of Summerhill

The Summerhill neighborhood in Atlanta, GA was my home for a year. Summerhill is located immediately southeast of downtown Atlanta, and was established after the Civil War to be one of three original African American settlements. This sixty-block community used to have 20,000 residents in the 1950's. Most of them were African Americans, but there was also a large Jewish community. The construction of interstate twenty through the middle of the neighborhood started a mass exodus of the population. Summerhill only had 3,500 residents left by the early 1990's, and nearly all of them were poor and black.[138]

Summerhill was the home of many prominent African Americans. One such individual is noted entrepreneur, philanthropist, and civic leader Herman J. Russell, Sr. One of seven children of Maggie and Rogers Russell, Herman Russell grew up in the 1930's when Summerhill was thriving. Herman began to learn his father's trade of plasterer when he was twelve, and purchased his first parcel of land at age 16 for $125. He later built a duplex on the property and used his savings to help pay his tuition at Tuskegee University. After graduating from the building program at Tuskegee, he returned to Atlanta to be a plastering subcontractor for his father.[139]

When his father died in 1957, Herman Russell expanded the company substantially.

He became the chairman/CEO of H. J. Russell & Co., which was now a conglomerate that included general contracting, construction/ program management, real estate development and property and asset management. The new company would have amazing success under Russell's leadership, becoming the fourth largest Construction Company in the U.S. with 700 employees and annual sales of more than $150 million![140]

What has Herman Russell done with his success? In November 1999, an Atlanta Inquirer told of how Russell donated $1 million each to Tuskegee University, Clark Atlanta University, Morehouse College, and Georgia State University for expanding their programs in entrepreneurship. This $4 million gift is largest given by an African-American for entrepreneurship in the nation's history. Each University has pledged to match the funds donated by Russell, meaning that $8 million will be invested in these Universities' entrepreneurial programs because of Russell's generous gift.[141]

---

[138]"Summerhill." Available online. April 29, 2003.http://www.arch. gate ch.edu/ imagine/Atlanta96/documents/city/atlantis/n-sh.htm

[139]"Herman J. Russell." Available online. April 29, 2003. http://www.the history makers.com/biography/biography.asp?bioindex=244&category= businessMakers

[140]ibid.

[141]"African American Millionaire Passes Torch of Entrepreneurship." *Atlanta Inquirer*. 11/13/1999. V. 39, N. 15 p. 14.

The money will be used for various things: funding scholarships, a lecture series, salaries for new entrepreneurial positions, the developing of new entrepreneurial curricula and constructing of a facility that will house an entrepreneurship program.[142]

Herman Russell has served in many capacities for numerous organizations. He is the Second vice Chairman of Tuskegee University's Board of Trustees. He has served on the boards of Citizens Trust Bank, Georgia Power Company, National Service Industries, Georgia Port Authority, and Central Atlanta Progress. He was also the former president of the Atlanta Chamber of Commerce. Russell has served also as a board member for civic organizations like the Allen Temple; Butler Street YMCA; Central Atlanta Progress; the NAACP Atlanta chapter; Midtown Improvement District and the Georgia State University Advisory Board.[143]

H. J. Russell & Co. has had a substantial impact on the Southeastern U.S., having done projects for the Atlanta Hartsfield International Airport (providing both program management and general contracting services), Birmingham Civil Rights Museum, Turner Field (previously Olympic Stadium, which is in Summerhill), Atlanta City Hall and the Georgia Dome. Privately, they have done projects for the headquarters of Georgia-Pacific, Wachovia Banks and The Village at Castleberry Hill. H.J. Russell & Company added Concessions International as a sub-company in 1978, which operates concession stands in various international airports. Russell Properties was added in 1991, an Atlanta-based real estate development company.[144]

Mr. Russell has received numerous entrepreneurship awards. He holds honorary doctorate degrees from two colleges and worked closely with Rev. Martin Luther King Jr., playing a leading role in the modern Civil Rights Movement. Russell is also the founder of the Herman J. Russell Entrepreneurial Scholarship Foundation for an Atlanta elementary school.

Herman Russell is an example to us all. His entrepreneurial vision made him successful; his generous nature and service makes him a role model. Although he and his wife, Otelia, now reside in midtown Atlanta, he got his start in Summerhill. Herman J. Russell Sr. is one of

---

[142]ibid

[143]"Herman J. Russell." Available online. April 29, 2003. http://www.thehistorymakers.com/biography/biography.asp?bioindex=244&category=businessMakers

[144]ibid.

many prominent African Americans who began their lives in the Summerhill neighborhood in Atlanta, Georgia.[145]

Joseph Sargent

Ramona Taylor

Ramona Taylor was born and raised in Philadelphia, Pennsylvania. Growing up she was never sure exactly what she wanted her profession to be as an adult. After high school, Ms. Taylor matriculated to the University of Pittsburgh and graduated in 1978. Ms. Taylor spent time working as a nurse before moving on to the University of Pennsylvania Law School. After graduating in 1982, Ms. Taylor served several offices on the state and national level. She was the Supervising Staff Attorney in Pennsylvania, an Immigration Attorney for the Department of Justice, both Assistant and Senior Assistant City Attorney for the cities of Suffolk and Virginia Beach in Virginia. After gaining valuable experience at these positions, in May 2000 Ms. Taylor was offered and accepted the position of Virginia Beach Juvenile and Domestic Relations Judge; making her the first female African American judge in the city of Virginia Beach.

Initially, Ms. Taylor admits that she was nervous feeling like a pioneer in her field. She was not sure whether her colleagues would see her as a "token" or if she would be held to a higher standard because she was essentially representing all future Blacks in her position. When asked about her impressions of her job, Ms. Taylor responded that she is happy with where she is, and will seek another term after her six-year tenure. Ms. Taylor added, though, that she feels lonely at times because there is a lack of people who she feels she can completely relate. While there is one other African American male in Virginia Beach who is a judge, Ms. Taylor noted that he was very helpful in acclimating her to the position in 2000 but has since proven little accompaniment.

Ms. Taylor cannot sense much movement within Virginia Beach toward more racial equity on the bench. When asked what steps she feels would help this process, Ms. Taylor suggested that there need to be more people pushing for equality with the power to actually cause changes. Virginia is a Republican state traditionally, and many people in the Republican Party are hesitant to see more Blacks as judges according to Ms. Taylor. To get where she is today, Ms. Taylor spent

---

[145]Publisher Note: In the November 10, 2003 issue of *Jet Magazine*, two full pages in the magazine's business section were devoted to the retirement of Herman Russell as CEO and the appointment.

time meeting and working Virginia Republicans, and she thinks that when it came to choosing a new judge, her connections propelled her over the other qualified applicants.

Kate Ofikuru

Clara Ofikuru

She well remembers the days when a Bachelors degree in Accounting would get you far. While it may not seem as if she has gotten far, she has in eyes of her appreciative children. Clara Ofikuru has achieved much in her time here in America. She arrived in the South Bronx just short of 25 years ago, leaving behind her homeland of Nigeria and her large family, and settling into a new life with her new husband – all the time striving for nothing but the best.

Her crowning achievements, in addition to her Bachelors degree, stand to be her three oldest children (three of four). The sacrifices she made to get them to where they are today stand the test of time as a mark of true dedication, love, and devotion as a mother. In this designation, she has girded herself with success that beneficiaries and all can acknowledge and applaud. Such sacrifices have not come without the resulting good in that her three oldest children now all currently attend competitive, four-year universities – her middle child attending Cornell while her oldest attends Pennsylvania State University, and her second youngest, preferring a state institution, attends SUNY Morrisville.

The path to success, her definition lying in the stability and achievement found embedded in her children, was highlighted by many hardships. Clara began her education, when the middle child was less than a year old, at Lehman College. After receiving her degree in 1987 she took on the title of breadwinner and City Tax Auditor while her husband resumed his work towards his own degree – all while her eldest son went through the rites if kindergarten. The most challenging of times would come in the year following the first birthday of her last child. Within this year, still recovering from the financial expense of taking the whole family back home to Nigeria for the summer, Clara lost her father just a few days after her birthday. Thus dealt a card to return to Nigeria, she struggled with and then accepted the fate that her three older children would have to remain at home.

Beyond the many sacrifices and struggles dotting the path, Clara continues to work hard and dedicate herself to her role as mother of four in the hopes that they will take from her determination to succeed and go a step above and beyond what she has done for them.

Selected Biographical Sketch of Contributors

Charles C. Fick is from Ithaca, New York. He is a sociology major with career aspirations to be an urban educator and activist. His hobbies include sports, music, art, and hanging with Jesus. He views the problem confronting the world as crappy urban schools and his solutions are total revitalization, new systems, and giving hope. The insight he gained from the book project was that he never knew that Herman Russell existed before the project.

Deven S. Gray is from Queens, New York. Her college major is Architecture, Art, and Planning. Urban and Regional Studies. She enjoys poetry as a hobby and views the pressing problem facing the world as the dawn of new technology. In her opinion, "people are forgetting how to be people. While everyone is sitting behind a computer instant messaging and emailing each other, they are lacking the skills to have simple human interactions. I think the ability to get along with other people and to just socialize in general is an educational process. The only way to learn is by doing. In connection with this problem is the idea that the people viewed to be the most intelligent are those people who are void of interpersonal skills, chemists, computer scientists etc. This makes me question our value system, why isn't the ability to hold a conversation and to be perceptive of the feelings and moods of those around, the main component of humanity lost in electronic interaction valued? The only solution I have to this problem is for people to realize that there is a certain function of electronic communication but also realize the value of human contact."

The insight she gained from the book project is the notion of questioning our value system. Why are some people well known and respected and others are not? What is it that we are really placing value in by glorifying some for what they do and ignoring others? Is a basketball player more important than your mother is or than your Pastor or any other community figure? These are the questions that we are inspired to ask ourselves.

Faith Harris is from Chicago, Illinois. She is a hotel administration major and has career aspirations in corporate law, writing, and entrepreneurship. Her hobbies are singing, dancing, and roller-skating. The insight she gained from the book project was that it made her think on how you appreciate people after the fact when you are not in their presence anymore.

Stefun Hawkins is from Dover, Delaware. He is undecided about his major; however, he aspires to be a lawyer/judge. His hobbies are baseball, basketball, tennis, ping-pong, and instrumental/vocal music. He believes the major issues confronting the world are a lack of minority political awareness and participation. The group project, according to Stefun "helped me realize that it was possible for individuals, especially Black ones, to pursue any and all types of aspirations they desired and that my people have mastered all genres that exist in the world and continue to excel in whatever they do."

Meredith Howell is currently a sophomore in the College of Architecture, Art, and Planning. An Urban and Regional Studies major, Meredith plans to pursue a career that will encompass the fields of city planning and law. Meredith believes that the career she intends to pursue will "improve the condition of the voiceless, oppressed and ignored and to this end will be for the betterment of the greater society."

She is actively involved in the Multicultural Living and Learning Unit, as a resident and part of the student staff. She also serves as the public relations representative for the Minority Undergraduate Law Society as well Cornell University Increasing Minority Applications and Gains in Enrollment (CU IMAGE). The Atlanta, Georgia native thoroughly enjoys being involved in campus life and exploring various educational interests.

Shari Tenielle Moseley, the author of the piece on Col. Alphronzo Moseley, is currently a student of Sociology at Cornell University and plans to seek a concentration in Africana studies for her own personal betterment. She decided to write about her father because she believes that one's history defines whom they are, where they have been, and where they are destined to go. She explored her father's contributions to the community to better understand her own family and the responsibility that she has in expanding the service that began generations before her time. This project showed her that community leaders are not just on television or written about in books, but they are in our churches, sororities & fraternities, and even in our homes. Her hope is that everyone who reads the biographies on community leaders is encouraged by what is written and takes it upon themselves to become active in their own communities.

Amanda Leslie Rabain is from Brooklyn, New York. She is a Human Development major with a concentration in Early Childhood and Elementary, Adolescence, and Africana Studies. Her career aspiration is to educate children (Teach), become a school administrator, and open a school or Learning Center. Her hobbies are reading, writing letters, and traveling. She sees the pressing problems of the world as too much concentration on wealth among many people in the world. According to Amanda, "I feel that there should be more focus on future generations. I believe that improvements in education and the environment should be put forth as primary priorities among world leaders and the people." The insight she gained from the book project was that sometimes we do not realize that the people around us affect so much and so many people. I realized that my mother did a lot to help the people of the Bronx through her work (She made me volunteer at the food stamp center that she helped manage in the South Bronx when I was 12). However, I just discovered the effort, energy, and aspirations that took place with her career and projects. I realized through this project that my mom's work is not just a job, it serves as a huge part of her fulfillment in life. My mother is proud of what she does and enjoys seeing the effect she can have locally within the Bronx.

Shelby Senzer grew up in Long Island, NY and graduated from Cornell University where she studied Industrial and Labor Relations. While a student, she was actively involved in programs that served both New York City children and the local Ithaca youth. She loves sports, music, traveling and art and did a semester abroad in Seville, Spain. After graduation, Shelby joined the Teach for America corps, and teaches in Atlanta, Georgia.. She is a member of Delta Gamma Sorority.

Catherine Soto is a sociology major with a career aspiration to be a health care professional. Her hobby is dancing. A pressing problem facing the world is racism, and I think part of the solution to this problem is providing truthful education. The insight she gained from doing the book project was that just because one did not deliver an "I Have A Dream" speech does not mean that a difference can't be made in this world. Even the smallest voices speak loud enough to be heard.

Phela Townsend is from Stafford, Virginia. She is an Industrial and Labor Relations (ILR) Major with the career goal of becoming either a Management or a Labor lawyer. Her hobby is playing soccer (she plays on the Women's Varsity team at Cornell). She believes a major problem facing the world is that it suffers from a disease of ethnocentrism, which has caused it to acquire enemies around the world. Once this country's leaders realize that there is a problem–that as this country gets richer, other countries are getting poorer—and learns to improve the disparity in diplomatic and non-violent ways, then the world will be a better place.

Kareen J. Waite is from Brooklyn, New York. She is in the College of Human Ecology where she majors in human development and pre-medical. She aspires to become a physician in either obstetrics or pediatrics and enjoys dancing, running, traveling, and reading. She reported several insights gained from doing the book project. According to Kareen, it "helped me to realize that there are role models all around us who we interact everyday of our lives; we are not to take them for granted. Also we can obtain history information just by asking people – we should not always resort to books." In her view, an important issue facing the world is a loss of culture. People must not forget where they came from. WE should be proud of who we are because it is the reason why we are the way we are today. Everyone should have a sense of cultural pride and instead of using cultural pride as a dividing factor, we should use it as a unification factor, especially among the Black community. A way to rectify this problem is to make sure that children and adults are educated on their culture.

Tara Leigh Wood is a rising junior in the College of Arts and Sciences at Cornell University. She is majoring in sociology with a concentration in business and organizational studies, with aspirations of attending graduate school at Cornell's Institute for Public Affairs. She hopes to study how educational policy affects today's youth, and what improvements can help develop an educational system that's enhances the chances of success for children across America. Tara also enjoys modern, ballet, and Caribbean dance, in addition to writing poetry about "love, life and everything in between."

Gerald G. Jackson

Afterward -Thank you and Beyond

This email is to provide a status report on the Unsung...book project, convey a note of respect, gratitude and appreciation for your timely contribution to this educational endeavor, and outline the book's future. Your essay imparts helpful knowledge and inspiration, your photographs a personal sense of reality and your biographical sketch a way of understanding and appreciating you and your icon better.

Before denoting the scope my plans, I will ensure that we are on the same page by reiterating where we have been on this project. The project was not only the culminating course requirement; it was the embodiment of the course itself, and the manifestation of its teachings about miseducation, world-views and notions of time. Our charge was to develop an electronic book for a hypothetical public school group. Our mission was to write a book, based upon real life people who have positively influenced you to aspire and achieve. Properly written, this book would make these students want to achieve in school and in life. Parenthetically, after I outlined the original project, I decided to add that your biographical sketch should accompany your materials. To organize this information, you may recall, I asked the class for a person to serve as editor, while I served as publisher, and Shelby Senzer quickly and singly volunteered.

In the final arrangement, each contributor had a high degree of autonomy. First, each decided upon whom he or she wanted to write. Second, each decided what type of prose they wanted to use, and last, held the decision on the format of the essay. All but two writers met the requirement of a submission for an electronic book, albeit some of the contributions were tardy and some folks had to be accosted in RPU to do their part. The submissions varied in content, length, focus, and inclusion of material. For example, some people provided short essays, while others had long ones, pictures of their icons, and more than one icon. In general, I was not perturbed by the differences among contributors because one of our project goals was to appreciate people who are different and value a difference. At the same time, however, I did find the additions respectful, evocative and appealing.

In any event, as editor Shelby took the material and designed the book. An exception to her rule was the professional staff. I had Shelby extend the administrative staff to include a writer for the preface and foreword and have such individuals come from the ranks of the prominent faculty of Cornell's Africana Studies and Research Center. She liked the idea and I took steps to secure the essays. Relatedly, the book cover reflects the expertise, timeliness and creativity of Dawn

Darby. Dawn was the only individual that responded to the request for book cover ideas. The overall design of the essays is the successful result of Shelby's time commitment, diligence, enthusiasm, devotion and willingness to continue to work after the course ended.

An unanticipated result stemmed from my request for additional contributions. The submitted innovations were so attractive that I became enthralled by an idea to publish a book that included these innovations in a uniform way. I subsequently requested pictures and biographical sketches (an oversight really). Regrettably, because of the confusion it caused, my role essentially shifted from educator to publisher and I became unnecessarily consumed with producing a publishable book. The tragedy is that it meant doing so even if it meant extending the original deadline and incorporating great ideas that were imaginable and achievable with a longer production timeline.

In hindsight, I should have stayed within the boundaries of the original mission and time constraints. Most relevant to the course design, I should have viewed the situation more Africentrically. This would have meant that the process was a continuously evolving one and the document should correspondingly grow by including the ideas and materials from my other Africana courses and perhaps other Cornell classes. Maybe even different schools and communities could be included in the book development mix. I envisioned, with this epiphany or practical realization, this as the backdrop to the status report. For instance, I had high expectations about the contributions of the Africana faculty; however, despite several appeals, the faculty has not produced the foreword and preface. In addition, at the rate requested photos and missing biographical sketches are being submitted, it would be another semester before a majority would be expected since some folks have either graduated or decided not to extend the time. A proposed need and goal, it will be seen, demand a much shorter period.

Moreover, I believe we would form a consensus in our belief that our current book is not representative of the best of the group and the high past academic achievement of its members, the class, University and icons. Similarly, since the whole cannot develop without all its parts, when people did not turn their essays in on time, they stifled the assessment of our book in time. This assessment would have included an analysis of the book's cover, essays, arrangements and pictures. We did not put, it must be recognized, the Africentric group concept in practice. Of equal importance, I believe my after-the-fact request violates the spirit of the original book project and the integrity of those individuals who took the time to make timely and creative submissions.

Therefore, I am halting the acceptance of additional information and will make an electronic book available that is based upon what we have to date. I will make a hard copy of this book and make it available for viewing in my office.

A more obtuse reason for not publishing the extant book is its paradox. Respect for the icons should have been testified by the production of the best-looking and reading book. Despite our admirable intentions, I do not believe we produced such a work. We made an earnest attempt but did not manufacture a stellar work. Our dilemma reminded me of a situation extending back to my Yale days as a youthful administrator. I produced a document, based upon how my undergraduate school inculcated in me to remember to "represent" excellence to your professors and eventually the outside world. I was pleased with the quality of the work I had produced. My reward was based upon my assessment of the standard I maintained from an elite Black University, Howard University. This work ethic and race consciousness paid off handsomely in the Yale environment.

One day I was approached by one of the Yale faculty working in our summer program and asked who produced the document. Sensing no disagreement, I calmly indicated that I had done the research, wrote the report and managed its production. He congratulated me on my product and said it reflected well on a great university. I did not know that my work would be assessed on how well it advanced an elite image of Yale. Alternatively, that as a member of this community it was my duty to produce work that adhered to a superior standard of excellence. His comment was truly a revelation and insight into what it meant to be Ivy League, and how to achieve some high marks.

During the year after the program, this faculty member would periodically visit my office and we would chat about a sundry of things. I was especially interested in his teaching philosophy and approach. His ratings by students had been outstanding. Students attributed magical powers to his ability to get them to read closely and enjoy writers such as Shakespeare. I was curious about this faculty member because I wanted to hire similar teachers. Surprisingly, he too had been assessing me. After one of our discussions, he asked me if I was a Fellow and I told him I was not. Several days later I received an official appointment as a Fellow of Ezra Stiles College of Yale University, where he was the Master. The appointment opened the door to the benefits of being a part of the elite of the elite. At our Fellows meetings, for example, I conversed and drank sherry with such notables as C. Van Woodard, an extremely prominent historian, and casually talked with the head of the Yale Medical School. This was important exposure to many of the top scholars in the world and a real endorsement of my ability by an individual who reputedly was the youngest person to be tenured at Yale. He became one of the few people I went to visit on and off campus and someone I came to regard as a friend. When I left Yale to become a dean at a Newark College, therefore, I continued to correspond with him.

I continued to keep in touch also with the Yale undergraduates I befriended as they graduated from the university. I was informed by one of my former Yale tutors that "my boy" was a dark horse for the presidency of the university. I thought to myself that he did not have a chance because it was the era of lawyer/college presidents. Shortly thereafter, Dr. A. Bartlett Giamatti became President of Yale University and our relationship never changed. We continued to correspond and he continued to serve as my trump card reference and one of my role model college professors. The experience reinforced an undergraduate shaping in going beyond the norms of expectations.

Thinking and behaving now as an Africentric educator, I am going to publish a book, a joint venture, that includes the Unsung book as a class project and working model. I will add a Publisher's perspective to introduce another educational dimension. This addition entails a pictorial essay of the people and events inside and outside of class that transpired during the course of the development of the book project, and puts it in relief. I expect that a subsequent version of this book will include a list of readings that support and enhance the writings, writing assessments, and additional essays with more uniformity about pictures and biographical sketches. If this Africentric cultural norm and process works, there will be a series of published books that incorporates input from college, high school, junior high and elementary school students and sources from different regions and types of educational institutions.

In closing, some may ponder if I imagined these outcomes from the outset. No, and reflective of the African based cultural norms you memorized for your world-view examination, this book has been an organic process, greatly motivated by you and the inside and outside class experience we had the spring, 2003 semester. Some of you inquired about my summer; well this is what I have been doing, and I have been enjoying myself immensely. I feel I have taken a final examination that has been given by you and on what happened in the end when we seek Africentrically to stop "miseducation." I would like an "A" and Amen for my submitted work.

Professor Gerald G. Jackson
AS&RC 172, Black Education
August 12, 2003

SECTION III
Afrospace Incubates Learning

An Africentric Learning Context

This section is analogous to learning about what occurred in the making of a film about a classroom of students taught at an Ivy League university. It involves viewing a moment from different angles of vision of different people, rather than an in-depth focus on one individual. This seemingly overwhelming undertaking is circumscribed by the social concerns of Black Studies. While some in the field may recommend the use of the MAAT[146] and others might propose the Husia,[147] it is the concept of Black Studies' social concerns, as espoused by Dr. Karenga,[148] and its incorporation of a positive concept of multiculturalism, that is followed. It should be kept in mind that from a Eurocentric dichotomous thinking mode, multiculturalism is viewed as the antithesis of American culture,[149] and therefore something to oppose.

Much of the "progressive" criticism of the anthropological definition of race have veiled presuppositions that are rarely admitted into evidence when attacking the concept of Afrocentricity. Some of them will be elucidated here because they provide insight into why a discourse on Afrospace is a crucial prerequisite to appreciating the symbolic and experiential relevance of the Harlem Experience. While the notion of "essentialism" is promoted as the rationale for abandoning the African-American reliance upon the notion of racial group solidarity, in reality, their position is premised on the suppositions that:

- Black is inferior to White, symbolically and practically;

---

[146]Jawanza Kunjufu (1993). *Hip-Hop vs. MAAT: A psychological social analysis of values*. Illinois: African American Images.

[147]Maulana Karenga (1984). *Selections from THE HUSIA*. California: Kawaida Publications.

[148]Maulana Karenga (2002). *Introduction to Black Studies*. California: University of Sankore Press.

[149]See chapter Issue 6 in chapter "Should Multiculturalism permeate the curriculum? In James Noll (Ed.) (1995). *Taking Sides: Clashing Views on Controversial Educational Issues* (pp. 82-99) (Eighth edition). Connecticut: Dushkin Publishing Group.

Gerald G. Jackson

-   Whites can not accept Black without seeing it as bad and Oppositional;

-   Black people and Black culture do not have redeeming value for Black, White, Brown, and Yellow people, and especially for people mixed with Black biology and

-   the presence of Blacks in a significant number contaminates the locale so that nothing valuable thrives or emanates from the physical setting.

Sections I, II, III, IV and V reveal portions of the film, the touted slice of life. A more complete image is a view that takes into account life events influencing the people in the film while it is being made. Africentrically, it is a relevant view of a cultural propensity to favor breadth in the characterization and exploration of events and people. In literature, it has meant producing and favoring works that give a panoramic view.[150] It is evident in the criticism of Spike Lee's movie call *Son of Sam*. Critics said he should have gone into depth about the characters rather than focusing superficially on what occurred in different places at the same time. It speaks to my broader concern about the domain of instruction. Should it be construed as simply the classroom? Should it be seen as something a teacher does and says? This section addresses these issues.

To reiterate, one epicenter of the book is the essays from the students. They were the products of an assignment that instructed them to write on Blacks back home, specifically, individuals that served as sources of inspiration in their lives. Overall, the students did pioneering and masterful work, and provided significant evidence of insight into a dimly recognized resource, that is, icons for group elevation and Africentric helping. The actions of these icons show that it is not enough to just work and do for self and family. The efforts of the students, however, did not occur in a vacuum.

Another avenue is the extension of the learning environment to out-of-classroom situations. One illustration is a group experience that allowed the abilities of the individual to be rewarded. Moreover, as the ensuing page on the First Year Writing Seminar reveals, program support and institutional resources are critical ingredients of successful education practices.

---

[150]Bonnie Barthold (1981). *Black Time: Fiction of Africa, the Caribbean, and the United States*. Connecticut: Yale University Press.

A Look at Cornell's First-Year Writing Seminars

"Hopeless Romantics." "Reporting from Hell." "Fantastic Spaces, Morphing Bodies." "Flexing Macho: Masculinity y US Latinidad."

Are these the titles of the next wave of reality TV shows?

Not quite. They are examples of First-Year Writing Seminars available to students in this year's freshman class.

Cornell's John S. Knight Institute for Writing in the Disciplines is one of the oldest and most comprehensive writing programs in the country. For freshman students alone, the institute offers over 150 seminar sections every semester, each with a maximum enrollment of 17 students.

Since all freshmen take writing seminars, the breadth of the course offerings needs to appeal to the wide variety of students at Cornell. More than 30 different departments—from anthropology to music to Spanish literature—teach seminars so students can focus on learning how to write for different audiences using different methods in different fields of study. Some of the most requested classes this semester were offered by the philosophy, anthropology, and mathematics departments.

A complete list of courses and detailed information about the First-Year Writing Seminar Program is located at: _www.arts.cornell.edu/knight_institute/_

 ## Seminar Teachers Talk About Writing

Tanya Matthews in the linguistics department is working to create a new writing seminar entitled "Language, Thought, and Reality: Like, Slang 101: Teens as Linguistic Innovators". The seminar will examine the use of slang in the English language and look at how slang evolves.

"Many people say slang is ruining English," Matthews explains, "but I want to work with this group of students at an age where slang is real for them and a huge part of how they talk to each other. I also want to give students a sense that they can write and that they can also enjoy writing."

Professor Gerald Jackson (left) has taught different writing seminars through the Africana studies department. He tries to get students to think in depth about writing – and even encourages them to seek publication. But he also gives students a real-life experience to write about.

"Last year, we took a group of students to Harlem and asked them to write essays about their experiences," he says. "A lot of students wrote about their fear – and many wrote about how they were able to confront one another about their beliefs and attitudes."

He also takes the group to the Johnson Art Museum on campus to view the permanent collection of African-American art. "This is the first time that many students have seen paintings of themselves," Jackson comments. "We can use that as a base to start students thinking about the 'self'."

Josh Greenberg in science and technology studies has taught several writing seminars and says they are the best teaching experience he's ever had. "I get to know all of my students in a more informal setting," he explains. "Students often come to me for advice on things unrelated to the class I'm teaching."

Through his seminar "Writing as Technology," Greenberg hopes to help demystify writing. "People sign up for my class who are willing to think about writing a little bit differently," he says. "They are interested in the history of writing and how it has developed."

Ultimately, all seminar instructors try to instill a love of writing in their students. "Once you get them to explore what is real and personal to them," says Professor Jackson, "they can really begin to enjoy their writing and use it to explore their own notions about things."

Gerald G. Jackson

Black History and Culture behind Educational Museum Experience

When the museum project was conceived, I did not have an idea of the knowledge and experience of my students with African-American art.[151] I presumed some familiarity on their part, given the Black art clearly displayed on the Cosby Show.[152] My purpose was two-fold. First, I wanted to give them additional exposure to some significant works in African-American art. Second, I wanted to reinforce writing and speech skills. I discovered a great deal more, and much of what I learned I gained through reading the essays written by students and reflecting on the powerful presentation given by Jeff Donaldson,[153] made possible by Donald Byrd and the Johnson Museum. A retrospective analysis of the entire experience has resulted in a discussion of the cultural context of the art and the experience of the students.

In a Eurocentric way of dichotomous thinking, art is apolitical. Consequently, in this mode it is quite common to hear a work criticized for being too political. In the African cultural paradigm, art is interrelated with all aspects of the community; therefore, it is expected that it should reflect the political life of the artist's community. To allow students to grasp this concept is no more propagandistic than teaching them that the artist should strive to convey apolitical art. An opportunity to teach this concept was presented by the Johnson Museum staff at Cornell University.[154] Seeing an opportunity based

---

[151] Sharon F. Patton (1998). *African-American art.* New York: Oxford University Press; Richard J. Powell (1997). *Black art and culture in the 20th century.* New York: Thames and Hudson.

[152] A book in the area of Whiteness Studies used essays and visual arts to demonstrate their use in getting Whites to learn about their racial preference and ponder issues around race. See Tyler Stallings, Roediger, D., Jones, A., Gonzales-Day, K. & Art, L. (2003). *Whiteness, a wayward construction.* California: Fellow of Contemporary Art.

[153] Dr. Jeff Donaldson died on March 9, 2004.

[154] The Herbert F. Johnson museum is named after a 1922 Cornell graduate that became the chairperson of S.C. Johnson & Sons. He was a lifelong enthusiast of art and an architect of achievement. The current art building was designed by I. M. Pei and contains reputedly the finest collection of art in New York State and is recognized as one of the most significant university museums in the country. Its permanent collection includes more than 30,000 works of art. Its African sculpture and textiles is considered a part of its

upon my belief that learning does not just transpire in the classroom, I took advantage of a unique program.

The program was unique in terms of the owner of the art and the artist; he elected to display their works. The introduction of African-American art in the Cornell community would not have been possible if not for the altruistic aims of Dr. Donald Byrd, an African-American man. From his private art collection, he provided works from such prominent artists as Henry Assawa Tanner,[155] Richard Barthe, Romare Bearden,[156] Jacob Lawrence,[157] Lois Mailou Jones, Ernest Crichlow, Charles White, James Lesisne Wells and Faith Ringgold.[158] In addition, he included the paintings and mixed media works of noted artists Paul Goodnight, Tyree Guyton and Jeff Donaldson.

Dr. Byrd shared his collection to honor the world of Black Art,[159] teach the beauty of Black art and inspire other affluent African Americans to share their collection with the public and African Americans. Who is such a man? Dr. Donald Byrd is a musician, composer, scholar, educator and collector and, to round off his personality, he is a member of Kappa Alpha Psi fraternity. He obtained from Columbia University two master's degrees and a doctorate in museum education. As a professor, he has served on the faculty of such

---

greatest strengths. It hosts approximately 80,000 visitors every year and presents special exhibitions annually and numerous tours, lectures and family programs.

[155] Marcus Bruce (2002). *Henry Ossawa Tanner a spiritual biography*. New York: The Crossroads Publishing Company.

[156] Romare Bearden & Henderson, H. (1993). *A history of African-American artists from 1792 to the present*. New York: Pantheon Books.

[157] Jacob Lawrence (1993). *Harriet and the promise land*. New York: Simon & Schuster.

[158] Faith Ringgold (1995). *We flew over the bridge: The memoirs of Faith Ringgold*. New York: Bullfinch Press Book; Faith Ringgold (1992). *The French connection*. New York: B. Mow Press.

[159] Duncan Clarke (1995). *African art*. New York: Crescent Books; Dallas Museum of Art (1989). *BLACK ART ANCESTRAL LEGACY The African impulse in African-American art*. New York: Harry M. Abrams Publisher; Robert Doty (1971). *Contemporary Black artists*. New York: Dodd, Mead & Company; Elsa Dine (1971). *The Afro-American Artist A search for identity*. New York: Holt, Rinehart & Winston; Crystal Britton (1996). *AFRICAN AMERICAN ART The long struggle*. New York: Smithmark Publisher; *Harlem Renaissance Art of Black America*. The Studio Museum in Harlem. New York: Abradale Press Harry M. Abrams Publisher.

universities and colleges as Queens College, Rutgers, Howard, North Carolina, Hampton and Cornell universities, and the Oberlin Conservatory of Music.

Illustrative of diunital thinking, Dr. Byrd has worn characteristically several hats. In 1940 his career started and he became a sought-after musician in the hardbop era. During this time he played and recorded with such icons as Charlie Parker, Thelonious Monk and John Coltrane. Many would have been satisfied with simply being a great musician; however, Donald would not allow himself to be bounded by one endeavor. He expanded his domain, achieved success as a composer, arranger and bandleader, and made a mark in the United States and Europe. Similarly, thinking syncretistically, he extended his margin into "jazz fusion," an amalgam of jazz, funk and rhythm and blues. Continuing his cultural propensity to be a vanguard, in the 1990's he collaborated with Hip-Hop artist GURU on Jazzmatazz Volumes 1 and 2 and has over sixty recordings to his credit.

The other noteworthy individual needing an introduction to the published student art is Dr. Jeff Donaldson, former Dean of Fine Arts at Howard University and Professor of Art. Dr. Donaldson has participated in over two group and fifteen one-person exhibitions in the United States and abroad. Many of Byrd's art pieces have musical subject matter. For Donaldson, music play is a prominent role in West African and African-American culture and serves as part of the philosophical base for his artwork. His work not only captures fragmentary sides of jazz musicians, he also arranges his paintings according to the qualities of the music itself. Even when his pieces are organized in a symmetrical fashion, he maintains a distinct jazz pattern by having a variation in form that parallels a jazz improvisation. This philosophical orientation is what he brought to the Black Arts Movement and an articulated view of African culture as the basis of Black Art. Doctors Byrd and Donaldson are learned men who understand the paradigm they sought to shift.

Both individuals are prototypical activist-scholars.[160] For example, in 1968 Jeff co-founded the African Commune of Bad Relevant Artists (AfriCobra). This progressive organization avoided the Eurocentrically oriented approach by focusing on bright colors, symmetry, improvisation and images, and patterns derived from African and African-American art and music. His work does not apologize for an African ancestry; it sought to celebrate the roots of African-American culture.

---

[160]See W.E.B. DuBois (1926). *Criteria of Negro Art*. (pp. 317-325). Republished in Kathryn Wilson (Ed.) (1999). *The crisis reader*. New York: Modern Library.

Highlights of Student Museum Learning

To repeat, a multicultural glimpse at art aesthetic appreciation is revealed in comments by several classes of my Cornell University students. Their thoughts were extrapolates from essays written in response to a viewing of an art exhibit of Donald Byrd's art collection, held at the Johnson Museum of Cornell University.[161]

African-American female, Africana Studies 100.4, 9/26/99

The Johnson Museum Of Art's 'Voyage of Discovery' expedition, however, proved to be the exception. I found in the pieces, to my utter bewilderment, a strong recognition, some mutual understanding. What was the source of this recognition, I could not be sure... was it de-ja-vu? Then, in the recesses of my consciousness, I felt something. First a sigh, then a flicker, a slight flutter, an agonizing shift, a strained deliberate movement, and then, at last, a realization ... I could actually relate to these artists. Accompanied with this sudden insight, came to mind the poignant words of Jeff Donaldson, "We strive for images inspired by African people/ experience and images without formal art training and / or experience...we try to create images that appeal to the sense-not the intellect." Intricately intertwined in the paints and brush strokes of these artists were my culture, depictions of my past and allusions to my future. Very simply, these paintings engaged my conscious, and no category was needed to comprehend that.

I found truly moving artwork by, to name a few, Faith Ringgold, Earnie Barnes, Benny Andrews, Henry Tanner, and Jeff Donaldson.[162]

---

[161]This was an extra credit assignment. Students who desired credit were instructed to submit an essay that relates the visual experience to the subject matter of the course. One course was based on the Black Family and the other was a first year writing seminar on Black Psychological Identity.

[162]The Jeff Donaldson painting referred to by students was titled "Victory in the Valley of ESU" (1970). It was the picture used in the brochure commemorating his life and including his obituary.

Gerald G. Jackson

African-American female, Africana Studies 100.4, 9/27/99

The second painting that I like was the direct opposite of the one I just described. This is a piece by Jeff Donaldson, the founder of the group AfriCobra. As an artist, Donaldson reportedly has said that he wanted to "create images that appeal to the senses-not the intellect." I loved his artistic style because of its vibrancy and color. It adds another realm to the painting.

The painting itself portrays his parents, as senior citizens and when they were in their prime. The amazing aspect that the couple aside from obviously being black, are made up of a compilation of different hues of green, yellow and red. The way in which the man has his hand draped over the woman's arm depicts the strength of the man and the strength of the woman to stand by her man. In addition, the man had what appears to be a tribal bracelet around his arm, which is a linkage to his own ancestry. This picture unlike the solitary man in the boat is more vibrant and depicts a different aspect of African Americans. This picture illustrates the stability and pride found within the homes of African Americans, as well as the strength that exists within the family bond. The way Donaldson portrayed his parents allows people, regardless of race to relate directly to the painting and the experiences behind which the painting is magnifying.

Puerto Rican female, Cornell University, Africana Studies 100.4, 9/26/99

Again, in another work, the attitude expressed examines another aspect of African American culture: glory and pride. Dignity is an undeniable characteristic of <u>Mother and Father</u>. Gold color stressed in this painting emphasizes the nobility of this king and queen who have battled life' struggles and survived; they've achieved the victory the artist has written at the bottom of the painting. The man wears a bracelet of nobility, and his huge hand extends around the shoulder of the mother figure, indicating respect for himself and his partner. The two exemplify triumph and accomplishment of goals.

Asian female, Africana Studies 171, 9/27/ 1999

It is difficult to explain the collection as a state of static significance in the African American family. Because the collection holds many works from different eras, saying that the African-American family is a specific way is unjustifiable. Moreover, the works and the artistic styles have shifted as reflections of the changing African-American family. Nevertheless, the collection symbolizes the overall values of the African-American family.

One of which is the importance of pride in oneself and pride in the family. A perfect example is the piece titled Mother and Father. In a subtle way, the artist portrays the couple as angels and heroes. The word "victory" is slightly visible as it blends with the vibrant colors of the background. "Victory" implies that there was some form of challenge in which it was overcome by the couple. Further, above the couple's heads seem to be colorful halos that represent goodness. In the center of the painting looks similar to Native art with a picture of a person. This feature of the piece illustrates the pride one feels towards its ancestors and heritage.

Biracial female, Africana Studies 100.4, 9/26/99

Later in the exhibit, I saw Jeff Donaldson's "Mother and Father." This picture is really a great portrayal of the strength and endurance of the African-American family. The picture is of the artists' parents in their later years. Although the picture is of two older adults, they appear to be strong, healthy, and proud to be Black. It seems that they have almost crowns of light radiating from their heads. The father's arm looks incredibly muscular and that again, shows the power of the Black man. The artist painted the subjects skin in many colors, not just different hues of brown, I think the different colors in the skin symbolized the distribution of people of African descent throughout the world. This picture also had the word "victory" at the bottom of it. From this picture, I concluded that victory meant that the subjects had overcome some sort of hardship and thus, they were stronger because of it.

African-American female, Africana Studies 171, 9/27/99

To me the painting of the elderly woman and man showed the strength of the black family to overcome oppression.

African female, Africana Studies 171, 9/27/99

All of these works of art, however, celebrate the community that is present within black culture. This emphasis on community is consistent with the African idea of extended family, which stretches to include neighbors, fellow church members, and beyond. Pictures entitled "The

Sisters" (Ernest Crichlow) and "Mother and Father" (Jeff Donaldson) are obvious depictions of family, be it nuclear or extended.

Belize female, Africana Studies 171, 9/ 27, 1999

My personal favorite of the works exhibited was Jeff Donaldson's "Mother and Father." This painting pays the ultimate compliment to the most influential persons in our lives, our parents. Donaldson's use of bright yet contrasting colors shocked then intrigued me. I began to wonder about what kind of upbringing Donaldson had as a child. This painting also made me appreciate my mother much more.

The Ensuing Section

It is on the creative milieu of the group project book. Its depiction explains why many educational projects that override the importance of context result in conceptual and theoretical inertia and plighted designs. In educational settings and mental health research, for instance, an environmental factor is omitted frequently from examination and therefore, from conceptualizations and interventions. Unless the environment is included as part of a field, such as environmental psychology, it is viewed Eurocentrically as a variable that can or cannot be included in a scientific investigation. In contrast, an Africentric framework defines it as an integral factor in human interventions and analyses. To correct this problem, a primarily pictorial account is given of classroom and outside events that occurred while the class was in the process of writing the book, and the period after the book's completion. This temporal dimension, coupled with a description of relevant people and events, has implications for individuals and groups working to adapt the process, and educational and mental health assessment.

Black Greeks – The self-knowledge cultural route[163]

My personal lens for viewing Black Greeks is African-American and Africentric. My first recollection of them as an entity extends back to my early years in Harlem. It was before elementary school and took place on St. Nicholas Avenue, around 145th Street.[164] I saw men lined up, as in a military stance, but without uniforms. I stared because I was curious about what I thought would be a problem, and maybe exciting. They seemed scared. Their subservient demeanor led me to conclude that they must really be big boys because men do not act that way. This appeared to be especially the case when I observed them being spanked with wood and not fighting back. I felt a degree of superiority because I reasoned that my mother had to hold me to give me a beating with a strap. Nevertheless, I asked my mother what was happening and she informed me that the group was a fraternity. The guys lined up, she followed, were trying to join the fraternity and what I saw was what they had to do to get accepted. She added that what you had to do to join a White fraternity was to swallow a goldfish, implying the Black thing was less foolish. I thought privately that these people were crazy for accepting spanking as a way to becoming a member of any organization and I definitely could not view myself swallowing anything that was alive. What monster, I pondered, would eat an adorable and live goldfish?

Fast forward to my first year at Howard University since the time between 1962 and my childhood experience. It revealed exposure to mostly White frats in movies doing silly things, during hazing and afterwards in the frat. I did see Black Greeks at the Penn Relays; while in high school, however, I saw them as an extension of my street gang, the *Enchanters*, and a threat to my coveted individualism. I paid, therefore, little attention to them as a role modeling agent.

I was in the Howard bookstore, enthralled by the campus, my educational and career prospects, and being in an alternative to what had become the doldrums of an East Harlem existence. So enamored was I with becoming a college-looking student that I almost bought some Black Greek paraphernalia. I made no connection to the group of guys getting spanked or acting "uncool" at the Penn Relays, behaving

---

[163]This African worldview axiology is experientially driven, as opposed to the Eurocentric orientation towards the accumulation of data (e.g., statistics, research studies).

[164]This street is almost as important as 125th and 135th streets. See Walter Dean Myers (2000). *145th Street Stories.* New York: Delacorte Press.

below the level of the smoothness of "Smooth." Besides, at the time I reasoned that I still had "my boys" back home, thus fulfilling my affiliative needs. As time progressed, however, and I spent more time in DC than New York, I started seeing some virtues in being in a recognized and respected campus gang. Every Friday the Black Greeks sang on campus and the women stood around and drooled over them. When the Black men greeted one other it had a majestic quality, a peculiar energy and power. The men carried themselves as if they had power, determination and answers to eking out a good existence in the United States. The lives of the Greeks determine campus rhythms.

I was learning about the Black privilege class[165] and its purported power to advance young Black men. Similarly, I felt at the time that I definitely needed a boost, especially after interacting at Howard with African Americans who had been great high school students, were well traveled and from affluent families. Here, my street coolness did not have a high salience. Seeking, therefore, to empower myself, a persuading factor in encouraging me to think Greek was my exposure to Alphas. The Dean of Men (Alpha), my dorm director (Alpha), and floor advisors (Alpha) were all Greek. Surrounded by Alpha Phi Alpha men and their propaganda about having the most influential Black men in their organization, I was headed towards becoming an Alpha man. My homeboy Emory cautioned me away from the Alphas by reminding me that New York was the home of the Omega Psi Phi fraternity. Tom Parker, my "running buddy," and later one of "my boys," advocated pledging Kappa. Tom was from Philly, a Kappa town, and argued that the Kappas were the real "mack" men and we needed, therefore, to be with a group that supported and advanced our "coolness" and way of life. I pledged Kappa; however, it was exposure to Kappa versus Alpha men that made the difference. It was Charlie Wilson that convinced me, and I convinced Glegg to pledge Kappa. The Chucker, as he was called, was Big, Black and apparently took "no shit" from anyone. He had invitations to parties in DC, Philly and New York, and he always had something to drink. He knew "the dirt" on everybody on campus. He

---

[165]See Tobb Boyd. (2003). *Young, Black, rich and famous.* New York: Doubleday; E. Franklin Frazier (1962). *Black Bourgeosie.* New York: Free Press; Lawrence Graham (1995). *Member of the Club.* New York: Harper/Collins; Lawrence Graham (1999). *Our kind of people: Inside America's Black upper class.* New York: Harper/Collins; George Nelson (2004). *Post-Soul nation.* New York: Viking; Leslie Goffer (December, 2003/January, 2004). "Blue blood brothers." *Savoy,* pp. 104-106, 108.

dressed like a **Peter Prep**[166] and allowed me to be my Harlem self in social situations. He also had knowledge of the White world and was willing to provide others with insight into how one might succeed in it, as a Black man. He was a positive role model during a time when great value was placed on being spontaneous, outrageous, smooth, daring, and sophisticated. Through Charlie, I learned the Kappa folklore. The Kappas had the women, dressed the best, were brilliant students when they wanted and had the hardest pledge period.[167] A part of me still had the East Harlem machismo and a morbid curiosity about whether I was still tough enough to make rank in another gang.

The six-week pledge period seemed like an eternity. In retrospect, it was one of the most meaningful growth periods in my life, akin more to an African-centered rite of passage,[168] similar in design and purpose to that provided Cinque. He received an African training for leadership and life that enabled him to take command of the Amistad, and subsequently earn enough money to free the enslaved Africans and return them to Africa. I remain indebted to the process the Kappas designed and implemented, especially after being a Big Brother and realizing how time-consuming and exhausting it is to "try and make the pledges right." Personally, I learned to override physical pain, listen closely to what is being said, how to surmount feelings of selfishness, envy, jealousy, and appreciate dimly-appreciated skills that I possessed. The "beasting" sessions are fondly remembered events at reunions and a major source of bonding with Black Greeks from the "old wood" days. I rediscovered what group loyalty meant and how my personal skills and ambitions can be realized via the growth and development of

---

[166]Group of young African-Ameican Harlem men who started dressing with clothes from Brooks Brothers and Paul Stuarts. This group challenged the more popular Black styles of the *Hustler* and *Continental* types. The former wore rep ties, buck shoes, pocket squares, blue blazer and grey slacks, and three piece suits, and aspired to college and professional careers.

[167]One guy pledged Alpha, after being scared almost to death during the Kappa interview of potential pledges. After he pledged Alpha I overheard him telling a Kappa that he pledged the wrong fraternity.

[168]See Paul Hill (1992). *Coming of Age: African American Male Rites-of-Passage.* Illinois: African-American Images; Richard Majors & Bilson, J. (1992). *Cool Pose: The dilemmas of Black Manhood in America.* New York: Lexington Books; Gregalan Williams (1997). *boys to men: Maps for the journey.* New York: Doubleday; Raymond Winbush (2001). *The warrior Method: A Program for Rearing Healthy Black Boys.* New York: Amistad.

the group. Most importantly, I learned, when necessary, how to be a leader, follower and team player.

Collectively, we learned about how arrogance can cause the group to be fooled into a false sense of security. It happened shortly after we became Kappas. Dr. Samuel Proctor, a Kappa and college President of a Virginia school, came to speak to us about being "a good Kappa." We went to hear him out of respect and deference but thought we would teach the frat something about the Immortal 32 way. Well, during the course of his remarks he noted that he had heard our line had taken more wood than any other pledge group. We thought, another accolade attesting to our greatness, and by a college President, and naively responded affirmatively. We expected another pat on the back when he declared alarmingly that paddling had been banned and should not have occurred. Busted, we relearned that more still could be learned from our elders about mistakes from our brazenness.

Contrary to the image of frat boys, I learned how to be truly successful with women. As a social fraternity, we received specific instructions during the pledge period on our mission to "please the ladies." What I discovered was not the obvious, it entailed more than giving great parties. It meant being a winner. It meant winning the intra-Greek basketball tourney, having the best pledge queen coronation, creating the best float for the homecoming parade, having the highest pledge line academic G.P.A., leading campus organizations, having the most varsity players on our line, being articulate, well-dressed and smooth. We named ourselves the Immortal 32 and thirty-one of us graduated. My line name was "Smooth" and I was teased about having a song named after me. It was called "The Boy from New York City," and it was by the Ad-Libs and I loved the tribute. Life as a young Kappa was grand, as depicted below in a picture taken at a H.U. Homecoming football game. I am on the right, Glegg Watson is in the middle, and Thomas Parker is on the left.[169]

My line turned out well, as revealed on the chart below. We were not, it has to be added, an anomaly, and this fact is partially revealed in a roster of accomplished Kappas appearing on the below chart. I did not

[169]Glegg published a major book, retired from a Vice President position at Xerox, and served on the Board of Trustees at several universities, including Howard. Tom did decades in corporate America, and before heading his own consulting firm, was the head speechwriter for the head of the Atlanta City Council. We all obtained advanced degrees. People referred to us back in the day as the Three Musketeers; we called one another Pope, Dragon, and Bengal.

Tom, Glegg & GGJ. Taken at Howard University Homecoming
football game in school stadium.

report in exactly the same way on the other Black fraternities but they
have a comparable number of great members There are also ways
where they are different. The Omegas have a disproportionate number
of Black astronauts and the Sigmas have a comparatively high number
of African leaders. To be a Black Greek, therefore, meant being more
than beer parties, hatred towards Blacks, and political dynasties.

Ultimately, we derived strength at Howard from the reality that
people like us were in conspicuous positions of power and authority, a
notion not needing a dissertation and reams of research to fathom. The
President, James Nabritt, was an Omega, the Dean of Student
Activities, Carl Anderson, was a Kappa, the head of my government
department Emmett Dorsey was a Kappa. They were our role models
and they imparted "tough" love. We saw a hard road, based upon their
example and reports, as a challenge and opportunity to demonstrate our
"manhood."

The modeling continued; when I arrived at Yale I met Dr. Houston
Baker, my former Kappa big brother at Howard and English professor
at Yale. I met Dr. James Comer, a dean in the Yale medical school, and
graduate of Howard University medical school. I interacted with Dr.

Banner,[170] a philosophy professor from Howard who was a visiting professor at Yale. I socialized with fraternity brothers and H.U. graduates pursuing degrees in law, medicine and architecture. I was not intimidated by the Yale elitist milieu because it was quite similar in feel to my Howard home environment. I was raised to feel confident to compete with the best and to have ambitions that meant reaching the real top of professional, economic, societal and political hierarchies.[171]

Similarly, my commitment to struggle and succeed in the United States was reinforced by seeing members of my gang succeeding in life. For instance, an article in *JET* magazine on a former Kappa big brother revealed the surgeon that successfully did the surgery on Reginald Denny, the White male brutally attacked after the Rodney King trial, was Dr. Madison Richardson.[172] Madison was not only a Kappa, he was a star football player during my Howard years, and line brother with Drs. Floyd Atkins, Alvin Chisolm and Houston Baker.[173] I

---

[170]William Banner (1968). *Ethics: An introduction to moral philosophy.* New York: Charles Scribner's and Sons and (1981). *Moral norms and moral order: The philosophy of human affairs.* Florida: University Presses of Florida.

[171]After I completed my first year as an administrator at Yale Summer High School and the program was deemed relatively successful, Houston asked me when I was going to publish my book on the program. He did not suggest that I get a doctorate, the traditional prerequisite step, he encouraged me to do the unconventional at my early career stage because of our undergraduate and fraternity training to go after the highest achievements.

[172]"Skill of Black Doctors Helped Save Life of L.A. Riot Victim Reginald Denny" (June 1, 1992), *Jet Magazine*, p. 51.

[173]The following works are especially applicable to and supportive of the notion advanced throughout this book of an African-American education facilitating an appreciation of multi-culturalism, multiracialism and class, gender, and generational differences. Houston Baker (Ed.) (1982). *Three American Literatures: Essays in Chicano, Native American and Asian American Literature for teachers of American Literature.* Modern Language Association; Houston Baker (1995). *Black Studies, Rap, and the Academy.* Illinois University of Chicago Press; Houston Baker (1989). *Modernism and the Harlem Renaissance.* Illinois: University of Chicago Press; Houston Baker (1990). Long *Black Song: Essays in Black American Literature and culture*; Houston Baker (1988). *Afro-American poetics: Revisions of Harlem the Black aesthetic.* Wisconsin: University of Wisconsin Press; Dana Nelson and Houston Baker (Eds) (2001). *Violence, the body and "the South."* Illinois: University of Chicago Press; Houston Baker, Alexander, E., and Redmond, P. (1993). *Workings of the Spirit: The poetics of Afro-American Women's Writing.* Illinois: University of Chicago Press; Houston Baker (2001). *Critical*

was not only impressed that he was still the man, from the same Kappa line as I was with Floyd Atkins, head of a medical department at Tufts before an early death, and Harry Simmons. Harry too was a former varsity football player, and became a head of an architectural firm in New York before an accidental plane death.

Motivation also stemmed from horizontal relationships. Seeing former Scroller brother John Brittain excel as a Civil Rights lawyer in Mississippi, although he was from Connecticut, and go on to be a Dean at the Thurgood Marshall law School. Glegg Watson, from DC and Jamaica, WI, who eventually became a Vice President during the "good ole days" at Xerox,[174] co-authored a pioneering book on Blacks in corporate America.[175] I was especially pleased, since he was one of *my boys,* to read how he not only talked the talk, he walked the walk.[176] In the same spirit, Dr. Therman Evans not only published several books on medical matters pertaining to Black Americans,[177] he and his family appeared on the cover of *Black Enterprise* magazine.[178] The picture represented an article on him and his family and revealed how they amassed millions of dollars by working as a team, and personified the Africentric concept of the group. The Mizell brothers, backed by Freddie Perren, ventured to Hollywood and excelled in the music industry. Barry Gordy said Freddie was his Think Tank, and I remember Freddie as a Big Brother who "made me" and the Mizell brothers. This is the cultural and social backdrop to my work on predominantly White College campuses and universities. It has included teaching and administrating at two Ivy League universities, teaching at a Catholic and State university and community college and

---

Memory: Public Spheres, African American writing, and Black fathers and sons in America. Georgia: University of Georgia Press; Joe Weeriman and Houston Baker (1988). *Studies in Black American Literature: Black Feminist Criticism and Critical Theory.* Florida: Penkevill Publishing Company.

[174]See Marjorie Whigham-Desir (December, 2003/January, 2004). "The files." *Savoy,* 90-94, 128.

[175]George Davis & Watson, Glegg (1982). *Black life in Corporate America.* New York: Doubleday.

[176]Barry Beckham (October, 1991). "Profile Glegg Watson Walking the Walk and Talking the talk." *American Vision,* pp. 52-54.

[177]Healthquest Editors & Evans, Therman. (2001). *Lighten up.* New York: Amistad; Sara Reese, Johnson, K. & Evans, T. (1999). *Staying strong: Reclaiming the wisdom of African-American healing.* New York: Avon Books

[178]The Evans Family Investment Club. (October, 1990). *Black Enterprise Magazine,* cover page.

LIST OF KAPPA LINE AND CAREER FOLLOW-UP

Immortal Thirty-two
1964 Pledge Line
Kappa Alpha Psi Fraternity
XI Chapter
Howard University

Name	Major	Varsity Sport	Career/Profession
Michael Amos*	Architecture		head/architect firm
Leonard Brinson	Business	varsity baseball	Corporate VP .
John Brittain	Government		Law School dean
Harold Brookins	architecture		architect
Richard Dale	Pre-med		medical doctor
Richard Ellis	Pre-med		medical doctor
Therman Evans	Pre-med		medical doctor
Claude Foggie	Pharmacy		lawyer/pharmacist
Carl Gaines	Psychology		social worker
Leonard Garrett	Business		Lawyer/bank Pres
Paul Gist .	Accounting	varsity basketball	Govt/accountant
Lawrence Gordon	Music		entertainer
Bobbie Graves	Pre-med		medical doctor
Raymond Hall	Business		lawyer
Thomas Hill	Business		manager
Wilfred Holland	Business	varsity basketball	corporate exec.
Michael House	Engineering	varsity football	businessman
Gerald Jackson	Government	varsity crew	college professor
William Lawson	Architecture	varsity basketball	architect
Robert Lee	Psychology	varsity basketball	college adminis.
Alphonso Mizell	Music		musical writer
Lawrence Mizell	Engineering		musical writer
Rodney O'Neal	Psychology		businessman
Theodore Primas	Pre-med		unknown
Otto Stallworth	Pre-med		medical doctor
Samuel Sullivan	Pre-med		medical doctor
Paul Thompson	Engineering	varsity football	college adminis.
Glegg Watson	Government	varsity soccer	corporate V.P.
Melvin White	Engineering	varsity track	head/engineer firm
Roland Williams*	Pre-med		medical doctor
Paul Whitt	Business	varsity football	Unknown
Sherman Wooten	Speech		college adminis.

*deceased

being a dean at a community college and state university. In addition, I have been a consultant, trainer and facilitator in the areas of human relations, diversity, multiculturalism, mental health and education for a large number of Institutions of Higher Education. I have enjoyed the differences and learned from the diversities.

Dispelling Myths and Advancing Positive Traditions

Today, we have too much bravado and intimidation. Suburban Black kids decry how they have been made *peripheral Blacks* but the cultural hegemony of urban Black culture continues.[179] This may be because suburbanization does not follow an adaptation pattern that is based upon an Africentric syncretism, and despite the shortcomings of Gangsta Rap, the urban cultural form is still culturally and contemporaneously rooted in a comprehensive Black reality. In contrast, many of the Black students coming to Cornell do not have much exposure to Black Greeks and frequently have internalized negative stereotypes of White and Black fraternities. The fact that five out of seven of the African-American faculty are Black Greeks and one that is not has a son that is a Kappa, does not deeply influence student perceptions. A personal belief about why there is this lack of knowledge is that the faculty does not "front" their affiliations, perhaps for the same reasons that the Black faculty had at Kean University.

At Kean College, currently Kean University, I learned that much of the Black Greek faculty and administrators purposely hid their Black Greek affiliation because the undergraduates embarrassed them. They expressed grave disappointment over the poor academic performance and lamented how they had associated membership with academic excellence, leadership, and community involvement and development. This is exhibited in the following well known **Omegas:** Hank Aaron, Clifford Alexander, Count Basie, Bill Cosby, Dr. Charles Drew, Earl Graves, Jesse Hill, Benjamin Hook, Langston Hughes, Rev. Jesse Jackson, Michael Jordan, Vernon Jordan, Percy Julian, Benjamin Mays, Tom Joyner, Earl "The Pearl" Monroe, Shaquille O'Neal, Carl Rowan, Joe Torrey, George Weaver, L. Douglas Wilder, Roy Wilkins, Sharpe James, and Dr. Carter G. Woodson. Similarly, the **Sigmas** can boast of such noteworthy individuals as Morris Chestnut, E.O. Jackson, John Lewis, Karl Malone, Clarence Meese, Rinaldo Nehemiah, Huey P. Newton, Barry Beckham, Kwame Nkrumah, Baba Olatunji, A. Phillip

---

[179]See, Maxine Moffett (January 16, 2002). "Rep your city…Myths of hood life." *The Hilltop*, 1.

Randolph, Herman J. Russell and Blair Underwood, to name a few. The negative stereotypes are just that because success in all areas runs through all the Black Greeks. As the tables reveal, Kappas are not "all Playas" and "pretty boys" and Alphas are not all "egg-heads" and "corny." The glue that unites is Black cultural humor, and one account will be given because these humorous relationships between Black Greeks can help gangsta gangs learn about not taking themselves so seriously that they kill one another, and consequently, diffusing their social consciousness and political clout.

The situation occurred at a Cornell social event. I was reminded how certain clothes color combinations signify certain groups, similar to street gangs, and that these distinctions can continue long after our undergraduate days. I was going to wear Crimson and Cream, the Kappa Alpha Psi colors but decided to not let fraternity rules dictate this particular evening's dress. Instead, I decided to wear my clothes from Ghana to symbolize the cultural unity between Africa and African Americans. Moreover, the black and gold I was styling was more in keeping with Ghana's gold and a Black nation status. I decided, therefore, to take a chance since there were few Black Greeks on campus to recognize the Alpha fraternity colors. I reasoned that Bob Harris, an Alpha, probably forgot the Black Greek color tradition, and liberated myself to wear what I wanted.

Later, as I strolled across the room receiving favorable nods and admiring glances about my attire, I felt reassured that I made a great culturally and politically conscious decision. A couple more steps to my table, I mused, and I would be exonerated for my bold step to dress in Alpha colors. I really thought I was home-free and then boom the embarrassment of the decade. Bob Harris called out and said, "I like your colors." Yes, I was busted and felt in my twenties again, being held responsible at all times for representing the frat. I even started imagining what I would say when confronted by the frat for looking as if I favored the Alphas' colors. At the same time, I felt closer to Bob because he invoked a connection that was exclusively in the realm of Black Greek tradition. The affiliate or spiritual bond, so much a part of the African world-view, has been exaggerated by gangs that have signs, color domains, dance steps and contests, similar to Black Greeks. Bringing the undergraduates in line, therefore, could yield some measures that would be applicable to non-college Black youth and encourage them to pursue careers.

List of Successful Members of Kappa Alpha Psi Fraternity

Activists Leaders
Dr. Rev. Ralph Abernathy – Civil rights leader, former president of SCLC

Astronaut Leader
Dr. Bernard Harris – First African-American to walk in space

Athletes and Leaders
Arthur Ashe – Tennis legend, humanitarian

Emmett Ashford – First Black umpire in major league baseball

Lem Barney – Former NFL Detroit Lion 1967-77; NFL Hall of Fame

Bernie Bickerstaff – Former Head Coach NBA Washington Wizards

Rolando Blackman – Former NBA Knick and Maverick

Larry Brown – Player, Dallas Cowboys, Super Bowl XXX Most Valuable Player

Ernest Brumer – Former NFL Baltimore Ravens

Wilt Chamberlain – Member, NBA Hall of Fame

John Chaney – Head basketball coach, Temple University

Eric Dampier – NBA Golden State Warrior

Eric Davis – NFL Carolina Panthers

Willie Davis – NFL Former Green Bay Packers, 1958-69; NFL Hall of Fame

Jon Drummond – World class sprinter, 1996 Olympic Silver Medalist

Alex English – Member, NBA Hall of Fame

Larry Finch – Former Head Basketball coach, Memphis State University

Robert Green – NFL Chicago Bears

Anfernee Hardaway – NBA Orlando Magic

Alan Henderson – NBA Atlanta Hawks

Jesse Hester – Former NFL Oalkland Raiders

Randall Hill – NFL Arizona Cardinals

Allan Houston – NBA New York Knicks

Sam Jones – Member, NBA Hall of Fame

John Henry Johnson – Former NFL Pittsburgh Steelers, 1954-56; NFL Hame of Fame

E.J. Junior – Former NFL Miami Dolphins

Kerry Tittles – NBA New Jersey Nets

Greg Lloyd – Former NFL Pittsburgh Steelers

Kenny Lofton – MLB Atlanta Braves

Derek Loville – Former NFL San Francisco 49ers

Danny Manning – NBA Phoenix Suns

Jim Marxhall – Former NFL Chicago Bears 1952-66; NFL Hall of Fame

Curtis McClinton – AFL-NFL, Former Kansas City Chiefs 1962-69

Guy McIntyre – Former NFL San Francisco 49ers

Glynn Milburn – NFL Detroit Lions

Johnny Newman – Former NBA New Jersey Nets

Chris Oldham – NFL Pittsburgh Steelers

Oscar Robertson – Member, NBA Hall of Fame

Bill Russell – Member, NBA Hall of Fame

Nolan Richardson – Head basketball coach, University of Arkansas

Gale Sayers – Member, NFL Hall of Fame

Bob Simmons – Head football coach, Oklahoma State University

Paul E. Smith – Head basketball coach, Dunbar High, Baltimore, Maryland

Aeneas Williams – NFL Arizona Cardinals

Bill Willis – NFL former Cleveland Browns 1946-53; NFL Hall of Fame

Darrell Walker – Former head coach, NBA Toronto Raptors

Steve Wallace – Former NFL San Francisco 49ers

Rudy Washington – Head basketball coach, Drake University; Former basketball Drake University; Former President of Black Coaches Association.

Educational Leaders
Samuel Proctor – former President of Virginia State University

Elected Public Leaders

John L. Conyers – Congressman, California, introduced legislation to make Dr. Martin Luther King's birthday a national holiday

George W. Crockett, Jr. – Congressman, Michigan

Sanford Bishop – Congressman, Georgia

Thomas Bradley – Past Grand Polemarch, Former Mayor of Los Angeles

Mervyn Dymally – Congressman, California

Richard Dixon – Former Mayor, Dayton, Ohio

Walter E. Fauntroy – Congressman, Washington, D.C.

Elihu Harris – Former mayor, Oakland, California

Theodore R. Newman – First Black Chief Justice, Washington, D.C., Court of Appeal

Carl Officer – Mayor, East St. Louis

Clarence Robinson – U.S. Representative (Bridge named in his honor in Chattanooga, Tennesse)

Carl Stokes – First Black mayor, Cleveland, Ohio

Bennie Thompson – Congressman, Mississippi

Nellington Webb – Mayor, Denver

Albert R. Wynn – Congressman, Maryland

Entertainment Leaders

Donald Byrd – Trumpeter and academian

Kenny Burrell – Jazz artist

Cedric the Entertainer – Comedian/Actor "Steve Harvey" Show

Jester Hairston – Actor, "Rolly Forbes" on "Amen" and "Pops" in "I'm Gonna Git You Sucka"

Whitman Mayo – Actor, "Grady" on Sanford and Son

Ray McCampbell – Music artis (The Mac Band)

Gregory D. Ridley Jr. – Artist

Billy Taylor – Jazz Piannist and scholar

Earnest Thomas – Actor, "Roger" on "What's Happening"

Gerald G. Jackson

Entrepreneur Leaders
Edward Gardner – President, Soft Sheen Products, Inc. and *Dollars & Sense* magazine

Robert Johnson – Founder and CEO, Black Entertainment Television (BET)

Reginald E. Lewis – Late CEO, Beatrice International Foods (largest Black-owned business, worth over $ 1 billion)

Maceo Walker – Insurance executive

Carl Ware – Vice president, Coca-Cola Company

Lawyer Leaders
John Brittain – Former Dean of Thurgood Marshall Law School

Johnnie L. Cochran, Jr. – Attorney

Robert L. Harris – Attorney

Alcee Hastings – Congressman, Florida

William Borders – Former President of the National Bar Association

Walter Sutton – Former President of the National Bar Association

Mass Media Leaders
Keith Clinkscales – Former President and CEO, *Vibe* magazine

Mel Reddick – Director, business affairs, CBS Sports

Percy E. Sutton – CEO, Inner City Broadcasting Corp.; owner, Apollo Theater

Travis Smiley – radio and television authority

Medical Leaders
Dr. Therman Evans – Medical doctor and author

Dr. Henry Foster – Surgeon General nominee

Dr. David Stacher – Director, Centers for Disease Control; former president, Meharry Medical School

Military Leader
Daniel James, Jr. – First Four Star Black general, USAF

Religious Leaders
Rev. Calvin O. Butts – Pastor, Abyssinian Baptist Church (largest Black church in the United States), New York City

Rev. Dr. Joseph H. Evans – First Black President, United Church of Christ

Scholars/writers leaders

Lerone J. Bennett, Jr. – Award-winning author, Executive Director, Johnson Publishing Company

Gerald G. Jackson – scholar/author

Leo Lawrence – Producer, "Living Color," "Hangin' With Mr. Cooper," "The Jamie Fox Show," winner 1994 Black Filmmakers Hall of Fame Festival

John Singleton – Director, "Boyz N the Hood," "Poetic Justice," "Rosewood," "Higher Learning"

Houston Baker – scholar/writer

List of Successful Members of Alpha Phi Alpha Fraternity

Activists

Frederick Douglas – Anti-slavery activist

Lester Granger – National Urban League

Dick Gregory – Activist

Martin Luther King, Jr. – Civil Rights activist

Thurgood Marshall – Civil Rights activist, Supreme Court Justice

Adam Clayton Powell – Civil Rights activist

Paul Robeson – Activist, scholar, singer, athlete

Athletes

Quinn Buckner – Former NBA player and coach

Todd Day – Former member of the Boston Celtics

Wes Chandler – Former San Diego Charger

Rosie Grier – Former member of the Los Angeles Rams

Charles Haley – Former member of the Dallas Cowboys

Jesse Owens – Olympic gold medalist

Fritz Pollard – First Black head coach in NFL history

Eddie Robinson – Winningest coach in college football history

Art Shell – Former NFL player and coach for the Oakland Raiders

Gene Upshaw – President, NFL Players Association

Wes Unseld – Former NBA coach and player for the Washington Bullets

Lenny Wilkens – Winningest coach in NBA history

Reggie Williams – Former player for the Cincinnati Bengals

Educational Leaders

James Cheek – Former President of Howard University

Frederick Patterson – Founder, United Negro College Fund

Dr. Ronald J. Temple – Chancellor, City Colleges of Chicago

Elected Public Leaders

Franklin Williams – Phelps-Stokes Fund

Marion Barry – Former Mayor, Washington, DC

Willie Brown – Former Mayor of San Francisco

David Dinkins – Former Mayor of New York City

Chaka Fattah – Congressman

Ernest Finney – Supreme Court Justice, South Carolina

Maynard Jackson – Former Mayor , Atlanta

Earnest "Dutch" Morial – First Black Mayor of ew Orleans

Marc Morial – Present mayor, New Orleans

Julius L. Chambers – NAACP Legal Defense Fund

Andrew Young – Former Mayor of Atlanta/ Former US Ambassador to the UN

Entertainment Leaders

Darryl Bell – Actor

Duke Ellington – Jazz musician and composer

Donny Hathaway – Musician and song writer

Lionel Richie – Singer

Entrepreneur leaders

Keenan Ivory Wayans – Comedian, producer

Doug Bush – Entrepreneur

William Gray – United Negro College Fund/businessman

Eugene Jackson – Black Entertainment Television

John H. Johnson – Owner, *Ebony* and *Jet* Publishing Company

Inventor
Garret Morgan – Invention – traffic signal

Mass Media Leaders
Tony Brown – Journalist/producer

Stuart Scott – ESPN Sports Center anchorman

Chuck Stone – *Philadelphia Daily News*

Medical Leaders
Dr. Lessall D. Leffall – President, American College of Surgeons

James Comer – psychiatrist

Louis Sullivan – Secretary, Health and Human Services

Military Leaders
Roscoe Cartwright – General, US Army

Fred A. Gorden – Brigadier General, US Army

Samuel Gravely – Admiral, US Navy

Benjamin Hacker – Rear Admiral, US Navy

Edward Honor – Major General, US Army

James McCall – Major General, US Army

Winston Scott – Commander, US Navy

Scholars/writers
W.E.B. DuBois – Writer, historian, civil rights activists

John Hope Franklin – Historian

E. Franklin Frazier – Sociologist

Dennis Kimbro – Author

Cornell West – Author

Gerald G. Jackson

Why African-American Fraternities?

An impediment to an increased presence of Black Greeks is the association made between them and the White Greek organizations. It is ironic that Black and White fraternities are viewed as synonymous because they both claim Greek names. To see them as the same, however, is equivalent to viewing African Americans as racially, ethnically, socially and politically identical to European Americans. The data challenging such a position is irrefutably axiomatic. Nevertheless, they have demonstratively distinct histories, based upon the operation of individual, group, and interpersonal and institutional racism. African-American history reveals that they were not warmly received by American institutions of higher education. In 1880 the first African American to attend West Point was dragged from his bed, gagged, bound, severely beaten, and then had his ears slit. The White cadets claimed the African-American cadet did the abuse to himself. Harvard professor Albert Bushnell advocated during a talk before the American Historical Association that lynching should be legalized.

White fraternities and sororities were not any more liberal. In 1923 at the University of Missouri, a lynch mob that included male and female students lynched a Black janitor at the University. One may argue that these schools did not represent the best of the best.[180] At Harvard University, arguably one of the best universities in the United States, in the fall of 1921 five African-American males applied, successfully passed the entrance examination, and were accepted into the first year class. When their racial designation was learned, the students were informed that the president of Harvard ruled that they could not live in the dormitory.[181]

As a consequence of such racist acts and mob behaviors, Black fraternities started as an alternative to the denial of membership in White ones, and as a means of preserving African and African-American cultural values and traditions.[182] The first Black fraternity

---

[180]Ralph Ginzburg (1988). *100 Years of lynching. Maryland*: Black Classic Press.

[181]Raymond Alexander (1823). "Voices from Harvard's own Negroes" (pp. 396–402). In Sondra Wilson (Ed.) (1999). *The opportunity reader: Stories, poetry, and essays from the urban league's opportunity magazine.* New York: Modern Library.

[182]Paula Giddings (1988). *In search of sisterhood.* New York: William Morrow; Lawrence Ross (2000). *The Divine Nine The history of African-American Fraternities and Sororities.* New York: Kinsinger Books.

started at Cornell University prompted by the inability of Black Cornell males to become members in the White fraternities. In a way that is more Africentrically syncretistic, their actions can be seen as a both/and response to institutional racism. They, on the one hand, formed their separate organization in reaction to the racist policy of the White Greek fraternities, and they followed Africentric symbolic models. The Alpha Phi Alpha fraternity used a distinguishing feature of Egyptian symbols to define its scope. If one looks at the roster of the Alpha fraternity, one sees men who spent their life fighting racism and group oppression. Additionally, these men created, invented, taught and managed affairs so that Africans and African Americans would receive justice and equality in the United States and the world.

Similarly, if we look at the roster of Black Greek fraternities, as revealed in several scholarly books,[183] it is apparent that it is a listing of a Who's Who of Black leadership, with a worldly magnitude. Its expanse includes political, social, business, academic, entertainment,and athletic realms. Research by Nikol Alexander-Floyd,suggests a current failure of Black Greeks in the production of political leaders.[184] Her work, however, is flawed by a reliance on Eurocentric concepts. For instance, Black fraternities and sororities need an analysis from an Africentric perspective that would include a look at the institutional and societal roles of African and African-American secret societies for men and women, based upon Eurocentric and Afrocentric culturalism constraints. Akin to the African family, they would be analyzed as a socializing agent, and evaluated in generating societal leaders.[185] This perspective would look also at Rites

---

[183]Lawrence Ross (2000). *The Divine Nine The history of African-American Fraternities and Sororities.* New York: Kinsinger Books; Paula Giddings (1988). *In search of sisterhood.* New York: William Morrow; Ricky Jones (2004). *Black Haze: Violence, sacrifice, and manhood in Black Greek letter Fraternities.* New York: State University of New York; Walter Kimbrough (2003). *Black Greek 101: The culture, customs, and challenges of Black Fraternities and sororities.* New Jersey: Fairleigh Dickinson University Press.

[184]Nikol Alexander–Floyd (2003). "Theorizing Race and Gender in Black Studies: Reflections On Recent Examinations of Black Political Leadership programming and the Alphas." *International Journal of Africana Studies, 9*(1), 57-74.

[185]This characteristic does not preclude them from operating politically as a group and fraternity. The Black Greeks initiated protest against B.E.T.'s Black images. See also Ashley Birt & Boyle, J. (April 29, 2004). "Kappa Alpha Psi stages rally in response to the Natrat material." *The Carnegie Pulse,* pp. 1–4.

of Passage and secret societies for women, and apply this knowledge to the African-American resilience experience.[186]

An Africentric scrutiny of Black leadership indicates a decline in Black male political leadership and other socio-economic indices. Something is amuck; however, it is patent in the arena of Black men. This is particularly the case when we examine the comparative college attendance and graduation rates of Black males and females. Before looking at the college and career situations, an instructive anecdote will give context. I was asked to conduct a workshop to help young Black males see the importance of education and subsequently excel in school and life. The Black male inspirational youth program was organized and conducted by the Black female sorority Delta Sigma Theta.[187]

I initially saw nothing at all wrong with Black women seeing a need and initiating change since I was partly reared by "take charge" Black women and had dated such women from the Alpha chapter of Delta Sigma Theta sorority. In fact, from my Africentric cultural perspective, I was actually pleased that they did not restrict themselves to female issues but operated instead from a more Africentric racial paradigm.[188] My view changed when I started talking to the other male group facilitators and learned they were primarily Black Greeks. How is it, I asked a frat brother, that we are a part of a program we should have been conducting through our "Guide Right" program? He had no definitive answer and we concluded the conversation with "it's a damn shame." The shame was on us and not the Deltas.

Roxanne Roberts (September 27, 2003). The sisterhood, taking on the old boy network

[186]See Nsenga Warfield Coppock (1994). *Images of African Sisterhood: Initiation and Rites of Passage to Womanhood.* Washington, D.C. Baobab Associates; Nsenga Warflied-Coppock & Bertram Atiba Coppock (1990). *Afrocentric Theory and Applications, Volume I: Adolescent Rites of Passage.* Washington, D.C.: Baobab Associates; Nsenga Warfield-Coppock & Bertram Atiba Coppock (1992). *Afrocentric Theory and Application, Volume II: Advances in the Adolescent Rites of Passage.* Washington, D.C.: Baobab Associates.

[187]Paula Giddings (1988). *In search of sisterhood.* New York: William Morrow.

[188]See, Paula Giddings (Ed.) (2002). *Burning all illusions: Writing from the nation on race 1866-2002.* New York: Thunder's Mouth Press. For an illustration of a racial paradigm see, Na'im Akbar (2000). Foreword. In Gerald Jackson's book *Precursors of an African Genesis model of helping.* New York: Global.

With rare exception, Black women comprise the majority of Black students at most co-educational colleges. According to the American Council on Education, barely a quarter of the 1.9 million Black men between the ages of 18-24 were in college in 2000, while 35 percent of Black women in the identical age group were enrolled in higher education. A similar dismal situation holds. Using the N.C.A.A. Division colleges as an example, in 1996 only 35 percent of Black men graduated within 6 years in comparison to 45 percent for Black women, 46 percent for Native American males, and 59 percent for White men. Black Greeks can alleviate these problems if people can get pass myths about them and ideological differences.

Beyond gender, in the 21st century African Americans continue to encounter discriminatory acts, psychological and physical violence, abusive behaviors by White fraternities and sororities, and Cornell is no exception. To help combat negative acts against African Americans, *The Journal of Blacks in Higher Education* maintains a column/section titled "Race Relations on Campus," reminiscent of the data collection that use to be maintained on the frequency of lynching Blacks. Akin to the lynching data, the section is national in scope and devoted to reporting racial incidents at the nation's institutions of higher education.

Black Greeks at a Predominantly White State University

When I entered Kean College (currently Kean University), as a dean in the Student Affairs area, it pleased me to learn that both of my associates were Black Greeks. This meant, I supposed, that they understood how Black Greeks aided the university's social, political, cultural and educational life. I learned that the Black Greeks on campus were in disarray and at odds with various groups. I expected conflict with the White fraternities and their system of governance; however, I did not expect conflict with the Black Student Union political leadership and altercations between Black Greek fraternities. I was baffled by the lenience of the administration, especially when a person could pledge. The frats did not have strong supervision and the thought of such a thing seemed alien. At Howard, you could not pledge until the second semester of your sophomore year and graduate-level and professional Big Brothers were always "spying" on pledges and monitoring induction process behaviors. To bring some immediate semblance of order to the campus milieu, my colleagues and I designed and implemented a variety of programs to resolve conflicts between and within frats. I went as far as writing to the *Black Collegian* magazine. Surprisingly, they published my inquiry, noted below.[189]

> …I am currently working with representatives of Black Greeks on Kean College Campus on ways of working more cohesively and constructively together in an effort to advance academic excellence among themselves and Black students. Your article will definitely facilitate the process we are currently undergoing…

> My primary reason for writing is to gain information on the "unity" plan you mentioned in your article. I would like the Black Greeks on Kean's campus to tie into such a constructive effort.

In the same issue of the *Black Collegian* were letters revealing a more profound subject that relates to the declining significance of Black Greeks. Members of the Malik Sigma Pi fraternity, with such alleged brothers as Dr. Yosef Ben-Jochannan, Gil Nobles (see Sect. I, group III for student essays) and Rev. Herbert Doughtery challenged the Black Greeks to stress their "Africanness" rather than Greekness. A similar critique, made twenty-one years later, suggests that the issue has not abated.[190] For instance, the Shemsu-Heru is viewed as an Egyptian fraternity whose members "strive to embrace the cradle of civilization in Kemet and unveil the mysteries and knowledge of Ancient Africa" (p. 1).

Suggestive even more of an Africentric thrust, an empowerment aim of the Shemsu-Heru group is to change themselves and their environment through group ideological solidarity. It is believed that its increasing popularity is based upon its call to activism and demand for a thorough knowledge of history.[191] Bespeaking much that has been attributed to diunital logic and the African world-view, the group's proposed forum entails:

---

[189]Gerald G. Jackson (February/March, 1982). "Dear Editor." *The Black Collegian*, pp. 26, 27. The situation had escalated to Black Greek altercations. Rather than being role models, the fighting reinforced negative stereotypes and *anti-self* and *alien-self disorders*.

[190]Candace Jones (October 14, 2003). "Shemsu-Heru: On Egyptian Fraternity." *The Hilltop,* p. 1.

[191]See, Khaila Edward (January 23, 2004). "Egyptian fraternity works to fly African flag on the yard." *The Hilltop*, pp. 1, 2.

collective problems and transcend cultural nationalism. The forum will pinpoint issues in the Howard community as well as on an international level. Attendees are also encouraged to bring ideas and comments that complement the issues addressed.

In an Africentric sense, therefore, it is possible to design an organization that fulfills affiliative needs and the criteria of Blackness advanced by Robert Williams. A non-political concern for some might be the appropriateness of the group in an educational institution. Namely, in what ways do such groups support the educational goals and objectives of Institution of Higher Education?

Black Greek Aesthetic as Education

In my days at Howard, the rivalry between the Black Greeks was the fodder that produced Campus Pals, student government leaders, clubs and organization leaders. The dynamic between the groups struggling for supremacy and future members created and instigated many campus social events. This meant the university did not have to pay students, as it is today, to run student programs. Several of these rituals have spilled over to the White campuses. One such event is the Step Show. I was asked to serve as a judge at a Cornell version and before the event commenced, I took pictures of the audience but especially the Kappas because they were not officially on campus.[192]

Specifically addressing the educational dimension, Deven, a student of mine at the time, expounds upon the learning underlying the event and advances the idea that Black Greeks are more than simply social organizations.

Deven S. Gray
April 13, 2003

---

[192]When I first arrived at Cornell, the Kappas were the group that was most visible and seemed to give most of the Black parties. Unfortunately, they committed a transgression that resulted in the National office removing them until 2008. The Kappa spirit is dauntless and Kappas have come from around the country to represent and embellish social and cultural events.

Gerald G. Jackson

Kappas at Greek Freak Night. Photo by Gerald G. Jackson.

Greek Freak - An Educational Experience in Disguise

Initially when planning to attend the 14th Annual Greek Freak Step Show I did not intend to write it up as an educational experience here on campus. However, after attending and seeing the display of the multi-cultural organizations that participated I realized that every experience is educational even if not in an academic setting. You just have to be seeking the messages that are displayed. The audience members, while only seemingly being entertained, were being imparted with academic knowledge both out directly and indirectly.

The most obvious educational information that was being displayed during the show was history. The Fredrick Douglass middle school team though the youngest of the performers where the richest in this aspect, along with being the best and most disciplined performers. They provided useful history about Fredrick Douglass that most people should know including his fight to end slavery and his publication of "The North Star." Other groups provided history on their organization including when they where founded, which I felt was important because it shows that this pride in being a Black women or a Black man is not newly founded, it has a legacy in all those that came before. This was also reiterated when I attended the unveiling show of the spring 2003 line of Cornell's chapter of Delta Sigma Theta Sorority, Incorporated.

I thought the boys' performance was remarkable. It appeared that these 12-14 year olds had practiced and prepared more than the 20-year-old Cornell students. I have to contribute this to the pride in them, in what they were doing and the pride in the history of the influential

Three KAPPAS from different chapters attending a
Cornell campus dance. Photo by Gerald G. Jackson.

African American man that their school was named. The question that
comes to mind when thinking of this group is, Does the visible lack of
preparation and discipline of some of Cornell's groups indicate a lack
of the same pride, appreciation or understanding of their history and the
history of those that came before them in the groups that they have
committed themselves to? As I sat in the audience the only explanation
that I could conceive is that Cornell academics may have stopped some
groups from preparing as much as they could. This to me brings to
mind the dichotomous attitude of the European worldview, it's either
you have good grades and a mediocre performance or you have a good
performance and your academics suffer. There is no dual success.

I also think of the Asian group that performed. They performed
extremely well at an event that in no way entails a portion of their
culture. This brought to mind the idea that was discussed in class about
what people's priorities are. Black students at Cornell always miss
events that would be beneficial because they claim they have no time.
They don't get involved in organizations because they are too busy.
The Asian group had more participants on stage than any of the other
Cornell fraternities or sororities. They even took time in their
performance to welcome back the Alpha's, that no other group did.
This seems to prove the point that Ivy League universities are preparing
scientists and engineers and not leaders. Though some leaders slip
through the cracks, as those two to three people who step up and
represent their organization, this is not enough.[193]

---

[193] She is referring to the Eurocentrically-based lack of participation by some
Black sororities. Some groups did not participate allegedly because they feared

I think that this event was very educationally beneficial for anyone to attend. It was a very good display of the dynamics of minority organizations on campus and although there was not as much representation of some groups as would be desired I hope that others who attended took this as motivation to get involved. There is no reason why a black organization should only have two or three members. People need to step up and commit to doing something other than making the grade.

I want to add to Deven's comments on the Asian participation because she overlooked membership inclusiveness in the Asian fraternity and the role of Black people in the Asian group's significant improvement over previous performances. I observed that the Asian fraternity had a Black male member and learned that the person that served as their choreographer was a Black female student. Reflecting a similar inclusiveness, Cornell Latinos have become members of the Kappa Alpha Psi, Phi Beta Sigma, and Alpha Phi Alpha Black Greek fraternities. Conversely, the Latino fraternities generally have not inducted African-American males into their fraternities.[194]

Strolling as a Black Administrator and Africana Faculty Member[195]

Being a Black Greek is a plus and minus when working with Black Greeks, as can be surmised in terms of diunital logic and Africentric perspective. At Kean, being a Greek enabled me to get creditability as

---

not performing in a superior fashion, thus catering to selfish, individualistic impulses. The Rhos, only two individuals deep, participated because they did not want the entire program to fold. They model the Black Greek and African notions of we-ness, collectivity, interdependence and extended affiliation.

[194]Similarly, at the University of Alabama, the Black Greeks have admitted Whites; however, no Blacks have been allowed into either the fraternities or sororities. On Cornell's campus, Latinos have become members of the Kappa, Alpha and Sigma Black fraternities but the reverse has not been true for the Latino Greeks. Black males have become members of the Asian and White fraternities. See also "Whites in Black sororities and fraternities" (December, 2000). *Ebony*, pp. 172-176.

[195]George Napper (1973). *Blacker than thou*. New York: Erdman Publisher; Anthony Orum (1968). "Black Students in protest." *ASA Publisher*; Joy Williamson (1999). "In defense of themselves." *The Journal of Negro Education*, 66(1), pp. 92–105; Jewelle T. Gibbs (1977). "Black students at integrated collleges: problems and prospects." In Charles V. Willie (Ed.). *Black brown white relations. Race relations in the 1970's*. New Jersey: Transactions Books.

an insider. Being a Kappa, however, had the other groups wondering if I would show favoritism. The passage of time removed doubt but the relationship with my undergraduate brother was more problematic. When a Kappa undergraduate made probation, for instance, speaking to him as a dean produced some strain. In particular, when I observed him informing potential pledges that Kappa stood for excellence, I privately asked him how he could espouse such a philosophy and be on academic probation? After our discussion, I frequently saw him in the library; however, he did not seem as close and stayed away from fraternity matters and functions. I would have hoped that he would have been able to do both, thinking diunitally, but it appears that he needed to dichotomize in order to be successful in his academic work.

As a faculty member at Seton Hall University, my Black Greek membership enabled me to broker in class a conflict between a White fraternity and Black fraternities. The space to discuss differences enabled the White frat male to say, at the close of the Black family class, that he would talk to his brothers about their offensive behaviors. He would do this based upon what he gleaned from the course material and class discussions. It is our charge, as faculty and administrators, to demonstrate what transcendence means in terms of involvement in programs and processes and affiliation with all Black Greeks. Our classroom should be a conscious vehicle for the promotion of the intellectual and cultural awareness of African-American contributions. In some cases the opportunity to inculcate and enlighten is giving as if a gift.

To illustrate, Dr. Robert Harris, Vice President for Faculty Development and Diversity and Associate Professor in Africana Studies at Cornell, asked if I would like the Martin Luther King Jr.

Robert Harris and Ozell Sutton. Photo by Gerald G. Jackson.

Gerald G. Jackson

Commemorative Lecturer to address my class. Following, mind you, an African-based temporal system that is fluid and flexible, I agreed for several reasons. First, the students would have the opportunity to pick the brain of a Black orator who had been with the Little Rock 9 when they entered Central High during the desegregation crisis. He marched with MLK in 1963 and was with Rev. King when Martin was murdered. Second, the selection of the class meant that an Africana class could be special. He was a big gun coming exclusively to lecture to our class.

Third, he was a past president of Alpha Phi Alpha fraternity. The Alphas were not only the first Black Greek fraternal organization, they started at Cornell; thus his presence, along with Bob's, modeled Black

Alpha monument rock at Cornell. Photo by Gerald G. Jackson.

Greek intelligence, mutual support and cooperation, key African world-view cultural attributes.

In Mr. Ozell Sutton's major talk he gave as a solution for the crisis in the Black community shorthand, which he called the four B's. They consisted of: (1) book – meaning education; (2) ballot – meaning political action; (3) buck – meaning reinvestment in the Black community; and (4) Black history – meaning learning about Black heritage in order to be inspired into action. He was not only an eloquent speaker[196] and class lecturer, he presented a controversial concept that

[196]For campus reports see, Franklin Crawford (February 6, 2003). "MLK lecturer inspires with his words and actions." *Cornell Chronicler*, pp. 1, 9; Amy Green (February 4, 2003). "Sutton Speaks on Racism, Human Rights." *The Cornell Daily Sun*, pp. 1, 8.

Cornell campus setting of Alpha monument rock.
Photo by Gerald G. Jackson.

stirred my students and provided a question on a subsequent prelim. He theorized that HBCU (Historically Black Colleges and Universities) were best at producing Black leaders and White schools were best at developing technological skills.[197]

The dichotomy he made between Black and White universities did not appear to alarm the students; however, in a follow-up classroom discussion they expressed grave disagreement. They appeared particularly vexed by the notion that White schools would not prepare them, competitively speaking, to be the best leaders. I knew that, for some, they found it difficult to conceive that a Black school could be superior to a White one in any realm. At the time, the issue was partially settled by having a question on the Prelim that tested their knowledge on the subject and permitted them to explore the notion in greater depth. If such a naturally occurring event had not come forth, I have had Black Greek graduate students present their organization's

---

[197]Viewing itself diunitally, Howard University believes it can do both. Examples: Barbara Murray (Winter, 2000). "Leading the World by Design. Howard University is preparing the next generation of leaders in technology." *Howard Magazine*, pp. 8-13; Ura Bailey & Morris, L. (2002). *One third of a nation: African-American perspectives.* Washington, D.C.: Howard University Press.

key virtues and enlighten the class on how their organization advances *extended self-affirmation* in the African-American community.

Leaving Safe Havens

At the beginning of the 21st century, dressing Hip-Hop is "in" and Black College students follow the trend. Back in the day, we had "Blocks" and "Hustlers" subculture styles but they did not dictate either Black College student fashion or decorum. I entreat my students to be pace setters and assert a leadership that is based on their socio-economic and experiential backgrounds. My campaign with Black Greeks meant the adoption of Africentric cultural and philosophical beliefs.[198] For example, when I was in the training process to become a professional counselor, I was adamantly told that counseling transpired in an office. I was given explicit direction on how to arrange my office for maximum counseling effectiveness. I was perplexed then when African-American students would approach me in the hallway, cafeteria and on the street and actively engage in a counseling dialogue.

I eventually realized that these students felt more comfortable in what was perceived as a neutral setting. My office was my haven and a problematic extension of the institution that was not necessarily their comfort zone. Analogously, I have not confined my instructional ends to the classroom and respond to outside classroom situations as educational extension opportunities. An invitation by Angela Brizant, the head of the local undergraduate AKA chapter, introduces my practice. She invited me to be the keynote speaker at the Skee Week 2003 program. The title of my talk was "Is Cornell's Leadership Effective," and it referred to campus student leadership. Moreover, I could not turn her down because she had been one of my most promising students, my former wife was an AKA, and some of my best dates had been AKA. I not only, therefore, had many connections to AKA but also respected the intellectual and professional drive of such women (e.g., Sharon Pratt, first female mayor of Washington, D.C.). The audience was composed mainly of Alpha Phi Alpha males, although they were not officially recognized on campus. I thought it important to relate to them as an older Black male Greek and accepted an invitation to have dinner with them and a group of AKAs.

I later went to a pre-party gathering and interacted with several pledge lines of Alpha men. It was enlightening and enjoyable. It was

---

[198]Ama Mazama (Ed.) (2003). *The Afrocentric paradigm.* New Jersey: Africa World Press.

GGJ with Alphas. Photo of Gerald G. Jackson.

interesting to observe how boundaries were maintained. They must have told each arriving Alpha that I was a Kappa because no one mistakenly gave me the recognition handshake and most mentioned during a respectful greeting that I was a Kappa. I teased several about them hiding their secret handshake and informed them that I could get their shake after the next line crossed. It was well established that girlfriends, after each pledge line of Black Greeks, would convince their boyfriends that sharing the secret handshake was the deepest admittance of love. All I had to do, I chuckled, was to wait for the next line and then canvas the girlfriends. The joke usually broke the ice because everyone knew it had a big kernel of truth that applied to all Black Greeks. These young men were solid and while they were not Kappas I enjoyed the moment and some even said they would contact me for some career guidance on college teaching.

The group convinced me to attend the party jointly sponsored with an Asian fraternity. I really did not want to attend. I felt, based upon my college days and chaperoning a party at SHU, that I would be perceived by my students as invading their personal space. Besides, I really did not want to sit around alone and watch a room full of people having fun, when I could be in my room studying the programs on B.E.T. It was a great party and I did spend a moment with an AKA faculty member. I pleasantly surprised my Betas and saw a number of students (White, female graduate students) that I did not imagine would be attending. I felt elated when Adrie told me a young man asked who I was and she replied, "he's Professor Jackson, and he's the man." The party also encouraged an Asian sorority to ask the AKA sorority to hold a slumber party with them. The request by the Asian sorority represents a soft approach to increasing intracultural communications and an appreciation of cultural differences and similarities.

Crossing Racial and Gender Boundaries

Cornell has had its share of racial situations, enough to make African Americans culturally paranoid from a "Black rage"[199] conceptualization. Most White Cornellians are not cognizant of the racial encounters experienced by Black Cornellians, and this doctrine of color-blindness is extended into the classroom. The doctrine of color-blindness or racism is confronted when such students enroll in an Africana course where they are the numerical minority. Outsiders perceive them as being in a tenuous situation. Given considerably less examination is the plight of the Black professor. It is common for Black students to note what race gets called on the most, is responded to more in depth and gets the choice assignments. The racial divide is compounded when the student is a White female and the professor is a "handsome" Black male.

In reaction to the campus racial divide, Black students can be led to claim the exclusive rights to the African-American faculty, feeling justified because they do not sense that they have access to the White faculty, to a large degree. It is not just the classroom that Black students expect loyalty, they expect Africana faculty to confine their time to Black programs and events. Being sensitive to the potential reaction of Black students, I accepted nevertheless an invitation to attend a tea given by a White female sorority.

GGJ & Shelby. Photo of Gerald G. Jackson.

Understandably, given America's propensities to segregate residentially, the sorority house was located down the street from the Africana Study building, but I had never really noticed it before because I had restricted myself to Afrospace. What I wanted to model to the class was that it was OK to venture out of one's Afrospace, akin to what I did when I lived for two years in Maine. To represent truth by

Cornell acapella singing group. Photo by Gerald G. Jackson.

example, that it is culturally and racially appropriate to socially interact with Whites, and affirm that such interactions could prove to be educational. I learned that White males appreciate Black music and singing (e.g, a cappella) enough to give performances in this mode.

I learned also that while the sorority was reputedly the "pretty girl" group, they had a page of community and campus development projects (see next pages). In particular, Shelby, who extended me the invitation, represented her classroom group in various roles. As a student in my course, she worked as editor of the electronic book reported in Section II, a member of the J.H. Clarke research project, and contributed as a member in The Future of Black Education group presentation (revealed through the journals of her group members).

---

[199]William Grier and Cobbs, P. (1968). *Black Rage*. New York: Basic Books.

Gerald G. Jackson

We appreciate all that you do as Cornell faculty membes. Delta Gammas give back to the Cornell community in many ways, either as leaders or members of many campus organizations:

Armenian Society
Arts and Sciences Student Advisors
Campus Insights Television Show
Cayuga Medical Volunteers
Cornell Hotel Society
Circle K
Cornell Alumni House
Cornell Coalition of Animal Defense
Cornell Daily Sun
Cornell Design League
Cornell Dining Ambassadors
Cornell EMS
Cornell Fitness Center
Cornell Fund
Cornell Hotel Society
Cornell Theater
Cornell Tradition
Food Science Club
Golden Key Honor Society
Ho-Nun-Do-Kah
Hotelies Volunteering Today
Hotel Ezra Cornell
Hotel School Admissions Crew
Hugh O'Brian Youth Leadership Organization
Human Ecology Alumni Board
Independent Film Makers
Institute of Biological Engineering
International Facility Management Association
Johnson Art Museum Intern
Kappa Omicron Nu
Lab and Teaching Assistants
National Society of Collegiate Scholars
New Living Voices
Order of Omega
Panhellenic Health Advisory Team (PHAT)

Panhellenic Council
Public Relations Society of America
Society for India
Society of Human Resources
Society of Women in Engineering
Student Government
Student Health Alliance
Varsity Athletics – Lacrosse, Equestrian
team, Swimming, Diving, Field Hockey,
Track, Soccer, Crew, Cheerleaders
Women in Business
Women in Communication

Thank you for attending our Faculty Tea. We understand that your time is limited and hope you can accept this event as a small token of our appreciation for your contributions to our lives!

Gerald G. Jackson

Black and Brown Together: Great Prospects

While greater attention is given nationwide to Black and Latino relationships, the subject is fraught with cultural biases. The predominant Eurocentric analytical thinking mode in the USA postulates conflicts and potential conflicts between the purportedly distinct groups.[200] Unaware of conceptual modes other than a Eurocentric one, a new generation of journalists, scholars and political writers are naively examining the topic of Black and Latino relationships. They do so, as if it were a topic that has just evolved, when proposals for successful human relations efforts are perennial,[201] especially in Black newspapers, magazines and journals.[202] The danger in this rediscovery of the subject is the way it is

---

[200]See Gerald Jackson (2004*). Njikoka: Towards an Africentric paradigm of helping*. New Jersey: Africa World Press.

[201]James Jennings (1994). "Changing Urban Policy Paradigms: Impact of Black and Latino Coalitions" (pp. 3-16). In James Jennings (Ed.). *Blacks, Latinos, and Asians in urban America.* Connecticut: Praeger; Manning Marable (1994). "Building coalitions among communities of color: Beyond racial identity politics" (pp. 29–44). In James Jennings (Ed.). *Blacks, Latinos, and Asians in urban America.* Connecticut: Praeger; Daniel Osuna (1994). "Blacks and Chicanos: Parallels in political and historical struggles" (121-128.). In James Jennings (Ed.). *Blacks, Latinos, and Asians in urban America.* Connecticut: Praeger; Juanita Tamayo Lott (1994). "Blacks and Latinos in the United States: The emergence of a common agenda" (pp. 47-56). In James Jennings (Ed.). *Blacks, Latinos, and Asians in urban America.* Connecticut: Praeger; Samuel Betances (1993). "African-Americans and Hispanic/Latinos: Eliminating barriers to coalition building." In Stanley Battle (Ed.). *The State of Black Hartford.* CT: The Urban League of Greater Hartford, Inc.

[202]Karen J. Carrillo (February 5 – February 11, 2004). "Black/Latino Caucus pushing for Afro-Latino Resolution." *The New York Amsterdam News*, p. 7; (December 18 – December 24, 2003). "Colombian Afro-Latinos offer rights alliance to African-Americans." *The New York Amsterdam News*, p. 2; (September 19 – September 25, 2002). "Last year's Miss Honduras says racism derailed her winnings." *The New York Amsterdam News*, p. 5.
They have been vanguard also in exposing racial struggles of Blacks in Brazil, Central America and Cuba. See David Hellwig (1998). "The African-American press and United States involvement in Cuba, 1902 – 1912" (pp. 70–84). In Lisa Brock & Fuertes, D. (1998). *Between Race and empire: African-Americans and Cubans before the Cuban revolution.* Pennsylvania: Temple University Press; Lamont Muhammad (October/November, 2001). "Invisible: Blacks in Mexico." *Black Diaspora*, pp. 26-27; Lori S. Robinson (1994). "the two faces of Brazil" (pp. 318-323). In George E. Curry (Ed.). (2003). *The best of emerge magazine.* New York: Ballantine Books. See Lori

packaged as a problem based upon numbers and not its philosophical base which is Eurocentric dichotomous reasoning.[203] Similarly, James Jennings, writing in *CRITICA*, the Journal of Puerto Rican Policy & Politics, wrote:

> Tensions among Black, Latinos and Asians are worsening, no question, but don't count on this news media to clarify and illuminate the real roots of racial and ethnic friction. In general, reports on race relations has only tended to reduce complex relationships to simplistic formulas that literally paint race relations in black and white terms.[204]

In actuality, even when numbers suggest an alliance,[205] a focus on numbers alone overlooks an African cultural base to an alliance model based upon a history of cooperation, especially between African Americans and Afro-Latinos.[206] Included in this Afro-Latino group would be Black Puerto Ricans, Afro-Mexican, Afro-Cubans, and other Afro-Latino groups.[207] Similarly, a Eurocentric dichotomous approach makes a split based upon the race of a group that is classified as ethnic.[208] Different in objective, an Africentric analytic mode is a

---

S. Robinson (1999). "Cuba and Blacks" (pp. 473-478). In George E. Curry (Ed.) (2003). *The best of emerge magazine.* New York: Ballantine Books.

[203] E. Ablorh-Odjidja (December, 2003). "USA Black power loses political base." *New African*, 62, 63; Mireya Navarro (January 17, 2004). "Blacks and Latinos try to find balance in touchy new math." *The New York Times*, pp. 1-4; Lori Robinson (January/February 2004). "Wedded to the Cause." *The Crisis Reader*, pp. 34-39; Van Gosse (1998) "The African American press greets the Cuban revolution" (266–280). In Lisa Brock & Fuertes, D. (1998). *Between Race and empire: African-Americans and Cubans before the Cuban revolution.* Pennsylvania: Temple University Press.

[204] James Jennings (July, 1996). "Cooling the heat in race relations." *CRITICA: Journal of Puerto Rican Thought and Policy*, p. 3.

[205] Lori Robinson, Cuadros, P. & Tate, A. (January/February, 2004). "Strength in numbers." *The Crisis Reader*, pp. 26-32.

[206] Juan Flores (January 2, 2003). "Afro-Latino cultures in the United States." http.www.Africana com/ Articles/tt.78.5htm., pp. 1-6.

[207] Lisa Brock & Digna Castaneda Fuertes (Eds.) (1998). *Between race and empires. Africans and Cubans before the Cuban revolution.* Pennsylvania: Temple University Press.

[208] Clara Rodriguez (2000). *Changing race. Latinos, the census, and the history of ethnicity in the United States.* New York: New York University Press;

problem-resolution one.[209] Specifically, this approach seeks solutions to contemporary problems based upon a historically, multidisciplinary and contextually based approach.[210] For example, people who have traditionally been links between Blacks and Latinos, such as Louis Reyes Rivera, are not given the opportunity to acquire prerequisite academic credentials. Mr. Rivera, who has been designated the Poet Laureate of Brooklyn, trained a cadre of students that subsequently went to Columbia School of Journalism; however, his application was rejected.[211] A more popularly known example is Amiri Baraka. He was denied a professorship at Rutgers-Newark, despite his international acclaim as a scholar. They are thwarted, therefore, from positions where they can earn a living as a professor that dispenses portions of Africentric knowledge.

As an alternative, Black Greeks have inducted Latinos into their organizations, and Latina sororities have inducted African-American women, formed campus political alliances, and coalitions. Few works have explored the role Greek organizations may play in the resolution of Black and Latino conflicts and in advancing institutions that affirm cultural differences and similarities. To elaborate, I first became professionally aware of Black and Brown situations when I was Associate Director of Yale Summer High School, at Yale University. The dilemma between these two groups was witnessed through either behaviors or expressions of Chicano students. The YSHS administration

---

Bernestine Singley (2002). *When race becomes real. Black and White writers confront their personal histories.* Illinois: Lawrence Hill. Juan Gonzalex (2000). *Harvest of Empire. A history of Latinos in America.* New York: Viking.

[209]See Robert Hill (1997). *The strengths of the African-American familes: Twenty-five years later.* Washington, DC: R& B Publishers.

[210]Juan Flores (2002). "Islands and enclaves: Caribbean Latinos in historical perspective" (pp. 59–74). In Marcelo Suarez-Orozco & Mariela Paez (Eds.). *LATINOS Remaking America.* California: University of California Press; John Florez (1971). "Chicanos and coalitions as a force for social change." *Social Casework,* 52(5), pp. 269–273; Charles Henry (1980). "Black-Chicano coalitions: Possibilities and problems." *Western Journal of Black Studies,* 4(4), pp. 222-231; Maulana Karenga (1997). "Black and Latino relations: Context, challenge, and possibilities" (pp. 189-204). In Ishmael Reed (Ed.). *Multiamerica. Essays on cultural wars and cultural peace.* New York: Penguin Books; Roberto Rodriguez & Gonzales, P. (1997). "Black/Brown relations: An unnecessary conflict" (pp. 246–256). In Ishmael Reed (Ed.). *Multiamerica. Essays on cultural wars and cultural peace.* New York: Penguin Books.

[211]Herb Boyd (January 8 – January 14, 2004). "The poet laureate of Brooklyn." *The New York Amsterdam News,* p. 28.

was made aware that programs based upon economics (poor whites) and race (Blacks) were not totally suitable for Chicanos.[212]

As Director of the Transitional Program at Yale, I was directly confronted by Chicano graduate student leaders who wanted, among a host of things, for the selection of students to be based solely on a national sample of students. This admission approach would have meant virtually no Puerto Rican students in future TYP programs. Later, there would be another confrontation; however, in this instance the Chicano students demanded a higher percentage of Chicano students. The issue here was not the traditional Black/White dichotomy but a Chicano/Puerto Rican split. I recognized that the Puerto Rican students selected from New Haven were not as strong academically as the Chicano ones but my decision was not based only on grades and traditional indices of achievement and need. In addition, I had been asked by local Puerto Rican leaders to secure slots denied them in the past. They bemoaned the low number of Puerto Ricans gaining access to Yale from the surrounding community and revealed how difficult it was to get students to remain in school through elementary school. This was my first exposure to the complexities involved even in Brown/Brown relationships but was not my first contact with Latinos.

The Latino community was a familiar area to me before coming to Cornell. I spent half my childhood living in a partly Hispanic East Harlem described by Piri Thomas[213] and partly in an Italian-American area written about by Robert Orsi.[214] In addition, I worked with Latino students as an administrator and counselor in compensatory education programs, as a college professor and Dean of Students at several institutions of higher education.[215] I did not expect that teaching in the Africana Studies Center at Cornell, however, would entail significant involvement with Latino students. I expected, given a spiritual

---

[212]See Alphonso Lopez (August 13, 1969). "Vacations are over...Are you Glad." *The Tower*. In Gerald G. Jackson (2000). *Precursor of an African genesis model of helping*. New York: Global Publications.

[213]Piri Thomas (1967). *Down these mean streets*. New York: Signet.

[214]Robert Orsi (2002). *THE MADONNA OF 115TH STREET Faith and Community in Italian Harlem, 1880-1950* (2nd edition). Connecticut: Yale University Press.

[215]At Kean University, for example, I received Certificates of Appreciation from the Puerto Rican Organization for Unity and Development and the Cuban Committee at Kean College.

connection to Latino Diaspora groups,[216] that a ceremonial and *simpatico* relationship might exist. This would certainly have been the case if it had not been for the intervention of Erika Ruiz into my life experiences and subsequent plans. Her actions and role may very well outline the concrete ways that African Americans, Blacks, Afro-Latinos and Latinos may build role modeling group and personal relations. In addition, her psychological identity growth and group solidarity behavior clearly reveal the potential of Black psychology models for Latinas and a heuristic value for American Africans and Diaspora Pan-African-Americanism.[217]

I am uncertain about how my crossing the subculture divide is viewed by Blacks, Whites and Latino males. My students typically know I am a Faculty Fellow for Omega Phi Beta sorority, Inc. but I have little idea why I selected to become one. After my selection, I was asked to assume a similar position with a Black sorority. More broadly, I can be seen at the annual Greek Freak Step Show judging the contest and supporting my Kappa undergraduate brothers. If one is focusing on me long enough, then one will see me embracing other fraternity and

---

[216]George Brandon (1997). *Santeria from Africa to the New World. The dead sell memories*. Indiana: Indiana University Press; Angel Jorge (1993). *La madama francesita: A new world Black spirit* (pp. 205-222). In Joseph E. Harris (Ed.). *African Diaspora* (2nd edition). Washington, D.C.: Howard University Press; Bennetta Jules-Rosette (1981). "Creative spirituality from Africa to America: Cross-cultural influences in contemporary religious forms." *Western Journal of Black Studies*, pp. 273–279.

[217]It helps such relationships to have Latino friends and colleagues that call you **Hermano** and Latino friends and confidants who are also scholars. Throughout the years I have been given a wealth of information by Dr. Wilfredo Nieves and exposed to the state-of-the-art thinking by Dr. Juan Flores, Dr. Marilyn Aquirre Molina and Dr. Lillian Comas-Diaz. For example, Lillian's work includes: (1994). "LatiNegra: Mental health issues of African Latinas." *Journal of Feminist Family Therapy*, 5, ¾, 35-74; (1992) "The future of psychotherapy with ethnic minorities." *Psychotherapy*, 29, 88-94; (1991) "Feminism and diversity in psychology: The case of woman of color." *Psychology of Women Quarterly*, 15, 597-609; (1988) "Mainland Puerto Rican women: A sociocultural approach." *Journal of Community Psychology*, 16, 21-36; (1987) "Feminist therapy with mainland Puerto Rican women." *Psychology of Women Quarterly*, 11, 461-474; (1986) "Puerto Rican alcoholic women: Treatment considerations." *Alcoholism Treatment Quarterly*, 3, 47-57; with Duncan, J. W. (1985). "The cultural context: A factor in assertive training with mainland Puerto Rican women." *Psychology of Women Quarterly*, 9(4), 463-476.

Betas steppin' on Slope Day. Photo by Gerald G. Jackson.

sorority members. I am not especially selective in my focus and aim to advance group cooperation. When I attended the Step Show, for instance, I applauded all groups including the Betas and the sole Kappa.

Epitomizing diunital thinking, I like all the groups for the peculiar cultural traditions they bring to the Greek rituals and relish their capacity to make their events both serious and joyous. For example, a day after the 2003 Greek Freak the Betas Cosponsored a cookout with a Black and Puerto Rican social organization called The LINK. It was fun viewing the inner-child of the students being revealed.

However, I was especially impressed with the panel on Life after Cornell. It consisted of Black and Latina Alumni who voluntarily returned to share their experiences and insights about the world of work. They provided invaluable first-hand information on the appropriateness of the preparation for work that they received from

Overview picture of Kappa steppin'. Photo by Gerald G. Jackson.

317

Gerald G. Jackson

Rosie jumping Double Dutch. Photo by Gerald G. Jackson.

Cornell. With humility they reported on their current career aspirations, based upon their job experiences. They not only provided relevant information but also fostered a belief in the interest of alumni in the growth and development of undergraduates.[218]

Consistent with the theme of the current section on Black Greek relationships and outside-classroom learning, I will discuss my relationship with Omega Phi Beta Sorority, Inc.[219] as an outgrowth of an Africentric cultural approach to self-knowledge and extended self. Before getting into the substantive material, let me keep it real about

---

[218]The VP for Undergraduate Education created and hired someone to direct an Alumni Student Mentoring Program. I hope that this person will take advantage of the student/alumni energy that already exists.

[219]According to the Nu Chapter of Omega Phi Beta Sorority, this chapter was "established at Cornell University by four women on May 28, 1999: Dawn 'Perseverencia' Brawley, Yadira 'Sabio' Perez, Dorothy 'Manicato' Rivera, and Marcy 'Apasionada' Lopez. They chartered the organization at Cornell because of the apathy towards Latinas and Women of Color on their campus. It is the first Ivy League Chapter of Omega Phi Beta." The cause of their chapter is **Child Welfare** and their signature events are: *Crayon Carnival* – program for children from Ithaca, a day of food, games, rides and performances that is free to the public; *Domestic Violence Brunch* – it is in honor of Domestic Violence Awareness month and the brunch is to bring awareness to this social disease. The proceeds from this event go to an organization that combats domestic violence; *Youth Leadership Conference*-high school students from NYC visited the campus and received admissions and financial aid workshops, campus tours and camaraderie. The aim of the conference was to empower underrepresented students to pursue a higher education; *Freaky Feast* – this annual October fundraiser provides home-cooked food and a scary movie.

Marcy at picnic. Photo by Gerald G. Jackson.

my age and race difference from the group. I had no ulterior motives, as a heterosexual Black male professor, scholar and diversity consultant. I will grant that I am good-looking but I am also an old Black male with a fatherly, political and social interest in the group. I am also brilliant, humorous, caring, hardworking, supportive and dedicated. What has maintained my affinity towards the group has been the way it personifies the concept of diunitality and its members freely express their affection for me and my role in the development of individuals. In addition, they allow me to experience diversity, a factor that enabled me to stay tuned to my philosophy. They can be artistic, as in a Step Show, and political and social, as in their program on violence and participation in a Washington, DC. March.

The Dominican group and Beta representative at DC March.
Photo by Kenneth Glover.

They are Latinas but not exclusively so.[220] They conduct programs with Ujamaa, a residential college for primarily Black students, the LINK, and Delta Sigma Theta Black sorority. They are bold, as when Marcy Lopez invited me to their national convention, the only male present, and receiving the honor. She did not hide me in the back but sat me at the chapter table in front of her podium. To remove any doubt about my presence, she declared to the group why this special man was present. The group's applauds, and the one-on-one personal thanks gave me a sense of gratitude that I will never forget. Participating in the program enhanced my desire to continue the struggle to get gender groups, races and ethnic groups to appreciate their differences and work harmoniously together.[221]

Marcy, GGJ and Jackie at Omega Phi Beta National Convention banquet.
GGJ first male invited to attend this august sorority meeting.

---

[220] I met African-American women members at their national convention and the organization had non-Latina founders. In their notes on the benefits of becoming a member they proclaimed: "As part of serving and educating through our diversity we embrace the cultural diversity in our membership. We learn to embrace our heritage and traditions as that of others."

[221] The Nu chapter leadership continued into the next year and Jackie co-chaired the 15th year National Convention. It was titled "Celebrating Our Past, Mapping Our Future," and included family and friends. The inclusion of family and friends reminded me much more of a Latino event. I sat at a table that included the keynote speaker, Sandra Guzman, author of the *Latina Bible*, Betas and dates, and the mother and father of Marcy Lopez. Watching her parents dance reminded me of the beauty of lasting marriages. Watching her mother joyously dance with Betas showed that generation differences in age can be surmounted. Watching a little girl dance playfully with a Beta, spoke to role models for youth of the subtle kind. The food, poetry, lectures and music were all great and indicative of a culture that speakers repeatedly noted as being the by-product of African, European and Indigenous cultures.

Beta group picture. Photo by Gerald G. Jackson.

I am not clear about why I was asked to be a Faculty Fellow.[222] What I know is the process leading up to the request and the experiences since becoming a member. I first met Erika in my First Year Writing Seminar entitled "Black Is, Black Ain't." The behavior she exhibited would have easily placed her in what Dr. William Cross, in his model of Black Psychological Identity,[223] called the Pre-Encounter Stage. For instance, she expressed delight in going to the Puerto Rican day parade and waving an American flag. At the same time, she was very open to discussing and writing about racism, colorism and the elevation of European phenotypic characteristics among Puerto Ricans, very touc hy subjects that many Puerto Ricans are not comfortable verbalizing.[224] My class benefited greatly from her openness and essay that included a famous poem about internalized

---

[222]In the faculty and staff support section of their brochure they wrote: "Professor Gerald G. Jackson, Faculty Fellow. Professor Jackson is an Assistant Professor in the Africana Studies & Research Center. He provides us with much guidance and support in our sorority activities and personal endeavors. He is also a brother of Kappa Alpha Psi Fraternity, Inc."

[223]William Cross (1991). *Shades of Black Diversity in African-American identity*. Pennsylvania: Temple University Press.

[224]For a detailed discussion, see Samuel Betances (1973). "The prejudice of having no prejudice in Puerto Rico: Part II." *The Rican*. 3, 22-37; Samuel Betances (1972). "The prejudice of having no prejudice in Puerto Rico: Part I." *The Rican. 2*, 41-54.

racism among Puerto Ricans.[225] It prompted much soul-searching and a lecture by an Afro-Puerto Rican graduate student on Afro-Puerto Ricans.[226] By being self-critical, she deepened the writing seminar and other students' introspection about their race and ethnic group identity. Specifically, she triggered discourses on the pervasiveness of racism and sparked discussions of internalized oppression among Africans, Jews and Asian students in the class.

At the close of the class, therefore, I had developed a high regard for her strength of conviction and willingness to write and be candid about herself and her beliefs. I did not perceive a mentoring relationship evolving from the course since I harbored more militant views about the plight of Puerto Ricans and did not want to falsely influence her outlook and stance. I gave her a conventional farewell and gave her an obligatory invitation to stop by and chat. I did not expect to see her in any additional Africana courses and believed our paths would only cross by accident.

The following summer, she later recounted, she had what I believe Dr. Cross would call an "Encounter." She worked at the Bronx zoo and proudly wore her Cornell Jersey. She mentioned the pain she felt when a customer noted that he had attended Cornell but did not make a personal connection to her, based upon the same alma mater. The comfort and fellowship she expected was granted not from a Cornellian but from a Yale Latina also working at the Bronx zoo. When she returned to school she informed me that she was no longer going to criticize people, meaning Puerto Ricans, which she did not know very well. She was moving, I ruminated, towards a love and appreciation of her people.

---

[225] In an article by Seth Kugel on the growing popularity of South Bronx spots, the power of this poem is revealed again. According to Kugel, "The first poem, performed in both Spanish and English (with translations by the associate director, Alvan Colon), was 'And Your Grandma, Where's She At?'" It told the story of a family ashamed of their dark-skinned grandmother. Mr. Merced mesmerized the crowd with an energy level so high that his eyes seemed ready to burst from his head. The audience chanted along with the Caribbeanized Spanish version of the title: 'Y Tu Abue a, A'onde Ehta?' Seth Kugel (January 30, 2004). "In the South Bronx, the Arts Beckon." *The New York Times.*

[226] After the lecture, Milagro Denis, a master's level graduate student in the Africana Research Center, revealed personal and observable cases of racism in Puerto Rico, and a feeling of alienation from the Latinos at Cornell. She is ABD at Howard University. For a more detailed look at the essays written by the students, see Gerald Jackson. *Njikoka: Towards an Africentric Paradigm of Helping* (2005). New Jersey: Africa World Press.

Marcy & Rahim. Photo by Gerald G. Jackson.

What I expressed though was elation at her insight and prodded her to keep me informed of her insights and progressive actions.

During the ensuing academic year, she became deeply involved in the Latino community at Cornell. She started writing articles that demanded a change in the definition of a Latina and her poetry developed to such an extent that she was invited to present at the Nuyorican Poets café in New York City. She became a member of the Omega Phi Beta sorority and one of its leaders. She took me for another course and had several of her sorority sisters take my course along with her.

Jackie in classroom observing Erika's group do their group presentation.
Photo by Gerald G. Jackson.

As a part of her group presentation requirement, she applied the Cross Model to her development since arriving at Cornell University. I was utterly amazed by how much her thoughts and actions paralleled and supported Cross' model of the "Immersion" Stage of psychological development. His model did not address Spanish-Speaking people of the Caribbean,[227] in particular, or Afro-Latinos, inclusive of Mexican and Latin Americans, in general. I did not presume a fit because of cultural differences practiced by Spanish versus English enslavers and African cultural destroyers. I was aware of an unmatched Afro-Cuban cultural heritage,[228] distinct consciousness of Afro-Puerto Ricans,[229] Latin American disdain for the form of Spanish spoken by Puerto Ricans, and increasing works on Blacks in Latin America and the Caribbean.[230] Similarly, I was well aware of the cultural prohibition

---

[227]David Geggus (2003). "The Influence of the Haitian Revolution on Blacks in Latin America and the Caribbean" (pp. 38–59). In Nancy P. Naro (Ed.) (2003). *Blacks, Coloureds and National Identity in Nineteenth-Century Latin America.* England: Institute of Latin American Studies; Franklin Knight (2003). "Blacks and the Forging of National Identity in the Caribbean, 1840 – 1900" (pp. 81–94). In Nancy P. Naro (Ed.) (2003). *Blacks, Coloureds and National Identity in Nineteenth-Century Latin America.* England: Institute of Latin American Studies.

[228]Louie Perez (2001). "Politics, peasants and people of color: The 1912 'Race War' in Cuba reconsidered" (pp. 171–194). In Emory Tolbert (Ed.). *Perspectives on the African Diaspora* (2nd edition, volume 1). New York: Houghton Mifflin Company.

[229]Juan Flores (2000). *From bomba to hip-hop: Puerto Rican culture and Latino identity.* New York: Columbia University Press; Juan Flores (1993). *Divided borders: essay on Puerto Rican identity.* Texas: Arte Publico Press; Alberto Sanchez (1997). "Puerto Rican identity up in the air: Air migration, I't a cultural representations, and Me 'Cruzando el charco.'" In Frances Negron-Muntaner & Grosoguel, R. (Eds.) *Puerto Rican Jam: Essay on culture and politics* (pp. 189–208). Minnesota: Univesity of Minnesota Press; Nancy P. Naro (Ed.) (2003). *Blacks, Coloureds and National Identity in Nineteenth-Century Latin America.* England: Institute of Latin American Studies; Ibrahim Sundiata (2001). *Puerto Rico and Africa: The ambiguity of Diaspora* (pp. 195-208). In Emory Tolbert (Ed.). *Perspectives on the African Diaspora* (2nd edition, Volume I). New York: Houghton Mifflin Company.

[230]Norman Whitten & Torres, A. (Eds.) (1998). *Blackness in Latin America and the Caribbean* (Volume I). Indiana: Indiana University Press; A Torres & Norman Whitten (Eds.) (1998). *Blackness in Latin America and the Caribbean* (Volume II). Indiana: Indiana University Press.

against discussing racism among Latinos.[231] It was not clear, then, if Black psychology models could be applied to Afro-Latinos' realities.

What was apparent was my return to thinking as an African-American psychologist. My Africana psychologist side kicked in and rather than continue to sit back and observe, as I had been taught by my Eurocentric psychology and counseling professors, I invited her to dinner. Erika accepted my invitation and asked if she could bring her sisters. I had no idea that I was being interviewed to be a Faculty Fellow. I learned her hidden agenda when she subsequently told me that the group wanted me to be its Faculty Fellow. I was flattered. I was transcending differences in age, race, gender, schooling, religion and income. I had no idea at the time that the group really expected me to be a part of them and do group and individual work. I attended their events and they bounced ideas off me from how to deal with all types of men, career strategies and how to attract members to the sorority.

Consistent with the Cross model for the Immersion Stage, Erika found the traditional classroom format was not enough and elected to pursue an independent research under my tutelage. In her statement of purpose, Erika wrote:[232]

> The topic that I would like to study independently is African-American women's self-image perception. I would like to delve into how women perceive their own and other

---

[231]Minority Rights Group (Ed.) (1995). *No longer invisible. Afro-Latin Americans today*. United Kingdom: Minority Rights Publishing Group. Richard Jackson (1997). *Black writers and the Hispanic canon*. New York: Twayne Publishers; Arlene Torres & Whitten, N. (Eds.) (1998). *Blackness in Latin America and the Caribbean* (Volume II). Indiana: Indiana University Press; Peter Wade (1997). *Race and ethnicity in Latin America*. Virginia: Pluto Press; Norman Whitten & Torres, A. (Eds.) (1998). *Blackness in Latin America and the Caribbean* (Volume I). Indiana: Indiana University Press; Norman Whitten (1998). "Ritual enactment of sex roles in the Pacific lowlands of Ecuador-Colombia." In Norma Whitten & Torres, A. (Eds.) *Blackness in Latin America and the Caribbean* (pp. 168-182). (Vol. 1). Indiana: Indiana University Press; G. Yager (Ed.) (1994). *Confronting change, challenging tradition: Women in Latin American history*. Delaware: A Scholarly Resources, Inc.; Silvio Torres-Saillant (2002). "Epilogue: Problematic paradigms: Racial diversity and corporate identity in the Latino community" (pp. 435–456). In Marcelo Suarez-Orozco & Mariela Paez (Eds.). *LATINOS Remaking America*. California: University of California Press.

[232]Independent study, "All the Drama: Black Hair in America," submitted May, 2002.

women's beauty. The focus I would like to take is on views of skin color, hair texture, and community surroundings. I believe these to be important factors in the perception of beauty for any woman, especially one of color.

There are many reasons why I have chosen this topic. One reason is that I identify with African-American women to some extent. I am often perceived as a woman with distinct African features even though I am Puerto Rican. In the Puerto Rican community there are similar feelings on straightness of hair and lightness of skin. Their peers see those who possess these features as more beautiful.

Another reason that I have chosen to study this topic is because I am curious about how black women see themselves as compared to other kinds of women. Black women are a minority in American society so therefore the standards of beauty in their society are not going to be modeled after the average black woman. The shape and image will be that of the average white woman. This particularly interests me because many statistics show that white women are more likely than black women to have eating disorders and have lower self esteem. So I would like to know more contritely what it is that makes the black woman feel beautiful and what makes others think that black women are beautiful.

I was impressed by her desire to include Black women as potential role models in her inquiry about identity, and good about the Africentric slant. Her trek reminded me of the monopoly game. She did not stop at the Latin American,[233] Lesbian/bisexual,[234] Puerto

---

[233]Daniel Balerston, & Guy, D. (Eds.) (1997). *Sex and sexuality in Latin America.* New York: New York University Press; D. Patai (1994). "Jorge Amado: Champion of women's sexual freedom." In G. Yeager (Ed.). *Confronting change, challenging tradition: Women in Latin American history* (pp. 55-65). Delaware: A Scholarly Resources, Inc.; Joel Streicker (1998). "Policing boundaries: race, class, and gender in Cartagena, Colombia." In Norma Whitten & Torres, A. (Eds.). *Blackness in Latin America and the Caribbean* (pp. 78-310) (Vol. 1). Indiana: Indiana University Press; Luis Urrea (1996). "Whores." In Ray Gonzalez (Ed.). *Muy macho: Latino men confront their manhood* (pp. 99-110). New York: Bantam Doubleday Dell.
[234]Daniel Balerston (1997). "Excluded middle? Bisexuality in Dona Herlinda y su hijo." In Daniel Balerston & Guy, D. (Eds.). *Sex and sexuality in Latin American* (pp. 190-199). New York: New York University Press; Gladys Jimenez-Munoz (1995). "Joining our differences: The problems of Lesbian

Rican,[235] or even Black Puerto Rican woman box.[236] Her stance, I speculated, was that she wanted to learn how African-American women concocted or defined a positive self concept in a land that rewarded women for having European physical features. Apparently struck by actual African-American women with positive self-concepts and African physical features, I conjectured that she wanted to know how they sustained themselves when they did not have the favored hair, nose, lips, buttock and skin color. I did not claim expertise on the matter, I supported her inquisitiveness and provided the space and opportunity for her to explore a monumental subject. I provided books, dialogues and even observations from attending workshops on Black women and hair.

The resultant paper was seminal and timely because of an increasing amount of literature in psychology on the psychological problems of Black women stemming from hair and the types of psychotherapy approaches used to assist them, and a political contest resulting from suing for being overcharged to get their type of hair fixed.[237] She pursued this subject and germane topics, experiences and

---

subjectivity among women of color." In Carole Davies (Ed.). *Moving beyond women's boundaries: Black women's diasporas* (pp. 112–124) (Vol. 2). New York: New York University Press\; Roger Lancaster (1997). "Gusto performance: Notes on the Transvestism of everyday life." In Daniel Balderston & Guy, D. (Eds.). *Sex and sexuality in Latin America* (pp. 9–32). New York: New York University Press; Juanita Ramos (1995). "Latin American Lesbians speak on Black identity" (pp. 57–77) (Vol. 2). In Carole Davies (Ed.). *Moving beyond women's boundaries: Black women's diasporas.* New York: New York University Press.

[235] Edna Acosta-Belen (1986). *The Puerto Rican woman Perspectives on culture, history, and society* (2nd edition). Connecticut: Praeger.

[236] Julia De Burgos (1995). "Ay Ay Ay for the kinky Black woman." In Roberto Santiago (Ed.). *Boricuas: Influential Puerto Rican Writing – an Anthology* (pp. 80–81). New York: Ballantine Publishing Group; Angela Jorge (1986). "The Black Puerto Rican woman in contemporary American society." In Edna Acosta-Belen (Ed.). *The Puerto Rican woman Perspectives on culture, history, and society* (2nd edition). Connecticut: Praeger.

[237] For example, see Milele Archibald (2003). "Why the hair styles of the 1940's?: More about hair" (pp. 197-200). In Daudi Azibo (Ed.). *African-centered psychology.* North Carolina: Carolina Academic Press; Kamau Imarogbe (2003). "Hair misorientation: Free your mind and your hair will follow" (pp. 201-220). In Daudi Azibo (Ed.). *African-centered psychology.* North Carolina: Carolina Academic Press; Ayana Byrd & Tharps, ??(2001). *Hair story.* New York: St. Martin's Press; Meri Banquah (2003). "Afro-Kinky

social interests without professing that she was Black, African-American or Afro-Latina. Despite the absence of a clear new racial group self-definition, she was stepping outside of her Latina comfort zone to acquire cultural knowledge from the Black/African-American experience. In her newly found collective self as a Beta, she extended her learning to include projects for the group, a clear manifestation of the Africentric notion of extended self.

One noteworthy event was attending a workshop conducted by Bobby Gonzalez, author of *Song of the American Holocaust*.[238] Afterwards we had coffee and he declared that he was really of Indian descent from Puerto Rico since studies of DNA among them prove that a majority are of mostly Indian DNA. I did not take his declaration seriously because of the widely held belief that the indigenous ancestry had been annihilated along with the group. However, several years later a major research study was reported that confirmed his notion of Indian DNA retention and dominance.

Another significant workshop delivered by an outside person was

Betas and Bobby Gonzalez.

by Tato Laviera, an Afro-Puerto Rican. I used a part of my fund from my Faculty Fellow position to co-sponsor his appearance and his

human hair" (pp. 83 – 91). In Greg Tate (Ed.). *Everything but the burden*. New York: Random House; Juliette Harris & Johnson, P. (Eds.) (1998). *tenderheaded*. New York: Pocket Books.

[238] Bobby Gonzalez (2001). *Song of the American Holocaust*. New York: Indio Bravo Press.

delivery was more than worth it. I not only learned from his lectures, I had my writing seminar students attend his workshop, and their essays revealed a great deal of learning about Puerto Rican culture and the art of writing.

In addition to receiving magnificent essays on their experience with

Tatto and group. Photo by Gerald G. Jackson.

him, he felt, according to Diane Hernandez, a doctoral student in sociology, "He truly enjoyed your students and was really impressed with their work and willingness to participate." I learned from Puerto Rican and Afro-Latino cultural authority Dr. Juan Flores, just how significant Laviera was. According to Dr. Flores, Afro-Puerto Rican Laviera, along with an elite group of other Latino poets, "incorporate a strong sense of black cultural identity in their proclamation of a U.S.-based Puerto Rican reality."[239]

Black Greekdom, Diunitality and the African-American Womanist Warrior

Some individuals expressed amazement that Kandis, pictured later in this section, a leading campus leader, would become a Delta. For them, she should have not needed such an affiliation. An Africentric diunital analysis would have found no such contradiction. The persons clearly did not understand the organization she elected to become a member, and how it shapes more than a STRONGBLACKWOMAN.

---

[239]Juan Flores (January 2, 2003). "Afro-Latino cultures in the United States." *http.www.Africana com/ Articles/tt.78.5htm.*, p. 5.

Morover, this could be because the notion of such a Black woman is controversial and can be elusive. Before many White Cornell students and Black students schooled by Whites understand the concept of diunitality, they defensively interpret Black affirmations as a White denouncement. This would be if we reasoned from a Eurocentric mode that favors dichotomies. The pattern is quite evident when we discuss the STRONGBLACKWOMAN. Interpreting the words literally, they propose their mothers as examples of strong white woman and believe they have invalidated the Black concept of a STRONGBLACKWOMAN. Eventually, they understand the concept and that it is not an attack on White women. An equivalent one might claim is the word "feminist," and while the term fits the White woman's experience it is no match for African-American women. To capture the African-American woman's experience and circumstances, Alice Walker invented the term "womanist."[240] We are not proposing a dichotomy; the feminist platform may not fit a model for many Jewish and Israeli students in the struggle for global humanity. For me, a group designation for them could be COURAGEOUS, [241] a converging point with the Africentric notion of service to the community.

An oblique measure of the Africentric cultural importance given to service is the beginning of the organization and what it has done with its comparative success in life. The DST founders were allegedly dissatisfied with the AKA commitment to service ideals. They left the organization and started DST. Some testament to the rightness of the cohort's decision is that, historically and contemporaneously, they are the largest Black organization among sororities and fraternities, and the largest African-American female organization. Continuing its commitment to scholarship, leadership, excellence and service, they gave Howard University one million dollars for its capital campaign.[242] Without a doubt, the group is composed of strong Black women dedicated to service and the advancement of Black women.

---

[240] Alice Walker (1983). *In search of our mothers' Gardens.* New York: Harcourt Brace Jovanovich.

[241] Examples: Shulani Aloni (June 6, 2004). "A remarkable Jewish woman speaks out." http//www.thehadndstand.org/arcives/may2004/articlesaloni; Jane Lazarre(1999). *Beyond the Whiteness of Whiteness.* North Carolina: Duke University Press; Bettina Apteker (1997). *The morning breaks* (2nd edition) New York: Cornell University Press.

[242] "Delta Sigma Theta presents $ 1 million to Howard University." (Winter, 2003). *Howard Magazine,* p. 3.

The STRONGBLACKWOMAN ideal that Michele Wallace[243] and Joan Morgan[244] castigated may need to be retired. A replacement model may be embodied in the Black female Greek. They replicate in successive generations of sorors what biology and nationalistic ideologies fail to do.[245] They make their accomplishments through peaceful means and in unparalleled discipline, humane regard and grace. During a time of Black male bashing, they remain resolute in their commitment to partner with them.

These women challenge the idea that African-American women are the arch rival or antithesis of Black men. Seeing African-American men in a positive light, progressive Black women promote a positive image of Black men and foster efforts to enhance their growth and development.[246]

They defy, through actions, behaviors and deeds, a Eurocentrically based classification that would force them to think and behave from one group designation. Exemplifying Joseph White's Black Psychology admonishment[247] that the norm for African Americans is to fit and be

---

[243]Michelle Wallace (1979). *Black macho and the myth of the superwoman.* New York: Warner.

[244]Joan Morgan (1999). *When chickenheads come home to roost.* New York: Simon & Schuster. See update, Toby Thompkins (2004). *The Real Lives of Strong Black Women: Transcending Myths, Reclaiming Joy.* New York: Agate Publishers; and Diane Brown & Keith, V. (2004). *Mental Health of African-American Women.* New York: Columbia University Press.

[245]See William Van Deburg (Ed.) (1997). *Modern Black nationalism. From Marcus Garvey to Louis Farrakhan.* New York: New York University Press.

[246]A significant number of constructive books on Black men have been written by Black women alone or in conjunction with Black men. See Tonya Bolden (Ed.) (1999). *Strong men keep coming.* New York: John Wiley & Sons; Nancy Franklin & Franklin, A. (2000). *BOYS INTO MEN Raising our African-American teenage sons.* New York: Dutton; Marita Golden (1995). *Saving our sons. Raising black children in a turbulent world.* New York: Doubleday; Kristin Taylor (2003). *Black fathers. A call for healing.* New York: Doubleday; Iyanla Vanzant (1996). *The spirit of a man. A vision of transformation for Black men and the women who love them.* New York: HarperCollins; Clifford Watson & Geneva Smitherman (1996). *EDUCATING African American males: Detroit's MalcolmX Academy solution.* Illinois: Third World Press; Delores Wilkerson & Taylor, R. (Ed.) (1977). *The Black male in America. Perspectives on his status in contemporary society.* Illinois: Nelson-Hall.

[247]Joseph White (1970). "Guidelines for Black psychologists." *Black Scholar,* 1(5), 52–57.

attracted to several group designations, a Delta comprises gender, race, age, profession, family, political and social identities, or simply an *extended self*. The context characteristically determines what identities may dominate a situation. Two cases illustrate the concept and their expression of the concept of diunitality among Black sororities.

One is a book and proposal for a series of books for children on Black Greeks by Audra Jackson. The author, a Delta, believes her book, *My Mommy is a Delta,* could serve as a source of collegiate aspirations for young people. It came after her discovery that there were not children books about Black fraternities and sororities, given the reality that these groups represent a large portion of the African-American educated population. In addition, she wants to dispel the myths about Black fraternities and sororities that have ensued from the negative stereotypes about hazing.

The diunital aspect's other goal is that she intends to write books not only about the Deltas but books that celebrate the achievement of Black Greek sororities and fraternities. There will be books, therefore, entitled:

> My Mommy is an AKA, My Mommy is a Sigma Gamma Rho, My Mommy is a Zeta and my Daddy is a Kappa, My Daddy is an Alpha, My Daddy is an Iota Phi Theta, My Daddy is a Phi Beta Sigma.[248]

The other is the political consciousness and involvement of Black sororities, three of which were founded on Howard University's campus. It is shown not only in terms of 500,000 women who work on the grass-roots level and stay involved for a life time; it can be seen in the attendance of AKA's for their Public Policy Conference the same week of the Congressional Black Caucus. They shared the space and time in DC town with the other Black sororities and during this period the AKA's:

> spread into the offices of their senators and representatives, gently but firmly reminding them who they are (college–educated professionals), what they do (organize, network and raise lots of money) and what they care about (education, health, equal and civil rights).[249]

---

[248]Charles Hamilton, Jr. (April 22 – April 28, 2004). *"My Mommy is a Delta* bring school spirit to a new generation." *The New York Amsterdam News*, p. 36.

[249]Roxanne Roberts (September 27, 2003). "The Sisterhood, Taking on the Old Boy network for Black women. Sororities are more about politics than parties." *Washington Post*, p. CO1.

Afrospace in Higher Education

Black psychology affirms that an ordered, in comparison to a disordered, identity has to be rooted in an Afrospace that includes educational institutions and the behavior of its alumni. To elaborate, just as Black Greeks may have a role in the amelioration of Black/Brown conflicts, historically Black Universities, the genesis of the majority of Black Greek organizations, play a part. Howard University, for example, has sponsored conferences that supported collaborative study and relationships between Afro-Latinos and African Americans. It has been reported also that Black colleges and universities are specifically recruiting Latino students. Some of the things they have done are:[250]

> open a multicultural affairs office,
> sponsor a Caribbean street festival,
> hold a salsa-meringue dance contest,
> hold an Afro-Latino week,
> recruit heavily along the Mexican border,
> offer scholarships, and
> recruit by mail in Texas and California

Efforts to provide an educational opportunity at such institutions for non-African Americans are not out of character, as revealed in the following remarks by Booker T. Washington in 1901:

> It was a constant delight to me to note the interest, which the colored students took in trying to help the Indians in every way possible. There were a few of the colored students who felt that the Indians ought not to be admitted to Hampton, but these were in the minority. Whenever they were asked to do so, the Negro students gladly took the Indians as roommates, in order that they might teach them to speak English and to acquire civilized habits.
>
> I have often wondered if there was a white institution in this country whose students would have welcomed the incoming of more than a hundred companions of another race

---

[250]Adrienne Schwisow (July 15, 2003). "Diversity looks different in historically Black colleges." *Associated Press.* http://www. washtimes. com/ metro/20030712 - 104204 - 2579r.htm. pp. 1–4.

> in the cordial way that these black students at Hampton welcomed the red ones. How often I have wanted to say to white students that they lift themselves up in proportion as they help to lift others, and the more unfortunate the race, and the lower in the scale of civilization, the more does one raise one's self by giving the assistance.[251]

Even more instructive is the reception of Afro-Latino students at Black institutions. Parenthetically, the relationship between African Americans and Latinos frequently cast as a Black/Brown is not a dichotomy. The Latino group includes Blacks just as the English group includes them. Their existence and connection is another illustration of how the Black/White racial divide is permeable and soluble. The first rebellious riot in New York City by Black people occurred when it was rumored that police had killed an Afro-Puerto Rican. Perhaps the first rebellion by Africans to enslavement occurred in Vera Cruz, Mexico by Gabon-born Gaspar Yanga in 1570, before Nat Turner in 1831, Toussaint L'Ouventure in 1791 and Zumbi in 1678. Unlike the other revolts, the Spanish signed a peace treaty with him and his maroon colony of 500 existed for thirty more years as an autonomous entity.[252]

Rather than camouflage sub-cultural differences, at Howard University diversity is defined differently. Associate Provost Alvin Thornton noted that the racial definition subscribed to by White institutions is not applicable to Black colleges and universities. At Howard, the mission is not reducible to skin color but entails course offerings and exposure to a multi-dimensional curriculum. Its mission, consequently, is to develop students "who are committed to the elimination of oppression and guaranteeing equal opportunity and access."[253] Afro-Latinos are allowed to organize and contribute to the knowledge base of its students. At H.U., this alliance occurs in a number of places and levels of operation. There is an Afro-Latino student organization. It was initially named the "Afro-Latinos Making Alliances" but was changed to "Cimarrones," after a group of Africans who emancipated themselves from enslavement and settled in Spanish

---

[251] Booker T. Washington (1901). *Up from slavery.* New York: Doubleday. Republished (1991) p. 73. New Jersey: Gramercy Books.

[252] Lori Robinson, Cuadros, P. & Tate, A. (January/February, 2004). "Strength in numbers." *The Crisis Reader*, pp. 26-32.

[253] Adrienne Schwislow (July 15, 2003). "Diversity looks different in historically Black colleges." *Associated Press.* http://www.washtimes.com/metro/20030712 - 104204 - 2579r.htm. p. 2.

and Caribbean countries. Somewhat different in thrust, the group at Howard University does not intend to impart Spanish culture to Black students; the club mission is to acknowledge all races of Spanish America and establish a cognizance of African culture in the Caribbean, Central and South America. What is strikingly similar is a drive to find a safe haven; that is, wrote Marta Vega:[254]

> In the late sixties and seventies our communities duplicated what the *cimarrones* (run-away enslaved people) did during colonization. We created safe places for nurturing our cultural and spiritual traditions. We empowered our communities, , while establishing locations for resisting Eurocentric cultural oppression. The ancient societies of our ancestors – the *quilombos* of Brazil, the *palenques* of Colombia and Cuba – became the Puerto Rican Traveling Theater, El Museo Del Barrio, Taller Boricua, Galeria de la Raza, Guadalope Cultural Center; Caribbean Cultural Center, Teatro Campesino, and other cultural-arts-education organizations too numerous to list. Artists and organizations united and/or collaborated with student movements like the Puerto Rican Student Union, the Young Lords Party, Brown Berets, Movimientos Pro la Independencia de Puerto Rico, and others.

Suggestive of an increasing disclosure by Afro-Latinos about racial conditions at home in Latin and Central America,[255] the students revealed that they experienced discrimination at home and in the United States. In a commendable diunital fashion, they do not seek to be either Latino or Black, they desire to keep their Black ancestry and Latino background.[256] In another sphere, Rosa Clemente is a self-

---

[254]Marta Vega (1993). "The purposeful underdevelopment of Latino and other communities of Color" (p. 104). In Marta Vega & Greene, C. (Eds.) (1993). *Voices from the battlefront Achieving cultural equity.* New Jersey: Africa World Press.

[255]Roberto Rodriguez (January 23, 1995). "Latinos explore & grapple with Black identity: Uruguay Parley finds racism all over the America." *Black Issues in Higher Education,* pp. 22–24; Peter Nicks (November, 1999). "Leaders call for action on plight of Latin-American Blacks," pp. 1–4. http://wwwlatinlink. com/opionion/97/0202hrilehtm.

[256]Kaneicia Brown ((September 26, 2003). "Afro-Latino students make alliances in Cimarrones." *The Hilltop,* 1,2.

proclaimed Black Puerto Rican who is a grassroots organizer, journalist, entrepreneur and graduate from Cornell's Africana Studies & Research Center. [257] It has been noted that "she is unabashedly proud of her Afro-Latin roots (and) has committed herself to making sure the voices and views of the 'hip-hop' generation are heard and taken seriously."[258] Reflective of her role and reception in a Black University setting, she was a panelist at a town hall meeting at Howard University School of Law. The event was covered on C-Span and her interview for the *Hilltop* newspaper consisted of responses to the questions regarding: (1) state of civil rights in the United States; (2) possibilities if the Supreme court decisions are against the University of Michigan affirmative-action policy and (3) the role of the youth in the fight for equality and justice for all.

Rosa is not a Black Greek and does not need to be one. What is serving her well is her understanding of her Black cultural heritage and its charges to resist, struggle and organize for one's people. This is in the credo of Black Greeks that may serve to better unite Black/Brown groups.

You do not have to be a Black Greek to be in an Africentric Orbit

My notion of student development is not confined to members of Greek organizations. Similarly, my pedagogical ideas are not restricted to the inclusion of my academic course content. The result of my approach is illustrated in a response I received from a former student. I had sent her a congratulatory email for being selected as one of the 25 students selected "The 25 Influential Cornellians." In a jestful manner, in acknowledgment of her increasing success at getting awards and political offices, I wrote: "When the time comes, you can count on campaign contributions, the energy of my students, and a charge to Cornell Alumni to join your election contest." In response, she wrote:

Dear Professor Jackson,

Thank you very much for your message, it really made me smile. We'll see about president of the united states, but

---

[257] Rosa Clemente (May 24, 2001). "Who is Black? A Puerto Rican Woman claims her place in the African Diaspora." *The Black World for Today*, pp. 2-2.

[258] David Johns (April 1, 2003). "Leading by example: town hall follow up." *The Hilltop*, pp. 1-4.

since you brought it up, does this mean I can count on you for a campaign contribution in the future? (Just kidding).

I want to thank you so much for your support of students of color at Cornell. Professors like you truly inspire us to be leaders. Although I know I have told you this before, your class truly changed my outlook on life. If you remember, I was a particularly shy freshman at first, but your class showed me that each and everyone of us has a responsibility to our community – and being shy just won't cut it if we are to see any progress.

Thank you again and I wish you the best in the coming New Year.

Sincerely Yours,
Funa[259]

When I was at Yale there was a frequent reference to a Community of Scholars. It made a connection between the various members of the faculty and during the 1960s, it could be seen as a protection against demands to serve the New Haven community.[260] In diunital thinking, both viewpoints can be true. Similarly, at Cornell Black students have the options of involvement in the Black Ithaca community and/or the Black Cornell community, usually interpreted to mean Ujamaa Residential College and Africana Studies and Research Center. Professor Abdul Nanji has opened another avenue, in recent times. He gets undergraduate and graduate students involved in the Africana Studies field community of scholars. Recognizing the importance of conference presentation skills in the academic career path of future Africana scholars, he has encouraged and influenced graduates and

---

[259]One of my aims for encouraging students to be verbal is to combat communication apprehension (CA). Black students in predominantly White classroom settings have been observed to ask fewer questions and give fewer answers than White students. See Marquita Byrd & Sims, A. (1987). "Communication Apprehension Among Black Students on Predominantly White Campuses." *The Western Journal of Black Studies*, 2(3), pp. 105-110.

[260]Years later I returned and consulted with the medical school on resolving a conflict between the doctors and the New Haven community. The split was based upon the doctors not identifying with the host community of the school, and the community was demanding more faculty sensitivity and involvement in New Haven.

undergraduates to become involved in all phases. Two of my students, Tiffany Mayhew and Deven Gray, worked at a statewide Africana Studies conference held in the Cornell vicinity.

Fast Tracking Black College Students

Working the table is not the only capacity we envisioned for our undergraduates. Just as brilliant White students are fast-tracked, we reserve the same right to contribute, in an informal program, intellectual and emotional support for Black students. Danielle Williams is one such student. She took all my courses during her first academic year at Cornell and I suggested she apply to the College Scholars program, based upon my experience with College Scholar students Tiffany Haliburton and David Ladd.[261] What attracted me to Danielle was her acceptance of an invitation made to her class to attend a weekend conference at Yale University.[262] Many students, caught up in the isolationism of Cornell, saw the request as an additional work that conflicted with their social time. Daniel saw the invitation as an opportunity, and I drew this conclusion from her synopsis of the experience. Danielle's essay is published below.

Danielle Williams
11/7/01
AS&RC 171

Black Solidarity Conference at Yale University
November 2-4, 2001

Last week I, along with fourteen other black Cornell students, attended the 7th annual Black Solidarity Conference at Yale University sponsored by their Black Pride Union (BPU) and Black Student Alliance at Yale (BSAL). Black Solidarity Day is observed on the Monday before Election Day to remind the nation, and especially African Americans, of their political power. In 1994, the Black Student Alliance at Yale expanded the observance of Black Solidarity Day into

---

[261] See David's discussion of the program and how he applies it to Africana. Tiffany Haliburton is quoted in Sect I and IV.

[262] "Perceptions of Self The Black Psyche in the 21st Century." *Seventh Annual Black Solidarity Conference. Black Pride Union & Black Student Alliance at Yale*. New Haven: Connecticut, November 2-4, 2001.

a weekend experience. In the last six years since its inception, the Black Solidarity Conference has been widely attended by students from colleges and universities across the United States. Students from Cornell, Texas A&M, Columbia University, Hampton, Harvard, Temple University, Spelman College, Swarthmore, University of New Haven, and Morehouse College are among the colleges and universities that represent 400 students who attend each year. The purpose of this conference is dedicated to providing a forum for African American college students to exchange ideas, opinions, and action plans. This type of forum encourages continuous discussion and the sharing of ideas in order to prepare us for the future.

Each year a central theme that focuses on black related issues is chosen. This year's theme was the Black Psyche. This emphasis on self-perception and the way we see each other is directly related to the progress of our race as a group. The two keynote speakers were Na'im Akbar and Kathleen Cleaver. Unfortunately, we arrived on Saturday and missed Mr. Akbar's lecture. Thankfully, we were able to catch the lecture presented by Kathleen Cleaver. Having known nothing of Ms. Cleaver before the conference,[263] I was very

---

[263]"Kathleen Neal Cleaver has spent most of her life participating in the struggle for human rights. As a sophomore, Ms. Cleaver dropped out of college in 1966 to work full time with the Student Nonviolent Coordinating Committee (SNCC). From 1967-71, she served as the Communications Secretary of the Black Panther Party, making her the first woman member of their Central Committee. She went into exile with her former husband Eldridge Cleaver and returned to the US in 1975. Professor Cleaver earned her B.A. Summa cum laude from Yale College in 1984, and her J.D. from Yale Law School in 1989. She devoted many years to the defense of Elmer "Geronimo" Pratt, a former Black panther Party Leader who won his habeas corpus petition in 1997 after serving 27 years in prison for a murder he did not commit. Professor Cleaver has taught at Emory University, Benjamin N. Cardozo School of Law, Yale University and Sarah Lawrence College. While at Emory, she served on the Georgia Supreme Court on Racial and Ethnic Bias in the Courts. She is co-editor of a new collection of essays entitled *Liberation, Imagination, and the Black Panther Party*. Most recently, Professor Cleaver was the executive producer of the International Black Panther Film Festival. She is currently teaching at Emory Law School (Perceptions of Self The Black psyche in the 21st Century, 7th Annual Black Solidarity Conference, November 2 – 4, 2001, Yale University, New Haven,

impressed by her dynamic personality, her wealth of knowledge on politics and American sociology, and her overall strength. Ms. Cleaver, who is now a professor at Emory Law School, spoke of the perpetuations of injustice in American society against African Americans. She emphasized the government's use of propaganda in order to fortify the oppression of blacks. At the end of her lecture, she took questions from the audience. The question-answer section took more than a half an hour, and I was very pleased to see that such an important woman would take time out of her schedule. She didn't appear impatient or tiresome from all of the questions; this proved to me that she was very involved in her work, but also in the education of the future black leaders of our country.

After the lecture, our group had lunch and then returned to campus for the workshops. There were four workshops offered: *The Psychology of Struggle, Illusion of Inclusion? Black on Black Liberation: Freedom from the Chains of Anti-Self Disorder,*[264] and *Deconstructing the Myths of the Independent Black Woman and "Good for Nothing" Black Man.* I chose to attend the workshop entitled *Illusion of Seclusion.* This workshop focused on the disenfranchisement of blacks in the American political system. We addressed such issues as black loyalty to bi-partisanship and why we are unable to unify to create the political power necessary to accomplish our political agenda.

Unlike the lecture, the workshop gave me the opportunity to interact with the other students at the conference. When we were broken up into small groups to discuss ways to achieve our political goals, I had the opportunity to share ideas with black students representing Swarthmore, Columbia, and upperclassmen from Cornell. While discussing a plan, I made a comment to the group that I thought it felt so good to be in a room of educated African Americans from a variety of schools.

Connecticut, Sponsored by Black Pride Union & Black Student Alliance at Yale, p. 9).

[264]This was my workshop. It was based upon Black/African psychology conceptualization of self-destructive disorders for Black people. For the source of the concept, see Na'im Akbar (1981). "Mental disorders among African-Americans." *Black Books Bulletin*, 7(2), 18–35.

The conference not only provided me with an opportunity to learn from my collegiate peers at other schools, it also gave me the opportunity to learn about my fellow Cornellians. Most of the students on the trip were upper-classmen whom I didn't know very well. I would say that after the trip I had a better understanding of their personalities, especially some of the goofier sophomores, juniors, and seniors. The long van ride back and forth from Cornell to Yale was filled with jokes and camaraderie that transcended arbitrary differences such as our respective graduation years. I felt a true sense of community when we made light-hearted jokes to one another and when we attended events together, such as the talent show and the party later that night. The trip to Yale last week made me aware of the efforts being made by other universities to create a stronger black student community with all universities and colleges. It also made me aware of how welcoming the black students are here on campus.

During her course work and our discussion, she developed a special interest in Afro-Mexicans.[265] Recognizing her potential to contribute to the embryonic stage of Afro-Latino studies in the Africana field, I supported her interest through several independent studies courses that resulted in several papers. As a consequence of her papers and demonstrated ability to work interdependently, Professor Nanji felt she was ready to present a scholarly paper at an Africana Study conference. He had her present in a panel I conducted as chairperson,[266] and she did a commendable job. So impressive was her work and scholarly comportment that he invited her to present at another Africana Studies professional conference.[267] The exposure we felt was good but it is not

---

[265] See Herman Bennett (2003). *Africans in Colonial Mexico. Absolutism, Christianity, and Afro-Creole Consciousness, 1570 – 1640*. Indiana: Indiana University Press; Lamont Muhammad (October/November, 2001). "Invisible: Blacks in Mexico." *Black Diaspora*, pp. 26, 27; Colin Palmer (1993). "Afro-Mexican culture and consciousness during the sixteenth and seventeenth centuries" (pp. 125–136). In Joseph E. Harris (Ed.). *African Diaspora* (2nd edition). Washington, D.C.: Howard University Press.

[266] Danielle Williams (April 3, 2003). "Non-traditional African Diaspora: Afro-Mexico." In Gerald G. Jackson, chairperson, *New Dimensions of the African Diaspora. Transnational Discourses in the African world*, 27th Annual Conference of the New York African Studies Association.

[267] Danielle Williams (November 7, 2003). "The Afro-Mexican influence in colonial Mexico." In Abdul Yussuf, chairperson, *The Afrocentric Paradigm:*

enough to produce a paradigm-shifting scholar. We knew, for example, what female reporters found as career blocks in the early days of male-dominated sports. They discovered that left out of the locker room meant that they could neither write a story on the players nor master the nuances of the game so they would be able to ascend the sports field hierarchy. Before these women, African Americans had been historically omitted from the inner circle of the scholars. In contrast, I remember my delight, as a faculty fellow at Yale, being able to converse with C. Van Woodard, also a faculty fellow and pre-eminent American history scholar, and learning some of his unpublished but insightful views. I brought this knowledge to the fast-track program operating for Danielle. She was invited to our circles where she met and conversed with the keynote speaker, Dr. Joseph Harris, a Howard University Faculty of Distinction, and early contributing scholar to the African Diaspora field.

Professor Joseph Harris conducting an informal talk with Danielle Williams, Abdul Nanji, Kenneth Glover, Rejane Frick, and Gerald Jackson. Photo by Gerald G. Jackson.

In addition, she was given the opportunity to spend hours with him. During this time she heard his distilled ideas, concepts and recollections and had the opportunity to pose questions.[268]

The Global Perspective. African Heritage Studies Association 36th Annual Conference, November 6-8, 2003. The Global Dimension of the African Diaspora and its relation to Africa. Holiday Inn, Philadelphia, Pennsylvania.

[268]Danielle would become a member of AKA sorority the winter of 2004 semester. Her work continues on confronting racial amnesia. See Ted Vincent

Faculty Fellow Program and Former Students
as Role Models

The understandable flakiness of residential undergraduates coupled to those who periodically feign deprecation can result in a patronizing stance by faculty who arrogantly see the classroom as being better than life. Generally, I try to make my classes a slice of life, and honor activities that promote the type of skills that contribute to a productive

A. Bartlett Giamatti lunching with students and a English department
colleague at Ezra Stiles College of Yale University.
Bart would later become the Master of Ezra Stiles College of Yale
University and ultimately president of Yale University.
Photo by Clyde Waite.

work life. The former posture can shortcut the skill and ability of students to imagine, design and implement programs that the University has difficulty conceiving and operationalizing. My membership in Cornell's Faculty Fellows program has helped me be a

(1999). "Racial Amnesia. African Puerto Rico and Mexico. *Konch Magazine,* pp. 1-9.

part of Co-curricula learning situations. My experience as an administrator in the Yale Summer High School program and as a Fellow at Yale University, the prototype of the Cornell program, provided me with some grounding.

In comparison, however, I find the Cornell program to be broader in scope and more focused on the student-faculty interaction. The encouragement, for example, to eat dinner with all students, rather than just students from one's residential college, has enabled me to extend the learning process beyond the period in which students are enrolled in my course. It is common, therefore, for me to meet with several former students for dinner and in addition to receiving progress reports, consider solutions to national and campus problems. This is the backdrop to the invitation presented by Hope Jamison and Nafis Smith, two of my former students.

We had lunch and the two Residential Advisors suggested a program to deal with domestic terrorism,[269] in the form of the lynching of a Black man. I agreed to serve as facilitator of this bold race relation's intervention and they presented me with the following program design.

---

[269]James Allen (2000). *Without Sanctuary: Lynching photography in America.* Twin Palms; W. Fitzhugh Brundage (2002). *Lynching the New South: Georgia and Virginia, 1880-1930.* Virginia: University of Virginia Press; Carroll Chase (1998). *The Slaughter an American Atrocity.* United States: FBC; Phillip Dray (2003). *At the Hands of Persons Unknown: The lynching of Black America.* Modern Library; James W. Loewen (1996). *Lies my teacher told me: Everything your American history textbook got wrong.* Touchstone Books; Ralph Ginzburg (1997). *100 years of lynching.* Black Classic Press; James H. Madison (2003). *A lynching in the heartland: Race and memory in America.* Palgrave MacMillan; Christopher Metress (Ed.) (2002). *The lynching of Emmett Till: A documentary narrative.* Virginia: University of Virginia; Leroy Phllips & Curriden, M. (2001). *Contempt of Court: The turn of the century lynching that launched a hundred years of federalism.* Anchor; Anne Rice & Wallace, M. (Ed.) (2003). *Witnessing lynching: American Writers respond.* New Jersey: Rutgers University Press; Mamie Till-Mobley & Benson, Christopher (2003). *Death of Innocence: The story of the hate crime that changed America.* New York: Random House; Ida B. Wells & Hill, P. (Ed) (1996). *The Anti-lynching campaign of Ida B. Wells 1892-1900.* Bedford/St. Martins; Laura Wexler (2003). *Fire in a Canebraker: The Last Mass lynching in America.* New York: Scribner.

A Town Torn by Hate
The Story of James Byrd's Killing
in
Jasper, Texas

Dinner & Discussion
with Professor Gerald Jackson

Tuesday,
March 4, 2003
7:00 p.m.
Balch Unit One Lounge

Sponsored by Balch Hall and Low Rises
Faculty Fellow
Format for Dinner and Discussion

6:30 p.m. – Set-up

7:00 p.m. Dinner

7:10 p.m. – Introduction and Greetings

Welcome
Extend Thanks/Recognize Faculty Fellows
Introduction of Professor Jackson

7:15 p.m. Professor Jackson

James Byrd Facts
Video Clippings

7:45 Discussion

8:30 p.m. Closing & Clean-Up

I perceived the program to be relevant to the content of my course and as an opportunity for students to increase their analytical and oratorical skills. I suggested, therefore, that they attend and submit a report for extra credit and possible classroom presentation.

Group looking at film. Photo by Gerald G. Jackson.

Group discussion. Photo by Gerald G. Jackson.

During the discussion period, the intensity of the subject overwhelmed a White female. In an attempt to inject optimism, she became overwrought by her sense of futility. The film had produced a similar pathos but did not foster crying in the Black students. I intervened with the student and she appeared comforted by my words and the support of Nafis and a White female peer.

What was most productive was an unexpected result from an intracultural exchange with a P.A. attendant. I informed the initially distraught P.A. that it is common in my human relations and diversity work to witness a divide between Blacks and Whites to the same visual stimuli. To support my contention, I related a training situation at Kent State between Black and White desegregation professionals. Whites thought the Blacks insensitive because they did not cry over the sharing of past racial encounters. Conversely, Blacks expressed disappointment with the Whites for not understanding the rage of Blacks who had to repeatedly experience the racist behaviors of Whites. Blacks noted also that they were not impressed with the crying of Whites because it was viewed as cathartic. Most importantly, the crying, in the viewpoint of Blacks, did not result in actions to abate racism. They proposed that

Hope & Nafis lecture. Photo by Gerald G. Jackson.

Whites cry less and act more. The P.A. thanked me for sharing the experience and mentioned that she gained an insight from our post-program dialogue. For the students that attended the event, it afforded them educational information and an opportunity to see me in a different professional capacity. I, however, wanted to extend the learning opportunity so I invited Nafis and Hope[270] to present an overview of their program to my Black Education class.

---

[270]Hope Jamison became a member of Delta Sigma Theta sorority after she co-directed the lynching program.

To further strengthen the learning I had Jamy Rodriquez and Tara Woods, who had submitted reports on their recollection and analysis of the program, read their papers in class. The evaluations they wrote are published below. Again, the learning I sought to promote was

Jamy Rodriquez reading the essay she wrote on lynching workshop. Photo by Gerald G. Jackson.

Africentrically inspired. I wanted the speakers to gain experience in public speaking and comfort in presenting to a primarily Black intellectually inclined audience.

Similarly, I wanted the audience/observers to see their peers in intellectual action, as competent allies to depend upon when they enter the world of work. For the moment, it was primarily an exercise in understanding collective responsibility and African-American values.

Jamy Rodriguez
ASRC 172

Two towns of Jasper

Two towns of Jasper was an in depth documentary on the 1998 racially motivated murder of an African American man in the small town of Jasper, Texas. James Bird Jr., on his way home late one night was strapped and chained onto a pick up truck by three white men who would then drag him for three miles. It was later confirmed that Bird was not unconscious during the heinous act, but that he attempted to ease his ordeal by leaning on his elbows until they were grinded to the bone. The lynching of Bird served as an awakening on the horrifying consequences of xenophobia in a racially divided America. Although slavery ended over a century ago, there are still incidents in America that occur purely because of racial discrimination.

The film is perhaps the first of its kind because it employed two different camera crews-one black the other white, to obtain the sentiments of a segregated community. This approach yielded candid responses from both the white and black residents of Jasper about their attitudes on the lynching of a black man by three white men for no apparent reason. Some of the white residents portrayed heartfelt sympathy towards the black community while others were blatant about their indifference and racist tendencies. The black community although deeply hurt, was not surprised about the crime, for the town of Jasper had already witnessed a number of hate crimes in the past, but none of such magnitude. As a result of the crime, a feeling of solidarity arose among the black and white sectors of the community, but some felt that this was a superficial sense of unity that was present only because of the recent tragedy.

I was personally disturbed after seeing the film. It made me feel a sense of helplessness and hopelessness as well. The notion of racism began in Africa with the European's colonization of an entire people and was later perfected in the United States with the systematic institution of slavery. Racism has been plaguing this nation since its beginning and it continues to be embedded in the conscience of many individuals. This type of discrimination determines the economics, politics, and psychology of every person of color in the United States. The notion of racism is what gives an uneducated white man the "right" to call a black professor a nigger. I am genuinely tired of hearing about incidents of young Black and Latino men getting shot in the back by white police officers and about women of color who are harassed by white males for no reason.

Today by means of social institutions Blacks, Latinos, and other minorities continue to experience racism. It has become a natural part of life, something we have to cope with since birth. The murder of Bird is not an isolated incident but part of a more general social pattern. These hate crimes occur on a day to day basis but we often forget to make the necessary connections. During the discussion, it appeared to me that some people disagreed with the comments of the Black Panther member who believed that blacks needed to rely less on European forces and more on each other for protection. I couldn't have agreed with him more. I believe that he's calling attention to something serious that's affecting our community and that is the lack of connection or interdependence that we feel for one another. We need not have a direct

Gerald G. Jackson

Tara reading essay written on James Byrd Lynching workshop.
Photo by Gerald Jackson.

correlation with someone to feel compassion for him or her. The Black Panther member was sending a message of activism to the black community; the ability to protest and mobilize against racist forces whenever any one member of the community becomes threatened.

Tara Leigh Wood
Africana 172
3/4/03

Essay on "Two Towns of Jasper"

This film was very eye opening for me. I think that it was very motivating and appropriate for this particular class on the education of Black Americans because some of the underlying feelings and themes in the movie have to deal with how people were educated and how they perceive different events. Connecting this tragic story to how people are educated and socialized in White communities compared to Black communities helps us to understand how and why people commit such horrific acts. I think it is important to look at the root of the problem and try to correct or at least find ways to deal with it.

The men that committed the acts were obviously estranged, mentally detached people who took their anger and frustration out physically on someone else. However, they are not alone in their thinking. I noticed that two of the three men were a part of some White supremacy group or hate group, which means there is a community that fosters this type of behavior. As a moral human being, I find it very hard to understand how one can brutally take another persons life-innocent or guilty-but in this case innocent. However, I think as a society, or even as a country, that is supposed to strive for morality I believe we need to address these issues not as something isolated and past tense, but as present and future problems if left alone. In addition, we need to look at how just a generation ago there was segregation and blatant hatred toward Blacks. Moreover, since the people who were in power, or even just supporting the cause at that time, are still alive their children have adopted the same views as them, which this case of racially motivated murder has clearly proven.

One of the most striking questions that this movie raised is "Why do we [Black people] always look to Europeans to solve our problems?" as the man who is a member of the New Black Panther Party clearly stated. He pointed out that Blacks are always looking to the law, or God, or some white force to handle our problems. He also asserts that we have a right to defend ourselves and stand up for our own problems in society. I completely agree with this statement because in this situation, no one really took matters into their own hands, they just waited around for a trial and hoped that it was a fair one. They prayed and conducted superficial relationships with White people at their respective churches, however nothing was really done to prevent this from happening again, and to assure that justice was served to those deserving. I speculate that this trial could have brought back a different verdict if the media and press didn't get so intimately involved. Although I don't have a direct solution to the problem and I'm not so optimistic to believe that White racists are just going to change their views, I do think that the American legal system or at least the people running it, do not cater to the needs of Black people. We need to recognize that and try to change it. Passive actions are such as bringing a cemetery together and praying in church on one Sunday is not going to get the job done.

One of the members of the community was very optimistic about the Black and White people in Jasper finally coming together, specifically stating that Jasper was "moving toward oneness." However, the father of the Catholic Church made a statement that "this is a tragedy in the Black community." This can completely contradict the first statement. In order to be moving toward a unified community, the first thing that must be done is realizing that there is only one community! The murder of a Black man in the community is not just a Black problem, it's everyone's problem. This further elaborates on the dichotomy of thinking in the Eurocentric point of view.

Watching this film invoked so many emotions that I had been ignoring because of my own personal problems. I think it was very important for all of us to see how racism in America still exists and although some may say it is covert, this is a blatant wake up call that it is not! With this Bush's upcoming war, and him trying to convince the world that America has the same beliefs as him, I think it is important to assert our opinions on issues concerning this country-whether they be about racism, war, terrorism, sexism etc. This discussion may have been the starting point for some people to get their voices heard in at least in a small setting, so that later on *in* a larger setting changes can be made.[271]

Giving back to the Cornell Community: Lecture by returning Alumni student from AS&RC 171, 172

It is easy in a predominantly Eurocentric environment, such as Cornell University, to slip into a Eurocentric-thinking mode and racially dichotomize what a commitment means to Africana Studies. It would mean to presume that only Black people believe in the institution of Africana Studies and, with the exception of *peripheral Blacks*, would devote time and energy to its elevation and maintenance as a place of scholarship. David Ladd, a Jewish (Reform) White male student with more than two dozen Cornell graduate relatives and a younger brother and sister following him to Cornell, affirms a diunital view. His work challenges the notion of a rigid color code to an Africana commitment. Be very clear, David, originally from the DC area, is no "wanna be" or "wigger," and this is a compelling plus to his creditability.

---

[271]The tombstone of James Byrd was vandalized subsequent to the writing of Tara and Jamie's essays. The authorities reported that racial epithet had been carved into the granite of the tombstone. Jamal Watson (May 13 – May 19, 2004). "Slain Byrd's Jasper tomb vandalized." *The New York Amsterdam News*, p. 6. Few mental health professionals, beyond Dr. Frances Crest Welsing, albeit psychodynamic, offer theoretical explanations for this example of the *Hatred of the Different*. See Frances Crest Welsing (1991). *The ISIS papers*. Illinois: Third World Press. Her trenchant analysis continues to be discounted by Eurocentric thinkers, propelled by *Eurocentric culturalism*.

David lecturing. Photo by Gerald G. Jackson.

He does not dress in Hip Hop attire, his girlfriends at Cornell were all White, and he was actively involved in a non-Jewish fraternity composed mainly of White males. His prowess is demonstrated in the kind of work he produces on African-American culture. Testimony to his vigor and ardor are the three years he devoted to creating a film on Africana studies (e.g., African cultural origin of Hip-Hop for portion of his group presentation). The essay by David is another celebration, though somewhat oblique, of the struggle of ordinary people who say, "we're not going to take it anymore." These are the people who built an institution to foster people and supportive scholarship to advance this idea. It exists, this book looks favorably on, because the dictate of a

Class learning about the scope of David's work.
Photo by Gerald G. Jackson.

literate culture could demand a written document, even if the accepted form was a visual presentation.[272]

David Ladd
College Scholar Program
Explanation of Honors Thesis Project

The Making of Africana Now

Carter G. Woodson, a prominent Black historian in the 1930's, once wrote that every man has two educations: "that which is given to him, and the other that which he gives himself. Of the two kinds, the latter is by far the more desirable. Indeed all that is most worthy of man he must work out and conquer for him. It is that which constitutes our real and best nourishment. What we are merely taught seldom nourishes the mind like that which we teach ourselves." These inspiring words will forever be ingrained in my head because they changed the course of my life. They are what motivated me to apply to the College Scholar Program and were the driving force behind the making of my documentary film on modem racism. To better understand these statements, and why I chose to organize my college curriculum around studying racism, I believe it is important to explain a little bit about my background and educational experiences.

I was raised in a reform Jewish household in a suburb of Washington, D.C. My temple has been very involved in social welfare programs in the local community for both Jews and non-Jews alike. It was impressed upon me at a very early age that I had the responsibility, as a Jewish person, to strive for the uplifting of my own community, and for the uplifting of my neighbors. My teachers explained that all social problems that existed within and between groups were interrelated, and because of this, by helping others we were simultaneously helping ourselves. Along with this philosophy, I was exposed to many films, speakers, and writings on the Holocaust. Unlike the rest of my religious school experience, this subject matter fascinated me. Trying to gain a better understanding of the flagrant prejudice and the hatred that embodied that time was an activity that held my interest from middle school onward. The major lesson I took away from studying the Holocaust was that if I saw any sort of injustice

---

[272]For a detailed look at the workings of Oral and Literate cultures, see Walter Ong (1982). *Orality and Literacy*. The technologizing of the word. New York: Methuen.

in the world, I must speak out against it and fight for change. I also learned that oppression of a people, like anti-Semitism, can exist on many different levels, come in different forms, and that the current problems we face with this social ill have, in part, been shaped and affected by its history.

While lessons about the Holocaust occupied my time at religious school, making videos on a wide array of subjects was a hobby I was incorporating into my public school experience. Whenever I had an opportunity to use a video camera for a class project, I jumped on it. In high school, I began working on the school news show, *Whitman Shorts,* and by senior year had worked my way up the ladder to the role of executive producer. After this experience, I knew that video production was something I wanted to pursue in some way during college.

On the social front, probably because of the area in which I lived, I had a wide variety of experiences and friendships with those of differing religious and ethnic backgrounds, and most especially with African Americans. Bessie Lucas, a housekeeper who has been with my family even before my birth, has always been considered our second mom for her role in helping to raise my siblings and me. She was the first African-American that I was in contact with, and I am sure that her presence significantly contributed to my current sense of identity and cultural polarization. My attraction towards R&B and rap music, my decision to play on an all-Black soccer team in 8th and 9th grade, and my interest in African-American history in high school and college, may all stem from my relationship with Bessie and from an intangible force around me growing up that stressed appreciating and learning from differences between people.

It might seem obvious that these influences and interests would one day all coalesce, but when I arrived at Cornell, I found myself lost. I spent my entire freshman year agonizing over what to study. I knew I wanted to pursue something in the social sciences and humanities that could then be practically applied, but settling on one major didn't appeal to me. I could not see the fields of psychology, sociology, human development, and anthropology as separate entities; to me, these subjects were all interconnected, especially when applied to the real world. When I signed up for *African Studies 172: The Education of Black Americans,* it was because I saw an opportunity to take a class that not only appealed to my interests but seemed to involve interdisciplinary study. After reading Carter G. Woodson's quote, it immediately hit me that I should find a way to tailor my Cornell education to my own needs. After a helpful hint from my advisor, Professor Maas, I found the College Scholar Program. My journey was far from complete, however. I still needed to figure out what I wanted to focus on in my studies.

One day while sitting in my Africana class, Professor Jackson asked a question that sparked the connection between my past interests and my current situation at Cornell. "How many of you," he inquired, "Will actually take your Cornell education and figure out how to apply it towards the betterment of the community you live in?" When I left the classroom that day my mind was racing with ideas about how I could apply my college education towards a greater good. For that to happen, I would need to tackle a deeply rooted problem in society, one that manifested itself on the surface in different ways. My mind immediately went back to my days in religious school, and the answer was clear: prejudice. I didn't want to focus on anti-Semitism, however. I wanted a different challenge. I wanted to study another form of oppression that not only was still a major problem in this country, but also one that would force me to introspect on my own life and role in society. It immediately came to my attention that, throughout my years of schooling, including my first year at Cornell, the subject of racism was rarely addressed. When it was, it was framed as a problem that exists predominately in the past, beginning with slavery, and subsiding with the civil rights movement. I knew, however, that there must be much more to the story than this. With Carter G. Woodson's quote in mind, I began making preparations to design a curriculum around the subject of racism and prejudice. With my acceptance into the College Scholar Program, I was able to follow through on this vision. My classes, extending into the disciplines of psychology, human development, government, education, sociology, anthropology, and Africana studies, all taught me about human culture and the ways in which individuals and groups think, act, learn and behave. The classes I took were specifically chosen because I felt each one individually had something to contribute to my understanding of racism, and also because they collectively allowed me to grasp the depth of the subject by providing a variety of different lenses through which to view it. I believe interdisciplinary study is essential for coming to terms with the causes, affects, and possible solutions to a problem that permeates every aspect of our society. I also believe that knowledge is useless unless it is applied, and so, while I was in the process of learning about racism and our understanding of it, I decided that making a documentary video on the topic would be the most beneficial and effective way to educate others and make a difference in society. Students in my generation want a more visually stimulating learning experience than reading provides, and a video, therefore, would draw the necessary attention to the topic of racism. In today's world, television is king, and this medium has the ability to influence and entertain in ways that the written word alone does not.

On a broader level, the underlying truth is that television, the popular press, and the film industry do a lot more than passively reflect the social and political reality of our times; these institutions actively define reality and give meaning to the history we have witnessed and experienced. By selecting which stories to cover, which shows to produce, and which films to release, these institutions actively define which topics and issues are important, relevant, and worthy of public consideration. In this way, the mass media acts as a filter through which our perceptions of the world around us are shaped. As technology has advanced, the media's reach and influence has grown. Television, for instance, provides viewers with easy access to news and information about the world around us, entertainment, and, by way of commercials, instructions on what products to use to make our lives better. American culture and the various ideologies we each hold dear to us, is consequently formed, in part, by what we see on television. Therefore, because of the decisions made by those who control the mass media, those who work within these institutions cumulatively wield enormous power. In many situations, this power is carried out with the best of intentions, aiming to perform a task well, objectively, and fairly. This has not always been the case, however. Throughout history, the various forms of media have been used by their controllers to manipulate and to persecute. African Americans, Native Americans, Jews, and women, to name a few groups, all unfortunately have been the targets of prejudice, discrimination, and outright bigoted attacks via the media. While overt racism in the media has declined, the scars have not been healed. There has been only minimal effort by the networks and their producers to use the media's power in a positive way to proactively combat the social ills in society to which they have historically contributed. As we enter the 21st century, the next generation of media personnel has the daunting task either to bring about significant reform, or to continue along with the slow-paced status quo.

My decision to create a documentary video on racism, therefore, stems from this understanding. Since what we see on our television screen reflects our current way of living, and at the same time, actively defines it for us, a video on modem racism seemed to be a great way to use the power of visual media for a good cause. It would also give students the most comprehensive and confrontational education possible, that is, one that taps into all of their perceptive abilities. A video that directly confronts the problem of defining racism could bring matters of race back into the public consciousness. For racism to end there must be an open and honest debate about how it functions in contemporary society. I wanted to create a film that not only looked at a debate, but also provided explanations and solutions for how to further the fight against racism.

My film, *Africana Now,* follows the present day push to legitimize the existence of the Africana Studies and Research Center on Cornell's campus,[273] as the issue of Africana's relevance opens up a discussion about the definition and nature of racism itself. Specifically, the video focuses on a protest rally organized by supporters of the Africana department to have the center receive more university funds. The Africana department has much to contribute to every student's education, but has been largely ignored and neglected by the university. The documentary follows this protest rally and the spontaneous debate it sparked between students immediately following its conclusion. It also consists of interviews with faculty and students on how they conceptualize modern racism and what it means to be Black or White in today's world. Intermixed throughout the film are clipsfrom many important scenes and speeches that took place in the civil-rights-era of the 1960's. I wanted the film to visually demonstrate how the past affects the present, and to challenge those watching to find their own way of joining in the fight against racism.

This three year endeavor has been the most profound educational experience I have ever encountered. Not only have I had to conduct the normal research associated with an honor's thesis, but I have also had to refine my skills in video production. Although I had experience filming and editing from high school, this project has required me to acquire new skills and learn on my own how to effectively use a digital

---

[273]David's work is much broader than he imagined. Since Woodson's miseducation thesis, there have been two developments aimed at eliminating the miseducation of Black people on the college level and ultimately all levels. One innovative effort was the Compensatory Education and the other was Black Studies. Often overlooked and approached by David's film is the cross-cultural basis of racial conflicts. See Ben Sidran (1971). *How the music of Black America created a radical alternative to the values of Western literary tradition.* New York: Holt, Rinehard and Winston; Thomas Kochman (Ed.) (1972). *Rappin' and Stylin' out. Communication in urban Black America.* Illinois: University of Illinois Press; Thomas Kochman (1981). *Black and White styles in conflict.* Illinois: University of Chicago Press. Geneva Smitherman (1994). *Black talk words and phrases from the Hood to the Amen Corner.* New York: Houghton Mifflin Company; Geneva Smitherman (1977). *Talkin and Testifyin The language of Black America.* Massachusetts: Houghton Mifflin Company.

camera and non-linear editing system. On a more personal level, making this film has afforded me the privilege to foster some incredible friendships with both students and professors at Cornell. The education I received just from talking with these individuals about the topic of racism has expanded my mind in ways I never thought possible. *Africana Now is* a conglomeration of my life experiences and my education from Cornell, and is my first step into the field of TV production that I will continue pursuing. Hopefully, this video will be analyzed on many levels by future students and faculty alike, and will keep the issue of combating racism at the forefront of academic thought. If so, I feel I have accomplished something worthwhile and lasting through my endeavors at Cornell.

Faculty Fellow Connection to Lecturer for Another Course

Those of us who have been in the academe for decades have learned to dread faculty socials and strained attempts to have faculty feel communal. The Faculty Fellow program at Cornell has shown me that this does not have to be the case. During one such social I happened to learn that Peter J. Davies, professor of Plant Physiology, had also been at Yale University. While reliving our Yale time, we discovered a mutual acquaintance, Richard Goldsby, currently at Amherst College. I remembered Dick as a biology teacher who devoted a summer teaching my Yale Summer High School students and published a monumental book on races.[274] Peter informed me that he was bringing Dick to the campus and his talk was titled "Is there a biology of race and races?" Just before Dick's arrival, Azaria Tests, a student at the time, did not know of my knowledge of Dick and his scheduled lecture, and wrote me: "it could very well be a stimulating experience for everyone. I will be attending, so I'll update you on it" (April 8, 2003 email). This was the second time Azaria had taken a course with me so he knew the drill and enthusiastically agreed to write a report. What follows is his report.

Azaria Tesfa
Africana 100.4 Black Is and Black Ain't
Professor Jackson
April 2003

---

[274]The course was titled "Relevant Biology" and dealt with the biology of races, drug addiction, sex, population explosion, and all from what Eurocentric science would say was a rigorous scientific point of view. Richard Goldsby (1971). *Race and Races*. New York: MacMillan.

Richard Goldsby. Photo by Gerald G. Jackson.

Biology of Races?

Dr. Richard Goldsby came to Cornell to speak at 9am on Wednesday, April 09 2003. He is currently at Amherst, and was a special guest lecturer to speak about biological differences between races. One of the first characteristics that struck me about Dr.Goldsby was his style of speaking to his audience. Rather than stand in one place behind a podium, he opted to walk around, pace and spice his talk with jokes. Although I found the topic, he was speaking about to be of personal interest, his style of public speaking captured my attention more effectively, especially in the early morning hours.

Dr. Goldsby defines race as a breeding population with characteristic frequencies of inherited traits. He added that there are certain factors that we can measure in a group of individuals. His first example to illustrate his point was of an experiment. Let's say that you have three different populations of people. One third traces their lineage to the West Coast of Africa, another third to east Europe and the last third to Japan. Each group will now be separately in three different rooms. If they cannot see out and you cannot see in, how will you be able to differentiate between the three different populations? He suggests that three different samples should be taken/experimented on these groups; earwax, blood sample and drinking a quart of milk on an empty stomach. Each of these has their own implications. Being able to differentiate earwax between sticky and adhesive as compared to dry and crumbly will tell the story of who is who. Real numbers indicate that East Asian Americans have an 85-98% of sticky earwax, while European Americans have approximately 15% of sticky earwax and African Americans have about 7%. The blood sample taken would tell the levels of each population that are Rh negative and therefore the solid numbers show that European Americans are 25-46% Rh negative, while 0-5% of East Asian Americans are Rh negative and about 4-29% of African Americans are. Finally, the test of drinking a quart of milk on an empty stomach allows us to figure out who is lactose intolerant. Because milk has lactose and the enzyme betagalacticyde helps ALL mammals to split lactose in their stomachs. However, as mammals get older, some lose this enzyme functioning and therefore become lactose intolerant. Hence, the condition of being lactose intolerant. In this case, numbers show that lactose intolerance is high in East Asian Americans at about 80-97%, while European Americans are level at 3-17% and African Americans at approximately 70%.

"Splitting hairs" when scientifically analyzing the differences between races is one of the only ways to be successful. Just because there is not a lot of difference does not mean there is NO difference. When comparing allele frequencies of residents in Utah versus Norway, we find a high correlation percentage and a strong 45-degree angle. The same situation in residents of Nigeria and Zimbabwe, however when comparing inhabitants of Utah and China, we find a scattered graph with no pattern nor correlation. In continuing his talk, Dr. Goldsby spoke about Vitamin D and that we need just enough, too much and too little can both result as problematic on the body. At this present time, getting Vitamin D in some form or fashion is not too difficult. With the existence of nutrition centers and grocery stores, we can find our way to a sufficient amount of Vitamin D. However, what about 50-100,000 years ago? At that time, we made it ... our bodies would produce enough Vitamin D to live efficiently. There is a correlation between Vitamin D presence and darker skin. The farther you move away from the origins of humans in East Africa, you find fairer skin and less sun in the environment. Generally speaking, the closer one is to the North Pole, the lighter the skin is and closer to the equator results in darker skin. The exception that exists is the Eskimos and they have darker skin because of their diet. It turns out that they had a heavy consumption of whale livers and fat.

Behaviors of individuals based on race are trivial for the most part. Although there is a strong correlation between blacks playing basketball, this is only a common result of having a population with a high concentration of tall individuals. Nothing more and nothing less. There is no influence in the Darwinian scheme of things. We will not care about these characteristics in 100 years. Pertaining intelligence, there is a relationship between genes and intelligence depending on how you define intelligence. Many individuals find that intelligence is strictly an IQ test. Countless studies have been conducted but the question will only be answered by performance. There were many articles and essays written about how blacks could not and would not constitutionally be able to play in a Major Baseball League with whites. When along arrived Jackie Robinson and Willie Mays who were able to disprove these myths and common thought. In the end, time will demonstrate otherwise in the long run on the ability and potential of blacks and other minorities. When Dr.Goldsby was asked about his thoughts on the homogenization of America, he answered, "In the past the races have been willing to exchange genes, of course now they're willing to exchange marriage vows as well."[275]

Reflections

Dick did not talk much about his small but powerful book on race. One of its thesis that is still not properly understood today because of the dominance of race definitions based upon the field of anthropology,[276] is that racial differences that make one group superior in one domain is canceled out by inferior abilities in other areas. His book advocated for the goodness of racial differences, grounded in a biological perspective of the environment as a causal factor in phenotypic differences. His claim that the comparatively successful performance of African Americans would change racist beliefs about

---

[275]Dr. Goldsby was invited back and received an extensive write-up in the campus newspaper. See, Neil Mukhopaohyay (April 29, 2004). "Goldsby lectures on the biology of race." *The Cornell Daily Sun*, pp. 9, 12.

[276]Les Back & Solomon, J. (Eds.) (2000). *Theories of Race and Racism: A reader*. New York: Routledge.

Black people overlooked the discipline of psychology. Hoberman,[277] for example, argued that the superior performance of Blacks as athletes was the cause of their problem because it preserved a dichotomous belief that intelligence and physical strength were incompatible in one person; therefore, if Blacks are physically strong they must be mentally weak. His analysis should have considered the Eurocentric culturalistic overlay to the idea.[278] It is the inability, from a Eurocentric perspective of crediting any distinct ability exhibit by a group perceived as oppositional, that is the psychological and intellectual culprit. A section of one of the premiere tests of intelligence was dropped from the final version because Blacks outperformed Whites. The test developers concluded that if Blacks outperformed Whites on intellectual tasks the section must not be a measure of intelligence.[279]

If, as Dick cautions, we do not use an anthropological definition, we can examine the policy implications and social justice programs harking racial disparities in diseases[280] and gnome research.[281]

Venturing off campus for an Investment in Learning

The town of Ithaca, akin to many places bordering prestigious institutions of Higher Education, is not seen by many students as a viable source for learning about self and others. Unfortunately, an elitist and ultimately isolationist view has contributed to a lack of significant involvement in the Ithaca Black community by a sizable number of Black Cornellians. Rather than stop at deploring elitism, I have sought to engage students by student lectures and workshops, revealed by the work of Hope, Nafis and David, lectures and events on campus, and promoting attendance at intellectual events in the community. One example of community learning is a lecture on the

---

[277]John Hoberman (1997). *Darwin's athletes: How sport has damaged Black America and preserved the myth of race*. Mariner Books.

[278]Ralph Wiley (1989). "the fixation on black athletic superiority: an idea whose time has gone." In George Curry (Ed.) (2003). *The best of emerge*. New York: Ballantine.

[279]Allen Thomas & Sillen, S. (1972). *Racism and psychiatry*. New York: Brunner & Mazel.

[280]Sally Lehrman (February, 2003). "The reality of race." *Scientific American*. comhttp://www.sciam.com/print_version.c-rm2articleID=0002A353　-C027-IEIC – 8B3B809EC55…

[281]Nicholas Wade (July 30, 2002). "Race is seen as real guide to track roots of diseases." *New York Times*, 1–6.

Kate and Shari picture at the Sanford talk.
Photo by Gerald G. Jackson.

subject "Parent Involvement in Reforming Education" that tied in closely to class discussions and videotape of parents challenging the Elizabeth, New Jersey school board. The lecture was symbolically held in the Beverly J. Martin Elementary School, named after a Black woman. Similarly, the speaker, a Black woman, was the New York State Regent Vice Chancellor Dr. Adelaide N. Sanford. Two students, Kate and Shari, attended and reported on the lecture, and their noteworthy recollections are published below.

Bringing 'Light' Into 'Dark Places'

Education of Black Americans call you "my beloved," I was confounded. She chose to stand in the midst of us, to connect with people flesh to flesh" rather than stand in a deceivingly distinguished place at the podium on the stage of Beverly J. Martin Elementary School's Library. It all started to come together. Regent Sanford did not come to Ithaca to conduct a forum on the parent's role in education, nor to debate the highs, lows, good and bad about the Board of Regents. Instead, she came to hear and to share, to impart wisdom as she has gained, to call us beloved because she has been loved.

Adelaide L. Sanford, currently Vice Chancellor of the New York State Board of Regents, has had numerous awards and scholarships conferred upon her and in her name. She chairs and/or is a member of several committees and organizations dedicated to affecting change in education (among which are the Regents' Committee on Low Performing Schools, Visiting Committee on Low Performing Schools, Committee on Closing the Performance Gap, and several regional and national organizations) and has worn many hats, including that of teacher and of principle of high achieving and highly recognized P.S. 21: the Crispus Attucks School in the Bedford-Styvesant section of Brooklyn (where she grew up). Also a graduate and honorary of several universities, this humble and refined educator, who works to "bring light into dark places" came to Ithaca for a visit.

The importance of attending this event, at which Regent Sanford was to speak on "Parent Involvement in Education Reform," first crossed my range of attention at church on Sunday – an occurrence which was not at all surprising to me as Calvary membership is comprised of a fair amount of educators. At the point, the thought of attending this event was just a possibility, lost in the fury of my schedule. Nevertheless I ended up sitting in the library and taking in the depth that was Regent Sanford.

She quotes Isaiah 40 as her purpose – that mountains and hills be made low and rough places made smooth (for our children); truly she is like the voice of one crying in the wilderness – and while she is not exactly crying "comfort, yes comfort my people," her voice projects passion and resolution, her analogies and anecdotes proclaim her dedication, devotion, and unrelenting ambition, her actions echo the Afrocentric principles often discussed in class. While the title of the discussion was "Parent Involvement in Education Reform," even I was empowered to take action (her response to me was "get that degree and the one after it if necessary ... you have to have power to be heard, an individual is easily overcome in the presence of authority"). Her discourse on presentation and appearance, on how "children need to value themselves, not too highly, and value others very highly" and how education allows us to create and environment where we can "be free and live free and create a climate in which others can be free" hit a resonating note in me and struck my concern for the declining quality of education and schooling in New York City.

On an enduring note, Regent Sanford addressed the link between children's health and academic success – citing the fact that there is a proven link between the two but that nothing is being done about it. "[Paraphrase] There are school nurses that check immunization but they don't check for lead poisoning...it is very easy for an individual school to create a partnership with a pediatric center and have children checked for lead poisoning, it is not very expensive at all," she noted, further "you can't heal a child without healing a family."

The audience reaffirmed the depth of Regent Sanford's discourse as they replied with a periodic "mmm" and "uh-huh." She pushed the point that parents have power, that parents should not be asking, "when will they..." but "when will we..." and that parents should see to it that their children are being taught stones that teach character and compassion and that build strength and courage. The challenges she presented to this unfortunately small crowd has resounded the call of the ancestors... "Prepare the way... I am encouraged, that is just what I hope to do."

Shari Moseley

A Night to Remember with Dr. Adelaide Sanford

The event held at the Beverly Jay Martin Auditorium tonight was well worth the venture from Cornell's busy campus to the more serene interior of children's library. Fitting with the academic atmosphere, the speaker for the night was Vice Chancellor Dr. Adelaide H. Sanford, an articulate communicator who displayed a sense of ingenious subtlety as she made plain the issues that are facing New York school systems and what parents, teachers, and faculty need to do in order to see changes in these institutions. Her speech was spoken in parables with each story relating to her main idea, yet, at the same time, maintaining a meaning of its own.

The overarching parables of her discourse addressed love, justice, joy, freedom, and hope. Beginning with the parable of love, her afrocentric concept of life was made apparent in connecting all people, calling us her "beloved." Though she has every reason to be bitter and hate, she "chooses to love." The concept of loving despite the trials was clarified when she referred to herself as "homeless." By using the imagery of homelessness, the audience was able to sense the experience of African Americans who were displaced from their native land through slavery. Sanford defined a home as, "[A place that] raises, protects, educates, and enhances her people." Without this support, African Americans are living in a country that considers them foreign inhabitants. The nodding heads of Whites in the room indicated that they agreed with the logic of being bitter and hateful in such a situation. Thus, the audience, whether Black or White, understood the concept of African American "homelessness" and embraced Sanford's decision to love in the midst of an unloving world.

Dr. Sanford's decision to love stems *from* her parable for justice identifying her afrocentric sense of spirituality and interdependence by quoting Isaiah 40: 4, 5:

"Every valley shall be exalted, and every mountain and hill shall be made low; and the rough ground shall become level, and the rugged places plain. And the glory of the Lord shall be revealed, and all mankind shall see it together. For the mouth of the Lord hath spoken."

In other words, she eloquently exposed that she cannot hold a grudge against the people who took her ancestors from their land, called them savages, and enslaved their bodies and minds because justice will prevail. The oppressor who exalts himself and values only his culture and practices will fall and the oppressed will be set on level ground with him. Thus, her afrocentric value for humanity endures because justice triumphs all oppression. She warned individuals holding "elevated positions" that their location is not permanent but cyclical and phenomenal meaning that they too must show their love for others because their destiny is uncertain. The only surety in the Sanford's address was that justice will be served.

Knowing that justice is coming intertwines with Dr. Sanford's parable for joy. She spoke about a five-year old that came home professing to his mother about how "beautiful" his new teacher was. After the mother saw that the teacher was not in particularly attractive, she asked her son, "What is beautiful about your teacher." He replied with excitement, "She looks at everything as if something wonderful is about to happen!" The speaker connected this parable with the audience by advising, "Radiate that you are expecting something wonderful to happen." One cannot go into a situation feeling defeated they must maintain their joy presenting themselves as loving and knowing justice will be served.

Upon the implementation of a more loving, just, and joyous environment, the parable of freedom will become reality. Dr. Sanford's parable for freedom was taken from Indigenous American saying:

"I have dug some wells I may not drink from. I have planted some trees that I may not use as shade."

In other words, the people of today must build a brighter future for those who come after us. Thus, she suggests that parents of school children need to use love and joy as a method to making things happen in the school system and they must know that they will see justice; however, they should not be inactive solely relying on those three concepts to attain their freedom. Freedom takes time and sacrifice. As my father once said to me, "Freedom was never free. Nothing is free." From Sanford's context, I feel she is expressing a similar concept. We all must work together to ensure the proper education of generations to come.

Finally, Dr. Sanford ended on a parable of hope. She described coming to Ithaca and seeing the cold, harsh snow covering the ground. However, in the center of all this ice and snow were blooming flowers. We need to be the blooming flowers that overcome the "cold mistrust" of our oppressors. If we all unite, we will not have to hope that our children will be the flowers in the center of the snow, but we can trust that our children will be flowers blooming in a garden of knowledge and success. Our children will be free, no longer being marginalized by inadequate school systems and simple "schooling," but they will be "educated" appropriately. For, like Shujaa in his book *Too Much Schooling Too Little Education,* Sanford juxtaposed schooling: "a prescribed physical sense of regurgitating facts" with education: "being free and living free with everyone learning about each other without anxiety or mistrust and making their world better."

As Dr. Sanford ended her thoughtfully constructed speech, I heard whispers and murmurs in the library and all around me saying "She is good" and "She is deep." When she was done with her speech, Dr. Sanford impressed the audience even further with her eloquence and knowledge as she answered questions that she in essence answered in her address. However, her calm was something to be applauded and her dedication outstanding. She revealed that her job as a New York City Regent is a non-salary position in which she must send in her receipts to be paid. She had no office at work, but maintains dedication to the cause saying, "You will not be paid for everything you do." 1 was encouraged by her presentation and am very grateful that I had the opportunity to hear her speak.

Kate Ofikuru

Intracultural Awareness and Communication is Necessary[282]

The divide is not a simple racial dichotomy because I was queried about attending a New York book party honoring the publication of a

---

[282]See Gary Weaver's monumental work that is used in over two dozen colleges and universities. Gary Weaver (Ed.) (1998). *Culture, Communications and Conflict: Readings in Intercultural Relations.* Massachusetts: Simon & Schuster.

Raquel Rivera at her book party in the Eastside
of New York. Photo by Gerald G. Jackson.

book on Hip-Hop. I mentioned my attendance to illustrate how I continued to seek out learning opportunities. Parenthetically, attending campus events shows interest; making time and spending money to attend off-campus events reflects a higher degree of commitment.

GGJ & Juan Flores at Rivera book party. Photo by Ingrid S. Hill.

The writer, Dr. Raquel Rivera, an Ivy League Brown University graduate, I exclaimed, was cited in my chapter dealing with Hip Hop[283] and her dissertation advisor, Dr. Juan Flores, was someone I really

---

[283]See chapter 10, "Njikoka: African-American Peace Initiatives" in G. Jackson (2004). *Njikoka: Towards an Africentric Paradigm of Helping.* New Jersey: Africa World Press.

respect as a scholar on subjects coinciding with my work, and as a person with *simpatico* for African Americans.[284]

Her book added immensely to the Africentric music literature.[285] It was the first to explore the participation of Puerto Ricans, not Latinos, in the development of Hip-Hop culture from the beginning to the present. Unlike other analyses that establish a musical tradition between Puerto Ricans and African Americans,[286] she determines a shared culture in terms of New York City history and in terms of an African Diaspora legacy in the Americas. This African legacy frequently escapes the purview of Black exponents of Hip-Hop so her Africentric slant fitted my Africentric cultural model quite well and added to its scholarly support of a cultural rung that is Pan-American.

Despite what I presented to the class, one student asked why I went to a Puerto Rican event and wanted to learn how they responded to my presence. I clarified that it was not an exclusive Puerto Rican event but one that celebrated a Puerto Rican advance. I noted that the event took place in my old neighborhood and I was not the only dark-skinned person present. In fact, people sported, I proclaimed, T shirts that declared that the wearer was an Afro-Latino. This digression was allowed because it allowed a moment to help students comprehend cultural similarities between African Americans and Puerto Ricans and cultural differences between Puerto Ricans and Latinos.[287] Marta Vega, president and founder of the Franklin H. Williams Caribbean Cultural

---

[284]See such works as examples: Juan Flores (2000). *From bomba to hip hop.* New York: Columbia University Press; Juan Flores (1993). *Divided borders: Essays on Puerto Rican identity.* Texas: Arte Publico Press; George Yudice, Franco, J. & Flores, J. (Eds.) (1992*). On edge: The crisis of contemporary Latin American Culture.* Minnesota: University of Minnesota Press; Cheryl L. Keyes (2002). *Rap Music and Street Consciousness.* Illinois: University of Illinois Press.

[285]See Eddie Meadows (1984). "African retentions in blues and jazz." *The Western Journal of Black Studies*, pp. 180-185; Robert Stephens (1986). "The study of music as a symbol of culture: The Afro-American and Euro-American perspectives." *The Western Journal of Black Studies.* 10(4), pp. 180-184.

[286]Ruth Glasser (1995*). My music is my flag Puerto Rican musicians and their New York communities 1917-1940.* California: University of California Press.

[287]Juan Gonzalez (2000). *Harvest of Empire. A history of Latinos in America.* New York: Viking; Marcelo Suarez-Orozco & Mariela Paez (Eds.) (2002). *LATINOS Remaking America.* California: University of California Press.

Center African Diaspora Institute, captures this essence between African Americans and Puerto Ricans when she writes:[288]

"The call for social justice, equity and parity carried with it the need for reclamation, reparation, repatriation (when desired), and equitable distribution of decision-making power and resources. Influenced by the Civil Rights and Black Power struggles, our cultural workers produced art that was culturally grounded in the traditions and histories of our people. These expressions gave first voice to our sheroes and heroes who had fought oppression before us. The images of Pedro Albizu Campos, Emiliano Zapata, Julia de Buros, Pancho Villa, and Emeterio Betances took their places alongside contemporary warriors like Lolita Lebron, Rita Kahlo, Cesar Chavez, Reuben Zalazar, Antonia Pantoja, and other articulators of a new, culturally grounded liberation vision for our communities"

African-American Socio-cultural Educational Events

The ensuing essay by Stefun,[289] is paramount for two reasons. First, he wrote it for my information, and not academic course extra credit. This was the period of his second course with me, and I was pleased to see how he had internalized the notions of *self-knowledge* and *reciprocity*. It typified my African-American belief that the modern Griot has to be capable of sharing history through ancillary writing. Stefun's adds a dimension to the event. He reveals the operation of diuntality. Unlike the split I strove to mend at Kean College between the Black Greeks and the B.S.U. (Black Student Union) leader, he notes that at Cornell the leader of the Black Student United was also a member of Delta Sigma Theta sorority. Africentrically thinking, her dual positions illustrate the successful extension of a Black Greek organization that started at a Black university, to nurturing leaders on a predominantly White campus.

---

[288]Marta Vega (1993). "The purposeful underdevelopment of Latino and other communities of Color" (p. 104). In Marta Vega & Greene, C. (Eds.) (1993). *Voices from the battlefront Achieving cultural equity.* New Jersey: Africa World Press.

[289]Stefun became a member of Omega Psi Phi fraternity after this writing.

Gerald G. Jackson

Stefun Hawkins
Africana Barbeque
Dr. Jackson
5/11/03

A Day of Cultural Reflection

Attending the end of the year barbeque at the Africana Center yesterday, May 11, 2003, was a cultivating and refreshing experience. Though very informal and planned to just be a good time and food for people to enjoy, I could not help but notice the academic pertinence of such a gathering. During the event, it was evident that many concepts of the Afrocentric worldview were being exemplified.

I first noticed cultural significance of this event when I observed the presence of three or four different generations and their interactions with each other. Despite the age, differences there were no divisions, cliques, or isolated groups among the crowd, the old, young, and in between were all mingling and enjoying the afternoon collectively. At this point, the communal concepts began to radiate from the bunch. Ideas, including the survival of the community, communal responsibility, and the perpetuation of young leadership all were exhibited. Undergrads listened to grad students give advice on what courses to take in order to be successful at Cornell, based on their own experiences. Professors were advising students to use their talents and intelligence to help out their peers and to be leaders that set positive examples for the black scholars of tomorrow, and represented an emphasis on the responsibility of the community to maintain it. Even the young children, who at times could be seen running around enjoying their youth, could also be seen sitting down being questioned and educated. I noticed some current students taking positive interest in the children and just taking some time out to let them know they were valuable and that if they remained focused on their goals and respectful they were destined for success.

Finally, at the end of the barbecue there was an awards presentation to recognize seniors and graduate students who were seen as very helpful and admirable people by the underclassmen. The idea alone to recognize those who were consistently there for others and who came through time and time again is Afrocentric based, not to mention the actions of the recipients all stemmed from a sense of giving back, the idea that they were only doing what many others did for them.

The Africana barbecue was overall an enlightening experience and I believe a very appropriate culmination of a year that I have spent

Kandis Gibson awarding graduating Black senior at BSU cook-out
ceremony at ASRC at Cornell. Photo by Gerald Jackson.

learning about my people, their profound heritage, and admirable
culture.

Stefun's essay gives evidence of what a student can realize about
the educational benefit of a Black social event when given the right
conceptual field and cultural configurations. The African world-view
he describes is the same framework that enabled Black intellectuals,
since slavery, to surpass racists beliefs, attitudes and practices and
contribute simultaneously to American society and the African-
American community.[290] The only area he omitted from analysis was
the predominant communication mode used in the setting. Had he done
so, he would have noted Ebonics and its functional uses as a mode of
communication, means of establishing and maintaining rapport and
measure to promote an African ethos.[291] This language and its culture
will atrophy when the social, political and economic circumstance of
African Americans equals that of European Americans. It maintains
itself as a survival mode, and dauntless in the face of ideological,
cultural and philosophical contamination and materialization. It is
embodied in the concept of Harlem and revealed in the Harlem
Experience, briefly describe in Section IV. Just as the European

---

[290]Williams Banks & Franklin, J. (1996). *Black intellectuals. Race and
responsibility in American life.* New York: W.W. Norton & Company.
[291]Molefi Asante (1990). "The African essence in African-American
languages" (pp. 233–252). In Molefi Asante & Asante, K. (Eds.). *African
culture.* New Jersey: Africa World Press.

Gerald G. Jackson

American does not have to reside in Europe to perpetuate a Eurocentric cultural system, the African American has created, in places such as Harlem, an Africentric cultural oasis.

The H.E. depiction makes tangible the meaning of black spirituality. It shows Africentric cultural creative energies in the arts, including culinary, literature, music, theater, and humanity—it demonstrates its appeal to a variety of ages, occupations, genders, races, and religions. It is not, therefore, an entity that can only be shared among black people.

SECTION IV
Harlem Experience Educational and Cultural Tour

Educational and Social Rationale

The book length intervention described in Section III also has a history that predates my more recent times at Cornell. This legacy needs recounting in a hyphenated form. It is a backdrop to my shift to environmental contingencies in the education of students about race, race relationship and racial harmony. Cornell University is a primarily residential campus that is home for a majority of its students. I perceive Cornell as my home, albeit temporary, and believe it should provide for students, regardless of skin color and culture, the physical and psychological comforts of a home. In contrast, historically I am of the age that remembers when Cornell's campus was the symbol of Black student protest and physical danger.

Those of us observing the event of the late sixties and early seventies realized that the gun-tooting Black students were afraid of harm. They were not, as the media publicized, the aggressors. Most honestly, they were the unfortunate victims of a psychologically abusive environment, reminiscent of a plantation governed by institutional racism.[292] Yet, when I mention to others that I teach at Cornell, I receive two typical questions that are obliquely related to the day to day campus life. From African Americans, I am asked why the Alphas are not on campus. From Whites I am asked if Cornell still has the Black dormitory. Before I can give an answer, I am informed that the person is opposed to the Black dorm and believes its existence is a form of reversed racism. Rarely asked are the questions, how do Black students experience being in predominantly White dorms, and made to feel about themselves in these environs. Eclipsed from view in the debate is just how good White Americans feel about living close to African Americans, and the extrapolation of who is really averse to

---

[292]Donald Downs (1999). *Cornell '69: Liberalism and the crisis of the American University*. New York: Cornell University Press; Harry Edwards (1970). *Black students*. New York: The Free Press; Charles White (Ed.). (1989). *The 20th Anniversary of the Willard Straight Hall Takeover Commemorative Book*. Ithaca: New York.

being in the presence of the other. It is a well-known fact that the most segregated time in the United States is during Sunday worship. To alter this behavioral practice, an African-American minister has offered to pay White people to attend and participate in his religious worship practices. In a number of predominantly White public schools the White students have voted to re-institute Black and White proms. One may wonder then why the onus for segregation is placed upon Black people? This is somewhat odd and disjointed especially when the main thrust of the African-American Civil Rights movement was integration with European Americans. Moreover, it is the power of the university to arrange and control living accommodations, and this power rests overwhelmingly in the hands of White people.[293]

The University's approach is typically to offer an opportunity to dialogue, in a cognitively driven fashion, on subjects on or related to race relations. An offshoot of the administrative or faculty-led discussion group is the student-designed and administered program. In 2002, another such program was given on the question of the need for Program Houses. Program house is a euphemism for the dwellings of "People of Color." Most of the "old Heads" at Cornell refused to attend the forums because they felt these events actually segmentalized, polarized and stigmatized more than they enlightened and unified. Most importantly, they did not emblazon what has and has not worked or produced workable program models for race relationship enterprises. I had my class attend the meeting as a form of intellectual edification and material for class writing projects. Predictably, they were enraged by the thinking of the opponents of the Program Houses and shortly excited about rallying the Left. This problem is the backdrop to the Harlem Experience reported in Section III.

Selection of Site

Starting from a personal space and time, I am a proud Harlemite, as others should feel gifted by their birthplace. I could be sensational and emphasize my bad experiences. I have not elected to do so because it was the Harlem environment and its people that propelled and compelled me to strive to be a better person and seek to serve human

---

[293] Some educators contend that the university is held to blame for solving the nation's race problems when the blame should be placed on society. See, Philip Altback & Lomotey, K. (Eds.) (1991). *The racial crisis in American higher education.* New York: SUNY Press. It is the main producer of the talented tenth that governs society and manages its main institutions.

beings. My portrayal of Harlem, therefore, is in contrast to the more popular view of Harlem from Claude Brown's depiction of his experience growing up in the area. I am not challenging what Black social scientists term a pathological model; I am asserting a concurrent viewpoint in an area of many outlooks.[294] I did many of the things Claude did and witnessed many of the deplorable things he described; however, I did not allow myself to be defined by bad experiences and disgusting people. My elementary school (P.S. 5) class conveniently walked up the street to visit the home of Alexander Hamilton. I was taught to swim, through the same elementary school, at the 135 street "Y," where much of the work of the Harlem Renaissance unfolded. During the lunch hour, I played in St. Nicholas Park.[295]

In all fairness to what felt like a sojourn, not all my pre-adult years were spent living in West Harlem. I lived in a predominantly Jewish area in the Bronx for a short while, a little longer in East Harlem when

---

[294] Lionel Bascom (1999). *A renaissance in Harlem: Lost Voices of an American Community*. New York: Avon Books; Herb Boyd (Ed.) (2002). *The Harlem Reader*. New York: Three Rivers Press; Stokely Carmicahel with Ekwueme Thelwell (2003). *Ready for revolution The life and struggles of Stokely Carmichael*. New York: Scribner; Mamdou Chinyelu (1999). *Harlem ain't nothin' but a third world country*. New York: Mustard Seed Press; Anna Swanston (2003). *Dr. John Henrik Clarke His life, his words his works*. Georgia: I am unlimited Publishers; Monique Taylor (2002). *Harlem between Heaven and hell*. Minnesota: University of Minnesota Press; John Jackson (2001). *Harlem world*. Illinois: University of Chicago Press; Michael Adams (2002). *HARLEM Lost and found*. New York: Monacelli Press. I am in the middle of a Harlem perceptual continuum. On the left is James Baldwin's nostalgic pine about the way Harlem use to be and on the right is Kevin Powell's portrayal of Harlem as a place that can foster "healing." James Baldwin (November, 1996). *Whose Harlem is this,anyway. Essence*, pp. 112, 202; Kevin Powell (December, 1999). "Manhattan Breakdown, Harlem Healing." *CODE*, pp. 52, 54. Craig Marberry & Cunningham, M. (2003). *Spirit of Harlem A Portrait of American's Most Exciting Neighborhood*. New York: Doubleday

[295] In 1970 I bought my first oil painting from an artist name Thomas Gunn. He was displaying his work on park benches in St. Nicholas Park, Harlem. I found his story about how he became an artist so compelling that I invited him to speak at the program I administered for pre-college youth at Yale University. As I suspected the students indicated that they found inspiring his self-discovery and career confidence. This experience took place thirty years after I played in the same setting.

the Italians dominated the area,[296] in the T Street, 14th street, and M street northwest and Anacostia sections of Washington, D.C. During this time, I visited relatives in Brooklyn, Amytville, Mount Vernon,

CCNY view from St. Nicholos park in Harlem.
Photo by Gerald G. Jackson.

and St. Albans, New York and New London, Connecticut. Harlem, however, remains my birthplace and major cultural frame of reference. It is where I attended churches in magnificent structures, rode elevators in luxurious apartment buildings, swam in the largest public pool (Colonial park, now called Jackie Robinson) in the city, became a member of the Cub Scouts and Minisink Cadets, watched major parades on Lenox Avenue and played in St. Nicholas Park, an area with City College as its background and almost one mile in length.

This is the same place that comforted Ralph Ellison.[297] Touchingly, David Taylor, in a book review, wrote:

> On the first leg from the Bronx across the Harlem River, my transport is the Bx 33. As I board, the driver waves me back to any seat. I choose, Jackson reports that Ellison savored such choices when he first arrived in New York from the segregated south. The bus then drops me off at St.

---

[296]See Robert Orsi (2002). *The Madonna of 115th Street*. Connecticut: Yale University Press.
[297]Lawrence Jackson (2002). *Ralph Ellison: Emergence of Genius*. New York: John Wiley & Sons.

Nicholas Park, which glows with a spring flush of grass, daffodils, and hyacinths. The sun is sliding down as a cold breeze kicks up. On early spring nights in 1938, the park benches here were a young Ellison's only shelter. He had just come from his mother's funeral in the Midwest, an orphan with no money and few connections.[298]

We had much in Harlem, even suburban-type backyards.[299] There was no place equivalent to 125th Street. I attended movies there, ate at fancy restaurants (e.g., Franks), played at the Penny Arcade, had my shoes shined in a parlor and dreamed of purchasing "very hip" clothes (e.g., A.J. Lester). The glorious Harlem recalled as an adult was based upon memories from my childhood and youth. This experience will serve as a revised first stage in the Cross-Model of Black psychological development, consistent with its African psychology critique.[300]After college I only frequented the place to be with my mother, who lived in East Harlem, and my father, who lived in West Harlem. It was conversations with professor Abdul Nanji that opened my eyes to a glorious Harlem from an adult point of view. West Harlem is still Nanji's "stomping grounds" and our discussions on the subject led to plans to sponsor a trip for Cornell University students. We both bemoaned how Black, Latino, Asian and White students spent 4 years at Cornell and never visited New York City, let alone the world-renowned Harlem. We theorized that the richness of Harlem would be an educational, interpersonal and enjoyable learning experience for a cross-section of students, staff and faculty. We believed it would appeal to a diversity of individuals, groups and ideologies. We believed

---

[298]David Taylor (July 17-23, 2002). "A walk through Ralph Ellison's New York Tracking the invisible man." *The Village Voice*, p. 1. http://www. village voice.com/issues/0229/taylor.php.

[299]Howard Dodson, Moore, C. & Yancy, R. (2000). *The Black New Yorkers*. New York: Schomburg Center For Research in Black Culture.

[300]Na'im Akbar (1989). Nigrescence and identity. *The Counseling Psychologist*, 17(2), *pp.* 258–263; Daudi Azibo (1998). "The distinction between African personality personologists and other African personality scholars: Implications and an entreatment for reconceptualization of racial identity issues" (pp. 207–215). In Reginald Jones (Ed.). *African American identity development*. Virginia: Cobb & Henry; Wade Nobles (1998). *To be African or not to be: The question of identity or authenticity – Some preliminary thoughts* (pp. 183–206). Virginia: Cobb & Henry; Wade Nobles (1989). "Psychological Nigrescence: An Afrocentric review." *The Counseling Psychologist*, 17(2), pp. 253–257.

Harlem's Blackness could be as universal as a Toni Morrison novel. For example, while Alicia Keyes was not born in Harlem, she identified with the site and in 2003 held a concert in Marcus Garvey Park, as a tribute to the historical site.

The publication of a book on the trip was designed to fulfill a myriad of needs. One need was professional, stemming from my training as a mental health professional. I had expertise to share with the group in Black psychology, cross-cultural psychotherapy, intracultural communication and diversity. Given an Africentric propensity for the experiential and historical, I believed a guided excursion by people who had grown up and lived in Harlem would engender better knowledge of African-American culture and foster functional intracultural and intercultural relationships. Similarly, my professional experiences suggested that the program could be expanded in a number of educational and mental health ways. These ideals also were tempered by the pragmatism of a cash economy. My plans and actions consequently had to calculate the payment for things costing my employer time, energy and money.

Another result of my professional experience was the recognition of the necessity to document efforts and accomplishments. As a former Student Affairs dean, I vividly recalled having to fight to justify our peer status with academic affairs. One of the things I was insistent upon during this period was documenting our actions and successes. This was to show not only why we should exist but why we should continue to do so and grow. As a kind of reflex action, therefore, I asked students at the close of the last event to write up the Harlem Experience. Participants also were my current students and I informed them that a submitted Harlem Experience evaluative essay would be used as extra credit. Understandably, the majority of social and professional essays emanated from current students. Another reason may be convenience. My current students had a ready-made mechanism for conveying their essays and receiving the rewards of extra credit and classroom praise for oral presentations.

Overall, this background resulted in my professional, as opposed to intellectual, need to document the positive aspects of the program. I wrote a small book on the Harlem Experience. The book was organic in nature and stemmed from an earnest desire to give order and respect to all the people involved. It was a means for expressing the picture students and I had taken of people and events. It was an outlet for expressing our elation over the awards received by the program, and confidence from our positive program evaluation that we would get future funding.

A telling program evaluation piece is the student essays and comments. Collectively, they reveal a profundity in thought and compassion that has been said to escape this Hip-Hop generation. For a broader circumference, one should pay particular attention to the observations of Rejane Frick, a graduate student from France who taught at Lincoln University, an HBU (Historically Black University), in 2001 and Cornell in 2002. She writes with the clinical eyes of a descendent of Alexis De Tocqueville[301] or his ghost. She alludes to a positive African-American culture, not ghetto experience, in her essay.

My afterthought to this work can be summed up in this way: the Harlem Experience should be any event that is *Africentric, inclusive, educational, enjoyable and collectively done. This is because of its symbolic significance, and it should be used to connote any educational cultural journey in the African Diaspora. Participants should bear in mind that it is not a thought that is ultimately dangerous to peace and tranquillity. Barriers to learning about self and others are thought patterns and processes. This is one of the main tenets guiding my pedagogical plans and actions. I give instruction and learning opportunities to assess problems and triumphs based on the culturally induced ways of structuring our perceptions of reality.*

Almost entire H.E. group taken in lobby of Schomburg.
Photo by Gerald G. Jackson.

---

[301]De Tocqueville, A. (1956). *Democracy in America* (specially edited and abridged by Richard D. Heffner). New York: The New American Library:

NOV. 16, 2002

1 BUS.
40 PEOPLE.

THE

HARLEM
EXPERIENCE

WITH PROFESSORS GERALD JACKSON
AND ABDUL GULU NANJI

A collaborative effort of Cornell Faculty Programs in Residential Communities,
Low Rises, and Ujamaa Residential College.

The Spirit of this Publication

How can the American Negro past be used? It is entirely possible that this dishonored past will rise up soon to smite all of us. There are some wars, for example (if anyone on the globe is still mad enough to go to war,) that the American Negro will not support, however many of his people may be coerced—and there is a limit to the number of people any government can put in prison, and a rigid limit indeed to the practicality of such a course. A bill is coming in that I fear America is not prepared to pay. "The problem of the Twentieth century," wrote W.E.B. Du Bois around sixty years ago, "is the problem of the color line." A fearful and delicate problem, which compromises, when it does not corrupt, all the American efforts to build a better world—here, there, or anywhere; it is for this reason that everything white Americans think they believe in must now be reexamined. What one would not like to see again is the consolidation of peoples on the basis of their color. But as long as we in the West place on color the value that we do, we make it impossible for the great unwashed to consolidate themselves according to any other principles. Color is not a human or a particular reality; it is a political reality. However, this is a distinction so extremely hard to make that the West has not been able to make it yet. And at the center of this dreadful storm, this vast confusion, stand the black people of this nation, who must now share the fate of a nation that has never accepted them, to which they were brought in chains. Well, if this is so, one has no choice but to do all in one's power to change that fate, and at no matter what risk— eviction, imprisonment, torture, death. For the sake of one's children, in order to minimize the bill that they must pay, one must be careful not to take refuge in any delusion—and the value placed on the color of the skin is always and everywhere and forever a delusion. I know that what I am asking is impossible. But in our time, as in every time, the impossible is the least that one can demand—and one is, after all, emboldened by the spectacle of human history in general and American Negro history in particular, for it testifies to nothing less than the perpetual achievement of the impossible. **James Baldwin, The Fire Next Time, 1963, p. 103.**

I believe fervently that we can learn potentially from everything and everybody, and from the living and the dead. This notion is amplified in a study of Harlem. Harlem is more than a geographical location and must be viewed from multiple angles. It readily encompasses the disciplines of psychology, sociology, education, anthropology, political science, economics, biology, philosophy or afrology. Less obvious, it includes engineering, architecture, urban planning, public health, and welfare, gerontology, linguistic, environmental studies and psychiatry. Most important, this document can be reread for a different angle of vision. The trip was cool, awesome, the bomb and all that. Enjoy the reading and pass the word.

Respectfully,
Gerald G. Jackson, See *The Boy from New York City by the Ad Libs*[302]

INTRODUCTION BY GERALD G. JACKSON

This publication, akin to the Harlem Experience that is evaluated herein, is organic in nature and based upon a voluntary effort and peace-initiative imperative. Since its pedestrian start, it has grown. It now encompasses a time that needs examples of an appreciation for world-view differences in cultural beliefs and practices. This report is one such illustration. It highlights an Africentric pedagogical approach to conventional program evaluation.

The text is the result of what was seen as a rudimentary assignment to gather insights for future cross-cultural and intra-cultural learning events. Briefly, as the bus was in the process of departing from Showman's, the last stop in our Harlem Experience, the college professor emerged. I requested students to submit, a day or so later, a commentary on the personal significance of the trip. For students enrolled in my fall, 2002 courses, I offered extra credit for an essay, and the opportunity and experience of reading their essay in class. All the essays are from my students and a majority are from the first year Knight writing seminar program. Ironically, given the limited sample of students included in the assessment, the students submitting essays do represent a diversity of voices that is not typically heard in positive assessments of Harlem.

By extension, Africana Studies is viewed in some circles as an area that nurtures "anti" sentiments, or the exclusion of groups based upon race, ethnic group, gender and age criteria. Overlooked in such assessments is the African Diaspora legacy of *peace*. This perspective is alluded to in my book on Africentric helping,[303] and reflected in the ideas and efforts of Dr. Ralph Bunche, Dr. Martin Luther King, Jr., Rev. Andrew Young, Bishop Tutu, President Nelson Mandela,

---

[302]Table of Contents omitted from this publication of the Harlem Experience.

[303]Gerald G. Jackson (2000). *Precursors of An African Genesis Model of Helping*. New York: Global Publications.

Diplomat Kofi Annan and Writer Walter Mosley.[304] This ancestry served as backdrop to an African American and African joining their energies to initiate a cultural experience for Low Rises 6 & 7 and Ujamaa students, in particular, and Cornell students, in general. The resulting program, the student evaluations will attest, was a successful diversity engagement that fostered intellectual growth and emotional intelligence.[305]

The photographs used in this document are another example of its organic nature. I was not thinking long-range when I shared the three Harlem Experience albums. Unexpectedly then, student viewers started contributing their photographs for the albums. I liked the idea and the processes of reliving and sharing the Harlem Experience. I contemplated, consequently, how I could share the album viewing experience in a broader context and more timely way. While reading the student essays, it dawned upon me that I could achieve my end by inserting photos in the student descriptive essays. Thus, the photographs would serve as a reminder for those who attended the educational tour and as an introduction to it for those interested in receiving an approximation of the experience.[306]

The Harlem Experience: Expression of an Extended Family[307]
By Gerald G. Jackson

This letter is intended as an overview of the Harlem Experience educational tour. The enclosed schedule informs you of what the educational experience will entail and the bibliography provides a source for additional insights and knowledge about Harlem, New York

---

[304]Walter Mosley's new book *What's Next* proposes that African Americans can have a voice and play a leading role in creating world peace. It challenges global capitalism which is viewed as profiting from the creation of war, hunger and death around the world.

[305]See Daniel Goleman (1995). *Emotional intelligence*. New York: Bantam; (1998). *Working with emotional intelligence*. New York: Bantam; and with Boyatzia, R., & McKee, A. (2002). *Primal leadership*. Massachusetts: Harvard Business School. See student evaluations on pages 22-39, 44,45.

[306]Many pictures were omitted from this version of the Harlem Experience.

[307]This discussion is the introduction in the package of materials given to participants. The package included, in addition, a bibliography compiled by librarian Eric Acree (e.g., pp. 8-13). The cover to this report was created by Jeanne Butler, map and organizational sketches by Kenneth Glover, and a Harlem magazine by Professor Nanji.

City. In addition, therefore, to a package that is rich with educational and social information, I want to include historical information on how this trip evolved and the cooperative efforts that ensured its reality. This backdrop captures a life-affirming energy that can be extended to other human relations areas.

The idea of a Harlem trip was a vision I shared with Professor Nanji every year since my arrival at Cornell. It took shape when Professor Ohadike recommended me to become a faculty fellow and Dr. Leslie Sadler, after consulting me about my interests, made my appointment to Low Rises 6 & 7. It took more shape when Samuel Reynolds asked me at an early faculty fellow staff meeting to express the program I wanted to contribute. I mentioned a desire to sponsor a trip to Harlem and his great enthusiasm, and that of the PA's and RA's, cemented my desire. In particular, Latossha's glee and quick decision to provide assistance for such a journey convinced me that the idea could come to fruition this semester. It took more to make this trip a reality than the outpouring of verbal support. It took the combined efforts of a Cornell family to put the idea of a Harlem Experience educational tour into practice. I think it fair to note the organizations and individuals that contributed freely their time and money.

I think the first group to be appreciated is the participant residents. Yes you, some may perceive your contribution as a nominal fee, but I prefer to see it as an educational investment in your intracultural learning. Of equal importance, kudos for the History department, CD, Minority Affairs, Ujamaa, Low Rises 6 & 7 and Alumni Affair offices and areas. In a similar vein, the following individuals are being acknowledged for their unique contributions to the Harlem Experience program and package: Latossha Tifre, Abdul Gulu Nanji, Lynette Logan, Zahirah Alleyne-Mcnatt, Samuel Reynolds, William Andrew Marler, Kenneth Glover, Mariely Rodriguez and Liana Fox. The last group that deserves mention is the Cornell Alumni who will be attending the Reunion event. It warmed my heart when I received confirmations soaked with great enthusiasms and appreciation. All this says something about the power of an extended family to unite diverse individuals and groups in an age of materialism.

Low Rises 6 & 7 Family[308]

Gerald G. Jackson teaches in the Africana Studies & Research Center, and he is a Faculty Fellow for *Low Rises* 6&7 and the *Omega*

---

[308]These biographical sketches have been written by the named individuals.

Phi Beta sorority. In addition, he is an authority on cultural diversity, cross-cultural psychology, and intra-cultural counseling and psychotherapy.

His environment has shaped much of what he strives to achieve in life. He is a proud Harlemite, reared in both West and East Harlem. Relatedly, the direction of his professional career was greatly influenced by the Black Social Consciousness Movement of the 1960's and the exposure he received, while a Howard University undergraduate, as a research assistant in the defunct Office of Economic Opportunity. His child rearing, combined with his formal education, compelled him to seek a job that would enable him to lessen poverty in the United States. Upon undergraduate graduation, therefore, he chose a Senior Resident Counselor position at a Job Corps Center for Women in Poland Springs, Maine. The locale and the nationally based sample of women sensitized him to their plight and made him cognizant of the complexity of providing vocational assistance to racially, ethnically and culturally diverse populations.

The Job Corps and related professional and community experiences deepened his appreciation for the empowerment that accompanies the acquisition of higher educational levels of formal education. It developed his attraction to non-traditional educational programs serving economically and culturally diverse students. He spent, therefore, several years directing programs at Yale University, and over a decade assisting community college and university students, as both an academic and student affairs dean. In an effort to strengthen a multicultural perspective of the learning process, he selected teaching positions at different types of educational institutions.

Throughout the years, he has attempted to augment his educational and psychological insights by providing services to professional organizations, community groups, institutions and agencies. He has served, for example, on the professional journal boards of the *Black Psychology, Counseling and Values* and *Cultural Diversity and Ethnic Minority Psychology* scholarly journals, and consulted with over 100 for-profit and non-profit institutions and agencies. He is one of thirty experts in Change Management that the Board of Governors of the American Society for Training and Development selected to help document existing practices in the field. Similarly, he was selected for membership in an international psychological group designing a postdoctoral curriculum for professional psychologists to intervene throughout the world in trauma situations and conflict-resolution of Ethnopolitical warfare.

Gerald is the author of *Precursors of An African Genesis Model of Helping* and two forthcoming books in a series on the Africana approach to helping. Summarizing his professional community involvement, he was appointed as *Associate Fellow* of Ezra Stiles College of Yale University and elected to *Outstanding Young Men of America* and *Who's Who in the East.* He has also appeared in the reference books: *American Men and Women of Science, Social Behavioral Sciences*; *Community Leaders of America; Dictionary of International Biography; Directory of Distinguished Americans;* and *International Who's Who of Intellectuals.*

Liana Fox is the Programming Assistant (PA) in the Low Rises 6 & 7 Complex. She is a senior in ILR. Liana grew up in rural Kansas and has never been to Harlem.

William Marler likes to consider himself from "the northeast." Having moved every 6 years since birth, and enlisted in the Navy at 18, there's no real location that he calls home, especially since his parents moved across the country to San Diego while he was at sea. Currently he is a junior Mechanical Engineer in the Sibley School of Mechanical and Aerospace Engineering, the server administrator (though not the webmaster) for the Cornell Lunatic humor magazine at www.cornell-lunatic.com, a member of the Cornell FSAE Race team (fsae.mae.cornell.edu), and a second-year RA.

Low rise staff group meeting in the Robert Purcell dinner hall.
Photo by Gerald G. Jackson.

Mariely Rodriguez: I am a sophomore, psychology major in Arts & Sciences. I plan to someday work for a forensics unit. I'm currently an RA for the Low Rises—and happy to be here, might I add. I currently live in NJ, although I've lived all over the place: I was born in the Dominican Republic, lived in NY for a while, then moved to NJ and lived all over the state. I'm proud to call Cornell my new home... it's the best place in the world!

Latossha Tifre: I am a senior Human Biology Health and Society major in the College of Human Ecology and I am from San Antonio, Texas. My extracurricular activities include The Cornell Tradition, Alpha Epsilon Delta Premedical Honor Society, Black Bio Medical Technical Association, Thakeneng Collective Saturday School, Black Southern Students Alliance, and Residential Advisor. After graduating from Cornell, I plan to attend medical school.

Ujamaa Family

Mwalimu Abdu Nanji was born in Tanzania, East Africa and came to the U.S. to further his education, attending SUNY and Howard University, majoring in African Studies. He started teaching Kiswahili (Swahili) Language, Literature, and Culture at Cornell in 1977. Before joining the Cornell faculty, he taught at SUNY at New Paltz, NYC Technical College, Hunter College, and Columbia University. His research and interests are in central and southern African languages and literature, languages of Africans in the Diaspora, and Pan-Africanism. He enjoys traditional and contemporary African music, jazz, blues, Caribbean music, salsa music, hip-hop, and rap.

Ujamaa (pronounced "oo-ja-ma") is a concept that is derived from the East African language, Ki-Swahili. There is no single word in English that fully conveys its meaning. The concept of "Ujamaa" is a process where all the members of a community work together as an extended family to build and maintain a cohesive community that nurtures and supports its residents. Those choosing Ujamaa as their home at Cornell will not only share a friendly, warm cooperative living environment, but also learn a great deal about the history, culture and forces that helped shape the lives of Black people in the United States, Africa and the Caribbean.

Zahirah Alleyne-McNatt: My name is Zahirah and I am a senior in the Africana Studies and Research Department. My family is originally from Trinidad and Tobago and I was born in the Lower East Side of New York City. I participated in the development of this trip to Harlem because it is important for the history and culture of an under-represented people to be brought to light. I hope you all enjoy your visit to Harlem and are able to share the knowledge you gain with your friends and family. It is important that we are able to dispel myths and uncover lies and share this information with others. Harlem is full of vibrancy and culture so I know you all will enjoy yourselves.

Lynette J. Logan is a psychology major in the college of Arts and Sciences. She plans to attend graduate school to obtain her Doctorate of Psychology in Child Psychology. Lynette is also the Program Coordinator for Ujamaa Residential College.

Ujamaa group. Photo by Gerald G. Jackson.

Kenneth Glover is the Ujamaa Residential College Director.

Since its founding in 1972, the mission of Ujamaa has remained steadfast – to create a living environment that celebrates the rich and diverse heritage of Black people, while promoting the integration of personal goals with academic and professional opportunities. This mission is supported through a variety of activities and events that include lectures from internationally renowned speakers, Black Women's History Month, faculty dinners, and the State of Black America Conference. Lively, engaging, and educational discussions on a variety of topics are never on short supply during the weekly student-organized forum called "Unity Hour."'

Consistent with its theme of working together to create a successful community, Ujamaa residents are very involved with several off-campus programs like Thakangeng (a community youth-education program), La Voz Boriken (a student social-action group), and the long-standing annual Festival of Black Gospel. Then there are the numerous, on-going social activities like movie night, bi-weekly dances, intramural athletics, and group dinners provide the opportunity to get to know other residents and form life-long friendships.

Friendships are not all that continue long after graduation, strong associations with Ujamaa often result in mentor-type relationships that are an appreciated extension of the entire living and leaning experience. This vast and loyal alumni network becomes a valuable resource for information and advice on academic decisions, career choices, and personal goals. It is much like an extended family that reaches far beyond the walls of Cornell.

Africana Studies & Research Center Family

Eric Acree is currently Director of the John Henrik Clarke Africana Library, Cornell University. He has been with Cornell University Library since 2002. Previously he worked at the University at Buffalo (UB) Undergraduate Library (1995-2002). He held positions at UB as the Head of Library Instruction for the Arts and Sciences Library; Coordinator of The Cybraries Teaching Center; and Reference/Instruction Librarian. He was also the Web Master of the Undergraduate Library's Web site. He also served on the peer-reviewed editorial board for the educational website MERLOT (www.merlot.org). He has an M.L.S. in library and information studies, B.A. in history. His research interests include Africana Studies and teaching.

The John Henrik Clarke Africana Library, also known as the Africana Library provides a special collection focusing on the history and culture of people of African ancestry. There are over 20,000 volumes in the collection. The library supports the curriculum of Cornell University's Africana Studies & Research Center. University-wide the library serves as a bibliographical reference and referral center by providing access to African, African American, and Caribbean resources available either in the Cornell University Library or in collections at other institutions.

History of the John Henrik Clarke
Africana Library

The John Henrik Clarke Africana Library is a special library located within Cornell University's Africana Studies and Research Center. The library is one of nineteen units of the University Library system, and offers a full range of services. Its collection of 15,000 volumes focuses on the social and political dimensions of the history and culture of peoples of African ancestry. It supports the curriculum of the Africana Studies and Research Center and sustained, independent study. Included here are basic books, complete collections of works of important writers, and highly selective research materials that complement the collections housed in Cornell University's research libraries. The Africana Library's documentation collection contains valuable primary source materials, including copies of rare monographs, manuscripts, newspapers, and journal publications on microfilm and microfiche. Those resources focus on especially important material on the American civil rights and Black Power movements.

The Africana Center was founded in 1969 following black student protests on the Cornell Campus. One notable event involved black students depositing hundreds of books at the undergraduate library circulation desk and denouncing them as irrelevant to their experiences. Historically, the faculty of the Africana Studies and Research Center has always had a strong commitment towards maintaining its own library. The Africana Center included a library when it was first established. Later, after its building was destroyed by arsonists (April 1, 1970), it garnered funds from the university and local community to replace materials lost from its library collection. Once it relocated to its present site, the library was prominently established near the building's entrance.

In the late 1970s, there was heated debate on campus about relocating the Africana Center once more. Because its location was some distance away from central campus (approximately 20 minutes walking time) and many of its courses were taught at the Center, some considered the Africana Studies program too segregated. A number of more central locations were proposed for relocation. In the end, these were rejected because they entailed substantial reductions in space. Ultimately, the Center's fledgling library benefited from this consequence. A reduction in space would have affected collection size and overall growth.

During 1984-85 the Africana Center and University Library reached an agreement to transfer the library administratively to the University Library. Faculty of the Africana Studies & Research Center named the library in honor of Dr. John Henrik Clarke during the summer of 1985. As a distinguished historian, Dr. Clarke was instrumental in establishing the Africana Center's curriculum in the 1970s and taught courses in black history at Cornell. Several years later, in 1990, the Africana Center and University Library collaborated to raise $50,000 to renovate the library's space and enhance the overall level of service. The John Henrik Clarke Africana Library now occupies most of the lower level of the Africana Center's three-story building. A third of this space is shared with a graduate student lounge and a computer lab. All of the holdings of the library are included in the University Library's online catalog, and the Africana Library itself houses several online catalog terminals, a circulation terminal, CD-ROM and various audio-visual equipment, and has access to numerous locally networked bibliographic databases.

Reprinted from: Black Caucus of the ALA Newsletter, vol. XXIV, No. 5 (April 1996), p. 11.

Bibliography on Harlem, New York

http://www.library.cornell.edu/africana/guidesharlem.html

Compiled by Eric Kofi Acree for The Harlem Experience Educational Journey

This bibliography list selective book titles and Web sites which reflect the rich experiences and traditions of Harlem, New York.

History:

23rd Precinct: The Job, Arlene Schulman, New York: Soho Press, Incorporated, 2002.

The Black Jews of Harlem: Negro Nationalism and the Dilemmas of Negro Leadership, Howard Brotz, New York: Schocken Books, 1970.

Black Manhattan, Johnson, James Weldon, New York, NY: Da Capo Press, 1991.

Black Organized Crime in Harlem, 1920-1930, Rufus Schatzberg, New York: Garland Publishers, 1993.

Communist in Harlem During the Depression, Mark Naison, New York: Grove Press, 1984.

Daydreams and Nightmares: Reflections of a Harlem Childhood, Horowitz, Irving L, Transaction Publishers, 1998.

Discovering Black New York: A Guide to the City's Most Important African-American Landmark, Tarrant-Reid, Linda, Kensington Publishing Corporation, 2001.

The Great Jazz Day, Graham, Charles, Da Capo Press; Kansas City, MO, 2000.

Harlem: A Community in Transition, Clarke, John Henrik, editor, New York: Citadel Press, 1964.

Harlem At War: The Black Experience in WWII, Brandt, Nat, New York: Syracuse University Press, 1996.

Harlem Churches: At the End of the Twentieth Century, Cynthia Hickman, Dunbar, Incorporated, 2001.

Harlem: Its Origins and Early Annals, James Riker, Upper Saddle River, N.J.: Literature House, 1970.

Harlem On My Mind: Cultural Capital of Black America, 1900-1968, Allon Schoener, Ed., New York: News Press, 1995.

Harlem, Lost and Found: An Architectural and Social History, 1765-1915, Michael Henry Adams, New York: Monacelli Press, 2002.

Harlem Style, Roderick N. Shade and Jorge S. Arango, New York: Stewart, Tabori & Chang, 2002.

Harlem, The Making of a Ghetto, Gilbert Osofsky, Chicago: Ivan R. Dee, 1996.

Harlem Today: A Cultural and Visitors Guide, Bailey, A. Peter, DIANE Publishing Company, PA, 1998.

Harlem, U.S.A, Clarke, John Henrik, Editor, New York: Collier Books, 1971.

A History of the Masjid Malcolm Shabazz: A Cultural Watershed in the Harlem and American Experience, United States: A.M. Mannan, 2000.

"Or Does it explode?" Black Harlem in the Great Depression, Greenberg, Cheryl Lynn, New York: Oxford University Press, 1991.

Sea Island to City: A Study of the Helena Islanders in Harlem and Other Urban Centers, Kiser, Clyde Vernon, New York: Atheneum, 1969.

A Short History of East Harlem, Donald Stewart, New York: Museum of the City of New York, 1972.

Showtime at the Apollo, Ted Fox, New York: Da Capo Press, 1993.

This Was Harlem: 1900-1950, Anderson, Jervis, New York: Farrar Straus Giroux, 1982.

What Made Harlem Famous, Kalamazoo, Mich.: On the Move Publishers, 1992.

When Harlem Was Jewish, 1870-1930, Jeffery S. Gurock, New York: Columbia Univerisity Press, 1979.

Social Conditions:

36 children, Herbert Kohl, New York: New American Library, 1967.

Blood relations: Caribbean Immigrants and the Harlem Community, 1900-1930, Irma Watkins-Owens, Bloomington: Indiana University Press, 1996.

Children Race and Power: Kenneth and Mamie Clark's Northside Center, Markowitz, Gerald E., Charlottesville, Va.: University Press of Virginia, 1996.

Dark Ghetto: Dilemmas of Social Power, Kenneth Clark, New York: Harper & Row, 1965.

From Abandonment to Hope: Community-households in Harlem, New York: Columbia University Press, 1990.

Growing Old in El Barrio, Freidenberg, and Judith, New York: New York University Press, 2000.

Harlem Between Heaven and Hell, Monique M. Taylor, Minneapolis: University of Minnesota Press, 2002.

Harlem World: Doing Race and Class in Contemporary Black America, John L. Jackson, Jr., Chicago: University of Chicago Press, 2001.

Manchild in the Promised Land, Claude Brown, New York: Macmillan, 1965.

One of the Children: Gay Black Men in Harlem, William Hawkeswood, Berkley: University of California Press, 1996.

A School of Our Own: Parents, Power, and Community at the East Harlem Block Schools, Tom Roderick, Teachers College Press, Teachers College, Columbia University, 2001.

Harlem Renaissance:

African-American Concert Dance: The Harlem Renaissance and Beyond, Perpener, John O, Urbana: University of Illinois Press, 2001.

Authentic Blackness: The Folk in the New Negro Renaissance, Favor, J. Martin. Durham: Duke University Press, 1999.

A Beautiful Pageant: African American Performance Theater, and Drama in the Harlem Renaissance, 1910-1927, David Krasner, Palgrave Macmillan, 2002.

Carl Van Vechten and the Harlem Renaissance: A Critical Assessment, Coleman, Leon, New York: Garland Pub. 1998.

Deep River: Music and Memory in Harlem Renaissance Thought, Anderson, Paul Allen, Durham, NC: Duke University Press, 2001

Double-Take: A Revisionist Harlem Renaissance Anthology, edited by Venetria K. Patton and Maureen Honey, New Brunswick, N.J.: Rutgers University Press, 2001.

Gay Rebel of the Harlem Renaissance: Selections from the Work of Richard Bruce Nugent, Richard Bruce Nugent, Duke University Press, 2002.

Grown Deep: Essays on the Harlem Renaissance, Long, Richard. Four-G Publishers, Incorporated, 2001.

Harlem Group of Negro Writers, Melvin B. Tolson; edited by Edward J. Mullen, Westport, Conn.: Greenwood Press, 2001.

The Harlem Renaissance, Wintz, Cary, Brandywine Press, Incorporated, 2001.

A Hubert Harrison Reader, Harrison, Hubert H., Middletown, Conn.: Wesleyan University Press, 2001.

Jean Toomer and the Harlem Renaissance, edited by Geneviève Fabre, Michel Feith., New Brunswick, N.J.: Rutgers University Press, 2001.

Renaissance in Harlem: Lost Essays of the WPA by Ralph Ellison, Dorothy West, and Other Voices of a Generation, Lionel C Bascom (Editor), Amistad Press, 2000.

This Waiting for Love: Helene Johnson, Poet of the Harlem Renaissance, Verner D. Mitchell, Ed., Amherst: University of Massachusetts Press, 2000.

To Make a New Race: Gurdjieff, Toomer, and the Harlem Renaissance, Woodson, Jon., Jackson: University Press of Mississippi, 1999.

Harlem Renaissance Reading List: Encyclopedia Smithsonian – http://www.si.edu/resource/faq/nmah/harlem.htm

Fiction:

Across 110th Street, Wally Ferris, New York: Harper & Row, 1970.

All Shot Up, Chester Himes, New York: Thunder's Mouth Press, 1996.

An Intimation of Things Distant: The Collected Fiction of Nella Larsen, Charles R. Larson, ed., New York: Anchor Books, 1992.

The Big Gold Dream, Chester Himes, New York: Thunder's Mouth Press, 1996.

Bird at My Window, Rosa Guy, Minneapolis, MN: Coffee House Press, 2001.

The Blacker the Berry, Wallace Thurman, New York: Scribner Paperback Fiction, 1996.

Blind Man with a Pistol, Chester Himes, New York: Vintage Books, 1989.

Classic Fiction of the Harlem Renaissance, William L. Andrews, New York: Oxford University Press, 1994.

The Complete Fiction of Nella Larsen, Nella Larsen, New York: Anchor Books, 2001.

The Conjure-man Dies: A Mystery Tale of Dark Harlem, Rudolph Fisher, Ann Arbor: University of Michigan Press, 1992.

A Conversation with the Mann: a novel, Ridley, John, New York: Warner Books, 2002.

Cotton comes to Harlem, Chester Himes, New York: Vintage Books, 1988, c1965.

The Crazy Kill, Chester Himes, New York: Vintage Books, 1989.

Daddy Was A Number Runner, Louise Meriwether, New York: Feminist Press at the City of New York, 1970.

Do or Die: A Mali Anderson Mystery, Edwards, Grace F. (Grace Frederica), New York: Doubleday, 2000.

A Feast of Fools: A Novel, Ebele Oseye, New York: Africana Legacy Press, 1998.

A Fling With a Demon Lover, New York: HarperCollins, 1996.

Friday Nights at Honeybee's, Andrea Smith, New York: The Dial Press, 2003.

Giveadamn Brown, Robert Deane Pharr, New York: W.W. Norton, 1997.

Harlem, Len Riley, New York: Doubleday, 1997.

The Harlem Knight, James Bovine, Brooklyn: L'écrivain, 1989.

Harlem Redux: A Novel, New York : Simon & Schuster, 2002.

The Haunting of Hip Hop: A Novel, Bertice Berry, New York: Doubleday, 2001.

The Heat's On, Chester Himes, New York: Vintage Books, 1988.

The Hit; and, The Long Night, Julian Mayfield, Boston: Northeastern University Press, 1989.

Home to Harlem, Claude McKay, Boston: Northeastern University Press, 1987.

If I should Die: A Mali Anderson Mystery, Grace F. Edwards, New York: Doubleday, 1997.

Infants of the Spring, Wallace Thurman, Boston: Northeastern University Press, 1992.

Jazz, Toni Morrison, Boston, Mass.: G.K. Hall, 1993.

Mumbo Jumbo, Ishmael Reed, New York, N.Y.: Atheneum, 1989.

Nigger Heaven, Carl Van Vechten, Urbana: University of Illinois Press, 2000.

No Easy Place to Be, Steven Corbin, New York: Simon and Schuster, 1989.

No Regrets, Mildred E. Riley, Columbus, Miss.: Genesis Press, 1998.

No Time to Die: A Mali Anderson Mystery, Edwards, Grace F. (Grace Frederica), New York: Doubleday, 1999.

Pinktoes: A Novel, Chester Himes, Jackson, MS: Banner Books, 1996.

Push: A Novel, Sapphire, New York: Alfred A. Knopf: Distributed by Random House, 1996.

Queen of Harlem, Brian Keith Jackson, New York: Doubleday, 2002.

Quicksand and, Passing, Nella Larsen, New Brunswick, N.J.: Rutgers University Press, 1986.

Satin Doll: A Novel, Karen E. Quinones Miller, New York: Simon & Schuster, 2001.

The Sleeper Wakes: Harlem Renaissance Stories by Women, Marcy Knopf, ed., New Brunswick, N.J.: Rutgers University Press, 1993.

S.R.O., Robert Deane Pharr, New York: W.W. Norton, 1998.

The Street, Ann Petry, Boston: Houghton Mifflin Co., 1991.

Tell Me How Long The Train's Been Gone: A Novel, Baldwin, James, New York: Dial Press, 1968.

A Toast Before Dying: A Mali Anderson Mystery, Grace F. Edwards, New York: Doubleday, 1998.

A Rage in Harlem, Chester Himes, New York: Vintage Books, 1989.

The Real Cool Killers, Chester Himes, New York: Vintage Books, 1988.

Requiem for Harlem, Roth, Henry, New York: Picador, 1999.

The Return of Simple, Langston Hughes, New York: Hill and Wang, 1994.

Rite of Passage, Richard Wright, New York: HarperCollins Publishers, 1994.

The Walls of Jericho, Rudolph Fisher, Ann Arbor, Mich.: University of Michigan Press, 1994.

Web Sites:

The Boys Choir of Harlem – http://www.boyschoirofharlem.org/

The Dance Theatre of Harlem –
http://www.dancetheatreofharlem.com/index.asp

Harlem – http://www.ny.com/sights/neighborhoods/harlem.html

Harlem 1900-1940: Schomburg Exhibition –
http://www.si.umich.edu/CHICO/Harlem/

Harlem: A History in Pictures –
http://www.newyorkmetro.com/metrotv/02/blackhistory_photos/

Harlem, New York: Africana.com –
http://www.africana.com/Articles/tt_020.htm

Harlem-Ontime – http://www.harlem-ontime.com/

The Harlem Renaissance –
http://www.unc.edu/courses/eng81br1/harlem.html

Harlem Spirituals & New York Visions Tours –
http://www.harlemspirituals.com/

The Harlem Theatre Company – http://harlemtc.com/

Malcolm X Boulevard –
http://www.nyc.gov/html/dcp/html/mxb/index.html

Morningside Heights Historic District Committee –
http://www.preserve.org/mhhd/mhhd.htm

Mount Morris Park Community Improvement Assocation –
http://www.harlemmtmorris.org./

Showtime in Harlem – http://www.showtimeinharlem.com/

The Studio Museum in Harlem –
http://www.studiomuseuminharlem.org/

Eric Kofi Acree, ea18@cornell.edu, (607) 255-5229
John Henrik Clarke Africana Library
http://www.library.cornell.edu/africana/harlem

More than a library name, Dr. Clarke's lingering classroom spirit

Black Studies was created to be a scholarship that was rooted in and directed towards social, intellectual and political activism. Dr. Clarke's life brilliantly symbolized this nexus and the library named in his honor follows his prescription for lasting change. Even his demise from one temporal plane to another is the source for student learning. *The Amsterdam News* cited several dozen individuals at his funeral as being noteworthy. Teams of Cornell students in my 172 class are required to write group developed essays on these individuals. The research is to determine why these individuals are special for the African-American community and reveal the relationship between these august individuals. This experience is a prerequisite to a class assignment to write a book on famous African Americans. This book, however, is based upon individuals who have impact the student personally. The goal of this book is to provide incentives for junior and high school students to succeed in life based upon the extraordinary work of ordinary Black individuals. Dr. Clarke, a Harlem resident, is an excellent role model for the task because he transcended humble origins to become a great historian, mentor, and intellectual leader.

Picture of famous 125th Street in Harlem

Photo by Gerald G. Jackson.

Gerald G. Jackson

African transcendence of space is embodied in the continuation
of Harlem identification from outside time and space.

Black New Yorkers:

Once a Harlemite, always a Harlemite

By **HERB BOYD**
Special to the AmNews

Standing at her kitchen window and pointing to the Polo Grounds housing units, Dr. Katherine Butler Jones steps back into the past.

"I remember how upset my mother was when they built those buildings," she began. "It completely destroyed her ability to see the Harlem River."

Dr. Jones may not be able to see the river from her 12th floor apartment at historic 409 Edgecombe, but she can see a river of memories that cascade from each riveting story she conjures. She moved from this cherished

ley Branithwaite, Roy Wilkins, Marvel Cooke and Rudolph Fisher are some of the famous residents she instantly recalled.

"Dr. Fisher used to live just above us on the 13th floor," Jones related. "He was a brilliant man, a real genius." Fisher was one of the major writers of the Harlem Renaissance. Among his most memorable short stories are "High Valley" and "The City of Refuge." "It was a shame he died so young (at 37) in 1934," she added.

In an essay that will appear in the anthology "The Harlem Reader," slated to be released later this month, Dr. Jones

But it hasn't been the confluence of these cultures that has snared most of Dr. Jones' time, it's spent delving into her father's ancestry, which she is able to trace back to the time of the African burial grounds in the early 18th century.

"I also discovered that members of my family were landowners in New York in the early 19th century and operated an Underground Railroad station in Keesville," she disclosed, making sure her guest was sufficiently supplied with tea, pretzels and deep memories.

Much of this history will seep

from chapters in her book "Deeper Roots," which is currently being shopped by her agent, Marie Brown. "I've done some more work on the manuscript, which I was advised to do, and it's just about where I would like it to be," Jones said.

Along with the obvious pride in her writing, Dr. Jones is also very pleased with a legacy she has left behind in Newton's education system, where a program she developed to enhance learning skills among the community youth is still in effect. "It's always good to leave something behind for others to build on,"

she smiled.

In a few days, after her husband, Hutto, returns from a trip to Cuba, Dr. Jones will be on her way back to Newton, but she promises to be back again in May to participate in an exhibition at the Museum of the City of New York. No doubt she'll journey up to Harlem to see some old friends, some of whom still reside at 409 and remember her as a youngster.

"It's always such a pleasure to run into some of the old-timers," Jones continued. "They help me to remember the past. Given her extraordinary sense of recall, she doesn't need too much help.

Katherine Butler Jones

ONE STREET DOWN FROM SUGAR HILL,
STILL EDGECOMBE AVENUE

GERALD AND BOYHOOD BEST FRIEND,
BOBBY HARRISON

Harlem landmark when she was 21, transplanting her roots to Massachusetts, where she completed her higher education, including her doctorate in education from Harvard University.

"We live in Newton, Massachusetts," Dr. Jones said, "but this apartment remains in the family." And the family includes her eight children and their spouses, who alternately spend time at a place that has changed little since Theodore and Mamie Butler, Dr. Jones' parents, paid the bills. Sentinels of antique furniture in fairly decent condition hover in the corners of a spacious living room.

When Dr. Jones was growing up, the building was a towering nest for Harlem's movers and shakers. At one time or another during her youth, she encountered the Black elite in the lobby and hallways. W.E.B. Du Bois, Walter

recalled her first moments at the famous address: "It was April, 1936, when my parents, Meme and Thede Butler, and I rode home to 409 in a cab from near by Columbia Presbyterian Hospital, where I had been born. My father carried me under the green awning emblazoned with the white numerals '409'; the uniformed doorman tipped his hat and opened the wrought-iron-framed glass door."

Since her mother was from Jamaica and her father an African-American with deep roots in New York, Dr. Jones was blessed with a unique perspective on the interrelations between native Blacks and immigrants from the Caribbean.

"In one of Fisher's short stories, I think it was called 'Ringtail,' he captures the dynamic and sometimes tension-filled relationships between the two

GERALD'S MOTHER   GERALD'S GRANDMOTHER

Photo A insert: Photo by Evely Harden.
Photo B insert: Photo by Ruby Harden.

East-West view of 135th Street.

James Baldwin or Claude Brown in the making.

Post High School of Commerce 41st Reunion.

African-American dancing knows no age, size or gender.

African American children are central to Harlem Festivities

Steel band introduced Caribbean Diaspora flavor.
Photos by Gerald G. Jackson.

Harlem children experiencing farm animals.

Playing chess, not basketball.

Wax figure of basketball great; we thought he was real.
Photos by Gerald G. Jackson.

Gerald G. Jackson

Harlem Experience by Carli Ball

When I first read the poster in Ujamaa I thought it would be a terrific experience for me, suburban girl meets big city. I saw that it was for only forty people and I thought there was no way I would find a place on the trip so I counted it as a loss. Alas! Professor Jackson made

Carli Ball. Photo by Gerald G. Jackson.

arrangements for his students that he thought would benefit from the experience, and low and behold I was one. After I had been signed up, my anticipation began to build for what I thought to be a unique experience. I felt comforted that my spot had been confirmed and I was definitely ready to head to Harlem. As the weeks progressed and the day grew near, I began to anticipate what type of experience I would have. Would I be scared? No, I do not fret easily. Would I be bored? Definitely not with this group of people, and in that City. Would I have fun? This is more likely to be the case for this is what I was determined to do. The Harlem trip exceeded my expectations.

The day had arrived and I had almost missed it. I called myself taking a nap, yet if it had not been for my roommate I may not have had a Harlem experience. With determination in my heart and fifteen minutes to spare, I showered, dressed, and left quickly as not to miss the bus. Upon the buses arrival in Harlem, I was so thankful that I had not awakened a moment later for I was definitely glad to be in Harlem. As points of interest were showed on the bus tour, I put myself back in the eras in which the streets were booming with political activism, cultural pride, and a strong sense of community. All this is hard to imagine if one only look at the littered streets, abandoned buildings, and destruction that lies in the streets of Harlem today. Yet, with a sense of Afro-centric time, which is cyclical, one knows that those streets will boom again.[309] As we rode through Sugar Hill, I imagined

Sugar Hill. Photo by Gerald G. Jackson.

being alive in the time when that street acquired that name. We were also shown the tomb of Ulysses S. Grant. The fact that a U.S. president was laid to rest just over yonder was pretty impressive. Riding pass the apartments where world renowned artists once stayed, slept, ate, and drank, made me think of the time when it was normal to see them walking down the street. They may have been heading to perform at a club or thinking of the verse that would one day rock the nation with its powerfulness. We were also given the chance to ride by Columbia University, Mount Sinai Hospital, and Harlem Hospital. All these things rekindled the memories of *The DitchDigger's Daughters.*[310] I pictured Yvonne walking to and from class, getting a bite to eat, or leaving the hospital after a long day. I thought, no I hoped that one day streets where I walked would be considered great because I was once there. Speaking of streets, walking on 125th St. lit a spark in my mind that once upon a time great man and women had once strolled the very street I was walking on. Everyone from Malcolm X and Marcus Garvey to Langston Hughes and Duke Ellington.

---

[309] A cross-cultural view of time that she learned in AS&RC 171 class on the Black family. For a view of what was recollected see Herb Boyd's article on page 19.
[310] A text used in AS & RC 171 Black family class dealing with surmounting great odds.

Schomburg Cultural Center. Photo by Gerald G. Jackson.

As far as the museums were concerned, they were different from any I had been in before. This time there were pictures I could relate to. Pictures of people with skin like mine and histories I could associate with. It was comforting to see the culture from whence I came being represented in art. At the Schomburg Cultural Center the exhibits depicted the art of Africa. At the Studio Art Museum the art was very unique and creative. Another interesting aspect about it was the children that were there analyzing the art. They were not fidgety or rambunctious but well-behaved, attentive, and quite intelligent. The teacher was very good at keeping them engaged and challenged. There was also a piece of art at this museum that was quite thought provoking. It was a busted piggy bank with African shells flowing out of it. It was explained to be a symbol of Black people, the shells, breaking out of the American thing that swallowed us up, the piggy bank. It was also exposing Americans real road to fortune, the slave economy. It carried much depth.

After leaving that museum, I was able to see the Hotel Teresa where Fidel Castro stayed when he visited America. It was said to be controversial because he opted not to stay in an affluent White area but among everyday minority people. During the lunch break, I was able to do some shopping and buy clothes that were not outrageously expensive which made me happy. It was also refreshing to get a taste of variety, which the suburban community from which I hail lacks. The next event on the itinerary was *Harlem Song* at the world famous Apollo Theater. The place was beautiful, although our seats were not the best in the house and the roof needed renovation. While I was

Photo of Malcolm X's 116 th street Mosque.
Photo by Gerald G. Jackson.

walking up all those steps, I was thinking about all the famous and talented people that had performed there. I again thought about the Thornton Sisters and their performance at the Apollo. As for the show, *Harlem Song,* it was fun and entertaining. It was very alive and expressive of the Harlem culture. Through the music, dance, and interviews it illustrated the atmosphere that Harlem exuded over the people that lived and visited there.

The final parts of the evening lead us to the Harlem markets to do some more shopping, Amy Ruth's for dinner, a book signing, and a jazz performance at a small club. The shopping was nice although it was raining. I saw African dress, materials, dolls, jewelry, and more. The dinner was nothing spectacular but the idea upon which the place was founded was inspiring and reminiscent. Reading the back of the menu, it was founded because a young girl used to always go down south to visit a relative and spent much time in the kitchen learning the art of southern cooking. I noticed that my waitress was not displaying that southern hospitality but the environment was still quiet and intimate. I noticed that all the dishes were named after Black people which was a nice touch .

After we finished dinner, we walked to a book signing, and on the way there, we saw the place where Malcolm X used to speak. At the book signing, we heard many messages for Black people. The author talked about how we need to be responsible for educating our children including basic reading and writing along with cultural learning. He talked about how there is no need for illiteracy with the free library system. There was also talk about how affluent Black people need to give back to Black communities and Black colleges. In addition to all these things, he talked about father and son relationships and how sons need fathers. He said mothers can not be fathers, and fathers are necessary in order to combat the streets in which their sons live. The things he said carried truth and depth.[311] The finale of our trip was the Jazz performance at Showman's. The performance was great, the atmosphere was very cozy, and family like. As the Jazz music played

Jazz picture. Photo by Gerald G. Jackson.

and I looked upon the wall at the musical greats, I thought about the past that this music carried. It has the ability to express the feelings of time and of people which is a very valuable capability in a time when our self-expression is constantly suppressed. In short, the jazz performance was genuinely enlightening and a wonderful, relaxing way to end the night off.

To sum up my Harlem experience it was a great one. It gave me a sense of the greatness and accomplishment of my people. It showed me that we can do great things despite the overwhelming doubt we are faced with. It is so comforting to be engulfed in so many things that validate your being when the daily life you live constantly discredits it. I enjoyed my Harlem experience and the hope and happiness it brought to light. I am thankful for Harlem and my experience there.

---

[311] The author referred to is Haki Madhubuti. See Joseph Sargent's essay in Sect. IV.

Harlem Trip Reaction by Joe Sargent

The last time I was in Harlem, I was a part of a group called Operation Understanding Hampton Roads. OUHR is a group of sixteen Black and Jewish teens that spends a year together learning about each other's culture. On our trip to New York City, we spent a few hours in Harlem, but I was disappointed when we drove through most of the area to "Jewish" Harlem, comprised of two or three blocks. All the Jewish kids in the group were excited to buy pickles from some world famous Jewish owned pickle shop, and to eat a famous kosher from a diner called Ratner's. I spent a majority of my time there wondering what made up the rest of Harlem; I knew that pickles and kosher dining couldn't be it.

I could tell things would be different during the initial bus tour that we took when we arrived in Harlem. Seeing famous spots from the Harlem Renaissance[312] was much more significant to me than the places I visited when I came to Harlem two years ago. Spending time walking 125th street gave me more perspective on what Harlem really is than an organized walking tour of the area. One of the greatest parts of the trip for me was the musical we watched in the Apollo. While the musical itself didn't really captivate me, rubbing the lucky tree stump and sitting in the same place that so many great performers made a name for themselves was memorable. I have watched *It's Show time at the Apollo* for as long as I can remember, and I have also heard many performers speak of the venue's legacy so being there is something that I will look back on for years to come. Overall, the trip was a positive experience for me because Harlem has been an important place in history, and I was glad that I had a chance to spend a day there to see it for myself.

Harlem Experience by Max Bushell

Upon first hearing of the Harlem Experience trip, I wasn't quite sure if it was worth the study time that would be lost. This compounded

---

[312]The original text had a composite essay on the Harlem Renaissance, also known as the **New Negro Movement and the Negro Renaissance.** Sources: *African American Desk Reference.* New York: Stonesong, pp. 337, 403, 441; Andrew, W., Foster, F., & Harris, T. (Eds.) (1997). *African American Literature.* New York: Oxford University Press, p. 340. In addition, see Sandra West (2003). *Encyclopedia of the Harlem Renaissance.* Houston Baker (1987); *Modernism and the Harlem Rensissance.* Illinois: The University of Chicago Press.

with the fact that it probably would not be offered to any student who was interested basically turned me off to the trip. I was still skeptical when I went to the first meeting in Ujamaa Residential College to check it out. Then, on the spur of the moment, I decided, considering my interest, even obsession with the civil rights movement, that this was a golden opportunity to go somewhere I had never been, experience something new, and learn more about African American History. Why not?

Group on walking tour of Harlem, stops in front of Liberation Book Store. Photo by Gerald G. Jackson.

The trip itself was pretty strenuous, possibly because I stayed up until I boarded the bus, though it was definitely worth it. It all began with a tour of Harlem in which we saw a variety of historical sights including the Harlem Hospital and Mt. Sinai Hospital. Then the group was dropped off at the Schomburg Center, a museum containing a variety of African art. Directly after the Schomburg, we walked a few blocks to the Studio Museum, another Art Museum. These Museums offered a varied look at African Culture and contemporary black art. This concluded the first half of the outing with greater things still to come.

After lunch, the group assembled at the Apollo Theater to see Harlem Song. Despite having the worst seats in the house, I was thoroughly impressed with the musical and the historical Theater, though it may have needed slight renovations on the roof. This was one of the highlights of the trip. After a short walk and a quick perusal of the African mart we adjourned to a delicious (anything would have been, I was so hungry) meal at Amy Ruth Restaurant. The menu included typical "soul" food, which was attuned to my taste, being from the South. After a short stop at a Harlem bookstore to see a widely published Black author, we convened at Showman's Bar. This part of the trip was my absolute favorite. A very normal looking man took the stage and began to play the most incredible live jazz I have ever heard. My experience with live jazz is not the most extensive to say the least,

Jazz musician Lonnie Youngblood.
Photo by Gerald G. Jackson.

but the band that played was brilliant. The experience of being in Harlem, the birthplace of jazz, and hearing this amazing music made the trip for me. I was sorrowful to leave and take the long bus ride home, but as the old maxim says, all good things must end. The trip was definitely worth whatever cost and it was truly a good experience; a Harlem experiences.

Harlem Experience Reaction by Kerby Samuels

My reaction to the Harlem Experience trip was a positive one. Before the trip, I didn't really know what to expect since I had never been to New York City for any other purpose than: for some form of work and I'm not from a big city or anything close to it since I'm from Wilmington, Delaware, and the suburbs at that. I didn't expect it to be a bad experience and didn't let the thought that Harlem was supposed to be a bad section of the city spoil my time because a lot of people say the same thing about Philadelphia, but I still enjoy going there. Feeling the energy of a busy city was a refreshing change of scenery from being in Ithaca.

As for the events of the day, visiting the museums displaying African-American art was interesting to me because I can't say that I have ever been to a museum that focused only on African art or post modem art by African Americans. Seeing "Harlem Song," which was a

"Harlem Song" show at Apollo Theater.
Photo by Adrie Ciccone.

high-energy show about the history of Harlem was appropriate for the purpose of the trip, to experience the culture of the city. Going to Showman's to hear jazz being played ended the evening perfectly since Harlem's the birthplace of jazz. Physically being in a place with so much history was something different for me since I'm from a state where it is not normal to see famous people or walk pass famous landmarks everyday.

Seeing where Langston Hughes lived on the bus tour, sitting in the Apollo where so many famous artists have performed and walking pass where Malcolm X used to speak gave me more of an appreciation for Harlem, and its contributions to our culture today. My only regret is that the weather was not as great as my day was, but if I have the opportunity next year, I would go again.

Harlem Experience by Stefun Hawkins

The trip that I attended to Harlem on Saturday was a fun, cultivating, and educational experience. Visiting the museums, the Apollo, various stores, and important historical sites all made the trip worthwhile. Despite the rough start to my day, I was able to endure and continue to absorb history that transcended the streets themselves.

Once we arrived in Harlem we remained on the bus and took a guided tour with the speaker pointing out various sites of importance and telling us about the economical status of the city and a lot about how it came to be. Due to biological difficulties, I was unable to concentrate and really listen to the portrayed information on this part of the trip. When the bus trip ended, we visited two museums. First was the Schomburg. This museum contained exhibits that ranged from African rugs to pictures of African children. Next we went to the Studio

Art museum, and saw many other more abstract exhibits. Following the museums, we split and had free time to eat, shop, and walk around by ourselves. Then we met at the Apollo and watched a musical entitled Harlem Song, which from what I saw was an excellent production that combined talent with history to make an excellent educational experience. After the show we ate at Amy Ruth's, one of Harlem's most popular restaurants. Having filled our stomachs, we went to Harlem's most prominent black owned bookstore. Finally, we went to a bar called Showman's. There we got to listen to some great jazz musicians, meet Cornell alumni, and end the trip.

My Harlem Experience by Rejane Frick

When I first discovered the Harlem Experience Trip flyer, I really felt like going. The only part of New York I had ever been to was Brooklyn, and I had spent most of my time at home with my hosts, who were too scared to let a White girl wander the streets. Harlem is quite famous in France. When we watch American movies, it is not rare to hear of this place, and I thought it would be great if I could see it with my eyes.

However, I did not ask Dr. Jackson for details. Actually, I was torn between my desire to go and the thought that as a White woman, some Afro-American students might feel uncomfortable having me around them in Harlem. After all, I remembered clearly Mrs. Durant's[313] warning. She was one of my first English teachers in France, and she had told us that it was not wise to go to Harlem, because it was Black people's domain, and despite some White people's good intentions, Afro-Americans did not want us there. Although I had some doubts about her claim, my former boyfriend's comments seemed to reinforce this argument. When I heard that he was going to spend three weeks at some friends' in Harlem, I told him that I would like to go with him. He explained to me that he could not take me, because this "black and white thing" was not even thinkable in Harlem. I was surprised by his answer – did we not both know that our relationship did not please everybody? Why would it be so different, or more dangerous in Harlem? However, I did not insist. When he went back to France, I asked him what it was like, his answer was: "It was so great to be in place where Black people were the majority. Each time I went out from Harlem, I saw more and more White people and it felt so weird to me.

---

[313]Pseudonym

That was a great feeling!" I weighed pros and cons for one week, and I finally concluded that I should not go.

Then, while Dr. Jackson and I were talking about my research, Danielle joined us. I briefly mentioned the Harlem trip, and asked them if it would be inconsiderate of me to go with the rest of the group. Danielle asked me what I meant by that, and I explained my concern about Afro-American students' potential discomfort about being in the street with a White girl. Danielle burst out in laughter and replied: "And so what! You'd be the first White to worry about what Afro-Americans might feel." Obviously, Danielle's answer was far from encouraging to me. Dr. Jackson told me that it was nice to take this element into consideration, but this trip was not reserved exclusively to African-American students. Actually, other White students were going. This time my mind was set: I was going to Harlem!

The next obstacle to overcome was the problem of space on the bus. The deadline for registration had passed, and I could only hope somebody would cancel her or his trip. I went to Ujamaa where a final meeting was organized to go over the last details. This was a wonderful

Rejane's picture at Ujamma.
Photo by Gerald G. Jackson.

experience. Three months after my arrival, I suddenly discovered that students did have a place to meet each other. So far, I would have qualified life on Campus as impersonal. People barely talk to each other; we cannot say that a family atmosphere reigns at Cornell. Yet, Ujamaa is the place where you can find this warm ambiance. People share stories, make jokes, and laugh, which was what I was longing for. It did not take me long to meet some people, some of whom even spoke French. I was so glad when at the end of the evening I finally had my seat on the bus with the rest of the group.

The next day, when I told my colleagues that I was going to Harlem, everybody was glad for me, except one older woman whose reaction left me speechless. She explained "This attraction for Harlem is so French. There's nothing great about that place, and yet French people keep wanting to go there." Although, I have never been there, I had heard about the Harlem Renaissance, and it seemed hard to believe that there was nothing of interest in such a place. I did not let her spoil my joy, and I simply told myself: "this woman (who ironically is French) is definitely Americanized!"[314]

By Friday evening, I was so excited about the trip that I did not sleep at all. I left home early enough to be sure not to miss the bus, and I was surprised to discover that it was snowing. Once at the RPCC bus stop, we all got on the bus quickly, since it was freezing! Danielle introduced me to her friends and we talked a while before falling asleep. When I woke up, we were already at McDonald's where we were supposed to have a quick breakfast. While I was in line waiting, two White men were talking behind me. One of them asked me what I was doing with this group! It did not take me long to understand what he meant by that. It was obvious that I had two genuine specimens behind me! When I replied that I was going to visit Harlem, they told me that nothing was to be seen there. I did not push this worthless conversation any further!

Once in Harlem, we had a bus tour of its major sites. Now I would be able to claim that those two bigots and this Americanized French woman were wrong. This tour was followed by the visit of the Schomburg Cultural Center. I really enjoyed it, because I attended a class in which we studied African women's power, and we talked a lot about the petty markets. Among the various pictures showing African women's art, such as housing design, weaving, and pottery, there was some portraying the petty markets. I also saw Courtney Clark's field report being exhibited; now I see what my professor meant by "field notes." It is not only words lay on paper; there are also some drawings. Then we went to the souvenir shop that sells a lot of cards representing Black leaders and African objects, which are quite difficult to find in the other parts of the US. Thanks to that, I could finally put a face on Langston Hughes. Just before leaving Schomburg Cultural Center, we met one alumnus who used to go to Cornell. We chatted a little while

---

[314]Herrick Chapman & Frader, L. (Ed.). (2004). *Race in France.*New York: Berghahn Books. In contrast, read Petrine Archer-Straw (2001). *Negrophilia: Avant-Garde Paris and Black Culture in the 1920s.* New York: Thames & Hudson.

with him, and he promised to meet us at Showman's in the evening. I was surprised by his enthusiasm, since we did not know him, but here again you could feel the strong bond that unites Afro-Americans.

Cornell alumni lecturing H.E. group. Photo by Gerald Jackson.

We continued our visit and we stopped at the Studio Museum in Harlem. I was impressed by some of the messages carried by some of Afro-American artists' pieces of work. The most powerful piece in my eyes remains the baseball bat covered with cotton. Nevertheless, what I liked the best through the SMH visit was the atmosphere itself. People from various ages come to enjoy artists' work in this place, and they interact with each other in what would seem as a unique way, according to the mainstream American vision. I was moved seeing some Black children, sitting in front of this huge canvas, trying to interpret the piece, and expressing their feelings towards it, under the guide's attentive ear. Some middle age Black women were listening carefully to thei guide commenting on each piece of work. Once the guide finished his tour, these women started to joke with him, teasing him and asking for his information. I had the feeling of being at the center of a family reunion, here in this museum, and it felt good!

After our SMH visit, we had some free time to see Harlem by ourselves and have lunch. Each of us was supposed to join the group we had decided to be in at the Schomburg Cultural Center. The person who at first was designed as our group leader, for having a cell phone, took her task very seriously. She was always checking that none of us was missing. Suddenly, the "Big sister image" we talked a lot about in class was taking on a concrete sense.[315] Our leader embodied this

---

[315] Refers to AS&RC 171 class on the Black family and discussions of African-American familial roles.

image. After a while, Danielle, Jamy, Greisy, and Angel and I finally left the rest of our group because Greisy and Jamy wanted to have their ears pierced.

We went to several jewelry stores to compare prices, and I had so much fun. One of the salesmen kept joking with us; when he showed the girls how he was going to pierce their ears, he took this big dirty steel bar out of the counter – it was awful, but of course it made us all laugh. But suddenly, Greisy and Jamy reactions changed – they decided to leave and go to another store, because this man was joking too much. I guess their reaction was justified; after all, I was not the one to get my ear pierced. Therefore, we went to another shop, and I was really disappointed by the way the saleswoman dealt with us. She was not friendly at all; she did not even take time to get down from her platform to pierce the girls' ears. She did it so quickly, and carelessly, that Greisy had to have it done a second time. It was so painful for her, even though she did not complain once, and she was bleeding. I was amazed to see that she did not hesitate to have it pierced again. After all these emotions, we were hungry and we only had few minutes before our next meeting. We decided to go to McDonald's.

When we entered only a few tables were available, and none of the girls wanted to keep one for us. I said that I would wait there for them. I did not understand why, but the girls did not seem to enjoy this idea, and they kept telling me they would do it. I insisted that I did not mind I would keep the table. Danielle told me: "OK, so what do you want to eat, I'll bring you your sandwich!" I replied that it was nice but I would get it myself. I guess I reacted this way because it is really rude in France to ask a person to get your food. Danielle insisted so much that I suddenly thought to myself: "Of course, it must be the reciprocity concept!"[316] I gave her the money and I waited for them. After a while, I saw that people of all ages were coming to McDonald's. There were some Moms and their children, some teenagers and some elderly people. It was really different from what I experienced at Cornell, where only teenagers seem to live. Students, children, and older people do not seem to interact, at least not in Collegetown or on the Commons. While these thoughts ran through my mind, I suddenly realized that everybody was looking at me. I was the only White person in

---

[316]Refers to African concept of reciprocity that she learned in AS&RC Black family class. For additional, see Niara Sudarkasa (1997). "African-American families and family values" (pp. 9–40). In Harriet McAdoo (Ed.). *Black families*. California: Sage; Joseph Holloway (Ed.) (1991). *AFRICANISMS in American culture*. Indianapolis: Indiana University Press.

McDonald's, and it did not enter my mind that some Afro-Americans could be surprised or angry to see me there. Here is a superb example of Réjane being blinded by her White privilege. It did not occur to me that my presence could be a problem. I was comfortable here, and I assumed that the people who surrounded me were too. My behavior was implying, in an unconscious way, that I expected to be welcomed! The girls joined me at the table, I forgot about it, and we started to eat and laugh.

One week later when I told Danielle what happened at McDonald's, she said: "Obviously! That's why we didn't want you to go get the table! And when you said that you wanted to get your sandwich after we came back, we weren't going to let you in line by yourself!" I suddenly realized that despite the fact that I had been blinded by White privilege, Whites in France and White Americans did not follow the same racial rules. Here in America, Blacks and Whites live in a racially divided world, and this is a tacit rule you must respect. If we have racism in France, it does not operate according to the same rules. French people of both "races," racists or not, are used to interacting with each other, at least in the cities. In America, the racial line is far more palpable. It is extremely difficult for me to translate my feelings into words, because this is something you feel but cannot properly express. To illustrate what I mean, I will give a simple example. I have noticed that the color line is so stark that it is visible and tangible to any White French outsider, racist or not. All French Whites who come to the USA mention this non permeable color line. It is in this country that I suddenly became aware of my White privilege, and it took me only 2 months. And yet, God knows how hard it is for White people to realize that they have those privileges! So many Whites go through life without noticing it. After my discovery of this American racial code of conduct, many things I experienced at Cornell, Harlem and Lincoln University took a new sense. Now I understand why some Afro-Americans say that I am "Black inside," that I must have "Black blood," or that I am not "White, but French." I do not follow the American racial rules, because I was not socialized in that sense. What appears to me as a natural interaction with Black people is perceived by Afro-Americans as a singular behavior. That is why when I walked into the Harlem bookstore with the rest of the group to hear the writer present his book, one Afro-American man asked me: "You're a journalist, aren't you?" For this man, this should be the most logical explanation. What would a White girl do in a Harlem bookstore?

Coming back to my Harlem itinerary, after our quick stop at McDonald's, we joined the rest of the group in front of the Apollo

Photo of Hue-man bookstore. Photo by Gerald Jackson.

Theater. This was what I liked the most about my trip to Harlem. I was sitting in front of the stage where the Ditch Digger's Daughters sung! The show was really powerful. The artists succeeded in transmitting to the audience their love for Harlem and its historical past. This was wonderful! When we left, it was raining a lot, and we had some time before dinner. Therefore, Dr. Jackson and Dr. Nanji decided to take us to one bookstore in Harlem where an author was presenting his book. I was so amazed by the number of books devoted to a Black audience that I did not hear much of the presentation. There were books for Black children everywhere. It is a shame we do not see more of them in mainstream American bookstores. I spent my whole time going through them. I do not know how long we stayed there, but I felt that it was not long enough. On the way to eat at Amy Ruth's, we stopped for a while at the African Market, where I found that some of the salesmen spoke French.

Once we reached Amy Ruth's, we were all cold and hungry. I had already had soul food, when I was in Lincoln University, but I had never tasted Southern Afro-American cuisine. I had a sugar-cured salmon filet with peach butter, and some cheesy grits, which was delicious! I realized that what was called "grits" was "la semoule au lait" that my mom used to give me when I was a child. Instead of melted cheese, she added some sugar and milk to it. We shared each of our dishes with the girls, so that we could have a taste of several dishes. Afterwards, we left for Showman's. Here we attended a live concert of blues and jazz music. I enjoyed it a lot; it seemed that all tiredness of the day disappeared. The place was filled with younger and older people. People were talking, laughing with each other as though this were a family reunion. The alumnus we talked to at the Schomburg Cultural Center kept his word and he met us there, as well as one of Dr. Jackson's former student and his girlfriend. When the bus came to pick us up, we did not feel like going back to Cornell. We had such a great time here in Harlem!

I would like to finish my narrative by emphasizing two points. The first one is that people who dare to tell that there is nothing to see in Harlem are obviously people who do not know the history of this city, and who did not take time or did not try to interact with its inhabitants. This is a place where people are so friendly that you feel at home. You can feel the whole extended family spirit running through you. The second point I would like to stress is that Harlem does not deserve the bad reputation that White people tend to give to it. During my visit, I never felt threatened or in danger. I know that I was not on my own, and that it is not wise to generalize based on one experience. Nevertheless, I advise you to go to Harlem and see it with your own eyes. I especially urge White Americans to go and see, for I am deeply convinced that these cultural experiences are the best way to learn about each other's cultures, and appreciate our differences. Avoiding places that have been considered to be Black people's domain reinforces the tacit color line rule and perpetuates the myth of the dangerous "Other."

The Interim Ending

The Harlem Experience day was exhausting. A reflection of the experience is captured in the student essays, formal evaluation report by William Marler, OTM November program award in the education category, and May, 2003 Diversity Program of the Year award from the Community Development Residence Hall Association for *The Harlem Experience, Ujamaa Residential College*. The evidence strongly suggests that the Harlem Experience should be continued and even expanded. Its duration could be from one day to two. Similarly, its location could include the Boston-Cambridge and Connecticut areas and Maryland and Washington, D.C.

Conceptually, the Harlem Experience is conceived of as an educational endeavor that encompasses both the cognitive and affective educational domains, more popularly described as thinking and feeling. As an amalgam of what is generally viewed as the academic and student affairs component of institutions of higher education, it was rightly housed in the Cornell Faculty Fellows program. On a more personal note, my observations and recommendations are extensions of my former posts as both an academic and student affairs dean. Similarly, it stems from my culturally and philosophically based conviction that a marriage is needed between the two spheres, and the advocacy of their complementary nature. It is consistent with the vision of Ezra Cornell and James Turner.[317] I inferred Ezra Cornell's vision from his words and the existence of Cornell University. James Turner's vision can be deduced from his legendary status in the Black Studies field and African-American Activist's Movement. It is visible in his perennial pictures and scholarly publications in the leading Black magazines, journals and books. I have observed it when he arduously works with and on behalf of Cornell students, leads campus human rights campus protests and injects wisdom in departmental, lectures,and colloquial discussions. It was under his tutelage that the Africana Studies & Research Center became a bastion of international Black scholarship and socio-psychological consciousness. He will remain a visionary and living legend until his demise. In short, it is from these perspectives of this unique program that my afterthoughts on the Harlem Experience program are based and prompted.

Biographical Sketches of the Children of the Village[318]

The now African cliché that "it takes a village to raise a child" leaves out the cooperative spirit idea that the process should include children. Reflective of this idea is my works on Black peer counseling[319] and human relations work.[320] I continued to be proud and inspired by students who "get involved." In this case, the students contributed their time and intellect in writing essays (e.g., Carli, Kerby, Stefun, Max and Rejane), submitting photographs (e.g., Jamie, Angel, Danielle, Rejane and Adrie), developing charts and proofreading (Danielle), and cropping photographs and formatting documents (Gerald Fils).

---

[317]The original text had a picture of the statute of Ezra Cornell and picture of James Turner.

[318]With the exception of two students, these biographical sketches have been written by the students.

[319]See Gerald G. Jackson (1972). "Black youth as peer counselors." *Personnel And Guidance Journal*, 51, 280-285.

[320]Cole, M. (December 7, 1968). "Panel would keep Black differences." *The Lewiston (Maine) Daily Sun*, p. 10; Cain. J. (April-May, 1996). "Are you on 'CPT' Time?" *Heart & Soul*, p. 74; N. Devidayal (Ocotober 3, 1988). "Breaking Barriers' Conference addresses campus race relations." *The Daily Princetonian*, p. 5; Golden, M. (February, 1986). "For single mothers: choosing a male role model for your child." *Essence*, pp. 134-135. "Multicultural Task Force hears speaker on role of black male." (February, 1991). *The Medical College of Virginia Hospital News*, p. 5; Pretti, E. (September 23, 1993). "WWPHS students participate in Human Relations Weekend." *The Pirate's Eye*, p. 1.

Gerald G. Jackson

The earnestness of these students grandly bespeaks the continued commitment of young people to the educational and cooperative process occurring outside of the classroom. For example, I asked Danielle to work up graphic representations of the numbers we gathered on the program's participants. She readily agreed to provide the assistance and when the work was completed, she enlightened me about the assistance she received from Greisy. Greisy is pictured in Sect. III, and has taken several of my courses. Danielle's computer malfunctioned and when she informally shared her plight with Greisy, the latter volunteered her computer and knowledge. Similarly, Gerald Fils volunteered an evening of work to the task of cropping photograph inserts and resolving formatting problems.

What is encouraging is how students are both receivers and givers. Gerald was a part of a Cornell Africana contingency that attended a Hip Hop conference at the Schomburg. Danielle was part of a group that attended A Yale University conference in which I presented and conducted a workshop.[321] A year later, and demonstrating how much she is a quick study, Danielle presented a scholarly paper.[322] The paper is a reflection of her scholar focus as a College Scholar with an Africana concentration. She and the other contributors give us all hope and grounds to still believe in a just world.

Carli Ball is from Wallingford, PA, which is about thirty minutes outside of Philadelphia, PA. Carli is a freshman and plans to double major in Africana Studies and Spanish. Her career ambition is to become a bilingual Pediatrician. She enjoys writing poetry, going to the movies, volunteering, and hanging out with her family and friends for fun. Carli sees some of the major problems of today as the lack of adequate and truthful American and African-American history being taught in schools, the destitution of Black people and their communities and the need to institute programs for hope, help, and opportunities for them to leave that state of destitution, and the need to change social and political policies so they are not so completely Eurocentric but take into

---

[321]Gerald G. Jackson (November 3, 2001). "Black on Black Liberation: Freedom from the Chains of Anti-self Disorder." In 7th Annual Black Solidarity Conference, "Perceptions of Self The Black Psyche in the 21st Century," New Haven, Connecticut. See Danielle's paper on the experience of the trip in Sect. III.

[322]Danielle T. Williams (2003). "Non-traditional African Diaspora: Afro-Mexico." In Gerald Jackson (chairperson), *New Dimensions of the African Diaspora*. In 27th Annual Conference of the New York African Studies Association, TRANSNATIONAL DISCOURSES IN THE AFRICAN WORLD, April 4th and 5th, Ithaca, New York.

account the worldviews of the minorities of America. Carli would like to see more minorities who are able to obtain higher education in the world and on Cornell's campus.

Max Bushell is from Greensboro, NC. Max is a first year student who is majoring in German. Max's career ambition is to live and work overseas and he likes to read and play cello for fun. Max sees the major problems and issues of today as very important and would like to see more diversity in the world and on Cornell's campus.

Adrieannette Ciccone is from Monterey Bay, California. Adrieannette is a senior student who is majoring in Urban and Regional Studies. Adrieannette's career ambition is to become an attorney/urban planner as an advocate for the African American Struggle and likes to travel, cook, shop and relax for fun. Arieannette sees the major problems and issues of today as and inequitable distribution of wealth based upon ethnicity and would like to see more equality and justice in the world and on Cornell's campus. Member of AKA sorority.

Gerald Fils is a Phi Beta Kappa graduate of Temple University and a graduating graduate student in the Africana Studies & Research Center. He is of Haitian descent and has been a primary mover at Cornell in supporting a cultural bond among Haitian students. Gerald is from Brooklyn, New York and consistent with his Caribbean cultural background, the thesis of his master is "From Sugar Cane to Computer Chip: The Political Economy of Information Technology in the Caribbean."

Réjane Frick is from France. Réjane is a graduate student who is majoring in American Civilization at the University of Paris XII. Réjane's career ambition is to teach at a University. She would like to be able to help several generations of students to challenge the all-too-often-stereotypical representations of Afro-American/White couples and biracial children. She likes to draw and write for fun, and hopes to publish some children's books. Réjane sees the major problems and issues of today as being linked to our ethnocentric values. According to her, people tend to establish their ways of being, doing, and thinking as the norm, and therefore they usually perceive differences as being bad. She would like to see more interactions between people in the world and on Cornell's campus. For her, this should help us to understand and respect each other's values, and so should challenge the "We versus Other" schema.

Stefun Hawkins is from Dover, DE. Stefun is a freshman student who is considering majoring in either Math or Africana. Stefun's career ambition is to practice law and he likes to play sports for fun. Stefun sees the major problems and issues today as the large number of uneducated, unemployed, and poverty-stricken blacks and would like to see more initiative on behalf of all the races to formulate solutions to these problems in the world and on Cornell's campus. Member of Omega Psi Phi fraternity.

Jamie Lavender is a junior from California. Member of DST sorority.

Kerby Samuels is currently a freshman at Cornell University. She is majoring in biology in the College of Arts and Science, and does not have permanent post college plans as of yet. Originally from Wilmington, Delaware, Samuels has found interests in choral music, running, and community service of all kinds. She views a lack of understanding and communication on all levels as a major problem in the world today, and in light of that would like to see more cooperation and interaction among different cultural groups in the world as well as on Cornell's campus.

Joseph Sargent, from Virginia Beach, Virginia, is a first year student at Cornell University. He is majoring in Business, and hopes to one day start and run a company. Joe loves basketball, and he plays video games for fun. Joe sees one major problem of today as the United States' policy in foreign lands, and would like to see more diplomacy in the world and at Cornell. Member of Omeg Psi Phi fraternity

LeRhonda J.A. Washington is from Fort Lauderdale, Florida. LeRhonda, also affectionately known as Angel, is a second year student who is majoring in Biology and Society/Behavior and Society. LeRhonda's career ambition is to lift young Black princes and princesses up to the level of excellence that they deserve and likes to read poetry and chill with friends for fun. LeRhonda sees the major problems, and issues of today as people losing connection with the past and would like to see more dedication to the community in the world and on Cornell's campus. Member of AKA sorority.

Danielle Terrazas Williams is from the San Francisco Bay Area. Danielle is a sophomore student who is majoring in Africana and Spanish. Danielle's career ambition is to become a successful historian and avant gard researcher and likes to play tennis for fun. Danielle sees the major problem and issues of today as equal access to opportunities and would like to see more understanding of ethnic diversity in the world and on Cornell's campus. Member of AKA sorority

Postscript

Officially, program obligations ended when the participants safely returned to the Cornell University campus. Since we had not contemplated a multi-tiered program, we had no human relations or diversity benchmarks to prescribe any post-program activities. I had no idea, therefore, that I would be writing a postscript. From the results I had reviewed, we had helped students see and take advantage of outside classroom learning. Similarly, the program provided opportunities for participants to apply their classroom learning and skills to events and circumstances outside classroom walls. In addition, the progenitors of the program were satisfied with the student reactions to the trip and the joyful subsequent campus encounters among participants. My personal experience in the event sharpened my relearning of the following:

African Americans have a culture that can be explained and understood by others,

differences within bio-social groups are just as significant as differences between them,

intra-group communication and cultural relationship are developed and maintained when such relationships are given time to grow and nurture,

African-American Cornell male students need racial- and gender-specific leadership training and clinical opportunities,

marketing plans need to take into account the White ethnic experience and class distinctions among White Cornell students, and

outside classroom learning should be conceived and perceived as collateral rather than as either ancillary or adjunctive.

As a backdrop to what I have done since the program, the first thing to make lucid is that the Harlem Experience was not designed to assess the long-range consequences of the program. This conceivable shortcoming, however, does not preclude noting some of the ways the experience has been capitalized on in the Cornell classroom learning experience. Both experiences took place in my AS&RC course on Black education and involved first year students who participated in the Harlem Experience.

The first case illustration is a direct educational application. The assignment was for groups of students to research the dignitaries reportedly attending the notable Dr. John Henrik Clarke funeral. My

Gerald G. Jackson

goal was to instruct them in the use of a group format for learning about Black people perceived as distinguished by African-American sources. Joe Sargent was assigned Dr. Haki Madhubuti. His response was to question who professor Madhubuti was and I reminded him that he was the author Joe had attended a book party in honor of during his Harlem Experience. Joe completed the assignment, revealed below, and commented that he had no idea that Haki Madhubuti was so famous.

Haki Madhubuti (aka. Don Lee) by Joe Sargent

Haki Madhubuti, born Don Lee in Little Rock, Arkansas in 1942, first made a name for himself in the literary world in the late sixties. Madhubuti's work, from his first to his most recent, has focused on various aspects of Black life in America, and is

Haki Madhubuti reading from his book at Book party at Hue-man bookstore in Harlem, New York. Photo by Jamie Lavendar.

even written in slang. Madhubuti can be described as a socially conscious poet as his work can be characterized by anger at social and economic injustices and rejoicing in African American culture. Madhubuti's mother, Maxine, who raised him in Detroit, died of a drug overdose when Haki was sixteen, and he still sites his mother as the driving force of his literary creativity.

In early adulthood, besides focusing his work on Blacks in America, Madhubuti also physically participated in groups aimed at fighting the social injustices prevalent during the civil rights movement. Madhubuti has participated in the Student Non-Violent Coordinating Community (SNCC), the Congress of Racial Equality (CORE) and the Southern Christian Leadership Conference (SCLC) proving that Haki has always had a great interest in helping the situation for all Blacks. Much has been said of Madhubuti's work. One critic says his work is "like a razor; it's sharp and will cut deep, not out to wound but to kill the inactive Black mind." Madhubuti's message is clear: if you are not for the betterment of society for Blacks then you are against it, plain and simple. A testament to his influence, Madhubuti sold about 250,000 books of poetry in 1971 alone that could be more than any other Black poets before him combined. After a short stint in the military, Madhubuti's literary career began to rise. Madhubuti earned professional degrees at several colleges, and moved on to teach his idea of a Black cultural value system as a guest professor at schools across the country. As a writer, Madhubuti has written nineteen books, and has reached out to other fledgling writers by founding the Third World Press. Some notable authors published by the independent press include celebrated playwright and essayist Amiri Baraka, scholar Chancellor Williams, and renowned poet Gwendolyn Brooks, who has published the second volume of her autobiography and several books of poetry with Madhubuti's press. Madhubuti has also helped to influence the education of young Blacks by helping to establish the Institute of Positive Education in Chicago, a school for black children, in 1969.

Joe's obvious gratefulness alleviated any trepidation I had about the practical side of the assignment. More, this experience reinforced Joe's writing and analytical skills. It did not provide a growth opportunity either for his interpersonal skills or emotional intelligence. Such learning flows from Harlem Experience activities. For example, Joe did not remember initially the names of the women he dined with at Amy Ruth. However, on April 18, 2003, a semester later, I met Joe and one of them dining at RPU. Such relationships can be augmented by classroom tasks that integrate outside and inside classroom activities. An essay written by Stefun illustrates such thinking and acting. Stefun's essay is based upon his experience in Washington D.C. at the

Affirmative Action Protest march. He voluntarily submitted the following essay for extra credit in my 172 AS&RC course.

Affirmative Action Rally by Stefun Hawkins

Stefun Hawkins
Africana Barbeque
Dr. Jackson
5/11/03

On Tuesday, April 1, 2003, I attended the March on Washington, for the preservation of affirmative action. This movement is by far the most powerful event I have ever witnessed or participated in, in my life thus far. Over 50,000 students from all over the United States gathered in the nation's capital to support Michigan and the minority community. Blacks, Latinos, Asians, and even a fairly good number of Whites were present to voice their opinions in defense of affirmative action.

The event began with a rally at the Supreme Court in which the hearings that day had begun. A plethora of speakers took turns at the microphone on the building's steps stressing America's dire need for affirmative action, and delivering the message that the community will not roll over and let institutions of higher learning re-segregate. Adopting the philosophy commonly associated with Malcolm X, **By Any Means Necessary**, the BAMN coalition was formed. BAMN was the main group responsible for the organization and implementation of the protest in DC. Cheers such as "They say Jim Crow? We say Hell no!" flooded the streets of our nation's capital.

I found it very inspirational that such a large group of strangers could come together, unite under one cause, and fight for not only their children but also the children of others. This is a prime example of the Black worldview because it exemplifies the concept of community. The march illustrated the Afro-centric notions of collectivism, interdependence, cooperation, and survival of the community. Marching down Constitution Avenue from the Supreme Court all the way around to the steps of the Lincoln Memorial the group showed its numbers and continued chanting various pro-affirmative action slogans.

Concluding with one final rally in the midst of the Lincoln Memorial, many more students and icons spoke to the masses. Judge Mathis also addressed the crowd stating that he, unlike some other judges (mainly Clarence Thomas), was not afraid to admit that he is a product of affirmative action, and that it is vital for it to be upheld and maintained. Although the rally was coming to a close, speakers made it very important to stress the fact that the fight has just begun and the call to action must continue to ring out in communities and schools across the nation until Brown vs. Board is upheld and minorities are given an equal opportunity to succeed.

To enhance the classroom learning, I devised a class presentation entailing Stefun reading his essay as an introduction to an interactive lecture by Funa Maduka. She is a Cornell senior and student trustee to the Cornell University Board who was a speaker at the event. Following her presentation, it was planned that Gerald Souders, a junior at Cornell and enrolled student in my 172 course, would show a video he made in Washington, D.C. that included Funa's speech.

I started thinking about what else should be set into motion when I reviewed some program statistics. We set out to attract an equal percentage of students from Low Rises 6 & 7 and Ujamaa and we accomplished this objective (figure 1). We did not, however, anticipate a great deal of diversity in terms of gender, race and residential housing. We were surprised, therefore, to learn that without a specific charge we had the following meaningful similarities and differences.

Attesting to the idea of differences being good (figure 2), Brian Kwoba, an African-American student from neither Ujamaa nor Low Rises, made the following post-program comments:

I would also like to give you my sincerest thanks once more for such a wonderful and educational experience. I learned a great deal and I am looking forward to going back to Harlem someday. Thank you very much for all your hard work in coordinating the trip (April 23, 2003).

Students came from a variety of living arrangements and Low Rises 6 & 7 and Ujamaa shared spots with a percentage of outsiders that exceeded percentages for either of the host residential communities. While the percentage of males and females attendees was not significantly different (figure 3), there are some noteworthy differences within and between residential colleges. The percentage of males and females between Low Rises 6 & 7 and Ujamaa are inversely related (figure 4). Donlon and Lyon had only male attendees and LLC, Dickson and Townhouses only had females. A retrospective student analysis may reveal some insights into the reported differences.

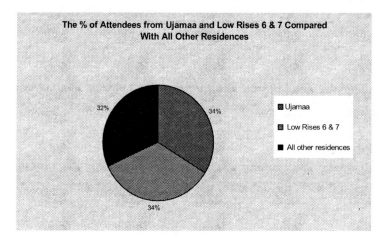

Figure 1

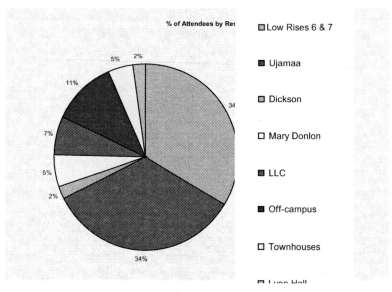

Figure 2

432

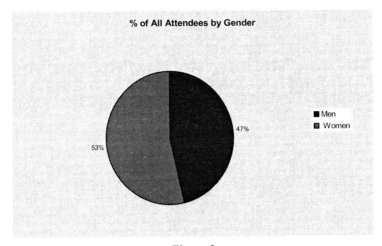

Figure 3

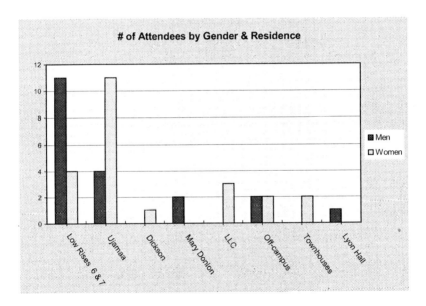

Figure 4

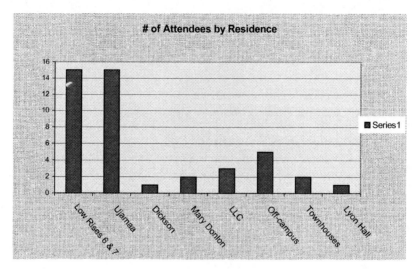

Figure 5

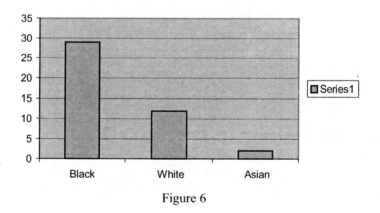

Figure 6

The Outsider

A basic premise of the Harlem Experience is to appreciate differences, and differences can include living quarters, gender, ethnic group, race or a combination of factors (figures 5 and 6). For example, a number of students who might be defined in the United States as either Black or of African descent identified themselves as either Dominican or Latina. Surprisingly, they did not subscribe to the more comprehensive or politically correct notion of Afro-Latino.[323]

Similarly, I wondered and continued to wonder about the Asian-American participants in the Harlem Experience. Fei Siu, for instance, self-identifies as an Asian American; however, my professional experience and research on the counseling implications of racial self-designation among Blacks[324] encouraged me to learn in the diversity field that there is much significance in whether a person calls himself or herself Chinese-born American or American-born Chinese. She was not a social isolate during the trip. Inside the theater, I sat close to her and observed a connection she made with Monique Horton, an Alumnae who participated in various aspects of the Harlem Experience program. At the Amy Ruth's dinner, however, Fei did not seem to relate personally to the various discussions. An essay by her could have been revealing and instructive.

Fear of Harlem Surmounted

An unfounded fear of Harlem was alluded to in several students'essays (e.g., Rejane and Kerby) and one student during the tour quizzed me about the whereabouts of the "bad" section of Harlem he had heard existed. He evinced chagrin when I informed him that he was in the reportedly terrible section. A belief in a Black racist environment is not race-specific, and can be seen in what is termed "internalized oppression." For example, after an earlier trip to the Schomburg the students asked if I could drive them to their car. Puzzled, I asked why their car was not in walking distance from the Schomburg and was informed that they had been told by an Africana faculty to park outside of Harlem where their car would be safe. This

---

[323]Minority Rights Group (Ed.) (1995). *No Longer Invisible Afro-Latin Americans Today.* United Kingdom: Minority Rights Publication; Rout, L. (1976). *The African Experience in Spanish America 1502 to the present day.* Cambridge: Cambridge University Press.

[324]Gerald Jackson & Kirschner, S. (1973). "Racial Self-designation and preference for a counselor." *Journal of Counseling Psychology,* 10, 560-564.

faculty member had neither been raised in Harlem nor born and reared in the United States but the power of his remark was so strong that he scared a student reared in Brooklyn, New York, no less!

In contrast, Yuval Shavit, a self-identified White Jewish student who was a Harlem Experience participant, shared the following "fun little anecdote."

> *Over winter break I visited a friend who goes to Manhattan School of Music, but by accident I took the A train instead of the 1-9, so that I found myself smack in the middle of Harlem on 125th. If it weren't for the trip, I'd have probably been pretty freaked out, but thankfully I knew where I was and that it was safe. So thanks! (April 23, 2003).*

Craig is a Jewish, White male alumnus. I recall him for several reasons. Most current, he met me at Showman's with his girlfriend (couple at the far right of the picture). When the group arrived at the club, he was comfortably seated waiting for us and did not appear frightened by the milieu, even though this was his first trip to Harlem. Then again, Craig was the only White student in a 172 course I taught

Picture of Craig, girlfriend Monique and students.
Photo by Gerald G. Jackson.

and one of the few such students that continued intra-cultural communication after the official conclusion of the course. His response, noted below, was given unsolicited a day or so later, after the Harlem Experience.

> *I had a great time, and my girlfriend (aka Andrea) was so happy to meet you. I've been talking you up so long, that I thought it was going to be tough for you to live up the billing, but you found a way. Thanks again for the invitation, as that*

was a rare cultural treat. It was my first real venture up to Harlem. It was nice seeing Monique, [325] and although most of the kids were exhausted, it was fun meeting them as well. We're on the edge of our seats waiting for the videotape, [326] can't wait to see it. hope the trip back to Ithaca was smooth."

In the same vein, a post program enthusiasm is reflected in the following comments by White Harlem Experience participants. These revelations were voluntarily given in response to a query about the racial and ethnic background of participants (April 2003).

Daniel J. Cohen is a White male of diverse ethnic background (English, Russian, German, and Jewish). Daniel noted:

By the way I wanted to say that I really loved going on the trip, it was a great experience. Will there be a way for me to be able to read the report once it is published? (April 23, 2003).

Jessica Goren identifies as a White American and noted:

The Harlem trip was great! It was an excellent opportunity and I really enjoyed the experience. (April 23, 2003).

Rachel Flynn identifies as a White American and her email not only conveys a program appreciation but a deep cross-cultural communication connection.

On another note, I'm the girl who told you that my father can speak Swahili, but I completely forgot to email you after the trip with his phone number so you could call him and test his ability ☺. His number is _____. I hope the report goes well; the trip was great (April 24, 2003).

---

[325]Craig, Monique, Sherry and Marsha were a group in my 171 course. They gave a moving presentation, a videotape of which is used every semester to illustrate the concept of Black Psychological Stage of Development theory, campus race relations, and interracial teamwork and cooperation. Marsha is currently in medical school and could not attend and Sherry was expected to come to Showman's.

[326]Videotape I made of their group presentation in my AS&RC course.

In essence, the Harlem Experience learning is not either a factor of time or place. The experience is expected to continue and extend into different areas. For example, Stefun emailed me an essay after a Black Student Union end-of-the-semester cookout.[327] I was elated to receive the essay for several reasons. As a Knight Writing program student, Stefun shared in class that his experience in my writing seminar fostered an enthusiasm about writing. Second, this essay was not written for a course credit; therefore, he has demonstrated a real commitment to writing and documenting his cultural heritage.

These findings have wide implications for future programs and the University's diversity imperative (e.g., Harris, 2003).[328] To strengthen subject programming, it is recommended that participants receiving a copy of this report should be requested to add instructive comments and return it to a Harlem Experience Steering committee. An analysis and report from this group should be a foundation for subsequent proposals. In closing, these applications of my professional diversity works into the classroom illustrate the nexus between distinct real worlds[329] and the pivotal role a Harlem Experience can play.

Some Notables of Harlem

William T. Andrews –Assemblyman
Josephine Baker – Dancer/actress/singer
James Baldwin – Writer
James Hubert "Eubie" Blake – Jazz Pianist and Composer
Julius C. (Jules) Bledsoe – Singer, Actor and Composer
Carroll M. Boyd – Pianist and Singer
Edward Boyd – Executive

---

[327]The essay was published in the original text in this place. The essay currently appears in Sect. IV.

[328]Robert L. Harris (February 27, 2003). "Preparing students for the changing world: Diversity and curriculum." *Cornell Chronicle*, p. 4.

[329]Badi Foster, Gerald Jackson, William Cross, Bailey Jackson, & Rita Hartiman, R. (1988). "Workforce diversity and business." *Training & Development Journal*, 42(4), 38-42; G.G. Jackson (1986). "Conceptualizing Afrocentric and Eurocentric mental health training." In H. Lefley & P. Pedersen (Eds.). *Cross-cultural training for mental health professionals.* Illinois: Charles Thomas, 131-149; Gerald Jackson (winter, 1987). "The implementation of an intracultural awareness coaching program." *Corporate Headquarters*, 9, 13, 30; Gerald Jackson (March, 1995). "Beyond the White male paradigm." *Cultural diversity at work*, 7-10.

Harry G. Bragg – Attorney
William Stanley Braithwaite – Poet, Literary Critic, Editor
Ronald Brown – U.S. Cabinet Member
Cab Calloway – Musician, Entertainer
Elmer A. Carter – Editor
Eunice Hunton Carter – Judge
Elizabeth Catlett – Artist
May Edward Chinn – Doctor of Science
Shirley Chisholm – Politician
Marvel Cooke – Journalist and Activist
Countee Cullen – Poet
Leonard De Paur – Choral Conductor
Aaron Douglas – Artist
Shirley Lola Graham Du Bois – Author and Composer
W. E. B. Du Bois – Historian and Sociologist
Paul Lawrence Dunbar – Poet
Dennis Edward, Jr. – Judge
Duke Ellington – Musician
Ella Fitzgerald – Singer
Marcus Moziah Garvey – Orator, Organizer and Black Nationalist
Althea Gibson – Tennis Coach
Alexander Hamilton – Statesman
W.C. Handy – Musician
Matthew Henson – Explorer
Billie Holliday – Singer
Harry Houdini – Magician
Langston Hughes – Poet
Jacob Lawrence, Jr.   American Painter
Jimmie Lunceford – Bandleader/Music Teacher
Thurgood Marshall – U.S. Supreme Court Judge
Claude McKay – Author
Florence Mills – Singer and Dancer
Jelly Roll Morton – Composer, Pianist, Jazz Bandleader
Charlie Parker – Alto Saxophonist, Composer
William Patterson – Civil Rights Attorney
Adam Clayton Powell, Jr. – Political Leader
Colin Powell – Military General
A. Phillip Randolph – Civil Rights Leader
Charles Rangel – Politician, Social Activist
Paul Robeson – Actor, Singer and Political Activist
James H. Robinson – Pastor
Luther (Bojangles) Robinson – Entertainer

Augusta Savage – Sculptor, Educator
Arthur Schomburg – Curator, Writer, Bibliophile
Hazel Scott – Pianist, Actress
Noble Sissle – Musician
Mamie Smith – Dancer, Singer and Pianist
Charles E. Toney – Judge
James Van DerZee – Photographer
Madame C. Walker – Entrepreneur, Philanthropist
Clarence Cameron White – Violinist and Classical Composer
Walter Frances White – Civil Rights Leader
Roy Wilkins – Civil Rights Leader/Editor
Richard Wright – Author
Malcolm X – Civil Rights Leader
Lester Young – Tenor Saxophonist

SECTION V
Only God is Perfect:
Elements of Engagements for Peace

As opposed to a Talented Tenth, I view college students as a part of a Talented Billion.[330] Within this sphere, college students are of central importance in Africentric helping because they comprise the bulk of persons who will make decisions affecting the health, welfare, education and defense of the modern world. The world they govern and manage will consist of people with diverse phenotypic and genotypic backgrounds, and racial and cultural heritages and experiences. As a diversity consultant on multicultural human resource management and development, I have spent decades designing and maintaining programs to correct the miseducation given to college students.

Experience has revealed, therefore, that consultation on the aftermath of students receiving schooling, not education, on human relations and leadership is not a sufficient prejudice reduction intervention. The college curriculum has to be suffused with an Africentric design and diunital logic to overcome cultural lethargy. Its participants for change would include staff, professionals, teachers, scholars, administrators and site designers, as learners who greatly influence the learning process of students.

Several books and studies have followed debates on the efficacy of an education either from a Black or White institution.[331] Frequently

---

[330]W.E.B. DuBois, based upon his study in the Germany of Albert Einstein, Karl Marx and Sigmund Freud that *U.S. News & World Report* said were the three minds that shaped the Twentieth Century, advanced the proposition that 10% of the race was superior, akin to other races, and should serve as leaders and benefactors for the less endowed 90%. Less elitist, my belief is that a multitude of leaders from all walks of life will have to be a part of a determined leadership hosting the survival and growth of humankind.

[331]Walter Allen, Epps, E. & Haniff, N. (Eds.) (1991). *College in Black and White. African American students in predominantly White and in historically Black public universities*. New York: State University of New York Press; Jacqueline Fleming (1984). *Blacks in college: A comparative study of students' success in Black and White institutions*. California: Jossey-Bass; Michael Nettles (1987). "Black and White College student performance in majority White and majority Black academic settings." In J. Williams (Ed.).

merited Black colleges and universities harbor a constellation of factors attributed to Blackness and African-American culture. For example, Regina Scott gives a wonderful story of how Black triumphs over racism. The story is of Judge Glenda Hatchett and the lecture she delivered at Bennett College. This historically Black College is headed by Dr. Johnetta Cole, renowned African-American anthropologist, and former pace-setting president of Spellman College. Dr. Cole assumed the presidency after technically retiring, and altruistically, seeking to enhance the performance of the college.

Judge Hatchett, in the crusading spirit of both Dr. Cole and HBCs, presented a personal account on how she confronted and overcame institutional racism in the segregated South of her youth. It was simultaneously a loss of innocence and discovery of a Black resolve from her father. The situation involved her observing her teacher pass by her because the page in her book she was supposed to read had been torn out. Not an uncommon reality for Black children receiving secondhand books from White school systems but unfamiliar to a young Judge Hatchett. The judge questioned the teacher and was informed "Everybody has an old book."[332] Not appeased by her teacher's response, she later asked her father for an explanation and he replied, "Get your crayons and write your own story." She closed by charging the Bennett students to "spread the good news. Excellence is the measure of the day. Take action, not lingering on the torn and marred pages."

As obvious as it may seem, few discourses on Africana studies have examined the issue of the preparation from these institutions of the leadership for Black communities, nations or a non-binary global world. This book was certainly not intended to answer these questions fully; however, afterthoughts have revealed issues that should be considered in an examination of how we might ensure a future for Black people and humankind, conceptually viewed as intertwined.

First, it would be myopic, and an anti-Africentric tenet, to confine the magnitude of what is being affirmed to a single goal of the elevation of African Americans. The United States is clearly not an island and African Americans are not an autonomous racial cohort within US borders. What follows then is a proposition based partly on the Africentric tenet of interdependence, and partly on scholarship that

---

Title VI Regulation of Higher Education: Problems and Progress. New York: Teachers College Press.

[332] Regina Scott (December 12 - 18, 2002). "'Write your story.' TV judge urges students." *The New York Amsterdam News,* p. 48.

reveals that Euro-American values are not sustainable of world hegemony, as they are currently defined and practiced.[333] African Americans are versed and strategically placed to do life-affirming cultural work, especially around maintaining spiritual connections, group identity and moral integrity.[334] Perceived in this efficacious manner, it is likewise conceivable for them to help in the development of identities that include Latinos, Afro-Latinos,[335] Asian Americans and Reform Jews. In this Africentric helping paradigm, African-American cultural workers/brokers would first heal themselves according to Africentric helping[336] and then engage in collaborative ventures that help manage historical pain, human violation and intracultural communication barriers.[337]

One simple deduction from the racial assessment of institutions is that they are limited in what they can do in the total development of Black leaders. Similarly, it is facile to argue that they are limited in their capacity and ability to disseminate knowledge that is pertinent to the political, social and economic advancement of Black people. To enhance these institutions, compensatory educational programs[338] and a

---

[333]Marcia Clark (1995). "Changes in Euro-American values needed for sustainability." *Journal of Social Issues*, 51(4), 63-82.

[334]Gerald G. Jackson (2005). *Delimits of American helping: Precursors of an African Genesis model of helping.* New Jersey: Africa World Press.

[335]See chapter six, "Towards a Self-definition," in Ilan Stavans (2001). *The Hispanic condition The power of a people.* New York: Harper/Collins.

[336]Kalamu ya Salaam (1993). "African American cultural empowerment: A struggle to identify and institutionalize ourselves as a people" (pp. 119-134). In Marta Vega & Greene, C. (Eds.) (1993). *Voices from the battlefront Achieving cultural equity.* New Jersey: Africa World Press. For a more detailed account of the concept and practice of a cultural broker see Harriet Lefley & Pedersen, P. (1986). *Cross-cultural training for mental health professionals.* Illinois: Charles C. Thomas.

[337]Bernice Reagon (1993). "Battle stancing to do cultural work in America" (pp. 69-82). In Marta Vega & Greene, C. (Eds.) (1993). *Voices from the battlefront Achieving cultural equity.* New Jersey: Africa World Press.

[338]Edmund Gordon & Wilkerson, D. (1966). *Compensatory education for the disadvantaged Programs and practices: Preschool through college.* New York: College Entrance Examination Board; Roosevelt Johnson (Ed.) (1974). *Black scholars on higher education in the 70s.* Ohio: Educational-Community Counselors Associates; Nathan Wright (Ed.) (1970). *What Black educators are saying.* New York: Hawthorne Books; Dyckman Vermilge (Ed.) (1972). *The expanded campus.* California: Jossey-Bass, Inc.

Black Studies discipline were advanced as modes for Black problem resolution. Contemporary analysis of the two approaches suggests that the former, while still in place, has been institutionalized and is no longer a source for curricular, institutional, structural, or ideological innovation. A similar analysis of Black Studies indicates that it is in a holding pattern on campus and peripheral in mass appeal and impact.

An innovative approach that has a great educational potential is the talk tour conducted by Dr. Cornell West (Alpha), Tavis Smiley (Kappa) and Dr. Eric Dyson.[339] The form is not new; there have been tours of Black women writers that reached out to all segments of the Black community to provide knowledge and inspiration. What is extremely pertinent is that African-American male scholars are going public, and inadvertently challenging the negative stereotype of Black males. They are courageously confronting the Black male invisibility syndrome,[340] by visibly competing with "thug" criminal and gangsta Hip-Hop subcultural styles. Other culturally grounded ways that African-American scholars are disseminating their knowledge beyond the academy is through video and audio tapes,[341] direct involvement in community organizations, and heading their consulting firms.[342] These sources seriously reduce the dependency on Eurocentric educational programs and structure to educate the African-American community and allow for African-American scholars to present their material in a way that is congruent with an African ethos and pedagogy.[343]

---

[339]Nikitta Foston (April, 2004). "Pass the mic! Talk tour educates, empowers and creates new dialogue." *Ebony*, pp. 84, 86, and 88.

[340]Anderson Franklin (2004). *From brotherhood to manhood How Black men rescue their relationships and dreams from the invisibility syndrome.* New York: John Wiley & Sons.

[341]Sample of audio tapes are: "Reclaiming the African character by Dr. Wade Nobles;" "The psychology of self hatred & self defeat" by Dr. Amos Wilson; "African education issues" by Dr. Asa Hilliard; and "African intellectual foundations" by Dr. Jacob Carruthers.

[342]See Dr. Akbar's company, Mind Production & Associates. Webpage address: www.mindpro.com. E-mail address: sales@mindpro.com.

[343]Kwame Agyei & Akoto, A. (2000). *The Sankofa movement.* Washington, D.C.: yoko Info(om Inc; Asa Hilliard (1997). *SBA: The reawakening of the African mind.* Florida: Makare Publishing; Asa Hilliard (1995). *The maroon within us.* Maryland: Black Classic Press; Mwalimu Shujaa (Ed.) (1998). *Too much schooling too little education.* New Jersey: Africa World Press.

They are daring to democratize scholarly concepts, as Black preachers have done for generations, and "teach" and "preach,"[344] the latter being the African-American oratorical style they use to convey their messages.[345] What they are in a position to do is getthe Black Greeks to be more politically, socially and economically involved, as are the Black Greek sororities. They are uniquely favored to do this because the majority have crossed the **burning sands**, have stellar Eurocentric academic credentials and have lost neither the willingness nor the ability to communicate to African Americans. What White institutions can provide is an understanding of the constructive ways of being White.[346] This approach entails all racial and ethnic groups accepting invitations to experience White, Asian, Latino and Indigenous cultures and people, as illustrated by my account of my involvement with a White female sorority function, a Latina sorority and South Asian students.

Current multicultural and diversity models have been perverted by *Eurocentric culturalism* and concomitant aggressive behaviors to maintain this culture. This means, among many things:

- White institutions are conducted according to the Doctrine of Colorblindness.Therefore, Black students are not consciously educated to combat, overcome or challenge obstacles based upon racism, Eurocentric culturalism, internalized oppression and colorism.

- White institutions of higher education are based upon paternalistic concepts of White male superiority and dominance in all major social, political, religious, education and business

---

[344]William Pipes (1997). "Old-time religion: Benches can't say 'Amen'" (pp. 41-66). In Harriet McAdoo (Ed.). *Black families* (3rd edition). California: Sage.
[345]Geneva Smitherman (1977). *Talkin and testifyin The language of Black America.* Massachusetts: Houghton Mifflin Company.
[346]Gary Howard (Spring, 2000). "Ways of being White." *The Diversity Factor*, pp. 20–24; Cooper Thompson, Schacfcr, E. & Brod, H. (Eds.) (2003). *White men challenging racism 35 personal stories.* North Carolina: Duke University Press; Michael Moore (2001). *Stupid White men.* New York: Regan Books; Richard Shenkman (1998). *Legends, lies & cherished myths of American history.* New York: William Morrow & Company; Andrew Hacker (2003). *Two nations: Black and White, separate, hostile, unequal.* New York: Scribber Book; Andrew Hacker (1997). *MONEY Who has how much and why.* New York: Scribner.

transactions. They conform to the beliefs and standards underlying a belief in the innate qualities of leaders by pre-selecting the best and honoring in the selection process the concept of White male legacy.

- White institutions provide Black people with an opportunity to imitate the practices and institutions that Western culture has determined to be the sources of its contemporary world leadership, without confering privileges to them of being White and the power to exercise them.

- Black institutions are not presumptively Africentric and naturally versed in preparing Africentric leaders. Their status is affirmed according to world-view criteria and perennial evaluation.

Consequently, their scope has been abridged so that they do not include problems and solutions that happen outside of conventional boxes. This is clearly the case with the 21st century problem of succession polity, and its implications for mental and physical health, employment, welfare and economic stability in the nation and the world.

Succession Politics in a Eurocentric Country

A major preoccupation for me has been the conceptual framework used to design and implement solutions to human conditions and human relationships books and disciplines. Marta Vega eloquently captures the essence of the goal of my frame when she wrote:[347]

Collectively, we defined, articulated, and insisted upon our fair share of resources, our right to our own culture, and our right to self-determination. We developed ethnic studies programs, Puerto Rican, African-American, and Chicano studies departments, and culturally grounded institutions that would reconstruct our histories, pass on our traditions, and make visible the creative genius in our communities. It

---

[347]Marta Vega (1993). "The purposeful underdevelopment of Latino and other communities of color" (p. 104). In Marta Vega & Greene, C. (Eds.). *Voices from the battlefront Achieving cultural equity.* New Jersey: Africa World Press.

was clear to us that it was necessary to dislocate the imposed *universal* Eurocentric hegemonic thought and practice by instituting what Temple University historian C. Tsehloane Keto calls a *pluriversal* cultural vision and practice that placed all of our histories and experiences on an equal level.

What we have been less great in doing is constructing disciplines that allow for a prosperous mix of cultural and racial heritages and social affiliations. The neat division established by sociologists frequently do not conform to the social realities of New York City. People today refer to Spanish-speaking people as Latinos; however, I lived for a while in what was called Little Italy and the Italians were more broadly recognized as the Latins. A Puerto Rican student informed me that she was told she is not Puerto Rican because she grew up in Florida and not either Chicago or New York. If we are going to teach, direct and correct such students so that they have a minimum of mental health problems and a maximum academic and career growth, more faculty and administrator training and education must be done to eliminate miseducation. A first step is the Africentric practice of self-exploration and self-knowledge.

What needs to be pinpointed further is a **susceptibility factor**, that is, those specific ideas, behaviors and threats that seduce an individual and group to take a **racial bribe**. Just as important are the people, places and things that support efforts to establish and maintain an alliance.[348] My place, as an African-American man, is one of relatively good human relations with Latinos. My concerns about African-American and Latino relations, therefore, do not stem from personal problems with this conglomerate. However, the general relationship between Blacks and Latinos is not as cordial as some suspect and project,[349] based upon a misdirection about commonalties; that is, that

---

[348]Roberto Rodgriquez & Gonzales, P. (1998). "Black/Brown relations: An unnecessary conflict" (pp.246–256). In Ishmael Reed (Ed.). *MultiAmerica. Essays on cultural wars and cultural peace.* New York: Penguin.

[349]Keith Jennings & Lusane, C. (1994). "The state and future of Black/Latino relations in Washington, D.C.: A bridge in need of repair" (pp. 57–78). In James Jennings (Ed.). *Blacks, Latinos, and Asians in urban America.* Connecticut: Praeger; Elizabeth Llorente (January 25, 2004). "Diverse and divided: One city, two communities." *North Jersey Media Group.* pp. 1–14; Elizabeth Llorente (February 6, 2004). "Minorities find suburbs offer no escape from bias." *North Jersey Media Group,* 1–6; Nicolas

they eviscerate group conflict, and social and historical differences. I believe, based upon my relationship with Latinos, that much human development greatness is possible if Latinos and Blacks concentrate on improving their relationship from a non-Eurocentric thought.[350] In an anticipation of the current struggle between Blacks and Latinos and wanting to head off such a catastrophic relationship in the future, I designed and implemented a conference in the 1980s that focused exclusively on Black and Hispanic needs and wants. I used only Black and Hispanic scholars, students, researchers and community leaders because I wanted solutions to be based upon experience and theories. In addition, I desired a cooperative model to be set in motion that would continue after the conference. Last, I wanted both the community and "experts" to learn to appreciate the strengths of the other group.

It was one of the first working conferences between just Blacks and Hispanics that aimed to generate solutions to their peculiar problems and establish an alliance to overcome comparable troubles.[351] The contrived socio-cultural and economic circumstances today demand actions of greater breadth and depth from the scholarly and academic communities. Touching upon the need and scope for such efforts, Franco Morales, a friend, colleague and speaker at my Hispanic and Black conference, proposed the following:

Vaca (2004). *The presumed alliance. The unspoken conflict between Blacks and Latinos and what it means for America.* New York: Rayo; Juan Gonzalex (2000). *Harvest of Empire. A history of Latinos in America.* New York: Viking.

[350] See, Roberto Rodriquez & Gonzales, P. (1998). "Black/Brown relations: An Unnecessary conflict" (pp. 246–256). In Ishmael Reed (Ed.). *Multiamerica Essays on cultural wars and cultural peace.* New York: Penquin; Maulana Karenga (1998). "Black and Latino relations: Context, challenge, and possibilities" (pp. 189–204). In Ishmael Reed (Ed.). *Multiamerica Essays on cultural wars and cultural peace.* New York: Penquin.

[351] See conference, Gerald Jackson, Valle, M. & Hill, I. (September 21, 1981). "Black and Hispanic Inner-City Families: Crisis and Solutions Conference." New Arena Consultants, East Orange, New Jersey. Since then there have been several conferences by academic institutions for academy. For example, in February of 2003, the University of Nebraska gave one that was entitled, "African and Latina/o Experiences: Cultural histories, identities & relationships in the Americas." Just the title, it will be seen, creates more confusion than a three day conference can resolve.

Dear Geraldo:

Attached is the rough outline which Casto and I developed. It's a sketch of some ideas, which I believe are long overdue and could contribute much to the unification and development of both the Black and Latino communities. It can of course help to ease tensions and avoid conflict which can be disruptive to say the least. We envision a five to ten year holistic social research plan inclusive of massive education effort on cultural, racial and ethnic histories, customs, social and economic problems, community development, employment opportunities and investment options, among others. The initial steering committee besides fund raising, planning and guidance must be totally inclusive and made up of people who have a vested interest in the Newark communities, based upon their personal histories or record of employment. Given your commitment toward improving Black/Latino relations combined with your academic writing, your input and guidance can be most beneficial, particularly as it pertains to the training components, seminars, etc. As you know, its not easy bringing people together with the goal of being fair, equitable and inclusive. Another key component is getting a group together. I believe that the Council of Higher Education in Newark (CHEN) can lead the social research aspect and ECC can be the motivating and unifying institution to prepare, house and play a leadership role, particularly given their role in Newark and the large Black/Latino students populations they serve. Let me know what you think.

Frank

I received Frank's email on August 21, 2003 while I was in the process of completing this book. Much of what follows is shaped by the needs unfolded by Frank and our friendship. The"pluriversal" cultural goal noted earlier by Dr. Vega was not only perverted largely by seductive Eurocentric institutions and individuals bent on maintaining their culture's elevated and dominant position, but also by an inarticulateness of what is Eurocentric and its reaches.

Gerald G. Jackson

The Racial Bribe Revisited

To illustrate, Gabriel Haslip-Viera claimed to review the appropriateness of Afrocentrism for Puerto Ricans, based upon an alleged concern about the increasing number of Puerto Ricans expressing an attraction to the thought.[352] His assessment entails an analysis of Afrocentric schools of thought that he invented, without either expertise or revealing scholarly work on the presented field.[353] His declaration of racial superiority affirmations by Afrocentricism theory and theorists is his imputation of racial superiority beliefs to Afrocentrism, not a genuine characteristic of the theory. His motivation, however, is only partially accounted for by the racial bribe concept. Theorectically, the concept is a U.S.A. phenomenon but a closer dissection of the notion reveals that it has a Western culture and European antecedent.[354] It is more than a racial bribe, it is a rite-of-passage activity for any aspiring White group to economic and social prosperity in America.[355]

It takes a world-view conceptual framework, however, to reveal this dimension. A world-view appraisal of his assessment reveals a use of an undeclared Eurocentric mode of thought and pathology attributed to Eurocentrism.[356] One might ask where his assessment was for Puerto Ricans using Eurocentrism, especially in light of all the different forms of racism used by a majority of its followers? I am not claiming a shortcoming based on the conspicuous absence of "balance". Rather, I wonder about whom and what he is attempting to protect. Certainly, it will be seen, not the concerns of Black/Afro-Puerto Ricans. A suggested rationale for his alleged inquiry can be seen in his subsequent attack on the research of Professor Ivan Van Sertima, the noted Black

---

[352]Gabriel Haslip-Viera (July, 1994). "Puerto Ricans and the Afrocentrism debate." *CRITICA: A journal of Puerto Rican policy & politics*, pp. 1, 6.

[353]Aisha Hakim-Dyce (August, 1994). "The Afrocentrism debate continues." *CRITICA: A journal of Puerto Rican policy & politics*, p.7 See, for example, Cecil Gray (2001). *Afrocentric thought and praxis: An intellectual history.* New Jersey: Africa World Press.

[354]John Hodge, Struckman, D & Trost, L. (1975*). Cultural bases of racism and group oppression.* California: Two Riders Press.

[355]David Richards (1999). *Italian American.* New York: New York University Press; Noel Ignatiev (1996). *How the Irish became White.* Connecticut: BrunerRoutledge.

[356]See Charles Ephraim (2003). *The pathology of Eurocentrism The burden and responsibilities of being Black.* New Jersey: Africa World Press.

scholar of Indigenous Indian and African ancestry.[357] What, I speculated, could account for the virulent attack, not scholarly critique, of Van Sertima? Professor Van Sertima merely gave evidence to show that Africans came to the Americas before the Europeans, strongly confirmed by the finding of a Little Lucy in Brazil.[358]

It was the implication that these Africans voluntarily returned to Africa, unlike the European, that is insightful. What type of family and land would propel men to leave them to establish permanent residence in another land and cohabitate with local women? Much deeper and closer to why Eurocentric Latinos might take up the gauntlet, Van Sertima's research has also revealed the African presence in the development of Spain. Both contentions undermine a Eurocentric view of racial, color and ideological superiority, hallmarks of the Eurocentric intellectual thrust that is no longer invulnerable to scrutiny,[359] and challenged by Afrocentrism.[360] In particular, a rebuttal by Professor Van Sertima exposes the fallacious approaches taken by Haslip-Viera and associates, and the inability of this group to transcend the narrow cultural script of Eurocentric paradigmatic thinking.[361]

A variant form of the Denial of African Significance is the application of creolization to transformations involving an African culturally-inspired syncretism. Why, for example, is the language spoken in Haiti called Creole when it could just as well be called Haitian? The European languages that are derivatives of Latin are called by the name of the country in which they developed. Similarly, when the African influence in Latin America is observed to be influencing the cultural mix, the process is defined as creolization,

---

[357]See Gabriel Haslip-Viera, Ortiz de Montellano, Bernard & Barbour, W. (1997). "Robbing Native American cultures Van Sertima's Afrocentricity and the Olmecs." *Current Anthropology*, 38, (3), 419 - 431.

[358](October 26, 1999). "Brazil challenges long-held theories." *The New York Times*, pp. F4, F5. Larry Rohter (October 26, 1999). "An ancient skull challenges long-held theories." *The New York Times*, pp. F1, 5.

[359] Ellis Cose (1997). *Color-Blind.* New York: HarperCollins.

[360]Molefi Asante (1999). *The painful demise of Eurocentrism.* New Jersey: Africa World Press; Molefi Asante (July/August, 1996). "Ancient truths. New attacks on Afrocentrism are as weak as they are false." *Emerge*, pp. 66–70.

[361]Ivan Van Sertima (2002). *Early America revisited.* New Jersey: Transaction Publishers.

Europeanization, but not Africanization.[362] A Eurocentric hegemonic cultural superiority is maintained by an intellectually lazy interpretation of Afrocentric as synonymous with Blackness, defined as a skin color and certain physical characteristics. No, I am not going to start with a sundry of citation of definitions; I will affirm my point by presenting an embedded definition that delineates the concept in practice. I teach in an Africana Studies Center; therefore, when beginning my study I viewed the Black/Latino situation. Similarly, my intellectual inquiry started in Africa, with an eye towards the Moorish cultural and racial influence in Spain.[363]

Understanding Afro-Latinos: An Africentric Journey

After a diversity training in San Francisco, an Afro-Puerto Rican Latina lesbian confided in me that she tended to overlook or downplay racism among Latinos and principally denounce the racism in Anglos. She indicated that the exchanges made during training had altered her approach. She would subsequently confront the racism exhibited by White Latinos towards Black ones. We gave little consideration to the "internalized oppression" that Black Latinos may carry for other Black Latinos and the racism Latinos may have towards African Americans. Although not discussed, our discussion resulted in me thinking about the shock and hurt I felt when informed that there was a derogatory term used by Latinos to characterize Blacks that was in addition to the conventional term "Nigger," or "Negrito." It was information gained in confidence and during a moment of a sharing of in-group racial and ethnic group secrets. I used the term "Moyeto," the derogatory term, to describe myself to a group of kids before my talk to them entitled "To be young gifted and Puerto Rican." Frank Morales, my friend made me give the talk. He charged, based on his belief that I liked to talk, was

---

[362] Jean Rahier (2001). "Blackness as a process of creolization: The Afro-Esmeraldian Decimas (Ecuador)" (pp. 315–321). In Isidore Okpewho, Davies, C. & Mazrui, A. (Eds.) (2001). *The African diaspora.* Indiana: Indiana University Press; Viranjini Munasinghe (March 10, 2004). "Theorizing world culture through the Caribbean: East Indians and creolization;" Thomas Morton (2000). "Palenge Awe/PalenqueHoy/Palenque Today: The Spanish Caribbean, the African Creole perspective and the Roia of San Basilo de Palenque, Columbia." *The Black Scholar*, 30(3&4), pp. 51–53.

[363] L. Harvey (1990). *Islamic Spain 1250 – 1500.* Illinois: The University of Chicago Press; Lane-Poole (1990). *The story of the Moors in Spain.* Maryland: Black Classic Press; Ivan Van Sertima (Ed.) (1992). *Golden age of the Moor.* New Jersey: Transaction Publishers.

good at it and the students needed inspiration. I wanted the kids to know that I was not trying to be Puerto Rican and that not all Moyetos were bad. They said my talk was good and gave Frank hell for not speaking in Spanish (he did not because he thought the kids did not know it well enough).

I felt foolish about learning of the existence of the term because I wondered how I did not learn of it during all my years dating, eating, sleeping, skating and fighting with and alongside Puerto Ricans in New York City. For example, at the age of twelve I was instructed to leave the Jefferson pool in East Harlem, because some "Spanish guy" called Nature Boy a Nigger. It did not surprise me to see Superman (Nuyorican) and Crazy (Jibaro) as part of the assembly outside the pool. In those times, being a member of the Enchanters street gang superseded racial, neighborhood and ethnic loyalty. Even the patrolman was a part of the deal and knew a gang fight was pending. He told us to take the fight across the street because that was not his beat.

Several years later the *Enchanter* empire fell and a new racio-ethnic group came to power and splinter-off Enchanter social clubs emerged in the East Harlem projects. Superman would switch loyalties and join the *Viceroy,* a Puerto Rican gang that did not reside in the projects. As a Viceroy, he crashed a party given by The Jokers, of Johnson projects, a former subdivision of Enchanters-turned-social club. According to folklore, he declared that he "was now a Viceroy and the "shit was on." He made no racial epithets. Even when my Boy Teddy Blackwell fought a Spanish guy for the right to walk Teddy's Puerto Rican girlfriend back from the Wagner project to her 119th street apartment (he won the fight), no unfamiliar derogatory term was used during the altercation. Even when Bourgois reported the following rage response of a Puerto Rican male towards Black people, no such derogatory word was used:

Philippe: She was white?

Caesar: [spinning into my face] It would not have made a
      difference if she was Puerto Rican, Portuguese or Spaniard. I
      was starving [shouting] I was: "Kill that motherfuckin' bitch!"
      If it had been a black woman, I would have fucked her up some
      more you know. Just because she was black; and I hate black
      people.
      Because I don't give a shit.
      I'm a racist motherfucker.[364]

---

[364] pp. 204, 205.

The seedbed of this intense feeling is not Anglo culture, it is more precisely European, in general, and Spanish, in particular. This origin was partially revealed to me by an Ecuadorian, during a corporate diversity training for Latinos, when he declared his hatred for the Spaniards. He announced that while he had a Spanish surname, he was Indian. He was angry, although living in the United States, because he recollected how Spanish domination in Latin America had meant that he could not speak his native Indian language in school and publicly manifest his culture.

According to research conducted by Samuel Betances, the derogatory term **moyeto** is a derivative of a Southwestern USA term called **Mayate,** literally meaning "an insect/bettle type animal which is black in color and is said to feed on animal and human excrement."[365] According to Black/African psychology thinking, the terms created by African Americans to describe Whites are a consequence of having a sense of oppression by Whites. A designation such as **Honky** is based also on the outrageous behaviors of Whites. African Americans have not applied the same process of name-calling to non-Whites but have typically accepted White American terms to convey prejudices. The legalistic approach taken to this subject by Guinier and Torres,[366] while illuminating, omits the psychological and Africana Studies dimensions of African Americans maintaining an alliance with a Latino group that has a European phenotypic ideal and a *Eurocentric culturalism* frame of analysis.

Claims predicated, therefore, on a Eurocentric dichotomous reasoning deny the significant number of Afro-Latinos (Spanish-speaking Black folks) in the Latino ranks and mask identity issues stemming from White racism. Frequently overlooked is the "invisible" Afro-Latino. This occurrence is not a slight but a culturally-induced systemic denial that has resulted in members of this group going to the White House, as a distinct group to give a briefing.[367] This person is not invisible to African Africans; however, the invisibility of them to Latinos exacerbates attempts at rapproachment between African

---

[365] Lani Guinier & Torres, G. (2002). *The miner's canary*. Massachusetts: Harvard University Press, p. 195.

[366] Lani Guinier & Torres, G. (2002). *The miner's canary*. Massachusetts: Harvard University Press.

[367] Jose Muhammad & Rodriguez, E. (December 21, 1999). "A First Ever White House invites Afro-Latinos for briefing." *The Final Call*, p. 17.

Americans and Latinos. African-American cognizance is illustrated in the following comments by Tiffany on a Latino Alliance initiative.

Here it is…your long awaited response to this letter. Sorry it took me so long, remember I'm not in the student mode anymore, but I still have it in me. Now don't try to grade this like a real paper, I didn't put a lot of time into it, but check it out. I am curious as to how you will respond to my response.

Although on the surface this letter appears to be supportive, I find many of its undertones to be very disenfranchising. The title of the letter makes it seem very broad and inviting, but it makes an informed reader ponder, whom are the Latinos writing to this very broad African American audience.

The Latinos writing this letter seem to be supportive of their African-American brethren in the struggle; however, closer analysis of their theory raises certain questions in the informed reader's mind. From the outset of the letter, the Latinos began to separate themselves from the African Americans whom they are addressing. The letter states:

As Latino/a teachers, activists, community people, students, artists and writers, we stand fiercely opposed to anyone making those statistics a reason to forget the unique historical experience of African Americans, the almost unimaginable inhumanity of slavery lasting centuries, the vast distance that remains on their long walk to freedom.

However, any reader versed in the history of Latin America, through either personal experience or academic study, knows that rather than being separately distinct, the history of many Latinos parallels that of African Americans. The quote noted above speaks as though inhumane slavery was only found in the United States. Some of the most brutal forms of slavery existed and continued to thrive in the Spanish Caribbean long after slavery was abolished in the United States. I do not make this statement to say that the U.S. is better than those countries for abolishing slavery first, I make that statement to say that both regions have a sordid and twisted past which is intricately intertwined by the exploitation of forcibly exiled Africans and their descendants.

As an informed reader, it makes me wonder, whom are these Latinos writing this open letter? Although numerous names appear at the bottom of the letter, I am forced to ponder their origins. Latino is an all-encompassing term for all Spanish-speaking people in the Americas. However, despite this unifying term, Latinos, are not all the same. Puerto Ricans differ greatly from Guatemalans, Cubans have a very different past from Peruvians, and so on, yet they are all united under the term Latino. The Latinos who wrote this letter cannot truly speak.

In their attempt to reach out to African Americans, these Latinos have alienated some of their fellow Latinos. By speaking as though people of African descent only have American origins, these Latino writers not only deny the rich history of the foundation of Latin America and the Spanish Caribbean, they illegitimate the Spanish speaking descendants of Africans who are also Latinos. These Latinos speak of America pitting Brown against Black as though Black does not exist in the Latino moniker. Before these Latinos can send an open letter of unity to African Americans, they must first unify their own people to ensure that their brethren of African descent are fully included in the Latino dialogue.

An illustration of the painful existence of Afro-Latinos is illustrated in the following essay by a Latina student who took my first year writing seminar. Yenifer's revealing essay debunks the notion of enchanted rainbow Latino families, and squarely raises a banner for Afro-Latinos and their distinct history and culture. Her essay gives a face to the waxing literature on the mental health struggles of Afro-Latinos stemming from what is depicted as White racism.[368] It appears that both African Americans and European Latinos may have to expand their definition of group membership to reflect a true sensitivity to Afri-Latinos who refuse to be invisible any longer[369].

I had requested Yenifer, as a student in my first year writing seminar, to write outside the "Latino/a equals White" box. She trusted me enough to do so, and reminds me of Rosa Clemente, another Cornell student that wrote and behaved outside the racial amnesia box. Had time permitted, I would have requested Yenifer to answer her own charge and provide the additional research on Afro-Latinos. What she did not know because, this book had not been published, was that I had

---

[368]Lillian Comas-Diaz (1996). "LatiNegra: Mental health issues of African Latinas" (pp. 167–190). In Maria Root (Ed.). *The multiracial borders as new frontiers.* New York: Sage Publications.

[369]Minority Rights Group (Ed.). *No longer invisible: Afro-Latin Americans Today.* England: Minority Rights; Norman Whitten & Torres, A. (Ed.). *Blackness in Latin America and the Caribbean.* Indiana: Indiana University Press.

done work in the area she will suggest needs additional development. Her essay, nevertheless, is a wonderful introduction to a growing student awareness and a foundation for promising scholarship by Afri-Latinas.

Racism amongst Latinos:
I am the Black Sheep of the Family by Yenifer Romero

May 18, 2004
Cornell University

Racism is a word that most people have heard at one point during the course of their life. However, there are those that don't only hear it but experience racism. According to the dictionary definition, racism is "a belief that race is the primary determinant of human traits and capacities and that racial differences produce an inherent superiority of a particular race." Though the forms of racism have varied from those in the past, it isn't astounding that racism is very much alive in the 21st century. Racism, however, doesn't only exist across racial and cultural groups. What happens when racism is prevalent within a culture? As much as it hurts me to admit a fact I cannot deny the truth; the Latino culture is a racist culture.

Latinos are a unique group of people. They represent about nineteen different countries, for example, Mexico, Cuba, Puerto Rico, and the Dominican Republic. Latinos can be of any race and range from various shades of color. Latinos may speak various dialects of the Spanish language. They may also differ in traditions; for example, "El Cinco de Mayo" is a Mexican custom not celebrated by other Latino countries. Therefore, with so many variations in the Latino culture, the fact that racism exist among Latinos should not be alarming.

Have one not ever observed a Puerto Rican or Dominican gets offended when mistaken for each other? Haven't one heard a Cuban say that they aren't Latino? How many times don't other Latinos mock Mexicans? How many times hasn't an Ecuadorian said that other Latinos are messing up the Spanish language just because they speak it a different way? How many times has one heard "oh Argentineans are the most proper and wealthiest Latinos?" However, the racism is not only common between different Latin American countries. Racism is present between Latinos of the same country and socioeconomic status. This kind of racism is most related to the racism that exists in the United States.

Latinos tend to deny their African ancestry. This is the root of the racism that pervades among different Latino groups and between Latinos of the same group. It wasn't until recent times that Latinos have begun to acknowledge their African heritage, or as Esdaille and Hughes (2004) noted: "It seems that if you relate yourself to being black its something negative" (p. 112). Afro-Latinos is a group among Latinos that has been kept silent for years.

The percentage of Latinos with African ancestry ranges or, according to Esdaille and Hughes (2004), "it has been "estimated that between 10% and 80% of Latinos who hail from countries like Cuba, the Dominican Republic, Colombia, Panama, Venezuela, Belize and the U. S. territory of Puerto Rico have African ancestry" (p. 111). Afro-Latinos has been a historically oppressed and neglected minority. Again, according to Esdaille and Hughes (2004), they "have been denied access to power, influence and material progress" (p. 111). Afro-Latinos is among the poorest people in the world. Their contribution to Latin American culture and society has been largely unacknowledged. Afro-Latinos has contributed to Latino food, music, dance, art, religion, and other cultural aspects. During the African Diaspora, countless numbers of African slaves were taken to North, Central, South, and the Caribbean. In early colonial time, 1570, Mexico's black population was about three times that of the Spanish. In 1646, it was about 2.5 times as large, and in 1742, blacks still outnumbered the Spanish. It was not until 1810 that Spaniards were more numerous. Therefore, it is evident that there is African ancestry in Mexico. However, Mexico still continues to deny its African ancestry, or as Esdaille and Hughes (2004) observed: "In Latino broadcasting [Afro-Latinos] are invisible because Latino broadcasting is Mexican-centric...for the most part, you won't see black people in anything Mexican" (p. 118).[370]

---

[370]Supporting Yenifer's contention, see Lamont Muhammad (October/ November, 2000). "Invisible: Blacks in Mexico." *Black Diaspora*, pp. 26–27; Colin Palmer (1993). "Afro-Mexican culture and consciousness during the sixteenth and seventeenth centuries" (pp.125-136). In Joseph E. Harris (Ed.). *African Diaspora* (2nd edition). Washington, D.C.: Howard University Press; Barbara Gonzalez (November 2, 1999). "The Mexican dark secret."

Nevertheless, Mexico shares this culpability with the rest of the Latino community and with both the African American community and the main stream media. In many Latin American countries, the Afro-Latino population is segregated. An example of this is in Ecuador in the city of Esmeralda. This region is completely Afro-Latino and they are discouraged from integrating with the rest of the Ecuadorian population. This resembles Joan Morgan's analogy of the "STRONGBLACKWOMAN" (Afro-Latinos) and step sister "MissSOUTHERNBELLE" (Latino community), "the two are permanently estranged, but they were once so close their existences depended on each other. Both sisters were bastard children of racism, sexism, and white male Mythmakers need for absolute dominance" (Morgan, 1999, p. 95). Conversely, it appears that the African American community as the Latino community fails to recognize the Afro-Latino, asking questions such as "you're not really black, are you?" (Esdaille & Hughes, p. 118) when they encounter an Afro-Latino. As stated in Black Enterprise Magazine (Oakley, 2001), main stream media fails to expose the Afro-Latino facet of the Latino culture. Gina Torres, for instance, an Afro-Latina actress, quoted in this article, said: "It has not been my experience thus far that the peoplethat have the power to make those those [casting] decisions are ready to embrace a Latina who is dark" Esdaille & Hughes, 2004, p. 116). It has been the norm that dark Latinos in the Latin media play roles of maids, nannies, or santeras. Today, however, in American media they are seen performing African American roles. According to Torres, the Latina that America is most comfortable with is a Jennifer Lopez image.

There are many Afro-Latinas, however, that have begun to change this comfortable image in mainstream media. Perhaps the most famous of these was Celia Cruz, a Cuban salsa diva. Her music is known for exposing the issues of the Afro-Latino community. Other famous Afro-Latinos include Dominican baseball player Sammy Sosa, Cuban Yankee pitcher "El Duque" and boxing Puerto Rican champ Felix "Tito" Trinidad. One Afro-Latino who is currently having an impact in the music industry is Tego Calderon. Through his

LatinoLink: http://www.latinolink.com/h10222e.html, p. 1–2; Herman Bennett (2003). *Africans in colonial Mexico*. Indiana: Indiana University Press.

music, this Puerto Rican native is raising political awareness among the Afro-Latino community.

Nonetheless, how does this issue affect the Latino family? How does a family function when there is a "negrito" or "negrita" in the family? Speaking broadly about negative characterizations, Esdaille and Hughes 92004), declared that "such disparaging terms as negrito (little black one), pelo malo (bad hair), or worse are commonplace for this group" (p. 112). Since Latinos range in color, many times families may have members that are darker than others. These members are stigmatized, and many times face discrimination within their own families.

I am the *black sheep* of the family. I mean the "negra" of the family. It was a nickname I was raised with; my aunt gave it to me. My father is known as "El Negro." My aunt also gave him that name. My brothers and my mother are light skinned. If you looked at a photograph of my family you would say we weren't related, yet we are family. If you looked at the photograph, you would only see a light skinned woman, three little light boys, and a brown skin girl. The absence of my father has made it harder for me to cope with the issue of color because I became the only "little black one" in the family. Growing up I hated being dark. I used to say how I was dark because I was born in the Dominican Republic. I wanted to be white just like my mommy. I wanted to be considered beautiful.

"you're black for nothing. You can't even braid."
"No I am not. I am brown. I am not black."

These are a few of the remarks my brothers would say, and oh would that piss me off so much. I was brown not black. Moreover, if I couldn't be white at least I had gotten "good hair." As I grew older being dark skinned didn't bother me as much; well of course I couldn't tan because I was dark enough. I had friends that were African American and this made it easier for me to identify myself as Latina. It was all about improving the race and dating people who were lighter. As I continued to further my institutionalized education, I learned more of the African American culture. However, the more I learned about it the more Latino centric I became. I knew that Africa had influenced Latin America tremendously, but subconsciously I denied it. Identifying as a Latina or Hispanic allowed me to break all bonds with Africa and to embrace the ties to Spain. I have always been proud of being Latina; it was not until college that this issue became so problematic.

> "How do you ethnically identify yourself?"
> The interviewer mentioned categories.
> "Hispanic" I responded.
> "With what racial group do you identify
> Yourself?" White, African-American,
> Pacific Islander, and other..." she mentioned
> everything except Hispanic.
> "Umm...what do you mean?" I couldn't
> answer the question.

This event made me realize that I have a real problem. I can easily identify ethnically with the Latino community. Yet, racially I can't because Latino isn't a race. Nonetheless I couldn't identify as African American because my experience has not been that of an African American and mainly because I was raised, detached from that identity. It was not until recent that I learned of Afro-Latinos. I had seen many dark skinned Latinos, but I did not identify them as Afro-Latinos. This newly surfaced group might be the answer to my problems and of many others.

Afro-Latinos is a group of people that have been marginalized and ostracized for many centuries. It has been recently that the Afro-Latino community has begun to voice their opinions and demand equality.[371] This group is the testimony of the African ancestry present throughout Latin America and the Spanish speaking Caribbean. However, the Latino community, racist as it is, has been trying to deny their existence. They have denied their contribution to the Latino culture. They have denied the Afro-Latino influence in music and dance. Dances such as Salsa, Merengue, Tango and Palo

---

[371] The notion of recency, we will see, is not so true; however, she is somewhat prophectic, for example, see Karen Carrillo (June 2 – June 9) "African-Americans/Afro-Latinos meet for 'Points of unity.'" *The New York Amsterdam News*, p. 3. and Karen Carillo (June 2 – 9). "For Afro-Venezuelans, Chavez is the only hope for change." *The New YorkAmsterdam News*, p. 2.

which all have African influence are an important part of the Latino culture. Worst yet, paralleling America, Latinos have deprived Afro-Latinos from any political, educational and economic power. Latinos have suffocated their own relatives. They have stigmatized Afro-Latinos as the Black Sheep of the Latino Family. More research should be done on Afro-Latinos in order to better their situation and to help the Latino community embrace that facet of its culture.

Africentric Outlook Applied to Afro-Latino Dilemma

Being Africentric is more than the affirmation of personal preferences, it holds promise as a method of analysis for an Afri-Latino group. One of its distinguishing differences is the way its adherents start an analysis from an African cultural, philosophical and historical base. To enrich my knowledge base on Afro-Latinos, therefore, I consulted the work of African Americans visiting and commenting on Spaniards and their culture.[372] In contradistinction to this approach, the first issue of *the Journal of Latino Studies* had three germane articles on Afro-Latinos, however, the articles contained a paucity of citations from African-American and Black scholars and Black journals and books on the subject. Had these sources been consulted, many of the questions left lingering by the authors for further work would have been answered. Of note was the use of the term Anglo-Black to refer to African-American, a usage that disconnects African-Americans from their African historical roots and the current African Diaspora, and smacks of Eurocentric imagination.[373] It reflects the pervasiveness of

---

[372]M. Weiff (1994). "Para Usted: Richard Wright's Pagan Spain" (pp. 212–225). In Werner Sollars & Diedrich, M. (Eds.). *the Black Columbiad.* Massachusetts: Harvard University Press; Richard Wright (1957). *Pagan Spain.* New York: Harper/Perennial.

[373]Silvio Torres-Saillant (2003). "Inventing the race: Latinos and the ethno-racial pentagon." *Latinos Studies*, 1, pp. 123-151; Tanya Hernandez (2003). "Too Black to be Latino/a: Blackness and Blacks as foreigners in Latino" *Latinos Studies*, 1, pp. 152-159; Anani Dzidzienyo (2003). "Coming to terms with the African connection in Latino Studies." *Latinos Studies*, 1, pp. 160-167. There is a rich scholarly and research history on African-American self-definition that is distinctive and instructive. It is relevant to a journal that is intended to be the cynosure of Latino Studies. See Barbara Collier-Thomas & Turner, J. (1992). *Race, class, nationality and color. The African American search for identity.* Philadelphia: Temple University Center for African American History and Culture; Gerald Jackson & Kirschner, S. (1973).

the Denial of African Significance, even writings focusing on its aftermath.

Speaking from an African-American cultural perspective, then, I found the Spanish cultural sport of bullfighting appalling and could not fathom Hemingway's, a European American, attraction to the event. Richard Wright, a famous African-American male writer, comparable to Hemingway, felt the same way I did, and wrote masterfully about it, or as Berry revealed, "No other writer in American literature, even Hemingway, has so artfully described a bullfight. Hemingway published twenty chapters plus photographs and a glossary in *Death in the Afternoon* on the technical and historical aspects of bullfighting, but the 'moment of truth' never rings as emotionally true as in Richard Wright's *Pagan Spain*."[374] At the same time, I perused scholarly articles in Black journals and books on Spain and the African Diaspora within its empire.[375] I even communicated with the acknowledged authority Martha Cobb.[376] When I initially made contact I did not

---

"Racial self-designation and preference for a counselor." *Journal of Counseling Psychology*, 10, 560–564; "African American or Black WHAT'S IN A NAME?" *Ebony*, pp. 77–78.

[374]Faith Berry (1995). "Introduction to the Harper/Perrential edition" (pp. xxi). In Richard Writing (1957). *Pagan Spain*. New York: Harper/Perennial.

[375]Examples, Martha Cobb (February, 1972). "An inquiry into race concepts through Spanish literature." *Black World* (formerly *Negro Digest*). pp. 32–40; Richard Jackson (1997). *Black writers and the Hispanic canon*. New York: Twayne Publishers; Richard Jackson (1979). *Black writers in Latin America*. New Mexico: University of New Mexico Press; Richard Jackson (1976). *The Black image in Latin American literature*. New Mexico: University of New Mexico Press; Richard Jackson (July, 1975). "The color crisis in Latin America 'Mestizaje vs. Black' identity." *Black World* (Formerly named *Negro Digest*), pp. 4–21; Gwendolyn Hall (1970). "The myth of benevolent Spanish slave law." *Negro Digest*, pp. 31–38; Robert Nodal (1986). "The Black man in Cuban society from colonial times to the revolution." *Journal of Black Studies*, 16(3), 251–267; Leslie Rout (February, 1970). "BRAZIL: Study in Black, Brown and Beige." *Negro Digest*, pp. 21–23, 65–73. The tradition continues and can be seen in *Emerge* magazine, e.g., Lori Robinson (April, 1998). "Cuba and blacks" (pp. 473–478). *Emerge Magazine*. In George Curry (Ed.). *The best of emerge magazine*. New York: Ballantin; Lamont Muhammad (October/November, 2000). "Invisible: Blacks in Mexico." *Black Diaspora*, pp. 26, 27.

[376]Martha Cobb (February 16, 1976). *Personal Communication*. Department of Romance Languages, Howard University, Washington, D.C. The foundational tree she established branched at Howard. Her most obvious legacy is the celebration of Hispanic Heritage Month (Nakia Hill, October 12,

realize her scope; however, I did learn something about her remarkability. She did her undergraduate work and master's at Howard University. To augment her academic work at Howard on African themes in Hispanic literature, she studied in France, Mexico, Spain, Puerto Rico, the Caribbean and Africa. In 1971, she inaugurated a post-graduate degree program in the field of Afro-Spanish literature and culture.

The perspective revealed in this material provided a backdrop for appreciating the concept of a Pan-African culture of resistance,[377] African-American contribution (18th century) to Pan-Africanism[378] and an analysis of the African-American and Latino situation prevalent in the Americas. For example, the situation in Latin America, especially Brazil, is often portrayed as an oasis of good race relations. However, in the assessment of Rosangela Maria Vieira, editor of the *Journal of Afro-Latin American Studies & Literature* at Howard University, as reported by Roberto Rodriguez "racism in Latin America against Blacks and indigenous people is worse than it is in the United States."[379] She affirmed that "They are in a pre-civil rights stage." In such a place, both Eurocentricism and White racism can be operative and destructive to Black Latino and Indigenous groups, just as they are in the United States.[380] Efforts aimed at the formation of an alliance

---

2004, "Hispanic Heritage Month Sheds Light On Latino Culture". *The Hilltop, pp. 1-2.* Less obvious is the presence and actions of the Cimmarrones, formerly Afro-Latin student organization. The group hosted a panel on the lives of Afro-Latina women that included Guatemala, Colombia, Peru, and Ecuador (Karen Lawrence, October 12, 2004. "Panel Explores the Lives of Afro-Latina Women" *The Hilltop,* pp. 1--2.

[377]Don Ohadike (2002*). Pan-African culture of resistance. A history of liberation struggle in Africa and the diaspora.* New York: Global Publication.

[378]Clarence Contee (February, 1970). "Afro-Americans and early Pan-Africanism." *Negro Digest*, pp. 24–28.

[379]Roberto Rodriquez (February 23, 1995). "Latinos Explore & Grapple with Black Identity Uruguay parley finds racism all over the Americas." *Black Issues in Higher Education,* p. 24; Lori Robinson (October, 1994). "the two faces of brazil" (pp. 318–323). In George Curry (Ed.). *The best of* emerge *magazine.* New York: Ballantine.

[380]The system has also been defined as a pigmentocracy. See Ellis Cose (1997). *Color-Blind.* New York: HarperCollins. This concept gets us closer but does not account for greater prestige given to hair texture. In addition to the Black psychologists professional and scholarly interest in the study of the significance of Black hair, Black Anthropologists are also investigating the subject. (See Evelyn Newman Phillips "Black Hair and Beauty in the African

between African Americans and Latinos can be sabotaged by the omission of a racial/cultural variable, in favor of an ethnic designation.[381] This is evident in a requested response I received from Tiffany, noted earlier, on her reaction to "An Open Letter to African-Americans from Latinos."[382] What it means in practice is captured in the essay by Yenifer. It continues because Latin Americans believe their concept of mestizaje is a superior to the prevalent Doctrine of Colorblindness form in the United States and as the best, does not need improvement, simply imitation.

In reality, the mestizaje concept aborts efforts to study ways of racially rewarding White and honorary White Latinos[383] so they will tear asunder the need and practices of privileges accorded European-descent physical features and status.[384] It weakens political actions by Afro-Latinos either around a social justice philosophy or by creating organizations that address their second-class status and an alien definition of physical and spiritual self. Translated into dualistic thinking this means sanctions against African-based religions and sabotage of women being beautiful who manifest Black features.

As suggested, most African Americans are neither oblivious nor ignorant of racial discrimination throughout the Americas. African Americans have noticed that the prototypical Cuban immigrant to the U.S. that gained U.S. governmental support was White. African Americans have also been disappointingly shocked to learn of the high percentage of Black Latinos in Latin American countries and their comparatively similar low socio-economic status and political impotence to African Americans. What they have been less cognizant of is that there are two world-views dominating this discussion. One is

---

Disapora". Journal of the Association of Black Anthropologists, 2(3). pp. 1—75.

[381] Nathan Glazer (1972). "Interethnic conflict." *Social Work*, 17(3), pp. 3–9.

[382] Tiffany Haliburton, Personal Communication,

[383] The way the Colored in South Africa and Mulatto in Latin America were differentially rewarded for being loyal to European domination.

[384] Neil Foley (2002). "Becoming Hispanic: Mexican Americans and Whiteness" (pp. 49–59). In Paula Rothenberg (Ed.). *Whiteness: The Power of the Past*. New York: Worth; Silvio Torres-Saillant (2003). "Inventing the race: Latinos and the ethnoracial pentagon." *Latinos Studies*, 1, pp. 123-151; Tanya Hernandez (2003). "Too Black to be Latino/a: Blackness and Blacks as foreigners in Latin America." *Latinos Studies*, 1, pp. 152-159; Anani Dzidzienyo (2003). "Coming to terms with the African connection in Latino Studies." *Latinos Studies*, 1, pp. 160-167.

African[385] and the other is European,[386] and what is problematic and politically dysfunctional for a democratic country promoting diversity, is the summing of all Spanish-speaking groups into a superordinant category. This is definitely the case with the Black/Latino dichotomy that may be too broad to be useful for African Americans seeking relationships with Caribbean, Central-American and Latin-American European Latinos and Afri-Latinos. There is a growing relation between African Americans and Afro-Latinos that does not fit the current Eurocentric use of a Black/Latino dichotomy model. Historically, Afro-Cubans have a long relationship with African Americans and have had concrete connections through sports, literature, music, politics, nationalist matters and religion.[387]

Conversely, a case illustration at Cornell reveals a dilemma for African Americans, Afro-Latinos, and the power of the racial bribe. It

---

[385]Richard Jackson (July, 1975). "The color crisis in Latin America: Mestizaje vs. Black identity." *Black World* (Formerly named *Negro Digest*), pp. 4–21.

[386]Lani Guinier & Torres, G. (2002). *The miner's canary Enlisting race, resisting power.* Massachusetts: Harvard University Press.

[387]Nancy Mirabal (1998). "Telling silences and making community: Afro-Cubans and African-Americans in Ybor City and Tampa, 1899-1915" (pp. 49–69). In Lisa Brock & Fuertes, D. *Between race and empire: African-Americans and Cubans before the Cuban revolution.* Pennsylvania: Temple University Press; Yvonne Daniel (1998). "Rumba: Social and aesthetic change in Cuba" (pp. 483–494) (Vol. 2). In Arlene Torres & Whitten, Norman (Eds.). *Blackness in Latin America and the Caribbean.* Indiana: Indiana University Press; Lisa Brock & Fuertes, D. (1998). *Between Race and empire: African-Americans and Cubans before the Cuban revolution.* Pennsylvania: Temple University Press; Rosalie Schwartz (1998). "Cuba's roaring twenties: Race consciousness and the column 'Ideales de una Raza'" (pp. 104–119). In Lisa Brock & Fuertes, D. (1998). *Between Race and empire: African-Americans and Cubans before the Cuban revolution.* Pennsylvania: Temple University Press; Kimberly Welch (2001). "Our hunger is our song: The politics of race in Cuba" (pp. 178–196). In Isidore Okpewho, Davies, C. & Mazrui, A. (Eds.) (2001). *The African Diaspora.* Indiana: Indiana University Press; Marta Vega (2000). *The altar of my soul. The living traditions of Santeria.* New York: Ballantine Publishing Group; Tomas Robaina (1998). "Marcus Garvey in Cuba: Urrutia, Cubans, and Black Nationalism" (pp. 120–128). In Lisa Brock & Fuertes, D. (1998). *Between Race and empire: African-Americans and Cubans before the Cuban revolution.* Pennsylvania: Temple University Press; Keith Ellis (1998). "Nicolas Guillen and Langston Hughes: Convergences and Divergences" (pp. 129-167). In Lisa Brock & Fuertes, D. (1998). *Between Race and empire: African-Americans and Cubans before the Cuban revolution.* Pennsylvania: Temple University Press.

involves the Director of the Latino Studies Program,[388] and gives evidence to support why Frank's proposal may be a more viable approach than engaging in academic departmental warfare in Institutions of Higher Education.[389] In a newspaper article describing her appointment, she revealed plans to enhance its academic connection to other "minority" programs. These programs included: "the directors of the Asian American Studies Program and American Indian Program as well as the vice provost for academic affairs on the development of comparative programs and resources that will further enhance all of these programs individually and collectively."[390] This is ironic since it was the African-American movements (Civil Rights and Black Power) that were the forerunners and role model for the subsequent Native American, Chicano, Latino, Asian and Women's Liberation ones.[391] Similarly, the Black Psychological Identity model, advanced and propelled by former Africana Studies & Research faculty member William Cross, was the precursor of identity models for women, gays, lesbians and disabled.[392] Is this the way to establish a Black/Latino alliance in an academic setting on a predominantly White campus? In

---

[388] A number of Black Studies scholars at a conference on the status of the field raised concerns about Latino Studies being a competitor, rather than an ally. See, Felicia Lee (February 1, 2003). "New topic for Black Studies debate: Latino." RaceMatters.org. http://www.racematters.org/newtopicblackstudies latinoshtm. The presenting situation supports the Black concerns and fears but does not confirm a widespread inevitability.

[389] Dr. Juan Flores, a Puerto Rican scholar, was not offered the position. Before the appointment, Silvio Torres-Saillant had observed: "Witness the stifling inability of Cornell University Chicano and Puerto Rican faculty and students to agree on a shared vision for the Latino Studies Program for over a decade." Silvio Torres-Saillant (2003). "Inventing the race: Latinos and the ethnoracial pentagon." *Latinos Studies*, 1, p. 126.

[390] Franklin Crawford (October 2, 2003). "Mary Pat Brady is appointed new Latino Studies Program director." *Cornell Chronicle*. p. 2.

[391] See Na'im Akbar (2000). Foreword. In Gerald Jackson, *Precursors of An African Genesis Model of Helping*. New York: Global; Gary Weaver (2004). Foreword. Gerald Jackson, *We're Not Going to Take it Anymore*. Maryland: Beckham Publishing Group; Maulana Karenga (2003). *Introduction to Black Studies* (3rd edition). California: University of Sankore.

[392] William Cross (April 12, 2004). *Theory & Research on Black Identity Before and After the 1954 Brown Decision on School Desegregation.* 2004 Femmie Kittrell Lecture of the College of Human Ecology, Cornell University.

the same period, the Africana Studies and Research Center received the following correspondence from Spain.

> I am Albert Roca, a lecturer of Cultural and Social Anthropology at the University of Lleida, and director of the review Studia Africana. I write you this brief note with the two issues of the review that I send you through Cesar Fernandez, a member of my own university that is making a research stage in Cornell University (nothing related with Africa). In this informal way, I would like to make a first presentation of the review. It is the leading publication on African research in Spain. It is an annual review and from number 13 and it is edited from Barcelona by ARDA, Grouping of Research and Teaching about Africa, a university network that links the main research teams on African studies in Spain. We want the review to be a Forum of exchange of information and research initiatives and we are broadening the scope of our interactions (till now, limits to Africa and Europe).
>
> So that is why we are writing you. We are interested in exchanging publications, information and in studying different ways of collaboration. In this sense, I'd try to send you information of the IVth Congress of African Studies in the Iberian World that we are celebrating in Barcelona, in January 2004. I hope this maybe a first step of a transatlantic connection. Thank you for your kind attention. We are looking forward to hearing from you soon.

The racial dilemmas in the Americas from Spanish and English sources are deep rooted and therefore are not resolvable by proffers based on class analysis or intellectual equality. Somewhat akin to the formulation of a race from a biological viewpoint, the ideology and military might of European nations created some New World beings. The Spanish and English, European powers and cultural group members, in particular, respectively created African Americans and Afri-Latinos. Neither of these New world groups asked to be developed, and indicative of the perception of their status, their ancestors fought to continue to be African and free.[393] Indicative of

---

[393]Herb Boyd (Ed.) (2002). *Race and resistance African Americans in the Twenty-First century.* Massachusetts: South End Press; Don Ohadike (2002).

mounted resistance to European assimilation, an African American is a functional entity, and an Afro-Latinos ostensibly exist in Brazil,[394] Cuba,[395] Ecuador[396] Mexico[397] and Venezuela.[398] Similarly, the concept of Blackness, espoused by African Americans as a cultural group manifestation, can be seen in the less acknowledged countries of Bolivia,[399] Chile,[400] Colombia,[401] Costa Rica,[402] Dominican

---

Pan-African culture of resistance. A history of liberation struggle in Africa and the diaspora. New York: Global Publication

[394] Hendrik Kray (Ed.) (1998). *Afro-Brazilian Culture and Politics.* New York: M.E.Sharpe; Nancy Priscilla Naro (2003). *Antislavery and Abolitionism: Thinkers and Doers in Imperial Brazil* (pp. 143–162). In Nancy P. Naro (Ed.) (2003). *Blacks, Coloureds and National Identity in Nineteenth-Century Latin America.* England: Institute of Latin American Studies.

[395] Pedro Sarduy & Stubbs, J. (Ed.) (1993). *AfroCuba.* Australia: Ocean; Jean Stubbs (2003). "Race, Gender and National Identity in Nineteenth Century Cuba, Mariana Grajales and the Revolutionary Free Browns of Cuba" (pp. 95–122). In Nancy P. Naro (Ed.) (2003). *Blacks, Coloureds and National Identity in Nineteenth-Century Latin America.* England: Institute of Latin American Studies; Jonathan Curry-Machado (2003). "Catalysts in the Crucible: Kidnapped Caribbeans, Free Black British Subjects and Migrant British Machinists in the Failed Cuba Revolution of 1843" (pp. 123–142). In Nancy P. Naro (Ed.) (2003). *Blacks, Coloureds and National Identity in Nineteenth-Century Latin America.* England: Institute of Latin American Studies.

[396] Carol Beane (1995). "Strategies of identity in Afro-Ecuadoran fiction: Chiriboga's bajo la piel de los tamores/Under the skin of the drums." In Carole. Davies (Ed.). *Moving Beyond Women's Boundaries: Black Women's Diasporas* (pp. 165-172) (Vol. 2). New York: New York University Press.

[397] Colin Palmer (1993). "Afro-Mexican culture and consciousness during the sixteenth and seventeenth centuries" (pp.125-136). In Joseph E. Harris (Ed.). *African Diaspora* (2nd edition). Washington, D.C.: Howard University Press.

[398] David Guss (1998). "The selling of San Juan: The performance of history in an Afro-Venezuelan Community" (pp. 244–28) (Vol. 1). In Norman Whitten & Torres, A. (Ed.). *Blackness in Latin America and the Caribbean.* Indiana: Indiana University Press.

[399] Madeline Leons (1998). "Stratification and pluralism in the Bolivian Yungas" (pp. 335–356) (Vol. 1). In Norman Whitten & Torres, A. (Ed.). *Blackness in Latin America and the Caribbean.* Indiana: Indiana University Press; A. Spedding (1995). "Bolivia" (pp. 319-344). In Minority Rights Group (Ed.). *No longer invisible: Afro-Latin Americans Today* England: Minority Rights Publication.

Republic,[403] Ecuador,[404] Guyana,[405] Honduras,[406] Mexico,[407] Nicaragua,[408] Panama,[409] Peru,[410] Uruguay[411] and Venezuela.[412] This

---

[400]William. Sater (1974). "The Black experience in Chile" (pp. 13–50). R. Toplin (Ed.). *Slavery and race relations in Latin America.* Connecticut: Greenwood Press.

[401]Nina Friedemann & Arocha, J. (1995). "Colombia" (pp. 47–76). *No Longer invisible: Afro-Latin Americas Today.* England: Minority Rights Publications; Peter Wade (1998). "The cultural politics of Blackness in Colombia" (pp. 311–334) (Vol. 1). In Norman Whitten & Torres, A. (Ed.). *Blackness in Latin America and the Caribbean.* Indiana: Indiana University Press.

[402]Philippe Bourgois (1998). "The Black diaspora in Costa Rica: Upward mobility and ethnic discrimination." In Norma Whitten & Torres, A. (Eds.). *Blackness in Latin America and the Caribbean* (pp. 110–132) (Vol. 1). Indiana: Indiana University Press; Kathleen Royal & Perry, F. (1995). "Costa Rica" (pp. 215–223). In Minority Rights Group (Ed.). *No longer invisible: Afro-Latin Americans Today.* England: Minority Rights Publications.

[403]Silvio Torres-Saillant (1995). "The Dominican Republic" (pp. 109–138). In Minority Rights Group (Ed.). *No longer invisible: Afro-Latin Americans Today.* England: Minority Rights Publications; Lauren Derby (2003). "National Identity and the Idea of Value in the Dominican Republic" (pp. 5–37). In Nancy P. Naro (Ed.) (2003). *Blacks, Coloureds and National Identity in Nineteenth-Century Latin America.* England: Institute of Latin American Studies.

[404]Norman Whitten & Quiroga, D. & Savoia, R. (1995). "Ecuador" (pp. 287–318). In Minority Rights Group (Ed.). *No longer invisible: Afro-Latin Americans Today.* England: Minority Rights Publications; Kathleen Klumpp (1998). "Black traders of north highland Ecuador" (1998). (pp. 357 376) (Vol. 1). In Norman Whitten & Torres, A. (Ed.). *Blackness in Latin America and the Caribbean.* Indiana: Indiana University Press; Norman Whitten & Quirogi, D. (1998). "To rescue national dignity Blackness as a quality of nationalist creativity in Ecuador." In Norman Whitten & Torres, A. (Ed.). *Blackness in Latin America and the Caribbean.* Indiana: Indiana University Press.

[405]Ralph Gomes (1998). "Race, class, and politics in Guyana: The role of the power elites" (pp. 146–159) (Vol. 2). {Guyana} In Arlene Torres & Norman Whitten (Eds.). *Blackness in Latin America and the Caribbean.* Indiana: Indiana University Press.

[406]Rachel Sieder (1995). "Honduras" (pp. 235–242). In Minority Rights Group (Ed.). *No longer invisible: Afro-Latin Americans Today.* England: Minority Rights Publications.

[407]Jameelah Muhammad (1995). "Mexico" (pp. 163–180). In Minority Rights Group (Ed.). *No longer invisible: Afro-Latin Americans Today.* England: Minority Rights Publications.

is why race, not ethnicity, is an issue in Latin America, and White racism is an identifiable problem in South,[413] as well as North America. The distinction, therefore, made between the English and Spanish colonial systems does not hold up to an Africentric scrutiny or any that is not persuaded by form versus substance. This is an Africentric assessment that is based upon a comparative study of the socio-economic and political conditions of African Americans and Afri-Latinos in Central and South America, and the Caribbean, including Cuba.

In both areas, Americans of European descent manifest *A Hatred of the Different* syndrome and the Americans of African descent adhere to a *Fear of Being Different* disorder.[414] Both disorders contribute to a

---

[408]Jane Freeland (1995). "Nicaragua" (pp. 181–211). "Afro-Latin Americans Today." In Minority Rights Group (Ed.). *No longer invisible: Afro-Latin Americans Today.* England: Minority Rights Publications.

[409]Darien Davis (1995). "Panama" (pp. 202–214). In Minority Rights Group (Ed.). *No longer invisible: Afro-Latin Americans Today.* England: Minority Rights Publications.

[410]Jose Luciano & Pastor, H (1995). "Peru" (pp. 271–286). In Minority Rights Group (Ed.). *No longer invisible: Afro-Latin Americans Today.* England: Minority Rights Publications.

[411]Alejandrina Da Luz (1995). "Uruguay" (pp. 319–344). In Minority Rights Group (Ed.). *No longer invisible: Afro-Latin Americans Today.* England: Minority Rights Publications.

[412]Eduardo Bermudez & Suarez, M. (1995). "Venezuela" (pp. 243–270). In Minority Rights Group (Ed.). *No longer invisible: Afro-Latin Americans Today.* England: Minority Rights Publications; John Lombardi (1974). "The abolition of slavery in Venezuela: A nonevent" (pp. 228–252). In Robert Toplin (Ed.). *Slavery and race relations in Latin America.* Connecticut: Greenwood Press; Winthrop Wright (1974). "Elitist attitudes towards race in Twentieth-Century Venezeuela" (pp. 325–347). In Robert Toplin (Ed.). *Slavery and race relations in Latin America.* Connecticut: Greenwood Press.

[413]Richard Graham (Ed.) (1990). *The idea of race in Latin America, 1870 – 1940.* Texas: The University of Texas Press; Leslie Rout (Ed.) (1976). *The African experience in Spanish America.* England: Cambridge University Press; Robert Toplin (Ed.) (1974). *Slavery and race relations in Latin America.* Connecticut: Greenwood Press.

[414]For discussion of concepts, see Gerald Jackson (2004). *Njikoka: Towards an Africentric paradigm of helping.* New Jersey: Africa World Press. In addition there are punishments attached to Blackness: FEAR OF FLYING – Cathy Harris (2001). *Flying while Black.* California: Milligan; LEARNING WHILE BLACK – Janice Hale (2002). *Learning while Black.* Maryland: John

denial of Blackness beliefs and practices, despite the evidence of the relevance of a racial category in determining the differential treatment of favoring European versus African looks and behaviors, typically called White racism.[415] From a diunital psychology perspective, we know that overtly aggressive behavior by one group towards another is based principally upon fear, undergirded by jealousy.[416] This has been at the hub of a sizable portion of the early Black psychologists and psychiatrists literatures.[417] A point a reader might ask now is where do we go from here, based upon the mountain of scholarship on the subject. Before going there, I would like to proclaim where our operational bases should be.

H. University Press; THINKING WHILE BLACK – Nat Irvin (May, 200). "Thinking while Black" (236–237). In George Curry (Ed.) (2003). *The best of* emerge *magazine*. New York: Ballantine; DRIVING WHILE BLACK – Marcia Davis (June, 1999). "Driving while Black" (pp. 262–271. In George Curry (Ed.) (2003). *The best of* emerge *magazine*. New York: Ballantine. In addition, see Katheryn Russell (1998). *The color of crime*. New York: New York University Press; Melvin Oliver & Shapiro, T. (1997). *Black wealth, White wealth*. New York: Routledge.

[415]Karen Carrillo (September 19 – September 25, 2002). "Last year's Miss Honduras says racism derailed her winnings." *The New York Amsterdam News*, p. 5; Barbara Gonzalez (November 2, 1999). "The Mexican Dark Secret." http://www.latin9olink.com/h10222e.html., pp. 1, 2; Nathaniel Nash (May 7, 1993). "Uruguay is on notice: Blacks want recognition." *The New York Times*; Eneid Routte-Gomez (December/January, 1996). "Racists????? A conspiracy of silence Racism in Puerto Rico." *Werner-Segarra*. pp. 55–58; Calvin Sims (November 2, 1999). "For Blacks in Peru, there's no room at the top." *The New York Times International*, p. 8.

[416]Na'im Akbar (2003). "Akbar paper in African psychology. Florida: Mind Productions & Associates." Daudi Azibo (Ed.) (2003). *African-centered psychology. Culture focusing for multicultural competence*. North Carolina: Carolina Academic Press; Kobi Kambon (1992). *The African Personality in America: An African-Centered Approach*. Florida: Nubian Nations Publications; Gerald Jackson (1979). "The origin and development of Black psychology: Implications for Black Studies and human behavior." *Studia Africana*, 1, 3, pp. 270–293; France Cress Welsing (1991). *The ISIS papers*. Illinois: Third World Press.

[417]Gerald Jackson (2005). *Sankofa Helping: The African genesis of an African-American model of helping*. New Jersey: Africa World Press.

Gerald G. Jackson

Pathways to Human Conflict Solutions

First, if a Legacy of Betrayal notion is understood, then when confronted by the demands of African Americans, the solution offered will not be for African Americans to return to Africa. It will be recalled that not only have African Americans been betrayed by successive waves of immigrant groups seeking Whiteness and resulting economic and social success, MLK was harassessed by the USA federal government for his philosophy, spirituality and revolutionary fervor.[418] Second, African Americans and Afri-Latinos do not need to go back to Africa to be African, and they have demonstrated admirable roles in the United States. This injunction does not mean that these groups should not provide assistance to Africa. The connection of these groups to Africa is imperative because it has been predicted that if political action is not taken at the highest level, within 25 years Africa will be empty of professionals.[419] Central to an African advancement cause, African Americans are identified as being central to getting an African assistance plan initiated. Bypassing the logistical, political and social reasons why the notion of returning to Africa permanently is inane, Harold Cruse,[420] in his characteristically blunt and direct manner, noted:

> So, the glorification of these Back-to-Africa movements has been overdrawn, uncritically heroized. By approaching the subject this way, we are neglecting to understand where the movements and leaders failed, why they failed, and what the consequences are for today. We can't afford that any

---

[418]David Garrow (1981). *The FBI and Martin Luther King, Jr. From "solo" to Memphis.* New York: W.W. Norton; Richard Burns (2001). *To the mountain top: Martin Luther King Jr.'s Sacred mission to save America.* California: HarperSanFrancisco.

[419]Rosalind Mclymont (July/August 2001). "Africa's brain drain." *The Network Journal*, p. 32; Matthew Scott (2001). "Creating a new Africa." *Howard Magazine*, pp. 14–19.

[420]Cruse is credited with a landmark analysis of Black intellectuals (Harold Cruse (1967). *The crisis of the Negro intellectual.* New York: William Morrow & Company). He is an important figure to consider Afrocentricity with even a guarded optimism. His hopefulness for the concept can be seen as an endorsement of Afrocentricity intellectual revolutionary potential in a time of Eurocentric intellectual blandness. See Moletif Asante (1999). *The painful demise of Eurocentrism: An Afrocentric response to critics.* New Jersey: Africa World Press.

more if we are talking about Afrocentricity–which requires a revival and reexamination of the ideas and contentions and intentions of these movements. And an understanding of why we are left having to pick up the reins at this late date. Unless we take these steps–from a philosophical, intellectual, and organizational point of view–Afrocentricity will not meet its goal of establishing a new critique in these matters.[421]

Not only does this mean that total solutions can not be found in traditional West African history and culture,[422] it also means that returning to Africa with dual citizenship, with nothing tangible to offer the continent, is not an acceptable outcome.

Shortcomings of the People of Color Concept

Second, meaningful alliances and coalitions do not stem from connections to groups that are impractical to manage, and their creation puts the most powerful and aggressive group in a non-negotiating and defensive posture. I am referring to People of Color (POC), the politically correct manifestation of a fantasy with little plausible history, ancestry or contemporary illustrations of success.[423] Quiet as it is kept, many White Latino/as immigrants and U.S. citizens are and enjoy being White. Many Asians believe they are the model minority. There are even a growing number of bi-racial people who no longer

---

[421]Harold Cruse (1993). "Afrocentricity: A philosophical basis for cultural equity battles?" (p. 11). In Marta Vega & Greene, C. (Eds.) (1993). *Voices from the battlefront Achieving cultural equity*. New Jersey: Africa World Press.

[422]This does not mean that serious scholarship should not include a study of people and groups that have returned to Africa. See, for example, S.Y. Boadi-Shaw (1993). "Brazilian returnees of West Africa" (pp. 421–440). In Joseph Harris (Ed.). *African Diaspora* (2nd edition). Washington, D.C.: Howard University Press; Solimar Otero (2000). "Rethinking the Diaspora: African, Brazilian, and Cuban Communities in Africa and the Americas." *The Black Scholar*, 30 (3&4), pp. 54-58. Rodolfa Sarracino (1995). "Back to Africa." In Pedro Sarduy & J. Stubbs (Eds.). *AfroCuba: An anthology of Cuban Writing on race, politics and culture* (pp. 67–76). Australia: Ocean; Robert Johnson (1999). *Why Blacks left America for Africa. Interwoven with Black repatriates, 1971 – 1999*. Connecticut: Praeger.

[423]Gregory Kane (April 29, 2004). "Commentary: 'People of Color' Solidarity a fictional bubble that may burst." Blackamericawet.com, 5/3/04, pp. 1-3

want to be classified as Black/African-American;[424] some have even declared that they are White.[425] The thrust of the writings here is my belief that alliances and coalitions need to be worked at and allowed to be dynamic relationships that are predicated upon an ongoing acceptance of reasonable struggle within and between groups.

As a trained clinical psychologist, it has long been apparent that struggle does necessarily mean physical. This is clearly evident in the way the European colonial period in Africa, the Caribbean, and Latin and Central America continues to negatively influence the political, social, and economic maturation of the countries in these areas. To elaborate, I was a member of a POC group charged to work with federal government agencies to change drug prevention research, programs and policies to be more in consonant with the needs of African Americans, Latinos, Native Americans, and Asian Americans. A Puerto Rican female who lived in Silver Spring, Maryland and was married to a White male, took offense to the group's self-description as a People of Color group. She claimed that she and other Puerto Ricans are White, not colored. In search of support, she asked each member to note if they saw their group as "colored." When each person identified himself or herself as "colored," she reminded the group that she and Puerto Ricans were White. Functionally, we never got beyond what to call the group and blew the two days allotted for us to problem-solve. Ironically, through the stand-off Bernard Redd asked why the group was using the term "colored," which African Americans had abandoned for a sundry of reasons, along with "Negro" "coon" and "Nigger." The profoundity of his question was not recognized by the group; however, the group did eventually call itself "the group of 10," rather than "people of color."

Viewed somewhat differently, Black students at Cornell conduct programs under the aegis of "People of Color." When I point out that the designation seems to be a misnomer because 99% of the attendees are Black, they offer the idea that the name is to encourage attendance by other groups. I contend that such simplistic formulations or designs do not materialize true alliances because they are not multiculturally based. The students rarely confer with the other groups to learn how to include culturally congruent strategies and agenda. The POC also presumes an equality in the reward structure for Indigenous, African

---

[424]Gerald Jackson (2005). *Njikoka: Towards an Africentric paradigm of helping.* New Jersey: Africa World Press.

[425]See Paul Tough (May 25, 2004). "The Black White supremacist." *New York Times Magazine*, pp. 42–46, 56.

Americans, American Africans, Latinos, American-born Chinese and Chinese-born Americans, and Asian Americans. The *racial bribe* or rewards and punishments for different racial and ethnic groups are different, and undeclared differences allow for group manipulation and rivalry. This is illustrated by the media accounts that link Asian and Latinos together and articles in the same vein.

I received an email that copied a Reuter report. The article was titled "The Hispanic and Asian American population in the United States are expected to triple by 2050." Shortly thereafter and coincidentally, I received a request by an Asian Executive Director of an organization to review an article written by a Japanese-American professor. The author, I was told, is examining the "ethnic political cooperation" between Hispanics and Asians. Flags went up when I read "ethnic," the same flag that went up when the new director of the Latino Studies department omitted Africana Studies from her list of groups she would extend herself to establish a professional relationship. Supposedly, she was turned off by the Africana Studies' position that it was not an ethnic group, in the traditional use of the term, and the acceptance of this designation was a trap.

The spirit of the law and not the letter propelled me. My concern about an unhealthy connection was justified when the letter-writer added "Where are black Americans in this 'ethnic cooperation?'" Yes, I might add, and note that ethnic has traditionally denoted Irish, Italian, Jewish, Polish or collectively non-White Anglo Saxon Whites. These groups also connote Whites who are not as good as people from White Anglo-Saxon stock. The proposed classification of minorities into the ethnic category is not an advance for African Americans, except as an ethnic member in an African Diaspora framework. It is an especial step backwards for groups advocating an appreciation of subculturally-based racial differences. Rarely, for example, do people explore Afro-Chinese from Cuba,[426] West Indians migrants in Central and Latin America,[427] and Africans in Asian history.[428] Such lines of inquiry

---

[426]Lisa Yun (May-June, 2000). "Africans & Asians Breaking boundaries What do we Asians and Africans know about each other? What do we know about ourselves?" *Black Issues Book Review*, pp. 58–59.

[427]Roy Bryce-Laporte (1998). "Crisis, contraculture, and religion among West Indians in the Panama Canal Zone" (pp. 100–118) (Vol. 1). In Norman Whitten & Torres, A. (Ed.). *Blackness in Latin America and the Caribbean.* Indiana: Indiana University Press; Roy Bryce-Laporte, assisted by Trevor Purcell (1993). "A lesser known chapter of the African diaspora: West Indians

would entail an appreciation of complexity, as an avenue to enhancing human relations.

A third roadblock is the casting of racial problems as a "Black problem."[429] Africans did not go to Europe and ask to be dispersed in the Americas. Africans originally came to the Americas before the Europeans, presumably interacted with the indigenous group, and returned to Africa.[430] Present-day African Americans, despite the horrendous treatment given to Blacks in America when attempting to think, drive, learn and fly while Black,[431] have been incomparably supportive of the military, and protective of their societies and ambassadors of Peace around the world. The resilience of African Americans should be praised and studied as a basis for human relations' enlightenment and spiritual guidance. Rather than scoffing African-derived spirituality and religiosity, as universal healing forms, they should be seen as viable alternatives to religions that allowed members to enslave other human beings.[432]

Fourth, is discounting drylongso (ordinary Black people)[433] in the design, implementation and evaluation of problems befalling Africans and their descendants. A case in point is two works by Professor Henry

---

in Costa Rica, Central America" (pp. 137-158). In Joseph E. Harris (Ed.). *African Diaspora* (2nd edition). Washington, D.C.: Howard University Press.

[428] Joseph Harris (1993). "Africans in Asian history" (pp. 325–338). In Joseph E. Harris (Ed.). *African Diaspora* (2nd edition). Washington, D.C.: Howard University Press.

[429] John Hoberman (1997). *Darwin's athletes: How sport has damaged Black America and preserved the myth of race*. New York: Mariner Books; David Shipier (1997). *A country of strangers: Blacks and Whites in America*. New York: Knopf; Tyler Stallings, Roediger, D., Jones, A. & Gonzales-Day, K. (2003). *Whiteness, a wayward construction: A wayward construction*. California: Fellows of Contemporary Art.

[430] Ivan Van Sertima (2002). *Early America revisited*. New Jersey: Transaction Publishers; Ivan Van Sertima (Ed.) (1987). *African presence in early America*. New Jersey: Tansactions Books; Ivan Van Sertima (1976). *They came before Columbus*. New York: Random House.

[431] See footnote 414 for references.

[432] For example, see Frances Bok with Edward Tivnan. (2003). *Escape from Slavery*. St. Martin's Press.

[433] John Gwaltney (1980). *Drylongso: A self-portrait of Black America*. New York: Random House.

Gates.[434] His criticism of Hip-Hop amounts to an assault that extends unnecessarily the conflict between the Civil Rights generation and the Hip-Hop one,[435] and contrasts with Manning's more conciliatory and facilitative approaches. The latter publishes scholarly accounts and intellectual dialogues in his journal, and assumes the role of researcher for the Hip-Hop industry. The Civil Rights Generation needs to learn why it is not dignified by some of its young, not broadly castigate a complex group that is relatively late in picking up the civil rights baton in the racially based relay race.[436] First, they collide with his own criticisms of the Duboisian notion of the Talented Tenth. Second, they minimize the critique, based upon a consideration of institutional, individual and group racism, of the failure of the War on Poverty. Most central, it simplifies the Black Studies field's attempt to include distinguishable movements and complexity into the 1960s and 70s.[437] While his department is recorded as a Black Studies one, his work tends to overlook and downplay the fields literatures, scholars and precautions . Addressing the issues approached here, Dr. Molefi Asante noted: "A lot of people falsely claim to be in Afro-American Studies, but they have never been to a conference or published in the *Journal of Black Studies* or the *Western Journal of Black Studies*, and don't have a dialogue with people in their field."[438] For example, an authoritative journal for comprehending Black and Latino relationships might be the *Afro-Hispanic* and the publishing firms might be Indiana University

---

[434]Henry Gates (2004). *America behind the color line: Dialogues with African Americans.* New York: Warner Books; Henry Gates (1998). *Thirteen ways of looking at a Black man.* New York: Vintage Books.

[435]For a fuller discussion, see Gerald Jackson's chapter "Chapter 10 – Njikoka: African-American Peace Initiatives" in *Njikoka: Towards an Africentric Paradigm of Helping.* New Jersey: Africa World Press.

[436]See chapter 10, "Njikoka: African-American peace initiatives" in Gerald Jackson (2004). *Njikoka: Towards an Africentric paradigm of helping.* New Jersey: Africa World Press.

[437]Maulana Karenga (2002). *Introduction to Black Studies.* (3rd edition). California: University of Sakore Press.

[438]E.R. Shipp (September, 1995). "Studying Black studies." *Emerge,* p. 48. See Maulana Karenga (2003). *Introduction to Black studies* (3rd edition). California: University of Sankore Press; William Banks & Kelly, S. (1997). "Guess who's coming to academia" (pp. 381–390). In Ishmael Reed (Ed.). *MultiAmerica Essays on cultural wars and cultural peace.* New York: Penguin.

Press and Africa World Press, not what individuals would call elite Ivy League universities and upscale publishing press.[439]

Lastly, the POC designation overlooks the concept of historical oppression, applicable to Jews and non-White Latinos.[440] Given racism among some Jewish intellectuals,[441] there are few other White ethnic or minority groups that can compile a list of illuminating scholars on Black concerns as Melville Herskovits,[442] Herb Aptheker,[443] Martin Bernal,[444] Irwin Katz[445] and Tim Wise.[446] A Jewish ally intellectual

---

[439]Variability exists among Ivy League institutions as well. Brown University appointed the first Black women to head an Ivy League school (see student essays in Sect. II). The publisher of this book is a Brown graduate, Raquel Riveria, pictured in Sect. III, is a Brown graduate; two out of the three authors writing in the first issue of the Journal of Latino Studies have Brown affiliations – Tanya Hermandez, a bachelor's degree, Anani Dzidzienyo – department chairperson. In addition, Juan Flores taught at Brown. With the exception of Howard University, no other institution has had as much scholarship reported in this book on the subject of Afro-Latinos. In addition, John Hope, a Brown graduate, was the first Black to be the president of Morehouse University. The great Black writer and poet, Sterling Brown is a Brown graduate. Lastly, Cooper Thompson, initiator and co-editor of the book *White men challenging racism: 35 personal stories*, is a Brown University graduate. Viewed as an anomaly, this subject deserves further investigation and insights.

[440]Edward Shapiro (1994). "Blacks and Jews entangled." *First Things* 45, pp. 1–10. Jane Lazarre (1999). *Beyond the whiteness of whiteness.* North Carolina: Duke University Press; Matthew Jacobson (2000). "Looking Jewish, seeing Jews" (pp. 238–256). In Les Back & Solomos, J. (Eds.). *Theories of Race and Racism A reader.* New York: Routledge; Sander Gilman (2000). "Are Jews white?" (pp. 229–237). In Les Back & Solomos, J. (Eds.). *Theories of Race and Racism A reader.* New York: Routledge.

[441]Sam Hamod (January 28, 2002). "Racism among some Jewish intellectuals." *Konch Magazine*, pp. 10-6.

[442]Melville Herskovits (1958). *the myth of the Negro past.* New York: Beacon; Melville Herskovits (1962). *The human factor in changing Africa.* New York: Alfred A. Knopf.

[443]Herbert Aptheker (2003). "Radical historian" (pp. 17–26). In Cooper Thompson, Schaefer, E. & Brod, H. (Eds). *White men challenging racism 35 personal stories.* North Carolina: Duke University Press. Herbert Aptheker (1993). "A few battles against racism." *The Black Scholar*, 26(21), pp. 3-6.

[444]Martin Bernal (1987). "Black Athena." *The Afroasiatic roots of classical civilization* (Vol. I). New Jersey: Rutgers University Press; Martin Bernal

tradition continues in my classes of progressive thinking, empathetic behavioral responses to racial oppression and desire to learn about the African-American experience. It has been manifested in the support and work of Nina Fant, Craig Altshuler, David Ladd, Shelby Senzer and Jared Wolfe, to name a few.[447] To illustrate, the student's revelation stemming from the Dr. Manning talk opens the door to an examination of Malcolm X's appeal and his relevance to multiculturalism, multi-nationalism and other social and ethnic groups. Yuri Kochiyama, an Asian, studied and reported on his influence and activism in the Asian American community.[448] Rosa Clemente, a Black Puerto Rican and panelist at the Schomburg Center, focused on Malcolm's impact on women and the Black Liberation Movement, and declared that "His autobiography inspired me."[449] Reflecting the activist-scholar tradition, Elizabeth Catlett, Afro-Mexican through marriage, "created a linoleum block print through which she tried to proclaim anew the cause of assassinated black nationalist Malcolm X." Her work, titled "'Malcolm Speaks For Us,' won a top purchase prize..." [and was] "Bought by the Instituto National de Bellos Arts...is now the property of the Mexican government. The following quotation shows her diunital thinking and activist-scholar perspective.

> Black people and Mexican people, my two people inspire me. The masses of neither black people nor Mexican people have either the time or the money to develop formal aesthetic appreciation. So I try to reach them intuitively because they

(1991). "Black Athena." *The Afroasiatic roots of classical civilization* (Vol. II). New Jersey: Rutgers University Press.

[445]William Katz (1997). *Black Indians A hidden heritage*. New York: Aladdin; William Katz (1997). *Black people who made the old West*. New York: Thomas Y. Crowell Company.

[446]Tim Wise. (2003) "Tim Wise"(pp. 152–163). In Cooper Thompson, Schaefer, E. & Brod, H. (Eds.). *White men challenging racism 35 personal stories*. North Carolina: Duke University Press.

[447]An example of Craig's, David's and Shelby's efforts are in this book.

[448]Yuri Kochiyama (1994). "The impact of Malcolm X on Asian-American politics and activism" (pp. 129–142). In James Jennings (Ed.). *Blacks, Latinos, and Asians in urban America*. Connecticut: Praeger.

[449]Herb Boyd (March 1, March 10). "Women hail Malcolm X's memory." *The New York Amsterdam News*, p. 31.

have an intuitive appreciation and thus help, if I can, their aesthetic development.[450]

Miss Catlett, who is deeply involved in what she calls the "worldwide drive for national liberation," urges artists to use their talent to further it. "I don't think that artists can remain aloof from the movement," says the militant sculptress, "I don't think we can still keep going to Paris and Rome to see what the last word is in art and come back to our desperate nations and live in intellectual isolation from what is going on in our countries and ghettoes."[451]

We can establish and maintain such divides if we elect to avoid thinking diunitally, feeling spiritually and believing Africentrically.

The African-American Diaspora Prototype

While the creation of an African-American racial group was based upon Eurocentric culturalistic norms that even called Africans *African Negroes,* a people has emerged with an immediate history in the United States and an African cultural legacy,[452] and a reciprocally helpful relationship with Africa.[453] Both cultural references serve as a special link to Afro-Latinos and pose a problem for alliances when the latter subscribe to Eurocentrically-based Latino notions about color and racial hierarchy. In Cuba, for instance, there are Blacks, Mulattoes and Whites. If this division were applied in the U.S.A., African Americans would be split apart because the Blackness defined by African Americans does not conform to the rigid phenotypic differences extolled in Latin, Central and Caribbean America. In contrast, African Americans are probably the only biogenetic group that includes individuals who could be phenotypically classified as "White." Less debatable maybe, they are the only group that lauds a member for not "passing as White" but declaring themselves Black/African-American/Negro or African-American and accepting such

---

[450]"My art speaks for both my peoples" (January 1970). *Ebony*, pp. 94–96, 98, 100, 101.

[451]"My art speaks for both my peoples" (January 1970). *Ebony*, p. 96.

[452]Paul Gilroy (2000). "The dialectics of diaspora identification" (pp. 490–502. In Les Back & Solomos, J. (Eds.). *Theories of race and racism: A reader.* New York: Routledge.

[453]W. Ofuatey-Kodjoe (1977). "The ideological triangle: Reciprocal ideological influences among Afro-West Indians, Afro-Americans and Africans." *Studia Africana*, 1(1), 1–16.

disadvantages as employment, housing and welfare discrimination.[454] At the same time, it is expected that one's lightness of skin will be used to aid African Americans in their fight against racism and Eurocentric culturalism. This behavioral ideal is illustrated in Walter Whites' non-fictional work on how he infiltrated White gatherings to obtain data to combat Black lynching and other nefarious crimes against humanity,[455] and the fictional work of Sam Greenlee.[456]

This outlook is decidedly West African and African-American, and impacted by colonialism and racism. If this situation between racial groups was simply a matter of skin color and other pronounced phenotypic differences, there would not be a rift between Africans and African Americans, especially Africans from East Africa. If it were only a matter of culture, there would not be gaps between Africans, American Africans, and African Americans. It is all of the above, in varying degrees and the factor of experience with European culture and White people. For instance, a disappointing similarity between North and South American fathers of their countries is the way their pronouncements about humanity do not extend to Africans and their descendants. We know that father George Washington owned and kept enslaved Africans. Less known are Simon Bolivar's, frequently called the George Washington of Latin America, racial ideology contradictions. Giuiner and Torres observed that at the commencement of the Latin American nationalist period, he understood that the emerging Latin American identity was an amalgam of peoples,[457] implying respect for differences and corresponding views of racial equality. This recognition, however, did not translate into his support of the Haitian revolution, a Black group fighting for emancipation from a European colonial power, with implications for rebellion in the Spanish-speaking Caribbean, Central and Latin America. He was not, in the final analysis, as colorblind and democratic as his fatherly and

---

[454]See Leroy Davis (1998), p. 5. (1999). "John Hope at Brown University: The Black man who refused to pass for White." *The Journal of Blacks in Higher Education*, pp. 121-126. For a discussion of how this concept is expressed in African and African-American literature, see Bonnie Barthold (1981). *Black time*. Connecticut: Yale University Press.

[455]Walter White (1918). "The work of a mob" (pp. 345-350). In Sondra Wilson (Ed.) (1999). *The Crisis Reader*. New York: The Modern Library.

[456]Sam Greenlee (1969). *the spook who sat by the door*. New York: Bantam Books.

[457]Lani Guinier & Torres, G. (2002). *The miner's canary*. Massachusetts: Harvard University Press.

politically-conscious title would make one assume. The legacy of Spanish domination continues to the present, despite the majority in many Latin American countries of people of African, Indian and Asian descent.

Eurocentric culturalism operates imperceptibly for many individuals reared on the concept of mestizaje. If one looks at the supposedly looser definition in Latin America of whiteness, one can see an inverse relationship between non-white peoples and the definition of whiteness. A rigid and binary racial system exists where the number and percentage of people is White. Whiteness and its variations are more acknowledged and honored in those places threatened by a sizable Black population. The Mulatto group existed and was bestowed privileges not granted Blacks; however, it was dissolved officially[458] when it became apparent and legal that Blacks would not pose a numerical threat.

Similarly, in the United States of the early part of the 21st century, predictions started surfacing that by 2050 White people would not be the numerical majority, despite the encouragement given to an Eastern European immigration. At the same time, the elastic definition started to expand to include South Asians, Latin Americans, North Africans, and Middle Easterners. Even some chapters of the Klu Klux Klan shifted their membership criterion to include anyone that looked White and supported White supremacy dogma. It is not surprising, therefore, to learn that even Fidel Castro's Cuba has been found to still have racism, and the Dominican Republic, clearly a Brown country due to its African ancestry, continues to deny this past and penalize Dominicans with Haitian (Black) ancestry.[459] The immediate challenge is a willingness to form and maintain relationships. The next section highlghts how relationships can be started.

Granted, the focus of this book has been overwhelmingly on Black College students. Contrary to the apparent focus, college students are not its intended exclusive beneficiaries. It is intended for learners and race, gender, age, occupation, income and education level, and religion do not delimit this diverse group. This dimension is illustrated in my teaching and training work in corporate America. This realm, as George Davis and Glegg Watson declared in their classic work *Black*

---

[458]See Stephan Talty (1987). *Mulatto America*. New York: HarperCollins.

[459]Eugene Robinson (November12, 2000). "Cuba begins to answer its race question." *Washington Post*, pp. 1–6.

Life in Corporate America,[460] the United States culture is synonymous with its corporate culture. The corporate experience therefore, serves, among several options presented in this book, as part of a multi-tiered solution.

Tales from the Corporate Hood: The Diversity Training Option

It was my professional experiences as a diversity consultant and multicultural trainer that encouraged me to return to teaching on the college level. As a prelude to my presentation of avenues to human relationship solutions, I will illustrate some of this work. This discussion also reveals the work companies have to do to compensate for what colleges and universities do poorly, and that is prepare its graduates for a diverse workplace.[461] It has taught me a number of things that are applicable to education, race-relations and mental health. It taught me, for instance, that the work setting alone was not the only source of stress for Black employees—a simple enough idea that is rarely incorporated into educational, employment and even mental health interventions, when the population to be served is African-American.

Moreover, I learned that a central ingredient of success is not the theory that prompts and underlies our efforts to teach great human relations concepts and impart skills, often unavailable to our conscious recollection, but the principal mode of thinking we are challenged presently to adopt. An article by Kristin Hibler illustrates this point about diversity training. The title of her article is "Is Diversity Training Anti-American"? Gleaned from her professional experience, she observed "diversity training challenges the worldview of U.S. American participants, particularly those who do not consider themselves a member of any minority group."[462]

---

[460]George Davis & Watson, G. (1982). *Black life in corporate America. Swimming in the mainstream.* New York: Doubleday.

[461]Gerald Jackson (Winter, 1987). "The implementation of an intracultural awareness coaching program." *Corporate Headquarters,* pp. 9–14, 30; Badi Foster, Gerald Jackson, William Cross, Bailey Jackson & Rita Hardiman (April, 1988). "Workforce diversity and business." *Training and Development Journal,* pp. 38–42; Gerald Jackson (March, 1995). "Beyond the White male paradigm." *Cultural Diversity at Work,* 7, pp. 1, 8, 9.

[462]Kristin Hibler (Winter, 2004). "Is diversity training anti-American." *Intercultural Management Quarterly,* pp. 7, 12; David Shipler (1997). *A*

Much of the contrast she makes is based upon the American bias favoring "individualism." However, to fathom many of the intracultural conflicts she identifies, she would need an African and European world-view model, identified in the chart in Section I. Diunitally-based logic can benefit the thinking of solutions to past, present and future problems. In this regard, the plight of African Americans makes them an illuminating group to examine for generating principles that are applicable to other biogenetic groups.

Armed with this knowledge, I conceptualized the Washington, DC area, and its cultural institutions as my training laboratory. It would be used to provide an opportunity to learn how social institutions can support cultural beliefs and practices. My first highlight deals with the combined uses of a Black City, university and cultural institutions to train and educate corporate managers. The trainees were responsible for designing, training and evaluating a diversity initiative for a manufacturing plant. These seasoned managers had been extensively trained and supervised in the conduct of workshops on diversity; however, the majority of this training and consultation had occurred on the plant site, a relatively isolated structure in a rural area.

Essentially, the exclusive use of the site, and location near the plant, removed environmental and social factors that frequently stifled work solutions to problem behaviors and attitudes. I proposed that the training site be shifted to Washington, DC and occur at Howard University's campus. In addition, the time required would be more comprehensive. Its scope would include a week and its depth would be a schedule including the morning, afternoon and evening. The proposal was accepted, and the group was housed at the then-Howard Inn hotel. The arrangements at Howard were facilitated by "my boy" Glegg Watson, Xerox executive and a member of the Howard University Board of Trustees. Had it not been for his involvement, I doubt if we would have been able to have college deans and facilities made available to us.[463] Similarly, if it was not for Maryanne Gayle, the

---

country of strangers: Blacks and Whites in America . New York: Alfred Knoft; Andrew Hacker (1997). *MONEY Who has how much and why*. New York: Scribner.

[463]Years later, Howard would be instrumental in facilitating intracultural learning. Nina Fant, a Jewish student of mine at Cornell, requested an opportunity for greater immersion in African-American culture. This request came after taking my First Year Writing Seminar course and several other Africana ones. She asked for a more intensive experience than those provided by Cornell. How intense her experience had been from my course is reported

Mehoopany plant manager for Procter & Gamble, it is doubtful that we would have been able to secure paid consultancies, training days and reimbursed expenses for the educational/training journey. These individuals are being identified because "key players" in administration and management are frequently omitted from social and behavioral sciences, human relations training models and psychological studies.

Psycho-Educational Training

Several noteworthy understandings occurred during the training week. Since Procter & Gamble is a business that hires a great deal of engineers, I had the group tour and meet department chairs and deans at the Schools of Engineering and Business. The exposure to ranking Howard educational leaders was a part of the cultural learning. Members of the training group shared that they waited, during these introductions, to meet the White person in charge. They eventually realized that no such person existed and the cultural expectation of the ultimate White leader was a cultural bias that could keep Blacks from rising to the top in the company. An unexpected learning occurred during lunch. I was originally going to accompany the trainees to lunch at the Howard University Blackburn Student Center building.

I ran into a schedule conflict that had the group eating lunch on its own, but still at the Blackburn building. When we reconstituted the training group after lunch, the group, in a jovial manner, asked me if my absence from their lunch in Blackburn was planned. Puzzled, I replied "no" and asked why they thought I would use such a ploy. They responded that when they walked into the dining area it seemed that every one seated stopped eating and starred at them. I asked if they experienced the stares as hostile and they responded no. If the Black people, I quipped, did not appear hostile to their presence, what was the problem? They replied that they became uncomfortably aware that they

---

in another one of my books (Gerald Jackson, (2004). *Njikoka: Towards an Africentric paradigm of helping*. New Jersey: Africa World Press). To surpass this experience, I believed entailed being in Afrospace. I suggested, therefore, that she spend a summer studying at Howard University and working in a DC urban charter school owned by Edward Pinkard, a frat brother and former Howard classmate. She followed my suggestions to the letter and her positive experiences appear as reflections in a forthcoming book. After graduating from Cornell, she returned to DC for employment, and served on the board of an adult education program in the community. She is contemplating law school at Howard University because of the specialty of the school in Public Interest law.

were the minority and had not been socialized to see themselves in what they perceived as a less powerful position.

The insight they gained was in how Blacks must feel at the plant and other overwhelmingly White populated places. They continued by noting that the feeling of discomfort followed them as they traversed the campus. A female manger group member, of Italian descent, expressed a different feeling and sense. She said she felt comfortable in the Black setting because the ambiance reminded her of her former all-women's college. It had an "at home" feeling to her. I interpreted her reaction to mean that the setting worked for people that were not a part of the dominant White male group of Anglo-Saxon descent. Overall, the experiences made the managers aware of unconscious fears, a degree of empathy with Black people on being a minority and the meaning of White privilege.[464]

To take them outside of their comfort zone, we purposely ate at West African, Ethiopian and African-American restaurants. The female managers appeared generally more relaxed in all of the eating places. At the African-American upscale club called *Tacoma Station*, only the White male of Italian descent seemed secure enough to leave the group's table space and engage a Black man in a private social conversation. Conversely, in our next day follow-up session, it was reported how another White male had asked another to accompany him to the bathroom. To minimize any misunderstanding about his intentions, he explained that he imagined trouble going to the men's room. His revelation opened the door to a discussion of gender differences and White male fears about Black men.

The women indicated that they did not have anxieties about being in the Club because they had made an assessment about its safety when they first arrived. They informed the men that women are socialized to be cognizant of surroundings because of the greater danger posed to them by sexual predators. One, in particular, expressed amusement when recalling the male asking the other male to accompany him to the bathroom. I did not anticipate this fear because I thought the group would feel comfortable when it observed the expensive cars outside the establishment, and the clothes worn by the patrons, clear status difference symbols for African Americans that would define levels of safety. I forgot that Whites could have their senses turned off when there are skin color differences. Besides, it was dark and almost

---

[464]Peggy Macintosh. (2002). "White Privilege: Unpacking the invisible knapsack" (pp. 97–102). In Paula Rothenberg (Ed.). *White privilege*. New York: Worth Publisher.

impossible for me to monitor everyone in this real-life laboratory situation.

Each of the restaurants taught something more about self and others and conveyed learnings that were transferable to work. The group learned about cultural difference in food preparation and eating styles, and temporal and class differences as well. After eating at the African restaurant, concern was expressed over the "waiting time." The group's view was that the meal was served "late." I subjected the experience to a cultural analysis. We were able to learn that the meal was not late, if regarded in an African cultural perspective, and we counted the interval between taking the order and serving the meal. I then asked the group to ponder a cultural difference. We were allowed to converse before eating so when the mean arrived we were not constrained to talk and eat at the same time. In a similar way, we learned to bring more than the managers into the training sessions and to go beyond the managers learning about how others needed training to remove scars.

I reasoned that the plant is not composed of just managers, and the training paradigm, therefore, had to include all members of the plant. Consequently, I included the bus driver in the training experience. I had been informed that he had been selected to drive our tour to DC because he was knowledgeable of the DC area. I was told also that when he was informed of the itinerary, he asked why they wanted to go to the designated part of town? He apparently believed the expected area to visit was dangerous, and feared for the theft of his bus. The hook, I imagined, that could bring him into the group would not be one of the traditional "isms." I decided to use his Vietnam vet status to educate and incorporate him into the group.

My strategy was not the consequence of convoluted thoughts. Before the trip, I had learned that many of the White males who had served in Vietnam had subsequent problems but were not allowed to form a work group that would receive multicultural-based diversity training assistance. The training we used included Vietnam vet status as one of the areas of oppression that the company needed to provide assistance, and a voice for its work-related problems. Many of our trainers had become skillful in helping Vietnam vets deal with the scars left from the experience. When our group, therefore, visited the Vietnam wall, we had facilitators who willingly coaxed the bus driver to visit the wall. He was initially opposed to visiting the wall but changed his mind when several of the men indicated that they would accompany and support him during his visit.

When we returned to the hotel, the bus driver was one of the first to depart from his vehicle. I thought his leaving was premature because the bus driver was usually the last person to leave a parked bus, akin to the captain of a ship. When he returned, therefore, I asked him if he was OK. He replied in the affirmative, and added that he had to call his wife and let her know that because of the experience he "could now go on with his life." He explained that one consequence of his Vietnam experience was that he was emotionally stuck in the Vietnam experience and could not be with either his wife or others. That evening when we went to eat at an African-American restaurant, we once again asked him to join us for dinner rather than waiting in the bus. This evening he smiled and said he would come and eat inside because he no longer cared about the bus. In an apparent state of elation, he announced he was feeling good in the setting. Suggestive of his anxiety-free state, he said they could steal the bus, for all he cared. At this point we took satisfaction from the fact that he was no longer simply a bus driver, paid to do a job, he was now a member of the group and included in the learning process.

In the end, it is not the multicultural and multiracial resources of a Black university that is illustrated. It is the driving conceptual belief in the curative powers of Blackness, viewed in terms of a city and area. Bearing this in mind, at my suggestion the group returned to DC for an additional training and educational experience. I suggested a visitation to the Holocaust Museum, and took responsibility for making group arrangements. A setback occurred, however, when I attempted to gain admission tickets. I was informed that it was a year's wait for admittance. Protracted patience is not one of my virtues, but going around obstacles is an attribute. Moreover, I believed the group would lose its interest and possible financial backing if we waited a year. Instead of accepting the stipulated time period, I contacted a former Howard classmate, Ms. Eileen Boyd, then Deputy Assistant Inspector General, Civil Fraud Division, Office of Inspector General, Department of Health and Human Services. She did not question why I was taking a group to a site that revealed the deplorable prejudicial experiences of a non-Black ethnic group; she freely provided help. She made the connection, and we were given tickets for the date the P&G group wanted.

There is a cultural legacy to this altruistic behavior in African-American history,[465] psychology[466] and philosophy,[467] testifying to the

---

[465]Molefi Asante (2002). *A journey of liberation* (2nd edition). New Jersey: The Peoples Publishing Group.

[466]Gerald Jackson (2005). *Njikoka: Towards an Africentric paradigm of helping*. New Jersey: Africa World Press.

profound and unique ways African Americans have influenced the moral development of the United States.[468] It marks the meaning of the word "minority," and through the ongoing Civil Rights efforts of African Americans shaped a country into the leading human rights nation in the world. [469] It continues to make the nation sensitive to managing struggles within its borders and a model for handling other countries' struggles for broad human rights. Because of Dr. Martin Luther King and Minister Malcolm X, who contributed to the turning of a concept into reality, it remains a paragon refuge for immigrants and paragon nation in the integration of diverse cultures within its borders.

They personify a group that has been successful because it was also led by the Fannie Lou Hammers[470] and Ella Bakers,[471] based upon the

---

[467]Fred Hord & Lee, J. (Eds.) (1995). *I am because we are. Readings in Black philosophy.* Massaachusetts: University of Massachusetts Press; Jesse McDade, Lesnor, C. & Wartofsky, M. (Eds.) (Winter, Spring, 1977-78). "Philosophy and the Black experience." *The Philosphical Forum A Quarterly IX,* (2-31, pp. 113–382); John Pittman (Ed.) (Fall-Spring 1992-93). "African-American Perspectives and Philosophical Traditions." *The Philosophical forum A Quarterly, XXIV,* (1-3) (pp. 3–296); Leonard Harris (Ed.) (1983). *Philosophy born of struggle: Anthology of Afro-American philosophy from 1917.* Iowa: Kendall/Hunt; Kwaku Person-Lynn (Ed.) (1996). *FIRST WORLD. Black scholars – thinkers – Warriors.* New York: Harlem River Press.

[468]Ralph Ellison (1986). "What America would be like without Blacks" (pp. 104–112). In Ralph Ellison. *Going to the territory.* New York: Random House. Dr. Martin Luther King models the Black spiritualist and moralist man. A dimension of him that is frequently eclipsed by his activist role is his scholar role in critiquing the social science and writing scholarly books. Martin Luther King, Jr. (1968). "The role of the behavioral scientist in the civil rights movement." *Journal of Social Issues,* 24(1). Republished, Monitor. American Psychological Association (January, 1999), pp. 1–5. I was reminded about the important aspect of his being during the Kevin Powell Black History Month talk noted in Sect. I. In addition, see Nikhil Singh (2004). *BLACK is a country.* Massachusetts: Harvard University Press.

[469]Ralph Ellison (1986). "What America would be like without Blacks" (pp. 104–112). In Ralph Ellison. *Going to the territory.* New York: Random House.

[470]Fannie Lou Hammer (1994). *Women of Hope: African-Americans who made a difference.* Knowledge Unlimited.

[471]Joanne Grant (1999). *Ella Baker: Freedom bound.* New York: Wiley; Barbara Ransby (2003). *Ella Baker and the Black freedom movement: A radical democratic vision.* North Carolina: University of North Carolina;

legacy of the Sojourner Truths,[472] Ida B. Wells[473] and Harriet Tubmans.[474] These are people that *were not willing to take it any longer and they gave rise to people who are not going to take it anymore.* Black universities have a place; the education fostered by Black colleges and universities strengthens a moral imperative for its graduates and guidelines for the nation and the world. They share a national responsibility with White universities to develop better programs and opportunities to exchange faculty, staff, curriculum and speakers.

A closing illustration that speaks to the cultural legacy of African-American oratory, symbolized by MLK, that can be spiritually and educationally uplifting, is the presence and words of Cornell University's 2003 Baccalaureate speaker Reverend Gardner C. Taylor. When Mr. Sutton spoke at Cornell, he mentioned that Black speakers

---

Shyrlee Dallar, Young, A. (1990). *Ella Baker: A leader behind the scenes*; Silver Burdett, Pr. Joy James (1998). *Race, woman, and revolution: Black female militancy and the praxis of Ela Baker.* Rowman & Littlefied.

[472]Olive Gilbert (1997). *The narrative of Sojourner Truth.* New York: Dover Publisher; Neil Painter (1996). *Sojourner truth: A life, a symbol.* New York: W.W. Norton and Company; Susan Taylor Boyd (1991).* *Sojourner Truth: The courageous former slave whose eloquence helped promote human equality.* Gareth Stevens Publisher; Catherine Bernard (2001). *Sojourner Truth: Abolitionist and Women's rights activist.* New York: The Horn Book Guide; Pat Mckissack (1994). *Sojourner truth: Ain't I a woman.* New York: Scholastic.

[473]Ida B. Wells & Duster, A. (Ed.). 1991) *Crusade for Justice: The Autobiography of Ida B. Wells* Illinois: University of Chicgo Press; Jacqueline Jones Royster. (1996). *Southern Horrors and Other Writings: The Anti-Lynching Campaign of Ida B. Wells 1892 – 1900.* New York: St. Martins; Elaine S. Lisandrelli (1998). *Ida B. Wells-Barnett: Crusader Against Lynching.* New Jersey: Enslow Publisher; Patricia A. Schea=chter (2001). *Ida B. Wells-Barnett and American Reform, 1880-1930.* North Carolina: University of North Carolina Press; Susan Davidson (20020. *Getting the Eeal Story: Nellie Bly and Ida B. Wells.* Washington: Seal Press; Linda O. McMurry (2000). *To Keep the Waters Troubled: The Life of Ida B. Wells.* New York: Oxford Univesity Press. Judith Bloom Fradin & Fradin, D. (2000). Ida B. Wells: *Mother of the Civil Rights Movement.* New Hampshire: Houghton Mifflin & Company; Miriam DeCosta-Willis (Ed.). (1995*). The Memphis Dary of Ida B. Wells.* Massachusetts: Beacon Press.

[474]Ann Petry (1996). *Harriet Tubman: Conductor on the Underground Railroad.* Harper/Trophy; Ann McGovern (1991). *Wanted dead or alive: The true story of Harriet Tubman.* New York: Scholastic; Catherine Clinton (20004); Harriet Tubman: The road to freedom,. New York: Little, Brown & Company;

should not be restricted to Black events. Reverend Gardner is one such person—a globalist, in the tradition of Dr. Martin Luther King, and a part of a long line of African-African Peace Advocates.[475] He did not profess to represent either an Africentric or a Black viewpoint; however, a perusal of his words would support either of these perspectives. His talk conveyed a special angle of vision; for instance, it addressed the power, responsibility and position of the United States that is consistent with a Eurocentric approach. Rather than being awed and satisfied with the ascendancy to power of the United States, he cautioned that its power "may be a threat to the whole world if used unwisely." Indicative of an Africentric philosophical point of view about interdependence, he defined a major problem of the U.S. as one involving "overreaching," and envisioned that in the U.S. "We are tempted as a nation today...to lose what I believe is an essential concern of individuals and Nation – a decent respect for the opinions of others."[476]

Using our Africentric Power to Define the meaning of education, it follows that the major element of success is the establishment of a culturally specific conduit for the housing, maintenance and assessment of human development and relationships.[477] The elder program outlined by Dr. Wade Nobles,[478] an authority and exponent on Black/African Psychology, is consistent with an Africentric Helping framework that views relationships as paramount in realizing human advances, and the capacity to maintain good ones as a hallmark of intelligence. The Black Greeks discussed in Section III are a socializing institution within Afrospace that is structurally and ideologically capable of providing the leadership and facilitation.[479]

---

[475]Gerald Jackson (2005). *Delimits of American helping. Precursors of an African Genesis model of helping.* New Jersey: Africa World Press.

[476]Linda Grace-Kobas (June 5, 2003). "Baccalaureate speaker warns the U.S. of the 'hazard of supremacy.'" *Cornell Chronicle*, 5, 8.

[477]This, embedded in the notion of driving, thinking, flying and learning while Black, is a form of racial barrier to African-American advancement.

[478]Wade Nobles (Nana Kwaku Berko I aka Ifagbemi Sangodare) (2002). "From Na Ezaleli to the Jegnoch: The force of the African family for Black men in higher education" (pp. 173-188). In Lee Jones (Ed.). *Making it on broken promises leading African American male scholars confront the culture of higher education.* Virginia: Stylus.

[479]See Robert Williams (1981). *The collective Black Mind: An Afrocentric theory of Black Personality.* Missouri: Williams & Associates; Louis Gates

Gerald G. Jackson

Relaciones, Relaciones, Relaciones – Personality and Cultural Dimensions

African-American Males

Starting on the personal level, Jacksone Consulting, my consulting arm, will create a specialty. Its goal will be the support of Black faculty and administrators in empowering Black men in culturally appreciative ways, and equipping them with practical skills, strategies and evaluation forms.[480] I am prone to do this because my firm is not bounded by the same socio-political considerations that mark Institutions of Higher Education.[481] Nor is it motivated by either a fear or insensitivity to the problems of White males.[482] My actions will be

---

(2004). *America behind the color line: Dialogues with African Americans.* New York: Warner Books.

[480]See following as some professional experiences and scholarship in this area: Gerald Jackson (March 11, 1980). "The influence of environmental factors on the sex role behavior of African-American males." Paper presented at the Black Psychology and Mental Health Conference, Atlanta Junior College, Atlanta, Georgia; Gerald Jackson (November 7, 1981). "The role of pre and post slavery temporal concepts on the current adjustment of African-Americans. In the African-American Male Experience. Is he still in chains?" Black Male Conference hosted at Essex County College, Newark, New Jersey; Kelsey, R., Jackson, G., & Anderson, L. (facilitator) (August 20-22, 1987). "Think Tank: Black men – At Risk in America." Twentieth Annual Convention of the Association of Black Psychologists, Atlanta, Georgia; Gerald Jackson (June 29, 1991). "Learning styles of African-American Males." Medical College of Virginia, Richmond, Virginia; Gerald Jackson (March 7, 1983). "Motivating Black males." Orange Public School System, Orange, New Jersey.

[481]One area is Black male and female relationships: Charlene Harper & Jackson, Gerald (January 29, 1986). "Can We Talk On Improving the quality of Black male/Black female relationships." North Carolina State University, North Carolina; Gerald Jackson (December 4, 1986). "Black male and female relationships." Bellcore Synergy II Conference, Bell Communications Research, Elizabeth, New Jersey; Gerald Jackson (April 7, 1987). "Black male and female workshop." Seventh Annual Black Psychology Theme Week Observance. Florida A & M University, Tallahassee, Florida; Valerie Batts, . & Jackson, G. (November 20, 2000). "Coalition building between men & women leaders of color workshop." Rocky Mount, North Carolina.

[482]Examples of assistance given to Whites, see Gerald Jackson (March 14, 1968). "Roleplaying as a method to improve interpersonal communications." Rural Youth Corp of Maine, Bangor, Maine; Gerald Jackson (November 16, 1994). "Hearing and interpreting from a cultural perspective: The White male

guided by a Howard motto that engenders leaders for the global community. It begets a Howard University tradition and spirits that dictate the current plans at Howard University for the education and empowerment of Black males.[483] Similarly, it conceivably shaped the ideas of Edison Jackson about his college's definition of community regard and academic excellence for Black males and females. This is attested partially by Howard's ranking recognition by Mother Jones as one of the most politically active campuses in the nation.[484] It is not all about activism either, and reflecting a diunital posture, Howard University was successful in recruiting and enrolling the largest number of National Achievement scholars of all colleges in the United States.[485] It is expected then, that a considerable amount of my consulting firm's time will be devoted to essential support areas. Namely, it will provide researching and writing on the subject, conduct workshops and seminars, and deliver mentoring and training for mental health professionals in the design and implementation of programs and research studies.

Latinas/Betas

On an organizational plane, I fondly refer to Omega Phi Beta sorority as *my Betas*; however, it is more likely that I am their professor. When it appeared, for example, that all the new Betas would be without upperclass leadership because of graduation, I was informed

---

voice in corporate America." Diversity Council Meeting of the American Society for Training and Development, New York Metropolitan Chapter entitled, "How to hear the voices of diversity in your organization," New York City, New York; Cooper Thompson & Jackson, G. (November 7, 1994). "White males in corporate America." AT& T Red Bank, New Jersey. Gerald Jackson (1987, winter). "The implementation of an intra cultural awareness coaching program." *Corporate Headquarters*, 9-13, 30.

[483]This does not mean that Howard will be unduly favoring men over women. A Black university such as Howard would shun dichotomously-based practices. See footnote 12 regarding the establishment of a Women's Studies program.

[484]Melanie R. Holmes (November 4, 2003). "HU Named Among Most Politically Active Campuses*." The Hilltop*, 1-2. Also, top college newspaper. Charreach Jackson (August 27, 2004). "The Hilltop Ranked Number One College Paper." *The Hilltop*, 1 – 2.

[485]Charreach Jackson (January 13, 2004). "Howard: Leader in Achievement Scholar Enrollment." *The Hilltop*. 1-2.

that I would be expected to guide them in being representative Betas. It was a *compliment* that I highly regarded but had no dream of receiving. I drew my satisfaction from seeing the members grow and prosper. They strike me as an untapped tour de force in Caribbean Latinas, in general, and Caribbean Afri-Latinas, in particular.

Erika initially wanted to be a successful lawyer. She completed a master's degree in public policy. Similarly, a number of graduates are obtaining advanced degrees in public health at prestigious universities. These women are not driven by money. They are not preoccupied with being pretty. The way the Betas are constituted, they will serve humankind and will be about people-saving. Despite claims by Latinos that they do not discriminate on the basis of color/race,[486] research and scholarship repeatedly shows a Eurocentric color caste system. This is not peculiar to Latinos; however, in terms of political alliances with other groups, it has been found that it can be manipulated in the United States to the disadvantage of dark-skinned and Black Latinos.[487] It is suggested here that Black and Latina Greeks may be a resource for surmounting racism and enhancing intracultural communication and collaboration; however, the success of this approach is contingent upon an acceptance and appreciation of an African-American culture and Africentric history. This entails a recognition and acceptance of a legacy.

Latina college and university students have been generally identified as a distinct group with peculiar problems and needs,[488] similarly, Puerto Rican women have specifically had their identity transformation process depicted in a unique way;[489] individuals and groups that are neither Latino nor Puerto Rican can give more assistance to Puerto Ricans. The uniqueness of this group does not mean, therefore, that an African-American male can not be a part of the psychological/identity transformation process, especially when it comes to the racism and colorism encountered by Afro-Puerto Rican

---

[486]See Lani Guinier & Torres, G. (2002). *The Miner's Canary*. Massachusetts: Harvard University Press.

[487]Neil Foley (2002). "Becoming Hispanic: Mexican Americans and Whiteness" (pp. 49-59. In Paula Rothenberg (Ed.). *White privilege*. New York: Worth Publisher.

[488]Felix M. Padilla (1997*). The struggle of Latino–Latina University students. In search of a liberating education* . New York: Routledge.

[489]Esmeralda Santiago (1993*). When I was Puerto Rican*. New York: Vintage Books.

females.[490] A key is taking into account the cultural dimension of a relationship with them. To illustrate, the temptation is great to attribute the remarkable space and time I share with Betas to a purely African cultural base. To do so would mean falling prey to wishful thinking. The reality is that their behaviors and attitudes influencing my positive regard are grounded in Latin American and Caribbean cultures. When I think of things the group has done to enhance my spirit or assist me in a project, I think of such words as *personalismo, confianza, simpatico, dignidad*, and *respeto*.

In terms of their meaning, in another work I mentioned these and other cultural characteristics as antecedents to intracultural communications and relationships.[491] To reiterate, *respeto* according to Abad, Ramos & Boyce, has no equivalent in reverence.[492] Christensen conveyed that it personifies respect but especially for authority, family and tradition.[493] Abad, Ramos & Boyce added that it applies to Puerto Ricans who have remained faithful to their cultural norms and values. It is recognition based upon the individual's personal attributes, and is not, therefore, dissuaded by wealth or position. In its application, it transcends social class and extends to children as well.

Similar in genre are the concepts of *dignidad* and *personalism*. The former is close to the American notion of "pride." It means that one cannot take the dignity of a person away from him or her in front of

---

[490] Angela Jorge (1986). "The Black Puerto Rican woman in contemporary American society" (pp. 180-188). In Edna Acosta-Belen (Ed.). *The Puerto Rican woman Perspectives on culture, history, and society* (2nd edition). New York: Praeger; Julia De Burgos (1995). "Ay Ay Ay for the kinky Black woman" (p. 80). In Roberto Santiago (Ed.) *Boricuas*. New York: One World; Juanita Ramos (Ed.) (1995). "Latin American lesbians speak on Black identity – Violetta Garro, Minerva Rosa Perez, Dibna, Magdalena C. Juanita" (pp. 57-78). In Carole Davies (Ed.). *Moving beyond boundaries Black Women's Diasporas*. New York: New York University Press; Clara Rodriquez (1995). "Puerto Ricans: Between Black and White" (pp. 81-90). In Roberto Santiago (Ed.) *Boricuas*. New York: One World; Marta Vega (January/February 2004). "Living at the margins of three worlds." *The Crisis*. p. 60.

[491] Gerald G. Jackson (2005). *Njikoka: Towards an Africentric paradigm of helping*. New Jersey: Africa World Press.

[492] Vicente Abad, Ramos, J. & Boyce, E. (1974). "A model for delivery of mental health services to Spanish-speaking minorities." *American Journal of Orthopsychiatry*, 44, 584 – 595.

[493] Edwin Christensen (1975). "Counseling Puerto Ricans: Some cultural considerations." *Personnel and Guidance Journal*, 53, 349–356.

others.[494] One can oppose another but to strip such a person of their pride is about the worse that can be done. In the same vein, *personalismo* is a general guide to an affective or feeling approach to life.[495] Basically, it is the belief that people are more trustworthy than institutions. Consequently, Puerto Ricans following traditional values show disdain for formal and impersonal institutional structures. According to Fitzpatrick, they are more likely to use those services that are readily accessible and relate to individuals who evince flexibility and availability (temporality) and usually, minimize time-consuming red tape.[496]

These cultural attributes, and others such as machismo, hembrismo, and vergüenza, are foundations to understanding tradition-dominant Puerto Ricans, Chicagoricans and Nuyoricans.[497] They vary in individual use, but still possess instrumental value for appreciating the behavior of many Puerto Rican and Latino students and professionals. For instance, I have found that Betas will attend events dealing with Black predicaments, when asked by me, and they will attend Africana social events because they enjoy being a part of the group, and the group respects and appreciates their presence and contributions.

One should be mindful also that Afro-Puerto Ricans are asserting a cultural identity,[498] and it is culturally congruent with the actual

---

[494]Edwin Christensen (1975). "Counseling Puerto Ricans: Some cultural considerations." *Personnel and Guidance Journal*, 53, 349–356.

[495]Michael Borrero, Cuadrado, L. & Rodriquez, R. (1974). "The Puerto Rican role in interest-group politics." *Social Casework*, 55, 94–99.

[496]Joseph Fitzpatrick (1971). *Puerto Rican Americans The meaning of migration to the mainland.* New Jersey: Prentice-Hall.

[497]Miguel Algarin & Pinero, M. (Eds.) (1975*). Nuyorican poetry An anthology of Puerto Rican words and feelings.* New York: William Morrow & Company; Lillian Comas-Diaz, Lykes, M. & Alarcon, R. (1998). "Ethnic conflict and the psychology of liberation in Guatemala, Peru and Puerto Rico." *American Psychologist*, 51(7), 778–792; Braulio Montalvo (1974). "Home school conflict and the Puerto Rican child." *Social Casework*, 55(2), pp. 100-110; Piri Thomas (1973). *Savior, savior, hold my hand.* New York: Bantam Books; Piri Thomas (1967*). Down these mean streets.* New York: New American Library; Frederico Tovar (1972). *The Puerto Rican woman.* New York: Plus Ultra Books; Henrietta Yurchenco, (1971). *¡Hablamos!* New York: Praeger.

[498]Victor Cruz (1995). "African things." In Roberto Santiago (p. 101) (Ed.). *Boricuas.* New York: One World; Julia De Burgos (1995). "Ay Ay Ay for the kinky Black woman" (p. 80). Willie Perdormo, (1999). *Nigger – Reecan blues* (pp. 91-92). In Roberto Santiago (Ed.). *Boricuas.* New York: One World.

psychohistory of Puerto Rico.[499] The point is that their use can result in mutually beneficial collaborative efforts and a complementary relationship. Viva las relaciones, they are needed contra viento y marea (against the stormy seas). In line then with reporting positive cultural interactions, I hope this piece spurs others to write about how they have helped and may help women. It is conceivable to me that one may write also on how to be helped by them. Such a discourse can also frame discussions on Black, Brown and Yellow, and new immigrant relationships,[500] and explain why racial group harmony may not result from conceptualizations that classify African-American issues as ethnic conflicts.[501]

One way of fighting either feeling drained by diversity work or falling prey to racial and class-based condescension is to allow for a contract of mutually beneficial assistance. For example, I asked some Betas, based upon their college major, psychological inclination and service interest, to review my section on Black-Brown Together. Jessica Lorenzo, a graduating Cornell senior responded:

Hi Professor Jackson,

I just finished reading your amazing and powerful section in your new book! I found some minor mistakes and I was wondering if you would like me to mail you the corrections, or is it too late?

Also your powerful writing and knowledge made me think that we should have a program discussing Black and Brown relations. The program could be part of our Week of

---

[499] Juan Cordero (1996). "AfroPuerto Rican cultural studies: Beyond cultura negroide and antillanismo." *CENTRO Journal of the Center for Puerto Rican Studies*, 8(1 & 2), pp. 57–77.

[500] Brenda Payton (1997). "Blacks, Browns, and Yellows at Odds" (pp. 213–217). In Ishmael Reed (Ed.). *Multiamerica. Essays on cultural wars and cultural peace*. New York: Penguin Books; Amritjit Singh (1997). "The possibilities of a radical consciousness: African Americans and new immigrants" (pp. 218-237). In Ishmael Reed (Ed.). *Multiamerica. Essays on cultural wars and cultural peace*. New York: Penguin Books.

[501] See Joe C. Fong (1997). "Ethnic conflict and harmony between African and Asian Americans in the United States" (pp. 309–318). In Ishmael Reed (Ed.). *Multiamerica. Essays on cultural wars and cultural peace*. New York: Penguin Books. For brief history of White ethnic groups and their defensive posture against Black human rights assertiveness, see Nathan Glazer (1972). "Interethnic conflict." *Social Work, 17*(3), pp. 3–9.

Illumination and it could be for the Café con Leche on Friday, April 2, 2004 at 6:30pm. I know that you go home for the weekend but this would be a great honor for us. This way we can incorporate the program you mentioned to us about hosting a book gathering. The students will be able to learn from your insights and about your new book release.[502]

Two outcomes occurred. First, I was elated by her assessment and reminded to do something more than publish the book. I had mentioned earlier a book party, and she asked what was a book party? I had no idea that she heard my response and, as a quick learner, would move to make the book party a quick reality. The learning for society is the significance of *Relationes*, the theme of the book party. I would add to the cultural list several Africentric cultural attributes that have aided and abetted my relationship with the Betas.

Support from African-American Women

First is my definition of a woman. It was not until I had become conversant with the African-centered notion of womanism that I came to appreciate the role my mother and grandmother played in my development.[503] My exposure at Howard to Black sororities that continues serving and giving to the present strengthened my convictions.[504] To illustrate, AKAs have continued to support my being and writing development. Dr. Gwen Grant, AKA, media psychology, lecturer and columnist for *Essence* magazine, years ago wrote me the following encouraging and somewhat prophetic letter:

---

[502]Jessica Lorenzo (March 7, 2004). "Section in Book & Book program." Email. Book party, Gerald Jackson (April 2, 2004). *"We're not going to take it anymore" – Black and Brown Relaciones*. Latino Living Center Lounge, Ithaca, New York, Cornell University.

[503]Joyce Ann Joyce (2001). "African centered womanism. Connecting Africa to the Diaspora" (pp. 538–554). In Isidore Okpewho, Davies, C. & Mazurui, A. (Eds.). *The African Diaspora.* Indiana: Indiana University Press; Catherine Acholonu (March-April, 2002). Motherism: The Afrocentric alternative. *Konch*, pp. 1–4.

[504]Shara Taylor (February 5, 2004). "Deltas host 12th woman to woman conference." *The Hilltop*. pp. 1, 2; Shara Taylor (January 16, 2004). "Deltas donate to campus closet." *The Hilltop*, pp. 1, 2; Danielle Scruggs (January 23, 2004). "AKAs raise $21, 000 for Africare." *The Hilltop*, pp. 1, 2.

February 24, 1977

Dear Gerald,

Thank you for the article. You are a very prolific writer. I have the feeling that one day you will be an internationally famous name in psychology.

I admire your theories and your ability to clearly state the essence of your thoughts. I am also speaking admirably of you to Katye from time to time. We agree!!

Your admiring colleague,
Gwendolyn (Grant – that is)

When those close to you and afar attempt to destroy your sense of self, purpose and resolve, letters such as Gwen's keep you going and believing in yourself, and, inferentially, in African-American women, and their time honored motherism.[505]

Adrie, two older AKA sorors and Angela.
Photo by Adrie Ciccone.

The Betas

More specifically, the Africentric ideas that fostered harmony and growth for me with the Betas are complementary of differences,

---

[505]Mary Kolawole (1997). *Womanism and African consciousness.* New Jersey: Africa World Press; Joan Morgan (1999). *When chicken-heads come home to roost A hip-hop feminist breaks it down.* New York: Touchstone.

reciprocity and spiritual essence.[506] Being a Faculty Fellow for the Betas has yielded me many non-tangible benefits. I have learned more about an evolving self-definition of a Latina, reflected in Erika's poem later in this section,[507] domestic violence on women, Latino history and culture, and self defense strategies for women—programs either conducted or sponsored by Betas. Parenthically, . Erika resides in Washington, DC so it is conceivable that she could be a helpful link to the HU Cimmarrones Club and the latter's work with Afri-Latinas. As an undergraduate at Cornell, Erika designed and participated in many programs that dealt with the problems of Afri-Latinas. As a corrolary of her scholarship, years after her undergraduate days the Betas sponsored a lecture on the African Influence in the Spanish-Speaking Caribbean. This lecture was a very progressive idea, and with immense mental health, curriculum and research implications. Dr. Lillian Comas-Diaz, an original writer on Afri-Latina mental health, also resides in Washington, D.C., Also in DC. is Milagros Denis, an ABD at Howard University, who lectured my class on Afro-Puerto Ricans and provided me with germane publications and leads on resource people.

Essentially then, an Africentric definition encouraged me to respond to Betas being strong and sensitive, smart and silly, and giving and receiving.[508] This is conveyed in some pictures of the moments we shared and in the diunitality present in Erika's poem To be Latina.

---

[506]Robert Hill (1997). *The strength of African American families: Twenty-five years later*. Washington, D.C.: R&B Publishers; Niara Sudarkasa (1997). "African American families and family values." In Harriette McAdoo (Ed.). *Black families* (3rd edition). California: Sage; Ann Wolf (1983). "A personal view of Black inner-city foster families." *American Journal of Orthopsychiatry*, 53(1), pp. 144–151.

[507]Ana Zentella (2002). "Latin@ languages and identities" (pp. 339-358). In Marcelo Suarez-Orozco & Mariela Paez (Eds.). *LATINOS Remaking America*. California: University of California Press..

[508]Daniel Mengara (2001). "Perceptions of African Feminism: A socio-historical perspective" (pp. 281–305). In Daniel Mengara (Ed.). *Images of Africa Stereotypes & Realities*. New Jersey: Africa World Press.

Table at Beta workshop on violence and its
prevention. Photo by Gerald Jackson.

Beta martial arts workshop. Photo by Gerald Jackson.

GGJ and Betas in NYC after having dinner in Little Italy.
Photo of Gerald Jackson

Gerald G. Jackson

GGJ & a founder of the Betas (Nancy).

Jackie, GGJ and June at Award Ceremony for Cornell Greeks.

To be Latina

By Erika Ruiz

To be Latina ...what does that mean?
Does that mean I have to know how to make a mean pernil?
Starch my husband's shirts even after he cheats on me?
Run around after multiple children yet be strong enough to climb up trees to get
quenepas for my family?
Does it mean I have to speak when spoken to, wash and clean after every man that
I encounter?

Or is it the other extreme of being a picante sex goddess, ready and willing to
show any man a good time as long as he says I'm pretty?
Is it to walk the streets in a tight red outfit showing mis curbas peligrosas?

You know what they say about Latin women---the Virgin Mary on their necks but
La Virgen Maria no son.
Hot blooded, fast speakers, heart breakers, soul shakers, money takers, baby
sitters, playa haters, fight breakers, slap takers, cold lovers, wage earners, baby
makers, orgasm fakers.
Both of these Latinas are victims of the man, y la mujer tambien.

We have no voice, we let it get robbed and we steal it from ourselves. We steal it
from each other, debilitate our neighbors.

It is all for him, not for us.
We feel no love, just work, another duty.
It's my job to cook those damned gandules.

We're damned if we do, damned if we don't.
Can't enjoy life, it is a sin to live.
One Latina dominates.
The other is dominated.
Both cry bloody tears because neither is loved for real.

You're a mother or a hooker, a cleaner or a flash dancer.
Is there room in the middle?
Can a Latina be feminist without being called a Lesbiana?
Can a woman enjoy men and booze without being labeled a susia?
Or can a woman not be a domestic without being a good for nothing?

We rob ourselves of choices—steal them from our hearts—old school thinking has
kept us in a place, a designated "our place."

Awaken sweet nenitas for soon we can be alive.
No more plantain grating, no more floor sweeping, no more street walking, no
more table dancing, no more wife beatings.
Feel my heart beating? Hear my fast breathing?
My eyes are open, it's starting.

During a focus group study for the Community Development area, the interviewer asked the faculty fellows what the intrinsic reward was they received for doing non-financially rewarded faculty fellow program work. I believe Marcy's email to me, published below, reflects what rewards me; that is, being appreciated for caring and being:

> Firstly, I want to say thank you. Thank you for always supporting my chapter and being there for us when we need you. I can tell you when I first was bringing Omega Phi Beta to Cornell I was not thinking long terms and what it would be, my main objective was to get it there and have people know of this great sisterhood. Now look at Nu Chapter, 5 years later how great it has become (part of me can relate to the feelings of our organizational founders).
>
> Secondly, I read the section of your new book and am "WOWed." I knew what you meant to us but did not know the extent of what we meant to you and now I am speechless. It is an honor to have this piece put in there and your words are amazing. You MUST let us know when the book is going to be released so that we can all be there in support of you.
>
> Lastly, you have my word that I am moving forward with my career and schooling. I am not letting the fear stop me and realize that I need to get over it quickly. I am not sure how well you know of my academic struggle at Cornell and that is what I hold on to all the time. I easily belittle the "overcoming" part of it and the pure fact that I am a graduate of an Ivy League institution. Thank you for always believing in me and pushing me to be the best. I will always hold that dear to my heart.
>
> Oh, one more thing :) I read in the footnote about the new initiative for minority alumni involvement and mentorship. This is something that I hold EXTREMELY dear to my heart and would love to be a part of. Who can I talk to so that I can be a helping hand in this initiative?

Marcy's email reveals why it is easy for me to be with Puerto Ricans and deal with most of their human complexities.[509] I sincerely

---

[509] Eileen Findlay (1999). *Imposing decency: The politics of sexuality and race in Puerto Rico, 1870 – 1920*. North Carolina: Duke University Press; Ramon Grosoguel, Negron-Muntainer, F. & Georgas, C. (1997). "Beyond nationalist and colonialist discourses: The Jaiba politics of the Puerto Rican ethnonation"

believe the concept of diunitality provides an intellectual solution to their problem of being between Black and White[510] and being both Black and Latino.[511] Diunitality or non-dichotomous thinking does not stop with Puerto Ricans but includes Asians as well.[512] Granted, I am not at the same place with Asians, although I have been abetted in a quest for greater cultural awareness and social contact by my supportive and professional relationship with Dr. Tina Tong Yee and Byron Kunisawa.[513] Both of them have made it possible for me to

---

(pp. 1–38). In Frances Negron-Muntainer & R. Grosfoguel (Eds.). *Puerto Rican jam: Essay on culture and politics.* Minnesota: University of Minnesota Press.

[510]Clara Rodriquez (1995). "Puerto Ricans: Between Black and White" (pp. 81–90). In Roberto Santiago (Ed.). *Boricuas: Influential Puerto Rican Writings – An Anthology.* New York: Ballantine Publishing; Angela Jorge (1986). "The Black Puerto Rican woman (pp. 180-188)" (2nd edition). In Edna Acosta-Belen (Ed.). *The Puerto Rican woman: Perspectives of Culture.* New York: Praeger Publishers.

[511]Roberto Santiago (1995). Black and Latino (pp. 93–95). In Roberto Santiago (Ed.). *Boricuas: Influential Puerto Rican Writings – An Anthology.* New York: Ballantine Publishing; Thomas Mathews (1974). "The question of color in Puerto Rico." In Robert Toplin (Ed.). *Slavery and race relations in Latin America.*

[512]Frank Wu (2002). *Yellow race in America Beyond Black and White.* New York: Basic Books; Harry Kitano (1969). *Japanese American The evolution of a subculture.* New Jersey: Prentice-Hall; Laura Uba (1994). *Asian Americans Personality patterns, identity, and mental health.* New York: Guilford; Stanley Sue & Wagner, N. (Eds.) (1973). *Asian-Americans Psychological perspectives.* California: Science and Behavioral Books; Vijay Prashad (2001). *The Karma of Brown folk* (2000). Minnesota: University of Minnesota Press; Vijay Prashad (2001). *Untouchable freedom A social history of a Dalit community.* New York: Oxford University Press.

[513]In the same spirit, see Vijay Prashad (2001). *Everybody was Kung fu fighting Afro-Asian connections and the myth of cultural purity.* Massachusetts: Beacon Press; Joe C. Fong (1997). "Ethnic conflict and harmony between African and Asian Americans in the United States" (pp. 309–318). In Ishmael Reed (Ed.). *Multiamerica. Essays on cultural wars and cultural peace.* New York: Penguin Books; Brenda Payton (1997). "Blacks, Browns, and Yellows at Odds" (pp. 213 – 217). In Ishmael Reed (Ed.). *Multiamerica. Essays on cultural wars and cultural peace.* New York: Penguin Books. Indicative of the elasticity of Africentric scholars, Dr. Karenga, a prime mover in the Africana Studies field, published a paper on Chinese psychosocial therapy. Maulana Karenga (1978). "Chinese psychosocial therapy: A strategic model for mental health." *Psychotherapy, theory, research and practice.* 5(1), pp. 101–107.

culturally appreciate and socially and intellectually connect with some Asian students. I did not grow up around Asians, as I did with Latinos, and learned about the latter primarily from the media.

Asian-American Students/Trainees as Mentorees and Allies

Broadly speaking, the media can scare us into believing that our age, political orientation, college status and race might dissuade us from being effective as educational agents for groups other than our

GGJ and Diane Seung. Photo by Gerald G. Jackson.

own. Most essential, it has helped forge a dichotomy between Africana Studies and other racial and cultural groups. Conflicts between African Americans and other groups are inevitable, more of a species inevitability, as are their resolutions. In this Africentric view, struggle can be a constructive force in dialogues, especially for Asians and African Americans.[514] Several cases will illustrate a diunital Africentric view. The first report or hypothesis, is the following email from a

---

[514]Amritjit Singh (1997). "The possibilities of a radical consciousness: African Americans and new immigrants" (pp. 218-237). In Ishmael Reed (Ed.). *Multiamerica. Essays on cultural wars and cultural peace*. New York: Penguin Books; Vijay Prashad (2001). *Everybody was Kung fu fighting Afro-Asian connections and the myth of cultural purity*. Massachusetts; Nikhil Singh (2004). *BLACK is a country*. Massachusetts: Harvard University Press. Vasant Rao (August, 1975). "African dynasty in India." *Black World*, pp. 78-82.

former first year writing seminar South Asian student. Her work will appear in forthcoming books because they model an Indian-American student gain from an Africentric approach, and at the same time provide insight for all to assist such students.[515]

Hi Professor Jackson,

This is Sonia from your Black is, Black Ain't writing seminar of last spring semester. How are you? Since I have not spoken to you in a while, I thought I might update you on my progress in discovering my niche here at Cornell. As I told you previously, it was my plan to join a sorority and I ended up doing so at the beginning of this semester. I still maintain my membership in the Indian organizations, and as a result, I think that I have finally achieved a satisfying balance of Indian and non-Indian friends. In my sorority, I have met African-American girls who too have achieved a similar balance between having white and non-white friends. I still believe myself to be a "Indian American" and therefore these two baskets of friends help me to achieve both my Indian and American identities. Its a difficult identity to balance, but after 1.5 years here at Cornell I think that I have finally done it. I am in a happy place right now, which is in contrast to several of the frustrated essays that I wrote last year. I just thought that I would let you know, and that I have kept what I learned in your class in the back of my mind the entire time as I struggled toward achieving a balanced friends' circle and finally solidifying my shaky identity.[516] Thanks again for an

---

[515]See Rupal Patel (2001). "Coalition building among People of Color" (pp. 275–277). In Vickie Nam (Ed.). *Yell-Oh – Girls*! New York: Quill. In 2002 she was selected as one of the top 10 Asian-American students. Source - Maria Tong & Liang, C. (October 10, 2002). "Big activists on campus. The top 10 Asian-American students (pp. 1–3). The Ammy Awards." http://www.aonline.com/print_article10,1124,2800 25480-1,00.html. Rupal was not a random selection. She spent a summer in a Berkeley program with my daughter and Melissa affirmed the breadth of Rupal's activism.

[516]In a research report on the attitudes of Asian Indians toward counseling, Panganamala and Plummer (1998) noted: immigrants often feel isolated and alienated from both the original culture and the American culture...culturally competent couseling could greatly aid in the acculturation process by providing a dependable source of support" Nancy Panganamala & Plummer,

amazing class. It's one of the only classes I feel that will affect me in future years. I hope to take another one soon!

Sonia Sabharwal

Another case illustration is based upon a paper by a South Asian-American male student. Sandeep Rao voluntarily submitted it at the end of my Black Family course. It is titled "Shades Apart: An Analysis of South Asian American – African American Relations." Of pertinence here, he wrote:

> A fact that I find personally more important than anything else: those South Asians who began to immigrate to the United States in the 1960s, a group that includes my parents and grandparents, benefited from and outright owe their place in this nation to the achievements of the African-American Civil Rights movement, although most of them did not actively participate.
>
> In addition to historical ties, these two communities share a much deeper bond – one that is unfortunately recognized by few. I myself did not become aware of underlying cultural similarities between African-Americans and South Asians until I took AS&RC 171. The foundations for both cultures are built upon themes of respect, reciprocity and a sense of family, community and communal good. A myriad of cultural practices serve as examples, but some that were highlighted in class as being typical of African Americans stood out to me as being typical also of South Asians. Respect for elders are a must, and when encountering an "Auntie" (for elders are never held on a first-name basis) one must always speak and do so with respect. I have found that Dr. Robert Hill's strengths of Black families correspond greatly to what many South Asians regard as their community's strengths as well, regardless of their origins. Family is of high importance to both peoples but it is also a large and flexible concept. Just as one might assume that the two groups would be natural allies in the U.S. Dr. Martin Luther King, Jr. and Mahatma Gandhi,

---

D. (1998). "Attitudes toward counseling among Asian Indians in the United States." *Cultural Diversity and Mental Health*, 4(1), pp. 55–63. An academic setting, as Sonia's email indicates, that allows for identity issues to be examined may also be an option.

icons of their respective group's struggles, shared a strong and deep camaraderie of ideals. Both believed in nonviolent resistance as the means to fight oppression and used their ideas to bring their people to freedom and equality. Actual collaboration existed between other civil rights leaders and Indian freedom fighters, such as Marcus Garvey and Harida T. Mazumdar, a Gandhian, Paul Robeson and Kumar Ghoshal, W.E.B. Dubois and his Indian counterpart Rabindranah Tagore. Many more alliances were also formed during the anti-colonial struggles, especially because of India's alliance with African and Caribbean decolonization movements (pp. 3, 4).[517]

Had his paper been a part of a discussion in one of my firm's Africentric training, the work of Karkar [518] might have been introduced to establish a cultural/philosophical link between an African and Eastern mind. For example, Karkar's argument about the relationship between the individual and society is very much like an African conceptualization, and the idea of diunitality. Both contend, in contrast to Western science, that the mind and body are not a dichotomy and cannot be separated from its society. The self, akin to the African-American concept of Blackness, is more than skin color and has many layers or concentric circles. The mode I would use would be Africentrically-based and beneficial to Asians, and perhaps against some forms of neoracism.[519] This is illustrated in a letter I received from an Asian participant in a training I conducted at the University of Wisconsin on the use of world-view differences in understanding and using racial differences in human relations work.

...The "Titanic" exercise was very exciting for me. Since I was born and raised in... I didn't exactly grow up in an Asian community. Yet in the exercise, my Asian heritage

---

[517]Sandeep Rao (2002). *Shades Apart: An analysis of South Asian American-African American Relations.* Research paper submitted to Gerald Jackson in AS&RC 171 – Black Family, Cornell University, Ithaca, New York.

[518]Sudhir Kakar (1998). Western science, eastern minds (pp. 348 – 254). In Gary Weaver (1998). *Culture, communication and conflict Readings in intercultural relations* (2nd edition). Massachuesetts: Simon & Schuster.

[519]Chetan Bhatt (2000). "The lore of the homeland: Hindu nationalism and indigenist 'Neoracism'" (pp. 573–593). In Les Back & Solomos, J. (Eds.). *Theories of Race and Racism A reader.* New York: Routledge.

pushed me to argue against the "age criteria," force me to defend the "senior citizens" in the group of cards. I cannot say that I have ever been put into a situation where I could clearly identity that my culture was conflicting with the commonly held "American" culture. (Ironically, my grandparents probably would have scolded me for disagreeing with a man older than me!).

I later discussed this experience with my father. He's a manager in the laboratory of a local hospital, and is usually very skeptical of "diversity training." When I first started to talk about the session, he scowled to another person at the table, "These new buzzwords: diversity, world views, bab!" However, as I related the exercise, and the other things we discussed, he, for the first time, showed interest. I think he, as well as I, appreciated that you talked not about right and wrong, but about respecting differences.

Thank you again for coming, and I hope I will have the opportunity to learn more with you in the future.

In the end, I try not to believe the hype inspired by Eurocentric ideology to denigrate differences between human beings. My outlook has allowed me, based upon the request of Asian corporate employees, to give a presentation on the Asian perspective of the corporate world. An Africentric outlook has also enabled me to deliver presentations and workshops for Black women sororities, conduct a workshop for Hispanics in Higher Education and be a part of a substance abuse prevention alliance with Native Americans, Chicanos and Asian Americans.[520] During the early part of the 21st century in the United States, it has afforded the ability to start to bond with students from

---

[520]Gerald Jackson (November 3, 1984). "Stress and survival strategies within a sorority community." Northeastern Regional Conference of Lambda Kappa Mu Sorority, Inc., Rochelle Park, New Jersey; Earl Braxton & Gerald Jackson (April 5, 1985). "The reflective mirror: The training of Blacks to work with other Blacks." Eighteenth Annual Convention of the Association of Black Psychologists, Chicago, Illinois; Gerald Jackson & Lenworth Gunther (March 16, 1985). "Hispanics in higher education: Observations of a friend." Seventh Annual Statewide Conference of the Hispanic Association of Higher Education of New Jersey, Essex County College, Newark, New Jersey.

universities other than my own.[521] Specifically, to be in a dialogue with a Rutgers University student for six hours in a New Jersey Dunkin' Donuts. He seemed enthusiastic at the close of our conversation; however, after weeks went by I started thinking that maybe I should have spent the time more wisely by completing this book. To my satisfaction, the Friday before submitting the final book draft he sent the following email:

> Dear Sir,
>
> I am the Indian kid that met you in a Dunkin Donuts in New Brunswick a few weeks ago. I would have wished to get in contact with you before but I was swamped by school. I was hoping you could give me some good references into African history or mythology. I would also like to read about your trips into the continent. I remember that you wanted to read about Indian history and mythology. I wouldn't mind lending you the mahabharat video set if you would like it. I would like to say the conversation that I had with you was an enlightening one.
>
> so drop me a line and let me know whats up
>
> Nirav Patel

Learning about the genuine greatness of our own culture and that of others is "waz up." Being able to share in the joys of the cultures of others is "waz up." Being "for real" is "waz up." Not taken stuff anymore is "waz up."

---

[521] This does not mean that the traditional Higher Education approach to learning is invalid. A 2000 conference titled "Blacks and Asians: revisiting racial formations," sponsored by the Institute for Research in African-American studies and The Center for the Study of Ethnicity and Race at Columbia University, is appropriate. What has to be included in the reasoning process is an understanding of the limitations of this type of intervention. Such a consideration would encourage alliances and coalitions to embrace a holistic human relations success. See Gerald Jackson (2005). *Sankofa Helping: The African genesis of an African-American Model of Helping.* New Jersey: Africa World Press.

EPILOGUE: AVOIDING THE POC TRAP IS EVENTUALLY MORE HUMANE

The shortcomings of the POC concept is revealed further through an investigation of the early negative treatment of Italians for living easily with African-Americans (lynching), punishment for political alliance with African-Americans (Vito Marcantonio and W.E.B. DuBois), socio-political involvement in the Civil Rights movement (raped and murdered), capacity to view the strengths of African-Americans and ability to not take themselves too seriously (Gomba). This ending discussion is to remind the reader that the fundamental battle is neither between Blacks and Whites nor between People of Color and Whites (presuming the skin color of European to be colorless).

My relationship with Italian-Americans, as an African-American male, had not been given much thought until reviewing several 2004 publications on the discrimination received by Italian Americans[522], and the perusal of the readings of a conference[523] dedicated to the exploration of anti-Italian discrimination. My introspection revealed myopia to just how close I have been with Italian-Americans but without giving great credit to the relationship between us. In graduate school in clinical psychology, one of my few outside classroom associations was with a blond Italian-American male from Jersey City. We shared a common urban experience and similar slight disdain for the absolute dominance of WASP (White, Anglo-Saxon, and Protestant) culture. During an extensive training and consultation at Bellcore, I developed a close professional/friendship relationship with

---

[522]Salvatore LaGumina (1999). *WOP! Anti-Italian Discrimination in the United States.* New York: Guerinca. Peter Vellon (2004). "'Between White Men and Negroes:' the Perception of Southern Italian Immigrants through the Lens of Italian Lynching" (pp. 37 – 43). In REAL STORIES: Discrimination and Defamation in The History of Italian Americans/ Booklet published by the Alberto Italian Studies Institute, Seton Hall University; Joseph Scelsa (2004). Affirmative Action for Italian Americans: The City University of New York Story. In REAL STORIES: Discrimination and Defamation in The History of Italian Americans/ Booklet published by the Alberto Italian Studies Institute, Seton Hall University.

[523]For example, see REAL STORIES. Discrimination and Defamation in the History of Italian Americans. December 4, 2004. A Conference presented by the Alberto Italian Studies Institute and UNICO National at Seton Hall University, South Orange, New Jersey.

Tony Buonocore, and at Procter and Gamble with Joseph DeMarco. Similarly, I felt closeness with Angela Guidice, of VISIONS, based upon African-American and Italian-American sub-cultures.

Ironically, I may have overlooked the significance of these Italian-Americans and others for the same reason that people generally overlook their families when contemplating extraordinary events and people. Their behavior was so comfortably familiar that they did not register as an anomaly. So what that I drank in a Newark bar, with an Italian-American who claimed that he knew enough about his Sicilian background that he would score first with a female graduate student peer. So what that Joe invited me to his home to dine with him and his family and left me alone with his son because he thought I was a great role model for his son to spend time. So what that Tony's daughters invited me to his surprise birthday party and I was the only African-American present. So what that Angela shared an observation, posed as a question, about how some people viewed my intellectual work. She asked me if I had been approached to do a book party in a certain area. So what that a young Italian-American engineer corporate trainee indicated a comfort at our Howard University training site because it gave a sense of security that she felt when she attended her all female undergraduate school. We shared candidly her perspective of the Howard Beach debacle, as an insider and the struggles of Italian-American youth to maintain their cultural heritage. She said her group had to claim a desire to speak to their grandparents as a justification for Italian to be taught in her high school[524]. Could I, an African-American, have internalized a view of Italian-Americans as gangsters, to such an extent that it overrode contradicting personal experiences?

Most painful, I had buried two relationships that guided my relationship with students of Italian descent at Cornell[525]. Thus, I had

---

[524]A struggle I thought ended thirty years earlier. At James Otis Junior High school in East Harlem, New York, Italian was the lingua franca for the smartest class. I wondered why it was even taught since most high schools in New York did not offer an Italian language sequence. I learned from a newspaper article that Principal Costello (Benjamin Franklin high school that housed James Otis) required the language to challenge the belief that Italian was not a worthy language to study in contemporary America.

[525]In a forthcoming book I will publish two essays written by Cornell students of Italian descent. These young men reveal how identity is still a prevalent issue for Italian-American men, even those with successful academic careers and attendance at an Ivy League university. In addition, they reveal a race/gender/ethnic interaction that is rarely given popular attention today.

denied a very central question to Peace work. What does it mean when an Italian-American says he is from the Mediterranean, and does so with an apparent realization that most Americans of Italian descent would say of European descent? I am not speculating but the person was president of a Catholic university, and he reminded me of another Italian-American president of an Ivy League university. I saw a cultural similarity because I had spent half of my formative years of schooling in East Harlem, at the time that the area was known as "Little Italy", and I had a sense of Italian descendants from Southern Italy. Both men modeled a respect for hierarchy and ability to be flexible about how to coordinate levels, people and ideas within an institutional structure. Their decidedly cultural approach enabled them to be relatively free of age, race, gender, occupation or class intellectual bondage. Neither denied the presence of group prejudice and racism as barriers for African-Americans and Italian-Americans, and neither overlooked ways of surmounting them. Both would probably claim to be politically conservative, however, neither would deny the advancement of African-Americans, based upon the latter's race and gender. Personally and culturally attractive to me, both rejected hypocrisy, respected loyalty and made career accomplishments in areas thought to be beyond their training and education.

Had I been educated in the history of Southern Italians in the United States[526], I would have appreciated and allied better with Dr. A. Bartlett Giamatti, someone who befriended me at Yale and afterwards. I would have more vigorously sought to aid Dr. John Petillo's plans for the growth and development of Newark, New Jersey, as a model urban center. John, who empowered me, when I was a consultant to Seton

---

[526]Even in an Italian run and dominated Junior High School, very little was taught about the achievements of Italians. We learned that General Garibaldi was great and in the Italian class that the language spoken in the neighborhood were dialects and not good Italian. We did not even learn that the Great Roman Empire was in present day Italy and based upon the ancestors of Italian-Americans. When I read the following books, I felt robbed of information that was an important backdrop to understanding the Italian youth that resented the migration of African-Americans and Latinos to Little Italy. See Philip diFranco (1988). *The Italian American Experience*. New York: Tom Doherty Associates, and Robert Orsi (2002). *THE MADONNA OF 115TH STREET Faith and Community in Italian Harlem, 1880 – 1950*. Connecticut: Yale University Press.

Hall, and I are still alive, and what the vehicle this book might engender is captured by Fred Gardaphe[527], when he wrote:

> When it comes to Italian-Americans, our image is out of control because we choose not to tell our story. In choosing to be silent, we have given up control of our culture, in choosing to remain invisible, we have chosen to leave our fate in the hands of others. As long as difference remains invisible it is impossible to see any similarities. It is unfortunate that when difference becomes visible, it overshadows similarities.

I believe the concept of diunitality, liberally discussed throughout this book, holds promise for the Italian-American dilemma around race, ethnic group and culture, as well as for other non-African-American groups at racial and ethnic intersections.

---

[527]Fred Gardaphe (2004). "Invisible People: Shadows and Light in Italian American Fiction (p. 81). In REAL STORIES: Discrimination and Defamation in The History of Italian Americans/ Booklet published by the Alberto Italian Studies Institute, Seton Hall University. One of my professor's at CUNY was of Italian descent. We developed a conversational relationship, based upon our realization of how our respective communities had been pitted against each other in Harlem and our fondness for a number of (White, Anglo-Saxon, Protestant) non-WASP ways of being. In some regards, his love of those things Italian included finding his wife in Italy and planning to live and work in the "old country." His behavior was not a radical departure from the conventional European immigrant literature on third generations' in the United States. However, the feelings captured recently by Italian-American scholars and researchers about being discriminated against and feeling a cultural loss may be a new phenomena. Richards, for example, argued cogently that Italians, akin to other European immigrants, had to embrace white racism tenets to gain white privileges and economic advancement (David A.J. Richards, 1999. *Italian American: The Racializing of an Ethnic Identity.* New York: New York University Press). In support of his contention, see the work of Thomas Guglielmo (2003). *White on Arrival: Italians, Race, Color and Power in Chicago, 1890-1945.*New York: Oxford University Press. Perhaps the concomitant demand to give up totally their previous culture and identity may be losing its appeal?

GLOSSARY OF AFRICANA STUDIES HELPING TERMS AND CONCEPTS:
Exercising the Power to Define[528]

African – African peoples on the continent of Africa and those in the Diaspora (African Psychology Institute, 1985). Being of, or descendent from, indigenous African/Black (Geo-historical Afrca) genetic-cultural origin expressed in discernible/overt biophysical traits (Kobi Kambon, 1998, p. 525).

African/Black Personality – The system of psychogenetic (spiritual, cognitive-emotional, biochemical) and behavioral traits that are fundamental to African people (i.e., of direct African descent). The African cultural (collective psychogenetic) reality manifesting itself in the basic psychological (spiritual, cognitive-emotional) dispositions and behavior of African people (Kobi Kambon, 1998, p. 525).

African/Black Psychology – A system of knowledge/philosophy, definitions, concepts, models, procedures and practice regarding the nature of the social universe from the perspective of African Cosmology/the African Worldview. African Cosmology provides the conceptual-philosophical framework for African Psychology (Kobi Kambon, 1998, p. 525).

African Nation-Building-Maintenance – The active participation in the conceptualization of, and/or planning and designing of, and/or operationalization and implementation of and/or practice and preservation of African-centered cultural institutions by African people. These institutions may be either modified old-traditional institutions or additional new ones, both ideational and material structures, which affirm, strengthen, and preserve collective African life, identity, and consciousness throughout the planet as an independent, self-determining and culturally distinct-world nation (Kobi Kambon, 1998, p. 526).

African Worldview – The conceptual-ideological framework derived from African Cosmology which projects African reality, history, culture, philosophy (ontology, axiology, epistemology-science etc.) as the center of the universe. It represents the African survival thrust of spiritualism, collectivism – interconnectedness, and harmony with Nature, inherent in African Cosmology (Kobi Kambon, 1998, p. 527).

Africana Studies – became more used as a designation for Black Studies (Maulana Karenga, 2002). See page 495 for definition of Black Studies.

African-American Focus of Black Studies – because it began as a self-defined and organized discipline or area of study among African-Americans, it tends to focus most heavily on the African-American initiative and experience. However, from its

---

[528]These definitions are verbatim quotations from the authority on the concept. I did not want to paraphrase the notions and forfeit denotative and connotative meanings.

beginning Black Studies Scholars have always defined and developed the discipline as inclusive of African peoples throughout the world African community (Maulana Karenga, 2003).

African Family – The basic unit of African people whose structural function is collective survival, perpetuation of Africanity and the procreation and protection of African life (African Psychology Institute, 1982, p. 13).

Africanity – The social theory of African people (African Psychology Institute, 1982, p. 13). Those unconscious and conscious, physical and spiritual qualities that define and manifest the fundamental nature of being African (Kobi Kambon, 1998, p. 527).

African Marriage – A union that is sanctioned by the community for the purpose of familyhood and which operates in accordance with the African social reality (African Psychology Institute, 1982, p. 13).

African Philosophy – the attitude of mind, logic and perception underlying the manner in which African people think, act or speak in different situations of life (John Mbiti, 1970).

African Psychology – a system of knowledge (philosophy, definitions, concepts, models, procedures and practice) concerning the nature of the social universe from the perspective of African Cosmology, "African Cosmology" thus provides the conceptual-philosophical framework for African (Black) psychology (Joseph Baldwin, 1980, p. 23).

African Psychology Development – What necessitated the development of African (Black) psychology was, first, the recognition that general psychology had failed to provide a full and accurate understanding of Black reality. In fact, its utilization had, in many instances, resulted in the dehumanization of Black people. Secondly, the philosophical basis of this body of theory and practice, which claims to explain and understand "human nature," is not authentic or applicable to all human groups. (Nobles, 1986, p. 64). African (Black) psychology has, from the discipline's inception in modern times, been enriched by the recognition of the need to grapple with an understanding of the fundamental nature of what it is to be human. Several Black psychologists and theoreticians (i.e., Wade Nobles, Cardric X, aka Syed Khatib, Na'im Akbar, Gerald Jackson, Joseph Baldwin, and Leachim Semaj) have in fact embraced a line of reasoning which views the behavior of African-Americans as having as its antecedents ancient African thought and philosophy. In this tradition Matthews has specifically noted that the African mode of thought has explanative import for understanding how African-Americans come to know and respond to their reality (Wade Nobles, 1986, pp. 54-55).

Africentric – (1) derived from but not exclusively West African culture. It is a worldview, therefore, that is steeped in African based languages, communication patterns, philosophies, behaviors, beliefs, rituals, temporal perspectives, and cosmos. For Diaspora descendants from West African nations forcibly transposed to the United States, it entails the inclusion of the African-American experience into its historical memory, conceptualizations of reality, and methods for ameliorating the effects of the

Mafia social, political and economic trauma. (2) An African cultural/philosophical orientation to reality (African Psychology Institute, 1982, p. 13). (3) Using the history, culture, philosophy, and collective experience of African people, the original, jet-black skinned people of the planet, as the frame of reference for organizing one's approach to reality-survival and understanding in the world. [The conceptual framework or orientation to reality (values, beliefs, definitions, rituals, customs, practices, etc.) based on the history, culture, and philosophy of African people (as a collective)] (Kobi Kambon, 1998, p. 525).

Africentric Culturalism – is the belief in the viability of people, customs, and behaviors emanating from the African continent, and is largely different from a Eurocentric approach in not posing itself as comparatively superior to other cultural systems (Asante, 1986) and not posturing a prototype physical type

Exponents of Africentric culturalism advocate: 1) African based languages; 2) collectivism; 3) cooperation; 4) Classical African based music, Blues, jazz and Hip Hop; 5) symbolic art; 6) traditional African religions; 7) African physical characteristics; 8) the affective-cognitive domains; 9) relational mode of thought; 10) spiral view of time; 11) the integration of time and space; and 12) diunital logic (Gerald G. Jackson, 2000, p. liv).

Afrocentric Axiology or value system – Afrocentric value system based upon a philosophical system such as the Nguzo Sabo developed by Maulana Karenga: 1) UMOJA – unity; 2) KUGICHAGULIA – self-determination; 3) UJIMA – collective work and responsibility; 4) UJAMAA – cooperative economics; 5) NIA – purpose; 6) KUUMBA – creativity; 7) IMANI – faith (Robert L.Williams, 1981, p. 118)

Afrocentric cosmology – is the world view underlying WEUSI formation. It is based on the belief that "SI SI Ki Ni Africa" (We are an African people). Further, the cosmology is based on the African ethos: "I am because we are; and because we are, therefore I am" (Mbiti, 197). It is the mental background, frame, and lens used to view the world. It lies at the foundation of all thinking, values, beliefs, attitudes and expectations within WEUSI. It would enable Black people to form a continuous network through which Black values and culture would be transmitted and perpetuated. The cosmology is responsible for one's feeling of identity and continuity. It prevents persons from feeling alienated or dissociated from their group (Robert L. Williams, 1981, p. 87).

Afrocentric Space – consists principally of a social system within the broader society through which the elements for the formation of a collective Black mind are transmitted or handed down from generation to generation. A social system is an organization of sub-systems united in some form of interaction and interdependence and surrounded by a boundary of social norms, which screens certain inputs from other systems. Within Afro-American society, these sub-systems are The Black family, Black community, and Black institutions (Robert L. Williams, 1981, p. 43).

Afrocentricity – placing African ideals at the center of any analysis that involves African culture and behavior (Asante, 1982, p. 2). The term centeredness means "the groundedness of observation and behavior in one's own historical experiences" (Asante, 1990, p. 12). Afrocentricity is "a methodology, orientation or quality of thought and practice rooted in the cultural image and human interest of African people" (Karenga, 1988, p. 403). As an intellectual concept, it contains both a particular and universal dimension.

Afrocentrism – is both a rediscovery and a reaffirmation of an ancient African wisdom, as well as a call to new ways of thinking and feeling. In its apparent etymology, Afrocentrism looks like recidivism to a naïve past but Afrocentrism is at once an affirmation of the latest thinking in contemporary cosmology and a return to the first recorded human philosophy (Charles Verharen, 1995, p. 67).

Agency – the study of African thinking, acting, producing, creating, building, speaking, problem-solving in their own unique way in the world or African agency is the treatment of Africans as active subjects of history rather than as objects or passive victims (Maulana Karenga, 2002, p. 47).

Alien-self Disorder – characterizes an individual who has been socialized to be other than themselves and in families with primarily materialistic goals and values and a preoccupation with social affluence and rational priorities (to the exclusion of moral imperative). They are encouraged to ignore the blatant inequities of racism and to view their lives as if slavery, racism and oppression never existed. They are a group whose very life represents a rejection of their natural dispositions, in favor of one dominated by material accouterments. As a result, they are asked to pretend that there are not forces of injustices threatening their collective survival. They are encouraged to always adopt the perspective of the dominant, even if it means a condemnation of self (e.g., suburban socialite, homosexual (Na'im Akbar, 1981, pp. 21-22).

Anti-self Disorder – not only identifies with the dominant group but essentially identifies with the projected hostility and negativism towards their group of origin. The dangerous aspect of this group is that, unlike the alien-self disorder, they feel quite comfortable with their alien identification. Most often, they exemplify the very epitome of mental health according to the standards of the "democratic sanity." They are unlikely, therefore, to seek help and be coerced into treatment by the legitimized authorities since they are the model of legitimized behavior (e.g., elected politicians who join any faction; elected leader who are more committed to the process than constituents, black police who beats Black heads; African-American scholar more concerned with scientific credibility than community facility, business people more concerned with personal solvency than about the community from which he or she came (Na'im Akbar, 1981, p. 22).

Axiology – It is that branch of philosophy that relates to the nature of values by which people live. By and large value systems are derived from the philosophical system of the society (Robert Williams, 1981, p. 79, 80). Axiology, therefore, is the study of the character of universal relationships and the rules and/or systems, which govern and/or define them (African Psychology Institute, 1982, p. 13).

Black Economics The interrelatedness of politics and economics which prompts some Black and radical economists to insist that the science of economics is best categorized as political economy...Political economy, then, can be defined as the study of the interrelationship between politics and economics and the power relations they express and produce. It focuses not simply on the economic process, but also on economic policy and the race and class interests and value judgments this suggests. Thus, the study of Black economics, of necessity, includes a study of the politics, which shape economics in both positive and negative ways (Maulana Karenga, 2000, p. 420).

Black Experience – that which was undergone or lived through Community – People linked by a common culture (African Psychology Institute, 1982, p. 13).

Black History – is the struggle and record of Africans in the process of Africanizing the world, i.e., shaping it in their own image and interests. As a particular people, Africans shape the world in a particular way, i.e., they tend to Africanize it, or shape it in their own image and interests (Maulana Karenga, 2000, p. 78).

Blackness – is the first and most distinctive Afrotypic feature of the WEUSI. A mullet-dimensional construct contains several constituents. The principal ones are cultural, genetic, psychological and spiritual (Robert Williams, p. 103).

A - Cultural – is the repository of all characteristics acquired through traditional Black institutions (formal and informal) such as the family, the church, the community, historically Black colleges, barber and beauty shops and the streets.

B - Genetic – is the basic constitutional makeup and identification of Black people in Africa and her Diaspora (p. 104).

C - Psychological – s a collective of attitudes, beliefs, preferences and behaviors undergirded by Afrocentric philosophy transmitted through the genetic, cultural and spiritual transmitters and bound together within a system by a natural rhythm. Psychological blackness is one's personal Black identity developed in Afro-space and expressed through Afrotypes (p. 107).

D - Spiritual – it is a feeling of unity and/or oneness with other Black people. It is a sense of togetherness, or rhythm. Rhythm in this sense means harmony, togetherness, and oneness (pp. 107-108).

Black Psychology – (1) Psychology technically means the study of the soul or spirit. Thus, Black psychology must be the study of the soul belonging to a particular group of people whose class membership is rooted in the historical and cultural experience of African people and who are euphemistically called Black (Wade Nobles, 1986, p. 47). (2) It is the study of human behavior conducted by Black people and for Black people. It is, therefore, concerned with the affirmation of Black people and not the negation of others. It is designed to provide a framework that will enable Black people to free our minds psychologically from oppression. It points out the problems and issues in such a way that it also has solutions attached. It is not a negatively oriented psychology; it is positively oriented. In fact, Black psychology must derive its energy from positive sources rather than from negative ones. Black psychology is not a protest psychology... It is more than a Black response to White racism. As many fields have been born out of protest, Black psychology did begin initially as a reaction to and a revolt against racism in mainstream and traditional psychology. But more importantly, it has evolved as an Africentric discipline that sets forth the appropriate frames of reference that sets forth the appropriate frames of reference, concepts and research strategies for Black Americans (Robert William's, 1981, pp. 64-65).

Black Psychology Task – It must concern itself with the mechanism by which the African definition of Black Americans has been maintained and what value its maintenance has offered Black people. It is to offer an understanding of the behavioral definition of African philosophy and to document what, if any modification, it has undergone during particular experiential periods. (Wade Nobles, 1986, p. 65).

Black Sociology is essentially the critical study of the structure and functioning of the Black community as a whole, as well as the various units and processes which compose and define it, and its relations with peoples and forces external to it. This includes study of family, groups, institutions, views, and values, relations of race, class and gender and related subjects. Moreover, Black sociology directs itself to the study of Black social reality from a Black perspective.As an emancipatory social science, Black sociology offers both critiques and correctives (Maulana Karenga, 2002, p. 299).

Black Studies – the critical and systematic study of the thought and practice of African people in their current and historical unfolding. It stresses and offers a dynamic portrait of African life in which Africans are not simply people swept up in the experience of victimization or passive encounter in the world, but rather are active agents of their own life, engaging their environment, each other and other people in unique, meaningful and valuable ways (Maulana Karenga, 2002, p. 3).

Conceptual Incarceration – The condition of African thought under the influence of the European Worldview. It refers to the conceptual universe or boundaries imposed on African cognitive-intellectual functioning by the internalization of the European Worldview. Consequently, such a condition reflects one which defines, i.e., limits/constrains or "imprisons," the conceptual universe of African thought under the influence of the European Worldview (Kobi Kambon, 1998, p. 527).

Cosmology – The study of the structure and origin of the universe (reality) (African Psychology Institute, 1982, p. 13). Refers to a people's world view, their concept of the supernatural, the basic nature of man and society and the way they organize these concepts to give meaning to their lives (Robert L Williams, 1981, p. 79).

Cultural Aspects – Comprised of a people's ethos, worldview and ideology (African Psychology Institute, 1982, p. 13).

Cultural Deep Structure – Cultural factors and cultural aspects (African Psychology Institute, 1982, p. 13).

Cultural Factors – Cosmology, ontology, epistemology, and axiology (African Psychology Institute, 1982, p. 13).

Culturalism – is the use of culture to define a biosocial group's spiritual, secular, and ecological reality. It affirms a belief in the viability of many cultural groups. It espouses that all bio-social groups will use their culture as a social and political construction of reality and grants them their right to continue to do so in the universe of all human beings, that is contingent upon their ability to exist reciprocally with other cultural groups. Furthermore, by prescribing the attitudes and behaviors of its members, it perpetuates its existence by defining what is a successful way to eke out an economic, social and political existence (Gerald G. Jackson, 2000, pp. l-li).

Cultural Manifestations – The surface structure of culture, e.g., language, customs, traditions, etc. (African Psychology Institute, 1982, p. 14).

Cultural Science – African Psychology (African Psychology Institute, 1982, p. 14).

Democratic Sanity – application of the social-political definition of majority rule to the definition of adequate human functioning. Consequently, the mental health practitioner determined insane behavior based on the degree to which it deviated from the majority's behavior in a given context(Na'im Akbar, 1981, p. 18).

Diaspora – Black people whose common origin is in Africa, but who have been dispersed or scattered throughout the world, i.e., in the Americas, the Caribbean and others islands of the seas, Europe and Asia (African Psychology Institute, 1985, p. 24). Refers to those Africans born and reared outside of Africa in non-African societies/cultures (Kobi Kambon, 1998, p. 528).

Dichotomization – A mechanism which accompanies objectification. It is the splitting of phenomenon into confrontational, conflicting parts. It facilitates the pursuit of power over other, and is therefore suited to the European Asili (Marimba Ani, 1994, p. xxviii).

Disorder – The process of change in opposition to Natural Order (African Psychology Institute, 1982, p. 14).

Diunital logic – means both/and. It is derived from the prefix "di" and unital, the adjectival form of the base word for "unit." When combined it means literally a single thing that forms an undivided whole. Diunital, therefore, is something apart and united at the same time. According to this logic, something is both in one category and not in that category at the same time and in the same respect (Vernon Dixon, 1976, p. 76).

Education – (1) The transmission of particular values, skills, knowledge, and understanding which: a) supports the process of transformation, b) results in the goal of mental liberation, and c) directs the attainment of self-knowledge (knowledge of self as an individual, as a member of a group, and as a cosmic being (African Psychology Institute, 1982, p. 14).

(2) The process of transmitting from one generation to the next knowledge of the values, aesthetics, spiritual beliefs, and all things that gives a particular cultural orientation its uniqueness. Every cultural group must provide for this transmission process or it will cease to exist (Mwalimu Shujaa, 1998, p. 15).

Epistemology – A system for determining how one knows what is real (African Psychology Institute, 1982, p. 14). It pertains to the theory or the source of knowledge. It asks the fundamental question: Where does the knowledge come from (Robert Williams, 1981, p. 80).

Gerald G. Jackson

Ethos – A set or sets of guiding principles which, as value codes, can be inferred from a people's Social Theory (African Psychology Institute, 1982, p. 14). The basic assumptions, code of values, or system of guiding beliefs inherent in a racial-cultural group's Cosmology (Kobi Kambon, 1998, p. 528).

Ethics of Sharing – is directed toward a sharing in seven basic areas: 1) shared status; 2) shared knowledge; 3) shared space; 4) shared wealth; 5) share power; 6) shared interests; and 7) shared responsibility for building the world we all want and deserve to live in – in a word the good world (Maulana Karenga, 2002, pp. 57-58)

Eurocentric – A European cultural/philosophical orientation to reality, which is typically dysfunctional when adopted by African people (African Psychology Institute, 1985, p.14).

Eurocentric Culturalism – is the belief in the comparative superiority of Anglo-Saxon culture, in particular, and European-American culture, in general, and the practice either directly or indirectly, consciously or unconsciously supporting the institution's philosophical beliefs, assumptions, and behaviors to ensure its comparative superiority over other cultural systems and its people. This approach assumes a hierarchial cultural group social and political order that decries the notion of cultural group equality and cultural differences as good qualities. What is normative, therefore, for groups who either occupy or descend from European lands are viewed as yardsticks for evaluating other culturally and geographically distinct groups.

Specifically, exponents and proponents of a Eurocentric approach ascribe comparatively greater value to: 1) Indo-European languages; 2) individualism; 3) competition; 4) classical European music; 5) representational art; 6) Judeo-Christian religions; 7) the cognitive domain; 8) analytical mode of thought; 9) Cartesian logic; 10) a linear-progressive view of time; 11) the separation of time and space; and 12) Nordic-typed physical characteristics (Gerald G. Jackson, 2000, p. liii).

Eurocentric Psychology – The study of behavior from a Eurocentric perspective (African Psychology Institute, 1982, p. 14).

Eurocentrism – an ideology and practice of domination and exclusion based on the fundamental assumption that all relevance and value are centered in European culture and peoples and that all other cultures and peoples are at best marginal and at worse irrelevant.

European – A group of people, generally classified as white, whose origins are in the Caucasoid mountains of Europe and whose basic bio-genetic characteristics is their lack of skin color due to the inability to produce melanin in sufficient quantity.

European/White – Being of, or descendant from, indigenous Caucasian/West Aryan-Nordic Geo-historical Western Europe) genetic-cultural origin expressed in discernible/overt biophysical traits (Kobi Kambon, 1998, p. 529)

European World-view – The conceptual-ideological framework derived from European Cosmology, which projects European-Eurasian reality, history, culture, philosophy (ontology, axiology, epistemology-science, etc.) as the center of the universe. It represents the European survival thrust of alienation, individualism, materialism, and control over Nature, aggression- violence, and White/Eurasian supremacy domination/anti-Africanness. Originated with peoples of pure Caucasian, mixed Caucasian-Asian, and Asian racial origins (Kobi Kambon, 1998, p. 530).

Extended self – the family, which includes the living, the dead, and those yet-to-be born, is the center. It is the focal point wherein the essence of the community is kept alive. The family or peoplehood thus becomes the source of our human definition. Psychologically, or in terms of social life, individual consciousness becomes such, that the family or peoplehood constituted the reference point wherein one's existence was perceived as being interconnected to the existence of all else. The individual was an integral part of the collective unity, i.e. the family. In recognition of this kind of awareness, it has been noted (Mbiti 1970; Nobles, 1973) that the traditional African view of "self" is contingent upon the existence of an interconnectedness with others (The Oneness of Being) (Wade Nobles, 1986, pp. 56-57).

Family – see definition of extended self

Fear of Being Different Complex – it is a cognitive and behavioral response to the oppression encountered because of their difference from Whites in looks, speech, dress, food, education, and concepts of civilize, spiritual, time, gender roles, social relationships, family structure, music and art. It is an African culturally based syncretistic approach to racial and cultural oppression, based upon a diunitally derived African ethos and worldview. It explains much of the accommodationist and assimilationist attitudes and behaviors of Blacks (Gerald G. Jackson, 2004).

Hatred for the Different Complex – it is based upon a Eurocentric dichotomous thought process that results in the oppression of people perceived as unfavorable or different in terms of physical characteristics, mental functioning, attitudes, beliefs, goals and objectives. It explains the segregationist proclivities of Whites in terms of housing, educational facilities, employment, and welfare resources (Gerald G. Jackson, 2004).

Human Order – The human expression of Natural Order (African Psychology Institute, 1982, p. 14).

Ideology – In cultural terms, it is a concept which represents an instrument for determining how a people should see their reality. It serves the process of knowing by providing a mental map which clarifies and gives perspective to the events and experiences of a people's socio-historical reality (African Psychology Institute, 1982, p. 14).

Liberation – The process by which a people regain the ability to actualize and implement their Social Theory in accordance with Natural Order (African Psychology Institute, 1982, p. 14).

Lineality – The interpretation of phenomena as being made of unidimensional, separate entities arranged in sequential order. This conception is necessarily secular and results in desacralization. It denies circularity and the spiral of organic development. It

Gerald G. Jackson

prevents transcendence of ordinary time and space, thereby denying ancestral ontological experience (Marimba Ani, 1994, pp. xxvii-xxviii).

Maafa – It is a "Kiswahilli" term meaning more or less a (prolonged) period of great disaster. It usually refers to the African Holocaust of Eurasian-European enslavement beginning in Africa under the Arabs and continuing through the so-called Western Europeans. It also sometimes refers to the approximately 2,500-3,000 years of continuous violent encroachment upon African civilization/African reality by Eurasians-Europeans beginning in Kemet (such as around 500 BCE or even earlier during the Hyksos invasion) and extending into the present (Kobi Kambon, 1998, p. 530).

Mentacide – the deliberate and systematic destruction of a group's mind with the ultimate objective being the extirpation of that group (Bobby Wright, 1973, p. 16). The psychological parity/equivalent to genocide. It is used both as a process and a psychological condition or state. As a state, Mentacide refers to the virtual depletion (or almost total suppression) of African cultural dispositions or prerogatives in African people. As a process, Mentacide refers to the actions of Eurocentric societal institutions in carrying out the cultural oppression, including miseducation of African people (Kobi Kambon, 1998, p. 530).

Mental Health – patterns of perception, logic, thought, speech, action, and emotional response in all areas of people activity (Economics, Education, Entertainment, Labor, Law, Politics, Religion, Sex and War) that reflect self and group respect, and respect for harmony in the Universe (Frances Crest Welsing, 1970 , p. 27).

Mental Order – The state at which mental processes are self-preserving in accordance with Universal Principles (African Psychology Institute, 1982, p. 15).

Miseducation – The process of the acquisition of Eurocentric/Eurasian-centered/White supremacy knowledge base about the world (i.e., its peoples, history, cultures, etc., including knowledge about African people specifically). It results in a false knowledge base/a false-superficial sense of enlightenment in African people that is Eurasian/European-centered and anti-African in nature perpetuated by the socializing and indoctrinating institutions of European society (Kobi Kambon, 1998, pp. 53 --532).

Multiculturalism – is a thought and practice organized around respect for human diversity. It expresses itself in four basic ways: 1) mutual respect for each people and culture; 2) mutual respect for each people's right and responsibility to speak their own special cultural truth and make their own unique contribution to society and the world; 3) mutual commitment to constant search for a common ground in the midst of our diversity; and 4) mutual commitment to an ethics of sharing in order to build the world we all want and deserve to live in (Maulana Karenga, 2002, p. 57).

Myth – when taken as concrete and analyzed symbolically can provide us with an important tool for understanding ancient African thought as well as contemporary African and African-American conduct (Wade Nobles, 1986, p. 40).

Natural Order – The state of life processes as they affirm and preserve themselves in accordance with Universal Principles (African Psychology Institute, 1982, p. 15).

Nature – The universal processes that operate independent of human intervention (African Psychology Institute, 1982, p. 15).

Off Track – Superficial exchange in which one's reaction is to the obvious aspects of the individual (Gerald Jackson, 2004).

On Track – Willing and capable of experiencing the totality of an individual and interact with the person in a way that supports and reinforces their essential greatness (Gerald Jackson, 2004).

Ontology – A system for defining the nature of being or reality (African Psychology Institute, 1982, p. 15). It is the branch of philosophy that pertains to one's being. It asks the fundamental questions "Where did we come from?" What is our purpose, our raison d'être? Ontological inquiries and issues related to the basic nature of man (Robert Williams, 1981, p. 80).

Order – The propensity of life processes to preserve themselves (African Psychology Institute, 1982, p. 15).

Pan African – thrust to include all Africans as subjects of study (African Psychology Institute, 1982, p. 19).

Pan-Africanism – The fundamental doctrine/belief and philosophy of global African racial-cultural hegemony. It advocates a unity of origin, nature, interest, and destiny among all African peoples of the planet. Sometimes Continental and Global Pan-Africanism distinctions are articulated. Continental emphasizes an African continent-wide focus, while Global emphasizes a planet-wide focus (Africa and the Diasporia) (Kobi Kambon, 1998, p. 531).

Peripheral African – Blacks socialized outside of Afrospace and adjusted to living by White European-American cultural standards and this culture's perception of acceptable Black behavior. Fragmented individual in constant search of self identity in a Euro-American group construction of reality (Gerald G. Jackson, 2004).

Philosophy – A method for examining and explaining the basic assumptions of a people's Social Theory (African Psychology Institute, 1982, p. 15). It refers to the common sense of a people as expressed through their collective consciousness and culture…[it] provides a framework for the construction of the common sense of a people. Philosophy is divided into four branches: a) Cosmology, b) Axiology, c) Ontology and d) Epistemology (Robert L. Williams, 1981, p. 79).

Power – The ability to define reality and to have others accept and/or respond to your definitions as if they were their own (African Psychology Institute, 1982, p. 15).

Principle of Oneness – Although in numbers we are many, in reality we are one. We are an African people. We are truly of one spirit, one substance, and one purpose. We are more similar to one another than we are different. An understanding, acceptance and internalization of this principle will re-awaken the hidden and dislodged belief in the realization of the Oneness of Black people (Robert L. Williams, 1981, p. 94).

Race – The unique biogenetic characteristics, which distinguish a cultural, group (African Psychology Institute, 1982, p. 15).
Racism – The deliberate systematic exploitation and oppression of a people solely based on race (African Psychology Institute, 1982, p. 15).

Reality – The phenomenon which the order of a people validates as being (African Psychology Institute, 1982, p. 15). That state or condition of experiences which the worldview/cosmology of a people validates as being, as existing or as real (Kobi Kambon, 1998, p. 532).

Reality for the ancients – was always conceived as the synthesis of the visible and the invisible, the material and immaterial, the cognitive and emotive, the inner and the outer. Accordingly, the phenomenal world was known through speculative thought as the representative of the subliminal (Wade Nobles, 1986, p. 36).

Rhythm – The synchronizing dimension of African reality (African Psychology Institute, 1982, p. 15).

Schooling – is a process intended to perpetuate and maintain the society's existing power relations and the institutional structures that support those arrangements (Mwalimu Shujaa, 1998, p. 15).

Science – An amplification and specification of a people's common sense. By way of a people's epistemology, it provides a reconstruction of reality by organizing and explaining experiences (phenomena) according to the cultural dictates of that people (African Psychology Institute, 1982, p. 15).

Self – The collective (I, We, Cosmic) representation of one's identity (African Psychology Institute, 1982, p. 15).

Self-Destructive Disorder – Most direct victims of oppression. Self-defeating attempts to survive in a society which systematically frustrates normal efforts for natural human growth (e.g., pimps, pushers, prostitutes, addicts, alcoholics, psychotics). These are the individuals who have, usually, found the doors to legitimate survival locked (Na'im Akbar, 1981, p. 24)

Slavery – The condition of inhumanity whereby all life sustaining institutions of one group are under the control of another group (African Psychology Institute, 1982, p. 15).

Social Theory – Those principles and concepts which determine the relationship of a people to each other and the world (African Psychology Institute, 1982, p. 15).

Speculative thought – is more akin to intuitive if not visionary modes of apprehension. Speculative thought attempts to explain, order, and above all else unify experience for and with the knower (Wade Nobles, 1986, p. 36).

Spirituality – (1) The apprehension of cosmic interrelationship. The apperception of meaning in existence, and the degree to which one is motivated by such meaning. Spirituality is one's ability to relate to the metaphysical levels of experience. It unites thought and feeling and thereby allows for intuitive understanding. This cognitive/affective sense is transmitted through collective ancestral relationship. The absence of spirituality is an ancestral legacy (Marimba Ani, 1994, p. xxviii). (2) The operational domain wherein a person/people experience and are informed by the constant presence and power of the Divine. Accordingly, it manifests itself as beliefs in Universal Laws and practices which reflect an understanding of the inherent natural growth potential of all beings in accordance with Natural (Divine) Law (African Psychology Institute, 1982, p. 15).

Symbolism – is the set of rules and methods for analytically interpreting ancient African thought. Through the use of symbols and symbolism the ancients' intuitive vision approached the world of knowing with an attitude which perceived all the phenomena of nature as symbolic writing, capable of revealing the forces and laws governing the material and spiritual aspects of the universe. The use of symbols and symbolism in ancient times was in fact the means for transmitting a precise and exact rational, if not supranational, knowledge which emerged from the ancients' intuitive vision (Wade Nobles, 1986, pp. 33-34).

Training – That process which conditions a person/people to accept certain values skills and practices (even in opposition to Natural Order). African Psychology Institute, 1982, p. 16).

Transformation – That natural process whereby human beings attain expanded manifestations and expressions of self from a state of innate knowledge to conscious self-knowledge (African Psychology Institute, 1982, p. 16).

Transubstantiation – A process wherein the meaning of reality, as seen and defined by one group of people (as determined by their cultural deep structure), is converted into the meaning of reality of another group of people (as determined by their cultural deep structure) (African Psychology Institute, 1982, p. 16).

Transubstantive Error – "Mistakes of meaning" which occur as a result of defining or interpreting the behavior, beliefs, actions, and other cultural manifestations of one people with "meanings" appropriate to and consistent with another cultural orientation (African Psychology Institute, 1982, p. 16).

Universal – Those phenomena that are not bound by time and space (African Psychology Institute, 1982, p. 16).

Values – The central dispositions, which influence the priority choices of a people (African Psychology Institute, 1982, p. 16). They are a set of commonly shared beliefs.

Gerald G. Jackson

The culture determines which values are to be transmitted and preserved and which ones are to be discarded. A value is a tendency to show preference for those factors intrinsic to one's culture (Robert L. Williams, 1981, p. 90).

Value System – Has three functions: 1) it gives some predictability of behavior; 2) it is an ultimate authority; and 3) it serves as a means of security (Maulana Karenga, 1968, p. 191).

Worldview – (1) represents the distinct unifying cosmological, ontological, epistemological and axiological principles representing a racial-cultural group's natural cultural (conceptual) orientation, outlook or perspective on and construction of reality (Kambon, 1998, p. 120). (2) A people's most comprehensive ideas about order (universal and human) (African Psychology Institute, 1982, p. 16).

REFERENCES FOR GLOSSARY

The African Psychology Institute Training Module Handbook. (1982). The African Psychology Institute, North Florida Chapter, The Association of Black Psychologists and Atlanta Chapter, The Association of Black Psychologists, pp. 1–49.

Na'im Akbar (1981). Mental disorders among African-Americans. *Black Books Bulletin*, 7(2), pp. 18–35.

Marimba Ani (1994). *YURUGU: An African-centered critique of European cultural thought and behavior.* New Jersey: Africa World Press.

Joseph Baldwin (1980). "The psychology of oppression." In Molefi Asante & Vandi, A. (Eds.). *Contemporary Black thought.* California: Sage.

Vernon Dixon (1976). "Worldviews and research methodology." In Lewis King (Ed.). *African philosophy: Assumptions and paradigms for research on Black persons.* California: The Fanon R & D Center.

Gerald G. Jackson (2000). *Precursor of an African genesis model of helping.* New York: Global Publications.

Gerald G. Jackson (2004). *Njikoka: Towards an Africentric Paradigm of Helping.* New Jersey: Africa World Press.

Kobi Kambon (19980). *African (Black) Psychology in the American context: An African-Centered Approach.* Florida: Nubian Nation Publication.

Maulana Karenga (2002). *Introduction to Black Studies* (3rd Edition). California: University of Sankore Press.

Maulana Karenga (1965). *Nguza Saba.* California: Kawaida Publications.

John Mbiti (1970). *African Religions and philosophy.* New York. Anchor Books.

Wade Nobles (1986). *African psychology: Towards its reclamation, reascension, and revitalization.* California: Black Family Institute.

Mwalimu Shujaa (Ed.) (1998). *TOO MUCH SCHOOLING TOO LITTLE EDUCATION A paradox of Black life in White societies.* New Jersey: Africa World Press.

Charles Verharen (1995). "AFROCENTRISM AND ACENTRISM A marriage of science and philosophy." *Journal of Black Studies*, 26(1), pp. 62–76.

Robert Williams (1981). *The collective Black mind: An Afrocentric theory of Black personality.* Missouri: Williams & Associates.

BIOGRAPHICAL SKETCH OF CONTRIBUTORS

Eric Acree is currently Director of the John Henrik Clarke Africana Library, Cornell University. He has been with Cornell University Library since 2002. Previously he worked at the University at Buffalo (UB) Undergraduate Library (1995-2002). He held positions at UB as the Head of Library Instruction for the Arts and Sciences Library; Coordinator of The Cybraries Teaching Center; and Reference/Instruction Librarian. He was also the Web Master of the Web site of the Undergraduate Library. He also served on the peer-reviewed editorial board for the educational website MERLOT (www.merlot.org). He has an M.L.S. in library and information studies, B.A. in history. His research interests include Africana Studies and teaching.

Ricardo Arguello. Born in 1982 in Granada Nicaragua, I emigrated from my native country with my parents at the age of two in order to escape the socialistic government at the time. For the first couple of years, my parents and I went from city to city in search of a brighter future. In the end, my parents decided to settle down in the south Bronx when I was six. Throughout my childhood my mother emphasized the importance of education and being a leader in your community. My mother would always tell me no matter where you go in life you must always remember your past, remember those who helped you, and never turn your back on those that need your help.

In September of 1996, I entered All Hallows High School where I met some of the most influential people in my life such as Mr. Brunell Griffith. While at All Hallows I excelled in my classes and continued to apply the lessons my mother instilled in me by helping tutor some of my classmates in various courses. Graduating valedictorian from All Hallows in May of 2000, I continued my academic career by attending Cornell University. While at Cornell I have learned the importance and the necessity of a good education for children of color. I have since joined La Unidad Latina, Lambda Upsilon Lambda Fraternity, incorporated in the Spring of 2002, became its treasurer and also the co-chair for the Latino umbrella organization, La Asociación Latina. In addition I have found the time to become a big brother for the Ithaca Youth Bureau, so that I can make a difference in the life of a child and tell him that his dreams, with a little bit of effort, can one day become his reality.

I will graduate this upcoming May 2004 with a Bachelor's degree in History with a concentration in Latino Studies from the college of Arts and Science. My plans are to enter corporate America and start a real estate company that will address some of the inequalities that are currently in place throughout the housing system of New York City. To summarize my view on education in a phrase would be an African proverb that states, "It takes a village to raise a child."He is a member of Lamda Lamda fraternity.

Carli Ball see biographical sketch.

Barry Beckham. Barry is a novelist and publisher. He began his first novel, *My Main Mother* (1969), while he was a senior at Brown University, completing it while living in New York City. He returned to Brown in 1970 as a visiting lecturer in English and, after being appointed to a professorship, remained there for seventeen years, several as director of the graduate creative writing program. In 1972, his second novel, *Runner Mack*, was nominated for the National Book Award, and his play *Garvey Lives!* was produced in Providence. In 1974, he was commissioned to write a biography of New York playground basketball legend Earl Manigault. The book was published in 1981 as a "novelized biography," *Double Dunk*. In 1987, Beckham moved to

Washington, D.C., teaching at Hampton University for two years. Partly because of difficulties with publishers over another of his projects, *The Black Student's Guide to Colleges* (1982), he has since dedicated himself to "developing a major black-oriented book company," Beckham Publications Group, Inc. He is a member of Phi Beta Sigma fraternity.

Herb Boyd is an author, activist, journalist, and teacher in New York City. His articles have appeared in numerous publications, including *The Amsterdam News, Essence, The Final Call,* and *The Network Journal.* He has published the book *Autobiography of a people: Three centuries of African-American history as told by those who lived it.,* and more recently a biography of Sugar Ray Robinson. aOf even more direct pertinence to this book, he edited *The Harlem Reader* (2002) and wrote *We Shall Overcome* (2004), a non-fiction book on the history of the Civil Rights Movement,. and *Race and Resistance* (2003) books. In 1995, with coeditor Robert Allen, Boyd received the American Book Award for *Brotherman: The Odyssey of Black Men in America*
    A noted authority in Black Studies, Boyd has been teaching African and African American history for nearly 40 years. He now teaches at the College of New Rochelle in the South Bronx. For the commemorative issue of the 50th anniversary of Brown vs. Board of Education, he published an article in the *Black Issues Book Review* magazine that chronicled the landmark decision.

Max Bushell see biographical sketch

Jeanne Butler has been the Campus Life graphic designer for the past 7 years. She is personally and professionally committed to increasing awareness of cultural diversity to the Cornell community. She feels that it is not just a nicety -- but a necessity --to the world outside of their "comfort zone." The feedback and enthusiasm she receives from students and staff continues to energize her!

Alexandra Carlin graduated from Cornell University in May of 2003 with a Bachelors of Science in Human Development. She was born and raised in the Bronx until she traveled to upstate New York for school but finds herself back in NY teaching in Manhattan at a New York City public school. The decision to teach can be attributed to many great Cornell classes.

Keith Cherry is a former Cornell University student.

Adrieannette Ciccone see biographical sketch

Keisha Cummings is a 2003 graduate of Cornell University.

Dawn Darby is born and raise in North Carolina during a time when integration was new and Black families who had a dollar more than the rest of their communities sometimes took flight and immersed themselves in this new and untapped experience of living and rearing children within the southern white lower middle class. She was fortunate to have been rooted in the African-American Church that remained the pillar and epicenter for the African-American southern culture. One of the most influential people in Dawn's life is her Grandfather; her contribution to the book, title and the cover design is a tribute to him.
    Dawn graduated from Salem College with a BA in International Relations and History. After experiencing the nefarious impact of receiving an education in a predominately Eurocentric university, she felt it time to migrate to the one center on the

Cornell Campus accurately portraying the world's ancestors, their contributions to this country while allowing a genuine acknowledgment of the African-American culture that has collectively shaped the USA. Her presence in this book, therefore, is directly related to her finding herself in the right place at the right time when she enrolled in a Cornell undergraduate course to refocus on the mis-education of today's African-American educational elite.

Dawn has studied and worked within Cornell for the past 6 years serving as chair of the Employee Assembly, member of the University Assembly, Student and Academic Services Human Resource Strategy Team, contributing editor to the Welcome to Cornell's new faculty and staff video, committee member and contributor to the Open Doors, Open Hearts, Open Minds, Cornell's Statement on Diversity and Inclusion document and is a community mentor and activist currently serving on the Board of Directors for the Tompkins County American Red Cross. The summers of 2002 and 2003, she worked as the program director and assistant camp director, respectively, for the New York City's Coalition for the Homeless' Camp Homeward Bound, a sleep away camp developed as a respite for children of the inner city shelter homeless.

Justin Davis was born in Atlanta, GA 9-19-84 and raised by his grandmother, Mrs. Beulah Davis. He graduated from high school with all honors and received several scholarships to attend Cornell University. His college major is psychology, with a premed focus. He intends to attend either Emory or Morehouse medical school. Enjoyment for Justin consists of playing baseball, swimming and mingling at parties. His more serious side involves Community service and he likes to help socio-economically challenged neighborhoods to attain equality amongst areas. Not surprising, given his full and rich schedule of activities and goals, his philosophy of life is that organization is key to success, along God's divine plan.

Rachelle Dubuche is a 2003 graduate of Cornell University.

Charles C. Fick see biographical sketch.

Gerald Fils see biographical sketch.

Réjane Frick see biographical sketch.

Kenneth Glover was born in Harlem and attended public schools in New York City. He attended City College where he obtained his Bachelors of Arts and majored in Black Studies. While an undergraduate student at City College, he worked with Black scholars such as John Henrik Clarke, Dr. Leonard Jeffries, Yosef-Ben-Jochannan and Edward Scobie. He also attended the community education forum called the First World Alliance and several conferences sponsored by the African Heritage Studies Association.

He became the Director of Ujamaa Resident College at Cornell University in September of 1988, after he worked as the Program Director of Southside Community Center in Ithaca, New York. Similarly, he is at the advanced master's degree level at Cornell University.

Sorbrique "Sorby" Grant is currently a sophomore in the College of Arts and Sciences at Cornell University. My intended majors are philosophy and government with a concentration in International Relations and Law and Society. I was born in Ft. Worth, Texas but I don't consider myself to have any ties to the large state. I have lived in the Bahamas, Florida, Canada, and most recently Ithaca. Even though I have spent most of my life in Florida, I consider myself to be a Jamaican, or, as I like to call myself a Jamerican. I owe much of my success to my mother who was born and raised in Jamaica. She has always been there for me with my bouts of attitude, and sometimes stubbornness----it is she who knows the true meaning of sacrifice. I know that nothing that I have achieved or will achieve could be done without my mother or my family in my life. My family has always had success, happiness, and education as top priorities and it is with those ideals that I have been able to excel, and accomplish my full potential. Hillary Clinton once said "it takes a village to raise a child" and after looking back at my short life, I completely agree. My family has always been there for me for pillars of support, guidance, and disobedience, and I am truly grateful and forever thankful. My greatest passion in life is life, and living it to the fullest may it be relaxing on Libe Slope or protesting for the rights of people that I will never meet; it is these things that allow me to feel alive. Where the road of life may take me I am not sure but I hope that I am happy. The ideal life would be one of power (everyone wants power), one that I would be able to help people with that power, but one that allowed me to remember the importance of family and raise a family of my own. The field of law and justice fascinates me, but I also think that is a result of the idealism and naiveté of youth. When thinking about the future I listen to the words of Marcus Aurelius "Never let the future disturb you. You will meet it, if you have to, with the same weapons of reason which today arm you against the present." Those words are the credence of my life and consequently I live life one day at a time and prepare simply for the present. I'm not a great mind like Albert Einstein but I do believe he was getting somewhere when he said he didn't concern himself with the future because it will come soon enough.

Deven S. Gray see biographical sketch.

Tiffany Lynn Haliburton was born and raised in Washington, DC. She is a product of District of Columbia Public Schools and subsequently graduated from Benjamin Banneker High School in 1998. Immediately following high school, Tiffany matriculated at Cornell University. At Cornell, Tiffany pursued an independent degree in the renowned College Scholar program. During her undergraduate career, Tiffany studied people of African descent with a focus on Latin America and the Caribbean. Tiffany's academic pursuit led her to study abroad in the Dominican Republic as well as completing several independent research projects and a Senior Thesis. Tiffany graduated from Cornell University in 2002 and is currently pursuing a career of public service with the District of Columbia's government.

Faith Harris see biographical sketch

Stefun Hawkins see biographical sketch.

Meredith Howell see biographical sketch.

Gerald G. Jackson see biographical sketch

Kimberly Jones is an organizational behavior and human resources major from Paterson, New Jersey. Her professional career aim is to become an entrepreneur, and the book project has made her appreciate Black heroes that could have gone unnoticed otherwise. Typifying an entrepreneurial drive and African-American social consciousness, she conceived a black-oriented newspaper for Cornell during the fall 2004 semester. She augurated a Cornell newspaper called, "The Black Perspective."

Jamie Lavender is a Cornell University graduate from California.

David Jayson Ladd was born on February 22, 1980 in Bethesda, Maryland and raised in a Reform Jewish household. Growing up, my parents always made an effort to expose me to diverse communities, cultures, environments, and activities. Therefore, my social and academic interests span across a broad spectrum. I graduated from Cornell in 2002 from the College Scholar Program, and the emphasis of my studies was in Social Psychology, Media, and Race Relations. I received Magna cum Laude for my honors thesis, "Africana Now," which was a documentary film about modern racism. This educational video was created with the hope that it would be watched, studied, and debated by future students and professors. "Africana Now" was my first real step into the world of film and television, and I am currently continuing my education in the field by pursuing a Masters Degree in TV production at Boston University. My goal is to one day become a producer and director. He is a member of Phi Delta Theta fraternity.

Marcy Lopez is a National Certified Asthma Educator at Bellevue Hospital Asthma Clinic in New York City. Hired under New York University, School of Medicine she also does extensive work on various asthma research studies conducted throughout the city. Ms. Lopez graduated from Cornell University in January 2002 with a major in Sociology and concentration in Latino Studies. Her dedications to serve, educate, and empower her community lies outside of her work environment as well. As a sophomore in the Spring of 1999, she became one of four chartering members of the first ivy league chapter in Omega Phi Beta Sorority, Inc. Five years later, she was elected National President for the 2003-2004 term and served as the sorority celebrated its fifteen year anniversary in March 2004. She is a member of Omega Phi Beta sorority.

Jessica Lorenzo was a senior at Cornell University, having graduated with honors in May of 2004, with a degree in Sociology and a concentration in Latino Studies. She pursues her MPH at New York University in Community Public Health. She hopes to pursue a career as a to executive within the New York Hospital system and provide her services to low-income based community health centers in the New York City region. Jessica is a Bronx native and graduate of the public school system of the City of New York. She is the oldest of three girls and serves as a mentor to her younger siblings and extended family members. Jessica is also a proud member of Omega Phi Beta Sorority, Inc., where she received a great deal of leadership and community service experience.

Shari Tenielle Moseley see biographical sketch.

Tracy Noisette is a 2003 graduate of Cornell University.

Kate Ofikuru – Kate Ofikuru
Birthdate: May 9, 1983
Junior, Industrial and Labor Relations

Kate is first generation Nigerian-American, the product of Clara and David Ofikuru. She is the second born of four, and respectively the second of three currently enrolled and attending college. While growing up "just making it" she has grown up with many riches – helping to raise her younger brother, attending a college preparatory school away from home, and being able to attend a prestigious and competitive four-year institution such as Cornell. With both a brother and sister in college, she certainly does not lack a source of encouragement nor an avenue to give it. Having changed her mind several times about her future career, she has now settled unwaveringly on

Education. After graduation in May of 2005 from the School of Industrial and Labor Relations, she hopes to attend Columbia University's Teachers College and pursue a Masters of Arts in Religion and Education.

Nirav Patel is a Rutgers University student in engineering .

Amanda Leslie Rabain see biographical sketch..

Sandeep Rao is a graduate of Cornell University.

Jamy Rodriquez. I am currently a junior in the college of Arts and Sciences majoring in Government. My parents are of Dominican background, but I was born and raised in Brooklyn, NYC. In the future I hope to go to law school and ultimately work in the criminal justice system. I want to dedicate most of my efforts towards youth criminal offenders. Due to the disproportionate amount young people of color coming into contact with the penal system, I believe that immediate action needs to be taken to investigate the source of this crisis; hence my desire to engage in this type of work.

Yenifer Romero. Currently, I attend Cornell University in the College of Human Ecology. I am very involved and active within both the Cornell and Ithaca community. I am a member of Sabor Latino Dance Ensemble, the only Latin dance troop on Cornell's campus and a proud sister of Lambda Theta Alpha Latin Sorority, Inc. However, there were numerous socioeconomic obstacles, which I had to overcome in order to be where I am today. I was born in the Dominican Republic, at age three I immigrated to the United States. I was raised in the Bronx, NY with three brothers in a single parent household. My mother has always encouraged me to do well in my studies. She is my motivation and inspiration. It is because of the experiences written in my essay that I have become the person I am. Thus, I hope to be the voice for a people that for a long time have been viewed as invisible.

Erika Ruiz is a Nuyorican from the Bronx. Having graduated from Cornell University with two degrees (Bachelors in Sociology and Masters in Public Administration). She is on track to make great contributions in her field of interest, affordable housing. While housing has become her passion, and current area of employment, Erika is very interested in racial and ethnic identity and relationships. Erika has partially fulfilled her hope to one day combine her interest in housing and ethnicty, with her current position in Washington, DC..

Sonia Sabharwal – I currently attend Cornell University in the College of Arts and Sciences. I am a premedical sociology major with a concentration in South Asian Studies. I am an active member of the Pi Beta Phi sorority. Furthermore, I am a proud member of the Cornell Bhangra dance team, which represents Cornell internationally in upbeat Indian dance competitions. My involvement in both the Indian and Greek communities at school reflects my dual identity as an Indian American. My essay in this book reflects my struggle to balance and integrate these two disparate cultural identities.

Kerby Samuels see biographical sketch.

Joseph Sargent, see biographical sketch.

Shelby Senzer see biographical sketch.

Catherine Soto see biographical sketch

Gerald Souders is a junior at Cornell University.

Phela Townsend see biographical sketch

Kareen J. Waite see biographical sketch

LeRhonda J.A. Washington see biographical sketch

Gary R. Weaver has been a member of the faculty of the School of International Service at American University for the last 35 years. During this time he has also been a consultant, lecturer and trainer to numerous government agencies, corporations and universities in the U.S. and abroad. Dr. Weaver's areas of expertise include: cross-cultural communication and adaptation, intercultural conflict resolution and multicultural management. He is author of the text Culture Communication and Conflict that is used in over thirty universities. He is a member of Alpha Phi Omega fraternity.

Diamaris Welch is currently a sophomore in the College of Arts and Sciences at Cornell University. My intended major is English. I was born in Brooklyn, New York, but at 6 months old my sister, who was two-year old, and I moved to Guyana, South America, to live with our grandparents.

I lived a very blissful life in this tropical country, with our retired grandparents and all of their friends who gave us an abundance of love and affection. Education was always stressed in my family as one of the most important aspects in our lives following family relations. Although my mother lived so far away, a week never went by when we did not speak to her and there was never a summer when we did not see her. She is a great person who understands the meaning of sacrifice. She sacrificed her happiness for eleven years, of not being able to see her children grow up, for our educational growth and happiness.

When I moved back to New York for sixth grade, I excelled at school, and once the teachers saw that they had a student with initiative, they pushed me even more. Everyone helped me out in any way that they possibly could. That lasted throughout my years of junior high school into my four years of high school,. and today I am where I am, on my way to a successful path. As long as I know that I am on this path because of the powerful influence in my life and the sacrifices that my mother made, I should not get side tracked. She is a member of Delta Sigma Theta sorority.

Thomas Weissinger is an Associate Professor of Library Administration at the University of Illinois at Urbana-Champaign. His prior appointments include service as Head Librarian of the John Henrik Clarke Africana Library (Cornell University), Instruction Coordinator (Rutgers University Library), and municipal reference librarian at the Newark Public Library in New Jersey. Weissinger has earned degrees from the State University of New York at Buffalo (B.A., 1973) and the University of Pittsburgh (M.A., 1978, M.L.S., 1980). He has been a consultant with the Board of Editors for the Black Periodical Fiction Project, the Arthur R. Ashe, Jr. Foreign Policy Library at TransAfrica Forum, and the African Centre for Development, Economic and Strategic Studies in Nigeria. Weissinger has also held various appointments in professional library organizations. These include service on the Executive Committee of the Africana Librarians Council, Secretary of the Cooperative Africana Microfilming Project, and Chair of the Publications Committee of the Black Caucus of the American Library Association. Recent publications include: "The New Literacy Thesis:

Gerald G. Jackson

Implications for Librarianship," portal: Libraries and the Academy 4 (April 2004), "Competing Models of Librarianship: Do Core Values Make a Difference?," *Journal of Academic Librarianship 29* (January 2003), "Black Studies Scholarly Communication: A Citation Analysis of Periodical Literature," *Collection Management 27* (nos. 3/4, 2002), and "Defining Black Studies on the World Wide Web." *Journal of Academic Librarianship 25* (July 1999).

Danielle Terrazas Williams see biographical sketch.

Jared Wolfe was born and raised in Queens, NY, before moving to Long Island when he was ten. He plans on earning a degree in Human Development from Cornell University in 2006. Jared's greatest passion in life is listening to music, where he could explore all the diversity and beauty that exists in the world through such life-changing albums as The White Album and Songs in the Key of Life. His career aspiration is to become a Civil Rights attorney, hoping to make a positive and significant contribution to society. He believes that diversity, whether ideology, art, or any other aspect of culture, is what makes life interesting and worthwhile; to live your life in just one cultural frame of mind is not really to live.

Tara Leigh Wood see biographical sketch

Rahim Wooley is a Cornell University student who is a member of the track team and Omega Psi Phi fraternity, Inc.